The Heritage of American Catholicism

A TWENTY-EIGHT-VOLUME SERIES DOCUMENTING THE HISTORY OF AMERICA'S LARGEST RELIGIOUS DENOMINATION

EDITED BY

Timothy Walch

ASSOCIATE EDITOR
U.S. Catholic Historian

A Garland Series

Early American Catholicism, 1634-1820

SELECTED HISTORICAL ESSAYS

EDITED WITH AN INTRODUCTION BY

TIMOTHY WALCH

Garland Publishing, Inc.
New York & London
1988

LIBRARY OF CONGRESS CATALOGING-IN-PUBLICATION DATA

Early American Catholicism, 1634–1820 : selected historical essays / edited with an introduction by Timothy Walch.
p. cm. -- (The Heritage of American Catholicism)
Includes bibliographies.
ISBN 0–8240–4075–9 (alk. paper)
1. Catholic Church--United States--History. 2. United States--Church history.
I. Walch, Timothy, 1947– . II. Series.
BX1406.2.E23 1988
282'.73--dc19 88-24515

DESIGN BY MARY BETH BRENNAN

PRINTED ON ACID-FREE, 250-YEAR-LIFE PAPER.
MANUFACTURED IN THE UNITED STATES OF AMERICA

Contents

INTRODUCTION

I THE SEARCH FOR A NEW LAND

R. J. Lahey, "The Role of Religion in Lord Baltimore's Colonial Enterprise," *Maryland Historical Magazine* 72 (1977), 492–511. **1**

Russell R. Menard, "Maryland's 'Time of Troubles': Sources of Political Disorder in Early St. Mary's," *Maryland Historical Magazine* 76 (1981), 124–140. **21**

II IF ALL THE CHURCH WERE MARYLAND

James Hennesey, "Roman Catholicism: The Maryland Tradition," *Thought* 51 (1976), 28—295. **41**

Gerald P. Fogarty, "Property and Religious Liberty in Colonial Maryland Catholic Thought," *Catholic Historical Review* 71 (1986), 573–600. **55**

III WITH PROMISE OF LIBERTY IN RELIGION

John D. Krugler, "Lord Baltimore, Roman Catholics, and Toleration: Religious Policy in Maryland During the Early Catholic Years, 1634–1649," *Catholic Historical Review* 65 (1979), 49–75. **85**

Thomas O'Brien Hanley, "Church and State in the Maryland Ordiance of 1639," *Church History* 26 (1957), 325–341. **112**

John D. Krugler, "'With Promise of Liberty in Religion': The Catholic Lords Baltimore and Toleration in Seventeenth-Century Maryland, 1634–1692," *Maryland Historical Magazine* 79 (1984), 21–43. **129**

IV THE CRUSADE AGAINST CATHOLICIS

Ronald Hoffman, "'Marylando-Hibernus': Charles Carroll the Settler, 1660–1720, "*The William and Mary Quarterly*, third series, 45 (1988), 207–236. **155**

Timothy W. Bosworth, "Anti-Catholicism as a Political Tool in Mid-Eighteenth Century Maryland," *Catholic Historical Review* 61 (1975), 53—563. **185**

Joseph J. Casino, "Anti-Popery in Colonial Pennsylvania," *Pennsylvania Magazine of History and Biography* (1981), 279–309. **210**

V Building an American Catholic Church

James Hennesey, "The Vision of John Carroll," *Thought* 54 (1979), 322–333. **243**

Thomas T. McAvoy, "The Catholic Minority in the United States, 1789–1821," *U. S. Catholic Historical Society, Records and Studies,* 39/40 (1952), 33–50. **255**

VI American Catholics and Religious Pluralism

Joseph P. Chinnici, "American Catholics and Religious Pluralism, 1775–1820," *Journal of Ecumenical Studies* 16 (1979), 727–746. **275**

Joseph Agonito, "Ecumenical Stirrings: Catholic Protestant Relations During the Episcopacy of John Carroll," *Church History* 45 (1976), 358–373. **295**

VII The Foundation of American Catholic Education

Charles J. Carmody, "The Carroll Cathechism—A Primary Component of the American Catholic Catechetical Tradition," *Notre Dame Journal of Education* 7 (1976), 7–94. **313**

Philip Gleason, "The Main Sheet Anchor: John Carroll and Catholic Higher Education," *Review of Politics* 38 (1976), 576–613. **323**

VIII The Stuggle Within Early American Catholicism

Patrick Carey, "The Laity's Understanding of the Trustee System, 1785–1855," *Catholic Historical Review* 64 (1978), 357–376. **363**

Patrick Carey, "Two Episcopal Views of Lay-Clerical Conflicts, 1785–1860," *Records of the American Catholic Historical Society* 87 (1976), 85-98. **383**

IX American Catholicism Turned Upside Down

Jay P. Dolan, "A Critical Period in American Catholicism," *Review of Politics* 35 (1973), 523–536. **399**

Introduction

America has always been a religious nation. From the biblical jeremiads used by the Puritans in the seventeenth century to the daily invocations by the chaplains of the U.S. Congress, Americans have repeatedly called on the Almighty to guide their nation. The motto "In God We Trust" appears on American coins, and the phrase "one nation under God" is part of the American pledge of allegiance. It is not an overstatement to say that religion is interwoven into the fabric of American culture.

Yet there is an ironic twist to the history of religion in America. Even though religious *practice* has always been a part of American history, religious *freedom* has not. For the first two centuries of American life—roughly from the foundation of Virginia in 1607 until the abolition of the state church in Massachusetts in 1833—religious freedom was inconsistently honored in what is now the United States. Americans were comfortable with the notion of being a Protestant nation and religious freedom was for those who accepted and practiced the Protestant faith. Other religious traditions were not welcome.

To be sure, the attitudes and laws of the nation changed gradually in the late eighteenth century. In fact, religious freedom was formally codified in the first amendment to the United States Constitution in 1791. But old prejudices die hard. It was not until the 1830s that the last of the state churches were abolished. And sectarian religious instruction remained a part of the public school curriculum in several states until the 1870s.

It is not surprising, therefore, that Catholicism did not thrive in early America. In fact, the few Catholics who settled in the colonies—most of whom were isolated in rural Maryland and Pennsylvania—did all that they could to be inconspicuous. It was not until after the independence that American Catholics enjoyed the luxury of practicing their faith in public without fear of reprisal. Even after they had won their religious freedom, the struggle was not over. Catholics faced the challenge of shaping a denomination that was loyal to both Rome and America. It would not be an easy task.

I

The practice of Catholicism in the British American colonies was a case study in persecution for much of the seventeenth and eighteenth centuries. Having outlawed the "popish religion" in the mother country, the British also did all that they could to keep Catholicism out of their colonies. In fact, virtually all of the colonial assemblies passed laws specifically proscribing the practice of Catholicism within their jurisdictions.

Given this institutional hostility, few Catholics chose to emigrate to the British colonies and those who did felt the lash of religious bigotry. If Catholicism did not flourish in America during these years, the faithful did manage to build a firm foundation in spite of the obstacles. It was the principal challenge of their faith.

The majority of the British Catholics who were brave enough to risk their lives on a perilous ocean voyage to the colonies chose Maryland as their destination. Conditions for Catholics were said to be different in that colony. Founded late in 1633, through a royal charter to Cecil Calvert, the second Lord Baltimore, the colony of Maryland was to have a large measure of governmental autonomy and religious freedom. Most notably, Catholics would be allowed to openly practice their faith in Maryland, something that they could not do in England at that time.

When the first colonists arrived on Maryland's shores in 1634, Catholics were on equal terms with Protestants, a situation that was unique in the British American colonies. Over the next fifteen years this denominational equality was codified by the Maryland assembly in several laws, culminating in the "Act Concerning Religion" of 1649. Although badly flawed, especially in its lack of respect for non-Christian denominations, the Act was an important first step in the struggle for religious freedom in this country.

Within this tradition of limited religious toleration, Catholicism built a foundation in America. Without question it was the Society of Jesus—the Jesuits—that formed the cornerstone of that foundation. Led by Father Andrew White, the first Jesuits worked among the colonists and the Indians who would listen to them preach the word of God. To support themselves, these priests and religious established a number of farms; in fact, they became planters and traders as well as missionaries. It was the Jesuit community, sending its members to all parts of the colony to minister to the faithful and at the same time to cultivate timber and tobacco, that gave the most visibility and identity to Catholicism during these early years.

Even though the Act of 1649 had codified Christian religious freedom, it did not guarantee it for long. A short five years later, the Puritan-dominated colonial assembly repealed the Act and this action set the Protestant community free to attack the Catholics. Some were put to death, others were forced to flee. The Jesuit farms were plundered and the priests fled in disguise to Virginia. Although the old order was restored in 1660, the Catholic community in Maryland had received a bitter lesson on the fragile nature of their religious freedom.

The Calvert family remained in control of the colony until the "Glorious Revolution" of 1688 when a Protestant was restored to the British throne. The Catholic Calverts were deposed and by 1691 Maryland had become a royal colony. The following year the Anglican Church was made the state church of Maryland; and all colonists, including Catholics, were obliged to pay taxes to support it. This was only the first of several laws that were offensive to Maryland Catholics. In later years, Catholics would be denied the vote, prohibited from practicing their religion in public, and prohibited from establishing schools for the instruction of their children.

Why did Catholics continue to live in a colony where they were an unwanted and persecuted minority? In large part because the alternatives—moving to another colony or back to England—would have subjected these Catholics to even greater hostility. Even though Maryland failed to become the haven for Catholics promised by the Calverts, the colony was marginally more tolerant of Catholicism than the mother country.

Maryland Catholics adjusted to the hostility of the Protestant majority by establishing insular communities. The typical Catholic community was rural and consisted of twelve to twenty families who lived within two miles of one another. Their common bond was their religion, making Sundays and holy days into social was well as religious occasions. Not surprisingly, then, Maryland Catholics trusted only one another; they intermarried, became business partners, and collectively supported the Church. They frequently met with their priests outside of church and invited them to participate in social occasions. Religion was at the center of the life of every Maryland Catholic during the seventeenth century.

Yet it also was true that the practice of Catholicism in colonial Maryland was very much of a private affair. Those faithful close enough to one of the Jesuit farms traveled there for Sunday Mass. The great Catholic plantation families built chapels and recruited priests to staff them. Other Catholic communities waited for a traveling Jesuit missionary who would celebrate Mass in one of the homes of the local Catholic farmers. Mass for these Catholics was a special occasion; on most Sundays these Catholics had to make due with their own services.

During the eighteenth century the Catholic communities in Maryland began to increase in size and visibility. Between 1700 and 1765, the number of Catholics in the colony increased from about 2,500 to approximately 20,000, a rate of growth substantially greater than that of the general population. The reason for this growth can be traced in large part to the large number of Irish immigrants arriving in Maryland during those years, a harbinger of future growth in the American Church. The increase in numbers led to the establishment of a public presence for the Church. Separate church buildings were constructed and formal parishes were established. By the eve of the American Revolution in 1776, the Catholic Church had become an institution in Maryland.

II

The history of Catholicism in other British colonies varied significantly from the Maryland experience. Small numbers of Catholics found their way into Virginia, Pennsylvania, and New York during the eighteenth century. Although there were no Catholics in New England, periodic rumors of an imminent Catholic invasion from Canada kept these northern colonies on their guard. Except for Pennsylvania and Rhode Island, colonial Catholics found little but hostility in the British colonies.

As the colony adjoining Maryland, Virginia was the logical colony to receive a few Catholic settlers. In fact, northern Virginia did provide haven for a number of Catholics during the anti-Catholic hostilities in Maryland in the 1650s. The Catholic families that journeyed across the Potomac river hoped to find a more hospitable colony than Maryland. What they discovered was an anti-Catholic hostility that isolated and limited Virginia Catholicism. There were never more than a few Catholics in Virginia and all of them in the northern part of the colony.

Catholics were tolerated only in Pennsylvania. Chartered in 1681 by the Quaker William Penn, Pennsylvania was committed to religious toleration in a manner only alluded to in Maryland. To be sure, there were a number of laws passed by the Pennsylvania general assembly in the eighteenth century that proscribed Catholics from full participation in colonial affairs, but there were no laws prohibiting Catholics from openly practicing their faith. It was a relative but real toleration that quite expectedly attracted Catholics to Penn's colony.

Those Catholics who chose Pennsylvania settled for the most part in the southeastern part of the colony. The largest congregation of Catholics lived in Philadelphia, where the colony's first parish was established in 1734. By the time of the American Revolution, there were an estimated 1,200 Catholics in the city. Other Catholics, primarily German farmers from the Rhineland and the Palatinate, settled in the Susquehanna, Schuykill, and Delaware river valleys. These rural Catholics were served for many years by two German priests who traveled the valleys on horseback. Both urban and rural Pennsylvania Catholics were able to practice their faith in the eighteenth century without much fear of a Protestant backlash.

New York also was the home of a small Catholic community. The presence of Catholics in New York can be traced to the proprietorship of James, Duke of York, brother of King Charles II and later king of England himself. James became a Catholic in 1672 and two years later instructed the governor of his colony that religion should not be a criteria for settling in New York.

Catholics accepted the duke's invitation to settle in New York. In fact, a number of Catholics held high office in the colony during the reign of King James II. The most prominent of these officials was Thomas Donegan, who became governor of the colony in 1683. Donegan fostered religious liberty during his short term as governor. As evidence of his ecumenical spirit, he welcomed Calvinists, Huguenots, and other dissenters. But this religious toleration was not to last. James was overthrown during the Glorious Revolution of 1688, Donegan deposed as governor, and religious toleration in New York quickly came to an end. By 1700, Catholics were a persecuted minority in New York as well as in Maryland.

There were few Catholic communities in the other colonies, but anti-Catholicism flourished nonetheless. In fact, it seemed as if the harshest laws were passed by colonies that had never had a Catholic resident. Hatred of all things Catholic was particularly intense in Massachusetts. The very idea of tolerating the presence of Catholics was regarded as a sign of weakness, a betrayal of English liberty, and a denial of the righteousness of the Protestant faith. Isolation, the lack of any contact with Catholics, and rumors of English Catholic plots and conspiracies all intensified and magnified the anti-Catholicism in that northern colony.

III

The American Revolution brought about a dramatic change in the status of Catholics in the former British colonies. The anti-Catholicism and legal restrictions of the colonial era were swept aside as a large segment of colonial society—both Catholic and non-Catholic—united to fight England. Protestants may not have liked Catholics, but for the sake of independence they were willing to tolerate the "papists." Protestant editors and clergymen turned their pens away from the "evils" of Catholicism and toward any and all who gave comfort to the detested "red coats."

More importantly, the legal restrictions that had kept Catholics from full citizenship were abandoned in the new state constitutions of the 1770s. Many states took the initiative of incorporating into their constitutions sections or statutes on the freedom of conscience and religion. Pennsylvania was among the first states to respond by passing a new constitution in September 1776. Maryland followed in November with a constitution that lifted all restrictions on the practice of Catholicism and on Catholics themselves. Catholics responded by fighting for independence side by side with their Protestant countrymen.

What accounts for this dramatic change in attitude toward Catholics and Catholicism? There are a number of factors involved, not the least of which was the assistance provided the rebellious colonies by Catholic France. A second reason was leadership. Men such as George Washington and Thomas Jefferson detested bigotry of any kind; they took every opportunity to attack religious prejudice in colonial society. If the colonies were to be a new nation based on the principle that all men were created equal, religious prejudice generally, and anti-Catholicism specifically, would have to be abandoned.

The Catholic community responded enthusiastically to the call for revolution. This commitment was symbolized in the important and highly visible contributions of Charles Carroll of Carrollton. A member of one of Maryland's wealthiest families, Carroll was as committed to liberty as he was to his religion. Writing in 1773 under the pen name "First Citizen," Carroll exposed the arbitrary rule of Maryland's former governor in a series of newspaper debates with a loyalist named "Antillon." Carroll's arguments were an important factor in swinging the assembly elections that year in favor of the patriots. Along with John Rutledge, Carroll was one of the two Catholics to sign the Declaration of Independence.

Other Catholics responded to the call for patriots. Daniel Carroll joined his cousin Charles as a member of the Continental Congress. Another Catholic, Thomas Fitzsimons, was one of the delegates from Pennsylvania in that body. Catholics also were among the men who fought and died for their new country. With Captain John Barry at sea and General Stephan Moylan in the field, even the most bigoted colonist would have found it difficult to criticize the patriotism of colonial Catholics.

With the end of the war in 1783, Catholics must have wondered if the freedoms they had been granted were permanent or if the nation would revert to the anti-Catholicism of the past. This uncertainty made Catholics apprehensive about their place in American society. For the most part Catholics wanted to fit in, to be inconspicuous, to accept the dominant Protestant culture in all things but religious beliefs.

The challenge facing Catholics in the post war years was religious freedom. Now that they were free to practice their faith, what sort of denomination would Catholics establish? Who would lead the Church in the United States? What sort of schools, hospitals, asylums, and seminaries were needed? Rome responded by leaving these matters in the hands of yet another member of the Carroll family. In 1784, Father John Carroll, brother of Daniel and cousin of Charles, was named by the pope as superior of the American Catholic missions.

Carroll knew that the American Revolution had created "a blessing and an advantage" for American Catholics. Catholics in this new nation were free of all foreign domination; no longer were they "colonials," they were "Americans." To symbolize and solidify this new identity within the Catholic community, Carroll petitioned the pope to appoint an American bishop to organize and lead the Church in this new nation.

Yet Carroll knew that this appointment of a native-born bishop would not resolve the major problem facing his denomination in America—a drastic shortage of priests. Since 1634, the few priests for America had been trained in Europe. This was sufficient to meet the needs of a small, somewhat persecuted religion. But freedom brought a renewed interest in Catholicism and many new parishes scattered around the country. European seminaries found it impossible to meet the demand for priests in America.

To nurture a native priesthood, Carroll proposed the establishment of a national Catholic academy and seminary in the United States. Carroll was well aware that it would take many years to fulfill his dream of enough American-born priests to staff every American parish. In the meantime, he was prepared to accept an alternative plan in which the laity would take a greater role.

IV

On November 16, 1789, the Vatican appointed John Carroll to become the first Catholic bishop in the United States. His elevation to the episcopacy was more than a symbolic gesture; it was the Vatican's recognition that Catholicism was no longer a persecuted denomination in the United States. Catholicism would survive—indeed, it might even prosper—in this new nation.

Being the head of the Catholic Church in America was not a position that Carroll had sought or wanted, and he accepted the position with a certain amount of resignation. It was most important, he believed, that an American be appointed the first bishop. If he refused the appointment, Rome might well send a foreigner to serve as the bishop. Thus Carroll reluctantly assumed responsibility for a national diocese based in Baltimore that included about 35,000 Catholics, most of whom lived in Maryland and Pennsylvania with small communities emerging in Massachusetts, New York, and Kentucky.

Even though there were a significant number of prominent Catholic families—the Carrolls of Maryland and the Fitzsimons of Pennsylvania, for example—most American Catholics at the end of the eighteenth century were poor farmers. They were simple people who were faithful to their religion but "lacked the fervor which is developed by constant exhortations to piety." Compounding this problem was the annual arrival of tens of thousands of Catholic immigrants from Ireland and Germany, many of whom were completely ignorant of their Faith. Carroll's task was to shape this motley collection of lay people into an American Church loyal to Rome.

As the first step in organizing his denomination, Carroll committed himself and his meager resources to the establishment of a school for the education of future clergy and lay leaders. Carroll vigorously worked for the establishment of Georgetown Academy (later University) in 1789 and called upon his flock to support the new institution. He was well aware that one academy could not possibly suffice for the growing number of American Catholics, but the new bishop argued that Georgetown would educate lay leaders who would return home and educate other Catholics both by word and example.

Behind his call for the laity to support Georgetown was the more important hope that the success of the institution would foster a significant increase in religious vocations. Carroll knew that cultivating vocations was only half the battle; he needed a seminary to formally train young Americans for the priesthood. In this regard Carroll looked to France where he himself had been educated in the 1760s. When a group of Sulpician priests arrived in the United States in the aftermath of the French Revolution, Carroll urged them to establish a seminary. In June 1791, he saw his wish fulfilled with the opening of St. Mary's Seminary. "All our hopes are founded on the Seminary of Baltimore," he wrote to the pope a year later.

There was a certain irony in Carroll's efforts to cultivate a native clergy. For all his work, the majority of priests in the United States during Carroll's tenure as bishop and archbishop were foreign-born. Even the graduates of his beloved seminary were foreigners and it was not until 1799 that Carroll had the satisfaction of ordaining the first American-born and American-educated priest. Even though the number of foreign-born, American-educated priests was increasing as Carroll had hoped, he worried about the loyalties of these men.

Yet he had no choice but to accept them. Like many American bishops who would follow him, Carroll was forced to accept foreign-born priests to meet the critical need in the parishes. During Carroll's tenure most of the foreign-born priests came from France and the influence of French priests was all pervasive during the years form 1789 to 1829.

Carroll had hoped that these Frenchmen would fill the demand for increasing numbers of priests. What the bishop learned after the fact was that such large numbers of foreigners precipitated the major crisis of early American Catholicism. Most of the foreign-born priests had a deep commitment to the European ideal of Catholicism. In Europe, bishops and priests made all of the decisions related to the Church at the diocesan and local levels; the laity were to obey without question. But this practice was very different from the more democratic traditions that had been a part of American Catholicism for more than a century. It was inevitable that bishops, priests and people would clash over who was to lead the Church in the first years of the nineteenth century.

The battlefield during these years was, of course, the parish. Canon law stated that bishops and their priests had the right to control Catholic parishes. But canon law did not mean much to Catholics who had pooled their funds to build churches and schools and hired teachers to educate their children. Many lay people saw little reason to consult with the bishop or even the local priest about the temporal affairs of their parishes. In fact, many parishioners expected the bishop to consult them about the appointment of pastors! During the years 1789 to 1829, lay people in Virginia, South Carolina, Pennsylvania, and New York fought with their bishops about temporal parish affairs. "Trusteeism," as it was called, proved to be the most significant internal conflict in American Catholicism in the years before the Civil War.

V

Even though lay clerical conflicts and shortages of priests and other religious were major problems, they did not seem to limit the growth of American Catholicism. The arrival of increasing numbers of Irish and German Catholic immigrants in Boston, New York, and Philadelphia underscored the need for more priests and more parishes. Moreover, it was clear to Carroll as early as 1792 that his diocese was too large. Finally in 1808, Baltimore was raised to the level of archdiocese and new dioceses were established at Boston, New York, Philadelphia, and at Bardstown on the frontier in Kentucky. In something of an autocratic fashion, Carroll nominated candidates for bishops of these dioceses without consulting either priests or laity.

The early histories of these dioceses reflect different problems and conflicts from those that plagued Bishop Carroll. In Boston, for example, the promise of rapid growth in the Catholic community never materialized. In 1820, the Boston diocese, which covered all of New England, had only 3,500 Catholics and 750 of those were Indians in Maine. In fact, the Boston diocese was so small that it was twice suggested that the diocese be merged into the New York diocese.

But the slow growth of Catholicism in Boston and the charm and diplomacy of the first bishop, Jean Cheverus, minimized the conflicts that would plague the Church in Boston and elsewhere in later years. Relations between Bishop Cheverus and the larger Boston community were extraordinary. The first Catholic cathedral was designed by the noted Federalist architect Charles Bulfinch and among the contributors to the building fund were John Adams, John Quincy Adams, Harrison Grey Otis, and other prominent non-Catholics. When Cheverus was transferred back to France in 1823, the city mourned his leaving.

Cheverus was succeeded by Benedict Fenwick who faced the traditional problems associated with the rapid growth of the Catholic community. By 1827, the number of Irish immigrants arriving in Boston was on the increase. The rise in numbers precipitated a need for more priests which, in turn, made the non-Catholic population uneasy. Poor peasants from Ireland, these new Catholics had none of the sophistication of Bishop Cheverus. Indeed, the non-Catholic population feared that this immigrant rabble would breed only crime and disease. This uneasiness and concern manifested itself in an anti-Catholic backlash in the 1830s.

The situation in New York was bad almost from the start. Catholics in New York struggled to provide for the spiritual and temporal needs of a deluge of new Catholics who arrived in the years form 1800 to 1830. At the turn of the century, the Catholic community in New York found it difficult to sustain even a single parish. But within a decade this parish was overwhelmed as the number of Catholics jumped from about 1,300 in 1800 to 15,000 almost a decade later.

Adding to Catholic New York's problems was a lack of leadership. To be sure, New York was made a diocese in 1808, but a resident bishop did not arrive until 1815. Bishop John Connolly arrived in that year to find about 15,000 Catholics, four priests, and two parishes. Connolly struggled to improve these statistics and recruited eighteen priests for the new diocese before he did in 1825.

During his tenure he also was able to build churches in other cities in his sprawling diocese—Brooklyn, Utica, Rochester, and Syracuse, among others. Connolly was succeeded by the saintly, but ineffective John DuBois, who would weather the same kind of anti-Catholic hostility in the 1830s that faced Bishop Fitzpatrick in Boston.

The bishops of Boston and New York had troubled but somewhat productive tenures during the first third of the nineteenth century, not so the first two bishops of Philadelphia. The tenures of Bishops Michael Egan and Henry Conwell were unmitigated disasters. It was ironical that the so-called "city of brotherly love," the city where Catholicism had flourished in the last quarter of the eighteenth century, would be the setting for an acrimonious battle of extraordinary proportions between Philadelphia's bishops, priests, and laity.

Bishop Egan was a saintly man, but a poor administrator. His four years in Philadelphia were one constant battle for the control of the principal parish in the city. The hardship and the heartache of this fight led to his premature death in 1814.

Egan was not replaced for six years and during this time the situation in Philadelphia deteriorated. After three other men had refused the appointment, the bishopric of Philadelphia fell to Henry Conwell, an elderly Irish priest with no experience in the United States. Conwell did no better than Egan in administering the diocese. Constant fighting led to chaos and before it was over, the conflict had involved the president of the United States, the secretary of state, the pope, the archbishop of Baltimore, and a host of lesser figures. Catholic conflict in Philadelphia had become and international scandal by 1830.

The new diocese of Bardstown shared some of the experiences of the eastern dioceses. Yet it also was true that frontier Catholicism had some unique features worth noting. Catholicism had come to Kentucky in the 1780s when Marylanders migrated into the future state in search of more fertile land. By 1815 there were a reported 10,000 Catholics in Kentucky with a majority in or near the settlement of Bardstown in the central part of the state.

Tension emerged within the Kentucky community over the issue of leadership. The lay Catholics who had established the parishes and built the churches were native-born, independent frontiersmen; they expected to share in the leadership of their Church. The new bishop and priests in the state were French for the most part; they remembered the excesses of the French Revolution and were suspicious of a laity that claimed "the extravagant excesses of Republicanism" in the governance of local Church affairs. The tension between clergy and laity festered in the 1820s and later resulted in "an emotional tempest that nearly tore the Church in Kentucky apart."

The conflicts between the clergy and the laity gave early American Catholicism a touch of chaos. This chaos was minor, however, in comparison to the revolution that was yet to come. Beginning in the 1820s, and for the next century, the American Church was besieged with endless waves of immigrant Catholics who were escaping poverty and political upheaval in Europe. By necessity, Catholic leaders had to devote virtually all of their time and energy to providing for the spiritual and corporal welfare of the legions of new communicants knocking on their church doors. In the years after 1820, American Catholicism would become a denomination turned upside down.

VI

The essays that follow underscore the theme that the first two centuries of Catholic life in America were a struggle for survival. To be sure, Catholics found a safe haven in Maryland for the first twenty years after the establishment of the colony in 1634. But toleration gave way to bigotry, and for the next century, Catholics were outcasts in the colonies. It was not until after the American Revolution that Catholics gained the right to practice their faith openly.

Religious liberty did not necessarily mean that American Catholicism was assured of survival in the new nation. Who would lead the Church—bishops, priests, laity, or a combination of the three? This and other questions were hotly debated over the next half century. For the first 150 years after their arrival in Maryland, Catholics had struggled for survival against *external* forces. But in the fifty years following independence, American Catholicism was threatened by *internal* forces.

Section one details the basic and persistent challenge faced by the Lords Baltimore in establishing a colony in British America that would accept Catholics. R.J. Lahey tells the story of Lord Baltimore's effort to establish a Catholic colony on Newfoundland. After this colony failed, Baltimore established a second colony, this time in Maryland. Russell Menard picks up the story by assessing the difficulties faced by Catholics in St. Mary's County, one of the first settlements in Maryland.

Section two provides an overview of the Maryland Catholic experience during the colonial period. There is no question that this colony and its religious traditions profoundly affected the future development of the Church in the United States. Two distinguished Jesuits, James Hennesey and Gerald Fogarty, explicate the foundations of Catholic traditions in this colony.

Section three discusses the contours of religious toleration and the rapid growth of intolerance in seventeenth century Maryland. Even though Catholic were among the founders of the colony and among its richest residents, they found themselves outcasts little more than two decades after their arrival. John D. Krugler and Thomas O'Brien Hanley discuss the fate of the Catholic founders and their families.

Section four concentrates on the growth of anti-Catholicism in the century before the American Revolution. Ronald Hoffman provides new insights into the precarious position of Catholics in the colonies by focusing on the life of Charles Carroll the settler, the grandfather of Charles Carroll of Carrollton and Bishop John Carroll of Baltimore. Timothy Bosworth and Joseph Casino detail the irrational anti-Catholicism that emerged in Maryland and Pennsylvania during the French and Indian War, 1754–1763.

Section five concentrates on the legacy of John Carroll, the "founding father" of American Catholicism. As the first Catholic bishop in the United States, Carroll struggled to lead and bring unity and identity to his small denomination. James Hennesey provides insight into Carroll's philosophy and Thomas MacAvoy shows how that philosophy was applied in the first years after independence.

Section six underscores the dramatic change in Catholic-Protestant relations in the early federal period. Eager to build upon the religious toleration that had been codified in the Bill of Rights, Catholics encouraged ecumenical communications with Protestants of all denominations. Joseph Chinnici and Joseph Agonito define the parameters of early American Catholic pluralism.

Section seven provides details on how Carroll hoped to use education to preserve the Catholic faith in a largely Protestant nation. He was convinced that through formal education, young Catholics would acquire a deep understanding and appreciation for their Catholic heritage. Charles Carmody discuses Carroll's catechism—the foundation document of Catholic religious instruction. Philip Gleason provides an excellent overview of Carroll's work in higher education.

Section eight concentrates on the leadership struggle within American Catholicism. From the time of the establishment of Maryland in 1634, lay people had always played a major role in leading the American Church. In most parishes during the colonial period, lay people served as trustees, providing for the temporary needs of the local Catholic community. These trustees were not always willing to turn over their power to their pastors and the end result was conflict. Patrick Carey analyzes this trustee controversy in great detail.

The final section is a chronicle of early American Catholicism turned upside down. Jay Dolan writes of a critical period in American Catholicism, the years from 1815 to 1865. The challenge of survival that so engrossed Catholics in the years from 1634 to 1820 would quickly become a challenge of coping with a rapid and sustained growth brought on by the massive immigration of Catholic peasants from Europe. Dolan masterfully details the transformation of Catholicism from a small, largely rural denomination in 1815 to the largest religious denomination in America by 1850.

It has been said many times that the true test of religious faith is the willingness to suffer for one's beliefs. There is no question that the small number of Catholics in this country during the years from 1634 to 1776 suffered for their faith. Persecution and prejudice were commonplace. So also, the generation that followed American independence suffered through the ordeal of establishing and nurturing a distinct religious identity in a decidedly Protestant nation. Even in 1820 it was not easy to be a Catholic.

The tenacity and endurance of these early American Catholics is to be applauded. It was this hearty band of survivors who layed the foundation for the extraordinary Catholic growth that was to follow over the next century. Their contributions to the heritage of American Catholicism have for too long been ignored. It is hoped that this volume of classic essays will help to remedy that oversight.

Timothy Walch

Acknowledgments

The editor and publisher are grateful to the following for permission to reproduce copyright material in this volume. Any further reproduction is prohibited without the permission of the copyright holders: The Maryland Historical Society for material in *Maryland Historical Magazine*; Fordham University Press for material in *Thought* © 1976 and 1979; Catholic University of America Press for material in the *Catholic Historical Review*; The American Society of Church History for material in *Church History*; *The William and Mary Quarterly*; The Historical Society of Pennsylvania for material in *Pennsylvania Magazine of History and Biography*; U.S. Catholic Historical Society for material in their *Records and Studies*; *Journal of Ecumenical Studies* and Temple Universiety for material in the *Journal*; University of Notre Dame for material in the *Notre Dame Journal of Education* and *Review of Politics*; American Catholic Historical Society for material in their *Records*.

I The Search For A New Land

The Role of Religion in Lord Baltimore's Colonial Enterprise

R. J. LAHEY

Among English efforts to settle Newfoundland in the early seventeenth century, Lord Baltimore's colony at Ferryland is commonly dis- 1
counted as a visionary affair. Perhaps the quasi-mythical aspects of the name Avalon, the title of his province, tend to obscure the seriousness of his purpose. In any case, it is fair to say that Baltimore's Newfoundland project has never been given the careful attention it merits and that even scholarly accounts sometimes further longstanding misconceptions. Of course, much of the documentation concerning the Ferryland colony does not appear to have survived the passage of time. Nevertheless, a considerable body has done so and is certainly sufficient to allow considerable new light to be shed on both the details of the venture and Baltimore's own actions and intentions in promoting it.[1]

Lord Baltimore's involvement in Newfoundland began in 1620. In that year Sir George Calvert, as he was then, one of two principal secretaries to King James I, purchased a lot in Newfoundland from Sir William Vaughan, whose own earlier efforts to plant there had not been successful.[2] Calvert's very motives frequently have been misunderstood. Even a recent and otherwise informative study of early Newfoundland settlement could state flatly: "Calvert's Newfoundland plantation was not intended as a cure for economic ills,

---

Dr. R. J. Lahey is an associate professor of religious studies at Memorial University of Newfoundland.

1. In addition to materials already better known, there exists a significant collection of documents of interest, hitherto apparently unexamined, in various Vatican archives. These documents cover the period between 1625 and 1631 and concern a proposal for a mission to Avalon to be staffed by English priests of the Carmelite order. With the exception of two pieces in the Ottobonian Collection of the Vatican Library (hereafter referred to as Vat. Libr., Otto. Coll.), the papers are housed in the Archives of the Sacred Congregation *de Propaganda Fide* (S. Cong. P.F.). There they are divided into three groups: the minutes or acts of the general congregations (*Acta*); letters formally referred to these general congregations, *Scritture Originale riferti al Congregazioni Generali* (S.O.C.G.); and letters otherwise dealt with, *Scritture Riferte nei Congressi* (S.R.C.).

2. Vaughan had purchased the whole southern part of the Avalon peninsula from the Newfoundland Company in 1616; he had planted a colony at Renews, immediately to the south of what was later Calvert's lot, the following year, but this lasted only a short time. At the same time as the sale to Calvert, Vaughan also sold the strip which included Renews to Henry Cary, Viscount Falkland, Lord Deputy of Ireland. Vaughan recorded that he sold a section to Calvert at the request of his brother, John Vaughan, later Earl of Carberry. See Orpheus Junior [William Vaughan], *The Golden Fleece . . . Transported from Cambrioll Colchos, out of the Southernmost Part of the Iland, Commonly called the Newfoundland* (London, 1626), inscription on map facing pt. I, p. 1, and also William Vaughan, *The Newlanders Cure* (London, 1630), Epistle Dedicatory (unpaginated), and pt. I, pp. 68–69.

. . . his colony seems to have been a personal, family undertaking—a refuge for the Calverts and their fellow Catholics."[3] This is the legend, and indeed the legend has a kernel of truth. At a later date Calvert probably did see his colony as a haven for Roman Catholics fleeing from the English penal laws. But it is in the first place to detract from Calvert's rightful place in the history of religious tolerance if this sentiment is confused with a desire to found a "Catholic colony." The standard version is equally wrong in theorizing about his initial motives from subsequent events. In fact, it is improbable that Calvert's original interest in Newfoundland settlement involved religious considerations of any kind, and even the assumption that these later dominated his thinking is much open to question. A careful perusal of the known facts provides a somewhat different version.

2 Calvert's mercantile interests are well established. Like so many Englishmen of his day, the secretary saw exploration and colonization as paths to substantial profit. As early as 1609 he was admitted as a member of the East India Company with the considerable investment of £1000.[4] He is known to have become a member of the Virginia Company that same year, and the New England Company by 1622.[5] His later interests extended to such disparate affairs as the silk trade[6] and a plantation in Ireland.[7] These other activities were purely commercial, and there is no reason to suppose that Calvert's original involvement in Newfoundland was any different. On the contrary, his own words, even when religion had entered into the picture, are assuredly those of a businessman. A letter he wrote to Sir Thomas Wentworth in 1627 gives perhaps the clearest indication of his personal preoccupations:

> It imports me more than in Curiosity only to see [Newfoundland]; for I must either go and settle it in a better Order than it is, or else give it over, and lose all the Charges I have been at hitherto for other men to build their Fortunes upon. And I had rather be esteemed a fool by some for the Hazard of one Month's Journey, than to prove myself one certainly for six Years by past, if the Business be now lost for the Want of a little Pains and Care.[8]

---

3. Gillian T. Cell, *English Enterprise in Newfoundland, 1577-1660* (Toronto, 1969), p. 92. The best account of the planting is Thomas M. Coakley, "George Calvert and Newfoundland: 'The Sad Face of Winter,'" *Maryland Historical Magazine*, 71 (Spring 1976): 1-18. Dr. Coakley also argues that economic motives were uppermost in Calvert's mind in the beginning, and he recognizes the religious purpose evolved through time. The present article is more precisely concerned with the nature of that evolving religious motivation, and uses the previously overlooked Vatican materials. Dr. Coakley's article, Dr. Krugler's in this issue, and the present article should be read together.

4. He increased this to £1600 in 1616 (*Calendar of State Papers, Colonial Series, East Indies, China and Japan, 1513-1616* [London, 1862], pp. 192, 273).

5. *The Genesis of the United States*, ed. Alexander Brown, 2 vols. (London, 1890), 2: 802-3, 841. See also Coakley, "Calvert and Newfoundland," pp. 2-3.

6. Baltimore to Sir Thomas Wentworth, April 17, 1628, *Wentworth Papers, 1597-1628*, ed. J. P. Cooper, Camden Society (London, 1973), p. 291. See also Sir Thomas Wentworth to Calvert, August 14, 1624, *The Earl of Strafforde's Letters and Dispatches*, ed. William Knowler, 2 vols. (London, 1739), 1: 23.

7. Calvert was first awarded lands in Ireland on February 18, 1622. He received a new grant, which took in a larger area (2,683 acres arable, 2,125 acres wood and moor) under more favorable conditions, on March 11, 1625 (*Calendar of the Patent and Close Rolls of Chancery in Ireland in the Reign of Charles the First, First to Eighth Years, Inclusive*, ed. James Morrin [Dublin-London, 1863], pp. 36-37).

8. Baltimore to Wentworth, May 21, 1627, *Strafforde's Letters*, 1: 39.

The second factor which necessarily must be taken into account in probing the reasons for Calvert's interest in Newfoundland is the state of his religious opinion in 1620. There is every reason, in fact, to suppose that he was still then a member of the Church of England. It is true that on the basis of the present evidence neither the time nor the circumstances of Calvert's conversion to Catholicism can be established precisely. Documentation hereafter considered would seem to suggest that the event took place in conjunction with the Spanish marriage negotiations, possibly in 1623 or 1624. In any case, however, the established facts would have to be contrived considerably to make Calvert a Catholic as early as the time of his acquisition of a Newfoundland lot.[9]

Calvert's original holding in Newfoundland was a narrow strip of land running east to west from the Atlantic seaboard to Placentia Bay; it was bounded in the north by Caplin Bay (now Calvert) and in the south by the 3
headland between Aquaforte and Fermeuse.[10] This lot included the harbor of Ferryland, and it was there that his first party of twelve colonists landed on August 4, 1621, under the command of Captain Edward Wynne, a Welshman and soldier.[11] The original settlers have been described as Puritans, but the

9. Much of the documentation relative to Calvert's conversion is treated in an article by John D. Krugler, "Sir George Calvert's Resignation as Secretary of State and the Founding of Maryland," *Maryland Historical Magazine*, 68(1973): 239–54. The author considers the evidence of Calvert's Catholic background, but argues against the theory that Calvert was all along a crypto-Catholic who showed his true colors only in 1625. Krugler himself suggests that the conversion took place at the time of, or after, Calvert's resignation in 1625, and that it was as a result of his loss of favor at court due to his having championed the unsuccessful negotiations for the Spanish marriage of the Prince of Wales. He further speculates that the conversion was brought about through the influence of Sir Tobie Matthew. The Vatican material which will be treated hereafter in the present article would leave the former part of Krugler's thesis tenable, although it does not really support it; however, it would make the latter conjecture highly unlikely. Perhaps the author's whole argument does not give sufficient weight to the implications of Calvert's support for the Spanish marriage as being indicative of his developing Roman Catholic sympathies; it should not be forgotten that he was committed to the proposal to the extent of wholehearted support also for civil liberties for English Roman Catholics. George Cottington, a familiar of Calvert and a member of his household from the time of his becoming Principal Secretary, certainly suggests that Calvert's conversion was a process which took place before his resignation: "His imployment long before his l[ordshi]p declared him selfe Catholick, I felt was little or nothing at all for me, during which tyme I discerned and palpably sawe his preparation to a new profession of religion . . . " (George Cottington to Sir John Finet, April 7, 1628, British Museum [hereafter BM], Sloane MSS, 3827, f. 124v).

10. See the inscription of Mason's map of Newfoundland found in Vaughan, *Golden Fleece*, facing pt. I, p. 1, and also Vaughan, *Newlanders Cure*, Epistle Dedicatory (unpaginated), pt. I, pp. [68–69]. Unfortunately, it is of little value to try to see the extent of seventeenth-century plantations from modern maps. Using Mason's map (1624), we can see that Calvert's lot was held to include the harbors of Aquaforte, Ferryland, and (in part) Caplin Bay in the east, and Placentia in the west. In terms of seventeenth-century cartography, it would have included the head of Conception Bay in the north but would not have been intersected by St. Mary's Bay, the whole of which was then thought to lie to the south of Calvert's territory. This would apply also, for example, to the map of Newfoundland included in [Samuel Purchas], *Purchas His Pilgrimes*, 4 vols. (London, 1626), 4: 1873.

11. Wynne to Calvert, August 26, 1621, printed as *A Letter Written by Captaine Edward Winne to the Right Honourable Sir George Calvert, Knight, His Majesties Principall Secretary: From Ferryland in Newfoundland, the 26, of August. 1621* (n.p., 1621), p. 1. Wynne said elsewhere that he spent the winter of 1620 in Newfoundland, and he spoke of "my several voyages and long staies" (See BM, Royal MSS, 17 A LVII, ff. 6v and 18. [This document has hitherto escaped attention. It is a lengthy treatise written later by Wynne to advocate the colonization of Newfoundland, and contains references to his experience at Ferryland. Wynne entitled it "The British India, or a Compendious Discourse tending to Advancement." No date is given, but internal evidence would suggest 1628.]).

assertion is not adequately supported. While the possibility cannot be excluded, especially in light of the Puritan migrations current in that period, contemporary reports afford it no real confirmation.[12] All that can be said with assurance of these first inhabitants of Ferryland is that they were largely Welsh and certainly not Roman Catholics, for one of Wynne's urgent appeals was for "a learned and a religious Minister."[13]

As did Wynne's other requests for personnel and supplies, evidently this one too received Calvert's favorable attention. Wynne records that on June 30, 1622, there arrived in the colony together a saltmaker, John Hickson, and "Master James." The latter, apparently, was Richard James, who in 1630 was said to have been "sent minister thither some nine years ago." James, who was something of an adventurer and an explorer and who later achieved fame as
4 librarian to Sir Robert Cotton, had thus the distinction also of being the first Anglican cleric known to have ministered in Newfoundland. His stay there, however, seems not to have been long; neither the saltmaker nor the minister are included in the list of those who were to remain for the winter. In any event, it is doubtful that James would have relished the idea, for the country left him unimpressed. He later described it as having "between eight and nine months' winter, and upon the land nothing but rocks, lakes, or mosses, like bogs, which a man might thrust a spike down to the buthead in."[14] Only in 1627 is James known to have been followed at Ferryland by another Anglican minister, although the presence of successors in the intervening years cannot be discounted completely.[15]

Under Wynne's leadership, Calvert's little plantation made marked progress. A new party of settlers in 1622 brought the population of Ferryland to thirty-three, including seven women. Buildings were constructed, crops sown, timber

12. The assertion is made by Lewis Amadeus Anspatch, *A History of the Island of Newfoundland* (London, 1819), pp. 86–87. Anspatch does not give his authority for the statement. The only evidence which lends any real support to his claim is the connection made in several of the Vatican papers between the Puritans and Newfoundland. See, among others, a report from the Nuncio in Brussels (whose jurisdiction included England), September 21, 1630, Vat. Libr., Otto. Coll., 2536, f. 158. However, all such references are found in secondhand reports and possibly arise from a confusion between New England and Newfoundland. (This is evident, for example, in a paper entitled "Nova Anglia sive Terra Recens Inventa," S. Cong. P.F., S.O.C.G., 259, f. 2.)

13. Wynne also asked for a surgeon and went on to suggest "that then your Honour may be pleased by God's assistance, not to doubt of a good and profitable successe in every respect, and a flourishing plantation, women would be necessary here for many respects" (Wynne to Calvert, August 28, 1621, in Wynne, *A Letter*, p. 20). As regards the presence of Catholics at Ferryland, a Vatican report makes it clear that there were at most but a handful of Catholics there even as late as 1625 (see "Relazione avuta dalli P.P. Carmelitani Scalzi," S. Cong. P.F., S.R.C., America Centrale, 1, f. 4^v). This report is unsigned and undated, but it appears to have been written by the English Carmelite superior, Father Bede of the Blessed Sacrament (John Hiccocks). If so, it likely was written between late summer, 1625, when Father Bede arrived in England, and late December, when he was arrested. This dating is corroborated by the internal evidence. For information on the author, see B. Zimmerman, *Carmel in England: A History of the English Mission of the Discalced Carmelites, 1615 to 1849* (London, 1899), pp. 61–94.

14. Wynne to Calvert, July 28, 1622, and list of settlers attached to letter of August 17, 1622, in Richard Whitbourne, *A Discourse and Discovery of New-found-land . . . As also, an Inuitation: and likewise certain letters sent from that country* (London, 1622), pp. 1 and 12 (letters paginated separately); Reverend Joseph Mead to Sir Martin Stuteville, January 23, 1629–30, *The Court and Times of Charles the First*, [ed. Thomas Birch], 2 vols. (London, 1848), 2: 53. On James' career elsewhere, see *Dictionary of National Biography*, s.v. "James, Richard."

15. The report of the English Carmelites to Rome in 1625 puts ministers in Newfoundland at that time, but it may not be reliable (S. Cong. P.F., S.R.C., America Centrale, 1, f. 4^v).

cut; even at that time there were in operation a quarry, a forge, and salt-making apparatus. Wynne was enthusiastic about the land and tolerant of the climate, and his reports to England reflected his optimism.[16] No doubt such accounts led Calvert to seek increased Newfoundland holdings and to strengthen his rights by means of a Royal Patent. (Until then, he had them only at third hand, through Vaughan from the Newfoundland Company.) Calvert's interest and influence at that point must have been considerable, for on December 31 of the same year he and his heirs were awarded by the Crown a grant to the whole island of Newfoundland.[17] So sweeping a concession clearly infringed upon the rights of the other Newfoundland patentees, and it was probably for this reason that it was quickly amended on March 30 to give Calvert only the additional land immediately to the north of his original lot, from Caplin Bay to the mouth of the river at Petty Harbour and stretching 5
west to Conception Bay.[18]

Finally, on April 7, 1623, there was issued the royal charter for the Province of Avalon, which comprised Calvert's somewhat extended territory. The charter in effect established Avalon as a palatinate, and to Calvert the king gave wide vice-regal powers to make laws, "provided allwayes that no interpretation bee admitted thereof whereby God's holy and true Christian Religion, or the allegiance due unto us, our heires and Successors may in any thing suffer any prejudice or diminution." The generality of this language must be contrasted with similar provisions of other contemporary colonial charters. The original grant to the Newfoundland Company in 1610, for example, provided that "we would be loth that any person should be permitted to pass that we suspected to affect the superstitions of the Church of Rome," and it specifically required the taking of the Oath of Supremacy, a measure unambiguously obnoxious to Roman Catholics.[19] By that standard, the absence of restriction on Roman Catholic colonization in the Avalon charter is indeed remarkable. The name "Avalon," too, had obvious religious connotations. The earliest recorded inter-

---

16. See Wynne's letters to Calvert, July 28 and August 17, 1622, in Whitbourne, *Discourse and Discovery*, pp. 1-4, 8-12. Equally enthusiastic were letters from Capt. Daniel Powell to Calvert, July 28, 1622, and from N[icholas] H[oskins] to W[ill] P[easley], August 18, 1622, *ibid.*, pp. 5-7, 13-15. Even in later years, Wynne's optimism about the prospects of Newfoundland settlement was maintained undiminished by his experience there. His unpublished treatise on Newfoundland is an unreserved call for colonization, dwelling on the advantages to be derived from the fishery, timber, and furs. He again mentioned his success in growing corn there and while he allowed that the winters were unpredictable, he found them comparable to those of Hamburg (BM, Royal MSS, 17 A LVII, ff. 17-19).

17. *Calendar of State Papers, Colonial Series, 1547-1660* (London, 1860), p. 35. A Vatican document suggested that Calvert's boundaries required the security of a Royal Charter for religious considerations (see "Nova Anglia sive Terra Recens Inventa," S. Cong. P.F., S.O.C.G., 259, f. 2 [This report seems to have been sent to Rome by the Nuncio in Brussels in September, 1630; there is no reason to suppose that the suggestion made therein came from other than hindsight]).

18. *Calendar of State Papers, Colonial Series, 1547-1660*, p. 41. This gave him the relatively small section of land between his lot and the St. John's lot, in effect (following Mason's map) increasing his territory by about 50 percent. It also seems to have clarified his boundary with the southernmost Conception Bay lot, called the "Sea Forrest" plantation, which had been granted by the Newfoundland Company to John Guy.

19. The Charter of Avalon is in the British Museum, Sloane MSS, 170. For the Newfoundland Company and other contemporary charters, see C. T. Carr, *Select Charters of Trading Companies, A.D. 1530-1707*, Sedden Society (London, 1913), pp. lxxxiv and 51-62.

pretation states clearly that Calvert named his province "in imitation of old Avalon in Somersetshire, wherein Glassenbury stands, the first fruits of Christianity in Britain as the other was in that part of America."[20] It should be noted, however, that the older Avalon was the cradle of *English* Christianity, and it cannot be assumed immediately that use of that title heralded Calvert's intent to make his colony a Roman Catholic establishment.

Nevertheless, there are indications that by this time Calvert might have developed Roman Catholic sympathies. Godfrey Goodman, a contemporary of Calvert, said that his conversion was brought about by the influence of Count Gondomar, the Spanish Ambassador (who left England in 1622), and Count Arundel (1st Baron Arundel of Wardour), whose daughter Anne later had married Calvert's heir, Cecil.[21] Goodman's relation tends thus to support the
6 version of the Vatican papers, which ascribe both Calvert's conversion and the naming of Avalon to Father Simon Stock (Thomas Doughty),[22] a Discalced Carmelite priest who was then the Spanish Ambassador's chaplain.[23] The two

20. David Lloyd, *State Worthies: Or, the States-men and Favourites of England from the Reformation to the Revolution*, 2nd ed. (London, 1670), pp. 750-51. See also a document drawn up by the Calvert family in 1670 on their colonizing efforts (BM, Sloane MSS, 3662, ff. 24-26 [" . . . called Avalon from Avalon in Somerset shire where Christianity was first receiv'd in England."]). It should be noted that a religious motive for colonization features strongly in Anglican works of this period. See Louis B. Wright, *Religion and Empire: The Alliance between Piety and Commerce in English Expansion, 1558-1625* (New York, 1965).

21. " . . . and as he was the only secretary employed in the Spanish match, so undoubtedly he did what good offices he could therein for religion's sake, being infinitely addicted to the Roman Catholic faith, having been converted thereunto by Count Gondomar and Count Arundel. . . . And, as it was said, the secretary did usually catechize his own children so to ground them in his own religion, and in his best room having an altar set up, with chalice, candlesticks and all other ornaments, he brought all strangers thither, never concealing anything, as if his whole joy and comfort had been to make open profession of his religion" (Godfrey Goodman, *The Court of King James the First*, ed. John S. Brewer, 2 vols. [London, 1839], 1: 379). The open profession of Catholicism by Calvert, to which Goodman refers, however, certainly does not seem to have taken place until after his resignation as Secretary.

22. Father Simon Stock of St. Mary was the religious name of Thomas Doughty, born in Plombley, Courty Lincoln, about 1574. Having been forced to flee England to escape persecution, he entered the English College in Rome in 1606. It was only after his priestly ordination in 1610 that he became a Carmelite monk. He returned as a missionary to England in 1615, and soon after his arrival there became chaplain to Gondomar, the Spanish ambassador. In this position he appears to have had not only immunity from prosecution, but also a relatively safe and regular channel of communication with Catholic authorities on the Continent. He retained this appointment until 1633, when he went to reside with the Roper family at Canterbury. He died in 1652 (see Zimmerman, *Carmel in England*, pp. 23-39). To avoid confusion, Doughty's religious name is used throughout the present article.

23. S'è scoperta dà Missionarii C. Scalsi d'Inghilterra una nuova Isola grande fertiliss[ima] e piena d'huomini sesati, chiamata da essi Avallonia, la qual è à mezo il camino da Inghliterra all'America settentrionala. S'è convertito già dalla gentilità un Sign. grande . . . " (Father Francesco Ingoli to Mgr. Agucchio, December 27, 1625, Vat. Libr., Otto. Coll., 2356, f. 45 [The reference to the discovery of the Island probably stemmed from a misunderstanding of the name *Newfound*land, or *Terra Nuova*.]). "Simonem Stochum Carmelitanum discalceatum in Anglia Missionarium ad fidem Catholicam convertisse quemdam magnum virum, et aliquot eius servos . . . " (Congregation of March 22, 1625, S. Cong. P.F., *Acta*, 3, f. 208ᵛ. See also Father Stock to [Father Ingoli], June 27, 1628, S. Cong. P.F., S.O.C.G., 102, f. 13, which more clearly identifies Baltimore as the person referred to). When Father Simon first informed Rome of Calvert's conversion is unknown, but his letter was answered on March 16, 1625 (see S. Cong. P.F., S.O.C.G., 101, f. 29). His letters took from two to six months to reach Rome, which would mean that his first report was probably written between September, 1624, and early January, 1625. The recipient of Father Simon's letters to Rome is unnamed; however, it was almost certainly Father Francesco Ingoli, Secretary of the Congregation of the Propaganda.

accounts obviously suggest a link between Calvert's decision to become a Catholic and his participation as principal secretary in the Spanish Marriage negotiations (the proposed marriage of the Prince of Wales, later Charles I, to the Infanta of Spain), which brought him into unusually close contact with the Spanish emissaries in England.[24] According to the Venetian Ambassador in London, Alvise Contarini, Calvert "managed the entire business."[25] In any case, he resolutely supported not only the marriage itself, but also the highly unpopular proposal, which had become attached to the marriage treaty, to abolish the penal measures against English Roman Catholics.

It was after the failure of the Spanish negotiations that there began to appear rumors of Calvert's impending resignation of his secretaryship. These circulated as early as April 1624,[26] but it was not until the beginning of the
new year that Calvert actually resigned his position and his espousal of Roman 7
Catholicism became known.[27] There are some signs that Calvert might have fallen from Royal favor;[28] nevertheless, he was retained as a member of the Privy Council and rewarded for his service by an Irish peerage and lands, becoming Baron Baltimore of Baltimore in County Longford.[29]

---

24. Zimmerman says that Father Simon made converts among prominent Englishmen with whom he had contact during these negotiations, although these men are not identified (*Carmel in England*, p. 32). The same idea is implicit in Goodman's statement about the conversion, for Arundel as well as Gondomar was closely involved in the Spanish marriage business (see Secretary Calvert to Secretary Conway, August 18, 1623, *Calendar of State Papers, Domestic, 1623-25. With Addenda.* [London, 1859], p. 58). While Goodman's statement as to Gondomar's influence upon Calvert's conversion accords with other accounts, it perhaps should not be interpreted too readily in its strictest sense, i.e., that Calvert became a Catholic before the Ambassador's departure from England in 1622. It should be noted too that Calvert had a similarly close relationship to Don Carlos Coloma, Gondomar's successor. In fact, a later tract by Calvert, L[ord] B[altimore], *The Answere of a Catholike Lay Gentleman to the Judgement of a Divine, upon the Letter of the Lay Catholikes to my Lord Bishop of Chalcedon*, was published in St. Omer in Belgium in 1631 appended to a work by Coloma, *The Attestation of the Declaration made by the lay Catholikes of England concerning the authority challenged over them by the Bishop of Chalcedon*.

25. Contarini to the Doge and Senate, March 12, 1627, *Calendar of State Papers, Venetian, 1626-28* (London, 1914), p. 147.

26. D. Carleton to Sir Dudley Carleton, April 4, 1624, *Calendar of State Papers, Domestic, 1623-25. With Addenda*, p. 208.

27. John Chamberlain to Sir Dudley Carleton, January 8, 1625, *The Court and Times of James the First*, [ed. Thomas Birch], 2 vols. (London, 1849), 2: 490. If Calvert were already a Roman Catholic before this time, the fact was certainly not obvious. Even as seasoned a court observer as Chamberlain was able to write to Carleton as late as February 26, 1625, that "Lord Baltimore (which is now his title) is gone into the North, with Sir Tobie Matthew, which confirms the opinion that he is a bird of that feather" (*ibid.*, p. 501 [Matthew was a prominent Roman Catholic who had been ordained a priest on the Continent.]). Similarly, another unnamed but usually well informed correspondent wrote to Rev. Joseph Mead on April 13, 1625: "It is said the Lord Baltimore . . . is now a professed papist" (*Court and Times of Charles I*, 1: 10).

28. These are well treated by Krugler, "Calvert's Resignation," pp. 239-54.

29. *Calendar of Patent and Close Rolls, Ireland, Charles I*, pp. 36-37. He was granted his title on February 16. He had earlier received from the king lands in County Longford, for which he was obliged to pay an annual rental; on March 11, having surrendered this grant, he was given an outright grant to a considerably larger area. The Secretary was also permitted to accept a substantial *douceur* from his successor as Principal Secretary (John Chamberlain to Sir Dudley Carleton, February 12, 1625, *Court and Times of James I*, 2: 498). It should be noted that Baltimore did not remain long as a member of the Privy Council; upon the accession of Charles I shortly thereafter, he was excluded, since he could not in conscience take the required oaths (John Chamberlain to Sir Dudley Carleton, April 9, 1625, *Court and Times of Charles I*, 1: 7-8).

Public life behind him, Baltimore was at last free to turn his interest to his Newfoundland and Irish plantations. It was the former which seems to have occupied his immediate attention, and following the business of his resignation his first thoughts seem to have been of personally inspecting his colony in the New World. On March 15, just four days after the finalization of his Irish land grant, he wrote definitely to Sir John Coke: "I intend shortly, God willing, a journey for Newfoundland to visit a plantation which I began there some few years since."[30] However, this voyage did not materialize, and by the end of May Baltimore had sought and received permission of the king to take up residence in Ireland.[31] His plans may have been forestalled by difficulties of transportation. Because of the war with Spain, the government would release for his use only two vessels, and these were obliged to return to England
8 within ten days of their arrival with a cargo of fish for naval use.[32] But perhaps this was not the only cause. A correspondent familiar with the Court suggested that religion might have been involved too: "Baltimore . . . is now a professed papist; was going to Newfoundland, but is stayed."[33] Whatever the reason, Baltimore's first visit to Ferryland had to be postponed and, as it transpired, did not take place for another two years.

That left Baltimore in 1625 with the pressing problem of securing a governor to succeed Edward Wynne, who had probably left his service not long before. Wynne has been charged with mismanagement.[34] However, this relatively modern accusation does not seem to square with the judgment of his contemporaries. Vaughan, for example, wrote in 1626 that Wynne was "much noted . . . for his personall abode and painefull care in settling the Plantation at Feriland . . . where for the space of 4 yeares hee did more good for my Lord Baltimore, then others had done in double the time."[35] Sir William Alexander, too, has suggested that in 1624 the colony was a thriving concern.[36] Neither does

30. Baltimore to Coke, March 15, 1625 (*Historical Manuscripts Commission, Manuscripts of the Earl Cowper*, 2 vols. [London, 1888-90], 1: 187).

31. The king to Lord Falkland, May 29, 1625, *Calendar of Patent and Close Rolls, Ireland, Charles I*, p. 36. The king asked that Baltimore be treated as "one who is parted from us with our princely approbation and in our good grace." The letter mentioned that it was Baltimore's intention to reside in Ireland for some time; apart from a visit to England in 1626 and journeys to England and Newfoundland in 1627, he seems to have lived in Ireland until leaving for Newfoundland in 1628. His residence, however, was not on his lands in County Longford, but at "Cloghamon," Ferns, County Wexford, where he purchased the estate of Sir Richard Masterman (David Roth, Bishop of Ossory, to Peter Lombard, Archbishop of Armagh, September 17, 1625, *Historical Manuscripts Commission, Report on Franciscan Manuscripts preserved at the Convent, Merchant's Quay, Dublin* [Dublin, 1906], p. 81).

32. Duke of Buckingham to Sir John Coke, March 17, 1625, *Historical Manuscripts Commission, Cowper*, 1: 187. Another account states: "The ships from the Western ports were forbidden to proceed to Newfoundland till sufficient mariners were provided for the King's service" (Secretary Morton to Secretary Conway, March 19, 1625, *Calendar of State Papers, Domestic, 1623-25*, p. 503).

33. Letter to the Reverend Joseph Mead, April 13, 1625, *Court and Times of Charles I*, 1: 10.

34. D. W. Prowse, *A History of Newfoundland: From the English, Colonial and Foreign Records*, 2nd ed. (London, 1896), p. 119.

35. Vaughan, *Golden Fleece*, pt. III, p. 20. See also Vaughan's *Cambrensium Caroleia* (London, 1625), sig. D6, where he states that Wynne spent four winters in Newfoundland.

36. "Master Secretary Calvert hath planted a companie at Ferriland, who . . . have done more than ever was performed by any in so short a time . . . and by the industry of his people, he is beginning to draw back yeerly some benefit from thence already" (William Alexander, *An Encouragement to Colonies* [London, 1624], p. 25. See also Richard Eburne, *A Plain Pathway to Plantations [1624]*, ed. Louis B. Wright [Ithaca, N.Y., 1962], p. 139).

Baltimore himself suggest impropriety on his governor's part. It is more likely that Wynne's departure was due to reasons of age or illness. In 1628 he spoke of his "wearie and overtoyled life" that had wrought "an unkinde and untimely effect upon my person, and faculties," and described himself as "now full of yeares and travailes."[37]

To replace Wynne, Baltimore chose another soldier, Sir Arthur Aston of Fulham in Middlesex.[38] It is here for the first time that Roman Catholicism appears to have become a factor in Baltimore's handling of his Newfoundland affairs, for Aston was not only a fellow Catholic but had been recommended for the governorship by Father Simon Stock.[39] Aston went to Ferryland in the spring of 1625, bringing with him a pass from the Privy Council "to transporte himselfe into Newfoundlande to provide hawkes and elkes for His Majesty."[40]
It was apparently intended also that a small party of fifteen Catholic settlers 9
should accompany the new governor "so that they might begin to establish the Church there."[41] Whether this came to pass is uncertain;[42] again, transportation might have proved to be a problem.

In this plan Father Simon's hand is much in evidence; the Carmelite priest was determined in his efforts to establish a Catholic presence in Baltimore's settlement and so to secure there for his Church a foothold in British America. When he wrote to inform Rome of Baltimore's conversion to Catholicism, he

---

37. BM, Royal MSS, 17 A LVII, ff. 10^{v}, 7^{v}, and 9.

38. Aston is an enigmatic figure. He was knighted on July 15, 1604, as Sir Arthur Aston of County Stafford (William A. Shaw, *The Knights of England*, 2 vols. [London, 1906], 2: 134). Later the same year he was given a licence for 41 years "to use and sell certain woods used in dyeing" (*Calendar of State Papers, Domestic, James I, 1603-1610* [London, 1857], p. 146). Little is known of his life until 1621, except that he spent time in Russia, when he was chosen to command the 8,000 volunteers which the Polish Ambassador was allowed to levy in England (Thomas Locke to Sir Dudley Carleton, April 23, 1621, *Calendar of State Papers, Domestic, James I, 1619-1623* [London, 1858], p. 249). This adventure landed him in trouble, for the Russian Ambassador was soon complaining to the English government of Aston's "several plots and practizes against the State of Russia discovered since his coming from thence." An order was issued for his immediate return to England, where he would receive "condeigne punishment." Sir Arthur proved very unrepentant, however, for on June 6, 1622, he was imprisoned in the Marshalseas for his "indecent behaviour" before the Russian Ambassador. Nevertheless, the Privy Council did not seem to take a too serious view of the whole situation, for his punishment was simply that in future he not serve the King of Poland or any other prince against Russia, and he was released from prison within a fortnight (*Acts of the Privy Council of England, 1621-23* [London, 1932], pp. 180–81, 244, 246, 252). After leaving Baltimore's service, he was engaged in the Duke of Buckingham's campaign in France in the autumn of 1627 and was killed in the retreat from the Isle of Rhé, October 29, 1627 (*Calendar of State Papers, Domestic, Charles I, Addenda: 1625-1649*, [London, 1897], p. 237). His widow was awarded a pension of £50 a year for life (*Calendar of State Papers, Domestic, Charles I, 1627-1628* [London, 1858], p. 525 [January 22, 1628]). His son, also Sir Arthur, was the Royalist governor of Oxford and commanded the forces opposing Cromwell at Drogheda in the Irish campaign of 1649.

39. "L'insula del quale ho scritto . . . da tanto gusto a quel cavaliero amico mio, che alla prima vera andavana la: che ci ha firmato la: et ho procurato che sia governatore di essa" (Letter of Stock to [Ingoli], October 30, 1625, S. Cong. P.F., S.O.C.G., 101, f. 27).

40. *Acts of the Privy Council of England, 1625-1626* (London, 1934), p. 20. The pass was issued on April 5, 1625.

41. " . . . ad novam Insulam Avalloniam, . . . alios quindecim catholicos profecturos esse, ut ibi ecclam. fundare incipiant" (S. Cong. P.F., *Acta*, 3, f. 218^{v}). The reference is to the minutes of the Congregation of May 2, 1625, reporting a letter received from Father Stock.

42. A report to Rome from the English Carmelites later the same year said that the only Catholics then in Newfoundland were Baltimore's agents (Relazione . . . ," S. Cong. P.F., S.R.C., America Cent., 1, f. 4^{v}). This report, however, need not be considered totally reliable. It is also possible that the small group referred to went out with Aston to manage Baltimore's affairs.

was eager to obtain formal approval for the establishment of a mission to Avalon. According to the proceedings of the Propaganda, Father Simon related that for this purpose Baltimore had requested priests of the Carmelite order "whom he would lead out with him to preach the Gospel to the heathens living there, and to thwart the English heretics who have already reached the said Island, lest they infect the people of those parts with heresey."[43] The minutes show that the Congregation of the Propaganda appreciated the significance of this request, for they issued an immediate order for the dispatch to Avalon of suitable Carmelite missionaries, or if these should be unavailable, Jesuits instead.[44]

"Many Catholic friends of mine will go there to live, if we had religious who would go with them," Father Simon told Rome.[45] What Father Simon really
10 envisaged for his Avalon, however, was not simply clergy to care for local needs, but a grand missionary design. Baltimore's settlement would be a missionary outpost halfway between England and the rest of the American colonies, to which priests could venture forth both to convert the Indians and to offset the increasing Puritan presence. Further still, the Carmelite was convinced of the existence of a Northwest Passage. Catholic missionaries established on the shores of Newfoundland would be in a strategic position to take advantage of this easier route to China, the Philippines, and the Indies, and could thus bolster the Church's missions already lodged in these parts.[46]

This alliance between colonization and evangelization was not a dream peculiar to Father Simon. In the early years of the seventeenth century many other Englishmen shared his vision of Newfoundland as England's chief asset in the New World, and this vision included the island's role as a cornerstone of Christianity. As Richard Whitbourne put it, "It is not a thing impossible, but that by meanes of those slender beginnings which may be made in New-found-land, all the regions neere adjoining thereunto, may in time bee fitly converted to the true worship of God."[47] In 1621 the king went so far as to command Whitbourne's book to be sent to every parish church in England, so as to better encourage the plantation in Newfoundland. Richard Eburne, too, a clergyman, argued along the same lines as did Whitbourne. He wrote of Newfoundland's importance to the conversion of America and set forth the doctrine that "our proper and principal end of plantations is, or should be, the enlargement of Christ's church on earth and the publishing of his Gospel to the sons of men."[48] Eburne spoke of going to plant there himself. Declarations such as these when

43. "Eundemque virum religiosos postulasse, quos secum illuc duceret ad predicandum Evangelium populo gentili ibi degenti, et ad impediendos Anglos Hereticos, qui iam ad dictam Insulam penetrarunt, ne Heresi populum ptum. inficerent" (S. Cong. P.F., *Acta*, 3, f. 208^{v} [Congregation of March 22, 1625]).

44. *Ibid.*

45. "Molti catolici amici mei anderanno per vivere la si havessimo religiosi a proposito per andare con loro" (Stock to [Ingoli], December 5, 1625, S. Cong. P.F., S.O.C.G., 101, f. 29).

46. See, for example, Stock to [Ingoli], March 7, 1626, S. Cong. P.F., S.O.C.G., 101, f. 17^{r}, and *Acta*, 3, f. 245–45^{v} (Congregation of July 21, 1625).

47. Whitbourne, *Discourse and Discovery*, p. 15. (The Royal Proclamation is printed at the beginning of the 1624 edition.)

48. Eburne, *Plain Pathway to Plantations*, p. 8. See also pp. 137 and 152–53. Eburne included a second dedicatory epistle to Calvert (p. 71). Edward Wynne struck the same note (BM, Royal MSS, 17 A LVII, ff. 31-31^{v}). On this whole matter see Wright, *Religion and Empire*, especially pp. 134–49.

combined with the Puritan migration to New England would certainly have created a climate for Father Simon's conviction as to the immediate importance of planting Newfoundland with Catholic settlers and missionaries and so denying it to Protestantism as a base.

The priest was no less in step with his times in suggesting the strategic relationship between Newfoundland and the supposed Northwest Passage. Both Whitbourne and Vaughan, for example, also mention this in their consideration of the island.[49] In any case, Father Simon was certainly taken seriously in Rome, which constantly pressed him for details as to the Passage, and directives went out from the Propaganda that the several religious orders should be encouraged to send missionaries to America, because of the possibility of easy transit from there to China and the East.[50]

In the end, Father Simon's plans for Newfoundland faltered only because the 11
few English Carmelites were unequal to the task. They simply had not the manpower for such a mission. One man, Father Elias of Jesus (Edward Bradshaw), actually did come to England from Flanders in the summer of 1625 for the purpose of going to Newfoundland. Father Elias, however, was soon afflicted by the terrible plague which then swept England, and his departure had to be postponed. Father Simon thought that in any event the faculties granted to his colleague were quite insufficient for a mission so far removed from the English bishop.[51] There were other obstacles to contend with as well. The Carmelite Vicar-Provincial for England, Father Bede (John Hiccocks), was dubious about the whole business. He reported to Rome that opposition from Protestants already in the colony would make the mission "completely unprofitable."[52] The immediate question of Father Elias's going, however, was resolved by another agency: in December he was arrested and several months later was deported from England.[53] By 1626 Father Simon alone was available to go to Newfoundland; two of his four fellow Carmelites were imprisoned, the other two ill.[54] Yet despite his advocacy of the mission, he was not prepared to set out under existing circumstances. His work in England would have to be abandoned, he said, for there was no one to replace him, and he felt that no priest should be obliged to travel alone to the New World. He told Rome that to go 2,000 miles without priestly company would be to risk losing his own soul; further, his present faculties would hardly allow him even to say Mass overseas.[55] He was disappointed that despite the Propaganda's directives and promises, sufficient missionaries were not made available; another spring had

49. Whitbourne, *Discourse and Discovery*, p. 16, and Vaughan, *Golden Fleece*, pt. III, pp. 41-47. Father Simon, of course, might well have been influenced by such accounts.
50. S. Cong. P.F., *Acta*, 3, f. 245-45^{v} (Congregation of July 21, 1625). See also *ibid.*, f. 284-84^{v} (Congregation of October 11, 1625).
51. Stock to [Ingoli], October 30, 1625, and December 5, 1625, S. Cong. P.F., S.O.C.G., 101, f. 27 and f. 29. On Father Elias, see Zimmerman, *Carmel in England*, pp. 95-107.
52. "Et anco quando vi andassero religiosi nostri, . . . gl' l'eretici s'opporranno, e se vi sarà alcun Cattolico non solo non potrà aiutare à ciò, mà averà che fare à conservare sestesso: . . . questa Missione debba essere del tutta infruttuosa" ("Relazione . . . ," S. Cong. P.F., S.R.C., America Cent., 1, ff. 4^{v}-5).
53. See Zimmerman, *Carmel in England*, p. 101.
54. Stock to [Ingoli], April 22, 1626, S. Cong. P.F., S.O.C.G., 101, f. 16^{v}.
55. *Ibid.*

come and gone, he complained that year, and still nothing concrete had happened.[56]

For Baltimore, too, this period saw slow progress. Like Wynne, Sir Arthur Aston seems to have been favorably impressed by Newfoundland, for Father Simon reported that the governor had written "marvellous things of that island and of the abundance of fish, an incredible thing. The natives are few and of a gentle nature, causing no harm to strangers, although they are all heathen."[57] Whether Aston was as effective a governor as was Wynne is another matter. Much less is known about the period of his supervision of the colony. Practically the only explicit comment, in fact, comes from the pen of Vaughan:

> 12 Sir Francis Tanfield, and Sir Arthur Aston, two generous knights, which to their imortall glory, doe imploy their times in building and manuring that new ground, cannot be spared from their Plantations lest the wild Boares breake into their Gardens.[58]

As a soldier, Aston apparently was well able to deal with the "wild Boares," the "piraticall rovers" who in the 1620s threatened the young Newfoundland settlements. There is evidence for doubting, however, that his general handling of affairs was equally competent. A letter of Baltimore indicates that Sir Arthur was still connected with the Ferryland colony in the spring of 1627; the proprietor wrote that Aston, who was then in England, was delayed from returning to Newfoundland only by the lack of a warrant releasing his ships from the wartime ban.[59] However, Aston ceased to be governor sometime that same year and was killed in October while serving with Buckingham's forces in France. It is not improbable that the governor's retirement and Baltimore's voyage to Newfoundland during the summer of 1627 were related. Baltimore appears to have been much preoccupied by the management of his business there when he determined that a personal inspection of his province could be postponed no longer. As he confided to his friend Wentworth, he was finally journeying to a place he had long wished to visit, but had only now the opportunity. However, it may well have been Aston's administration which prompted him to add: "It imports me more than in Curiosity only to see [it]; for I must either go and settle it in a better Order than it is, or else give it over

56. Stock to [Ingoli], March 7, 1626, S. Cong. P.F., S.O.C.G., 101, f. 17ᵛ.

57. "Et scrive cose maravigliose de quella Insula et dell' abundanza de pesci cose incredibile. L'inhabitanti sono poci, et di naturà benigna, senza fare male alli strangeri, ancorche sono tutti idolatri" (Stock to [Ingoli], October 30, 1625, S. Cong. P.F., S.O.C.G., 101, f. 27).

58. Vaughan, *Golden Fleece*, pt. III, p. 20. These pirates were also referred to as Dunkirkers and were likely French privateers. Pirate activities in this period are also referred to by Wynne (BM, Royal MSS, 17 A LVII, ff. 19ᵛ-20). Tanfield was governor of the nearby colony of Renews, resettled in 1623 under Lord Falkland's patronage. There is reason to suspect that in the case of piracy, Calvert's lack of trouble may have been a case of his using fire to fight fire. He is on record as having sought clemency for the notorious pirate John Nutt, referring to him as "a poore man that hath been ready to doe mee and my associates courtesies in a plantacion wch. we have begunn in Newfoundland, by defending us from others wch. perhapps in the infancy of that worcke might have done us wronge." (Calvert to Secretary Conway, July 28, 1623, *Calendar of State Papers, Domestic, 1623-1625*, pp. 82-83.)

59. Baltimore to Edward Nicholas, April 7, 1627, PRO, CO 1/4, 19. (In the *Calendar of State Papers, Colonial, 1577-1660*, p. 83, this is dated incorrectly as 1626.)

and lose all the Charges I have been at hitherto. . . ."[60] That this was so is supported by words of Robert Hayman, who was in Newfoundland during this period as an agent of the Bristol interests and who wrote in 1628 that Baltimore adventured personally to his plantation "after much injurie done him."[61]

Baltimore's voyage of 1627 also seems to have marked the beginning of concrete efforts to make his new province one in which Catholicism was fully represented. Dr. John Southcote, the archdeacon of the English Roman Catholic bishop, Richard Smith, was conscious enough of the significance of the moment for his Church to record in his notebook for that year: "The first mission into New found land was begun by Mr. Anthony Smith and Mr. Thos. Longville priests of the secular clergy who put to sea the 1 of June and landed there the 23 of July with my lord of Baltimore."[62] The Carmelite mission to Newfoundland
had by then failed to materialize. In fact, these first priests to go to Ferryland 13
belonged to no religious order, but as Southcote noted, were seculars or "seminary priests"; their mission to the island was most likely arranged not by Father Simon but perhaps by Southcote himself, who at that time resided with Lady Aston.[63] Baltimore remained in Newfoundland only for the summer months, and when he returned to England, Father Longville[64] sailed with him.[65] However, his companion, Father Anthony Pole[66] (Smith was an alias),

60. Baltimore to Wentworth, May 21, 1627, *Strafforde's Letters*, 1: 39.
61. This is contained in Hayman's proposals for Newfoundland settlement (BM, Egerton MSS, 2451, 164–169[v]). It is also the version given in a Calvert family document of 1670 recounting their colonizing ventures: "In the yeare 1627, his Lordp. transports him selfe from England to Avalon being dissatisfied wth. the Management of his affaires there" (BM, Sloane MSS, 3662, ff. 24[v]–25).
62. "Note-book of John Southcote, D.D., from 1623–1637," *Catholic Record Society, Miscellanea I* (London, 1905), p. 103. One of the Vatican documents said that the priests who went with Calvert were "Dmus. Antonius Rivers et R. Dmus. Thomas à Longavilla," but the former name is certainly incorrect, at least as regards the voyage of 1627 (S. Cong. P.F., S.O.C.G., 259, f. 2).
63. *Cath. Rec. Soc., Miscellanea I*, p. 98. Father Simon, however, certainly knew of their going and reported this to Rome (see Stock to [Ingoli], June 27, 1628, S. Cong. P.F., S.O.C.G., 102, f. 13).
64. Thomas Longville was born near Stony Stratford, Buckinghamshire, in 1598, of well-to-do Anglican parents, Sir Henry Longville and Elizabeth (daughter of Sir Robert Cotton). However, after his father's death, his mother married Sir William Windsor, a Catholic; after the banishment of his stepfather from England, Thomas became a Catholic and was educated in St. Omer's College in Belgium. He entered the English College in Rome in 1617 and was ordained a priest in 1626, leaving Rome to return to England the following year. In 1632–33 he seems to have acted as an agent for Bishop Richard Smith in the latter's dispute with the Jesuits, for whom Longville had no liking. Little is known of his later life, although there is one report that in 1640 he acted for the English government in the arrest of the Jesuit, Henry Morse (See *Records of the English Province of the Society of Jesus*, ed. Henry Foley, 7 vols. [London, 1880], 4: 284; *Cath. Rec. Soc., Liber Ruber Venerabilis Colegii Anglorum de Urbe* [London, 1940], p. 185; *Cath. Rec. Soc., The Responsa Scholarum of the English College Rome*, 2 vols. [London 1962], 1: 310–11; Joseph Gillow, *Biographical Dictionary of the English Catholics*, 5 vols. [London, 1885–95], 4: 327–28; *Cath. Rec. Soc., Miscellanea I*, p. 103; Philip Hughes, *Rome and the Counter-Reformation in England* [London, 1942], pp. 411–12; Philip Carman, *Henry Morse: Priest of the Plague* [London, 1957], pp. 22–23, 24, 142; Godfrey Anstruther, *The Seminary Priests* [Great Wakering, England, 1975], 1: 202–3).
65. Examination of Erasmus Stourton, October 9, 1628, PRO, CO 1/4, 59.
66. Anthony Pole was born of non-Catholic, middle-class parents in London about 1592, but as a youth he went to Belgium and there became a Catholic. Like Longville, he studied at St. Omer's College. He then went on in 1610 to prepare for the priesthood at the English College at Valladolid in Spain. However, he left there in 1613 to enter the Society of Jesus, which he joined in 1614, probably in Belgium. It is known that he was near the end of his theological course in Liège in 1621, and that by 1623 he was back in England on the Yorkshire mission. At that stage, however, he apparently left the Society and functioned as a secular priest. A warrant for the

stayed behind at Ferryland, thus to become the first Catholic priest to be engaged in a regular ministry in the British territories of America.

Baltimore must have been reasonably content with what he saw at Ferryland in 1627, for soon after his return he made the decision to take up residence there. Royal permission was obtained; in his letter of authorization the king informed Lord Falkland that Baltimore's purpose was to stay there for some time so as to be able to supervise his plantation's growth.[67] In fact, Baltimore's probable intention was to reside in Newfoundland permanently. On this voyage his wife and all his children except Cecil, his eldest, went with him, as did his sons-in-law, William Peasely and Sir Robert Talbot.[68] Before leaving he put his affairs in order. Wentworth was designated as his executor and was reminded of a promise he had made to visit Newfoundland, "though you never meane to
14 performe it." Baltimore's parting words to his old friend reflected this air of finality surrounding his move to the New World. "God send us a happy meeting in heaven," he told Sir Thomas, "and in earth yf it please him."[69]

Baltimore arrived in Newfoundland sometime during June 1628, and brought with him, besides his family and another priest named Hacket, a party of about forty fellow Roman Catholics.[70] The origins of these colonists and their motives for settling in the New World are unknown to us. They probably

---

arrest of a "Father Smith" was issued on January 7, 1626. Pole was imprisoned in the New Prison in London, probably until about December, 1626. He was released at the intervention of Marshal Bassompierre, the Ambassador Extraordinary of France, who came to England to conclude arrangements for the marriage of King Charles I to Henrietta Marie. As part of the marriage arrangement, the Marshal had sought the release of Catholic priests who had been arrested. After Pole's return from Newfoundland, he seems to have gone to France for a short time. During 1630–31 he lived in London at the house of the French Ambassador, where he, again like Longville, had by now become anti-Jesuit and active in the campaign of the secular clergy against them. He is the reputed source of the accusation that the Jesuit, John Gerard, was involved in the Gunpowder Plot. Pole returned to France in 1631, and thereafter the details of his career are unclear. He appears not to have maintained contact with his ecclesiastical superiors, for in April 1633 Southcote wrote to Bishop Richard Smith: "I hear no more of Anthony Smith. God send him to be constant in his purpose." Later there exist only rumors of his scandalous conduct, including one that he continued to exercise his ministry as a priest, despite the fact that he had not one wife but two, one a Protestant and the other a Catholic (See *Cath. Rec. Soc., Registers of the English College at Valladolid, 1589-1862* [London, 1930], pp. 107–8; *Records, English Province, S.J.*, 7: 609; *Cath. Rec. Soc., Miscellanea XII* [London, 1921], p. 179; *Calendar of State Papers, Domestic, Charles I, 1625, 1626*, [London, 1858], p. 215; *Calendar of State Papers, Venetian, 1626-28*, p. 63; A. F. Allison, "John Gerard and the Gunpowder Plot," *Recusant History*, 5 [1959–60]: 43–63).

67. The King to the Lord Deputy, January 19, 1628, *Calendar of State Papers, Ireland, 1625-1632* (London, 1900), p. 305.

68. BM, Sloane MSS, 3662, f. 25.

69. Baltimore to Wentworth, April 17, 1628, *Wentworth Papers*, p. 291.

70. Examination of Erasmus Stourton, October 9, 1628, PRO, CO 1/4, 59. The identity of "Hacket" is something of a mystery. Stourton called him a seminary priest; this accords with Father Simon's account that another secular priest went with Baltimore in 1628 (Stock to [Ingoli], June 27, 1628, S. Cong. P.F., S.O.C.G., 102, f. 13). However, there does not appear to be any English secular priest of the period of this name, or for whom "Hacket" is an alias of record. If a report to Rome of 1630 can be credited, then one of the secular priests who went with Baltimore was "Antonius Rivers" (S. Cong. P.F., S.O.C.G., 259, f. 2). If that were the case, "Hacket" was conceivably Anthony Whitehair, for whom Rivers is a known alias (see Anstruther, *The Seminary Priests*, 2: 354–55). That Hacket was Irish is another possibility, for there were contemporary Irish priests of that name. For example, see Father Paul Raget to Cardinal Sordi, February 12, 1625 (*Historical Manuscripts Commission, Franciscan Manuscripts, Merchant's Quay*, p. 79).

included Yorkshire recusants;[71] it is possible, at least, that some of them might have been Catholics recruited by Baltimore in Ireland, as his voyage to Newfoundland was made from there.[72] Most likely, however, they were English, for Father Simon wrote that they included several of his "spiritual children."[73]

From beginning to end, Baltimore's residence in Newfoundland was marked by misfortune. As early as August he wrote to the king that he was meeting great difficulties in that "remote wilde part of the worlde."[74] As a result of the war with France his colony had been harassed by French men-of-war. To the Duke of Buckingham he put it succintly: "I came to builde, and sett, and sowe, but I am falne to fighting with ffrenchmen."[75] Fortunately, fighting Frenchmen was a problem that Baltimore appeared to handle with relative facility, as he also recorded that he had captured six enemy prize ships at Trepassey.

More of his troubles were of a religious nature. It seems to have been the 15
Baltimore policy in Ferryland, as it later was in Maryland, that Roman Catholics, who in any case were a minority, and members of the Established Church should live side by side. Not only had he his priests, but by this time his colony had also its own resident minister. It is probable that the Reverend Erasmus Stourton, described as "Preacher to the Colony of Ferryland," like Father Pole, arrived there during the summer of 1627.[76] As the Nunciature in Brussels reported to Rome in 1630, not without a somewhat scandalized tone: "As to religious usage, under one and the same roof of Calvert, in one area Mass was said according to the Catholic rite, while in another the heretics carried out their own."[77] Nor would Catholics alone have been shocked by such

71. Apart from family and clergy, only two persons are mentioned by name as being with Baltimore in Newfoundland in 1628-29, Thomas Walker and a man named Gascoyne (*Southampton Record Society, Book of Examinations and Depositions, 1622-1644*, ed. R. C. Anderson, 2 vols. [London, 1931], 2: 38-91). Walker was from Yorkshire, and Gascoigne was a prominent Yorkshire Catholic surname. On his 1627 voyage, Baltimore was accompanied by William Robinson of Tinwell in Rutland, Esq. (R. H[ayman], *Quodlibets, Lately Come Over from New Britainiola, Old Newfoundland* [London, 1628], Book II, p. 36.)

72. The King to the Lord Deputy, January 19, 1628, *Calendar of State Papers, Ireland, 1625-1632*, p. 305. Baltimore had royal permission to depart from any port in Ireland and to take with him whatever he wanted. Previously (December 31, 1627), he had been given a pass by the king to return to Ireland with his family (*Acts of the Privy Council of England. 1627 Sept.-1628 June* [London, 1940], p. 216). This departure from Ireland is confirmed by the family account of 1670 (see BM, Sloane MSS, 3662, f. 25). Baltimore's letter to Wentworth of April 17, 1628, just prior to his departure, was written from his home "Cloghammen" (*Wentworth Papers*, p. 291).

73. "Li dui ch'andavano l'anno passato furano sacerdoti seculari: et questo anno sono andati delli alt[ri] et con loro quello dal quale ho scritto quando prim[o] scrivena . . . da questa missione et altri fig[li]loli mei spirituali, et li ho dato avisso che stabilita poco la missione . . . " (Stock to [Ingoli], June 27, 1628, S. Cong. P.F., S.O.C.G. 102, f. 13). A report to the Vatican in 1630 said that those who went with Baltimore did so to avoid the wave of persecution in England (see S. Cong., P.F., S.O.C.G., 259, f. 2).

74. Baltimore to the king, August 25, 1628, PRO, CO, 1/4, 56.

75. Baltimore to the Duke of Buckingham, August 25, 1628, PRO, CO, 1/4, 57. See also Coakley, "Calvert and Newfoundland," pp. 12-14.

76. Stourton took his M.A. at Cambridge in 1627; however, he seems well acquainted with Newfoundland events of that same summer. For a biography, see *Dictionary of Canadian Biography*, I, s.v. "Stourton, Erasmus."

77. "Quod ad usum religionis attinet sub eodem tecto Calverti, in una parte Missa Cathco. ritu fiebat; in alia haeretici sua peragebant" (S. Cong. P.F., S.O.C.G., 259, f. 2ʳ). Baltimore's "mansion house" has been the subject of some speculation (see J. R. Harper, "In Quest of Lord Baltimore's House at Ferryland," *Canadian Geographical Journal*, 61 [1960]: 106-13). It is

co-existence. Among verses included in the *Quodlibets* addressed from Newfoundland in 1628, Robert Hayman has one dedicated to "my Reverend kind friend, Master Erasmus Sturton, Preacher of the Word of God, and Parson of Ferry Land in the Province of Avalon in Newfound-land":

> No man should be more welcome to this place,
> Than such as you, Angels of *Peace*, and *Grace*;
> As you were sent here by the *Lords* command
> Be you the blest *Apostle* of this Land;
> To Infidels doe you Evangelize,
> Making those that are *rude, sober* and *wise*
> I pray that *Lord* that did you hither send,
> You may our *cursings, swearing, jouring* mend.[78]

16 At the same time Hayman included in his work numerous and vitriolic anti-Catholic lines, among which were the following dedicated "To a Jesuit":

> Art thou a *Jesuite*, yet dost us reproach
> With want of *Faith*, ere Luther did his broach?
> Your race was raiz'd, since he preach'd: your new errors
> Are odious to your owne, to others terrors.
> A hated race, spew'd in these latter dayes
> Though fathers cal'd, y'are the *Popes Roring boyes*.[79]

It is little wonder that with attitudes like these prevalent on both sides, Baltimore's noble experiment could not succeed. Perhaps Baltimore himself did not always honor its spirit, as Stourton was to imply later. Perhaps, on the other hand, as "Parson of Ferryland," Stourton was genuinely shocked by the open practice of Roman Catholicism there in defiance of English law. It may have been instead that the colony's patron and its preacher clashed over matters other than religious; Baltimore said vaguely that the minister had been "banished the Colony for his misdeedes."[80] Whatever the reasons, shortly after Stourton arrived back in England in September 1628 he swore out a deposition roundly denouncing the profession of Popery at Ferryland:

> About the 23rd of July last these twelve months the Lord of Baltamore arrived in Newfoundland and brought with him two seminary priestes one of them called Longvyll and the other called Anthony Smith which sayd Longvyll returned againe for England with the sayd Lord and afterwarde in this June *1628* my Lord

---

pictured in a manner relatively close to Wynne's description of it in an inset on Auguste Fitzhugh's map of Newfoundland (1693; British Museum Add. 5415 [30]), although the siting of it is obviously fanciful. Its location is likely shown with accuracy on a plan of Ferryland drawn by James Yonge in 1663, where it is described as Lady Kirke's (*Journal of James Yonge, 1647-1721, Plymouth Surgeon*, ed. F. L. N. Poynter [London, 1963], plate facing p. 81). Although it is clear from Yonge's map that the present shoreline is somewhat different from that of the seventeenth century, the house is close to the position which Harper posits for it. It is very possible that Baltimore's house was levelled by the French in their destruction of Ferryland in 1696 (See *Calendar of State Papers, Colonial, America and the West Indies, 1696-1697*, p. 427).

78. Hayman, *Quodlibets*, Bk. II, p. 102. Hayman was then governor of the plantation of Bristol's Hope (Harbour Grace) in Conception Bay, first settled in 1618.

79. *Ibid.*, Bk. II, p. 11.

80. Baltimore to the king, August 19, 1629, PRO, CO, 1/5, 27.

> of Baltamore arrived there agayne and brought with him one other seminary prieste whose name is Hacket with the number of forty papistes or thereaboute where the sayd Hacket and Smith every Sunday say the Masse and doe profess all other the ceremonies of the Church of Rome in the ample manner as tis used in Spayne. And this deponent hath seene them at Masse and knoweth that the childe of one William Poole a Protestant was baptized according to the orders and customs of the Church of Rome by the procurment of the sayd Lord of Baltamore contrary to the will of the sayd Poole to which childe the said Lord was a witness."[81]

Stourton's charges could have proved damaging to Baltimore's fortunes. They were referred by the king to the Privy Council, and Baltimore took them seriously enough to file a formal defense with that body. To the king he
contented himself with writing that "those who go about to supplant and 17
destroy me are persons notoriously lewd and wicked. Such a one is that audacious man who . . . did the last wynter . . . raise a false and slanderous report of me at Plymmouth."[82] (Elsewhere Baltimore referred to his accuser as "that knave, Stourton."[83]) Lord Baltimore feared especially that these reports might harm his chances of obtaining a new grant of land in Virginia, but this proved not to be the case, and in fact, the Council seems not to have acted upon them.

From the apparent inhospitality of land and climate, however, and not from religion, came Baltimore's greatest trials in Newfoundland. The winter of 1628–29 began early. Baltimore described it as lasting from mid-October to mid-May; he said that both land and sea were so frozen the greater part of the time as not to be penetrable.[84] Adequate provisioning may well have been wanting, for as early as February a request had reached the Privy Council from Baltimore asking permission, "in regard of the scarsetie of corne" in Newfoundland, to export thither of "14 lasts of Wheate, and the lyke quantitie of Maulte for the releefe of those of that Plantacion."[85] Baltimore reported later that his house had been a hospital all winter; of his hundred settlers, as many as fifty, including himself, had been sick at one time, apparently from scurvy, and that nine or ten had died.[86]

---

81. Examination of Erasmus Stourton, October 9, 1628, PRO, CO, 1/4, 59. The document also notes that Stourton was chaplain to Lord Anglesea, Christopher Villiers, and had gone to attend on the Privy Council. In the later legal dispute between the Calvert and Kirke families over the claim to Ferryland, a William Poole, who had been in Ferryland in Baltimore's time there, but who was then resident in Renews and aged 60, testified that he favored the Kirkes, "by reason Sr. David is a protestant and my Lord of Boltomore a Papist" (Deposition of William Poole, August 24, 1652, in Lewis D. Sisco, "Testimony taken in Newfoundland in 1652," *Canadian Historical Review*, 9 (1928): 246).

82. Baltimore to the king, August 19, 1629, PRO, CO, 1/5, 27. Unfortunately, Baltimore's defense addressed to the Privy Council does not appear to be extant.

83. Baltimore to Sir Francis Cottington, August 18, 1629, in Lawrence C. Wroth, "Tobacco or Codfish: Lord Baltimore makes his Choice," *Bulletin of the New York Public Library*, 58 (1954): 527.

84. Baltimore to the king, August 19, 1629, PRO, CO, 1/5, 27.

85. *Acts of the Privy Council of England. 1628 July–1629 April* (London, 1958), p. 343 (February 25, 1629).

86. Baltimore to the king, August 19, 1629, PRO, CO, 1/5, 27. It was Sir William Vaughan who declared the illness to have been scurvy (*Newlanders Cure*, pt. I, p. 67).

"In this part of the worlde crosses and miseryes is my portion." So Baltimore summarized his residence in Newfoundland, to which he referred as "this wofull country, where wth. one intolerable wynter we were almost undone. It is not to bee expressed with my pen what wee have endured."[87] Baltimore could take no more. At the end of the summer of 1629 he sailed southwards for Virginia and sought from the king a grant of land there with the same palatine privileges as he had for his province of Avalon.[88]

Even in departure from Ferryland Baltimore and his settlers were not free of religious troubles. Although his colony in Newfoundland was not abandoned (Baltimore left it under the command of an agent named Hoyle[89]), it seems that all the Catholic colonists, at least, left there simultaneously with their patron.[90] Some of them went with Baltimore and his wife to Virginia, where
18 John Pott, the governor, refused to receive them as planters, since "being of the Romish religion" they would not take the requisite oaths.[91]

---

87. Baltimore to Sir Francis Cottington, August 18, 1629, Wroth, "Tobacco or Codfish," p. 527. It is not uncommonly suggested that it was the choice of Ferryland in particular which led to Baltimore's misfortune and that had his settlement been in a less exposed harbor, he would not have suffered such ill effects. In fact, Vaughan affirmed that this was Calvert's own thinking at the time of his original purchase and that for this reason Calvert himself was insistent upon the inclusion in the purchase of the more sheltered harbor of Aquaforte (about two miles south), in addition to Ferryland. Vaughan said that Calvert was persuaded by some "who had more experience of Fishing than of Wintering" to build at Ferryland instead, "the coldest harbour in the Land" (Vaughan, *Newlanders Cure*, pt. I, p. 68). However, even as late as 1628, Wynne, who had spent at least three winters at Ferryland, recorded his impressions of the Newfoundland winters as being variable, but not hard, one with "scarce anie Ice or Snowe at all." He singled out Ferryland as being pleasant in summer "but bleake in winter," yet still suggested it as one of the three principal harbors for Newfoundland settlement (with St. John's and Trinity) (See BM, Royal MSS, 17 A LVII, ff. 18 and 21^{v}). It is probable that in addition to its merits as a fishing station, Wynne found Ferryland attractive because of its good and easily defended harbor and especially the availability there of large pasture lands. In fact, Baltimore's troubles seem not to have come so much from his choice of site as from what must have been, from his description, an uncharacteristically hard winter, coupled with inadequate supplies and a consequently poor diet, which led to illness. Immediately afterwards, Vaughan could write, "Let me intreate you to conceive charitably of our New-Land Plantation, which by one hard Winter, among many more tolerable, is likely to suffer" (*Newlander's Cure*, pt. I, Epistle Dedicatory [unpaginated]).

88. Baltimore to the king, August 19, 1629, PRO, CO, 1/5, 27. This is surely Baltimore's initial request for land in Virginia, and the memorial concerning this from Baltimore to Secretary Dorchester (undated), PRO, CO, 1/4, 62, is certainly incorrectly dated in the State Papers as December 1628. It was probably written instead in February 1630 (See Mr. Pory to Rev. Joseph Mead, February 12, 1630, *Court and Times of Charles I*, I, p. 54, and Wroth, "Tobacco or Codfish," p. 530). It is a matter of speculation only whether the king's initial reluctance to give Baltimore the grant in Virginia and his advice to the latter to desist from planting and to return to his native country had anything to do with Stourton's charges (see the king to Baltimore, November 22, 1629, PRO, CO, 1/5, 39).

89. Depositions of John Steephens and William Poole, both August 24, 1652, in Sisco, "Testimony in Newfoundland," pp. 242, 245.

90. Baltimore put the number going with him to Virginia at forty (Baltimore to the king, August 19, 1629, PRO, CO, 1/5, 27). In addition, some of his children, Peasley, and Father Pole are known to have returned to England. In 1639 Sir David Kirke implied that no Catholics remained in Newfoundland. "The ayre of Newfoundland agrees perfectly well with all God's creatures," he wrote, "except Jesuits and Schismatics. A great mortality amongst the former tribe so affrighted my Lord Baltimore that hee utterly deserted the country" (Sir David Kirke to Archbishop Laud, October 4, 1639, PRO, CO, 1/10, 40).

91. Governor John Pott, etc., to the Privy Council, November 30, 1629, PRO, CO, 1/5, 40. See also Rev. Joseph Mead to Sir Martin Stuteville, January 23, 1630, *Court and Times of Charles I*, 1: 53. Apparently Baltimore accepted the oath of allegiance, but refused the oath of supremacy.

Religion, too, ensured that the return of some of Baltimore's more prominent Catholic colonists to England was not uneventful. A complaint was sworn out in Southampton against Father Anthony Pole (Smith), who had smuggled himself into England under the new alias of Gascoyne, on the grounds that he was "a Seminarye Priest and hath exercised that Office."[92] Obviously, Pole's practice of Roman Catholicism at Ferryland had been quite open. Another relator amplified that "hee knoweth the said Smith to bee a popish priest for that hee saw him bury a dead Corps with burning tapers."[93]

The elusive "Smith" escaped the authorities, but they were able to apprehend an unfortunate named Thomas Walker, "heretofore a Minister of the Church of England," of whom it was charged "that hee was now become a Popish Priest, and . . . that in the voyage outwards while the Companie of the said Shipp were at prayers the said Mr. Walker did whoope and make a noyse to the 19
greate disturbance of the said Companie."[94] When examined, Walker confirmed that "Smith" was indeed a Catholic priest, "out of the new prison in London about 2 yeares since released by Mounsieur Bassampeire and that then hee went to the Newfoundland and there he remayned until now of late." Walker, however, utterly denied the charges against himself. He stated that he was indeed an Anglican deacon but emphasized as strongly as he could "that hee is noe priest neither seculer or Reguler nor Jesuite nor Semynarie nor of any order or degree whatsoever by any authoritye derived or pretended to bee derived from the Pope or from the Church or See of Rome."[95] Despite his denials Walker was bound over to appear within the year before a member of the Privy Council in London, and Leonard Calvert and Will "Pasley" [Peasley] were obliged to post a £100 bond on his behalf.[96]

With Baltimore's departure, the hope of a haven for Catholicism in Avalon and the vision of a Newfoundland colony turned landwards rather than to the sea died together. To reckon Baltimore's Newfoundland venture a complete

---

92. Relation of Stephen Baker, September 14, 1629, *Southampton Rec. Soc., Examinations and Depositions, 1622-1644*, 2: 38-39. What happened to the other priests who went with Baltimore to Newfoundland is unknown. Not only is "Hacket" unaccounted for, but Father Simon Stock reported to Rome in 1629 that two Jesuit priests had also gone there that year (Letters of July 2, 1629, and August 9, 1629, S. Cong. P.F., S.O.C.G., 131, ff. 341 and 343^v). These priests may, of course, have gone with Baltimore to Virginia. It is interesting to observe that although the first priests to go with Baltimore to Newfoundland were secular priests, the priests who went to Maryland were Jesuits and that in the violent dispute which in this period raged between the secular clergy and the Jesuits, Baltimore later publicly sided with the Jesuits (See L[ord] B[altimore], *The Answere of a Catholike Lay Gentleman*, which was published in 1631).

93. Relation of William Huntresse, September 14, 1629, *Southampton Rec. Soc., Examinations and Depositions, 1622-1644*, 2: 40.

94. Relation of Steven Day, September 14, 1629, *ibid*. Some of the basis of the charge against Walker seems to be that he was known to have frequented Baltimore's house at Ferryland. Walker acted as Baltimore's agent in seeing that the proprietor received his rightful share of the fish taken by one of the ships. The extent of Baltimore's involvement in fishing activities is unclear.

95. Examination of Thomas Walker, September 14, 1629, *ibid*. Walker was the son of a grazier from Giggleswick in Yorkshire. He had taken his B.A. at Cambridge in 1610–11 and had been ordained a deacon by Dr. Harsnett, Bishop of Chichester (1609–19). One of the same name was later rector of Sudborough, Northants., 1631-33, and Vicar of Leamington Priors from 1633 (see John Peile, *Biographical Register of Christ's College, 1505-1905*, 2 vols. [Cambridge, 1910], 1: 264).

96. Proceedings of September 19, 1629, *Southampton Rec. Soc., Examinations and Depositions, 1622-1644*, 2: 41–42. The outcome of his case does not appear to be recorded.

failure, however, is a mistake. It is often forgotten that his colony at Ferryland, though reduced in numbers and no doubt battered in spirit, remained intact, even after his own departure. In fact, Ferryland (and indeed the whole southeastern region of Newfoundland) can trace its settlement in an unbroken line from Wynne's first establishment in 1621 to the present day. As Baltimore himself feared, though, another was soon to reap the profit of the expensive foundation that he had laid there—in this case Sir David Kirke, who received a Royal patent for Baltimore's lands in 1637.[97]

In the long term, perhaps Baltimore's experiment in Newfoundland can be reckoned as profitable in a much more significant manner. For his religious policies there, so out of step with that time, were a harbinger of the future. Baltimore had shared in sounding the death-knell for the prevailing axiom:
20 "*Cuuis regio eius religio.*" In accepting the practice of more than one expression of Christianity under the same civil government, he had taken one of the first positive steps in the English-speaking world towards recognition of the individual's right freely and openly to profess his religious beliefs. The description of Baltimore's personal convictions in Lloyd's *Worthies* was true also of his public policy: "Though he was a catholick, yet kept he himself sincere and disengaged from all interests; and though a man of great judgment, yet not obstinate in his sentiments, but taking as great a pleasure in hearing others opinions as delivering his own."[98] It was unfortunate that the application of these maxims in Newfoundland was both turbulent and short-lived, and that they were rendered nugatory when the Catholic population departed the island. Baltimore himself died before a new attempt could be made to give effect to them, but the principles he stood for did not. Transplanted by his heirs from Ferryland to Maryland, there they survived, and in a later day flourished.

---

97. With Kirke the patentees were the Marquis of Hamilton, the Earl of Pembroke, and the Earl of Holland (see PRO, CO, 1/9, 76 [November 13, 1637]). Kirke forcibly seized the mansion house in Ferryland from Capt. William Hill, the agent there of the second Lord Baltimore, in 1638. Sir David resided there until the time of his death in 1654. Despite several rounds of litigation and a clear recognition of the Calvert claim from 1661 to 1665, the property seems, in fact, to have remained in the hands of the Kirke family throughout the remainder of the century, ending up by 1708 in the hands of Mary Benger, whose first husband had been Sir David's son, David Kirke (see *Acts of the Privy Council of England, Colonial Series, 1680–1720* [London, 1910], pp. 539–41). The amount spent by Baltimore on the Ferryland plantation has been subject to various estimates, from that of Philip Davies who swore "that the said Sr. George Calvert did expend 12000 ll. as she hath heard the sd. Lord Boltomore speake himselfe" (Examination of Philip Davies, August 24, 1652, in Sisco, "Testimony in Newfoundland," p. 247) to that of £20,000 made by the second Lord Baltimore in 1637 when he asked for protection of the family's rights in Newfoundland (Memorial of Cecil, Lord Baltimore, 1637, PRO, CO, 1/9, 43).

98. Lloyd, *State Worthies*, pp. 750–51.

Maryland's "Time of Troubles": Sources of Political Disorder in Early St. Mary's

RUSSELL R. MENARD

"ALL OF THE SETTLERS IN WHATEVER COLONY," BERNARD BAILYN HAS 21
observed, "presumed a fundamental relationship between social structure and political authority. Drawing on a common medieval heritage, continuing to conceive of society as a hierarchial unit, its parts justly and naturally separated into inferior and superior levels, they assumed that superiority was indivisible; there was not one hierarchy for political matters, another for social purposes."[1] If the settlers of early St. Mary's shared these attitudes, they were not disappointed. There was no confusion over the nature of leadership, no uncertainty about the identity of leaders in the province. The men who held positions of power in the colony's government were the men who dominated the local economy, whose names were distinguished by titles of respect, and who had the benefits of a classical education. Leonard Calvert, Giles Brent, Thomas Cornwallis, John Lewger, John Langford, Thomas Gerard, and William Blount monopolized wealth, education, social position, and political power in early Maryland. Their political authority was but a particular expression of a generalized social authority. As representatives of the upper levels of English society, they were well equipped to create a traditional polity in Maryland, one in which ordinary settlers would defer to the new society's natural leaders.[2]

By placing power in the hands of such men, recent scholarship on colonial politics suggests, Lord Baltimore met an essential requirement of political stability and took an important step toward implementing his vision of a hierarchic, stratified, well-ordered society in early St. Mary's. However, the first decade of Maryland's history was marked by nearly continuous conflict culminating in a complete political collapse in the mid-1640s. Most prominently, Lord Baltimore fought for the survival of his colony against a diverse group of merchants and planters associated with Virginia, a battle that centered on the contest with William Claiborne for control of Kent Island. Calvert also engaged in a long, bitter struggle with the Jesuits over the rights of the Church in Maryland, and fought with other adventurers over constitutional issues, the fur trade, and Indian policy. Religious hostility between Catholics and Protestants also flared up occasionally at St. Mary's. In addition, the colony was plagued by struggles

---

Professor Menard has published numerous articles about early Maryland in this and other historical journals.

MARYLAND HISTORICAL MAGAZINE
VOL. 76, NO. 2, SUMMER 1981

among the gentry for power, profit, and preeminence and between the government and the more ordinary settlers over a variety of issues, particularly Indian policy and taxation. These conflicts were not minor disagreements occurring within an essentially stable political order. Rather, they were disruptive, debilitating struggles that often shook the government to its foundations. At the end of the first decade of settlement, Maryland's survival as a distinct political entity was not assured.

Why was the polity so fragile? Why were political struggles so intense, so disruptive of daily life? What made the anarchy of the mid-1640s possible? These are difficult questions and fully satisfying answers are perhaps unobtainable. However, such questions do suggest useful lines of inquiry that can reveal much about the social basis of politics, the nature of political legitimacy, and the sources
22 of tension in a New World community.

Political stability—"the acceptance by society of its political institutions, and of those classes of men or officials who control them"—was rare in the preindustrial West.[3] Even Stuart England with its firmly rooted traditions and relatively stable social structure was racked by violent political strife, revolution, and civil war. Political stability was not the normal social condition; it is not surprising that colonists found it difficult to create "well-ordered" communities, that it took time for stable government to emerge along the Chesapeake.

The newness of the society militated against political stability in early St. Mary's. Men previously unknown to each other found themselves thrown together in a colony, forced to organize a community and maintain social discipline in a strange environment. Their experience as Englishmen guided their actions. They had long traditions and firmly established customs that governed relations among men to draw upon. In the main, that experience served them well; it accounts for much of the success they did attain. Paradoxically, however, in certain respects their experience was not well suited to the tasks confronting them.

In seventeenth-century England social behavior was legitimated largely by tradition. The political order, the institutional structure, and the rules governing human relationships were seen as timeless: men behaved as their forebears had since time immemorial. It was also a society of rapid change and innovation. Families rose and declined, old institutions were altered and new ones created. But change was not elevated into a positive ideology. Social mobility took place along established lines without undermining the hierarchial organization of society or the deference owed those at the top by those at the bottom. Innovation in institutions and changes in political behavior were justified by the introduction of precedents and by appeals to a more perfect past.[4]

Marylanders may have expected to order their lives in a traditional fashion, but it proved difficult to transplant traditionally sanctioned institutions to a colony. To do so they had to make a series of conscious decisions about a complex pattern of relationships that could be taken for granted in England. They had to agree on what traditional behavior constituted; they had to erect old institutions anew in an unfamiliar setting. Tradition, in short, had to be interpreted. Small wonder the colonists soon fell to arguing.

The need to interpret and transplant tradition led to a vast expansion of the role of government in society.[5] What had evolved gradually over centuries in

England had to be created almost overnight in Maryland. In the issues they considered, the Assemblies of the first decade were more like constitutional conventions than simple legislative meetings. Issues as fundamental to daily life as the organization and administration of justice, church-state relations, the sources of law, the system of inheritance, debtor-creditor relations, land policy, the regulation of tobacco production, and relations with the Indians were discussed and voted upon. Indeed, the very structure of government, particularly the powers of the Assembly and the rights of the proprietor, became the subject of contention. The stakes were high and the issues hotly contested.[6]

It was necessary that the settlers of early St. Mary's work together if the process of creating a well-ordered society was to succeed. Without widespread agreement it was nearly impossible to implement decisions, for the Governor and Council possessed only a limited ability to enforce unpopular policy. Perhaps it 23
was in recognition of the need for cooperation that several of the early Assemblies were opened to attendance by all resident freemen. Those institutions, procedures, and policies on which there was general consensus worked effectively. The method of adjudicating debtor-creditor relations, for example, a crucial matter in an economy that relied heavily on credit, operated without serious problem, as did the systems of land distribution and probate. On other matters, such as tax assessment and collection and Indian policy, disagreements among the settlers made the enforcement of decisions difficult.[7]

Religious differences among the settlers of early St. Mary's helped make cooperation elusive. However, relations between Protestant and Catholic *within* the colony were surprisingly smooth during the first decade. Protestants, who made up about three-fourths of the population, may have resented Jesuit successes in converting "heretics" and Catholic domination of the government, but their resentment seldom surfaced before the middle 1640s.[8] There were a few minor incidents, occasional incendiary rumors (that the Jesuits wished the Indians success in "cutting off virginea," for example), and some rash statements, but none of these disrupted public life in the colony. The government acted with vigor and intelligence to contain potential conflict, particularly to insure that the rights of Protestants were not violated.[9] Essentially, however, they were engaged in a holding action. The government suppressed conflict but did nothing to encourage cooperation except insofar as the fair treatment of Protestants in St. Mary's served to demonstrate that Catholics could be trusted with power. Eventually, teaching by example did have some success, but it was a slow process, far from complete in the 1640s. Protestant-Catholic conflict remained a potentially disruptive force in Maryland politics at the end of the first decade.[10]

Relative harmony between Protestant and Catholic did not mean an absence of religious conflict, however, for there was a serious division among Maryland Catholics. Although Lord Baltimore did not have a fully developed position on toleration and church-state relations in the 1630s, he was clearly in the tradition of spiritual or sectarian Catholicism, emphasizing the private aspects of his faith and rejecting the temporal claims of the Church.[11] The Jesuits, on the other hand, perhaps more firmly than any other group of English Catholics, still upheld the exclusive, churchly pretensions of the Counter-Reformation. A bitter conflict ensued—more bitter because neither side realized at first the extent of their disagreement and both felt betrayed—as the differences between Baltimore and the Jesuits gradually emerged in the New World. As a result of the conflict, which produced, incidentally, a debate as sophisticated and far reaching as any conducted in New England, Baltimore, with the help of his Maryland Secretary, John Lewger, brought new precision to his understanding of the proper relationship between church and state.[12]

A full description of the controversy is beyond the scope of this essay, but the source of the conflict and the aims of the contestants can be stated briefly. The Jesuits had no intention of accepting the status of a minority sect without special privileges in a colony governed by Catholics, but that was precisely the role Baltimore planned for them. They had more grandiose hopes for the Church in Maryland, visions of a semi-autonomous Catholic community of English colonists and Indians living on Jesuit-owned manorial estates governed by ecclesiastical
24 courts and exempt from the taxation and much of the jurisdiction of the civil government. Baltimore, infuriated by what he considered "demands of very extravagant priviledges," quashed the vision, in part because it limited his sovereignty, threatened his precarious political position in England, and promised to inflame anti-Catholic sentiment among Protestant colonists, but also because those hopes violated his sense of the role of religion in public life.[13]

The conflict began even before the *Ark* and the *Dove* sailed for Maryland and lasted for more than a decade. Once amicable partners in an effort to serve their shared faith soon became bitter enemies. The Jesuits threatened Baltimore and any official who violated the divine rights of the Church with excommunication, and organized the laity in support of their position. Baltimore countered by threatening expulsion and sending secular priests to the colony.[14] By the early 1640s, all semblance of mutual trust and respect had vanished. The Jesuits, once ardent supporters of the Maryland mission, planned to close it permanently. Calvert accused the order of planning "my destruction," either by organizing the colonists or, failing that, by conspiring with the Indians for an armed attack on the province.[15] The Jesuits finally accepted the role Baltimore insisted upon, apparently deciding that their ministry to the Indians and to English Catholics in the colony was more important than loyalty to their grand design. Calvert need only "give us souls," the Vicar-General wrote in November 1644, "the rest he may take to himself."[16]

Unfortunately for the peace of the colony, the conflict was not an internal matter concerning only Calvert and the priests. Religious affairs in Maryland affected Baltimore's relationships with English officials, London merchants, and Virginia planters. The controversy also touched the lives and interests of lay Catholics associated with the colony, drawing them into conflict with the proprietor and each other. Thomas Cornwallis, for example, the largest investor in the Maryland enterprise, felt Baltimore's policy contrary to "Gods Honor and his Churches right," and threatened to leave the colony rather than "Consent to anything that may not stand with the Good Contiens of a Real Catholick."[17] Even family relationships were strained. The controversy led to "a bitter falling out" between Baltimore and his sister and brother-in-law Peasely and to some harsh words between Cecilius and Leonard Calvert.[18] One writer has suggested that the conflict created a deep party division within Maryland with the Calverts and a few of their clients on one side and most of the first adventurers and the Jesuits on the other.[19] This overstates the case, but the controversy did heighten tensions between Baltimore and the colonists and did have an impact on strictly secular issues.

The problems facing the colonists, aggravated by religious differences, were compounded because disagreements could not be resolved, solutions adopted, or policy determined entirely within Maryland. The proprietor's desires and interests had always to be considered. Baltimore did delegate extensive authority to his brother Leonard, but he retained the ultimate power in his hands. Decisions reached in Maryland were subject to his review and the dissatisfied were not reluctant to appeal. Despite efforts to keep himself well informed, Baltimore long remained insensitive to the special problems presented by life in a new settlement. Even Leonard Calvert complained that his elder brother's proposals contained 25
"many things unsuteable to the peoples good."[20] Baltimore invested the "greatest part" of his wealth in the colony, turning a once substantial inheritance into a "weak fortune."[21] Financial difficulties and his position as Maryland's apologist before sometimes hostile English officials provided him with a perspective that often differed from that of the colonists. Instead of serving as a stabilizing influence, proprietary intervention in provincial affairs was often resented as an unwelcome intrusion. Had affairs in England permitted Baltimore to settle in his plantation, the process of establishing a new colony might have proved less tumultuous.

The ultimate authority in Maryland was possessed by neither the colonists nor the proprietor, but by the Crown. Royal officials seemed little interested in Maryland, but they did create difficulties. Vacillation by the crown was in part responsible for the length of the struggle over Kent Island and the fur trade. The possibility of appeal to Whitehall made it impossible for decisions taken in Maryland to appear final, while the failure of English officials to develop a clear policy toward Chesapeake affairs contributed to the uncertainty of political life in the colony. English political controversies were also carried to the province, particularly with the outbreak of Civil War, where they increased the emotional intensity of local struggles. Political instability in the home country contributed to disruptions in Maryland throughout the seventeenth century.[22]

Marylanders had to adapt traditional English institutions to a new environment without the power to make or enforce basic decisions on policy and procedure. Even under ideal conditions their task would have been difficult; the hostility of the colonists' new neighbors made it awesome. A war with the Susquehannah placed a heavy financial burden on the young settlement, while fear and suspicion of the Indians on the part of many settlers led to a strong, emotional reaction against the rational and relatively peaceful policy urged by the Calverts.[23] The Indians did not pose a serious threat to the colony's survival, but they did increase the difficulty of building an orderly community.

Maryland's English neighbors proved more troublesome. From the 1630s to the 1660s, Baltimore struggled with a diverse group of merchants and planters associated with Virginia for control of his colony. Baltimore eventually won the struggle with the "Virginia interest," although not without first making several concessions to their demands. In the meantime, the question of whether Maryland would remain a separate colony distinct from Virginia remained open. The struggle diverted energy and resources from the task of building a stable community along the Bay and contributed to the general political uncertainty of the colony's early history.

The "Virginia interest," a combination of London merchants and Chesapeake planters, consisted of obscure, ambitious, fiercely competitive men who had risen to power in colonial affairs following the destruction of the Virginia Company and the withdrawal of established London merchants from the tobacco trade. The new merchants were a diverse group. Most were born outside of London, younger sons of the lesser gentry, minor merchants, or prosperous yeomen. Often they worked as small retailers, domestic merchants, sea captains, and planters in Virginia or the West Indies before entering colonial trades. By the 1630s family
26 and business associations were turning these men of varied origins into a self-conscious group capable of collective action both political and commercial.[24]

The line between merchant and planter was thin and often crossed: merchants ran plantations and wealthy, aspiring planters engaged in trade. Recruited from the same mold, both groups consisted of men of undistinguished origins actively engaged in the pursuit of wealth and power. Whether merchant or planter, preeminence in the Chesapeake depended not on inherited wealth, status, or education, but on entrepreneurial talents, the ability to wring wealth out of the colonies. Despite the fiercely competitive character of their enterprises, success required cooperation. The planter needed the merchant's capital and English political connections; the merchant depended upon the planter's experience and influence in the colony. The men who dominated Virginia's political life in the post-Company period through their positions on the Council—William Claiborne, Samuel Mathews, William Tucker, and George Menefie, for example—were closely bound to the leading tobacco merchants—Maurice Thompson, Thomas Stone, William Cloberry, and others—through a complex set of tightly woven business and personal connections. By the 1630s the merchant-councillor faction had become a "nearly irresistable power bloc" in Chesapeake affairs.[25] Virginia, in the words of a contemporary observer, was "wholy depending on the Wills and counsailes of Men of Trade."[26]

The merchant-councillor group was in firm control of the Virginia economy when the Calverts first became interested in Maryland. They had acquired almost unlimited access to land and had assumed direction of the process of growth in the colony. They were in an expansive, optimistic mood and opposed Baltimore's project which would restrict Virginia's growth and their control of the developing Chesapeake economy. The immediate focus of the conflict was Kent Island, a small planting and fur-trading settlement recently established well within the bounds of Lord Baltimore's patent by members of the group led by William Claiborne.[27]

Claiborne, younger son of a minor English merchant, was appointed surveyor for Virginia in 1621, shortly after leaving Pembroke College, Cambridge. He was an ambitious man of considerable abilities and his career advanced rapidly in the New World. By the mid-1620s he had obtained a seat on the Council and the lucrative post of Secretary of State for the colony. He used this newly acquired power to launch a grandiose mercantile venture that would, he planned, dominate the colonial fur and provisions trade from the Chesapeake to Canada. Kent Island, which Claiborne had discovered while on a fur trading expedition in 1627, was to serve as the center of his empire.[28]

Claiborne could not launch a venture of such magnitude alone. He understood the trade, was familiar with the region, and had the necessary influence in Virginia, but he lacked the capital and the political connections in England that the project required. In 1630, he found the support he needed in London among traders to the American colonies. Claiborne would supply the experience and the Chesapeake connections and supervise New World operations. His London partners, William Cloberry, Maurice Thompson, Simon Turgis, and John de la Barre—men already active in the colonial trades—would provide the capital. Cloberry also promised to secure a patent from the crown.[29]

An agreement was signed on May 24, 1631, and Claiborne sailed for Kent Island 27
on the *Africa* with twenty servants and over £1300 in provisions and trading goods on May 28. Despite a disastrous fire in 1631, the new settlement prospered, although not on the scale of Claiborne's initial vision. By 1634, when the *Ark* and the *Dove* landed at St. Mary's, the partnership employed forty-four men on the island in the fur trade and in raising tobacco and provisions. They constituted a formidable barrier to Calvert's control of his newly acquired territory.[30]

No narrative of the intense, occasionally violent struggle between Baltimore and the merchant-councillor alliance need be offered here; an adequate reconstruction of the events has been provided by others.[31] Rather, the focus will be on the strategy Calvert pursued to gain a victory over Claiborne and to integrate the Kent Island settlement into the province of Maryland. Both victory and integration were only temporary, but they reveal the considerable political abilities that enabled Lord Baltimore to survive this struggle and those that followed, and still retain the Maryland proprietorship.

The merchant-councillor connection was powerful, but it was not invulnerable. Calvert's attack focused on three specific weaknesses. In the first place, colonial merchants had not yet attained the power in English politics they would achieve by the middle 1640s. Before the Civil War, Calvert possessed at least equal, perhaps greater, political influence and he used his connections well. Second, the merchants and councillors were closely bound together, but they were not inseparable. In particular, the merchants were more concerned with trade than proprietary rights, while many of the Virginians reversed those priorities. The members of the merchant-councillor group, furthermore, were singularly ambitious men not unwilling to desert a partner in pursuit of their own advantage. Baltimore exploited these characteristics to divide the opposition. Finally, the success of the Kent Island venture depended upon the loyalty of the employees settled there by the partnership, a loyalty that could be undermined. Calvert combined these tactics with a judicious use of force to produce a strategy that proved successful against imposing odds, at least in the short run. Given the precarious foothold he had established in the New World, the short run counted, for each year that he held his patent meant more colonists and a stronger claim.

Both Baltimore and the merchant-planter group knew that their fate would ultimately be decided in England. The merchant-councillors tried first to prevent the grant to Baltimore, then to have it revoked. Failing that, they worked to

obtain a royal charter for Kent, a license to trade in the Chesapeake, or at least an order that Baltimore not interfere with their operation. Calvert, for his part, fought to obtain the patent, then to keep it, to prevent a royal charter or license to the Claiborne–Cloberry group, and to secure an order that they either submit to his government or withdraw from his territory. Whether because of official incompetence, a reluctance to make a decision that would inevitably offend someone, a hope that the parties would reach a compromise on their own, or because the contestants were so evenly matched, the crown vacillated. Proclamations were issued, orders dispatched, and letters written favoring first one side and then the other. Finally, nearly six years after the Maryland patent was issued, on April 4, 1638, the Lords Commissioners for Plantations declared "the Right & Tytle of the Ile of Kent & other places in question to be absolutely belonging
28 to the Lord Baltimore, & that noe plantation or Trade with the Indians ought to be within the precincts of his Pattent without Lycence from him."[32]

Calvert not only used his court connections to obtain a favorable decision on his charter; he also, with the help of his constant ally, Secretary of State Windebank, launched an attack on merchant–councillor control of the Virginia government. Crown endorsement of his patent was critical, but the cooperation, or at least neutrality, of the Virginia government would make the task of establishing a colony much easier. Far from being cooperative, Governor John Harvey pointed out, the Virginia Council intended "no less then the subjection of Maryland."[33]

Harvey was the only official in Virginia friendly to the Calverts when the *Ark* and the *Dove* arrived. Baltimore cultivated Harvey's friendship by obtaining letters of support and encouragement and attempted to place others favorable to Maryland in positions of power in the Virginia government. His first success was a spectacular one. In December 1634, Richard Kemp arrived in the Chesapeake with a commission as Secretary, replacing no less a foe than William Claiborne![34]

In part because he supported Baltimore, Harvey was "thrust out" of office and the colony by the Virginia Council in May 1635. The Council then chose one of its own, Capt. John West, governor pending orders from the crown.[35] At the same time, perhaps realizing that deposing royal governors was risky business, the councillors adopted a more conciliatory attitude toward Maryland. The conflict over Kent and the fur trade had recently erupted in violence. The council made a sincere effort to avoid "further unnatural broiles" by promising the Marylanders "all fayre correspondencie on the behalfe of the Inhabitants of the Ile of Kent untill wee understand his Majesties further pleasure."[36]

The "thrusting out" of Governor Harvey offered Calvert an opportunity to increase his influence in the Virginia government. The merchant–councillor faction had discredited itself in the eyes of royal officials by their rebellion. Baltimore petitioned the crown to summon "the Prime actors in the late Mutenye," John West, Samuel Mathews, John Utie, and William Pierce, to England to answer for their treatment of Harvey. He also asked that Harvey be recommissioned and that his friend Windebank write Harvey's instructions.[37] Most of his requests were granted; by early 1637 Baltimore had attained a dominant influence in Virginia's government. Harvey was again governor and most of the old council—including Claiborne—had been replaced by more pliable men. Richard Kemp was still Secretary, while Jerome Hawley had been appointed Treasurer. Hawley's younger brother, Gabriel, George Reade, brother of Windebank's assistant, George Donne, son of the poet, and Robert Evelin rounded out the Calvert connection. Baltimore even had the audacity to suggest that he be appointed Governor of Virginia! Windebank was to inform the King that, although "Lord Baltimore hath no ambition or affection" for the office, he would accept it out of a sense of duty for a mere £2000 a year.[38]

Baltimore did not retain this influence for long. Harvey was replaced in 1639 and the members of the old council gradually returned to power. But he held it long enough. The merchant-councillor faction's power in the Virginia government was neutralized at a critical point in the struggle; in fact, official Virginia became for a time Calvert's active partner. When Sir Francis Wyatt, the new governor, arrived in 1639, the Claiborne-Cloberry partnership had dissolved in a bitter 29
dispute and Baltimore's authority had been reluctantly accepted by the inhabitants of Kent.

Compared to obtaining a favorable decision on the charter and neutralizing the Virginia government, creating dissension between Cloberry and Claiborne proved easy. Even before the *Ark* and the *Dove* left England, Cloberry, Thompson, De la Barre, and other London merchants approached Calvert without Claiborne's knowledge. They "made somewhat slight of Cap: Clayborne's interest" in the partnership and asked for a grant of Kent Island and a license to trade. Baltimore realized that Claiborne was the central figure in the Kent venture; he lived on the island, understood the fur trade, commanded the loyalty of the settlers, and would make a useful ally. Leonard Calvert was to inform Claiborne of the merchants' approach and also that Baltimore, "lest he might prejudice him by making them any grant," postponed an agreement until he "could truly understand from him, how matters stand between them, and what he would desire of his Lordship." If Claiborne would accept Maryland's sovereignty, Baltimore promised "all the encouragement he cann to proceede" with the development of Kent Island.[39]

The course of the negotiations between the partners and Baltimore is now obscure, but it is clear that Claiborne and the merchants soon became too suspicious of each other to mount an effective opposition. Cloberry failed to send adequate supplies to Kent, while Claiborne refused to render an accounting of the firm's income and expenses. Both entered into independent negotiations with Baltimore and each accused the other of preventing an amicable settlement. Calvert, of course, cultivated their mutual suspicions at each opportunity. Thompson, Turgis, and De la Barre soon dropped out of the venture. They were replaced by David Moorehead and George Evelin, men without the wealth or the political influence of the earlier partners.[40] Evelin, in fact, destroyed the Claiborne-Cloberry partnership once and for all.

Evelin, whose younger brother Robert was one of Calvert's men in the Virginia government, may have reached an agreement with Baltimore before joining the partnership. At least he wasted little time in betraying the firm's interests. Cloberry sent Evelin to Kent in late 1636 to examine the accounts and take over management of the joint-stock. At first, Evelin was "very ernest in speaking severall times against the pretended right of the Marylanders to the said trade and plantacion, and did speake ill language of the Governor of Maryland." However, as soon as Claiborne left for England, Evelin began negotiations with Leonard Calvert. He helped Calvert take the island by force, took a commission as Commander of Kent, persuaded the inhabitants to accept Baltimore's authority, and converted much of the firm's property to his own use. What remained was seized by Governor Calvert. The joint-stock was dead, the partners left to settle their differences in a bitter court fight.[41]

It remained only for Baltimore to convince the Kent Islanders to accept a *fait accompli* and become good citizens of Maryland. This proved difficult. One of Claiborne's most impressive talents was an exceptional ability to command personal loyalty. However, the inhabitants of Kent did have interests of their own. They were not merely followers of Claiborne and employees of the company,
30 but men with families to support, plantations to run, and ambitions to pursue. Leonard Calvert worked intelligently to achieve his brother's goal. He combined a judicious use of force with a general pardon and promises of secure titles and easy terms for land Claiborne had distributed. He recruited some of the island's officials from among Claiborne's supporters, while sending men of more certain loyalty from St. Mary's to live on Kent, hold the critical positions of power, and safeguard his interests. The strategy worked. By 1640, the inhabitants had accepted, albeit reluctantly, the legitimacy of Calvert's claim to the island. They held their land from Baltimore by patent, paid him quit rents on it, participated in the island's government under his commissions, paid taxes, and sent representatives to the Assembly at St. Mary's.[42]

Lord Baltimore had won the first round in the struggle with the "Virginia interest." His patent had been upheld, his opponents had lost their firm grip on Chesapeake affairs and had fallen to fighting among themselves, and the inhabitants of Kent had been integrated into his government. But the victory had been costly, diverting energy and resources away from the process of building an orderly community and contributing to the general climate of political uncertainty. Nor was the victory permanent; Baltimore had won a battle, not a war. Cecilius Calvert had not heard the last from William Claiborne, the London merchants, or the Isle of Kent. They would again pose a threat to Maryland's survival in the near future.

The men who held high office in early Maryland possessed the characteristics traditionally associated with political leadership by Englishmen. They were gentlemen by English standards, distinguished from the majority of settlers by birth, education, and wealth. Despite these qualifications, they contributed to the instability of public life in the province. The gentry of early St. Mary's were men whose opportunities in England were limited because of their religious persuasion and their rank within their families. They were Roman Catholic younger sons with restricted career possibilities at home who saw in Maryland a chance to earn fortunes and make a mark in the world. Lord Baltimore encouraged their ambitions; the promotional campaign raised expectations to unreasonable levels.[43] Maryland did not turn out to be an economic paradise, a fact that created tensions between the proprietor and the provincial gentry and tested the strength of the gentry's commitment to Maryland.

Their commitment proved weak. One of the differences between the gentry

and the majority of settlers lay in their attitude toward migration. For most settlers the decision to emigrate was irrevocable. They lacked the capital to return, while their confinement within a largely oral culture limited their contacts with family and friends in England once they had crossed the Atlantic. For the gentry the decision to migrate was not necessarily permanent. They possessed the capital to return home if they wished. They could also maintain contact with England through letters and mercantile connections. They could, having made their fortune, having had their fill of adventure, or having found that Maryland did not meet their expectations, return home. Many did. The persistence rate among the local gentry was low, a fact with important political consequences.[44] It hindered the emergence of a stable, permanent governing elite whose personal interests were firmly identified with the success of the Maryland adventure. The men who held high office in Maryland were well qualified as individuals, but as 31
a group they were too transient to develop the sense of common purpose, social responsibility, and loyalty toward the province necessary for the creation of a well-governed, orderly community.

The ambitions of the gentry had political consequences similar to their transience. Those who came to Maryland in search of wealth, office, or personal aggrandizement pursued those ends with a single-minded willfulness that disrupted public life and led to conflict among themselves and with the proprietor. Jerome Hawley, for example, deserted Maryland for an office in Virginia, where his ruthless pursuit of wealth heightened hostility toward Roman Catholics in general and Catholic Marylanders in particular. Giles Brent and John Lewger engaged in a bitter, disruptive struggle for political pre-eminence, while Brent tried to use his marriage to an Indian "princess" to carve out a vast landed empire in Maryland that rivaled that of the proprietor. Brent was also accused of using his position as chief judge of Kent for personal profit and then of subverting an expedition against the Indians out of indignation over his removal from the bench. Thomas Greene used a brief term as Governor to advance his personal interests at the expense of the public welfare. Thomas Cornwallis threatened to leave Maryland if his demand for a share of the fur trade was not met, and later resigned his position on the Council because of a disagreement with the Calverts. Thomas Gerard used the opportunity afforded by the collapse of government in the mid-1640s to forcibly collect an outstanding debt. Leonard Calvert almost undermined an expedition against the Susquehannah by insisting that he be exempted from the levy and his servants from the march.[45] Maryland's gentry lacked the cohesiveness, the loyalty to the proprietor, and the interest in the well-being of the province to successfully defend the colony against serious attack.

The ambitions of ordinary settlers contributed to the general instability. Although the pace of property accumulation was too slow for the local gentry, Maryland was "a good poore man's Country" during the middle decades of the seventeenth century.[46] The full social impact of opportunity was not felt until after Ingle's Rebellion. In the early 1640s, Maryland society was clearly divided into dominant and dominated groups. However, signs of a forthcoming social transformation were already in evidence. Men who had arrived without capital were establishing households with ease. Twenty to twenty-five men who arrived

in Maryland as servants or poor free immigrants had become freeholders by 1642, suggesting that manorial lords would soon find it difficult to keep tenants on their estates. One former servant, John Hallowes, had achieved success in the Indian trade and emerged as one of the leading creditors of early St. Mary's. Two men of middling status and limited means, Nicholas Harvey and Richard Gardiner, neither of whom could sign his name, had become Lords of Maryland Manors. Several ordinary settlers had won election to the Assembly or appointment as a justice, militia officer, or sheriff; although none yet wielded great power and most only held office briefly, they were precursors of a time when small planters would play a major role in the government of Maryland. The social structure of early St. Mary's approximated Lord Baltimore's vision of a hierarchic, stratified community, but the dynamic of opportunity was beginning to undermine the "well-
32 ordered" society that migrated to Maryland on the *Ark* and the *Dove*.[47]

Opportunity led to heightened expectations and these, in turn, may have contributed to political disorder. Deference to "natural leaders" in political affairs was the rule in early St. Mary's, but it was not universal. Men who expected improvement would perhaps be unlikely to view the social division between leaders and led as natural or to behave with proper deference toward their social superiors, particularly if religious differences provided ideological justification for their resistance. Ordinary settlers did not always follow the gentry's lead in the Assembly, nor were they reluctant to protest vehemently policies with which they disagreed.[48]

Maryland society possessed several characteristics which perhaps encouraged the disruptive political consequences of social mobility. The age and sex structure of the community and the peculiar shape of households in early St. Mary's may have contributed to political unrest among small planters. Men predominated. There were few women in the society—roughly one for every four men—and even fewer children. Further, most of the women and children were attached to the gentry; the great majority of small planters were childless bachelors. Moreover, they were young: roughly two-thirds of those of working age were under thirty. And they quickly left the initial settlement cluster at St. Mary's City to scatter along the Potomac and Patuxent rivers, often living alone or in households in which all residents were young, unattached males.[49] A young man not yet burdened by family responsibilities could afford the consequences of political assertion more easily than an older man with wife and children to support.[50] The dispersed pattern of settlement, the fragility of the new institutions, and the limited police power at the disposal of proprietary officials made it difficult for the gentry to deal effectively with unrest.

It is perhaps impossible to rank the several factors that contributed to political instability. The political immaturity of the gentry, ambition and opportunity, fundamental issues, sex and age patterns, the structure of households, dispersed settlement arrangements, religious tensions, limited police power, fragile institutions, hostile neighbors, Lord Baltimore's absence, vacillation in Whitehall, English political strife, and the sheer difficulty of the task of constructing a well-ordered community all contributed to political disorder in early St. Mary's. It would be misleading to single out one and call it fundamental, although some—in particular, religious tensions, hostile neighbors, the political immaturity of the gentry, and the awesome character of the task—seem more important than others. The important point is that they reinforced each other, worked together rather than at cross purpose. It is not surprising that the whole structure collapsed into anarchy when Richard Ingle challenged the Maryland political order in early 1645.

By 1644, Maryland's government was on the brink of collapse. Leonard Calvert was in England from April 1643 to September 1644. During his absence, Giles Brent, the acting governor, and John Lewger struggled for pre-eminence in provincial affairs, a contest culminating in Brent's removal of Lewger from the office of Secretary. Maryland suffered some humiliating defeats at the hands of the Indians and many settlers refused to pay taxes or serve on another expedition. The conflict with the Jesuits, brought to a head by Baltimore's effort to suppress
a public chapel, had embroiled the gentry in a bitter legal struggle resulting in 33
the refusal of local officials to serve process, Cornwallis' resignation from office, and Brent's arrest. Further, the government at St. Mary's had begun to lose its hold on Kent. William Claiborne returned to the island in late 1644 to see if he could detach it from Maryland; he nearly succeeded in persuading some of the inhabitants to seize the government. Nor did things improve when Leonard Calvert returned. Calvert found himself almost hopelessly entangled in the chapel affair, in the Brent-Lewger controversy, and in a separate dispute growing out of Brent's recent marriage to Calvert's former ward, the Indian Mary Kitomaquand. Calvert, furthermore, was helpless in the face of growing discontent with proprietary rule at Kent, afraid that anything he did would provoke open rebellion.[51] When Richard Ingle marched on St. Mary's in early 1645, Calvert and the gentry were unable to mount an effective resistance.

Ingle, a veteran ship captain employed by the prominent London tobacco merchants Thomas Allen and Anthony Pennyston, first appeared in St. Mary's in early 1643. Although he was later accused of making inflammatory statements against Charles I, the voyage was uneventful.[52] On his return to the province in early 1644, however, Brent and Lewger arrested him for treason. Despite persistent efforts, Lewger was unable to assemble a jury that would return an indictment. Cornwallis, fearful of offending parliamentary forces, helped Ingle escape, contributing further to the deterioration of relationships among the local gentry. Ingle left Maryland with a threat "to assault & beate downe the dwellin houses of divers the inhabitants of this colony."[53] He returned the next year to make the threat good.

Ingle arrived at St. Mary's in late February 1645. Because Leonard Calvert was exercising "a tyrannical power against the Protestants, and such as adhered to Parliament," Ingle attacked the settlement. The details of what followed are now lost. Baltimore's supporters apparently surrendered without a fight; Leonard Calvert abandoned the province for refuge in Virginia; Ingle and his men ("most rascally fellows of desperate fortune," Lewger called them) burned some houses, looted others, sent several priests to England in chains, and returned to London with Giles Brent and other Catholics as prisoners, leaving the settlement in the hands of a small group of mercenaries recruited in Virginia. For nearly two years Maryland was without government: the colonists were terrorized, their lives disrupted, their estates despoiled. Later, when peace had been restored, settlers who had remained at St. Mary's in 1645 and 1646 referred to the period as the "time of troubles" or "the plundering time."[54]

It is not certain that the leading London tobacco merchants helped plan Ingle's attack on St. Mary's, or even that they knew of his intentions, but when he returned to England they came out in force against Baltimore's charter.[55] They nearly succeeded. While Charles I was in power, Cecilius Calvert's influence at court at least equaled, if it did not surpass, that of the colonial merchants. In the 1630s he could afford to refuse any concessions to their demands. By 1645, however, the London merchants clearly held the upper hand. A new strategy was called for, and Baltimore responded accordingly. The new policy is clearly evident in the appointments of William Stone as governor and of Job Chandler and Edward Gibbons to the Council; it may also have influenced Baltimore's decision
34 to offer refuge to dissenting Virginians and to insist that the Assembly pass legislation to guarantee religious freedom for all Christians. The effect of Calvert's conciliatory attitude was soon evident: by 1650 he could call on several leading London merchants, men who had petitioned against his charter as recently as 1647, to testify in his behalf before parliament.[56]

However, a firm grip on the charter and the full support of the London merchants took Baltimore longer to obtain. He lost control of the government again in the mid-1650s, but he continued to cultivate friendships with the merchants. With the Restoration he again acquired influence at court, while his appointment of men of trade to positions of power and his offer of large land grants on easy terms earned support among London tobacco merchants. By 1660, Baltimore had created a position strong enough to keep the charter in Calvert family hands for thirty years. Cecilius' son Charles, by then Lord Baltimore, lost the charter in the aftermath of the Revolution of 1689, in large part because he had failed to cultivate and maintain the friendship and support of the leading merchants that his father had slowly built up during the middle decades of the century.[57]

Leonard Calvert returned to Maryland in early 1647. Slowly over the next two years, Baltimore's authority was restored. By late 1648, despite Leonard Calvert's recent death, peace and regular government had returned. The colonists deserved a rest. The structured, hierarchic society of early St. Mary's was now a shambles. Most of the gentlemen who had been charged with providing leadership were gone; plundered homes, some burned, others vandalized, and abandoned fields remained as testimony to their failure.

The decline of population provides striking evidence of the destructive impact of Richard Ingle. The anarchy and disruption of daily life that marked the "time of troubles" created an extensive emigration as settlers left Maryland for more tranquil regions. It is not certain how low the population fell in 1645 and 1646, but in 1648, after the arrival of some new immigrants and the return of many who had fled during the "plundering time," there were fewer than 250 people at St. Mary's. Certainty is impossible, but it is likely that the population of St. Mary's fell well below that of the first year of settlement, to perhaps as few as 100, during Ingle's Rebellion.[58] The decline underscores the precarious existence of the original settlement. More than a decade after the charter was granted, the survival of Lord Baltimore's colony as a distinct political entity was by no means certain. Quite literally, Maryland experienced a death crisis in the mid-1640s. The province recovered, but the society that emerged in the 1650s and 1660s bore slight resemblance to the stratified, hierarchic community planned by Lord Baltimore for early St. Mary's.

REFERENCES

1. Bernard Bailyn, "Politics and Social Structure in Virginia," in James Morton Smith, ed., *Seventeenth-Century America: Essays in Colonial History* (Chapel Hill, 1959), p. 91.
2. For biographical data on Maryland's early leaders see Russell R. Menard, "Economy and Society in Early Colonial Maryland" (Ph.D. diss., University of Iowa, 1975), pp. 36–47, 87–89, and Harry Wright Newman, *The Flowering of the Maryland Palatinate* (Washington, D.C., 1961).
3. J.H. Plumb, *The Growth of Political Stability in England, 1675-1725* (Baltimore, 1969), p. 12.
4. I am here relying primarily on Peter Laslett, *The World We Have Lost: England Before the Industrial Age* (New York, 1965).
5. Bernard Bailyn, *The Origins of American Politics* (New York, 1968), pp. 101-104. 35
6. The contests can be followed in William Hand Browne, *et al.*, eds., *Archives of Maryland* (Baltimore, 1883–), I: 1-198, and in the following works dealing with politics in early Maryland: Thomas Hughes, *History of the Society of Jesus in North America, Colonial and Federal*, 4 vols. (London, 1907), I (text): 348–564; Matthew P. Andrews, *The Founding of Maryland* (Baltimore, 1933), pp. 75-93; Bernard C. Steiner, *Maryland During the English Civil Wars*, Johns Hopkins University, *Studies in Historical and Political Science*, vol. XXIV, no. 11-12, vol. XXV, no. 4-5 (Baltimore, 1906–1907); Thomas O'Brien Hanley, *Their Rights and Liberties: The Beginnings of Religious and Political Freedom in Maryland* (Westminister, Md., 1959); John Leeds Bozman, *The History of Maryland, From Its First Settlement in 1633, to the Restoration in 1660*, 2 vols. (Baltimore, 1837), II: 23–291; Charles M. Andrews, *The Colonial Period of American History*, 4 vols. (New Haven, 1936), II: 274–324.
7. For disagreements over Indian policy and tax assessment see, for examples, *Archives of Maryland*, I: 130–131, 139, 140; IV: 173, 176–177, 182–184, 230, 235, 248–249, 250, 260, 360.
8. For the proportion of Protestants in the colony and Jesuit successes in converting them see Hughes, *History of the Society of Jesus*, I (text): 496.
9. *Archives of Maryland*, I: 119; IV: 35–39, 279.
10. For both the limited success of teaching by example and the continuing disruptiveness of Protestant-Catholic conflict see Lois Green Carr and David W. Jordan, *Maryland's Revolution of Government, 1689-1692* (Ithaca, 1974).
11. For Calvert's position on toleration see Menard, "Economy and Society in Early Colonial Maryland," pp. 39–44, and Wilbur K. Jordan, *The Development of Religious Toleration in England from the Convention of the Long Parliament to the Restoration, 1640-1660* (London, 1938), pp. 437–465.
12. The best account of Lord Baltimore's controversy with the Jesuits is, despite its curious partisanship, Hughes, *History of the Society of Jesus*, I (text): 141-564. See also Edwin W. Beitzell, *The Jesuit Missions of St. Mary's County, Maryland* (n.p., 1959), pp. 2-31, and Bradley T. Johnson, *The Foundation of Maryland and the Origin of the Act Concerning Religion*, Maryland Historical Society, *Fund Publication*, no. 18 (Baltimore, 1883).
13. The quotation is Cecilius Calvert's marginal comment on a letter from Thomas Copley, the head of the Jesuit mission in Maryland, to him, Apr. 3, 1638, "Calvert Papers," Maryland Historical Society, *Fund Publications*, no. 28 (Baltimore, 1889), I: 157.
14. Annual Letter of the Society of Jesus, 1642, in Clayton C. Hall, ed., *Narratives of Early Maryland, 1633-1684* (New York, 1910), pp. 139–140; Copley to Cecilius Lord Baltimore, Apr. 3, 1638, *Calvert Papers*, I: 157–169; Cecilius Lord Baltimore to Leonard Calvert, Nov. 21–23, 1642, *ibid.*, 212, 216–221; Hughes, *History of the Society of Jesus*, I (text): 489ff; Rev. George Gage to Rev. Richard Smith, July 21, 1642, *Maryland Historical Magazine* 4 (1909): 262–265.
15. Father Ferdinand Poulton to Mutius Vitelleschi, May 3, 1641, in Hughes, *History of the Society of Jesus*, I (documents): 119–121; Cecilius Lord Baltimore to Leonard Calvert, Nov. 21–23, 1642, *Calvert Papers*, I: 217.
16. Quoted in Hughes, *History of the Society of Jesus*, II (text): 45.
17. Cornwallis to Cecilius Lord Baltimore, Apr. 16, 1638, *Calvert Papers*, I: 172, 176.
18. Cecilius Lord Baltimore to Leonard Calvert, Nov. 21–23, 1642, *Calvert Papers*, I: 217.
19. Hughes, *History of the Society of Jesus*, I (text): 377.
20. Leonard Calvert to Cecilius Lord Baltimore, Apr. 25, 1638, *Calvert Papers*, I: 189.
21. On Baltimore's financial difficulties and Maryland investment see Menard, "Economy and Society in Early Colonial Maryland," pp. 29–30.

22. For the impact of instability in England on Maryland politics see Stephen D. Crow, "'Left at Libertie': The Effects of the English Civil Wars and Interregnum on the American Colonies, 1640–1660" (Ph.D. diss., University of Wisconsin, 1974), and Carr and Jordan, *Maryland's Revolution of Government.*
23. On the reaction see, for examples, *Archives of Maryland,* IV: 173, 176–177, 180–184.
24. Robert P. Brenner, "Commercial Change and Political Conflict: The Merchant Community in Civil War London (Ph.D. diss., Princeton University, 1970), pp. 72–144.
25. *Ibid.*, pp. 94-97; Bailyn, "Politics and Social Structure in Virginia," pp. 90–98.
26. T.H. Breen, ed., "George Donne's 'Virginia Reviewed': A 1638 Plan to Reform Colonial Society," *William and Mary Quarterly,* 3rd Ser., 30 (1973): 460.
27. Brenner, "Commercial Change and Political Conflict," pp. 108–109.
28. For Claiborne's career see Nathaniel C. Hale, *Virginia Venturer: A Historical Biography of William Claiborne, 1600-1677* (Richmond, 1951).
29. Brenner, "Commercial Change and Political Conflict," pp. 97-103. The history of the Kent Island venture can be followed in the case of *Claiborne v. Cloberry,* heard in Admiralty in 1639. Most of the papers from this case are printed in *Maryland Historical Magazine* 26 (1931); 27 (1932); and 28 (1933).

36

30. *Maryland Historical Magazine* 4 (1909): 188-189; 26 (1931): 389; 28 (1933): 183–185; Hale, *Virginia Venturer,* pp. 152–153.
31. Hale, *Virginia Venturer,* pp. 130ff; Brenner, "Commercial Change and Political Conflict," pp. 118–125.
32. *Archives of Maryland,* III: 71–73.
33. Harvey to Secretary Windebank, July 14, 1635, *ibid.*, pp. 38–39.
34. Cecilius Lord Baltimore to Secretary Windebank, Sept. 15, 1634, *ibid.*, pp. 25–26; Windebank to John Harvey, Sept. 18, 1634, *ibid.*, pp. 26–27; Hale, *Virginia Venturer,* p. 192.
35. On the rebellion see J. Mills Thornton, III, "The Thrusting Out of Governor Harvey: A Seventeenth-Century Rebellion," *Virginia Magazine of History and Biography,* 76 (1968): 11–26; Thomas J. Wertenbaker, *Virginia Under the Stuarts, 1607-1688* (Princeton, 1914), pp. 60–84; Richard L. Morton, *Colonial Virginia,* 2 vols. (Chapel Hill, 1960), I: 130–146.
36. Samuel Mathews to Sir John Wolstenholme, May 25, 1635, *Archives of Maryland,* III: 37; John West to the Lords Commissioners for Plantations, Mar. 28, 1636, *ibid.*, III: 41.
37. William N. Sainsbury, et al., eds., *Calendar of State Papers, Colonial Series, America and West Indies* (London, 1860–), I: 217; *Archives of Maryland,* III: 40.
38. Cecilius Lord Baltimore to Secretary Windebank, Feb. 25, 1637, *Archives of Maryland,* III: 41–43; Breen, ed., "George Donne's 'Virginia Reviewed," 449–466; Secretary Windebank to Sir John Harvey, Jan. 10, 1637, *CSP, Col.*, I: 243; George Reade to Robert Reade, Feb. 26, 1638, *ibid.*, p. 264; Richard Kemp to Robert Reade, Mar. 20, 1638, *Virginia Magazine of History and Biography,* 10 (1902): 268–269; Leonard Calvert to Cecilius Lord Baltimore, Apr. 25, 1638, *Calvert Papers,* I: 188–189; Richard Kemp to Cecilius Lord Baltimore, Apr. 25, 1638, *ibid.*, I: 152–155; *CSP, Col.*, I: 244; Morton, *Colonial Virginia,* I: 141–143.
39. "Instructions to the Colonists by Lord Baltimore, 1633," in Hall, ed., *Narratives of Early Maryland,* pp. 18–20.
40. The firm's problems and the negotiations with Baltimore can be followed in the case of *Claiborne v. Cloberry* cited above, note 29, and in Hale, *Virginia Venturer.*
41. *Maryland Historical Magazine* 27 (1932): 26–27, 346–352; 28 (1933): 260–265; *Archives of Maryland,* III: 59; Hale, *Virginia Venturer,* pp. 210–224.
42. Leonard Calvert to Cecilius Lord Baltimore, Apr. 25, 1638, *Calvert Papers,* I: 182–189, 193; *Archives of Maryland,* I: 30–31, 143–144; III: 62–63, 75, 80–82, 88–89, 95, 96; Patents, I: 75–95, Maryland Hall of Records, Annapolis.
43. On the promotional campaign and the adventurers it attracted see Menard, "Economy and Society in Early Colonial Maryland," pp. 24–47, 451–454.
44. *Ibid.*, pp. 70–71.
45. Leonard Calvert to Cecilius Lord Baltimore, Apr. 25, 1638, *Calvert Papers,* I: 188–189; Richard Kemp to Cecilius Lord Baltimore, Apr. 25, 1638, *ibid,* I: 152–155; Elizabeth Rigby, "Maryland's Royal Family," *Maryland Historical Magazine* 29 (1934): 212–223; Thomas Cornwallis to Cecilius Lord Baltimore, Apr. 16, 1638, *Calvert Papers,* I: 176; *Archives of Maryland,* I: 173, 179, 182; III: 148–151, 162–163; IV: 125, 126, 128–129, 133–134, 353, 357, 363–364; X: 33.
46. The phrase appears in *Archives of Maryland,* V: 145.
47. William T. Buchanan, Jr. and Edward F. Heite, "The Hallowes Site: A Seventeenth-Century Yeoman's Cottage in Virginia," *Historical Archaeology* 5 (1971): 38–48; *Archives of Maryland,* I: 2, 3, 28; Patents, I: 62, 129–130; AB&H, 77; Russell R. Menard, "From Servant to Freeholder: Status Mobility and Property Accumulation in Seventeenth-Century Maryland," *William and Mary Quarterly,* 3rd Ser., 30 (1973): 37–64.

48. See, for examples, *Archives of Maryland*, I: 8–9, 22; IV: 173, 176–177, 180–184.
49. Menard, "Economy and Society in Early Colonial Maryland," pp. 73–77.
50. Edmund S. Morgan has assigned such men a central place in the political history of the Chesapeake colonies. "Slavery and Freedom: The American Paradox," *Journal of American History* 59 (1972): 5–29. However, there is reason to believe that he has exaggerated their role. See Carr and Jordan, *Maryland's Revolution of Government*, pp. 192–193, and Lois Green Carr and Russell R. Menard, "Immigration and Opportunity: The Freedom in Early Colonial Maryland," in Thad W. Tate and David L. Ammerman, eds., *The Chesapeake in the Seventeenth Century: Essays on Anglo-American Society* (Chapel Hill, 1979), pp. 235–238.
51. Hale, *Virginia Venturer*, pp. 252–254, 256–259.
52. *Archives of Maryland*, IV: 189, 197, 233–234; Brenner, "Commercial Change and Political Conflict," p. 160.
53. *Archives of Maryland*, III: 165–171; IV: 231–234, 237–241, 245–248, 250, 251, 252, 258, 261.
54. Hale, *Virginia Venturer*, pp. 259–266; Brenner, "Commercial Change and Political Conflict," pp. 159–161. For references to the "time of troubles" and the "plundering time" see *Archives of Maryland*, IV: 357, 362, 395, 396, 421, 422, 423, 424, 427, 429. The quote from Lewger is in Chancery 24/690/14. f. 509, Public Record Office, London.
55. Brenner, "Commercial Change and Political Conflict," pp. 161–162. *37*
56. Leo F. Stock, *Proceedings and Debates of the British Parliaments Respecting North America*, 5 vols. (Washington, D.C., 1924–1941), I: 194–195; *CSP, Col.*, I: 333; Brenner, "Commercial Change and Political Conflict," pp. 545–551.
57. Carr and Jordan, *Maryland's Revolution of Government*.
58. Menard, "Economy and Society in Early Colonial Maryland," pp. 145–146.

II If All The Church Were Maryland

Never the dominant model for church-state relationships, the Maryland tradition of toleration echoes in Catholic thinkers who find native political forms compatible with religious freedom.

ROMAN CATHOLICISM: THE MARYLAND TRADITION

JAMES HENNESEY

ROMAN CATHOLICISM HAS A HISTORICAL IMAGE. Torquemada, Inquisition, St. Bartholomew's Day, Syllabus of Errors. Perhaps you have other favorites. Take your choice. And on the American scene? A student of mine, outlining a series of lectures he plans, put this as a topic-heading: "Roman Catholicism as a religion does not conform to the American pattern: Democracy vs. Autocracy." Paul Blanshard in his heyday could hardly have put it better. So I make a proposal: that a general apprehension of the incompatibility of Roman Catholicism and genuine toleration has considerably skewed, if not totally impeded, appreciation by historians of what happened among the Roman Catholic community in Maryland between 1634 and the American Revolution.

What was the Maryland Roman Catholic tradition of the 17th and 18th centuries? Who colonized Maryland? Why? What did they intend in the matter of religion? Was there a clever hidden design for establishment of Roman Catholicism as the state church? Was there mere opportunism, making the best of the bad deal that it was to be a papist in Stuart England? Or was something else happening, developing? Was there a practice of religious toleration hardly matched elsewhere in its day? Then, was there a theory behind the practice—confused, frequently unarticulated, conditioned by the limits of consciousness of the era—but still discernible? Where do we look for practice and theory? To the successive Calverts, Lords Baltimore, "true and absolute lords" of the proprietary colony? To something indigenous, happening among the gentlemen adventurers in Maryland itself? Was there a broader context? To what extent did painful self-reflection forced upon Roman Catholics by their minority situation in England foster development of practice and theory that can be properly identified as English and then English-American?

First a time-frame. June 20, 1632. King Charles I, in the seventh year of his reign, granted Caecilius Calvert (c. 1605–1675), second Baron of Baltimore, a charter for the proprietary colony of Maryland, a crown fief, a medieval seigniory modeled on the county palatinate of the Bishop of Durham at the 14th century apex of its independence.[1] Baltimore's powers were second only to those of the king himself. His colony was to have a large measure of autonomy. Its laws, by Charter, were to be

> . . . consonant to Reason and be not repugnant or contrary, but (so far as conveniently may be) agreeable to the Laws, Statutes, Customs and Rights of Our Kingdom of England.

The Charter set out the purposes of the colony, political, mercantile,
42 religious. It was founded from "a laudable and pious Zeal for extending the
Christian Religion, and also the Territories of our Empire."

Passengers boarded the 360-ton *Ark* and the 60-ton pinnace *Dove* at London in November, 1633. Before sailing, they took "a corporal oath upon the evangelist" that the king was "the only supreme governor of this realm" and of all his other dominions and countries, "as well as in all spiritual or ecclesiastical things or causes, as temporal. . . ."[2] The Oath of Supremacy. The *Ark* and the *Dove* sailed down the Thames to Cowes on the Isle of Wight, where more passengers boarded. Then, with a gentle east wind filling their sails, they turned into The Solent, only to anchor opposite Yarmouth Castle, near the southwestern tip of the island. It was a critical moment. Let one of the passengers tell the story:

> Here we were received with a cheerful salute of artillery. Yet we were not without apprehension; for the sailors were murmuring among themselves, saying that they were expecting a messenger with letters from London, and from this it seemed that they were contriving to delay us. But God brought their plans to confusion. For that very night, a favorable but strong wind arose; and a French cutter, which had put into the same harbor with us, being forced to set sail, came near running into our pinnace. The latter, therefore, to avoid being run down, having cut away and lost an anchor, set sail without delay; and since it was dangerous to drift about in that place, made haste to get farther out to sea. And so that we might not lose sight of our pinnace, we determined to follow. Thus the designs of the Sailors, who were plotting against us, were frustrated.[3]

The writer was Andrew White. Priest, Jesuit, Roman Catholic. The passengers who boarded at Cowes were Roman Catholics. They thus avoided taking the Oath of Supremacy. If White's apprehensions about the messengers from London were founded, that favorable but strong wind off Yarmouth deserves a footnote in the history of religious toleration in America. Maryland was a unique English colony. Its first ministers of

---

[1] Henry Steele Commager, ed., *Documents of American History* (7th ed.; New York: Appleton-Century-Crofts, 1963), pp. 21–22; John Tracy Ellis (Ed.), *Documents of American Catholic History* (rev. ed.; 2 vols.; Chicago: Henry Regnery, 1967), I, 95–98.

[2] Henry Bettenson, ed., *Documents of the Christian Church* (2nd ed.; London: Oxford, 1970), p. 235.

[3] Translation of White's *Relatio itineris in Marylandiam*, in Ellis, pp. 100–108.

religion were three Jesuits. It began with a substantial Roman Catholic element in its population, including the Governor, the youthful Leonard Calvert, brother of the Proprietor; John Lewger, who was to be Secretary of the Council; and the military captain, Thomas Cornwaleys. The Catholic gentlemen adventurers were never, from the beginning, a majority, but they represented something unique in the entire history of Roman Catholicism in English America: they were the political and social elite of Maryland. Religious attitudes which grew in that context were inevitably nuanced in a way different from attitudes that grew in a community which intruded, as did later and less well endowed immigrants, upon an established and hostile homogeneity. It is a difference that must be kept in
mind as we study the course of events in the land of the Chesapeake and 43
Potomac.

Lord Baltimore's instructions to the colonists, dated November 13, 1633, set the tone that prevailed in Maryland for a decade. The Governor and the Commissioners were to

> . . .be very carefull to preserve unity and peace amongst all the passengers on Shipp-board, and . . . suffer no scandal nor offense to be given to any of the Protestants, whereby any just complaint may heereafter be made, by them, in Virginea or in England, and . . . for that end, . . . cause all Acts of Romane Catholique Religion to be done as privately as may be, and . . . instruct all the Romane Catholiques to be silent upon all occasions of discourse concerning matters of Religion; and . . . treat the Protestants wth as much mildness and favor as Justice will permit. And this to be observed at Land as well as at Sea.[4]

We have here a 17th century Roman Catholic "true and absolute lord" writing to his Roman Catholic officials. Whatever the relative religious population aboard the *Ark* and the *Dove*, the Catholics clearly controlled the expedition. The situation was anomalous. Their charter was from a Protestant king, their mission to extend the territories of his empire. The religious laws of England gave them short shrift. Baltimore's instructions proceed from that context. Peace is to be preserved, disputation outlawed, religious practice kept in low key, Protestants favored so long as justice remained even-handed. The facts are clear enough. The reasons are harder to discern. The Calverts were not philosophers, which later led John Courtney Murray to refer to their thought as "somewhat impenetrable."[5] But I am not so sure.

The story of religious toleration in Maryland is not limited to the Calverts. It has a subsequent American dimension in the acts of the Maryland assembly and afterwards, and a background in the distinctive, independentist, Anglo-American Catholicism which survived well into the 19th century on both sides of the Atlantic until driven back into the subconscious by immigrant inundation in both Britain and the United

---

[4] Ellis, pp. 98–100.

[5] John Courtney Murray, S. J., *We Hold These Truths: Catholic Reflections on the American Proposition* (New York: Sheed and Ward, 1960), p. 59.

States and by a renaissance of ultramontanism projected on to the universal church as a result of essentially continental European preoccupations in the wake of the French and industrial revolutions. The ultramontane understanding of church won the day, paradoxically perhaps more in Anglo-Saxon countries. That does not mean that there were never other understandings, like that born in Maryland.

Charles M. Andrews has written of George Calvert (c. 1580–1632), first Lord Baltimore and original petitioner for the Maryland Charter, that he was no great statesman or civil servant, nor was he an advanced thinker, "excepts perhaps in religious matters." In these he found him tolerant, sympathetic, benevolent rather than liberal, and cited from a letter of
44 Calvert to Thomas Wentworth, later Earl of Strafford:

> . . . .your lordship sees that we Papists want not charity toward you Protestants, whatsoever the less understanding Part of the world thinks of us.[6]

Caecilius Calvert's 1633 instructions are another link in the chain. For Andrews they

> disclose better than any formal document of authority the deeplying desire of the proprietor to erect a colony free from religious animosity and contention in which Roman Catholics and Protestants might live together in peace and harmony.[7]

That the tradition noted by Andrews was so understood in the Calvert family is clear frôm the historical musings in 1675 of Charles, third Lord Baltimore and last of the Catholic proprietors:

> Many there were of this sort of People who declared their Wyllingness to goe and Plant themselves in this Province soe they might have a Generall Toleračcon settled there by a Lawe by which all of all sorts who professed Christianity in Generall might be at Liberty to worshipp God in such Manner as was most agreeable with their respective Judgm^{ts} and Consciences without being subject to any Penaltyes whatsoever for their soe doing. . . . Without complying with these condičons in all probability This Province had never been planted.[8]

The intentions of the Calverts and their execution are one thread in the Maryland story. They will be seen again in conflict with the assembly and with the Jesuits. But perhaps enough has now been said to suggest that the Signer and early constitutional authority James Wilson (1742–1798) was right when he complained of the "ungracious silence" which deprived the Lords Baltimore of recognition for their part in building the American understanding of religious toleration.[9]

The role of the Maryland assembly is important. Its first meeting took place in 1635. Baltimore's broad lawmaking powers were, by Charter, to be exercised

---

[6] Charles M. Andrews, *The Colonial Period of American History, The Settlements*, II (New Haven: Yale, 1936), 280.

[7] Ibid., p. 290.

[8] Ibid., p. 291

[9] James DeWitt Andrews, ed., *Works of James Wilson* (Chicago: Callaghan, 1896), I, 4–5.

of and with the Advice, Assent and Approbation of the Free-Men of the same Province, or of the greater Part of them or of their Delegates or Deputies, whom We will shall be called together for the framing of Laws, when, and as often as Need shall require, by the aforesaid now Baron of Baltimore. . . .[10]

The Free-Men of Maryland proved to be no rubber stamp, and so an element of conflict between them and their distant lord was introduced. Legislative scope, as Thomas O'Brien Hanley has pointed out, was broadened in this corner of the empire just at a time when men still remembered well how James I had prorogued Parliament and when Charles I was refusing to summon it. The Maryland Free-Men not only made provision for regular triennial meetings of their assembly, but they proceeded to make law and shift the functions of advice, assent and 45
approbation from themselves to the Proprietor.

Early legislative and judicial acts touch the religious issue. In 1638 the pirate Thomas Smith was sentenced to death. When officials denied him clerical ministration the assembly granted it and made the right into law. Priests who were property owners were excused from attendance at the assembly, but by law and not in recognition of medieval clerical immunity.[11] When Governor Calvert used a priest to serve a warrant on Indian livestock rustlers the assembly responded with a law prohibiting such confusion of church and state in the future.[12] William Lewis, lay overseer of the Jesuit estates, was fined for proselytizing Protestant indentured servants, and his employers gave him no sympathy. Father Copley instead "blamed much Mr. William Lewis for his contumelious speeches and ill-governed zeal and said it was fit he be punished."[13] Another layman, and member of the Governor's Council, Thomas Gerrard, was fined for taking away the key to the Protestants' chapel on his estate, and the nice touch was added that the fine be held in escrow until the arrival of the first Protestant minister and then used for his maintenance.[14]

The evidence of practical toleration justifies Matthew Page Andrews's judgment that there is in early Maryland history no record of "any persecution or prosecutions of any group, sect, or individual because of any religious belief or lack of belief."[15] Only those who attempted to carry over into America the conflict-practices of the Old World ran foul of the law. That this was understood by contemporaries is attested by no less a

---

[10] Thomas O'Brien Hanley, S. J., *Their Rights and Liberties: The Beginnings of Religious and Political Freedom in Maryland* (Westminster: Newman, 1959), pp. 81–82.

[11] Ibid., pp. 85–86.

[12] Ibid., pp. 87–88.

[13] Ibid., pp. 83–85.

[14] Celestine Joseph Nuesse, *The Social Thought of American Catholics*, 1634–1829 (Washington: Catholic University of America, 1945), p. 21.

[15] Quoted by Joseph Blau, *Cornerstones of Religious Freedom in America* (New York: Harper and Row, 1964), p. 33, from Matthew Page Andrews, *The Founding of Maryland* (New York: Appleton Century, 1933), p. 144.

personage than the Puritan Governor of Massachusetts Bay, John Winthrop, who recorded in his diary:

> The Lord Bartemore being owner of much land near Virginia, being himself a papist, and his brother, Mr. Calvert, the governor there being a papist also, but the colony consisted both of Protestants and papists, he wrote a letter to Captain Gibbons of Boston, and sent him a commission, wherein he made tender of land in Maryland to any of ours that would transport themselves thither, with free liberty of religion, and all other privileges which the place afforded, paying such annual rent as should be agreed upon, but our Captain had no mind to further his desire herein, nor had any of our people temptation that way.[16]

The next phase in the history of religious toleration in Maryland
46 developed in two conflicts: Proprietor versus assembly and Proprietor versus Jesuits. Out of the first conflict emerged an American solution to church-state relationships; out of the second a clearer nuancing of that solution.[17]

Battle was joined between Proprietor and assembly in 1638/9 when Governor Calvert presented the Free-Men with a code of laws drafted and sent over by his brother. The assembly overwhelmingly rejected the code and framed instead a briefer text adopted on February 25. The Maryland emphasis was on parliamentary initiative and laws based on the natural rights and liberties guaranteed by Magna Carta, the citizen's rights as man. Baltimore had proposed that the rights proper to "any natural born subject of England" be limited to Christians. The assembly text read: "The Inhabitants of this Province shall have all their rights and liberties according to the Great Charter of England." It did not distinguish Christians and non-Christians. Only the police power of the state was affirmed: the obligation to keep the peace if religious dissent disturbed it. Slowly but surely, foundations were laid for growth in understanding what freedom of individual conscience means. The code of 1639 was an important building-block in the process.

Seventeenth-century Englishmen were also concerned about the rights of church as moral body. Thomas Cornwaleys, who led the revolt against the Proprietor, put his conviction strongly:

> I will rather sacrifice myself and all I have in defense of God's honor and his Church's right, than willingly consent to anything that may not stand with the conscience of a real Catholic.[18]

In the final text, the Free-Men replaced the Lord Proprietor's assertion of the rights of "Holy Church" with the apparently ungrammatical and certainly ambiguous "Holy Churches within this Province shall have all

---

[16] James K. Hosmer, ed., *Winthrop's Journal* (New York: Charles Scribner's Sons, 1908), II, 150.

[17] Hanley, pp. 79–108.

[18] *Fund Publications*, (37 vols.; Baltimore: Maryland Historical Society, 1867–1901) No. 18 (1889), Calvert Papers, p. 172.

her rights and liberties."[19] What church? Or churches? The code of 1639 does not say. Given the anomalous situation of Maryland within England's empire, the ambiguity seems deliberate. There was recognition of the existence of "Holy Churches" as autonomous entities. Details would become clearer in the conflict with the Jesuits. But the general Maryland picture was that described by 20th century commentator Joseph Blau:

> While this was a proprietary colony under the Roman Catholic Calverts, the largest measure of religious freedom was allowed to the various Church denominations.[20]

Proprietor, assembly and Jesuits did not think alike on all matters. They all did contribute to the development of a climate in which religious freedom
was possible. And it was not done mindlessly. As one of the early Jesuits 47
put it,

> Conversion in matter of religion, if it bee forced, should give little satisfaction to a wise state of the fidelity of such convertites, for those who for worldly respects will breake their faith with God doubtlesse will do it, upon a fit occasion, much sooner with men.[21]

During the crisis of 1638–9, questions were raised with the Proprietor about issues which did not die with the code of 1639.[22] Attempts were made to transfer European solutions, arrived at out of medieval European problems, to problems raised in the new environment of Maryland. Men worried whether Baltimore was not obliged to model himself on continental Catholic sovereigns and grant exemptions to the clergy which had been the product of the medieval European experience and which had, in the minds of some, become normative. The same issue arose in Baltimore's subsequent conflict with the Jesuit missionaries. Thomas Copley succeeded Andrew White as superior of the Jesuit mission. His reaction in the case of William Lewis has already been noted. But his position on other matters was not always consistent with the large-mindedness he displayed then. He objected to omission in the Proprietor's proposed 1637 code of specific clerical immunities: exemption from jurisdiction of civil courts, from payment of quit-rents in corn, from assessments for military purposes, and, for the priests' servants, from military service. Copley was even more distressed that the code adopted in 1639 made no mention of clerical immunities.[23]

Matters came to a head in the dispute over lands given to the Jesuits by

---

[19] For the code drawn up in the Assembly, see William Hand Browne, ed., *Archives of Maryland* (32 vols.; Baltimore: Maryland Historical Society, 1883–1912), I, pp. 82–84; see pp. 41–2 for Lord Baltimore's proposals.

[20] Blau, p. 33.

[21] "Objections answered touching Maryland," in Thomas A. Hughes, S. J., *History of the Society of Jesus in North America, Colonial and Federal* (4 vols.; London: Longmans, Green, 1907–1917), Documents, I, I, 11, and Text, I, 257.

[22] *The Calvert Papers*, Fund Publication No. 28 (Baltimore: Maryland Historical Society, 1889), 157–221.

[23] Ibid., p. 157–169.

Indian chiefs.[24] Baltimore denied that such gifts conferred valid title on the Jesuits, since, by the Maryland Charter, all property was in the Proprietor's gift. Copley reminded him of the excommunication that fell on those who confiscated church property. Baltimore denied that the lands were church property. The dispute was finally resolved in the Proprietor's favor by the General of the Jesuit Order, Mutius Vitelleschi, in a decision which recognized, whether or not it fully understood, that Maryland was not old Europe, and that there were new ways of preserving the rights and liberties of "Holy Church." The Jesuit General ordered his men to claim no rights that they would not have in England, and he warned them:

> 48 I should be very sorry indeed to see the first fruits which are so beautifully developing in the Lord, nipped in their growth by the frost of cupidity.[25]

Historian William Hand Browne has said of Maryland, "Before Claiborne's rebellion we scarcely hear of religious differences."[26] The Puritan Revolution changed that. Disputes with Puritan Captain William Claiborne of Kent Island in the Chesapeake began in 1635 and flared again in 1644–8 when sparks from the English Revolution ignited in Maryland, where the original Anglican and Catholic settlers had been joined by Puritan refugees from Virginia. From 1648–52 the colony had its first Protestant Governor, William Stone, who swore on taking office that

> I will not by my self nor any Person, directly or indirectly trouble molest or discountenance any Person whatsoever in the said Province professing to believe in Jesus Christ and in particular no Roman Catholick for or in respect to his or her Religion nor in his or her free exercise thereof within the said Province so as they be not unfaithful to his said Lordship or molest or Conspire against the Civil Government Established here under him.[27]

The very need for such an oath suggests a change in climate. The Maryland Act Concerning Religion (1649) confirms this. It restated themes from the colony's early tradition when it declared

> . . . whereas the inforceing of the conscience in matters of Religion hath frequently fallen out to be of dangerous Consequence in those commonwealths where it has been practised, And for the more quiett and peaceable government of this Province, and the better to pserve mutuall Love and amity amongst the Inhabitants thereof. Be it therefore . . . enacted . . . that noe person or persons whatsoever within this Province . . . professing to believe in Jesus Christ, shall from henceforth bee any waies troubled, Molested or discountenanced for or in respect of his or her religion nor in the free exercise thereof within this Province . . . nor in any way compelled to the beleife or exercise of any other Religion against his or her consent. . . .[28]

---

[24] Ibid., passim. See also Hughes, Text, I, 390–446, and Gilbert J. Garraghan, S. J., "Catholic Beginnings in Maryland," *Thought*, 9 (1934–35), 5–31; 261–285.

[25] Mutius Vitelleschi, S. J., to Edward Knott, S. J. [Provincial Superior of the English Jesuits], Rome, December 5, 1643, in Hughes, Documents, I, I, 31.

[26] William Hand Browne, *Maryland: the History of a Palatinate* (Boston: Houghton, Mifflin, 1884), p. 70.

[27] Nuesse, p. 22.

[28] *Archives of Maryland*, I, 244–247.

Penalties were set for those who contravened this part of the act—treble damages, fines, whipping and imprisonment. More out of character with Maryland's previous historical development were other passages in the Act which have led historians like Henry Steele Commager to dismiss it as "this so-called toleration act."[29] Those who blasphemed or denied the Trinity or the divinity of Christ were subject to the death penalty and forfeiture to the Proprietor of all lands and goods. Penalties were assessed for contumelious references to other religions. None of this was in the text submitted to the assembly by Baltimore. Nor is it consonant with the whole early approach of that body itself. Rather they are the contribution of the Puritan element in the assembly, echoing acts in the home country like that of May 2, 1648 against heresies and blasphemies.[30] 49

After the Act Concerning Religion, the situation in Maryland worsened. In 1651, Acting Governor Thomas Greene, a Roman Catholic, recognized Charles II as king. Parliament responded by setting up a board of commissioners, among them William Claiborne. Governor Stone was ousted, the assembly repudiated the Proprietor's authority, repealed the act of 1649 and, "in the Name of his highness the Lord Protector," prohibited exercise of the Catholic religion. Persecution of papists followed.[31]

With restoration of Proprietary rule in 1660 the act of 1649 was once more in force, but its age had passed. Commercial change challenged a feudal economy, growing political consciousness reacted against limited suffrage and nepotism in government, an Anglican missionary complained of the activities of Quakers and Catholics and termed the colony "a Sodom of uncleanness and a Pest house of iniquity."[32] Anti-proprietary movements broke into open rebellion in 1676 and 1681. Support for the old ways was strongest among Anglicans and Catholics, but by 1676 they made up only 1/6 and 1/12 of the population respectively. The rest of Maryland's 20,000 settlers were mostly Puritans.

The definitive end of the colony's early period came in 1689, in the aftermath of the Glorious Revolution. The Proprietary government of Charles, third Lord Baltimore, was overthrown, and in 1691 Maryland became a royal province, its Charter annulled. A year later the Church of England was by law established. In 1695 the capital was transferred from Catholic St. Mary's City to Protestant Annapolis. Then followed what John Tracy Ellis has called "a dreary process," a succession of penal laws directed at Roman Catholics.[33] Items included compulsory attendance at

---

[29] Commager, p. 31.

[30] See Andrews, *Colonial Period*, II, 311.

[31] *Maryland Archives*, I, 340–341; Ellis, *Documents*, I, 114–115, and, for an account of the persecution, 115–116.

[32] John Yeo to Archbishop [Gilbert Sheldon] of Canterbury, Pesuxent River, Maryland, May 25, 1676, in *Archives of Maryland*, V, 131.

[33] John Tracy Ellis, *Catholics in Colonial America* (Baltimore: Helicon, 1965), p. 345.

services of the established church, a Test Act the phrasing of which effectively barred Catholic participation in public life, the usual kind of penalties against those who refused the oaths of supremacy and allegiance: they might not bear arms or keep ammunition, or own a horse worth more than £5, they were denied the right to vote, banned from the legal profession, incapable of inheriting or purchasing land. Priests could be banished or sent to prison for life. Informers were paid. The laws were fierce; it is a fact that they were not generally enforced strictly, largely because the Anglican gentry effectively moderated the zeal of the assembly.[34] But the net effect was painful enough that landowners like Charles Carroll, father of the Signer, thought seriously of selling out and
50 moving to French Louisiana.

Queen Anne intervened in 1705, and after that private Catholic worship was allowed, which accounts for chapels still to be seen, built as part of old manor houses. Lord Baltimore continued to support his co-religionists as best he could, but that ended with his death in 1715 and the succession of Benedict, fourth Baron Baltimore, his son and a Protestant. Benedict Calvert died a few weeks after his father and in the same year the proprietorship was restored to his son Charles, so that until the end of the colonial period Maryland's Proprietor was a Protestant.

The general reading of the Maryland Catholics after 1689 is that they developed a quiet introverted religion not unlike the "Garden of the Soul" variety of their English cousins. Thomas O'Brien Hanley contests this: he thinks they were a counter-revolutionary generation, critics of existing institutions and protagonists of the original Maryland freedoms. In Charles Carroll of Carrollton (1737–1832) he has a prime example for his thesis. Carroll came of an Irish family that had prospered despite the penal laws. From 1748–1767 he was educated abroad, in the Jesuit colleges at St. Omers in Flanders, at Bourges and in Paris at the Collège Louis-le-Grand, and then in London at Westminster and the Temple. He was a man of the Enlightenment, introduced by his Jesuit tutors to Locke and Montesquieu.[35] By the 18th century the Jesuit tradition had moved far from its original inspiration in the medieval *respublica christiana* and the dream of European political unity under papal suzerainty. In 1763 young Carroll wrote his father that he regarded "Jesuites [to be] men of Republican principles who will not fail to inspire the youths with a love of liberty,"[36] and his later adversary Daniel Dulaney wrote in exasperation that the English Jesuit college at St. Omers was "the best seminary in the universe of the champions of civil and religious liberty," which, he predicted with dismay, would finally lead to church disestablishment.[37]

---

[34] Thomas O'Brien Hanley, S. J., *Charles Carroll of Carrollton: the Making of a Revolutionary Gentleman* (Washington: Catholic University of America, 1970), pp. 16–21.

[35] Ibid., pp. 32–33.

[36] Ibid., p. 133.

[37] Ibid., p. 254.

Charles Carroll of Carrollton held civil liberty dear. It was "that greatest blessing," and he condemned traditionally acknowledged Catholic countries like France and Spain as bereft of it. But he was no less critical of England and its empire, and he did not, he wrote in 1759, understand how a Catholic could live under English rule because of the lack of religious liberty:

> Now where is the man of spirit that can behold the rod lifted up, tremble, and kiss the hand of him who holds it?[38]

In Carroll's thought, religion and state policy should be separated, though society and religion could not be separated. Religion, he argued, was distorted by its connection with the state: *51*

> Ye savage wars, ye cruel massacres, ye deliberate murders committed by law, under ye sanction of Religion, have not reformed ye morals of men.[39]

To Anglican friends he wrote:

> I could wish, and I believe you wish with me, that ye unhappy differences and disputes on speculative points of Theology had been confined to divines; or that the happiness of mankind had been ye object of these disputes. . . .

and:

> Were an unlimited toleration allowed and men of all sects were to converse freely with each other, their aversion from a difference of religious principles would soon wear away.[40]

The choice of religion was not, however, an indifferent matter to him:

> Do you advise me to quit a false religion, & to any false belief; & this merely to honour and humour the prejudices of fools or to be on a footing with knaves? I have too much sincerity & too much pride to do either, even if filial love did not restran me. . . .
> I am a warm friend of toleration. I execrate ye intolerating thirst of ye Church of Rome, and of other Churches—for she is not singular in that designing.[41]

During his literary debate in 1773 with Daniel Dulaney, Charles Carroll summed up his attitude:

> That the National Religion was in danger under James 2nd from his bigotry and a despotic temper, the dispensing power assumed by him, and every other part of his conduct evince. The nation has a *right* to *resist* and so secure its civil and religious liberties. I am as averse to having religion crammed down people's throats as a proclamation. These are my political principles in which I glory, principles not hastily taken up to serve a turn, but what I have always avowed since I became capable of reflection.[42]

---

[38] Ibid., p. 70.
[39] Ibid., p. 200.
[40] Ibid., pp. 200–201.
[41] Ibid., p. 202.
[42] Kate Mason Rowland, *The Life of Charles Carroll of Carrollton, 1737–1832* (2 vols.; New York: G. P. Putnam's, 1898), I, 126.

Ideas like these are an expanded articulation of the earliest Maryland tradition. In their formulation they were helped by attitudes Carroll assimilated as a student at Jesuit colleges in Europe. And they were not unique to him.

Apropos of the First Catholic Relief Act (1778), Charles Carroll's cousin, the future Bishop John Carroll, wrote to his English fellow ex-Jesuit Charles Plowden:

> I am glad to inform you . . . the fullest and largest system of toleration is adopted in almost all the American states. I am heartily glad to see the same policy beginning to be adopted in England and Ireland; and I cannot help thinking you are indebted to America for this service.[43]

52 Explaining the same situation to a correspondent in Rome in 1783, John Carroll reminded him that Roman Catholics had to make sure that they avoided even the appearance of subservience to a foreign temporal ruler, and that their only concern in regard to the Pope had to be for that which was essential to their religion: "an acknowledgement of the Pope's spiritual supremacy."[44] Three years later, writing as "Pacificus" in the Philadelphia magazine *Columbian*, he again praised the spread of toleration, which he attributed to the "genuine spirit of Christianity:"

> Freedom and independence acquired by the united efforts and cemented with the mingled blood of Protestant and Catholic fellow-citizens, should be equally enjoyed by all.[45]

Plainly, we have not dealt here with a finely worked-out body of political theory. We have seen a development in process. It was a Maryland process which bore fruit in early toleration and in settled and more sophisticated convictions of heirs to the tradition like the two Carrolls. But the process also fitted the larger context of developing Anglo-American Roman Catholic self-understanding in a changing environment which had abandoned the unitary medieval image and replaced it by distinctively Anglo-Saxon pluralism in politics and religion.

Maryland developments had both origins and parallels in the English Catholic scene. In a chapter on "The Catholic Protest," J. W. Allen has studied the English Catholic phenomenon perceptively.[46] Under Elizabeth I, papists were forced to clarify the grounds of their faith. Thomas More, Reginald Pole, John Fackenham, William Allen had all taken the stance that if the church on earth had no one head, there was no church universal.

---

[43] John Carroll to Charles Plowden, February 28, 1779, in Annabelle M. Melville, *John Carroll of Baltimore, Founder of the American Hierarchy* (New York: Charles Scribner's Sons, 1955), p. 55.

[44] John Gilmary Shea, *History of the Catholic Church in the United States*, II, (1763–1815) (Akron: McBride, 1888), 211.

[45] Melville, p. 86.

[46] J. W. Allen, *A History of Political Thought in the Sixteenth Century* (London: Methuen, 1960), pp. 199–209.

They, and those who followed them, believed in a church universal. They could not in conscience accept that any political sovereign had real authority in matters of faith. At the same time, there was among them no one commonly accepted theory on the relationship of papal power and secular rulers. Robert Bellarmine's claims for the papacy sat uneasily with French Gallicans and English cisalpines. There were differences among the English Catholics, particularly between those who remained in the island and those who lived on the Continent. The former tended to be more English, and out of their Englishness and their Catholic allegiance fashioned an independentist stance that hardly fit well with the growing ultramontanism of the Continent. William Watson and the other priests involved in the "stirs at Wisbech" put it strongly when they declared that 53
they were "thoroughly persuaded that Priests of whatever order soever ought not by force of arms to plant or water the Catholic faith,"[47] but even that redoubtable papalist, Robert Parsons, insisted that every man was duty bound to put his personal religion before everything else, and that in matters of conscience sovereigns and laws were incompetent. That these thoughts were part of a development that sharpened modern Anglo-Saxon ideas on freedom of conscience and separation of church and state might well have been incomprehensible to these men—or most others—of the 16th and 17th centuries. But, reflexively or not, patterns were developing in England and in America, where Maryland made its substantial contribution.

The orientation taken by the Maryland Catholics did not die with them, although their successors had to struggle constantly and not always successfully against imposition of norms in church-state relationships born of the European experience and then broadcast as universally applicable. A fuller study of the Maryland tradition theme finds it recurring at regular intervals: in Bishop John England with his diocesan constitution and conventions,[48] in Bishop John Baptist Purcell and his declaration that American Catholics wanted in religious matters only "a free field and no favor,"[49] in the consternation among American bishops at the 1864 Syllabus of Errors[50] and, at the First Vatican Council, in their opposition to pronouncements on church and state and to a definition of papal infallibility.[51] Later generations saw the thought of Isaac Hecker flower among the Americanists of the turn of the century[52] and the decisive

---

[47] Ibid., p. 207.

[48] James Hennesey, S. J., "Councils in America," in *A National Pastoral Council Pro and Con* (Washington: U.S.C.C., 1971), 48–50.

[49] Id., *The First Council of the Vatican: The American Experience* (New York: Herder and Herder, 1963), p. 132.

[50] Id., "The Baltimore Council of 1866: An American Syllabus," *Records of the American Catholic Historical Society of Philadelphia*, 76 (1965), 161–165.

[51] Id., *The First Council of the Vatican*, and, "James A. Corcoran's Mission to Rome: 1868–1869," *Catholic Historical Review*, 48 (1962), 157–181.

[52] Margaret M. Reher, "Pope Leo XIII and Americanism," *Theological Studies*, 34 (1973), 679–689; Thomas E. Wangler, "John Ireland and the Origins of Liberal Catholicism in the

influence of John Courtney Murray in Vatican II's Declaration on Religious Freedom.[53] There was always the darker side, and it shaped the predominant model, but in the United States it has never, since 1634, gone unchallenged by thinkers within the Roman communion who accepted their native political forms as good and who were convinced that they offered a viable way of being Roman Catholic in the world in which they lived.

United States," *Catholic Historical Review*, 56 (1971), 617–629; "John Ireland's Emergence
as a Liberal Catholic and Americanist," *Records of the American Catholic Historical Society
of Philadelphia*, 81 (1970), 67–82; "The Birth of Americanism: 'Westward the Apocalyptic
54 Candlestick,' " *The Harvard Theological Review*, 65 (1972), 415–436; and Gerald P. Fogarty,
S. J., *The Vatican and the Americanist Crisis* (Rome: Pontifical Gregorian University, 1974),
represent a new look at the turn-of-the century situation.

[53] John Courtney Murray, S. J., *The Problem of Religious Freedom* (Westminster: Newman, 1965); Thomas T. Love, *John Courtney Murray: Contemporary Church-State Theory* (Garden City: Doubleday, 1965); Richard J. Regan, S. J., *Conflict and Consensus* (New York: Macmillan, 1967); Donald E. Pelotte, S.S.S., *John Courtney Murray: Theologian in Conflict* (New York: Paulist, 1976).

PROPERTY AND RELIGIOUS LIBERTY IN COLONIAL MARYLAND CATHOLIC THOUGHT

BY

GERALD P. FOGARTY, S.J.*

The historiography of colonial Maryland has frequently reflected 55
denominational bias. Catholic historians have often been defensive of the fact that Catholics in Maryland had a practice of religious toleration.[1] Non-Catholic historians imposed on Maryland the Catholic practice of France or Spain and concluded either that Maryland Catholics had no choice than to develop toleration or that they were in fact intolerant.[2] More recently, historians have shown how Maryland Catholics developed their tradition of religious liberty. James Hennesey has provided a useful overview of the consistency of that colonial tradition up to the Revolution.[3] John D. Krugler has investigated the practical motives behind Lord Baltimore's innovative enterprise to increase his colony's profits by making religion a private matter. He has persuasively argued that Baltimore achieved his purpose by making Maryland "a manor writ large."[4] No one to date, however, has investigated the interrelationship between religious

*Father Fogarty is a professor of religious studies in the University of Virginia. He read an earlier and shorter version of this article on March 3, 1985, as the annual Catholic Daughters of the Americas Lecture at the Catholic University of America, where he was visiting professor from January to May of that year in the chair endowed by the Catholic Daughters for American Catholic history. Publication of this article has been financed by a grant from the same endowment.

[1]John Tracy Ellis, *American Catholicism* (2nd ed.; Chicago, 1969), pp. 26-27, and his *Documents of American Catholic History* (Chicago, 1967), I, 112.

[2]See Sydney E. Ahlstrom, *A Religious History of the American People* (New Haven, 1972), p. 332. Others hold that the policy embodied in the Act of 1649 was intolerant since it excluded non-Christians; see Jacob R. Marcus, *The Colonial American Jew: 1492-1776* (Detroit, 1970), I, 448-449.

[3]James Hennesey, S.J., "Roman Catholicism: The Maryland Tradition," *Thought*, LI (September, 1976), 282-295.

[4]John D. Krugler, "Lord Baltimore, Roman Catholics, and Toleration: Religious Policy in Maryland during the Early Catholic Years, 1634-1649," *Catholic Historical Review*, LXV (January, 1979), 49-75, especially p. 74.

liberty and property rights in Catholic colonial theory. If Maryland was a manor writ large, the manor itself with all its rights was the basis on which Catholics, and especially the Jesuits, would argue for their civil rights and religious liberty. The situation of the Jesuits as property owners in colonial Maryland stood in marked contrast to England where priests usually lived as tutors or schoolmasters in the homes of the gentry and were frequently treated as little more than servants.[5]

This essay will trace the significance of the Catholic Church's never having been established under the Catholic Calverts and of the clergy owning their own property. Property was the basis for civil rights and was
56 the proper sphere of the State's competence. In the Maryland Catholic theory, the State was not to deprive one of civil rights merely because of one's religion. When the State did pass laws against Catholics, they became increasingly conservative and revolutionary. At the time of the Revolution, Maryland Catholics joined the patriotic party, but for conservative reasons. Their thought developed through three phases. First, from 1634 to 1689, they had to work out in practice the relationship between Church and State. Second, from 1690 to 1718, they had to contend with increasing anti-Catholic laws, which forced them to defend their tradition. Father Peter Attwood, S.J., became their spokesman and produced the first written reflection on that tradition. Finally, from the 1750's, Catholics faced even harsher laws, which imposed on them a double tax for their religious beliefs. This time it was Father George Hunter, S.J., who wrote a pamphlet defending the Maryland tradition. The Catholic view that property was the basis for civil rights and that religion was a private matter led them not only to embrace the revolutionary cause, but also, after the adoption of the Constitution, to join the Federalist Party.

I. Development of a Practice: 1634-1689

> Conversion in matter of Religion, if it bee forced, should give little satisfaction to a wise State of the fidelity of such convertites, for those who for worldly respects will breake their faith with God doubtlesse will doe it, upon a fit occasion, much sooner with men; and for voluntary conversions such Lawes [demanding conformity] would be of no use.[6]

In these words did an anonymous pamphleteer defend the innovative proposal of Cecil Calvert, Second Lord Baltimore, to establish a colony with religious liberty. The pamphlet was written either in the early 1630's to

[5]John Bossy, *The English Catholic Community: 1570-1850* (London, 1975), pp. 250-277.

[6]"Objections Answered," in Thomas Hughes, S.J. (ed.), *History of the Society of Jesus in North America: Colonial and Federal* (London, 1908), *Documents*, I-I, 11.

advertise the Maryland colony or in the 1640's to defend Baltimore's practices.[7]

The English Catholics who settled Maryland could no longer remember when Catholicism was the established religion of England, and neither George Calvert nor his son, Cecil, thought that it should be. They and other English Catholics had been loyal to the crown and simply accepted the *de facto* government. In their mind, government should exist only to protect civil rights, which were derived from property, and should not interfere with religion or use it as the basis for the enjoyment of civil rights. They rejected the concept of *cuius regio eius religio.*[8] Unlike the Puritans who escaped from the English penal laws intentionally to establish their own form of intolerance,[9] the Maryland founders denied the right of government to intrude into religion, provided that religious practice was kept a private matter.

Lord Baltimore stated his policy succinctly in the instructions he gave to his brother, Leonard Calvert, the governor, and to his commissioners. He required them to see to it that

> in their voyage to Mary Land they be very carefull to preserve unity and peace amongst all the passengers on Shipp-board, and that they suffer no scandal nor offence to be given to any of the Protestants, whereby any just complaint may heereafter be made, by them, in Virginea or in England, and that for that end, they cause all Acts of Romane Catholique Religion to be done as privately as may be, and that they instruct all the Romane Catholiques to be silent upon all occasions of discourse concerning matters of Religion; and that the said Governor and Commissioners treate the Protestants with as much mildness and favor as Justice will permit. And this is to be observed at Land as well as at Sea. . . .

Upon landing, Baltimore's representatives were to send a messenger, who was a member of the Church of England, to Sir John Harvie, the Governor of Virginia, with King Charles I's charter of Maryland and a personal letter from Baltimore to Harvie. They were likewise to send a Church of England messenger to Captain William Claiborne, a Virginia Councillor and trader who had already established a settlement on Kent Island in the Chesapeake Bay within the territory of Maryland.[10] Religion, then, was to be a private

[7]See Krugler, *op. cit.*, p. 56n. for the arguments for the later date.

[8]*Ibid.*, p. 60. R. J. Lahey, "The Role of Religion in Lord Baltimore's Colonial Enterprise," *Maryland Historical Magazine*, 72 (Winter, 1977), 511. Cf. Thomas O'Brien Hanley, S.J., "Church and State in the Maryland Ordinance of 1639," *Church History*, XXVI (December, 1957), 327-329.

[9]Perry Miller, *Errand into the Wilderness* (New York, 1964), p. 145.

[10]Given in Ellis, *Documents*, pp. 98-99.

matter. Lord Baltimore was so convinced of the value of his bold experiment that he invited Massachusetts Puritans to settle in Maryland and share in full religious liberty.[11]

Calvert's was a novel plan and he may well have been naïve in thinking that others like the Puritans would accept it. But how was the plan to be put into practice? Calvert and his colonists had no precedent on which to build. Like typical Englishmen, they developed their practice first and only in the early eighteenth century did subsequent colonists derive a theory from the early practice. The problem the Maryland founders confronted was to provide religious liberty without making the State secular or hostile to
58 religion. The means they chose was to separate Church and State by separating the spiritual and temporal. Religion was essentially a private matter, an inherent right prior even to the rights which the State might either acknowledge or grant. The State, on the other hand, was to be concerned primarily with the public life of the inhabitants, with the civil rights which were derived from property.

The right to property was a principle of English law worked out during the Middle Ages under the influence of both Anglo-Saxon and ecclesiastical law. The hereditary right to own property and the right to buy and sell it meant the recognition of rights independent of the King's grant or dominion.[12] Early in the seventeenth century, Edward Coke argued that the laws of England were the finest legacy of Englishmen because they safeguarded the right to property. But Robert Persons, S.J., argued that Englishmen had a right even prior to and more ancient than the laws of England, for not all Englishmen owned property. This prior right, he stated, was "their right to Catholic religion." Denying the State's right to determine religion, he declared that no man could give his conscience to the State.[13] A generation

[11] James K. Hosmer (ed.), *Winthrop's Journal* (New York, 1908), II, 150, quoted in Hennesey, "Roman Catholicism: The Maryland Tradition," p. 187.

[12] Donald W. Hanson, *From Kingdom to Commonwealth: The Development of Civic Consciousness in English Political Thought* (Cambridge, Massachusetts, 1970), pp. 54-57.

[13] A Catholicke Devine [Robert Persons], *An Answer to the Fifth Part of Reportes Lately Set Forth by Syr Edward Cooke Knight, the Kinges Attorney General* (n.p., 1606), Vol. 245 of *English Recusant Literature* (London, 1975), p. 16. See also J. W. Allen, *English Political Thought: 1603-1660* (London, 1938), p. 154; J. W. Allen, *A History of Political Thought in the Sixteenth Century* (New York, 1928), pp. 208-209.

Two other strands intertwine to weave the intellectual tradition of English Catholics who settled in Maryland. First, Robert Bellarmine's separation of ecclesiastical and political power with the latter being immediately derived from the people. Second, there is the strong possibility that Thomas More's *Utopia* and, in particular, his emphasis on religious toleration helped shape the attitude of these Catholics. More's great-grandson, Henry, became the

later, the founders of Maryland applied to their new situation the tradition of property rights they had inherited from England. On the basis of those rights, they provided for religious liberty by keeping the spiritual and temporal separate.

Cecil Calvert received the proprietary charter to Maryland in 1632. It gave him the right to make laws with the consent of the freemen of the colony and to establish churches.[14] The former he set out to do, but the latter he did not. Instead he applied to the English Province of the Society of Jesus to send over priests. They came as settlers like any of the laymen. Among the first settlers in 1634 were Fathers Andrew White and John Altham (*alias* Gravenor) and Brother Thomas Gervase. Father Thomas Copley (*alias* Philip Fisher), who became the superior of the Jesuit Mission, arrived in 1636. Like other settlers, they took up land in the new colony in their own names, because mortmain, the right of the Church or a religious order corporately to own property, was not recognized in England or in Maryland. The Jesuits and their legatees, therefore, became property owners.[15]

Treating the clergy like any other settlers had the effect of keeping Church and State separate, for the priests were to receive no public support. The Maryland State was concerned only with settlers; it drew no distinction between the clergy and laity and between Catholics, Anglicans, and dissenters. All were property owners and property was fundamental to all other civil rights.

Maryland's pragmatic approach to the separation of Church and State, however, developed only after tension was resolved between the Jesuits, the settlers, and Lord Baltimore. Each party presented a different line of argument. The Jesuits claimed certain traditional church immunities and rights based on canon law. The occasion for their assertion of this right was their receiving from the Indians the use of land for missionary purposes, which Baltimore claimed was a violation of his exclusive right to grant land.[16] The second line of argument was Lord Baltimore's broad claim to

---

Provincial of the English Jesuits in 1635 and was a principal negotiator with Cecil Calvert in the disputes between the proprietor and the Jesuits. See Thomas O'Brien Hanley, S.J., *Their Rights and Liberties: The Beginnings of Religious and Political Freedom in Maryland* (Westminster, Maryland, 1959), pp. 49-55, and "Church and State," pp. 327-329.

[14]Hughes, *Documents*, I-I, 13-14, and *Text*, I, 257-259.

[15]Joseph Zwinge, S.J., "The Jesuit Farms in Maryland," *Woodstock Letters*, XXXIX (1910), 376; Hughes, *Text*, I, 333-334. See also Edwin Warfield Beitzell, *The Jesuit Missions of St. Mary's County, Maryland* (2nd ed.; Abell, Maryland, 1976), pp. 11-14.

[16]Hughes, *Text*, I, 380-384.

exclusive jurisdiction, both civil and ecclesiastical, which he embodied in his code of laws presented to the assembly of Maryland on January 25, 1638. There his claims were represented by John Lewger, the governor's secretary, who sought to intrude into such ecclesiastical matters as jurisdiction in marriage and disinheriting any woman with a vow of virginity.[17] Baltimore's code occasioned the final line of argument as the settlers demanded that no laws be passed without their consent. They had already broached this question at an assembly in 1635, the records of which are now lost.[18]

This meeting of the assembly provides the initial glimpse of the way in
60 which the clergy and other settlers regarded their roles within the colony. The minutes for the first session recorded the list of all those present and then added: "After were summoned to appeare by vertue of writts to them directed: mr. Thomas Copley, Esq., of St. Maries hundred mr. Andrew White mr. John Altham, gentlemen of the same hundred. Robert Clerke appeared from them & excused their absence by reason of sickness."[19] On the next day, the three Jesuits were again absent and were again summoned, but "Robert Clerke made answere for them that they desired to be excused from giving voices in this Assembly, and [their excuse] was admitted."[20] The priests, though freeholders, claimed an exemption from sitting in the Assembly with other freeholders for two reasons. First, the assembly also acted as a court imposing the death penalty which was forbidden to priests by canon law.[21] Second, they argued for the right corporately to own property as the Church in Maryland, a position which Baltimore was compelled to reject. Lord Baltimore and the Jesuits now entered into a prolonged and tedious debate over the status of the priests and their right to property in the colony.

On April 3, 1638, Copley explained to Lord Baltimore the absence of the Jesuits from the assembly. "It was not fitt that we should be there in person," he wrote, "and our proxis would not be admitted in that manner, as we could send them and therfor as we weare excluded thence, Soe we did not intermeddle with them there."[22] Copley had written Baltimore to

[17]For some of Calvert's proposals which pertained directly to ecclesiastical affairs, see Copley to Lord Baltimore, April 3, 1638, in *The Calvert Papers, Number One* ("Fund Publication No. 28 [Baltimore, 1889]), p. 165, and Hughes, *Documents*, I-I, 170-171.

[18]Charles M. Andrews, *The Colonial Period of American History*, Vol. II: *The Settlements* (New Haven, 1936), p. 300.

[19]*Archives of Maryland* (71 vols.; Baltimore, 1883-1970), I, 2.

[20]*Ibid.*, p. 5.

[21]Hughes, *Text*, I, 380-384.

[22]Copley to Lord Baltimore, April 3, 1638, in *Calvert Papers*, p. 158.

defend the right of the Jesuits to receive land from the Indians. In his argument, he cited the papal bull *In Coena Domini*, issued annually on Holy Thursday, which asserted the right of the Church as a corporate body to own property.[23] The Jesuit was still envisioning Baltimore as a Catholic prince with an obligation to safeguard church rights. Despite their earlier agreement with the proprietor to come as other settlers, the Jesuits were now trying to claim the status they would have enjoyed in a European Catholic State. Baltimore, for his part, seems to have been vague on his precise intentions in regard to the relationship between Church and State.

Part of Baltimore's code called for each manor to set aside 100 acres for glebe land to support pastors. Copley reacted: "If then the intention should 61
be to bind them to be pastors who enjoy it [the glebe land], we must either, by retaining soe much even in our owne land undertake the office of Pastors, or less even in our owne Mannor maintaine Pastors, both whch. to us would be very Inconvenient."[24] Though Copley was arguing from canon law to assert the right of the Church to own property, nevertheless, he was also arguing for the clergy to be independent of public support as well as to be exempt from sitting in the assembly.[25]

Within the assembly, the Jesuits had their supporters for the recognition of church property, notably Captain Thomas Cornwaleys.[26] Even Lord Baltimore's brother, Governor Leonard Calvert, seemed at times to side with them. In 1641, Copley and the other Jesuits officially applied for grants to the land they were already using in accordance with Baltimore's Conditions of Plantation. The governor issued the grants, but received a reprimand for his action from his brother.[27] To safeguard against any possible confiscation, however, the Jesuits had already placed the property in the hands of lay trustees.[28]

The debate continued on both sides of the Atlantic. Both Lord Baltimore and the English Jesuit provincial appealed to Rome. The former succeeded

[23] *Ibid.*, pp. 165-166.

[24] *Ibid.*, p. 165.

[25] The uniqueness of the Maryland tradition can be seen when contrasted with Puritan Massachusetts. In Maryland the clergy were land owners in their own right but refused to sit in the assembly; yet, the Church received the protection of, but no support from, the State. In Massachusetts the clergy could hold office but in fact did not and the Church was both protected and supported by the State; cf. Edmund S. Morgan, ***The Puritan Dilemma: The Story of John Winthrop*** (Boston, 1958), pp. 162-166.

[26] Cornwaleys to Lord Baltimore, April 16, 1638, in ***Calvert Papers***, pp. 171-173.

[27] Lord Baltimore to Leonard Calvert, November 23, 1642, ***ibid.***, pp. 219-220.

[28] Hughes, ***Text.***, I, 484-485.

in having introduced into Maryland two secular priests, only to find them turn against him in regard to the Jesuits' arguments for jurisdiction over strictly ecclesiastical affairs. Ultimately, the dispute was settled with both sides compromising. Baltimore gained recognition that only he could grant land and the right in the future to approve any Jesuit sent to the colony.[29] The Jesuits won the right to own property, but only in their own names and not in the name of the Church or their religious order. They also won certain immunities, traditionally granted the clergy in canon law: exemption from serving in the assembly, from military service, and from the taxation of those parts of their estates used for religious or educational
62 purposes.[30] But they gained these immunities from the civil law of the assembly and not from the canon law on which they had originally based their claims.[31] Maryland's tradition of the separation of Church and State was off to a shaky and acrimonious start, but it would develop from these early precedents.

While the Maryland colonial government was not to establish or support any church, it was still concerned about church rights in other areas. Baltimore had proposed a bill on church immunities in his code of 1638,[32] but the assembly adopted its own law, which read: "Holy Churches [*sic*] within this province shall have all her rights and liberties."[33] It was a vague statement. To which church did "Holy Churches" refer? In 1661, Father Francis Fitzherbert argued that the act had stated nothing about "what Church is there meant." For him, the subsequent act of 1649 had the effect of saying that "every Church professing to believe in" the Trinity "is accounted Holy Church here."[34] Maryland, therefore, made no attempt to distinguish between various Christian churches and establish one, but it acknowledged the "rights and liberties" of each. The colony was not to be secularist.[35] On October 23, 1640, the assembly expanded on its earlier act

[29]*Ibid.*, pp. 534, 544, and *Documents*, I-I, 194-196. For the arguments of Edward Knott, S.J., the English provincial, see *ibid.*, pp. 168-172. For a critical evaluation of Hughes as an historian, particularly in his portrayal of Cecil Calvert, see Robert Emmett Curran, S.J., "From Saints to Secessionists: Thomas Hughes and *The History of the Society of Jesus in North America*," in Nelson H. Minnich, Robert B. Eno, S.S., and Robert F. Trisco (eds.), *Studies in Catholic History in Honor of John Tracy Ellis* (Wilmington, Delaware, 1985), pp. 239-259.

[30]Thomas J. Scharf, *History of Maryland*, Vol. I: *Colonial Period 1600-1770* (Baltimore, 1879), I, 168.

[31]Hanley, *Rights and Liberties*, pp. 85-87.

[32]*Archives of Maryland*, I, 40.

[33]*Ibid.*, p. 82. Though "her" was an ancient form of the third-person plural, possessive pronoun, it seems more likely that this was a grammatical error.

[34]*Archives of Maryland*, XLI, 566-567.

on Church liberties by stating "Holy Church within this Province shall have and enjoy all her Rights liberties and Franchises wholy and without Blemish."[36] But still, it had done nothing to specify which church it meant.

Maryland's assembly also advanced beyond Baltimore's code in providing for the rights and liberties of individuals. The proprietor proposed that all Christian inhabitants of Maryland, except slaves, have all the rights of subjects of England, according to common law or statute.[37] The assembly declared that "the inhabitants of this Province shall have all their rights and liberties according to the great charter of England."[38] The act was a far-reaching acknowledgment of liberty and not merely a grant of toleration. It recognized that Maryland was different from England and that not all parliamentary statutes were binding in the colony.[39] It was to these acts of 1639 that Father Fitzherbert appealed. For him the Act Concerning Religion of 1649 had merely specified what the assembly had meant by "Holy Churches" ten years before. In eighteenth-century Catholic thought, as will be seen, however, the acts of 1639 and 1649 would become conflated and confused.

Maryland's Act Concerning Religion in 1649 was a response to a concrete political crisis in the colony. In 1645, Protestants overthrew Baltimore's government. Two priests fled to Virginia where they died in hiding. White and Copley were taken in chains to England where they were charged with entering the kingdom illegally. No priests remained in Maryland. In 1647, Baltimore regained his rule, and Copley returned to re-establish the mission. Two years later, at the proprietor's request, the assembly passed the Act Concerning Religion. It granted toleration to all who believed in the divinity of Christ and the Trinity. It also imposed severe penalties on those who engaged in public name-calling or blasphemy.[40] Inasmuch as it specified toleration for Christians only, it was more restrictive than the act of 1639.[41] The imposition of penalties, according to Charles M. Andrews, "was an amendment added by the Protestant-Puritan assembly in the colony to accord with the spirit of the act of the Long Parliament of May 2, 1648, punishing heresies and blasphemies."[42]

[35]Cf. Hanley, *Rights and Liberties*, pp. 105-106.
[36]*Archives of Maryland*, I, 96.
[37]*Ibid.*, p. 41.
[38]*Ibid.*, pp. 82-84.
[39]Hanley, *Rights and Liberties*, p. 86.
[40]*Archives of Maryland*, I, 244-247.
[41]Hanley, "Church and State," p. 337.
[42]Andrews, *op. cit.*, II, 310-311.

While the new act was intolerant by comparison with the act of 1639 and represented a step away from Maryland's original recognition of liberty, it sought to avoid the type of civil conflict over religion which led to the overthrow of the proprietary government. It thus granted toleration to all Christians, who, in fact, comprised the majority of the colonists. For Catholics, the act was more tolerant than the laws passed in Virginia and Massachusetts Bay in the 1640's. Even for Jews, Maryland toleration in practice was broader than the letter of the law, for, in the 1660's, under the Calverts, a Jew sat on juries and was given license to trade with the Indians.[43] The new act, however, failed to end religious controversy.

64 In 1652, Commissioners of the Commonwealth from Virginia used the pretext of a boundary dispute to invade Maryland, overthrow Baltimore's government, and proscribe Catholics. In 1654, the Protestant-dominated assembly declared that no Roman Catholics could enjoy the protection of the laws of England or of Maryland. Other Christian dissenters, however, were granted toleration.[44] Fundamentally, the issue at stake was whether Baltimore and Maryland Catholics had property rights. The recognition of those rights by Cromwell himself was another important factor in the development of the Maryland tradition. Essentially a middle-class man, Cromwell defended property rights. His attitude was particularly manifest after he dissolved the Rump Parliament in 1653.[45] In January, 1655, he wrote Richard Bennett, Governor of Virginia, about the invasion of Maryland. "At the request of Lord Baltimore and divers other persons of quality here, who are engaged by great adventures there," he ordered Bennett and those under his authority to cease disturbing the government of Lord Baltimore and the people of Maryland, until he could personally examine the matter.[46] Cromwell referred the case to the Committee for Trade,

[43]Susan R. Falb, "Advice and Ascent: The Development of the Maryland Assembly, 1635-1689" (unpublished Ph.D. dissertation, Department of History, Georgetown University, 1976), p. 297. For the laws in Virginia and Massachusetts Bay against Catholic priests, see Ellis, *Documents*, I, 110-112.

[44]*Archives of Maryland*, I, 340-341. It was during this period that the only recorded case of a Jew being charged with blasphemy occurred. Richard Preston, a Puritan, accused Jacob Lumbrozo of blasphemy in a conversation with Josias Cole, a Quaker; *ibid.*, XLI, 203.

[45]Perez Zagorin, *A History of Political Thought in the English Revolution* (London, 1954), pp. 149ff.

[46]Wilbur Cortez Abbott, *The Writings and Speeches of Oliver Cromwell* (Cambridge, Massachusetts, 1945), III, 570-571.

which, on September 16, 1656, recommended that Baltimore be restored to power and that he sign a treaty with Bennett.[47]

On the strength of Cromwell's recognition, Calvert instructed his governor, Josias Fendall, on October 23, 1656, to see to it "that the Law in the said Province, intitled, An Act concerning Religion and passed heretofore there with his Lordship's Assent whereby all Persons who profess to believe in Iesus Christ have Liberty of Conscience and free Exercise of theyr religion there be duly observed in the said Province."[48] Calvert, therefore, considered the recognition of his proprietary right to Maryland by Cromwell as justification for his reinstatement of the Act of Toleration of 1649.[49]

With Baltimore's restoration, Maryland Catholics reverted to their previous status. From 1660 to 1689, they built most of their few public churches. Many, if not most, were wealthy. Their social status and support of the proprietors, who were growing increasingly imperious, contributed to the lower-class reaction which led to the Maryland version of the Glorious Revolution.[50] In England, the Catholic King James II was overthrown; in Maryland, Baltimore's rule was ended. Maryland became a royal colony. Between 1692 and 1702 laws were passed to establish the Anglican Church.

[47] *Archives of Maryland*, III, 324-325, 333. On very slim evidence, unconfirmed elsewhere, Hughes argued that Cromwell issued Cecil Calvert a new charter, based on the original charter of Charles I, but omitting any allusion to royalty or feudal oaths. Instead, the charter considered Calvert to be a landowner, entitled to exact oaths of fealty from any of his tenants. Had such a charter been granted, however, it would certainly have been later used by crown attorneys against the Calvert claims. See Hughes, *Text*, II, 56, 638-639. For pointing out the difficulties of Hughes' interpretation, I am grateful to Dr. Lois Green Carr.

[48] *Archives of Maryland*, III, 325. Part of Maryland remained in rebellion, however, and Lord Baltimore's government was completely restored throughout the whole colony only on March 20, 1658. This resulted from an agreement he signed on November 30, 1657, with Richard Bennett and the commissioners for the Commonwealth. Included in the agreement was Baltimore's promise "that he will never give his assent to the repeale of a lawe established heeretofore in Maryland by his Lordships Consent & mentioned in the said Report of the Comtee for Trade" guaranteeing freedom of conscience to all Christians. See *ibid.*, p. 334; Scharf, *op. cit.*, p. 229.

[49] Lord Baltimore, however, was not immediately restored to complete control of the colony. Governor Fendall and the lower house of the assembly challenged his authority from February 28, 1659, to December 11, 1660, when Baltimore's brother, Philip Calvert, was sworn in as governor. See Scharf, *op. cit.*, pp. 266-268.

[50] See Michael G. Kammen, "The Causes of the Maryland Revolution of 1689," *Maryland Historical Magazine*, LV (Winter, 1960), 293-333; Lois Green Carr and David William Jordan, *Maryland's Revolution of Government: 1689-1692* (Ithaca, New York, 1974), pp. 1-45. See also Andrews, *op. cit.*, pp. 325-378.

II. Challenge to the Tradition and Peter Attwater's Reflections

After 1690, Catholicism in Maryland became increasingly subject to penal laws, but never to their harsher aspects. When the assembly attempted to pass penal laws similar to those in England, Catholics again articulated their basic rights to property as inextricably woven to their right to religious liberty. Government existed to protect property rights and should not violate them solely on the grounds of religious belief. This argument usually won the support of the Protestant property owners. Whenever the lower house of the assembly passed a law against Catholics, it was usually vetoed or at least modified by the upper house, the wealthier
66 and more propertied body of the assembly.[51] Though convinced of their inalienable rights, Maryland Catholics came increasingly to depend not on the protection of the law, but on the benevolence of the upper house, or the crown, or, after the restoration of proprietary rule in 1715, on the Calvert family. They became counter-revolutionaries, but, as either or all of their benefactors failed them, they began to develop a political theory which transformed them into conservative revolutionaries. Their theory would lead them to embrace the movement for independence and, after the Revolution, the Federalist Party.

Only gradually, however, did the Catholic alliance with the upper house develop, as the colonial government began imposing penal laws. In 1696, for instance, the Governor and his Council, the upper house, questioned whether Catholic priests should be allowed to officiate at marriages and whether Catholic-Protestant marriages should be tolerated, but the assembly decided that the existing laws were sufficient.[52] At the same time, the Governor and Council asked whether Catholics should be disarmed, but the assembly saw no reason.[53] But in the early years of the eighteenth century, the new royal governor, John Seymour, sought to curtail Catholic activity.

In September, 1704, Seymour had brought before him two priests, Robert Brooke, the first native-Maryland priest, and William Hunter, the Jesuit superior. Brooke was charged with saying Mass in the chapel at St. Mary's City during court time and Hunter with having consecrated an altar. Their attorney, Charles Carroll, accompanied them, but he was refused admission. Brooke acknowledged his charge, but invoked the precedent that others had said Mass at St. Mary's before him. Hunter denied his

[51]See Thomas O'Brien Hanley, S.J., *Charles Carroll of Carrollton: The Making of a Revolutionary Gentleman* (Washington, D.C., 1970), pp. 16-18.

[52]*Archives of Maryland*, XIX, 303, 316, 340.

[53]*Ibid.*, p. 389. Cf. also *ibid.*, XXVI, 44-45.

charge, since he was not a bishop. He acknowledged that he had said Mass wearing the vestments of a priest at the place mentioned in the charge, but he stated that this had occurred fourteen months before the governor's arrival. Seymour delivered a harangue, for which he was praised by the lower house.[54]

It was precisely this overt practice of Catholicism that Seymour wished to stamp out. At his direction, the assembly passed an Act to Prevent the Growth of Popery on September 30, 1704. It forbade priests to exercise their ministry. For a first offense, the penalty was a fine of £50 and six months in jail; for a second offense, a priest was to be deported to England where he would be made subject to the penal laws passed under William III. These laws included life-imprisonment.[55] The Catholics would later argue for the significance that Seymour, a royal governor, did not presume to apply to Maryland the penal laws of England.

For the time being, however, the issue of penal laws was a dead letter. On December 9, 1704, the assembly reconvened. Since, it said, "the intent of the said Act was only to restrain some exorbitant accons," it was suspending the clause prosecuting priests as long as they said Mass in private homes. The suspension was to last for eighteen months or her Majesty's pleasure. On January 3, 1706, Queen Anne, on the advice of the Lords Commissioners, called upon the assembly to enact the suspension without limit of time.[56] The assembly left no minutes of its discussion of rescinding the penalties against priests. It is, therefore, impossible to discover its precise motives or whether it acted under any pressure from the upper house. The provision for tolerating Catholic worship in private

[54]Most Catholic historians have focused on Seymour's abusive harangue; see, for instance, John Gilmary Shea, *History of the Catholic Church in the United States* (4 vols.; New York, 1886-1892), I, 354. But they have failed to consider the dismissal of charges because it was a first offense. Brooke's family was prominent. Hunter, as superior of the mission, was surely well known as a priest. The case may well have involved "plea-bargaining" and be an instance of the wealthier Protestant class exercising its influence to mitigate the anti-Catholic hostility of the lower classes.

[55]*Archives of Maryland*, XXVI, 340. The law of 11 and 12 William III is given in *The Statutes at Large from the tenth year of King William the Third to the end of the Reign of Queen Anne* (London, 1763), IV, c. 4, pp. 41-42. It did not contain any clause explicitly extending the laws to the plantations. In Seymour's time, some Maryland judges argued that such statutes did not extend to plantations without a local law. Seymour was, therefore, intent on having the assembly pass such a local act.

[56]*Archives of Maryland*, XXVI, 431; Shea, *History*, I, 361. Shea, unfortunately, leads the reader to believe that Queen Anne initiated the suspension clause and thus was personally responsible for allowing Mass in private homes.

homes, however, is directly related to property. The law was not to interfere with what one did in the privacy of one's own home. Since the priests too were property owners, their estates and homes could also be used for private worship. They were to continue to enjoy manorial rights. The assembly and Queen Anne's public recognition of the right to private worship became another step in developing the Maryland Catholic theory.

The Catholic situation remained quiet for almost another decade. In 1715, the Calvert family, which had conformed to the Anglican Church, regained its proprietorship, but John Hart, the former royal governor, was retained in office. Under him, the Catholic question again came up. In 1715,
68 he issued a proclamation against Catholics speaking openly of the Stuart rebellion. On July 28, 1716, the upper house passed an act forbidding one to hold a public office if he attended Mass. It made exception for anyone who collected the proprietor's rents.[57] The house had in mind Charles Carroll, the agent for the Calverts.

Carroll, like his son and grandson of the same name, became the Catholic spokesman for civil rights. He argued that, according to the original charter of Maryland, Catholics were not to be disqualified from holding office. With others, he petitioned the Lords Commissioners complaining of Hart's conduct and the anti-Catholic laws. But the Lords sustained Hart, who, therefore, felt justified in saying that the Catholics had not considered:

> that the Circumstances of this Country is happily Changed for these thirty Years past Who have so long tasted of the Lenity & Liberty of a Protestant Government, that if I may Judge from the many good laws that have been made in this Province, And the Profession of so great a Majority of this People, they are firmly Resolved never more to give way to a Popish Administration.[58]

The issue of course was not the establishment of a "Popish Administration," but whether papists could exercise civil rights. These Hart set about to curtail.

At the assembly of 1718, a law was proposed forbidding Catholics and Quakers the right to vote. The upper house queried whether this was repugnant to the laws of England. William Bladen, the attorney general, assured the house that, far from being repugnant, the act was consonant with the laws of England and especially the laws of 7 and 8 William III, which required that all office holders and practitioners of the law take the Oath of Supremacy.[59] The assembly passed the act because "all measures

[57] *Archives of Maryland*, XXX, 520.

[58] *Ibid.*, XXXIII, 120-123.

[59] *Ibid.*, p. 144. The act of 7 and 8 William III is in *Statutes at Large*, III, c. 24, p. 614.

that have been hitherto taken for preventing the Growth of Popery within this Province" had been ineffectual. The assembly also repealed the earlier Act to Prevent the Growth of Popery of 1704 and the subsequent suspension clause, on the grounds that "by one Act of Parliament made in the Eleventh and Twelfth Year of the Reign of his late Majesty William the Third, Chap. 4, there is good Provision made to prevent the Growth of Popery, as well in this Province, as throughout all others his Majesty's Dominions, and that an Act of Assembly of this Province can in no ways alter the Effect of that Statute."[60] The assembly had done more than disenfranchise Catholics; it acknowledged that English statutes were binding in Maryland. 69

Two separate, but interlocked, issues, therefore, confronted the colonists: whether Catholics had the right to vote and hold office in Maryland and whether Maryland itself was subject to English statute law. These issues provided the occasion for the earliest extant Catholic reflection on the significance of the colony's entire history. Father Peter Attwood (1682-1734), then the superior of the Maryland Jesuits, took on the task of refuting the assembly's claims in a treatise entitled, "Liberty and Property or the Beauty of Maryland Displayed."[61]

Attwood's argument was similar to Persons' a century before. Property was to be the basis for civil rights, but the right to religion was prior even to property. Religious freedom, Attwood said, was the "fundamental" and perpetual law of Maryland on which rested the enjoyment of all other rights and privileges, including the right to property. Furthermore, against Hart and the assembly, he stated that Maryland's religious practice under the Calverts from 1634 to 1690 was publicized and recognized in England. He began his treatise by tracing the origin of the charter granted to Cecil Calvert, a known Catholic, who published

> a declaration, throughout all England and other the King's dominions, that whosoever of his Majesty's subjects would go and settle in Maryland, should not only have a considerable Tract of land granted unto them gratis, but should there enjoy all Rights and Privileges equally and without distinction.[62]

[60] *Ibid.*, pp. 287-289.

[61] The original of this treatise is at Georgetown University. It was published by Shea in the *United States Catholic Historical Magazine*, III (1889-1890), 237-263. Although the document is unsigned, the author's handwriting coincides with Attwood's; for this identification, the author is grateful to Martin Barringer of the Georgetown University Library. Shea wrongly dated the document as late seventeenth century, a date impossible from internal evidence. In the page references below, however, Shea's published version will be used.

[62] Attwood, p. 238.

The "general liberty in the enjoyment of each one's religion and property," continued Attwood, "was a great encouragement to the first adventurers" who sought to insure this liberty to all their successors by passing at their assembly of 1639 an act "whereby liberty of conscience is allowed to all that profess to believe in Jesus Christ."[63] Like many subsequent historians, Attwood had thus confused the Act of 1649 with that of 1639.[64] But it is significant that he did recognize that the assembly of 1639 had passed some kind of act of religious liberty.

Liberty of conscience, said Attwood, was not a political ploy to woo people away from England to populate the Maryland colony. It was enacted
70 by law, "religiously observed from the first settlement of this Province, for above sixty years without the least alteration," and was "approved of by the Crown," inasmuch as it "was printed in and diffused thro' all England, to encourage people to come and reside in this Province." It was "made so publick," he asserted,

> that all authors writing of Maryland mention the same . . ., and yet it never met with any countermand, check or opposition from the crown or government of England, no not even in the days of Oliver Cromwell, who, altho' he used his utmost endeavours to extirpate, both the Church of England and Popery out of the whole kingdom, did nevertheless permit both to enjoy their ancient privileges here in Maryland.[65]

In addition to arguing that freedom of conscience was permanently guaranteed by Maryland law and usage, Attwood also argued from the right of property. From the beginning, he said, Maryland colonists enjoyed not only religious liberty but "also an entire liberty and full enjoyment of all other rights, privileges and immunities for all subjects of Great Britain," to buy and sell, bequeath, inherit, or profit from their property. As a result,

> Clergy and Laity of all persuasions have taken up land of his Lordship, bought of and sold to each other and succeeded to Estates by bequest or Inheritance, without doubt or scruple, and the Lord Proprietary has not only allowed thereof but acted therein, in and from the infant years, as I may say of their Province, as it appears upon our Records . . . where land is granted to Thomas Copley, or according to his assignment the said Copley having Rights . . . to twenty-eight thousand Acres of Land for servants imported into this Province, though the said Thomas Copley was known to be both a Priest and a Jesuit, and such did publickly profess himself.[66]

[63] *Ibid.*, p. 239.

[64] *Ibid.*, pp. 244-248. Here Attwood quotes the Act Concerning Religion of 1649 as being passed in 1639, but he omits any of the penalties attached to blasphemy, etc.

[65] *Ibid.*, pp. 242-243.

[66] *Ibid.*, p. 250.

Attwood, of course, was merely articulating what every eighteenth-century Englishman took for granted: that the right to property was inalienable. But for him it was premised in Maryland on "a fundamental and Perpetual Law, the law of religion, where . . . it is enacted 'that no one shall be any ways troubled, molested, or discountenanced for or in respect of his or her religion.'" But the penal laws of William III forbade Catholics to inherit, buy, or sell property. On this point, Attwood could only query whether there could "be a more severe discountenancing, or a more disagreeable molestation, or a more sensible troubling, than to deprive a man of his birthright, to rob him of his subsistence, and render him incapable to buy, sell, or enjoy any estate whether real or personal, and this 71
upon account or in respect of his Religion."[67]

On the issue of prohibiting Catholics the right to vote, Attwood approached the language of the patriots fifty years later. Laws, he said, were to be made with the consent of the governed; it was unjust that "neither Quakers [who were finally enfranchised in the law] nor Roman Catholics are allowed to have a vote in the making of any law, tho' they and their late posterity must be bound by the same."[68] In Attwood's interpretation of Maryland history, the Glorious Revolution had introduced "Governors that were strangers to our constitution, and unconcerned for our prosperity . . . who . . . when no other crimes could be detected, made the Religion of some high treason, or at least a mark of disgrace, and a hindrance not only to promotion, but to the usual common and undoubted Rights and Privileges of a Marylandian."[69]

But Attwood was arguing for more than rights for Catholics. He warned all his fellow "Marylandians," whether Catholic or Protestant, of the general danger in the assembly's acceptance of English statutes as binding in Maryland. Here, he may well have gone beyond the political thinking of his contemporaries in his perception of the relationship between the Maryland Assembly and Parliament. It was "for seventy years and more the opinion of all in Maryland in courts and out of courts," that the penal laws did not apply to Maryland. Now a new situation had arisen. In his analysis,

> Tho' some of late to secure w[ha]t may be justly deemed an Englishman's birthright, the enjoyment of all beneficial laws, or laws of Privilege, w[hi]ch were made in England before our first settlement, have unwarily advanced too much, in claiming all the Laws of Great Britain: for should we examine into

[67]*Ibid.*, p. 251.
[68]*Ibid.*, p. 252.
[69]*Ibid.*, p. 254.

> necessary consequences thereof so extensive a claim might be found to be not beneficial, but highly prejudicial to, if not destructive of our constitution. But to leave the more exact and convincing solution of this difficulty to the gentlemen of the gown, I shall only observe we can rationally desire no more than to bring with us the Laws of Privilege; the others being rather a burden on, and hinderance to a new Colony, than any benefit or advantage: and to have a power of making Laws, for ourselves and consequently of re-enacting here such laws as either have been (since our first beginning to make laws) or shall be made from time to time in England, w[hi]ch we shall judge agreeable to our constitution, and for our advantage; whilst others that may be repugnant to or inconsistent therewith, are void and of no force.[70]

72 Attwood made no attempt to distinguish between Parliamentary statutes which specifically mentioned the colonies and those which did not. Whether through carelessness or ignorance of the law, he was taking a far more radical position on the rights of the Maryland Assembly than most of his contemporaries.

Attwood reasoned that it was no "wonder" that laws repugnant to Maryland "should pass in England, since the Parliament is neither knowing of nor interested in our affairs." "An unprejudiced person" could easily determine "whether it is better for us who are so highly concerned in improving this Colony, and so feelingly sensible of our own interest, to make our own laws or to leave them to be made by such who are strangers to our constitution, and not only ignorant of but perchance unconcerned for our advantage." This position was for him so clear that he believed

> most will join with me, in advising such as will still insist for all the laws, to supersede this claim, till they have obtained two things from the Crown; the first is, that our province may be freed from the unnecessary trouble and expence, of having Assemblys, for if all the laws of England should extend hither and we are not allowed to contradict the same, or to make laws contrary to them, as by our charter we are forbid to do, to have Assemblys, would be an unnecessary charge and a superfluous trouble. The second is to obtain leave that our freeholders may chose a sufficient number of delegates from among themselves that may be Representatives, and both sit and vote in the British Parliament, for w[ha]t can be more reasonable, than that we ourselves should have a vote in those laws that are to bind us: and yet whether either of these would be granted by the Crown, or if granted, would be beneficial to this Province, I leave the disinterested and impartial to be judges.[71]

[70] *Ibid.*, p. 251.
[71] *Ibid.*, pp. 251-252.

In short, Attwood argued—perhaps inaccurately—that Maryland had its own assembly, impowered to pass its own laws, even if they ran contrary to Parliamentary statutes.[72]

Aside from his view of the Maryland constitution, however, Attwood argued on a more pragmatic basis from Maryland usage. Citing the Act to Prevent the Growth of Popery and the subsequent suspension clause, he inferred,

> that neither Governor Seymore [*sic*] nor our Assembly were of opinion that the penal laws of England extended hither, for to what end should they trouble themselves, or risk such a severe check, as they had from the Crown by making
> a law for that for which the Laws of England had more severely provided, had 73
> they dreamed they had Laws ready made, in force and more severe.[73]

Attwood further argued that Queen Anne's approval of the right of private worship acknowledged that, whatever the law in England, Catholicism was not treason in Maryland. She and George I in no way wished to deprive Maryland Catholics of their right to religion, for, just as toleration had originally encouraged people to settle in Maryland, penal laws would "depopulate this Profitable Colony." In summary, the Queen's action meant for Attwood "that the will of the Crown is a Law to Maryland, as well as to the rest of the Plantations, which are therefore governed by the Prerogative, and not by the English Parliament and that we have power to make laws for ourselves, is a grant of the Crown and no inherent right, or such, as is independent of the Royal Pleasure."[74] Attwood argued, therefore, that from the time Charles I issued the charter to Cecil Calvert, the crown had granted Marylanders the right to make their own laws. The establishment of either a royal government or of a Protestant proprietary government in no way abrogated that right.

Attwood premised his interpretation of the Maryland tradition on the principle that religious toleration was the "fundamental law" of Maryland. From that was derived the right of all colonists to their property. Conversely, no one could be deprived of either his property or a right accruing

[72]Constitutionally, it would have been more accurate for Attwood to have argued that since the penal laws of 11 and 12 William IV did not specifically extend to the plantations, Maryland was free to pass its own laws. Legally, the assembly could pass laws which did not conflict with those of England and could pass a local law making inoperable any act of Parliament which did not specifically extend to the plantations. Attwood, however, went beyond this constitutional principle in arguing his position. For the above distinction, I am grateful to Lois Green Carr.

[73]*Ibid.*, pp. 255-256.

[74]*Ibid.*, p. 257.

to it simply because of religious allegiance; recognition of property rights guaranteed one the freedom necessary to live out one's religious convictions. The way Maryland had publicly worked out its practice since the establishment of the colony in 1634 gave that practice the force of law. In light of Maryland's history, he, therefore, concluded that there could be no just legislation without representation and that Maryland was independent of Parliament.

Governor Hart, however, read the Maryland tradition differently. Addressing the Maryland assembly in 1720, he denied that "Maryland was granted an asylum [to the Papists] from the Rigour of the penall Laws in
74 England" for Cecil Calvert "cou'd not give greater powers than he had." Charles I, who granted the charter to Cecil, was a Protestant "and Certainly could not intènd this Proviso [calling for respect for "God's holy and truely Christian religion"] in favour of any other Religion than that of which he was a Zealous Professor."[75] Hart simply rejected either the facts of history or the validity of what had happened in Maryland under the Catholic Calverts. Whereas the Catholics argued that the crown could act independently of Parliament outside Britain, Hart and the assembly under his control would simply subjugate Maryland to parliamentary jurisdiction to which, in turn, the crown was subject in terms of granting toleration. Hart and Attwood represented two conflicting mentalities which would ultimately lead to the American Revolution.

There is no record of Lord Baltimore's action on the assembly's act of 1718. Since he did not disallow it, however, he approved it and it became law. In 1722, in regard to another act, he informed the assembly that it could not accept English statutes which did not specifically mention the plantations, but had to "enact them De Novo" whenever it found them convenient.[76] More importantly, at the end of 1720, probably as a result of continuing Catholic complaints, Hart was removed from office and replaced by Charles Calvert, the uncle of the proprietor.[77] For the time being the question of the English penal laws was dead.[79] In 1727, the Maryland Catholics wrote George II expressing their happiness "to see your Majesty peaceably succeed to the crown of your great Father." In 1733, Charles Calvert, Lord Baltimore, was the first Protestant proprietor to journey to Maryland; he came to settle the border disputes with Pennsyl-

[75] *Archives of Maryland*, XXXIII, 572-573.

[76] *Ibid.*, XXXIV, 492.

[77] *Ibid.*, XXXIII, 603-605. Scharf, *op. cit.*, pp. 390-391.

[78] The assembly also passed laws against importing Irish servants, cf. *Archives of Maryland*, XXXVI, 175.

vania. The Catholics again expressed their loyalty to the Hanoverian family. Calvert, in reply, noted his pleasure "with that dutiful regard which you express for his Majesty and the royal family, the continuance of which, will always secure to you my favour and protection."[79] But the lingering suspicion of Catholic support for the Stuarts remained.

The 1740's ushered in a new wave of anti-Catholic laws. Colonial economy, the proprietor's rights to rents, fear of the French on the frontier, and the lurking specter of Bonnie Prince Charlie ready to reclaim the British throne—all these were contributing factors to the anti-Catholic feeling. In 1744, the Governor's Council ordered all Catholics dismissed
from the militia and the removal from them of all public arms.[80] During 75
Charles' abortive invasion of England, Maryland priests were accused of perverting Protestants from their religion and of alienating them from their loyalty to King George.[81] The list of accusations was long and imaginative: conspiring with the French and Indians on the frontier, inciting slaves to revolt, perverting slaves and others to popery, and in general being a menace to Maryland society. Between 1751 and 1755, the assembly passed several bills to enforce the penal laws of William III; each time the upper house vetoed them. In 1754, the lower house passed a bill to confiscate the property of the Jesuits, which the upper house rejected. The following year, the lower house passed a bill compelling non-property-owning priests to register and making it illegal for them to obtain property; this too the upper house rejected.[82]

Each of the bills, proposed by the lower house, concerned either property rights or the application of English statutes. The upper house, representing the wealthiest landed gentry and the proprietor's interests, would reject any law which touched upon the basic right of property, even if owned by Catholic priests. But by 1756, the Catholic question was coming to a head and prepared the way for the final expression of the Catholic tradition before the Revolutionary period.

III. Catholic Reflections on the Eve of the Revolution: George Hunter

General Braddock's defeat brought fear to Marylanders on the frontier and made necessary increased contributions to support the British army. In 1756, both houses of the assembly passed an Act for Granting a Supply of

[79] Shea, *op. cit.*, I, 379-380.

[80] *Archives of Maryland*, XXVIII, 314, 340.

[81] *Ibid.*, p. 363.

[82] Timothy W. Bosworth, "Anti-Catholicism as a Political Tool in Mid-Eighteenth-Century Maryland," *Catholic Historical Review*, LXI (October, 1975), 558-559 *et passim*.

Forty Thousand Pounds for his Majesty's Service. It imposed a tax of one shilling on every hundred acres of land. For Catholics, this tax was doubled on the grounds that they did not serve in the militia, from which they had been excluded.[83] While the bill was pending before the upper house, the Catholics, led by Charles Carroll of Annapolis, petitioned the house to reject the bill. After Braddock's defeat, they said, they demonstrated "that We had the Welfare of our Country and the Defence and protection of our Protestant fellow subjects as much or maybe more at Heart than the warmest of Our Patriots or the most inveterate of Our Enemies." When a subscription was raised to defend the frontier, Catholics "countenanced it,
76 they promoted it, they subscribed generously & paid their subscriptions honorably... beyond their proportion to an aid so seasonable & necessary." Nevertheless, this double tax was now placed on Catholics. Equal taxation they were willing to accept, but "We conceive such a Tax or any Particular Tax on us to be unjust and unreasonable."[84]

On this issue, Governor Horatio Sharpe played a double game with the Catholics. His secretary, John Ridout, replied to the petition on May 12, 1756. In the name of the governor, he denied knowledge of any such bill then pending before the upper house and advised the Catholics to petition the lower house if they learned of such a bill.[85] The act was actually passed by both houses on May 15. The Catholics then petitioned the governor to veto the act,[86] but he failed to do so. Subsequently, Sharpe told Frederick Calvert, Lord Baltimore, that the Catholics were asking him to take extraordinary action by vetoing the act. They had failed to petition the lower house when they knew the bill was pending. If he vetoed an act already passed by both houses, he would be accused of favoring popery.[87]

Charles Carroll was furious at the governor's betrayal. He told Lord Baltimore that he considered the governor's suggestion that the Catholics could have petitioned the lower house while the bill was pending nothing else than to "make the Upper House and Govr Cyphers." He believed that the governor was simply too weak to see that the lower house, like similar bodies in other colonies, was seeking to usurp all the prerogatives of

[83] *Archives of Maryland*, LII, 508-510. Bosworth, *op. cit.*, pp. 558-559.

[84] Archives of the Maryland Province of the Society of Jesus (hereafter cited as AMP), Petition of Charles Carroll *et al.* to upper house, May 12, 1756.

[85] AMP, John Ridout to Charles Carroll *et al.*, May 12, 1756 (copy).

[86] The petition, "The Address of the Roman Catholics . . .," is published in the *United States Catholic Historical Magazine*, III (1889-1890), 201-215.

[87] Sharpe to Calvert, May 27, 1756, in *Archives of Maryland*, VI, 419; see also pp. 496-497.

government.[88] But not only was the power of the lower house increasing; the anti-Catholic feeling in Maryland was growing. On September 22, 1756, Father James Beadnall was arrested for saying Mass in a private home and for trying to proselytize a Quaker. When he came to trial in April 1757, the second charge was dropped because of lack of evidence and the first because the practice was allowed by Queen Anne's order.[89] That order should, of course, have been repealed by the act of 1718, imposing the penal laws. As was seen, it was originally only the royal approval of the assembly's own suspension of a clause in the act of 1704, which the act of 1718 repealed. Since the Maryland courts in 1757 accepted Queen Anne's order as a defense for a priest saying Mass, they seem to have recognized that the prevailing usage in Maryland upheld that order, independent of its origin. Whatever may have been the courts' argument, the Beadnall case contributed to the Catholic reaction to the new laws.

The question of double taxation touched on many of the sensitive issues which would create an independent nation within twenty years. It also occasioned the second historical reflection on the meaning of the Maryland tradition, this time by George Hunter (1713-1779), the superior of the Jesuit mission. His treatise probably was intended to accompany the dossier of documents which Charles Carroll and the Catholics were sending to England in hopes of having Lord Baltimore veto the act. Many of his arguments were reminiscent of those of Peter Attwood.

Hunter, like Attwood, considered freedom of religion to be the "fundamental" and perpetual law of Maryland and linked it to the right to property. With the act of 1756, he wrote, Catholics

> were burthened with a tax the double of that of their fellow subjects, a thing never before practised in the Province, and, consequently, contrary to the

[88] AMP, List of Documents sent to England, 1751-1756. Carroll, who compiled the list, added at the end: "Oh, the Sagacious, Merry & Witty Govr. who ordered his clerk to write to me & others at 40 miles distance from him to oppose a law which past the House the Day Mr. Ridout wrote his letter, if Maybe before the letter was out of his hands. Most Governrs. find their Lower Houses of Assembly assuming Power and encroaching on the Rights of Governmt. and instead of encouraging them, they are always attentive to restrain attempts of this sort, but Our Sagacious Governr. says You or they may & ought before you make application to any other Branch of the Legislature concerning it present a Petn. to the Honble. the Lower House and desire to be heard on the Subject Matter of such Petition. This is a Doctrine which would make the Upper House and Govr. Cyphers. For by a Parity of Reason, if you cannot apply by Petition to the Upper House and Governor against a Bill past by the Lower House unless you at 1st applyed to the Lower House against that Bill, the Upper House and Governor ought not to reject any Bill past by the Lower House."

[89] "Indictment of Father Beadnall," *Woodstock Letters*, X (1881), 21-22.

> Royal Orders to all Governors of other Colonies, by which they are ordered not to suffer to pass into execution any *new law affecting the property of the subject.*

Reiterating Carroll's argument against unequal taxation, Hunter urged the proprietor to veto the bill and to issue an order "that no new law henceforward touching the religion or property of the Roman Catholic, uncommon to his fellow subject be passed into execution without the previous consent of the Crown and Proprietor."[90]

Hunter adapted two of Attwood's other arguments. First, he said, penal laws and the new double tax would depopulate the colony and some
78 Catholics were already thinking of leaving.[91] Second, the English penal laws did not apply in Maryland or else the assembly would not have tried to pass them "by Bills brought in for this purpose at each session for these six years past."[92] The act of 1718 had been "only supposed" to introduce the statutes, "which error they seem expressly to acknowledge in the preamble to the bill from the Lower House."[93] In other words, Hunter was arguing that, at least in Maryland usage and in the terminology of the assembly itself, the Parliamentary statute did not apply in Maryland.

Most of all, Hunter regarded the double tax as a breach of promise, for

> Notwithstanding all the hardships and restraints the Roman Catholics were laid under by these several Penal Laws, contrary to the solemn promises made to their ancestors, which induced them to quit their native soil in order to settle in that new Colony, and secure to their posterity a peaceable, quiet habitation, in the free exercise of their religion at the expense of their lives and fortunes; they patiently submitted to all whilst allowed the exercise of their religion, though deprived of many means of advancing their fortunes common to their fellow subjects.[94]

The anti-Catholic laws had been unjust, but they had not touched property. Now the act of 1756 attacked their property, only because of their religion. The governor's own investigation, he noted, had proven the Catholics

[90]George Hunter, "A Short Account of the state and condition of the Roman Catholics in the Province of Maryland, collected from authentic copies of the provincial records and other undoubted testimonies," original in AMP; published in *Woodstock Letters*, X (1881), 10-11. All references will be to the published text.

[91]*Ibid.*, pp. 19-21.

[92]*Ibid.*, pp. 11-12.

[93]*Ibid.*, p. 15.

[94]*Ibid.*, pp. 15-16. The earlier petition to the governor had said: "however grievous and oppressive the laws heretofore against us are they touch not our Property in any other manner than by subjecting us to the payment of 40 £ Poll to the established Clergy"; "Address of the Roman Catholics," p. 208.

innocent of any disloyal activities, and they had publicly professed their loyalty both to King George II and to the proprietor.[95] They simply accepted the *de facto* government as long as their rights to property and religion were not violated.

While the Catholics were petitioning Lord Baltimore, Governor Sharpe was explaining to the proprietor why he had to accept the act.[96] Two years later, he again wrote the proprietor that the Catholic claims to rights were erroneous. He found, however, that, after two investigations, the charges of Catholic disloyalty were groundless. So loyal were the Catholics, he concluded, "that if I was asked . . . whether the Conduct of the Protestants or Papists in this Province hath been most unexceptionable . . . I should not hesitate to give Answer in favour of the Latter."[97]

But the constitutional question was paramount. Sharpe told his brother that the penal laws of England actually did apply in Maryland and that, if Lord Baltimore vetoed the act, Maryland would be thrown into political upheaval.[98] In retrospect, the double-tax bill was a critical turning point in Maryland history. Sharpe and Frederick Calvert, the proprietor, were faced with the growing revolutionary spirit of Maryland's lower house and its antagonism for the proprietor. The Catholics, however, had always sustained Baltimore's claims and depended on him for their safety. But in this case, Baltimore approved the act.[99] Moreover, in reply to a petition from Beadnall, Calvert declared "that the Method in the prosecution of Roman Catholicks on Religious Concerns in Maryland is by known Laws not only of the Province But also, by Acts of Parliament throughout his Majesty's Realm." While he himself would not initiate prosecution, he wrote Sharpe, if any Catholics were brought before the courts, "on Conviction they are to be punished."[100] The Catholics had lost their last source of protection. But Calvert had also now lost their political support.

As Hunter had predicted, some Catholics did think of leaving Maryland. Charles Carroll seriously considered selling his estates—thus losing £100,000—and moving to Louisiana "to procure ease to myself by flying

[95]Hunter, p. 16. The petition to the governor also included the Catholics' earlier public protestations of loyalty to George II and Lord Baltimore; "Address of the Roman Catholics," pp. 211-214.

[96]*Archives of Maryland*, VI, 419.

[97]*Ibid.*, IX, 318.

[98]Horatio Sharpe to John Sharpe, October 10, 1756, *ibid.*, VI, 496-497.

[99]Sharpe to Baltimore, June 30, 1757, *ibid.*, IX, 34.

[100]Calvert to Sharpe, April 7, 1757, *ibid.*, VI, 539-540.

from the pursuits of envy and malice."[101] Carroll, however, did not leave. In 1758, the upper house of the assembly argued against imposing still more taxes on Catholics. It used many of the arguments of the Catholics: Maryland had been given as an asylum to Catholics and the imposition of the double tax was a breach of promise made to their ancestors, which would force many to flee the colony.[102] Two years later, on the advice of the upper house, Sharpe convened the assembly which relieved the Catholics of the unequal tax.[103] By then, however, the proprietor had lost the trust of the Catholics. In 1761, Charles Carroll was still bristling at Baltimore's failure to reject the act. To his son Charles, then studying in England, he
80 wrote: "I do not care to mortify Mr. Calvert, who can urge nothing to excuse his Family's ingratitude to the Roman Catholics."[104] For Carroll, Calvert had betrayed the trust of Catholics in him and his ancestors.

Maryland Catholics after 1689 have been described as a counter-revolutionary force within the colony.[105] Calvert's breach of trust began turning them into part of a new revolutionary movement. Under the Catholic Calverts, Catholics enjoyed full civil and religious liberty and extended it to others; all settlers had the civil rights premised upon property. Under the royal government and the Protestant Calverts, they were disenfranchised. They accepted the *de facto* government and obeyed, but they asserted the fundamental rights to religion and property and denied the justice of laws made without their consent. For protection of their rights, they depended upon the upper house, or, failing that, the crown and proprietor. Always they claimed that Maryland was different from England and had the right to make her own laws independent of Parliament. When the double-tax act was passed, they ceased to depend on either the upper house or the proprietor for protection. Yet they clung to their theory and were now ready for a type of government which would not merely tolerate, but acknowledge the rights they held to be fundamental.

Nine years after the double-tax act, the colonies were in turmoil over the Stamp Act. Charles Carroll of Carrollton, who had returned to Maryland, wrote:

[101] Kate Mason Rowland, *The Life of Charles Carroll of Carrollton, 1737-1832* (2 vols.; New York, 1898), I, 31; see also pp. 32-33, and Horatio Sharpe to William Sharpe, July 6, 1757, in *Archives of Maryland*, IX, 46.

[102] *Archives of Maryland*, LV, xliii, 507-511.

[103] Sharpe to Calvert, October 12, 1760, *ibid.*, IX, 453.

[104] *Unpublished Letters of Charles Carroll of Carrollton, and of his Father Charles Carroll of Doughregan*, edited by Thomas Meagher Field (New York, 1902), p. 59.

[105] Hanley, *Charles Carroll of Carrollton*, p. 18.

> there are certain known fundamental laws essential to and interwoven with the English constitution which even a Parliament itself cannot abrogate: such I take to be the allowed maxim of the constitution that invaluable privilege from birth of Englishmen of being taxed with their own consent: the definition of freedom is the being governed by laws to which we have given our consent, as the definition of slavery is the very reverse.[106]

The position was not new to Maryland Catholics. In 1756, the petition to the governor had stated that by the penal laws, "we are almost reduced to the level of our Negroes not having even the privilege of voting for persons to represent us in the assembly."[107] It was also the position taken by Attwood in 1718. When the patriots began arguing for no taxation 81
without representation, no laws passed without the consent of the governed, and no parliamentary jurisdiction over the colonies, they found ready allies in the Maryland Catholics who had been expressing the same theory since 1634.

Maryland Catholics were conservative and aristocratic. The penal laws which did apply in Maryland paradoxically reinforced their conservatism and consciousness of English rights. Barred from receiving advanced education in the colony, young Maryland boys attended the English Jesuit college of St. Omer's in Flanders. They studied not only with other English Catholics but also with the young men who would serve the Maryland mission as Jesuit priests. They thus became more English in their mentality than their counterparts in other colonies; moreover, both the laity and clergy came from the same social class and received the same intellectual formation. Twenty years before the Revolution, Governor Sharpe noted that many Catholics tended to be "Men of considerable fortunes." [108]

Property had a twofold influence on Maryland Catholic thought. On the one hand, it was the basis for political and civil rights, none of which should be curtailed because of religion. Charles Carroll of Carrollton stated the Maryland tradition succinctly in 1767: "No persecutions have ever been found effectual in suppressing any religious Sect." He rejected such persecution whether perpetrated by his own or any other church.[109] His position echoed the pamphlet "Objections Answered," published in 1633. On the other hand, after the Revolution, Carroll and most Maryland Catholics

[106] *Ibid.*, p. 99.
[107] "Address of the Roman Catholics," p. 208.
[108] Sharpe to Calvert, July 9, 1755, in *Archives of Maryland*, VI, 240.
[109] *Unpublished Letters*, p. 143.

joined the Federalists who wanted to see some type of property qualifications for citizenship.[110]

This conservative tradition in regard to property led them to adopt a practical program for the separation of Church and State. Government was concerned with preserving property and the common good, while religion was fundamentally private; the clergy received no State support and, at their own request, were uninvolved in legislative actions. After the Revolution, the Catholic clergy added a corollary to the tradition: if the State had no jurisdiction over religious matters, the Church had none over temporal ones. In 1773, Pope Clement XIV suppressed the Society of Jesus. The
82 Maryland Jesuits became secular priests subject to the Vicar Apostolic of the London District. His jurisdiction was impractical before the Revolution and impossible after independence. In 1782, John Carroll emerged as the leader of the Maryland ex-Jesuits. He argued, and the rest of the clergy agreed, that the pope, as spiritual leader of the Church, had no control over property. The papal act of suppression of the Jesuits in no way touched the ownership of the estates, which "still continue to be held by the former members of that body."[111] Once the civil law permitted, Carroll, who had been elected the first Bishop of Baltimore, called on "all Clergymen of this State [Maryland], Citizens thereof" to submit written opinions on the incorporation of their property. One of Carroll's motives was to prevent possible papal confiscation of or ecclesiastical encroachment upon the property, which for him, as for his ancestors, was the basis of civil rights. For him, no one exercising spiritual authority—superior, bishop, or pope—should by the fact of that office have any jurisdiction over temporalities.[112] The ecclesiastical policy of John Carroll was as radical as his distant cousin Charles' political one—both were rooted within the Maryland tradition.

[110]Celestine Joseph Nuesse, *The Social Thought of American Catholics: 1634-1829* (Washington, D.C., 1945), pp. 72-74.

[111]AMP, 2 N 1, Hughes, *Documents*, I-II, 610-614.

[112]AMP, 2 N 9, Proceedings of the General Chapter. May 11, 1789. See also James Hennesey, S.J., *American Catholics: A History of the Roman Catholic Community in the United States* (New York, 1981), pp. 85-86.

III With Promise Of Liberty In Religion

LORD BALTIMORE, ROMAN CATHOLICS, AND TOLERATION: RELIGIOUS POLICY IN MARYLAND DURING THE EARLY CATHOLIC YEARS, 1634-1649

BY

JOHN D. KRUGLER*

In large measure the religious policies established in early Maryland resulted because Cecil Calvert, the second Lord Baltimore and 85
first proprietor of the colony, was a Roman Catholic. However, the relationship of Catholicism to Maryland and its role in the religious settlement has not been properly understood. In analyzing that relationship, historians have worked from a very limited appreciation of what it meant to be an English Catholic in the early seventeenth century. As a result they have left a bundle of contradictory interpretations, none of which satisfactorily established the relationship between Catholicism, the proprietor, and the colony. Lord Baltimore's religious motivation has especially been subjected to a number of conflicting interpretations. One interpretation described him as moved by the noblest religious idealism. His intention was to establish a haven for persecuted English Catholics. Conversely another interpretation presented him as a bold opportunist driven by the basest pecuniary motives. Religious considerations had little importance.[1]

*Mr. Krugler is an associate professor of history in Marquette University. He wishes to acknowledge the financial support he has received from the Marquette University Committee on Research and to express his appreciation to Professor Athan G. Theoharis for his helpful criticism of this article.

[1] The role of religious idealism reached its most exaggerated form in ***Maryland: The Land of Sanctuary: A History of Religious Toleration from the First Settlement until the American Revolution*** (Baltimore, 1907) written by the Catholic bishop William T. Russell. T. K. Rabb in ***Enterprise and Empire: Merchant and Gentry Investment in the Expansion of England*** (Cambridge, 1967), p. 38 n., argued that the involvement of the Baltimores in colonization was an exception because of their religious purposes. On the other hand, the Episcopalian minister C. E. Smith in his ***Religion Under the Barons Baltimore. . . .*** (Baltimore, 1899) saw the Calverts as men who manipulated religion for their own benefit. Alfred Pearce Dennis, "Lord Baltimore's Struggle with the Jesuits, 1634-1649," ***Annual Report of the American Historical Association, 1900*** (2 vols.; Washington, 1901), I, 112, likewise argued against any religious motivation on the part of the Calverts. Some historians simply combine the two without trying to

Some studies represented Baltimore as devoting his life to an experiment in religious toleration as a result of either the teachings of the Catholic Church or the influence of the Utopian concepts of Sir Thomas More. Still another study concluded that Baltimore had little to do with the religious settlement but was forced into it by the Catholic freemen of the colony.[2] In terms of his personal religious commitment, some authors argued he was a devout son of the Roman Catholic Church. Another believed he transgressed against the Church because of his Protestant upbringing. Finally, one severe critic thought Baltimore only "posed as a Catholic."[3]

The difficulty in interpreting the Catholic Lord Baltimore is that
86 some of his behavior appears to be anti-Catholic. This study proposes to resolve some of these inconsistencies and contradictions by getting back to the basics. What did it mean to be a Catholic in seventeenth-century England? How did Lord Baltimore reflect this experience in his handling of the religious situation in Maryland? All too frequently the interpretation of these questions has been based on an assumption of what a Catholic ought to be and Lord Baltimore's actions have been judged in the context of this definition. Those sympathetic to the proprietor found excuses for his behavior; those hostile to him either condemned or used his behavior to demonstrate the absence of any religious commitment. Any judgments about his behavior as a Catholic and his subsequent handling of lay Catholics and members of the Society of Jesus in Maryland must be rendered against the reality of the seventeenth-century world in which he lived and not against some idealistic standard.

---

weigh their relative importance or assessing their relationship. See Thomas T. McAvoy, *A History of the Catholic Church in the United States* (Notre Dame, 1969), p. 9.

[2] Matthew Page Andrews, "Separation of Church and State in Maryland," *Catholic Historical Review*, XXI (July, 1935), 170-171. Thomas O'Brien Hanley, S.J., *Their Rights & Liberties: The Beginnings of Religious & Political Freedom in Maryland* (Westminster, Maryland, 1959), also saw Utopia as profoundly influencing Maryland but through the freemen in Maryland and the Jesuits in England (ch. 1).

[3] William Hand Browne believed Baltimore to be a sincere Catholic. *Maryland* (Boston, 1895), p. 69. The Jesuit H. S. Spalding excused Baltimore's blunders because he was a convert. *Catholic Colonial Maryland: A Sketch* (Milwaukee, 1931), p. 95. Thomas Hughes, S.J., was less charitable. *History of the Society of Jesus in North America, Colonial and Federal* (2 vols.; New York, 1908-1917), I, 435, 456, 509. Hughes made the most extensive analysis of Calvert's religious commitments and left the distinct impression that Calvert was a "bad" Catholic at best. See his "Appendix E," II, 671-675.

Resolving doubts about Baltimore's religious commitment is complicated by the absence of hard information on his spiritual life. The eldest son of George and Anne Calvert was baptized in the Church of England in 1606. Named for his godfather, the influential secretary of state Sir Robert Cecil, almost nothing of substance is known of his religious life before 1624. Baptism in the Church of England did not confirm that he would be reared as a Protestant. His father, a schismatic, had been reared a Catholic but at about the age of twelve responded to external forces and conformed to the state church. During the years he served King James, the elder Calvert was at least a nominal Protestant, making it difficult to determine the point at which he chose to instruct his children in the Catholic religion. The not entirely reliable Bishop Godfrey Goodman reported "it was said" at the time of the Spanish marriage negotiations (c. 1620-1623) that Calvert, who was "infinitely addicted" to the Catholic faith, "did usually cathechize his own children so as to ground them in his own religion." Goodman's description cannot be considered entirely accurate. It may be that Calvert began educating his children in the Catholic religion sometime before he came to a final resolution of his own religious doubts in late 1624. By this time, however, Cecil was already a young man.[4]

By young adulthood Cecil most certainly had become a Catholic. About a year before the elder Calvert came to the resolution to live and die as a Catholic, Cecil received a pass to travel overseas. In spite of the perfunctory injunction not to visit Rome he evidently went there and made a profession of his faith. Sometime after his return to England, probably in the autumn of 1628, he married the daughter of Thomas, Lord Arundel of Wardour. Marriage into this

[4] Cecil was baptized March 2, 1606, in Bexley, Kent, in the Archdiocese of Canterbury. John Bailey Calvert Nicklin, "Some Notes Concerning Sir George Calvert (1579-1632), First Lord Baltimore and his Family from the English Records," *Maryland Historical Magazine*, XXVII (December, 1932), 335. Goodman, *The Court of King James the First*, ed. John S. Brewer (2 vols.; London, 1849), I, 376. In 1629 three of George Calvert's sons were sent to study at the College at St. Omer under the charge of Jesuits. Hughes, *Society of Jesus, Text*, I, 206. On the symbolic importance of St. Omer for both English Protestants and Catholics, see A. C. F. Beales, *Education Under Penalty: English Catholic Education from the Reformation to the Fall of James II, 1547-1689* (London, 1963), p. 158. For the elder Calvert, see John D. Krugler, " 'The Face of a Protestant, and the Heart of a Papist': A Reexamination of Sir George Calvert's Conversion to Roman Catholicism," forthcoming in *Journal of Church and State*, and R. J. Lahey, "The Role of Religion in Lord Baltimore's Colonial Enterprise," *Maryland Historical Magazine*, 72 (Winter, 1977), 494-498.

prominent Catholic family established his credentials in the Catholic community. Throughout the remainder of his life, and in defiance of the attacks made upon him because of his religion, Cecil Calvert remained a Catholic.[5]

As a Catholic, Baltimore identified with a persistent minority of Englishmen. He displayed certain traits common to that group. The transformation and revival of Catholicism in the face of strong opposition is an exceedingly complex historical problem, one to which historians are at long last giving serious attention.[6] It now appears that the early seventeenth century witnessed a revival of Catholicism. In spite of the oppressive penal legislation designed to constrict the
88 Catholic community, Catholicism demonstrated remarkable staying power. In some areas Catholicism undoubtedly increased in number during the reign of James I. By the time of Charles I, concentrations of Catholics were to be found throughout England and were duly noted by suspicious Protestants. Undoubtedly English Protestants exaggerated the growth of Catholicsm. Nevertheless, reports such as the one in March, 1637, from Baltimore's parish in London, St. Giles in the Fields, of "the greate increase of those of the Romish Church" contained the essential truth that Catholicism was on the increase.[7]

For Catholics London offered many advantages and conveniences such as ready access to foreign chapels and their priests so necessary for their spiritual well-being and to professional classes necessary for

[5] Acts of the Privy Council, Public Record Office, PC 2/32/235. The pass was issued on January 31, 1623/4. General Mutius Vitelleschi to the English Provincial Edward Knott, October 31, 1643, in Hughes, *Society of Jesus, Text*, I, 558. On April 17, 1628, his father asked Thomas Wentworth to look after Cecil's marriage, seeing that Cecil selected a wife that was fit for him. *Wentworth Papers, 1597-1628* (London, 1973), p. 291.

[6] John Bossy, *The English Catholic Community, 1570-1850* (New York, 1976). Keith Lindley, "The Part Played by the Catholics," in *Politics, Religion and the English Civil War*, ed. Brian Manning (London, 1973), pp. 127-176. Keith Lindley, "The Lay Catholics of the Reign of Charles I," *Journal of Ecclesiastical History*, XIII (July, 1971), 199-221. Martin J. Havran, *The Catholics in Caroline England* (Stanford, 1962). Anthony Henry Forbes, " 'Faith and true allegiance': The Law and External Security of England, 1559-1714: A Study of the Evolution of the Parliamentary Legislation and the Problem of its Local Administration and Enforcement" (unpublished Ph.D. dissertation, University of California, Los Angeles, 1960).

[7] John Bossy suggested that the Catholic community grew from 35,000 in 1603 to 60,000 in 1640 indicating that those who thought popery was increasing were right. "The English Catholic Community 1603-1625," in *The Reign of James VI and I*, ed. Alan G. R. Smith (London, 1973), pp. 101-102. PRO SP16/349/228.

their material well-being. Catholic survival in London under the shadow of Parliament encouraged the significant Catholic revival in the countryside among the nobility and gentry. Here, in what has been described as Catholic enclaves, the recusancy laws were rendered less effective and the religion survived. By sheltering priests on their manors, by supporting financially the proselytizing activities of the missionary priests, and by protection of their servants from persecution, the Catholic nobility and gentry ensured the continued survival of Catholicism.[8]

Through the support of the nobility and gentry, the number of priests, guilty of treason by their very presence in England, increased 89
rapidly during this period. The most notable increase was in the number of Jesuits. From a few at the beginning of James's reign to 152 by the end of the reign, this figure remained fairly constant until the restoration of Charles II. More important than the numbers themselves was the change in attitude that the Jesuits underwent. There is no need to recount here the struggles that went on between the Jesuits and the secular clergy over jurisdiction and the appointment of bishops. This division within the Catholic community reflected, as A. F. Allison noted, "a wider conflict common to the whole post-Reformation Church. Behind it lay the legacy of medieval disagreement over the rights and powers of the Pope in relation to local churches and hierarchies." The supporters of a bishop sought to restore traditional church order in England. Those opposed were willing to make adjustments in the traditional order to accommodate Catholicism to new realities.[9]

The Jesuits opposed the appointment of a bishop. They took the

[8] A document in the PRO detailing the arrests of London Catholics indicates they were able to pursue a rich variety of occupations. SP16/495. Lindley, "Lay Catholics," p. 206. Howard S. Reinmuth, Jr., "Lord William Howard (1563-1640) and his Catholic Associations," *Recusant History*, 12 (April, 1974), 232. Havran detailed the devastating effect of the penal laws on the lower classes (*op. cit.*, ch. 6).

[9] *Records of the English Province of the Society of Jesus*, ed. Henry Foley, S.J. (7 vols.; London, 1877-1882), VII, pt. I, clxviii (I). There was a steady increase during the 1630's with 193 Jesuits in England in 1639 and 1644. This undoubtedly accounted for some of the anti-Catholic hysteria of this period. For one English Protestant's view, see the speech of Sir Edwin Sandys given in Parliament on May 4, 1621. *Commons Debates 1621*, ed. Wallace Notestein, *et al.* (7 vols.; New Haven, 1935), V, 141. A. F. Allison, "Richard Smith, Richelieu and the French Marriage: The Political Context of Smith's Appointment as Bishop for England in 1624," *Recusant History*, 7 (January, 1964), 149, 157, Bossy, *Catholic Community*, pp. 49-58.

position that the laity should be free to admit into their home priests of their own choosing, a position which undoubtedly enhanced their appeal among the gentry. They recognized that a bishop in England was not in step with the realities faced by the laity. The Jesuits were sympathetic with the "Lay Catholics of England" who protested that the authority which the recently appointed Bishop of Chalcedon, Richard Smith, attempted to exercise over English Catholics imperiled not only their property but their safety. Especially sensitive to the needs of the laity, the Jesuits made accommodations to them, such as providing individual priests for gentry households. During the early seventeenth century English lay Catholics asserted greater con-
90 trol over their own religious affairs, frequently with the encouragement of individual Jesuits. The Catholic nobility and gentry in particular had grown accustomed to exercising greater independence in their dealings with the clergy. Baltimore certainly reflected this trend in his dealings with the clergy in Maryland.[10]

Catholic survival constitutes a record of remarkable achievement and, in no small part, it is the achievement of the gentry. But survival was not without its price. To survive as Catholics, the gentry learned to be pragmatic and not philosophical, flexible and not dogmatic about their Church. Without effective clerical leadership and uncertain of their own status within the Church, they had to fend for themselves. In their struggle Rome provided little assistance, and they developed a sense of self-reliance and independence that made their survival as Catholics possible. That their Church was important to them goes without saying, but English Catholics learned that survival frequently dictated that religious considerations must be subordinated to more worldly concerns. Baltimore mirrored these characteristics in his dealings with the clergy in his colony.[11]

[10] Lay Catholics of England to Richard Smith, Bishop of Chalcedon (1627) in Hughes, *Society of Jesus, Text*, I, 204-206. The Catholic "Gentry may have actually preferred laws enabling them to harbor priests, who were subject to execution, since that allowed them to control their confessors as well as use the priests to tutor their children and in some cases to handle their legal affairs." Susan R. Falb, "Advice and Ascent: The Development of the Maryland Assembly, 1635-1689" (unpublished Ph.D. dissertation, Georgetown University, 1976), p. 294.

[11] Lindley, "Lay Catholics," p. 206. Hugh Aveling gives many examples of how Catholics survived on their cunning and wit: *Northern Catholics: The Catholic Recusants of the North Riding of Yorkshire, 1558-1790* (London, 1966), ch. 3. For the effects of an episcopal church without bishops, see Daniel J. Boorstin, *The Americans: The Colonial Experience* (New York, 1958), ch. 21.

As a Catholic, Baltimore was also heir to a different perspective on religious uniformity than other Englishmen. Catholics rejected the dominant concept that the religious faith of the subjects must be the same as the rulers. Their sincerity was questioned by many Englishmen. However, after the passing of the militant phase of the late Elizabethan period, English Catholics labored to demonstrate that spiritual loyalties and temporal loyalties were not mutually exclusive. Certainly Baltimore recognized that men could divorce their religious sentiments from their loyalty to the state. His father's willingness to subordinate his religious sentiments to his political career could not have been lost on Cecil. Further, he had witnessed English Catholics who maintained their religion in private and still worked at the highest levels of government. Whether they took the oath of allegiance or not, and there is reason to believe that many English Catholics did, in practice they were willing to limit the temporal powers of the pope.[12] It was within this context that Baltimore sought to establish a colony in which a diversity of religious opinions existed. Baltimore acted upon the assumption that religion was essentially a private matter and that the settlers would be able to overcome their religious differences for the greater good of the colony and the lord proprietor. Unlike Massachusetts Bay, where society was posited on the necessity of religious unity, Baltimore sought unity by appealing to secular loyalties.

Baltimore was not so naïve as to believe that religious differences could merely be swept aside. From the very beginning his enterprise was under constant attack. Had the Calvert family been content to colonize their frozen lands to the north, the religious question would not have loomed so large. Upon abandoning his Newfoundland colony, George Calvert visited Virginia, where he immediately saw the great potential for a colony of his own. The Virginians, however, viewed him with suspicion from the very first and feared that he might disrupt their situation. To express their displeasure, Virginia authorities imposed the oaths of supremacy and allegiance. Baltimore suggested an alternate form of the oath of supremacy but the Virginia authorities remained adamant that no exception could be made. Soon thereafter he departed for England to secure a charter for what be-

[12] Clarence J. Ryan, "The Jacobean Oath of Allegiance and English Lay Catholics," *Catholic Historical Review*, XXVIII (July, 1942), 159-183. Maurus Lunn, "English Benedictines and the Oath of Allegiance, 1606-1647," *Recusant History*, 10 (October, 1969), 146.

came the Maryland grant. This marked the opening of the sparring between the representatives of the defunct Virginia Company and the Calverts.[13]

In England forces representing the defunct Virginia Company labored to prevent the Calvert family from securing their charter. Couched in language that appealed to the prevailing anti-Catholic sentiments of the English people, these attacks on Baltimore because of his religion provided a convenient way of moving against the colony. The attacks put Baltimore on the defensive, necessitating the preparation of a paper entitled "Objections Answered Touching
92 Maryland." Among other things, these critics charged that in Maryland where Catholics "may have free liberty to their Religion" the penal laws would not be able to work "their conformity to the Protestant Religion"; that giving Catholics leave to go would seem "a kind of toleration of (at least a connivance at) Popery"; that the King's revenues would be impaired by the loss of recusancy fines; and that the establishment of Catholics in Maryland would endanger Virginia and New England. A persistent theme was that somehow the Catholics, if allowed to go to Maryland, would "bring in the Spaniards or some other forraigne enemy to supresse the Protestants" already in English America. While it is doubtful that the "Answers" did much to alleviate Protestant fears, they do indicate Baltimore's precarious position with regard to religion.[14]

[13] Dr. John Pott (acting governor of Virginia) *et al.* to the Privy Council, November 30, 1629, *Archives of Maryland*, ed. William Hand Browne, *et al.* (70 vols. to date; Baltimore, 1883-), III, 16-17. Rev. Joseph Mead to Sir Martin Stuteville, January 23, 1629/30, in *The Court and Times of Charles the First*, comp. Thomas Birch (2 vols.; London, 1848), II, 53. The first Lord Baltimore believed when James dissolved the Virginia company in 1624 he "understood it to be damned for ever" and acted on that basis. George, Lord Baltimore, to the Earl of Middlesex, March 28, 1632, in "Unpublished Letter of the First Lord Baltimore," ed. Matthew Page Andrews, *Maryland Historical Magazine*, XL (June, 1945), 90-91.

[14] The "Objections" as reprinted in Bradley T. Johnson, *The Foundation of Maryland and the Origins of the Act Concerning Religion* (Baltimore, 1883), pp. 24-30. The "Objections" could not have enjoyed wide circulation. There are only three known copies and they were printed in 1646 as part of another pamphlet. On the problem of the dating and authorship, see Lawrence C. Wroth, "Maryland Colonization Tracts," in *Essays Offered to Herbert Putnam* . . . (originally 1929; reprint, Freeport, New York, 1967), pp. 542, 550-551. Lathrop Colgate Harper suggested that the "Objections" might have originally been drawn up for the private instruction of Lord Baltimore in defending his charter in its passage of the Great Seal. "A Maryland Tract of 1646," in *Bibliographical Essays: a Tribute to Wilberforce Eames* (originally 1924; re-

A last desperate effort to scuttle the initial expedition, made just before Baltimore's ships prepared to sail during the fall of 1633, demonstrated how religious rumors could be used against Baltimore. Writing to Sir Thomas Wentworth, a family friend who, on more than one occasion, used his considerable influence to ease some of the expedition's difficulties, Baltimore confided that he was troubled by his adversaries in many ways. He lamented that his expedition was delayed by those carrying vicious tales to the Privy Council. According to Baltimore, the council had been informed "that I intend to carry over Nuns into Spain and Soldiers to the King" of Spain. While the councillors scoffed at the charge, the other charges that his people left "in Contempt of all Authority," that they had abused the king's
officers, and that they had refused "to take the Oath of Allegiance," led to the recall of the *Ark* and *Dove* before they could make open sea. This necessitated that Baltimore appear before the Council to repudiate these charges. Only after much expensive delay were Baltimore's ships restored "to their former Liberty." The anti-Catholic sentiment used to attack Baltimore's enterprise at home spilled over into Virginia and was instrumental in the thrusting out of Governor John Harvey in 1635.[15]

Clearly, the Catholic Lord Proprietor, although possessing absolute powers under his charter, was vulnerable on the matter of his religion. Admittedly, Baltimore did not act mainly out of religious considerations nor was his colony planted only to further religious ends.

---

print, Freeport, New York, 1967), p. 146. On the persistent fear of Catholicism, see Carol Z. Weiner, "The Beleaguered Isle: A Study of Elizabethan and Early Jacobean Anti-Catholicism," *Past and Present*, No. 51 (May, 1971), 27-62, and Robin Clifton, "Fear of Popery," in *The Origins of the English Civil War*, ed. Conrad Russell (London, 1973), pp. 144-167.

[15] Cecil, Lord Baltimore, to the Privy Council, "The humble Declaration of the Lord Baltemores proceedings in the procuring & passing of his Pattent of the Province of Maryland adjoyning to Virginea, and of severall unjust molestations which some of the old dissolved Company of Virginea have given him both before & since, to his great prejudice," *The Calvert Papers* (3 vols.; Baltimore, 1889-1899), I, 221-229. Baltimore to Wentworth, January 10, 1633/4, *The Earl of Strafforde's Letters and Dispatches . . .*, ed. W. Knowler (2 vols.; London, 1739), I, 178. For litigation against Baltimore over the additional expenses incurred see High Court of Admiralty, Instance and Prize, Libels etc., Public Record Office, HC 24/91/114, 134, 154. Edward Watkins, searcher for London, to Privy Council, October 29, 1633, *Maryland Historical Magazine*, I (December, 1906), 352-354. Sir John Harvey to Lords Commissions for forraigne Plantations (1635), *Virginia Magazine of History and Biography*, I (April, 1894), 425-430.

Nevertheless, religious considerations were always a factor with which he had to reckon. In marked contrast to Massachusetts Bay Colony, where the Puritan leadership desired to be "a City upon a Hill" with the world recognizing its example, Baltimore eschewed publicity and sought to plant his little colony as unobtrusively as possible. For him the guiding principle was that religious disputation was a potentially destructive element in Maryland. As the colony's chief civil authority, he recognized that the colony's survival depended on removing religious considerations from the political arena. Taking little interest in fostering the growth of religious institutions, Baltimore labored to prevent religious controversies from becoming notorious and thereby polarizing society.[16]

In addition to his vulnerability because of his religion, other circumstances dictated that Baltimore labor to keep religion in the background in order to prevent religious strife from destroying his enterprise. A principal factor was the religious affiliations of those settlers willing to venture to Maryland. Baltimore devoted some time to scrutinizing the prospective settlers. According to Robert Wintour, who was closely associated with the initial recruitment, Baltimore was both cautious and wary in his selection of settlers. He admitted no one to the Maryland enterprise without good recommendations. The backbone of the settlement were the master adventurers whom Wintour described as gentlemen, wellborn, of noble education, and good friends. What Wintour did not indicate was that these gentlemen were for the most part Roman Catholics who generally came from families who had long been interested in colonization or had connections with the Calvert family. Baltimore's enterprise had its greatest appeal for the younger sons of the English Catholic gentry who saw in Maryland the opportunity to better themselves without having to compromise their religion. As younger sons in England,

[16] John Winthrop, "A Modell of Christian Charity," *Winthrop Papers* (5 vols.; Boston, 1929-1947), II, 282-295. See also John D. Krugler, "Puritan and Papist: Politics and Religion in Massachusetts and Maryland before the Restoration of Charles II" (unpublished Ph.D. dissertation, University of Illinois, 1971). Cf. Lahey's perceptive analysis of the role of religion in Newfoundland (*op. cit.*, pp. 492-511). Father White deftly spun the spiritual and secular threads together in Maryland's first publicity tract, *A Declaration of the Lord Baltemore's Plantation in Maryland, nigh vpon Virginia: Manifesting the Nature, Quality, Condition, and rich vtilities it contayneth* (London, 1633), p. 5. Baltimore undoubtedly approved of the conceptualization for he corrected the text before publication. White to Baltimore, February 20, 1638/39, *Calvert Papers*, I, 209.

they had little chance of inheriting the family estate. Their religion made it extremely difficult for them to seek careers in the professions or in politics. Maryland was a rejection of the proposition that new plantations were no more than a refuge for lost men, courses of much danger and little profit which were fit only for desperate fortunes and those who could not live in their own country. Maryland offered to young Catholic gentlemen an alternative to dissipating themselves in the service of foreign princes.[17]

Baltimore also paid close attention to those settlers who went as servants. The workers brought by the gentlemen were not idle vagabonds promiscuously taken from jails or outlaws forced to flee their country. They were either servants to the gentlemen or to their friends who were secure before they went to perform their contractual obligations. Unfortunately for Baltimore, not all the servants fell into this category. Increasingly he was forced to rely upon unknown quantities who had neither religious nor familial ties to the Calvert family. The result was, in the words of Baltimore's son and successor, that he had to depend upon such as for "some Reason or other could not lyve with ease in other places. And of these a greate parte were such as could not conforme in all particulars to the severall lawes of England relating to religion." From the beginning, then, Maryland was composed of individuals representing a variety of religious persuasions: Roman Catholic, Church of England, Englishmen with Puritan leanings, and undoubtedly a number who were indifferent toward religion.[18]

Baltimore's policy toward religion was conditioned by three realities. The first was that he and his fellow Catholics were a distinct minority within Maryland, albeit a dominant one in the beginning. The second reality was that the majority of the settlers reflected traditional hostilities toward Catholicism. The last was his relative weakness as an "absolute" proprietor who had to labor within the confines of a militant Protestant country. His policy reflected not so much a philosophical commitment to religious liberty as a pragmatic one.[19]

[17] *To Live Like Princes: "A Short Treatise Sett Downe in a Letter Written by R. W. to His Worthy Friend C. J. R. concerning the New Plantation Now Erecting under the Right Honorable the Lord Baltimore in Maryland,"* ed. John D. Krugler (Baltimore, 1976), pp. 12, 38. Russell R. Menard, "Economy and Society in Early Colonial Maryland" (unpublished Ph.D. dissertation, University of Iowa, 1975), pp. 32-36.

[18] *To Live Like Princes*, ed. Krugler, p. 39. *Archives of Maryland*, V, 267-268.

[19] There will probably never be any resolution as to the intellectual origins of the Calvert's colonization schemes. As strong an argument as those in favor of Sir Thomas

Experience had taught English Catholics in general, and the Calvert family in particular, that civil harmony need not be posited on the concept that the subjects' religion must be the same as the ruler's. R. H. Lahey very succinctly made this point in assessing George Calvert's activities in Newfoundland:

> For his religious policies there, so out of step with that time, were a harbinger of the future. [George] Baltimore had shared in sounding the death-knell for the prevailing axiom: *'Cuius regio eius religio.'* In accepting the practice of more than one expression of Christianity under the same civil government, he had taken one of the first positive steps in the English-speaking world towards recognition of the individual's right
> 96 freely and openly to profess his religious beliefs.[20]

Conditioned by both experience and practical necessities, Cecil Calvert rejected the notion that his settlers must be of the same religious persuasion as he was. He believed that religious ties were not the only way to achieve secular loyalty. Given the religious animosities of the early seventeenth century, Baltimore's effort to colonize with a heterogeneous religious population was no mean undertaking. Maryland marked a significant break with the dogmas of the age. However, it must be emphasized that religious toleration was not the purpose of the founding of Maryland. Religious toleration was the *modus operandi* of the "Maryland Design."[21]

Although Baltimore intended to embark for Maryland as soon as

---

More's influence can be made for James I. Given George Calvert's close association with the king, he was no doubt influenced by his thoughts and actions. In some important ways the policy in Maryland paralleled the Protestant king's policy toward his Catholic subjects with his attempts at securing their loyalty through the oath of allegiance. Obviously the Catholic Calverts went far beyond James in their attempts at separating religious and secular loyalties. See Krugler, "Puritan and Papist," ch. 1. The Calverts undoubtedly drew, perhaps without any conscious effort, from many diverse sources in formulating their policy.

[20] *Op. cit.*, p. 511.

[21] Wintour used the term "Maryland Design" frequently to describe Baltimore's enterprise. See John D. Krugler, "Captain Robert Wintour and the Maryland Design, 1633-1638," in *To Live Like Princes*, pp. 6-23. Maryland historians have frequently reversed the order of Baltimore's priorities. E.g., Edwin W. Beitzell wrote that "Lord Baltimore was venturing to advance religious freedom during a period of religious upheaval. The attempt was complicated by the fact that the undertaking had to be financially successful or his family would be reduced to pauperism." "Thomas Copley, Gentleman," *Maryland Historical Review*, XLVII (September, 1952), 214. Obviously both were an integral part of the Maryland Design. Baltimore's emphasis was on the latter, however, and not the former.

the colony was established, conditions in England never permitted him the opportunity. As a result he attempted to control events thousands of miles away in distance and months away in time. To execute his policies he relied on written instructions to his subordinates. Initially this proved successful. Baltimore carefully detailed his policy toward religion in the instructions he issued for the governor and commissioners in November, 1633. Both on the voyage to Maryland and after landing, the proprietor ordered that they should be very careful "to preserve unity & peace amongst all the passengers on Shipp-board, and that they suffer no scandall nor offence to be given to any of the Protestants, whereby any just complaint may hereafter be made, by them, in Virginia or in England." To prevent discord, he ordered his officers that "they cause all Acts of Romane Catholique Religion to be done as privately as may be, and they instruct all Roman Catholiques to be silent upon all occasions of discourse concerning matters of Religion." Finally the Protestant settlers were to be treated with as much mildness and favor as justice would permit. From these instructions two points are salient: Baltimore's fear of "just complaints" to Protestant Virginia or England and, an easily overlooked point, that the burden of implementing this religious policy rested squarely with the Roman Catholic settlers.[22]

During the first decade, two incidents tested Baltimore's policy. Both involved Protestant complaints against Catholics. The Protestant majority lived virtually free of any organized religious experience. With the exception of Kent Island, where there was an Anglican priest in 1634, there was no ordained minister in Maryland until about 1650. Religious services, when held, were no doubt conducted by lay readers or by occasional visiting clergymen from Virginia. The Protestant majority, for the most part drawn from the servant class in England, proved incapable of creating its own religious institutions.[23]

The Protestant settlers were sensitive to the religious situation, and disputations over religious matters took place. One such incident involved William Lewis, overseer of the Jesuit plantation of St. Inigoes. The tensions which flared in this 1638 case may have resulted from the successful proselytizing of the Jesuits. In their Annual Letter of

[22] *Calvert Papers*, I, 132-136.

[23] Lawrence C. Wroth, "The First Sixty Years of the Church of England in Maryland, 1632-1692," *Maryland Historical Magazine*, XI (March, 1916), 1-41. George B. Scriven, "Religious Affiliation in Seventeenth Century Maryland," *Historical Magazine of the Protestant Episcopal Church*, XXV (September, 1956), 220-229.

1638 the Jesuits recited their successes. Not only was the attendance on the sacraments large but "the most ignorant have been catechized" and the sick and dying "have been assisted in every way, so that not a single person has died without sacraments." Nor were the Protestants forgotten. Unable to secure a "station among the barbarians," i.e., Indians, the Jesuits were able to devote themselves "more zealously to the English" and boasted of their accomplishments in bringing numerous Protestants to the Catholic faith.[24]

Against this background the Lewis case emerged. Lewis, on the first Sunday in July, 1638, reported that some of his servants intended to circulate a petition to the governor of Virginia in chapel that morn-
98 ing. The petition was to inform the governor of "the abuses and scandalous reproaches which God and his ministers doe daily suffer" from Lewis. The Protestant servants claimed that Lewis said

> our Ministers are the Ministers of the divell; and that our books are made by the instruments of the divell, and further saith that those servants which are under his charge shall neither keepe nor read any booke which doth appertaine to our religion within the house of the said william Lewis, to the great discomfort of those poore bondmen which are under his subjection, especially in this heathen country where no godly minister is to teach and instruct ignorant people in the grounds of religion. And as for people which cometh unto the said Lewis. . . [he] taketh occasion to call them into his chamber, and there laboureth with all vehemency [,] craft and subtlety to delude ignorant persons.

The Protestants concluded their petition with a plea that the Virginia governor ("you who have power") do what he could to relieve them of "these absurd abuses and herediculous crimes." Quite obviously this petition threatened the very foundations of Maryland's existence, for the last thing the proprietor and his officials in Maryland wanted was outside interference from Protestant Virginia.

This dispute, having come to the attention of the government, was treated seriously. Similarly to the Massachusetts cases of Roger Williams and Anne Hutchinson, Maryland authorities moved quickly to prevent the social fabric from being torn apart by religious disputation. But with a curious twist. In this instance the dominant element moved quickly against one of its own who had violated the principles enunciated by Baltimore in his Instructions. A warrant directed the sheriff to bring Lewis and the Protestant servants into court where three Catholics—Governor Leonard Calvert, Commissioner Thomas

[24] Foley, *Records*, III, 370-371.

Cornwallis, and the newly appointed secretary to the colony and recent convert John Lewger—heard the particulars.

According to Lewis, his servants had been reading from a book of sermons by an Elizabethan Puritan minister, "Silver Tongued" Henry Smith.[25] When he entered the room "they read it aloud to the end he shoulde heare it, and that the matter being much reproachfull to his religion," Lewis responded by branding the book a "falsehood," charging it "came from the Divell, as all lies did, & that he that writt it was an instrument of the divell." Two witnesses testified that Lewis had also charged that Protestant ministers "were the ministers of the divell" and another that Lewis had forbidden Francis Gray, a freeman who evidently conducted lay services, to read Smith's book of sermons in the house nor any other "such base fellowes as he [Smith] was." Lewis's case was not aided by the fact that Gray's testimony about a conversation with Father Thomas Copley on the matter went unchallenged in court. Gray reported that Copley, entrusted with the secular affairs of the Jesuit mission, "had given him good satisfaction" and "blamed much William Lewis for his contumelious speeches and ill-governed zeale and it was fitt that he [Lewis] should be punished."

The court found Lewis guilty of disturbing the peace. Lewger found him guilty of "offensive & indiscrete speech" and that he had exceeded his authority in forbidding the Protestant servants "to read a booke otherwise allowed & lawfull to be read in the state of England." Although acquitting Lewis of the charge that he had forbidden his servants to use Protestant books in his house, the secretary found that Lewis's "unseasonable disputations" on religion tended "to the disturbance of the publique peace & quiett of the colony" in direct disregard of a "publique proclamation sett forth to prohibite all such disputes" (the public reading of the Instructions in 1634?). Lewger fined him 500 pounds of tobacco as did Cornwallis, who found him guilty of acting against the proclamation "made for the suppressing of all such disputes tending to the cherishing of a faction in religion." The court then put Lewis on bond of 3,000 pounds of tobacco until "tenth of November next" and ordered him not to "offend the peace of this colony or the inhabitants thereof by injurious & unnecessary

[25] "Silver Tongued" according to Thomas Fuller, who published his collected sermons. His sermons were frequently reprinted. William Haller, *The Rise of Puritanism* (New York, 1938), pp. 29-30. According to Paul S. Seaver, Smith was "a very paragon of Puritan religiosity." *The Puritan Lectureships: The Politics of Religious Dissent, 1560-1662* (Stanford, 1970), p. 136.

arguments or disputations in matters of religion," or use "any ignominious words or speeches touching the books or ministers authorized by the State of England."

For Maryland the threat from hostile authorities and enemies in England loomed very large. With Baltimore's enemies only awaiting an opportunity to undermine the charter, every effort had to be made to deprive them of ammunition. And the victim of this policy seems to have been the overseer of St. Inigoes, William Lewis, a man of "ill-governed zeale." His servants could sneer that "the Pope was Anti-christ" and that the Jesuits were anti-Christian but he could not
100 answer. To do so promoted "faction in religion." The Lewis case clearly indicates the Catholic leadership's recognition of the precariousness of their foothold. Determined to avoid any charges that it had come to plant "the Romish religion," no breach of the peace over religion (regardless of a case's merits) could be tolerated. Nor would the leadership even countenance suppressing a book which ran directly counter to its religious beliefs as Catholics.[26]

That this policy was adhered to and that Protestants could seek redress in Maryland is seen in another case involving Thomas Gerard, a physician and in 1642 a Catholic. This incident, which came before the Assembly in March, 1642, involved the use of the only house of worship in Maryland. At this time, Maryland Catholics shared the chapel with Protestants who evidently conducted lay services there. For reasons unknown, Gerard took away the key to the chapel and removed the Protestants' books from the edifice. This prevented the Protestants from holding services. Through David Wickliff, a Protestant and a delegate from St. George's Hundred, the Protestants petitioned the Assembly for redress. The Assembly found Gerard "Guilty of a misdemeanor," ordered him to return the key and books, and fined him 500 pounds of tobacco to be used "towards the maintenance of the first minister as should arrive." As the Assembly was still dominated by Catholics, it is evident that they were still willing to punish their own for violating Lord Baltimore's policy.[27]

Significantly, during this same period there is no record of any Protestant charged with breach of the peace in matters of religion.

[26] *Archives of Maryland*, IV, 35-39. Father Copley did not challenge the validity of the words attributed to him. This does not mean that Gray's recital was accurate.

[27] *Ibid.*, I, 119. Some Catholic clerics were scandalized by George Calvert's efforts to hold both Catholic services and services for the "heretics" under the same roof in Newfoundland. Lahey, *op. cit.*, p. 506.

Nor were any religious qualifications imposed on freemanship or office holding in Maryland. Although the appointive offices with few exceptions were held by Baltimore's co-religionists, in many instances relatives or family friends, political office was open to Protestants. Father Copley lamented in a 1638 letter to the proprietor that the office of sheriff was occupied by one "who hath formerly bin a persevante, and is now a chiefe Protestante."[28] During the formative years, Maryland differed from the other English colonies founded before her to the extent that religious diversity was encouraged even at the expense of the dominant Catholic element in Maryland.

Baltimore's Maryland was unique in another respect. In the three colonies founded before Maryland the civil government actively pro- 101
moted religious activities, especially in Plymouth and Massachusetts Bay, where religion had been the principal reason for their founding. In both Anglican and Puritan thought, magistrates were the "nursing fathers" of the church, having a special role to foster and protect the religious institutions. Although described by historians as a paternalistic feudal lord who concerned himself with all aspects of his settlers' lives, Baltimore certainly does not fit the image of a "nursing father" in religion. If anything, he appeared indifferent.[29] As shown, he did nothing to foster or prevent the growth of religious institutions for his Protestant settlers. But what of Catholic institutions? In his confrontation with the Society of Jesus in Maryland, Baltimore demonstrated his attitude toward religious institutions.

There were many reasons for associating the enterprise with the Jesuits beyond the obvious one of providing for the spiritual needs of some of the settlers. Baltimore's father had worked closely with the

[28] Copley to Baltimore, April 3, 1638, *Calvert Papers*, I, 163. Many English pursuivants worked for the government searching for undiscovered Catholics. Some were blackmailers and extortionists. Havran provides an excellent analysis of their illegal activities (*op. cit.*, ch. 7).

[29] John Jewel, a foremost Anglican theorist, put it most succinctly: "For princes are nursing fathers of the church, and keepers of both tables. Neither for any great cause hath God willed governments to exist, then that there might be always some to maintain and preserve religion and piety." *Epistola ad Scipionem* in *The Works of John Jewel, Bishop of Salisbury*, ed. John Ayre (4 vols.; Cambridge, 1845-1850), IV, 1125-1126. For the similar thoughts of a Massachusetts minister, John Norton, *The Answer to the Whole Set of Questions of the Celebrated Mr. William Apollonius, Pastor of the Church of Middelburg* . . . trans. Douglas Horton (Cambridge, 1958), p. 161. Norton's work was written in 1645 and published in Latin three years later. Cf. Thomas O'Brien Hanley, "Church and State in the Maryland Ordinance of 1639," *Church History*, XXVI (December, 1957), 338.

Society during the last years of his life. But beyond this familial association, the Jesuits were well organized and disciplined. They had contacts throughout England which could be utilized to disseminate information about Maryland. The Society actively recruited settlers for the colony. This was as much for their own welfare, however, as for Baltimore's. The proprietor also had a close working relationship with Father Andrew White, who wrote Maryland's first colonization tract. In addition, Baltimore undoubtedly saw the dedicated Jesuits as a useful instrument in pacifying the native population of Maryland. They would fulfill one of the major stated goals of the colony, namely, Christianizing the Indians and would also aid in the devel-
102 opment of what hopefully would be a lucrative trade with the Indians. Baltimore was not, however, in any position to accord special privileges to the Society. He undoubtedly viewed the acquiring of their services in much the same manner as if he were securing a priest for his own household. Jesuit sources claim that he sought the assistance of the Society for his colony. This may have been at the urging of certain Jesuits who were predisposed to venture to Maryland. Whatever the circumstances, Baltimore drove a hard bargain in acquiring their services. Unable to persuade the proprietor to provide any contribution to support their work, either from his own funds or from any common source, the Society agreed to accept "the same conditions, agreements and contracts as the rest of the colonists, and act accordingly." In the allotment of lands it was agreed the Society "should accept a portion tallying with the conditions and agreements." The Jesuits thought this a "hard condition," not in conformity with their role as priests. The initial understanding between Baltimore and the Jesuits was that in Maryland they would have to fend for themselves with little or no assistance from the proprietor. His willingness to allow members of the Society to emigrate on the same terms as the other gentlemen was as far as Baltimore would or could go in providing for the spiritual needs of his Catholic settlers.[30]

The Jesuits in Maryland soon proved to be a greater problem than Baltimore had foreseen. Under the leadership of Father Thomas Copley, who had arrived in 1637, the Jesuits launched a campaign to secure a greater recognition of their position. Their demands went far beyond what had been agreed upon to secure their participation. The three Jesuits in Maryland had managed to win some recognition of

[30] Father Edward Knott, Provincial, to Papal Nuncio in Belgium, in Hughes, *Society of Jesus, Text,* pp. 255-256. Foley, *Records,* III, 363-364.

their priestly office by gaining a special exemption from the 1638 Assembly. Soon after the Assembly adjourned, Copley wrote to Baltimore concerning the laws just passed. He objected that there had been no effort made "to provide or to shew any favor to Ecclesiasticall persons, or to preserve for the church the Immunitye and priveledges which she enjoyeth every where else." After urging the proprietor to take the good advice of the Church in all things concerning the Church, he entreated Baltimore privately to authorize the Society to enjoy certain privileges while the government was Catholic. Disregarding the initial agreement between Baltimore and the Society, Father Copley now raised the perplexing question of what obligation Baltimore as a Catholic had to the Church. Could the civil authorities deny the Catholic Church in Maryland the rights and privileges she enjoyed in other Catholic countries?[31]

For the Catholic proprietor, Copley's letter posed a delicate, almost embarrassing problem. Certainly Baltimore had no desire to insult his Church. However, the issue raised was central to the survival of his colony. By merely allowing the Jesuits to go to Maryland he had taken a major risk. Now they demanded more than he could allow. His marginal notation on Copley's letter reflected his initial anger over such demands as a tax-exempt status for the priests and their servants. Characteristically, Baltimore attempted to avoid a direct confrontation over this issue. As a result the matter dragged on for years before final resolution was achieved. Baltimore's thinking on this point probably coincided with that of his newly appointed secretary, John Lewger. In an attempt to resolve the issue, Lewger composed a series of twenty "cases." He concluded that the Catholic Church as represented by the Society must subordinate her interests to those of the colony. Baltimore, however, was not in a position to push this point.[32]

Baltimore had compelling reasons for avoiding a confrontation. The last thing he wanted was to have this disagreement become public. It could only have a damaging effect on his efforts to attract settlers for his little colony. Further, having invested all his money in the enterprise, he was at this time completely dependent on his father-in-law. He also needed the priests in order to satisfy the

[31] *Calvert Papers*, I, 162-168.

[32] *Ibid.*, p. 165. The fullest exposition remains Hughes, *Society of Jesus*, *Text*, I, 255ff. Lewger's "Cases" were published by Johnson, *op. cit.*, pp. 73-78, and in a slightly different form by Hughes.

spiritual needs of the Catholic settlers already there and to attract new Catholic settlers. In addition, he was in many ways beholden to the Society. Father Copley tersely reminded him of this. In the peopling and planting of Maryland, he noted, "I am sure that none have donne neere soe much as we, nor endeed are lykly to doe soe much." Nor was the Society without its supporters in the colony. Thomas Cornwallis, one of the original councillors and now one of the colony's most prominent inhabitants, besought Baltimore "for his sake whose honor you and wee do heere pretend, and whoe at Last must Judg with what Sincerety wee have discharged it," that he permit nothing to pass which was prejudicial to "the Immunettyes and
104 Privildges of that Church which is the only true Guide toe all Eternal Happiness." He urged that the differences between the Church and his government be reconciled as quickly as possible. Baltimore, concerned that his own rights be recognized, that his enterprise not be undone before it had a fair chance, and that an open rupture with the Jesuits in Maryland be avoided, attempted to negotiate a settlement with the Society in England.[33]

During the summer of 1638, Baltimore worked out what he thought was an understanding with the Society, whose English provincial, Father Henry More, was more favorably disposed to reaching an understanding than were the Jesuits who labored in the colony. Baltimore, probably as a result of the accord, then sent a sharp rebuke to Maryland, censuring both the governor and the secretary for the errors committed against the Jesuits. As Baltimore's letters of July 30 and August 2 are no longer extant, the exact nature of the settlement he thought he had worked out with Father More and the nature of the rebuke to his officers in Maryland remain unknown. In January, 1639, Lewger wrote to the proprietor on behalf of the governor and himself. He protested that they knew not what errors they had committed against the priests, having thought they had implemented his will. He denied any evil intentions against the Jesuits. In this same letter Lewger informed Baltimore that he had acquainted the newly arrived replacement for Father Copley with what the proprietor had written in his previous letters concerning some instructions

[33] Thomas, Lord Arundel, to Secretary of State Windebank, February 17, 1638/39, PRO SP16/413/17. Copley to Baltimore, April 3, 1638; Cornwallis to Baltimore, April 16, 1638, *Calvert Papers*, I, 168-171. Cf. Falb's contention that by openly arguing with the Maryland Jesuits, Baltimore and his deputies increased Protestant confidence in the proprietorship (*op. cit.*, p. 302).

and directions "to be sent out of England" for the future conduct of the Society in Maryland. Father Poulton, however, disclaimed any knowledge of the instructions. He desired "a note of what was written concerning them that they might conforme themselves to it in all points so far as in conscience they might. . . ." Poulton did, however, refuse to believe that the provincial would concede that "a Catholique magistrate may in discretion proceed here, as well affected magistrates in like cases doe in England." Whatever the nature of the understanding between the leader of the colony and the leader of the Society, it was not finding a friendly reception in Maryland.[34]

A further blow to any accord agreeable to Baltimore came from the *105*
Assembly which convened shortly after Lewger wrote his letter. The Assembly passed as part of the Ordinance of 1639 an "act for Church liberties." This act probably was not in the package of laws Baltimore sent over for approval and which were rejected by the 1638 Assembly. Jesuit historians are undoubtedly correct in attributing the act to the freemen in Maryland. The question is why they chose at this particular time to champion the liberties of the Church. Although there is no direct evidence to link Father Copley with the act, it is possible that he used his influence with the legislators to gain from the Assembly what he could not convince Baltimore to grant.[35]

The act itself is sufficiently vague and ambiguous, allowing for a number of interpretations. As adopted, it read, "Holy Churches [*sic*] within this province shall have all her rights and liberties." And although the act was renewed by the 1640 Assembly, only experience could determine what it meant in practice. In practice, and in keeping with Baltimore's intent, these "rights and liberties" would be circumscribed to the point where the blanket guarantee meant little. The 1639 Assembly enacted at least one piece of legislation directly infringing upon the rights "she hath in other Catholick countryes" when it placed the proving of wills and granting of administrations in the hands of the secretary of the colony. Since Maryland had no ecclesiastical court system to fulfill this function, too much should not be made of this point. This action, however, presaged the direction Baltimore wished his little colony to take. More important, the Jesuits failed to secure independence in the areas of their greatest concern,

[34] Lewger to Baltimore, January 5, 1638/39, *Calvert Papers*, I, 194.

[35] *Archives of Maryland*, I, 83, 40. Hughes, *Society of Jesus, Text*, I, 446, and Hanley, "Maryland Ordinance," pp. 325-341. By 1642 Baltimore was convinced the Jesuits were actively lobbying among the lay Marylanders. *Calvert Papers*, I, 217.

namely, their dealings with the Indians, tax privileges, and acquisition of land. Baltimore saw the Society as a threat not only to his prerogatives and financial well-being, but to the very existence of the colony. Initially he had hesitated to move directly against the Society and had sought accord. After 1640 he moved away from reconciliation.[36]

In so doing he clarified his thinking on his and the colony's relation to the Society. On the issue of acquiring land in Maryland he remained adamant and recognized no superior, the Catholic Church notwithstanding. Having failed to win support for this position in the Assembly, he issued new "Conditions of Plantation" in November,
106 1641. The new conditions consisted of six articles. Only the first four, which were similar to, but less generous than, the previous conditions, were published in the colony. The remaining articles were directed at the Society and introduced significant changes. The fifth stipulated that no ecclesiastical or temporal body shall have the benefit by the preceding conditions "of possessing or enjoying any lands" without "special license first had and obtained for this end under the hand and seal of his Lordship." With the sixth article, the proprietor attempted to introduce the English statute of mortmain.[37]

Seeking recognition of his position, Baltimore prepared a statement consisting of four points which he desired the English provincial to issue in the Society's name. Had this document been accepted, the Society would have forthrightly recognized Baltimore's superiority. The statement stipulated first that the Society would relinquish all claims "directly or indirectly [to] trade or traffique with any Indian or Salvage [*sic*] without the speciall licence of the Lord Baltimore" or his governor. Second, the Society would relinquish any legal right to land in Maryland unless Baltimore granted it. The provincial was to "disavow and disannull all purchase whatsoever of any such land made by any of our Community or Society" not acquired in a lawful manner. Baltimore's third point was extraordinary and indicated how far he was willing to go with the clergy. He asserted that the laws of

[36] *Archives of Maryland*, I, 96. Also passed by the 1640 Assembly was "An Act touching Marriages" which closely paralleled Lewger's thinking as expressed in Article II of this "Cases" (*ibid.*, p. 97). Hughes, *History of the Society of Jesus in North America, Documents* (one volume in 2 parts; Cleveland, 1908-1910), I, 160.

[37] *Archives of Maryland*, I, 41, 42; III, 100. The fifth and sixth articles were in the papers relating to the Society of Jesus in Stoneyhurst College. In Latin, they are translated in Johnson, *op. cit.*, p. 67.

Maryland "doe binde all persons whatsoever as well spiritual as lay" and added:

> Considering the dependancie which the Gover[n]ment of Maryland hath upon the State of England, unto which it must be (as neere as may bee) conformable, no ecclesiasticall person whatsoever, inhabiting or being within the said Province, ought to pretend or expect, nor is the Lord Baltimore or any of his officers (although they bee Roman Catholiques) obliged in conscience to allow unto the said ecclesiasticall persons, inhabiting or being within the said Province, then what is allowed by his Majestie or any of his officers or magistrates to like persons in England.

He concluded by asserting that he and his officers could proceed 107
against ecclesiastical persons, lands, and goods "for the doeing of right and justice to any other person" or, more importantly, "for the mainteyning & preservation of all the rights, prerogatives and jurisdictions granted to the said Lord" just as they may do against the laity "without committing any sinne or incurring the censure of Bulla Coenae for soe doeing."[38] The final point concerned "causes testamentarie, probate of wills, granting of letters of administration, &c., and the granting of licenses for marriages" which ecclesiastical courts handled in Catholic countries. Until such courts were established ("with the Lord Baltemores consent"), such cases were to be heard, determined, and punished only by the officers authorized by Baltimore.[39]

Not unnaturally, the Society resisted this bold attempt to circumscribe their role in Maryland. Negotiations stalled; Baltimore slapped an embargo on Jesuits intending to go to Maryland until "all matters are agreed and perfected before they goe," and took steps to replace the remaining Jesuits in Maryland with secular clergy. When the Society sought to have members of Baltimore's family intercede to have the embargo lifted, there was a "bitter falling out" between Baltimore and his sister and her husband. Only Baltimore seemed to have recognized the threat posed by an uncontrolled Catholic clergy to Maryland's survival.[40]

[38] The bull *Pastoralis Romani Pontificis* or *Bulla in Coena Domini* published by Pope Urban VIII in April, 1627, provided excommunication for specific transgressions against the Church. The fifteenth, eighteenth, and nineteenth were most relevant to the Maryland situation. Hughes, *Society of Jesus, Text*, I, 436-437. Father Copley made direct reference to this bull in his letters to Baltimore in April, 1638. *Calvert Papers*, I, 166.

[39] Hughes, *Society of Jesus, Documents*, I, 166-168.

[40] "The Fathers of the society do purposely withhold from subscribing to what the

Exasperated by the Society's dilatory tactics and refusal to acknowledge his superiority and provoked by communications from his brother counselling moderation, Baltimore vented his anger in a letter to the governor in November, 1642. "I am (upon very good reason) satisfied . . . that they doe designe my destruction," he lamented. He had good cause to suspect the worst. If they cannot "make or mainteine a partie" among the English settlers "to bring their ends about" they will, Baltimore asserted, "endeavour to doe it by the Indians within a verie short time by arming them &c. against all those that shall oppose them and all under pretence of God's honor and the propagacon of the Christian faith, which shalbee the maske and viz-
108 ard to their other designes." The Jesuits in Maryland, according to Lord Baltimore, were no longer serving the religious needs of the colony; they had become a subversive force. Baltimore then took the opportunity to enlighten his brother on the nature of the relationship of the individual to the clergy.

> If all things that Clergie men should doe upon these pretences should bee accounted just and to proceed from God, Laymen were the basest slaves and the most wretched creatures upon the earth. And if the greatest saint upon the earth should intrude himselfe into my howse against my will and in despite of mee with intention to save the soules of all my family, but with all give mee just cause to suspect that hee likewise designes my temporall destruction, or that being already in my howse doth actuallie practise it, although with all he doe perhaps manie spiritual goods, yet certeinlie I may and ought to preserve myselfe by the expulsion of such an enemy and by providing others to performe the spiritual good hee did, who shall not have anie intention of mischiefe towards mee. . . .

When the priests failed to serve Baltimore's needs, no matter how much spiritual good they may have done, they had to go. He would tolerate no more from "those of the Hill," as he contemptuously referred to the Jesuits, whose actions were of "dangerous consequences" to him and to his colony. As to the threats of excommunication, threats that evidently tempered his moves for years, Baltimore no

---

baron exacts of them, because they consider some of the points quite adverse to ecclesiastical immunity." Knott to the Nuncio Monsignore Rosetti, November 17, 1641, in Hughes, *Society of Jesus, Text,* I, 417. Lord Baltimore to William Peasely, September 30, 1642; William Peasely to Mr. Gervits, S.J., September 30, October 1; Mrs. Peasely to Gervits, October 5, "Applications for the Maryland Mission—1640," *Woodstock Letters*, IX (1880), 91-93.

longer seemed concerned. After a long digression about the "princes of Italie" and their war with the pope, Baltimore demanded his brother to remain strong, asserting that if he were excommunicated it would have no validity. No matter what inconvenience might result, he admonished Leonard to act "according to what you shall understand to be my mind. . . ."[41]

How are Baltimore's strong words to be interpreted? As a Catholic, Baltimore had severely limited options available to him. To have acquiesced to the Society of Jesus would have been suicidal and Baltimore had no desire to destroy his little colony before it had been given a fair chance to succeed. The events of 1633-1634 could not have failed to make a firm impression on his mind. He was vulnerable because of his religion. If he overreacted in his feelings toward the Jesuits it was because he acutely perceived the situation and the threat. Baltimore was not about to allow his colony to be destroyed by the Jesuits and he took steps to replace them with priests more willing to subordinate themselves to his will. In so doing he followed a policy that had been sanctioned by the Jesuits themselves.[42]

Historians have assigned Cecil Lord Baltimore a role which does not fit him. Simply put, he was not involved in founding a Catholic refuge as such. At no time did he ever put the interests of the Catholic Church above the interests of his colony. Uppermost in his mind was the establishment of a colony that would return some dividend on the family investment. He hoped to achieve this through his Maryland Design which he thought "when rightly understood will not want un-

[41] *Calvert Papers*, I, 217-219. Baltimore chided his brother for his misguided loyalty to the Jesuits. You would, he wrote, have no reason "to love them verie much if you knew as much as I doe concerning their speeches and actions here [in England] towards you." Father Hughes was especially hard on Baltimore at this point. His reaction, however, came largely from misunderstanding the purpose of the colony. If Baltimore's purpose had been to found a Catholic refuge in which English law had no meaning, and where Jesuits were to enjoy all the privileges and immunities of Catholic countries, then Hughes's interpretation would have some validity. For a recent statement of Maryland as a Catholic refuge, see Falb, *op. cit.*, p. 301.

[42] Baltimore had taken the position that he would allow no one "to set out for Maryland who [held] opinions adverse to him." Knott to the Nuncio Rosetti, November 17, 1641, in Hughes, *Society of Jesus, Text*, I, 505-506. The Jesuits were attempting to delay the granting of permission for secular priests to go to Maryland. George Gage to Richard Smith, Bishop of Chalcedon, July 21, 1642, in "Catholic Clergy in Maryland," ed. Henry F. Thompson, *Maryland Historical Magazine*, IV (September, 1909), 263. In their Annual Letter of 1642 the Jesuits reported from Maryland that the secular priests failed to support Baltimore's exalted claims. Foley, *Records*, III, 385.

dertakers."[43] This did not mean that Baltimore was indifferent to religion. Lord Baltimore was a Catholic who maintained his religion throughout his life. His colony reflected that in many ways, not the least of which can be found in the names of the principal settlements, rivers, bays, and manors of Maryland. Because he was a Catholic, he and his colony were exposed to the anti-Catholic sentiments prevailing in England. His primary concern was not to violate too openly the existing laws of England. This concern determined both his government's actions against William Lewis and his move against the Society of Jesus in Maryland. Until conditions in England changed, Maryland Catholics would have to accept this hard reality.

110 However, Baltimore was not entirely indifferent to the problems faced by his co-religionists. He sought to build a successful colony, one where Catholics would have as much security as they had in England, perhaps in time more. Still, it must be asked, why were no formal attempts made to protect Catholics until 1648? In 1633 Baltimore evidently believed that no legal enactments would be necessary. The means by which security was to be achieved is to be found in Baltimore's feudal charter. In emphasizing its feudal characteristics, historians have overlooked a fundamental point. Catholic survival in England was in large part tied to the manor. Here enclaves of the outlawed religion survived and sometimes prospered. The manor, if successfully transplanted, would avoid the necessity of formal laws to protect Catholics; it would provide the necessary privacy and safety. Maryland was to be the manor writ large and Catholic survival in Maryland would take place in the same manner as it had in England. What Baltimore attempted was to recreate as much as possible that which had ensured Catholic survival in England. To have gone further would have undermined his Maryland Design.[44]

Events both in England and Maryland soon forced modifications in his policy. The continuing hostilities between Parliament and forces loyal to King Charles I altered the circumstances considerably. De-

[43] *To Live Like Princes*, ed. Krugler, p. 38.

[44] The point needs further exploration. Baltimore's primary interest was in the economic advantages of the manor but he certainly could not have overlooked its advantages for social control, especially for keeping religion a private matter. For the internal proceedings of a court-leet held at St. Clement's Manor (1659-1672) see *Archives of Maryland*, XLIII, 627-637; *Calvert Papers*, I, 172-173. By allowing the Jesuits to establish manors on the same terms as the other gentlemen, Baltimore thought he could provide for the spiritual needs of the Catholics. As they came to be one of the largest landowners, Baltimore had second thoughts and moved to curtail further land acquisitions.

spite the proprietor's best efforts, Maryland was sucked into the vortex. In the words of Father Henry More, the English provincial of the Society of Jesus, some "enterprising heretics, thinking to gratify the Parliament, invaded the colony of the Catholics." The attack by that "villian" Richard Ingle in 1644 came very close to destroying Baltimore's little colony.[45] Eventually, Governor Calvert would restore control but Maryland would never be the same. After the death of his brother in 1647, Baltimore effected a revolution in his government by appointing a Protestant as governor. Unable to migrate himself, unable to attract Catholic landowners in any significant numbers, and faced with a dwindling but religiously pluralistic population, Baltimore made the necessary adjustments. Through an oath for his appointed officials in 1648 and by a legislative enactment in 1649, Baltimore moved to protect in a formal manner his co-religionists. The Act Concerning Religion protected all Christians.[46]

In seeking to found his Maryland Design and prosper by it, Baltimore moved ahead of many of his contemporaries. He was an English Catholic who was sufficiently daring or foolish to believe that a colony could be founded where religion would be essentially a private matter. In this he was compelled neither by the teachings of the Society of Jesus nor the Catholic gentlemen of Maryland, both of whom misunderstood Baltimore's intentions and provided unexpected opposition. The religious policy pursued by Baltimore until 1648 reflected the hard realities of being a Catholic in the early seventeenth century. The pragmatic attitudes which enabled Catholicism to persist in England served Baltimore well in his struggles to maintain his colony. Nevertheless, the Act Concerning Religion of 1649 was an admission that the original policy had failed. Not even in the free air of the New World could Englishmen put aside their religious differences.

[45] Hughes, *Society of Jesus, Documents*, I, 125-126. On Ingle, *Archives of Maryland*, III, 166; IV, 231, 237-239, 241, 245-248, 251-252, 258, 262. Henry F. Thompson, "Richard Ingle in Maryland," *Maryland Historical Magazine*, I, (June, 1906), 132, 137.

[46] Petition of William Arundell (March 26, 1642) that a writ *ne exeat regio* be granted against Baltimore to prevent him from going to Maryland. Two days later, Baltimore petitioned to have the writ stayed until he presented his case to the House of Lords. He also attached an affidavit that he had no intention of *suddenly* leaving the kingdom. Historical Manuscripts Commission. *Fifth Report of the Royal Commission on Historical Manuscripts*, "The Manuscripts of the House of Lords" (2 parts; London, 1876), I, 14. Russell R. Menard, "Population Growth and Land Distribution in St. Mary's County, 1634-1710," unpublished report of the St. Mary's Commission (May, 1971), Hall of Records, Annapolis, Maryland. *Archives of Maryland*, I, 244-246; III, 108-116, 201-214.

CHURCH AND STATE IN THE MARYLAND ORDINANCE OF 1639

THOMAS O'BRIEN HANLEY, S. J., *Marquette University*

With justification American historians emphasize the rise of democratic government during the Colonial Period. The will of the colonists to determine their own affairs grew with greater force after their departure from the mother country. Within the colonies themselves they successfully demanded greater liberty in their political institutions.[1]
112 Free representation was strengthened by the plea for free conscience in a common effort to transform the outward political forms which they had left behind in seventeenth century England. In this process new understanding of the State was developing.

Maryland is characterized in this drama as a contributor to religious toleration, a crucial element of the constitutional ideal in which the State is subordinated to the spiritual life of its citizens. A single enactment, the Toleration Act of 1649, has consequently become a landmark in the Colonial Period, of importance both for Maryland and the new nation. It is a detailed and specific pronouncement on the rights of conscience.

As a matter of fact, however, in the words of an eminent historian of Maryland, "The Act of 1649 only formulated the policy which had ruled the province from the very beginning."[2] The Lords Baltimore, Proprietors of the Province, contributed considerably to the creation of this policy, but the most noteworthy legal action and formulation was achieved by the Maryland Assembly in 1638 and 1639. After a critical struggle with the Proprietor, the assemblymen created a basic set of laws, which was named The Ordinance of 1639.[3] Unlike the Toleration Act, this document was not detailed in its reference to toleration, but contained only broad principles concerning the rights of man, the Church and the State. An analysis of this enactment of 1639 and its contemporary context reveals the basis of toleration, whose quality is so largely determined by such principles.

What is so striking in the Ordinance of 1639 is that it implies a toleration more extensive and rich than what the Toleration Act of 1649 suggests. By comparison, the latter would seem to be a departure from the policy dictated by the Ordinance. The Toleration Act also seems to suppose principles which are at variance with the foundations of toleration contained in the Ordinance. It is thus that a close consideration of the Ordinance creates an historical problem which is not adequately solved by the accumulated literature on the Toleration

Act of 1649. A step toward a satisfactory solution of this problem is possible by a study of the Ordinance of 1639; (which is helped by the fact that the assembly of that year possessed a homogeneity of thought not to be found in any great measure in the Assembly of 1649).

I

The members of the first Maryland Assemblies, who formulated
the Ordinance of 1639, were souls living in an era of historical transition and politico-religious ferment. Out of this background developed
two events in England which directly affected Lord Baltimore and the
legislators of 1639. There was the Catholic Remonstrance of Grievances which the English Catholic laity formulated and signed in 1625; 113
better known was Robert Bellarmine's debate with James I over his
oath. The first political leaders of Maryland adhered to the party of
the Remonstrance and opposed the Oath of James I.

What is the justification for singling out these two instances which concerned only the Catholics of England? It is true that the majority of the Maryland settlers were Protestant. But as one Maryland historian has said, "The physical power was Protestant, the intellectual and moral and political control was Roman Catholic."[4] One need not attempt to credit exclusively any sect for Maryland toleration, which was, after all, the happy achievement of many elements and circumstances in the colony; notably, a common English political tradition, which antedated the rise of sectarianism, was a profound force. But since the "intellectual and moral and political control was Roman Catholic" in Maryland, this segment of background in England claims primary consideration. It will appear how this factor combined with English political traditions and the simple circumstances of Maryland polity to produce a clearer vision of guiding principles in the realm of Church and State.

What was the intellectual content of this "Roman Catholic control"? It has been said that toleration was not a Catholic, nor an Anglican, nor a Puritan *principle,* though in Maryland it was a *practice.* There is abundant evidence in Europe in the seventeenth century that toleration was not a *practice.* This fact is revolting to our own generation and it might make one hasty in assuming that there was no *principle* of toleration in the residue of Christianity from which all the sects drew their light. To our own purpose here, it can be said that the intellectual content of Maryland's first Assemblies did have such principles from their experiences in England.

We find some of these principles in the Catholic Remonstrance of Grievances of 1625. For a number of years the Catholic Church in

England was deprived of the administrative machinery which was common in Catholic countries. Its re-establishment would have risked severe penalties for Catholics and as a consequence authorities at Rome did not urge English Catholics to press such rights to ecclesiastical functions.

In the years immediately preceding the 1625 Remonstrance, the lack of a bishop was keenly felt. It was at this time that Dr. Richard Smith was sent to England, possessed of the episcopal powers of the See of Chalcedon. Large numbers of the Catholic laity, however justified, became fearful that the prelate would proceed to organize tribunals and other ecclesiastical features such as would be found in Cath-
114 olic countries. It was in this situation that the Remonstrance of Grievances was drawn up and signed by more than three hundred of the laity, among whom was George Calvert.

The Remonstrance forcefully states what might be expected from a hostile government should any change be made in the present *modus vivendi.* The problem that then remains for the laymen is to justify theologically their acquiescence in the present Church-State arrangement. In proceeding to this they declare their orthodoxy and obedience. They profess the right of the Church to tribunals, legislation for marriage and other matters of a mixed temporal and spiritual nature. The fact of these rights is a matter of dogma. The precise manner in which they are respected in time and place is something else again. The latter is disciplinary, not dogmatic, and can be adjusted with the different temporal authorities involved. The Remonstrance itself expresses this line of reasoning as follows:

> Controversies of this kind appeal to a mixed power, being partly temporal over our property and fortunes; and, as such, this authority has by our laws and statutes been made the subject, in varying circumstances, of various ordinances, confirmations, and alterations, no less in the reigns of Catholic than of Protestant kings, as seemed expedient in the eyes of ecclesiastical and political powers here.[5]

We find a more radical discussion of Church-State principles in Robert Bellarmine's writings against the Oath of James I and the Divine Right rationale. As Luigi Sturzo says, Bellarmine "brought back under discussion two acute problems that had never found solution either in the minds of jurists or in popular consciousness—that of the international unity of Christendom and that of the supremacy of the Pope over civil power."[6]

The starting point of Bellarmine's thinking was the ancient Gelasian formula of two distinct powers. "The Christian Republic," he wrote, "was instituted by Christ; its purpose is the attainment of eternal life; its laws are God-given; its magistrates are bishops and the pope; and the rites by which it is bound together are the seven

Sacraments. The civil State, on the other hand, took its origin from human agreement; its purpose is temporal peace; its laws are the creation of human reason, and vary according to circumstances. . . ."[7]

Heartening to those who sought toleration were the conclusions which Bellarmine drew from these premises on the nature of Church and State. "Since," he explained, "this great distinction divides the two Republics, your Majesty's prudence will tell you that, in Christian Kingdoms, the civil ruler has authority over his subjects in their civil capacity, but not in their capacity as *cives sanctorum* and *domestici Dei* (fellows with saints and those of God's household); while, on the other hand, the ecclesiastical rulers have authority over the same men in their character as Christians, but not in their character as citizens."[8] 115
The most important factor which complicated the historical condition in which Bellarmine had to discuss his problem was the international unity of Christendom in which a spiritual power, the Pope, had through medieval times come to play a leading role. The national states had not yet developed the momentum which was to stun Europe and displace from her mental construct this medieval notion of unity. As John Courtney Murray has observed: "The principles could only with difficulty be seen in their clarity and purity; indeed it may be said that their clarity and purity never appeared in any act because every act had a context that tended to obscure its inspiration."[9] By coming to the New World, the Marylanders were able to escape the major source of these obscurities.

From the standpoint of English political thought, Bellarmine's formulation of the nature of the State was of importance, particularly among the Catholic population. In essence he had declared for a State which was integral; he was able to justify a society and its civil State which "took its origin from human agreement." In vindicating the power of common consent of a people against a king, he does more than appeal to the mediation of Christendom and its spiritual head. He categorically denies on the grounds of natural law the divine right theory and tells James that as a sovereign of the people he can be deposed by them.

Such reasoning as this on the nature of the State has no affinity with that Puritan view which calls the godly to rule the corrupt masses; nor the Hobbesian policeman who must deal with a social organism which is unreasonable and recalcitrant by nature. At the same time, Bellarmine had averted any secularistic interpretations which might have been read into his view of the State as a healthy, functional whole. By reckoning with the historical fact of a universal Christendom, he established the primacy of man's spiritual life over his political existence and led one to accept the fact of a middle zone of mixed spiritual and temporal matters, a thing congenial to man's spirit-matter reality. Affinities with Bellarmine, as well as the Remonstrance, in these matters are evident in the Ordinance.

II

In the late days of feudal England, there was a common saying, "What the King was without, the Bishop of Durham is within." The Palatinate of Durham in the North of England had extended beyond the Tyne since medieval times and as a remote province possessed unique autonomy which it had not lost by the time of Henry VIII. The principality served as a model for the proprietary colonies which
116 the King of England established in North America. Durham had in time become more subject to the crown but a unique clause in the Maryland Charter provided that this colony should possess all privileges which Durham had "heretofore ever enjoyed."

Explanation of this breadth of autonomy is found in the intentions of those who formulated the Charter. As Charles M. Andrews says of Baltimore: "He was under the impelling influence of motives and obligations that were more imperative than those of a mere colonizer—among which was the sacred duty of finding a refuge for his Roman Catholic brethren, an obligation which had been felt by the Arundel group for many years."[10] Respect for this purpose was not wanting in King Charles, who in accepting a Charter providing such broad freedom of growth was granting something more than commercial benefits to a friend.

"With the assent and approbation of the freemen," is a clause that recurs as a dominant theme in the background of the Charter, as the way is opened to the creative growth of new laws, greatly freed by Durham privileges from obligation to those of England. In an age of political ferment in England, with Parliament striving to broaden its age-old privileges, the Maryland counterpart of this spirit would in its Assembly even more boldly expand the activity of self-government.[11] It was to all this that the bent for religious freedom in Baltimore and the Arundel group was to lead.

Against this general outline of the Maryland government in the Charter, Maryland clearly approximates what can be defined as a quasi-sovereign state. The concept of the State as we have been discussing it has adequate meaning in reference to the colony, since Maryland possessed a political unity and institutions suitable for procuring the common temporal good according to the classic definition, a perfect and integral society. Consequently we can speak of the nature of the State as understood by the Marylanders and that of the Church as indicated in the relationships which they came to recognize in the State.

English law has been characteristically capable of broad interpretation and application. In the case of the Charter, which was in the tradition of English law in this respect, the advantages of this fact were important to the colonists. The general references to rights of Englishmen were thus capable of broad extension, ultimately to the fulfillment of religious toleration in Maryland. It was the misfortune of the English, particularly of Catholic Englishmen, that Elizabeth had in her own terms fixed the meaning of these rights in reference to toleration. In the Charter no explicit mention was made of toleration for Catholics, but it was clearly implied, however, in the general rights of Englishmen and of Christians, which were mentioned. These elements of the Charter together with the privileges of Durham which 117
the colony possessed combined to give Maryland the privilege of rejecting the Statute Laws of Elizabeth and their misrepresentation of English tradition.

Aside from the roots of toleration to be found in the rights of Englishmen as Englishmen, we find a passage which treats of religion as an institution, explicitly the Christian religion. In it Baltimore's power to interpret the Charter favorably to himself is granted, but "provided always that no interpretation is made by which God's true and holy Christian religion . . . would suffer any prejudice diminution or curtailment."[12] There is a tradition here from the principle of liberty of the human person to that of the religious institution; the personal entity as distinct from the moral entity which embodied many persons. In the Charter's passage this unity is recognizably integral from the State's viewpoint, and its function and subsequent growth beyond the power of the State to control.

"God's true and holy Christian religion," as a Charter term, creates considerable ambiguity. To some it would seem to imply only the official Church of England. In that case it would not necessarily follow that an identical reproduction in Maryland of the Church-State arrangement in England was demanded by the Charter.[13] Apparently the privileges of Durham would free the Maryland government from this obligation. Others would argue that the privileges of Durham gave Baltimore the power to establish the Roman Church, since the generic term, "Christian Religion," included this possibility.[14] It would not be realistic to attach either explanation to the intention of Baltimore and Charles. If a passage in the Charter conclusively held the possibility of establishment as it existed in England, Maryland would hardly offer a solid hope for those who were dissatisfied with conditions in the mother country, and from whom Baltimore intended to draw the nucleus of his colonial settlement. On the other hand, it was inconceivable that establishment of Catholicism was hoped for in the face of a numerically Protestant population in Maryland, and under grant from a ruler in opposition to Rome. Understanding all these aspects Baltimore, as well as the King, shrewdly and in the spirit of English law, did not attempt to resolve such circumstances of the Charter. The result was as George Petrie concludes in his monograph: "Historical forces were at work, and these, in connection with the policy of the administration and the temper of the colonists, were, after all, to determine the relation of Church and and State in Maryland."[15]

Lord Baltimore's own writings and actions are a valid source of commentary on the Charter which was formulated by him. There is, first of all, little doubt that Calvert understood the powers which the
118 privileges of Durham gave him. Baltimore's jealous rivals in Virginia were quick to protest. Governor Pott and others, in a statement to the Royal Government, made specific reference to the singular extension of the Durham rights: "There is intended to be granted the Liberties of a County Palantine and there is noe exception of Writts of Error, or of the last appeale to the King as by law ought to bee." The protest then attacked the key phrase in the Charter which removes possibility of the usual limitations of these liberties—*"prout aliquis Episcopus Dunelmensis infra et unquam entehac habuit vel habere potuit* (insofar as any Bishop of Durham thus far ever held or could have held)." The Virginians thought that this was "to Genrall and incerteine because it doth not name any one certeine Bishop of Durham to whom it may referr; and the County Palantine of Durham was altered 27.H.i.c.24 that the Justices must be made in the King's name and by his authority."[16]

The King referred these complaints to the Privy Council. Its report agreed with the Virginia group, criticizing categorically the "Royall and Imperiall Power which is granted in all things of Sovraignty saving only allegiance to the Kings Majestie . . ." Among other departures from the practices of England, the Council decried, "the power of giveing Honors, Lands, Priviledges and other Franchises to such as shall take of him." The end result would be "to people his (colony) with persons of all sorts whatsoever different from the other Colonies in Religion Assertion or otherwise." Such a colony "haveinge power in themselves to manage their affaires free from all dependency on others" presents a temptation to colonists from Virginia and creates a "very dangerous" condition.[17] When the King left the Charter unchanged in the face of these criticisms, he made it clear that Maryland was not compelled to the system of law which governed his subjects in England and in the other colonies of America.

A further matter of significance regarding the King is found in the liberty which he gave the Marylanders in taking the oath of allegiance. Before the colony was ever proposed Charles had personal experience of the attitude of George Calvert and in the situation did not urge him to the oath which was in current practice, but, on the contrary, expressed admiration for Calvert's courage and honesty as a recusant.[18] Calvert was but reflecting a conviction which had persisted among the Catholics of England in the wake of Bellarmine's conflict with James I over the oath. When the planting of the Maryland settlement was under way, Charles respected the mind of these recusants and permitted them to modify the oath in keeping with their consciences. As a consequence, the nature of monarchy possessed a different, non-Stuart construct in the minds of the Marylanders.

The framers of the Maryland Charter managed to keep their pur- 119
poses a secret until the document had received its seal. Then they openly affirmed that the document was correctly understood regarding the liberty granted in Maryland. Something of an official *apologia* for the Charter was formulated under the title, *Objections Answered.* It seems that among Baltimore's advisers Andrew White, the missionary, was largely responsible for this tract, which was a popular approach to the very profound problem of principles involved in Church-State matters.

One commonly urged objection was the "sin of permission," of which the Massachusetts Bay Puritans were to make so much. If Marylanders were put outside the discipline of English laws touching religious practice, the Royal Government would be "permitting" the spread of heresy and would be relinquishing that charitable concern for the citizen's soul which is a ruler's most sublime responsibility. To this *Objections Answered* moderately responds: "Conversion in matter of Religion, if it bee forced, should give little satisfaction to a wise State of the fidelity of such convertites, for those who for worldly respect will breake their faith with God doubtless will do it, upon a fit occasion, much sooner with men."[19]

In dealing with another objection, the author reveals how the Maryland project clearly departed from European Church-State arrangements. The charge was similar to the one found in the Virginia appeal to the King against the Maryland Charter. "The said Roman Catholiques," reads *Objections Answered,* "will bring in the Spaniards or some other forraigne enemy to suppresse the Protestants of those parts, or perhaps grow strong enough to doe it themselves..."[20] The immediate answer to such an objection was the *reductio ad absurdum* which followed from a realistic statement of circumstances in the New World and the projected colony.

More fundamentally, however, the objection rested on the common belief of the time that religious uniformity was essential to the well-being of the State, and, many would say, of the Church. The Marylanders, however they were able to couch their answer, must deny this principle; for the government they planted in America could not be justified in terms of national states and national religions. Religious dissent among Protestants was rising fast in the 1620's in England and when the Marylanders questioned the rigors of religious conformity, a hearing was in reach. From this standpoint the Maryland government was truly an experiment in new foundations and structure. Its principles were a European heritage, but a more ancient one, one washed by an ocean voyage of the tarnish which in Europe obscured its meaning.

120

III.

The broad and often ambiguous terms of the Charter took on more precise meaning in the minds of the first Maryland political leaders. The first Assemblies in Maryland unfold in their records some fundamental notions of the State which were expressed by Bellarmine. The legislative activities of the Marylanders leave no doubt that they believed that civil authority derived from God and that its repository was not a royal bosom, as James had said, but the people. The vital force which such a premise gave to representative government was striking in the first Assemblies. It led to disagreement with Baltimore.

Without explicit order from Lord Baltimore, the first Maryland Assembly convoked in 1635. The assemblymen did not delay in formulating certain laws by which they intended the colony should be governed. The Proprietor immediately took aggressive measures to resist their action. Baltimore denied that the Charter gave the assemblymen authority to initiate legislation. By the time the 1637 Assembly had convened, Baltimore had made his own Code of Laws, on the presumption that the Assembly would consent to them.

The assemblymen did not admit that the Proprietor alone had the power to initiate legislation nor that Baltimore's Code was suitable. From several standpoints, Baltimore did not deem it advisable to continue opposition to the assemblymen. He first tried to win a reconsideration of his Code; and, when this failed, he sought revisions and compromises in its wording. The latter attempt likewise failed and the Proprietor was forced to see the assemblymen proceed to formulate their own set of laws. They were more definitive than the earlier legislation and were entitled the Ordinance of 1639.

Thus it is that the Code of Baltimore, as external evidence, gives us a better understanding of the much briefer formulation of 1639. It would not be correct to say that all that was rejected of the Code was denied in principle by the assemblymen. Instances of substitution under a specific topic, however, do offer significant evidence. Beyond radical disagreement in some cases, there is the more important modification which reveals a clearer insight into essential principles and their application. It was this latter boon which a viewpoint in the New World had brought about.

In the First Act of the Ordinance of 1639 the spirit of self-government was formulated in the following terms:

> All acts and ordinances assented unto and approved by the said house or by the Major part of the Persons assembled and afterward assented unto by the Lieutenant Generall in the name of the said Lord Proprietarie . . . shall be adjudged and established for Laws to all the same force *121*
> and effect as if the Lord Proprietary and all the freemen of this Province were personally present and did assent to and and approve the same.[21]

This passage of the Ordinance substantially modifies the Code of Baltimore where it touches on the same topic. Baltimore agrees that the Maryland Assembly should have "like power . . . as the house of Commons . . . had used or enjoyed. . . ." To this he also adds the significant phrase, "or of right ought to have use or enjoy." However, in the interest of his own power, he includes strictures on the democratic processes on which the colonists were bent. He wished to hold the power of veto over enactments of the Assembly. "All acts," one passage reads, "shall be of force untill the Lord Proprietarie shall Signifie his dissassent to the same. . . ."[22] In connection with felonies, unlawful assembly was mentioned and any "exercising within the province any jurisdiction or authority which ought to be derived from the Lord Proprietary without lawful power or commission from or under him." Regarding the liberties of the people, he declared that none shall be imprisoned nor dispossessed except "according to Laws of this province saveing to the Lord Proprietarie and his heirs all his rights and prerogatives by reason of his domination and Seigneiory over this Province and the people of the same."[23] There is little wonder that such legislative proposals were rejected by an Assembly which had heretofore functioned in such free style.

It is noteworthy that the Ordinance did not mention the Statute Laws of England. Baltimore had not only mentioned them but also outlined the order and function of authority in English courts, officials, etc., which were to be the pattern for those in the Colony. Baltimore's directions in his Code generally implied that these English forms were to be followed as nearly as possible. The Maryland Government would be free to depart from them in specific instances, but only by definite legislation which the Assembly would pass. The Ordinance, on the other hand, implied that a specific Statute Law would have to pass the

Assembly before it had force. In brief, the Code of Baltimore tended to impose a detailed pattern for Maryland, whereas the Ordinance left the assemblymen the task of constructing the course of the Colonial Government according to New World conditions, with the broad general norms of English tradition and Common Law only as a point of reference.

One vital root of an Englishman's law was the Magna Carta. From its broad statement of principle, their positive law derived as from a consideration of human nature. Appropriately, then, the Second Act of the Ordinance made explicit reference to this political birthright of Englishmen. "All Inhabitants of this Province shall have all their
122 rights and liberties according to the great Charter of England."[24] The assemblymen had avoided a long legal document by presupposing the Maryland Charter; so now they did not enter into a detailed discussion of rights which, after all, must live by a spirit and tradition.

This simplicity again contrasted with Baltimore's Code. He entitled one act "for the liberties of the people," but he limits its force. "Being Christians" entitled them to liberty, slaves were explicitly excluded by a parenthetical reference, and liberties were to be by force of "the common law or Statute Law of England (saveing in such Cases as the same are or may be altered or changed by the Laws and ordinances of this Province)." He does not fail to insist on "his domination and Seigneiory over this Province and the people of the same."[25] This Act for the Liberties of the People, as it is entitled in the Code, possessed little authentic relationship to the Magna Carta, as the assemblymen must have been quick to note.

The outline of the notion of the State, as we see upon analysis, begins to emerge from the Ordinance. It was for the people to designate in whom the civil authority, which God created in human society, should be exercised. Under this conviction the Marylanders logically emphasized representative government.

IV

In addition to the origin and exercise of civil authority, we find enlightening considerations on the limitations of civil authority in the Ordinance. Not only in references to the rights of Englishmen as human persons, but in a passage on the ancient rights of the Church as a moral person, we find evidence of clearly conceived principles.

In the simplest terms the Ordinance states that the Church "shall have all her rights and liberties."[26] Its wording varies little from what we find on the same topic in Baltimore's Code. The language, in tone as well as formulation, is in accord with a long line of famous English charters dating back to the Magna Carta. A textual difficulty, however, has given rise to a discussion which has uncovered the deeper significances of the apparently commonplace dictum.

The Act which we find in the Ordinance does not say Holy Church but rather Holy *Churches*. The question arises in the face of an obvious error of the scrivener, must *her* be changed to *their,* or should *Churches* become *Church* in correcting the text, "Holy Churches within this province shall have all her rights and Liberties."[27] The textual difficulty is easily resolved because the Maryland Assembly in the year following the Ordinance corrected the phrasing by its own modification of the
1639 Act of the Ordinance. The singular, *Church,* was used in the re- 123
vision. It would seem that the 1639 scrivener, before being distracted, had in mind the seventeenth century possessive singular of Church, which is *Churches,* evidently intending to couple the word with "rights and Liberties" in a construction with the passive voice.

The reasoning contrary to this which led to positing the plural of Church seems plausible to us today. The assemblymen were trying to adapt the phrasing of the traditional English charters but between the Ordinance and these charters stood the disruption of religious unity with the rise of Protestantism. There was not one Church but many. The legislators intended that Marylanders of whatever faith or church should enjoy the traditional liberties of these charters according to a new adaptation suited to this historic change. All churches should enjoy the rights and liberties accorded the one Church before Henry VIII's break with Rome.

The suppositions, however, are too simple for the early seventeenth century Englishmen, whether in England or America. These people had a living memory of religious unity in Europe from which they were not many years removed. It would be safe to say that each sect believed that there was but one Church. Diversity arose only from disagreement about the outward form of the Church and all were zealously bent upon winning proselytes to their view of what that form should be. To the Anglican, for example, this form meant the proper order of worship (the *Book of Common Prayer*) and the King as head of the Church. It was on all sides a question of dealing with recalcitrants or the heterodox. The legislators seemed to be clearly aware that there were many views about the true nature of the Church, and did not with their terse statement pretend to remove by force of law any of this diversity. The singular, *Church,* was indeed ambiguous, but it was an honest ambiguity.

Where, then, is provision made for freedom of conscience, which

defenders of the plural form have found in this passage on the liberties of the Church? There is an ill-advised supposition in this question; individual freedom is not likely to be found in a passage which purports to deal with freedom of a moral person such as the Church. It is true that freedom of the Church implies and indirectly provides freedom for the member. But such an indirect approach leads to the conclusion that membership in the Church is a requisite for the enjoyment of toleration and freedom of conscience for the individual. Nor is this reasoning faithful to the understandings of Englishmen. According to their tradition freedom of conscience was directly provided for as distinct from those accorded the moral persons such as the Church. This dis-
124 tinction we see in the historic charters and in imitation of these the Ordinance places two separate Acts, one for the rights of the Church and another for those of the people. In the broad provisions of the latter act we should place the right of freedom of conscience of the individual.

Among other changes which the Ordinance made in the Code's Act for the Liberties of the People, was one touching the phrase, "being a Christian." Baltimore proposed "that all the Inhabitants of this Province being Christians (Slaves excepted), Shall have and enjoy all such rights liberties immunities priviledges and free customs within this Province as any naturall born subject of England hath or ought to have."[28] The Ordinance dropped all the qualifications which we find in the first part of the Code's passage and added the reference, "according to the Great Charter." It is on such a broad foundation of personal liberty that we must base the toleration which was practiced in the early Maryland.

On the basis of the Ordinance, then, we cannot say that one had to be a Christian in order to enjoy toleration or the religious liberties referred to in this passage. Omission of the phrase, "being Christians," has this force. The Ordinance safely avoided the danger of misinterpretation when it omitted all reference to *Christian.* At the same time it took a firm stand against the oversimplification of the secularist when it gave special reference to the spiritual society, the Church, and to her rights and privileges as a moral entity, distinct from individual persons and their specific rights.

The simplest and clearest evidence of what we are saying here is found in the fact that a Jew was a member of the Assembly a few years after the Ordinance was passed. There is another instance at a later date.[29] Such a practice is not legally validated by the ambiguous passages of the Charter and, much less, by the Toleration Act of 1649, which clearly extends its benefits only to Christians. On the basis of written law, the non-Christians could appeal only to the Ordinance of 1639, and its Act for the Rights of the People.

It is suggestive to find *immunities* added to the general reference to the rights of the Church in Baltimore's Code, and to observe that the term is dropped in the Ordinance's Act for the Liberties of the Church. The feudal structure of medieval times, the national state, these and other European circumstances provided certain privileges by which the Church could exercise her rights and liberties in pursuit of her divine mission. The Church did not need these practices to safeguard her liberty in Maryland. In their new condition and the viewpoint which it provided, the Marylanders were able to see how many of these practices in Europe tended to defeat their purpose of freedom for the 125
Church, and, in other cases, how they degenerated into clerical venality and bureaucracy. Marylanders would seem to have freed themselves of such traditions, especially if they believed that some of these immunities usurped the legitimate function of the State, or obstructed the course of freedom of conscience. At the same time, there is ample evidence from the *Proceedings of the Assembly* that a secularistic view of religion was far from the legislators when they dealt with the specific situations, for example, the right of condemned to access to clergy, or the exemption of clergy from the role of civil negotiators with the Indians.

In contrast with the Marylanders, Baltimore seemed to desire all the consequences of a full-blown, medieval Palatinate. An extremely personal character of feudal authority supposed that the religious life of the individual prince would overflow into his civil offices, thus producing the basic problem of medieval rule out of which grew the dangers of lay-investiture. A vestige of this order of things may be found in the years following the Ordinance, when Lord Baltimore took a direct hand in the replacement and selection of the clergy for ministry in his Palatinate.

The Ordinance differed greatly regarding the religious felonies which we find enumerated in Baltimore's Code. Sacrilege and sorcery are mentioned by him and he states that "it Shall be adjudged felonie within this Province to commit Idolatry which is the worshipping a false God or to commit blasphemy which is accursing or wicked speaking of God. . . ."[30] Penalties are severe. In his Act for the Authority of Justices of the Peace, cursing is specifically called to the attention of those who are to execute justice. The whole passage reminds one of the medieval prince who was the personal guardian of his people. Under the pressure of Calvinistic theology, such laws as these found growing support in the England of Calvert's day. The Puritan theory of them, however, unlike Calvert's, derived less from the notion of feudal government than from the economy of the Chosen People of the Old Testament.

The Ordinance refers to felonies only briefly, and the implication for religious felonies differs greatly from Baltimore's Code. "The Leiutenant Generall or any one of the Councell . . .," it said, "shall or may Command and appoint all power and means necessary or conducive to the apprehending of felons or keeping of the peace. . . ." This does not refer directly to religious felons. Conceivably, blasphemy and other such matters, which Baltimore had designated felonies, could come into court in consequence of this. If blasphemy were such that it dis-
126 turbed the public peace, then the civil magistrates were empowered to act. They do not decide the nature of sorcery or judge one's guilt of blasphemy. These are essentially spiritual matters of which the Church, a spiritual society, and her ministers are the competent judges. Thus, according to the Ordinance, a religious felony would not be so judged, but, rather, as a breach of public order because of public contempt for the religious beliefs of others.

Happily the Assembly was saving itself and its courts much grief by the approach which it took to felonies. One need only look to the conditions brought on by the opposite course in seventeenth century New England, where civil courts developed a casuistry dealing with many religious topics. In Europe both Protestant and Catholic countries were caught up in similar schemes which invited all the disorders of which fanaticism, bigotry and personal enmity are capable.

In this substantial departure from Baltimore's Code, it should not be supposed that the Maryland government was neutral with regard to the religious life of its citizens. There was no personal patronage of religion such as we find in medieval times and in reflected form in Baltimore's thinking on Maryland. The representative nature of Maryland government precluded this. The distinctness of the two societies, which emerges in such clear lines in the Ordinance, would likewise suggest that this concept of personal patronage was passé. Nevertheless, the Maryland government gave evidence that it hoped to effect one end envisaged by the devout prince, reverence for God as the source and foundation of political life. We have instances of this intention in the Assembly's legislation. Clearly the course to its fulfillment was not in the direct feudal manner which unavoidably confused the temporal and spiritual realms. Instead, the contribution of the State would liberate the Church in pursuit of her spiritual mission and liberalize the view which the State took of mixed matters.

Another passage of Baltimore's Code which the Maryland

Assembly entirely rejected was an oath of allegiance. It differed from that of James, but must have had some questionable clauses which prompted the assemblymen to postpone a final formulation. A partial explanation may be found in the Act of Treason which is closely related to the oath, and which was likewise omitted from the Ordinance. Of the offenses classified as treason we find this: "to . . . adhere to any forreine prince or State being a professed and declared enemy of his Majesties in any practice or attempt against his said majestie."[31] It would seem best to explain Baltimore's position in terms of his general policy, which was to reproduce in his colony the political forms of the mother country, making modifications in favor of religious liberty
where he thought that it was endangered. The assemblymen must have 127
remembered the attempts in English history to apply the terms of treason laws to the Pope. When one observes that the practice of informing on the treasonous was included in Baltimore's oath, one can further understand why both topics were untouched by the laconic formulation of the Ordinance.

Laconic speech becomes the forthright assemblymen of Maryland. They were not anxious to multiply ramifications of the few radical principles for which they spoke. They may have volubly spoken with historical hindsight of the gross failures of European governments in discerning and applying those principles. For themselves and their immediate problem of statecraft, however, they seemed to realize full well the very limited clarity with which contemporaries of the historical moment must be content in making their decisions.

This brevity borne of conviction and humility, which we see reflected in the Ordinance of 1639, was blessed by the providential circumstances of the New World. In the remarkable concurrence of events, the Marylanders, as we view them in historical retrospect, demonstrated an impressive mastery of their own historical moment.

1. "It is through a broad and thorough study of this conflict," wrote Herbert Osgood, "that we shall discover the main trend of events within the provinces themselves, and at the same time note the preparation of forces which were largely to occasion the revolt of 1776." Cf. "The Proprietary Province as a Form of Colonial Government, Part I," *American Historical Review*, II (1896-1897), 654.
2. William Hand Brown *et al.* (eds.), *The Calvert Papers No. 1*, Maryland Historical Society Fund Publications No. 18 (Baltimore, 1889), p. 35
3. In the *Proceedings of the Assembly*, ordinance implies all the force of the term, *law*, but designates a specific period of time for which it binds.
4. Bradley T. Johnson, *The Foundation of Maryland and the Origin of the Act Concerning Religion of April 21, 1649*, Maryland Historical Society Fund Publication No. 28 (Baltimore, 1883), 31.
5. In the *History of the Society of Jesus in North America, Text* (New York, 1917), I, 204-205, by Thomas Hughes.
6. *Church and State* (New York, 1939), 249-250.
7. Xavier M. La Bachelet (ed.), *Auctarium Bellarminianum* (Paris, 1913), 235; the translation followed here is that of James Brodrick, *The Life and Work of Blessed Robert Francis Cardinal Bellarmine 1542-1621* (London, 1928), II, 166.

8. *Ibid.*
9. "St. Robert Bellarmine on the Indirect Power," *Theological Studies*, IX (Dec., 1948), 503.
10. *The Colonial Period of American History* (New Haven, 1937), II, 279; I, 79.
11. Mary P. Clarke, *Parliamentery Privilege in the American Colonies* (New Haven, 1943).
12. William Hand Browne *et al.* (eds.), *Archives of Maryland* (Baltimore, 1883—), III, 12; hereafter referred to as *Archives.*
13. George Petrie, *Church and State in Maryland,* Johns Hopkins University Studies in History and Political Science, Vol. X, No. 4 (Baltimore, 1892), p. 11.

14. William King, "Lord Baltimore and His Freedom in Granting Religious Toleration," *American Catholic Historical Society Records,* XXXII (December, 1921), 298.
15. *Church and State in Maryland,* 11-12.
16. *Archives,* III, 18.
17. *Ibid.*, 19.
18. Florentine Ambassador to the Grand Duke of Tuscany; in C. M. Andrews, *Colonial Period,* II, 277-278.
19. Hughes, *op. cit., Documents,* I, 11.
20. *Ibid.*, 13.
21. *Archives* I, 82.
22. *Ibid.*, 75.
23. *Ibid.*, 41.
24. *Ibid.*
25. *Ibid.*
26. *Ibid.*, 83.
27. *Ibid.*
28. *Ibid.*, 40.
29. Matthew Page Andrews, *History of Maryland: Province and State* (New York, 1929), 95-96.
30. *Archives,* I. 71-72.
31. *Ibid.*

"With promise of Liberty in Religion": The Catholic Lords Baltimore and Toleration in Seventeenth–Century Maryland, 1634–1692

JOHN D. KRUGLER

THE ORIGINS AND NATURE OF TOLERATION in Maryland were once controversial historiographical issues. Essentially, Maryland historians have put forth two mutually–exclusive interpretations concerning toleration. The more popular interpretation credited the Calverts with founding religious liberty in the New World. Indeed, religious liberty became Maryland's *raison d'être*. Generally, this interpretation maintained that as a Roman Catholic, George Calvert, the first Lord Baltimore (?1580–1632), sought a religious haven for his persecuted Catholic brethren. In seeking his goal, he reflected Catholic thinking on religious toleration, most notably Sir Thomas More. Historians who argued for this interpretation seemed concerned with molding the events to fit the pre–conceived notion. Calvert's career in England was treated in a cursory fashion; it was sufficient that he had become a Roman Catholic. Relying primarily on the self–serving testimony of Catholic priests and noting the apparently destructive penal legislation which aimed at curtailing Catholic activity, they presented a bleak picture of Catholic life in England. The Lords Baltimore founded Maryland as a refuge for their fellow Catholics who were, in the words of one priest, "persecuted, proscribed, and hunted to death for their religion." In this interpretation, Maryland was primarily a "Land of Sanctuary."[1]

A strongly contrasting interpretation also emerged. This interpretation denied any religious motivation on the part of the Calverts. These historians, frequently pro–Protestant and usually hostile to the Calverts, played down the importance of religious toleration, ascribing it to mere expediency on the part of Lord Baltimore (as if doing something expedient were bad). In some instances, they attributed toleration to sources other than the Calverts.[2]

Neither interpretation of Maryland toleration is entirely satisfactory. But if the passions of the earlier polemics have dissipated, it is not because the contending disputes were resolved. Rather, Maryland historians turned their attention to other issues.[3] This essay explores how and why, and with what degree of success, the Catholic Lords Baltimore became involved in the struggle to free the religious conscience from the dictates of the civil government. By examining not only the history of events in Maryland, where the policy of toleration was worked out, but also the history of events in England, where the Calverts formulated their policy, an interpretation emerges that takes into consideration their religion and their economic interests.

John D. Krugler is Associate Professor of History and Assistant Chairman of the History Department at Marquette University. He completed his Ph. D. in 1971 at the University of Illinois, writing a dissertation on "Puritan and Papist: Politics and Religion in Massachusetts and Maryland Before the Restoration of Charles II." Earlier essays on religious history have appeared in the *Maryland Historical Magazine*, the *Journal of Church and State*, *The Catholic Historical Review* and *The Historian*. Dr. Krugler's other publications include his edited and annotated work, *To Live Like Princes: "A Short Treatise Sett Downe in a Letter Written by R. W. to His Worthy Freind C. J. R. concerning the New Plantation Now Erecting under the Right Ho[nora]ble the Lord Baltemore in Maryland"* (Baltimore: The Enoch Pratt Free Library, 1976). He is presently working on a book *"The Maryland Designe": Lord Baltimore, His Maryland Colony, and English Catholics.*

MARYLAND HISTORICAL MAGAZINE
VOL. 79, NO. 1, SPRING 1984

130

Cecilius Calvert (1605–1675), Second Lord Baltimore (1632–1675), and First Lord Proprietor of Maryland. Mezzotint from life, Abraham Blooteling, 1657. (Courtesy, The Maryland Historical Society.)

A Contemporary Description of Cecil Lord Baltimore, 1635

[H]e is a man of excellent parts, who thoughe young hath given testimony to the world of a ripe judgm[en]t approved worth and solid vertue, noble, reall, courteous, affable, sharpe and quickwitted but not willfull, of a singular piety and zeale toward the conversion of those people, in his owne particular disinteressed, but strickly sollicitous of the common good, an excellent Master of his passions, of an innocent life and behaviour, free from all vices, nobly conceipted of the businesse, one that doth not with vaine ostentations and empty promises goe about to entice all sorts of adventorors to make prey or benefitt of them, he knowes such a designe [for Maryland] when rightly understood will not want undertakers, but rather cautious and wary whom he admits into so noble a society without good recommenda[ti]ons and knowledge of them to be free from any taints in life and manners, yet to those he thinke worthy he freely imparts him selfe and fortunes, making them so far as he can, his companions and free sharers in all his hopes: in fine such a man as all the adventorors may promise themselves with assured confidence all content and happines under this gov-erm[en]t wch to confirme he entends to crowne their wishes with his presence by transporting into those parts his owne person wife and children wth a number of noble welborne and able gentlemen that know by experience both how to obey and command, every one fitted with a brave adventure of choice men well fitted, cattell, and all other necessaries to settle such a colony as so worthy a designe deserves[.]

— From Robert Wintour's "Short Treatise . . . concerning the New Plantation Now Erecting under the Right Ho[nora]ble the Lord Baltemore in Maryland" (1635), modern edition edited by John D. Krugler.

Neither George Calvert, the first Lord Baltimore, nor his son and successor Cecil (1605–1675), envisioned Maryland primarily as a Catholic refuge. Both Lords Baltimore fully expected that life for Catholics going to Maryland would be better than it had been in England; but they also expected that this would hold true for their Protestant settlers. Colonization, after all, could hardly be sold on the basis that the settlers would be less well off than they had been in England. As Catholic gentlemen, the Lords Baltimore set out to achieve a goal, namely, to found a successful and prosperous colony, first in Newfoundland and then in Maryland. They achieved this goal, only after years of struggle against overwhelming odds, by making toleration a reality in their colony.[4]

In their colonizing efforts, the Catholic Lords Baltimore were not attempting to implement a philosophical position for which they took their cues from Sir Thomas More or Cardinal Robert Bellarmine.[5] Toleration was not so much a philosophical posture as a practical one.[6] In the context of the alternatives they had, the Catholic Lords Baltimore saw religious toleration as a means to accomplish their goal of founding a successful colony, not as an end in itself. To succeed as Catholics, the Calverts recognized that every effort had to be made to minimize religious differences, and especially those which would call attention to their Catholicism. The Catholic Lords Baltimore sought to found a colony where Catholics and Protestants worked together to achieve an economically viable enterprise. In attempting this, they ran counter to the prevailing sentiments of their age.

Maryland was for most of the seventeenth–century a refreshing oasis in an age in which the state or civil authority advocated coercion and persecution to achieve religious uniformity. In England, as elsewhere in post-Reformation Europe, civil peace and political stability rested on the belief that the subjects' religion must conform to that of the ruling monarch (*cuius regio eius religio*). After vacillating between Catholic and Protestant establishments under Elizabeth I in 1559, the English government sought to impose a degree of uniformity on the religiously-splintered nation. Parliament, through a series of laws, decreed that all English men and women must worship in the *Ecclesia Anglicana*. The broadly based national church created by the Elizabethan religious settlement embraced some of the theology of the more radical Protestant reformers, but also maintained much of the polity of the Catholic Church. Failure to comply with the religious penal laws subjected the violators to penalties ranging from small fines, to confiscation of property, to, in extreme cases, loss of life. Roman Catholic priests by their very presence in England were guilty of treason, a crime punishable by death. With the accession of James I in 1603, Parliament passed, at the first opportunity, the entire body of Elizabethan penal laws. After the Gunpowder Treason in 1605, Parliament added new laws, including the notorious oath of allegiance.[7]

Closely related to the principle of religious uniformity was another major tenet of Christian thinking, namely, that it was the duty of the magistrate, i.e., the monarch, to protect the true faith. Under English law, the monarch was the "supreme governor" of the church and was responsible for maintaining the church as it was established by law. It was the duty of kings, James I lectured his fellow monarchs in *The Trew Laws of Free Monarchies* (1598), "to maintaine the Religion presently professed within theire countrie, according to their lawes, whereby it is established, and to punish all those that should presse to alter, or disturbe the profession thereof." In this way the ruler intimately bound together the religious and civil institutions.[8]

Not all parties in England accepted religious uniformity as the norm. The onus of the penal laws notwithstanding, a significant minority of English men and women refused to accept the necessity of worship in the established church. Some persisted in worshipping as Catholics, while zealous Protestants, i.e., Puritans, agitated for greater reformation than provided for by the Elizabethan settlement. But the con-

THE OATH OF ALLEGIANCE, 1606

I [name] do truly and sincerely acknowledge, profess, testify, and declare in my conscience before God and the world, That our Sovereign Lord King James is lawful and rightful King of this Realm and of all other his Majesty's dominions and countries; and that the Pope, neither of himself, nor by any authority of the Church or See of Rome, or by any other means with any other, hath any power or authority to depose the King, or to authorise any foreign prince to invade or annoy him in his countries, or to discharge any of his subjects of their allegiance and obedience to his Majesty, or to give licence or leave to any of them to bear arms, raise tumult, or to offer any violence or hurt to his Majesty's Royal Person, State, or Government, or to any of his Majesty's subjects within his Majesty's dominions. . . . And I do further swear, That I do from my heart abhor, detest, and abjure, as impious and heretical, this damnable doctrine and position, that princes which be excommunicated or deprived by the Pope may be deposed or murdered by their subjects or any other whatsoever: And I do believe and in my conscience am resolved that neither the Pope nor any person whatsoever hath power to absolve me of this oath or any part thereof, which I acknowledge by good and full authority to be lawfully ministered unto me, and do renounce all pardons and dispensations to the contrary: . . . .

This oath of the reign of James I (1603–1625) was very similar in wording to that required of the first Maryland colonists before their departure from England in November 1633.

tending parties, with few exceptions, did not advocate that all religious doctrines had a fundamental right to coexist with theirs. Rather each sought to establish the supremacy of its own brand of religion. Even among the groups that decried the established religion's supremacy, there existed no particular quarrel with the concepts of religious uniformity and the magistrates' duty to enforce the true faith.[9]

For toleration to flourish, the concept of religious uniformity, and its concomitant belief that it was the magistrates' duty to protect the true faith, had to be broken. The struggle for religious toleration persisted throughout the seventeenth-century. Like a great tidal basin, there were ebbs and flows as the tide for toleration came in and then rushed out. Those who sought to break the hold of religious uniformity were a disparate lot. Some wrote ponderous philosophical treatises to justify religious toleration but with small effect. Others, more practically minded, sought toleration through political activities. There were some successes. However, unlimited toleration was not to be established in the seventeenth-century. As demonstrated by England's 1689 Act of Toleration, passed as part of the settlement ending the Glorious Revolution, the gains were ephemeral. In some respects that statute marked a step backwards from the desperate practices of the abortive reign of the Catholic James II.[10]

Lord Baltimore's little colony in Maryland became part of the seventeenth-century struggle to establish religious toleration in the Western world. Maryland was the first permanent colony founded by the English to be based on the concept of toleration. The Lords Baltimore rejected *cuius regio eius religio* because they were English Catholics. Given the intense anti-Catholic prejudices of their age,[11] they knew that they could not establish Catholicism in Maryland and certainly evidenced no desire to do so. But beyond this they knew, based on the career of George Calvert, that political loyalty was not necessarily conditioned by religious preference. From his experience, the Lords Baltimore concluded that other means besides religious preference could be used to secure political loyalty.[12] In order to understand Maryland toleration, the Calverts must be viewed as hard-nosed pragmatic Catholic entrepreneurs who were attempting to prosper in a world that was predominately Protestant.[13]

The condition of the English Catholic community on the eve of colonization was one of the important factors which brought the Calverts to their policy of religious toleration. Given the nature of the penal legislation that sought to ensure religious uniformity in England, it is perhaps remarkable that Catholicism survived at all. But contrary to the traditional picture presented by many Maryland historians, the English Catholic community was not a beaten and subdued minority looking only for a way to escape England. To be certain, the penal laws exacted a heavy toll. To dwell endlessly on this factor, however, is to overlook the remarkable transformation and viability of the Catholic community. Not only had Catholics survived the onslaught of the penal laws and the destruction of their Church, but their numbers grew significantly during the reigns of James I and Charles I. For example, a recent study indicated that the number of recusants (Catholics) may have almost doubled between 1603 and 1640. The community flourished to such an extent that one historian concluded that "English Catholicism would not experience such expansion again until the nineteenth-century." In casting their lot with Catholics, the Calverts joined a viable, rejuvenated community that had come to terms with its situation in England.[14]

Equally important was where and how Catholicism survived. For all intents and purposes, the penal legislation destroyed the Catholic Church in England. But to destroy the Church was not, as historian John Bossy so ably argued, to destroy Catholicism. With its hierarchial structure in shambles, English Catholicism survived as a sect. Individual Catholics, demonstrating great wit and cunning, survived because they were able to adapt to the new conditions in England. One reason that the Society of Jesus became the backbone of Catholic survival is because Jesuits recognized this development and became missionary priests.[15]

Functioning like itinerant preachers, the Jesuits carried their priestly office to the scattered families where the ancient faith had survived, notably among the gentry and nobility. For the most part Catholic survival was a function of social and economic standing. Among the lower social and economic elements, Catholicism disappeared. The exceptions were London, where in the very shadow of Parliament, Catholics pursued a rich variety of occupations, and in the countryside where many of the faithful survived in the service of the Catholic gen-
134 try or nobility. In these Catholic enclaves in the countryside, the gentry neutralized the impact of the penal legislation and made Catholic survival possible.[16] In turn, their sons, educated overseas, returned as priests to nurture the religion among the gentry, who protected them in their clandestine practices. Caroline M. Hibbard, in assessing the many local studies in recent years, concluded that the great value of these studies was to demonstrate how mistaken was the traditional picture of Catholic life in England and "how normal, even uneventful, was the life led by many English Catholics." A long tradition of civility and tacit understanding existed between Protestant and Catholic. Friendship and social standing prevented the penal laws from having full effect. Thus, while the occasional persecutions were real, they were not particularly effective against the gentry. On the eve of colonization, Catholics had made the necessary adjustments to survive. Their continued existence as Catholics was no longer in doubt.[17]

That Catholicism survived mainly among the gentry and nobility was of particular significance for the Calverts and the Maryland colony. Early in the seventeenth-century an English Jesuit noted the problems involved in attracting Catholic settlers to colonization. Father Robert Parsons (Persons) thought that it would "be a very hard matter" for Catholics to be drawn into a colonial enterprise because "the better and richer sort, in respecte of theire wealth and commodities at home and of the love of the countrey and feare of the state, will disdayne commonly to heare of such a motione." Recognizing "the poor sort" were dependent on their betters, he argued that they would not be an effective source for potential colonists either. The demography of Catholic survival worked against attracting significant numbers of settlers from the Catholic community. The inability to attract many Catholics to their colony profoundly influenced how the Calverts would manage their "Maryland designe." It meant that whatever their preference might have been, the Catholic Lords Baltimore would have to rely on Protestant settlers to succeed in the design.[18]

Only Charles Calvert, the third Lord Baltimore (1637–1715), made a direct statement concerning the origins of toleration in Maryland. While his 1678 assessment does not provide a full explanation, and is incorrect on at least one important matter, Calvert's statement merits a detailed examination. Replying to a set of queries from the Lords of Trade, he fairly described the situation his father confronted:

> . . . at the first planteing of this Provynce by my ffather Albeit he had an absolute Liberty given to him and his heires to carry thither any Persons out of any of the Dominions that belonged to the Crowne of England who should be found Wylling to go thither yett when he came to make use of this Liberty he found very few who were inclyned to goe and seat themselves in those parts But such as for some Reason or other could not lyve with ease in other places . . . .[19]

During the eighteen months between the granting of the charter (20 June 1632) and the sailing of the *Ark* and the *Dove* (22 November 1633) from Cowes, Cecil Lord Baltimore actively recruited investors and settlers from his house in the predominately Catholic Bloomsbury district in London. Father Andrew White, S.J., who earnestly sought the opportunity to conduct an overseas mission, ably assisted Baltimore and wrote Maryland's first colonization tract in 1633.[20] Although the major effort concentrated on men and women with capital available for investment, considerable attention was given to attracting yeomen, artisans, laborers, and other poorer men who would provide the vast majority of immigrants. In spite of a seemingly attractive set of inducements, the campaign was not particularly successful in attracting Catholics. Those who responded were primarily the younger sons of gentry families. Because of their position in their family and because there was little prospect of employment in England, they opted to join Baltimore. The presence and financial backing of those seventeen Catholic gentlemen and their retinues were significant for launching the Maryland design. However the bulk of the settlers would differ from the proprietor in the critical matter of religious beliefs.[21]

Venturing to America with a Catholic Lord Proprietor gave non-Catholics reason to pause. As Charles Calvert related

> And of these [who considered throwing in their lot with the Catholic Baltimore] a great parte were such as could not conforme in all particulars to the severall Lawes of England relating to Religion. Many there were of this sort of People who declared their Wyllingness to goe and Plant themselves in the Provynce so as they might have a Generall Toleracion ....

He then added, almost parenthetically, that unless certain conditions concerning toleration were met by his father, "in all probility This Provynce [would have] never beene planted."[22]

Several points made later in the century by Charles Calvert need to be explored, namely, the reliance on a heterogeneous religious population in order to secure the necessary settlers; the assertion that the impetus for toleration came from the people who "could not conforme in all particulars;" and that the idea that toleration was a precondition for emigration.

A precise statement of the religious affiliation of the early settlers is not possible. Lord Baltimore did not even know the exact number of settlers who sailed with the first expedition. He reported in January 1634 that he "sent a hopeful Colony into Maryland" with "two of the Brothers gone with near twenty other Gentlemen of very good fashion, and three hundred labouring men well provided in all Things." Baltimore was either misinformed or unduly optimistic, for the actual number falls far short of his estimation. Edward Watkins, searcher for London, reported that immediately before the departure of the *Ark* and the *Dove*, he tendered the Oath of Allegiance "to all and every the persons aboard, to the number of about 128." Down river, the ships picked up some additional Catholic settlers, including two Jesuits. The most accurate count to date yields a range of between 132 and 148 settlers who participated in the founding of Maryland.[23]

Although English Jesuits reported to Rome that "under the auspices of a certain Catholic baron, a considerable colony of Englishmen, largely Catholics," had been sent to America, it is certain that the majority of the settlers were Protestant. Some of the settlers during the early years were Puritan leaning (i.e., those who "could not conforme in all particulars"). For example, the first significant dispute concerning religion involved the Catholic overseer of the Jesuit plantation and one of his servants. The servant had been reading aloud from the sermons of "Silver Tongued" Henry Smith, a particularly virulent anti-Catholic Elizabethan Puritan minister. Protestantism was strongest among the lower social and economic element in Maryland, while the leadership of the colony was predominately Catholic and would remain so until Baltimore appointed a Protestant government in the late 1640s. Governing a colony with a religiously mixed population in an intolerant age was no mean feat and pushed the resources of the Catholic Lords Baltimore to their limits.[24]

While it is doubtful that Cecil Calvert had a fully developed plan for governing his colony in the early 1630s, it would be incorrect, as Charles Calvert did, to attribute toleration to the dissenters. However imperfectly perceived, toleration was the foundation of the Calverts' overall strategy. The means by which toleration was to be accomplished must be viewed as having an evolutionary character. A number of points must be stressed. The first is the novelty of the "Maryland designe": a Catholic colony founded "by the good grace and authority" of a Protestant monarch. The second is that, with the death of George Calvert in April 1632, execution of the design rested squarely with a young Lord Baltimore who not only lacked his father's long experience in government and colonization, but was untested as a leader. Finally, Cecil Calvert had intended to move with his family to Maryland, where he expected to exercise close control over the conduct of affairs, especially as they related to religion. As it was, his "Adversaries" strenuously fought his effort to found the colony and forced him to remain in England. Having to exercise authority from England complicated Lord Baltimore's task and made all efforts at implementing toleration tentative.[25]

Initially Cecil Calvert thought in terms of keeping toleration as informal as possible.[26] By not relying on formal legislation,
136 the Lord proprietor perhaps thought he could avoid any possible scrutiny of his practice of toleration, which ran contrary to the laws of England. Thus he implemented toleration through executive fiat. The substance of what Lord Baltimore promised Protestant settlers was embodied in the Instructions he issued to his brother Leonard, who was to govern the colony in his absence, and the Catholic commissioners, Jerome Hawley and Thomas Cornwallis. These Instructions, issued on 13 November 1633, required the Catholic leaders to be "very carefull to preserve unity and peace amongst the passengers on Shipp-board" and

> ...[to] suffer no scandall nor offence to be given to any of the Protestants, whereby any just complaint may hereafter be made, by them, in Virginea or in England, and that for that end, they cause all Acts of Romane Catholique Religion to be done as privately as may be, and that they instruct all Romane Catholiques to be silent upon all occasion of discourse concerning matters of religion; and that the said Governor and Commissioners treete the Protestants with as much mildness and favor as Justice will permit. And this is to be observed at Land as well as at Sea.[27]

Whether or not Governor Calvert read his Instructions to the settlers, he apparently treated them as if they had the full force of law. During the first decade only two cases involving disputes between Catholics and Protestants became public. In both cases the Catholic government ruled in favor of the Protestants at the expense of the Catholics, who violated the intent of Baltimore's Instructions. In addition, Baltimore's government assiduously avoided any taint of a religious test for voting or holding office. All male residents, excluding servants and Jesuits, were eligible.[28] These practices were contrary to developments taking place in the Massachusetts Bay colony. There, for example, the General Court passed a law which made political freedom an attribute of membership in one of the churches. In that colony the magistrates took seriously their role as "nursing fathers" of the religious institutions. In common with the Anglicans in Virginia, the

---

AN EARLY CONTROVERSY OVER RELIGION

On Sunday the first of July, william Lewis informed Capt: Cornwaleys that certaine of his servants had drawen a petition to Sir John Hervey [Harvey, governor of Virginia]; & intended at the Chappell that morning to procure all the Protestants hands to it. . . . The writing was of this tenor

> *Beloved in our Lord &c This is to give you notice of the abuses and scandalous reproaches wch God and his ministers doe daily suffer by william Lewis of St Inego's, who saith that our Ministers are the Ministers of the divell; and that our books are made by the instruments of the divell, and further saith that those servants wch are under his charge shall keepe nor read any books wch doth apperteine to our religion within the house of the said william Lewis, to the great discomfort of those poore bondmen wch are under his subjection, especially in this heathen country where no godly minister is to teach and instruct ignorant people in the grounds of religion. . . .*

— The Processe agst William Lewis . . . , June/July 1638, Proceedings of the Provincial Court

Bay colony Puritans moved toward religious uniformity and an established religion.[29]

Under the Catholic Lords Baltimore, Maryland would not have an established religion. The charter was written in such a way that the Calverts could have played a role similar to that of the English monarch, or for that matter, the governor of Virginia. The charter granted Baltimore "the Patronages and Advowsons of all Churches, which ... shall happen hereafter to be erected: together with license and power, to build and found Churches ... in convenient and fit places." within the colony. However, the Catholic Calverts made no effort to establish religious institutions, undoubtedly because the charter required that all churches be consecrated according to the ecclesiastical laws of England.[30]

In implementing his toleration strategy, Baltimore acted wisely. He recognized from the beginning that for Maryland to succeed, religious disputes must be avoided at all costs and that religion must be kept as private as possible. Rather than following the accepted pattern of establishing religious uniformity, Baltimore moved to the other end of the spectrum by attempting to use his authority to remove religion from the body politic. From the beginning, and without hesitation, he moved to implement this policy. For a Catholic founding a colony under the auspices of a Protestant nation, no one was more ideally fitted for the task than Cecil Lord Baltimore. A moderate man with a pragmatic outlook, he conscientiously rejected the role of protector of the "true faith." Baltimore survived because he recognized that, if he were to recoup the family fortunes in Maryland, provide an opportunity for Catholics to worship without fear or burdensome laws, and still attract a sufficient number of settlers, he had to keep religion out of politics. The degree to which this could be accomplished would determine the success of his "Maryland designe."

Although Baltimore made one unsuccessful attempt during the first decade of settlement to legislate in religious matters (his proposed "Act for Felonies") and the Assembly passed an ambigious "Act for Church Liberties" in 1639, the proprietary government did little to provide for the spiritual needs of the colonists. In marked contrast to the other colonies, religion was considered to be a private matter, of concern to the proprietor only if it became disruptive. As a result, the development of religious institutions in Maryland lagged far behind those of the other English colonies.[31]

Father White and the other Jesuit priests, whose presence in the colony was as a result of their own efforts, provided for the spiritual needs of the Catholic settlers. Cecil Calvert allowed the Jesuits to emigrate under the same conditions afforded the other colonists. Although the priests thought Baltimore drove a hard bargain in acquiring their services, they accepted his terms and sought private solicitations to finance their "pious undertaking." Many Catholics "showed great liberality," contributing both money and servants to secure a Jesuit presence. Once in Maryland, the priests quickly learned they could not expect "sustenance from heretics hostile to the faith nor from Catholics [who are] for the most part poor." In addition, the Jesuits, especially Father Thomas Copley, did not appreciate fully Baltimore's delicate position regarding toleration and pushed him for special privileges as Catholics. Risking alienation from some of his coreligionists, Cecil Calvert steadfastly refused and took steps to replace the Jesuits with secular priests.[32]

Nothing was done to provide for the special religious needs of the Protestant settlers. Although having full freedom to provide their own religious institutions, they lacked the means to do so and lived without benefit of formal religious institutions during the first decade. With the exception of Kent Island, where an Anglican minister briefly served the needs of William Claiborne's settlers, there were no clergymen from the Church of England in Maryland until 1650. Evidently some of the Protestants conducted lay services in the Catholic chapel at St. Mary's City. However, lacking an institutional basis, a number of Protestants succumbed to the proselytizing activities of the Jesuits and were converted to Catholicism.[33]

Considering the potential for religious animosities among the religiously diverse population, the first decade was remarkably free of religious disputations. There were tensions; but the government ably diffused them. It is not possible to tell where Baltimore's novel experiment would have taken him had he been left to govern his colony in peace. Between 1645 and 1660 events over which he had little or no control intervened to destroy the harmony he sought. In order to maintain his policy of toleration, new tactics were needed.

Robert Wintour declared in 1635 that Baltimore "knowes such a designe when
138 rightly understood will not want undertakers." He was wrong, and optimism soon gave way to despair. Writing from Maryland three years later, Father Copley lamented that "here certainly nothing is wanting but people." In the four years since its founding, Maryland's population had increased only slightly. Baltimore, having committed all his funds to colonization, was living off his father-in-law's generosity. His creditors brought suit against him at home, and his colony, racked by dissention, showed little prospect of profit.[34]

Throughout the 1640s Baltimore's greatest challenge was to get people to his colony. When his efforts to attract settlers from the mother country did not produce the required numbers, he turned his attention to other English colonies. What attracted him to New England, described by the Jesuits in their annual letter in 1642 as "full of Puritan Calvinists, the most bigoted of the sect," cannot be known. In 1643 Baltimore commissioned Cuthbert Fenwick to journey to New England in search of settlers. He carried a letter and a commission to Captain Edward Gibbons of Boston. As reported by Massachusetts Governor John Winthrop, Baltimore offered land in Maryland "to any of ours that would transport themselves thither, with free liberty of religion, and all other privileges which the place afforded, paying such annual rent as should be agreed upon." To Winthrop's obvious relief, "our captain had no mind to further his desire herein, nor had any of our people temptation that way."[35]

The English Civil War (1642–1649), a power struggle between King and Parliament, sidetracked Baltimore's efforts to attract settlers from other colonies. The polarization between Royalists and Roundheads, between those Anglicans and Catholics who supported the King and those Presbyterians and Independents who supported Parliament, spilled over into the American colonies. In this charged religious atmosphere, Baltimore's task was rendered more difficult. His bold experiment with religious toleration received a severe testing, as his enemies plundered his little colony. When Baltimore lost control of the colony, toleration disappeared.

Using Maryland's close identification with Roman Catholicism and Royalism as a rallying point, "that ungrateful Villaine Richard Ingle," invaded Maryland in 1645 under letters of marque from Parliament. Driving Gov. Leonard Calvert from the colony, the captain of *The Reformation* came close to destroying the budding society that had been nurtured during the past decade under the Catholic leadership. Ingle's destructive machinations, later called "the plundering yeare," were aimed primarily at prominent Catholics, who, in addition to suffering the heaviest property losses, were dragged back to England. As a rationale, Ingle claimed that most of the people in Maryland were "Papists and of the Popish and Romish Religion" and supporters of the king. The invasion of Ingle's "enterprising heretics," as English Jesuit Provincial Henry More styled them, left Maryland in a sorry state and the Catholic proprietor open to legal attack against his charter in England.[36]

Leonard Calvert returned near the end of 1646 to restore some semblance of order in the wake of the anarchy that followed Ingle. His death in June 1647 left Baltimore without his primary agent in the colony. Temporarily, leadership went to a Catholic councilor, Thomas Greene, whom Leonard Calvert had designated as his successor. But the winds of change blew briskly through Maryland. Baltimore, in an effort to outmaneuver his adversaries in Parliament, fostered a revolution in his own government. In 1648 Baltimore commissioned a Protestant governor, William Stone, to replace Greene, gave the council a predominately Protestant composition, and appointed a Protestant secretary. Although Protestants had held lesser offices in the colony, the governor, councilors, and the secretary had been Catholics.[37]

Why did Lord Baltimore revolutionize his government at this time? Originally, he had relied on Catholic gentlemen and especially on his brother for leadership in the colony. These two elements, religion and family, were noticeably absent in the wake of Ingle's invasion and Leonard Calvert's premature death. But of greater importance, Stone, as a Virginia Protestant and a supporter of Parliament, mitigated the chances that English authorities would step in to seize control of the colony. With changes made by Ingle against his colony still pending before Parliament, Cecil Calvert strengthened his position with that body by appointing Protestants to the major offices.

But equally important in naming Stone was Lord Baltimore's desire to build up the population of his colony, which had been dispersed with Ingle's invasion. As Stone's commission read, he "hath undertaken in some short time to procure five hundred people of British and Irish discent to come from other places and plant and reside within our said province of Maryland for the advancement of our Colony." Baltimore envisioned that his policy of toleration and the lure of rich lands would serve to attract those who suffered from intolerance in other colonies.[38]

That Stone's commission coincided with unrest among Puritans in Virginia was no doubt instrumental in their coming to Maryland. Virginia had passed a law against dissenters in 1639, "though as yet none" lived there.[39] Within three years a congregational church was formed and an appeal was made to New England for clergymen. In 1642 the new governor, Sir William Berkeley, executed his instructions "to be careful that Almighty God is served according to the form established in the Church of England." Under his leadership the Virginia Assembly required the conformity of all ministers to the "orders and constitutions" of the Church of England, and in 1643 compelled all nonconformists "to depart the Colony." In 1648 Berkeley again raised a "persecution against them" and dispersed the congregation at Nansemond. Some of these nonconformists were the first of many who would seek refuge in Maryland under the encouragement of Governor Stone. As one of the Puritan emigrants put it, "In the year 1649, many, both of the congregated Church, and other well affected people [i.e., supporters of Parliament] in Virginia, being debarred from the free exercise of Religion under the Government of Sir William Barkely removed themselves, Families and Estates into the Province of Maryland, being thereunto invited by Captain William Stone, then Governor for Lord Baltimore, with promise of Liberty in Religion and Priviledges of English Subjects."[40]

With Protestants filling most of the principal offices, and with an influx of settlers 139
traditionally hostile to his religion, Baltimore confronted a new problem, namely, how to protect his co-religionists in the exercise of their religion without jeopardizing his increasingly positive relationship with Parliament. As long as the colony was in the hands of Catholics and family members, there had been no special need for formal legislation. Events after 1645 dramatically altered the situation. Baltimore now sought more formal guarantees for his policy.

Baltimore first moved to secure safeguards for Maryland Catholics through a series of oaths to be administered to all of his principal office-holders, most of whom were now Protestant. Although religious considerations were not apparent in the many previous oaths required by Baltimore, their increasing importance was reflected in the new oaths prescribed in 1648. The governor, for example, had to swear not to "trouble molest or discountance any Person whatsoever in the said Province professing to believe in Jesus Christ and in particular no Roman Catholic for or in respect of his or her Religion nor in his or her free exercise thereof within the said Province so long as they be not unfaithful to his said Lordship or molest or Conspire against the Civil Government Established here." In addition the governor had to attest that he would not "make any difference of Persons in Conferring of Offices Rewards or Favours proceeding from the Authority which his said Lordship has conferred . . . in Respect of their said Religion Respectively," but merely as they are found "faithful and well deserving of his said Lordship." The governor also was to use his "Power and Authority" to protect

Christians in the free exercise of their religion from molestation (without Baltimore's "consent or Privity") by any other officer or person in the province.[41]

These oaths articulated the basic policy that Baltimore wanted to follow. The government would not interfere with the free exercise of religion on the part of Christian Marylanders, especially Roman Catholics; the government would not discriminate on account of religious preference in appointing persons to positions of authority; and the government would protect Christians
140 from being harassed in the free exercise of their religion. All was posited on loyalty to the proprietor. As long as Marylanders remained faithful to his government, they could enjoy religious freedom.

Having dealt with his major appointive officers, Lord Baltimore turned his attention to the remainder of the inhabitants, who were to be dealt with through the assembly that convened 2 April 1649. The vehicle was "An Act Concerning Religion." This act, popularly known as the "Act of Toleration," had its origin in the same circumstances that produced the oaths. In part the Act also was a response to the growing anti-Catholic sentiments expressed during the second half of the decade. The will of Thomas Allen, a poor Protestant, exemplifies the fear and distrust evident in society. Although he left his children with little estate, he willed that "for the disposall of my children I would not have them to live with any Papist." Whether based on fear or on cupidity, there was a rising anti-Catholic sentiment in Maryland.[42]

The 1649 Act Concerning Religion was clearly the work of the proprietor. Although the Act may have been modified by the assembly, it originated in the same imperatives that led to the oaths for the governor and council. Cecil Calvert submitted "a body of laws ... conteining sixteene in Number" to the first assembly under a Protestant governor. He desired that the whole body be passed without alteration, declaring that the new code of laws would replace all existing laws for the colony. However, the assembly, asserting its independence, refused. Eventually the legislators passed a code of twelve laws, the first being "An Act Concerning Religion," which they undoubtedly lifted from Baltimore's code.[43]

The Act was in keeping with the policy the lord proprietor had assumed from the beginning, namely, to use all means available to hold down religious disputes. This Act resulted not from the needs of the Protestant settlers, as Charles Calvert incorrectly suggested, but grew out of the necessity to reassure Baltimore's fellow Catholics. He still sought to keep religion out of politics, but with the altered nature of Maryland government and the heightened tensions regarding religious matters thoroughout the English world, formal legislation, as opposed to the informal "Instructions," was necessary to secure peace in the province. Baltimore wanted to unite the people of Maryland "in their affection and fidellity to us" while avoiding those things which tended toward factionalism. He sought the unanimous "and cheerfull obedience to the Civill Government . . . that as wee are all members of one Body Politique of that Province wee may have also one minde in all Civill and temporall matters." Herein lies the novelty of the "Maryland designe." Nothing was said about uniting all Marylanders in religion. What was important was loyalty to the head of the civil government, not to a religious doctrine. As Cecil Calvert summed up his thinking in 1650: "It being a Certaine and true Maxime which tells us, that ... By Concord and Union a small Collony may growe into a great and renouned Nation, whereas by Experience it is found, that by discord and Dissention Great and glorious kingdomes and Common Wealths decline, and come to nothing." The Act of 1649 was designed to remove, as far as was humanly possible, religion from politics.[44]

Whether the assembly lifted "An Act concerning Religion" verbatim from Baltimore's original code or supplemented it according to its own needs, the legislation imposed severe penalties in an attempt to quell religious disputes. Any person under the authority of the "absolute Lord and Proprietary of this Province" who shall "blaspheme God," or "deny Jesus Christ to be the Son of God, or deny the Holy Trinity, or utter reproachful speeches against the Holy Trinity" was to be punished with death and forfeiture of all lands and goods to Lord Baltimore.[45]

In similar vein, any person who used or uttered "any reproachfull words or Speeches concerning the blessed Virgin Mary the Mother of our Saviour or the holy apostles or Evangelists" was subject to fines and whippings, and for a third offense, banishment. The Act provided similar penalties for reproachfully calling any person a "heretic, schismatic, idolater, Puritan, Independent, Presbyterian, Popish Priest, Jesuit, Jesuited Papist, Lutheran, Calvinist, Anabapist, Brownist, Antinomian, Barrowist, Roundhead, Separatist," or any other disparaging epithet relating to religion. In addition, the Act made it an offense punishable by fine for profaning "the Sabbath or Lords day called Sunday by frequent swearing, drunkennes or by any uncivill or disorderly recreation, or by working . . . when absolute necessity doth not require it."[46]

The Act concluded on a more generous note. Because the "inforceing of the conscience in matters of Religion hath frequently fallen out to be of dangerous Consequence," and in order to procure more quiett and peaceable government of this Province . . . and . . . to preserve mutuall Love and amity amongst the Inhabitants thereof," the Act proclaimed that no one "professing to believe in Jesus Christ, shall from henceforth bee any waies troubled, Molested or discountenanced for or in respect of his or her religion nor in the free exercise thereof." In Maryland no person was in any way to be compelled "to the beleife or exercise of any other Religion against his or her consent." The only condition imposed on this freedom was that the residents "be not unfaithfull to the Lord Proprietary, or molest or conspire against the civill Government."[47]

Lord Baltimore offered freedom of worship to Christians in return for their obedience to him and the civil government instituted by him. The reorganization of the government in 1648 and 1649 strengthened his belief that religion and religious disputes could only frustrate his efforts at controlling the colony. By imposing very severe penalties with regard to what the inhabitants of Maryland could do or say about another's religion, Cecil Calvert intended to remove religion from politics. At the same time, by offering all inhabitants the free exercise of their religion, he insured the Catholics would be protected in their own religious worship.

Regarding the new Puritan emigrants from Virginia, Baltimore's policy was quickly put into effect. He promised liberty of religion and conscience in return for political obedience and land on the same terms given others, in return for a yearly rent and subscription to an oath of fidelity. If a 1650 document signed by the leading Protestants, including Puritan elder William Durant, means anything, the proprietary government fulfilled the bargain. An incident involving Walter Pakes, who accused Protestant Secretary Hatton of speaking evil about "Roman Catholickes," indicated that the Proprietor leaned over backwards to avoid trouble. He absolved his Secretary of any wrong doing, once again supporting a Protestant against a Catholic. In addition, Baltimore's officials erected a new county (Anne Arundel) to encompass the Virginia Puritans, allowed them to choose their own officers, and to hold their own courts.[48]

These extraordinary measures, however, proved insufficient to insure the civil peace Baltimore so much needed for his colony to prosper, as once more outside forces intervened to disrupt the colony. In 1651 Parliament, which had defeated and executed Charles I in the Civil War, dispatched a commission to reduce Virginia to the obedience of the Puritan Commonwealth. After accomplishing their mission in Virginia, the Commissioners, taking a broad interpretation of their instructions, decided to reduce Maryland to obedience also. Between 1652 and 1655, intermittent war raged between the commissioners and their supporters, mainly the recently arrived Puritans from Virginia, and Governor Stone and Calvert loyalists. When Governor Stone capitulated in 1655 and submitted to the presumed authority of the commissioners, Baltimore was again deprived of his province without benefit of legal proceedings.[49]

Having gained control of Baltimore's

Freedom of Conscience Monument, St. Mary's City

Designed by Baltimore sculptor Hans Schuler and erected by the counties of Maryland in 1934 to commemorate the 300th anniversary of the state, this large limestone statue honors the tolerant Act Concerning Religion of 1649. The figure, seemingly caught between a rock and a hard place, nicely symbolizes Maryland's geographical position in the 17th century, between the intolerant Anglicanism of Virginia to the south and the intolerant Puritanism of Massachusetts to the north. In another sense, the monument reminds us that the 1649 toleration act was philosophically and historically a midpoint between the successful, de facto Calvert policies of the early years and the drastic, restrictive era for Catholics from 1689 to the American Revolution. (Courtesy, The Maryland Historical Society.)

province, the Puritans set about to undo his policy of toleration. The "Act concerning Religion" of 1654, passed in an assembly that excluded all inhabitants who had supported the proprietor or who were Roman Catholic, stands in marked contrast to Cecil Calvert's 1649 Act. Considerably shorter than its predecessor, the 1654 Act differed in two significant ways. It dropped the extreme provisions against blasphemy and it excluded Catholics explicitly and Anglicans implicitly from protection in the profession of their faith. It is inconceivable that Lord Baltimore, the extensive grant of power he received in his charter notwithstanding, could have operated in a similar fashion by using religion as a basis for excluding persons of a particular faith from the full enjoyment of political privileges.[50]

Acting within the context of the anti-Catholicism of their time and sensing that Lord Baltimore's toleration policy reflected his weakness within the English Protestant world, the Puritans forgot their promises of fidelity and unseated the proprietor. At this point, supported by the commissioners and religiously in accord with the dominant elements in Parliament, the Puritans acted from a position of strength. What they did not reckon with was Baltimore's political genius and his ability to manipulate the Puritan government in England based on his legal right to Maryland. Much to their surprise, Cromwell eventually came out in support of the Catholic proprietor. By 1657 Calvert had reestablished control of his province. One of his first priorities was to ensure that the 1649 Act Concerning Religion was thereafter "inviolably observed both in the Provinciall and all inferior Courts of the Province." He returned to oaths as a means of insuring the religious freedom of the inhabitants, ordering justices in St. Mary's County, where most of the remaining Catholics lived, to swear not "to trouble molest or discountenance" any person "professing to believe in Jesus Christ for or in Respect of his Religion" nor in the free exercise of that religion.[51]

Of great significance is the provincial court case involving Father Francis Fitzherbert, S.J., who arrived in 1654. A "zealous missionary" who brought "aggressive leadership" to the Maryland order, the attorney general charged him in 1658 with four counts of "practising of Treason & Sedition & gyving out Rebellious & mutinous speeches" and endeavoring to raise distractions and disturbances within the colony. Two of the counts charged him with attempting to seduce and draw certain inhabitants from "their Religion," while another accused him of threatening Catholic Councillor Thomas Gerard with excommunication. His behavior, the attorney general maintained, was contrary to "a knowne Act of Assembly." The case was not settled until 1662. Father Fitzherbert entered a plea to dismiss the suit on the grounds that although the charges may be true, they were insufficient to sustain the claim. Basing his demurrer on the 1639 Act for Church Liberties and the 1649 Act Concerning Religion, he argued that active

THE "SECOND" ACT CONCERNING RELIGION, 1654

It is Enacted and Declared . . . by the Authority of the present Generall Assembly That none who profess and Exe[r]cise the Popish Religion Commonly known by the Name of the Roman Catholick Religion can be protected in this Province by the Lawes of England formerly Established and yet unrepealed nor by the Government of the Commonwealth of England Scotland and Ireland and the Dominions thereunto belonging[.]

. . .

. . . Liberty [of religion] be not Extended to popery or prelacy nor to such as under the profession of Christ hold forth and practice Licentiousness.

— **"An Act Concerning Religion," Proceedings of the Maryland Assembly, 20 October 1654.**

preaching and teaching was "the free Exercise of every Churchmans Religion." The court sustained his plea.[52]

The period thus ushered in, from Cecil Calvert's restoration in 1657 to his death in 1675, was perhaps the calmest period in terms of religious disputation in seventeenth-century Maryland. In 1666 Baltimore instructed his son and governor, Charles Calvert, to "most strictly and Carefully observe keepe and Execute and cause to be observed kept and executed" the 1649 Act Concerning Religion. This Act served
144 as the basis for preserving the peace after 1660 and was in no small way responsible for the remarkable growth of the colony after that date. It is perhaps no coincidence that also in 1666 George Alsop, in a fit of hyperbolic exuberance, wrote that in Maryland "the Roman Catholick, and Protestant Episcopal, (whom the world would persuade have proclaimed open wars irrevocably against each other) contrary wise concur in an unanimous parallel of friendship, and inseparable love intayled unto one another." Further, he noted that the "several Opinions and Sects that lodge within this Government, meet not together in mutinous contempts to disquiet the power that bears Rule, but with a reverend quietness obeys the legal commands of Authority." If Alsop exaggerated, he did not err. Lord Baltimore's Maryland design finally began to grow and prosper in the fashion he had envisioned.[53]

It had taken Baltimore twenty-seven years to establish religious toleration on a firm basis, from the time he issued his Instructions in 1633 until he reaffirmed the 1649 Act Concerning Religion in 1660. For about the next twenty-seven years, religious toleration formed the basis of a flourishing society. There were two major success stories, involving the two most despised religious groups in the English-speaking world. Of all the Protestant sects, the Quakers were the most scorned and least welcomed in both England and the American colonies. Roman Catholics, increasingly a symbol of political absolutism, continued to excite fears among the English, and like the Quakers, were proscribed in their activities in England and in all the colonies but Maryland. These two disparate groups gained the most from Lord Baltimore's policy, and, in turn, provided much of the leadership of the colony after 1660.

In 1677 Charles Calvert, the third Lord Baltimore, estimated that the "greatest part of the Inhabitants of that Province (three of four at least) doe consist of Praesbiterians, Independents, Anabapists and Quakers." Of all Protestant groups named, the Quakers were the most numerous. Entering Maryland in the turbulent late-1650s, the Quakers tested the substance of Baltimore's restored policy of toleration. Persecuted and expelled from other colonies, Quaker principles had yet to find a home in America. Initially, Maryland seemed to fit the intolerant pattern established in the other colonies. Maryland Quakerism began with the work of Elizabeth Harris, who in about 1656 succeeded in gaining converts among the recent Puritan immigrants. Other missionaries soon followed and enjoyed equal success. This rapid growth of the Quaker community, coupled with the unsettled condition of the government in 1658 and 1659, produced a brief but heavy persecution of that notorious sect. One of the problems was the Quakers' refusal to take oaths. Given the great emphasis Baltimore placed on oaths as a means of insuring loyalty, the move against the Quakers is not surprising. However, the persecution quickly abated as Cecil Calvert's government sought an accommodation with them.[54]

After 1660, Baltimore viewed the Quakers as less of a political threat, especially after they made concessions regarding attestations of their fealty to him as lord proprietor. As the Society of Friends rapidly increased in numbers and gained adherents among influential settlers, Calvert and his officers in Maryland saw them as a potentially useful addition to society. In extending toleration to the Quakers, Baltimore may have sought to gain their support in establishing his claim to disputed territory on Maryland's Eastern Shore. Whatever the basis of the accord, it worked to the benefit of both parties.[55]

The Quakers, zealous missionaries who were able to organize more effectively than other Protestant sects, increased rapidly under Baltimore's tolerant policy. When the first Maryland General Meeting took place in 1672, Quakerism was wide-spread, with adherents in the majority of counties. In return, the Quakers provided much needed political leadership in the colony, serving through to the end of Cecil Calvert's proprietorship (1675) in all levels of government. During this period, Quaker representation on the governor's council was especially noticeable.[56]

The Quaker experience in Maryland was not without its rough edges, however. Questioning their previous acceptance of political oaths, Quakers began to withdraw from political office early in Charles Calvert's proprietorship. In the 1680s Quakers were markedly absent from the council. The lord proprietor turned against the Quakers in 1681, making their exclusion, partly voluntary, complete. However, as political circumstances changed in the late 1680s, Charles again courted the Quakers, indicating a willingness to accommodate their particular political scruples. The Quakers, having flourished under the Calverts' generally lenient policy of toleration, continued to support the proprietor. In the Protestant movement that overthrew proprietary government in 1689, Quakers were conspicuous by their absence. They also strenously opposed the establishment of the Church of England in the 1690s.[57]

The other major beneficiary of Maryland's restored toleration policy were Roman Catholics, who after 1660 were able to enjoy the security of conscience and prosperity for which they had emigrated. Although they were the first to establish religious institutions in Maryland, Catholics still comprised only a small portion of the population during the second half of the century. Charles Calvert in 1677 estimated that they had the fewest numbers of all the many denominations in the colony.[58]

In keeping with past practices, Cecil Lord Baltimore did little after 1660 to provide for the needs of his fellow Catholics. He did, however, expect the Church hierarchy to do so, and was irritated by the weak effort put forth on behalf of Maryland. When Claudius Agretti visited Baltimore "at his villa near London" in 1669, the proprietor angrily repudiated the impression that he opposed the presence of religious orders in his colony. He criticized the Holy See, which, influenced by this false impression, had consigned no missionaries to Maryland in the course of twenty-four years. Baltimore lamented that there were but two ecclesiastics for about two thousand Catholics and that efforts to secure diocesan priests had been stymied because Maryland had been reserved for the Jesuits. After this meeting, Propaganda Fide sought to reach an accord with Baltimore in order to send "pious ecclesiastics" who met with his approval.[59]

Despite a flurry of activity as a result of 145
Cecil Calvert's complaint, Maryland remained a Jesuit province. On board from the beginning, the Jesuits had persevered through the various disruptions and maintained their mission. In their annual letters they continued to claim converts among the Protestants, and in spite of their small number, to serve the needs of Maryland's Catholics. Roman Catholics, in accordance with the governing principles, were expected to maintain their own clergy without support of the government.[60]

If Catholics were a small minority of the population, they nevertheless had an importance which transcended their actual numbers. As was the case in England, Maryland Catholics tended to be found in the upper social stratum. After 1660, they assumed a political role far beyond what their numbers suggested, although never to the extent of the 1630s. With the appointment of his son Charles as governor in 1661, Cecil was able to reestablish a network based on familial and religious ties. In this way he expected to build a following that would remain "faithful" to him. Obviously there was a strain of thinking, although never institutionalized, that religion was a method of determining loyalty. Charles Calvert expected Catholics to vote as a block in the assembly in support of the proprietor as a matter of "their own interest."[61]

Unlike his father, Charles Calvert, as second lord proprietor, was not as sensitive to keeping his support as broadly based as possible. Under his leadership, the composition of the council changed from one having a significant Protestant representation to one dominated by Catholics and a few

Protestant relatives of the Calverts. Of the ten appointments made by Charles between 1677 and 1684, only one went to an unrelated Protestant. By confining his appointments to a relatively small portion of Maryland's population, namely, Catholics or Protestants who had married into the family, Baltimore made Maryland vulnerable to attacks from England. This was increasingly true in the wake of the Popish plot (1678) and the anti-Catholic Exclusion Crisis (1679–1681) in England, which attempted to eliminate James, Duke of York, 146 who was an avowed Catholic, as heir to Charles II. Maryland was not lacking in disgruntled subjects who were willing to raise a hue and cry in England. Ironically, in the case of the Catholic population, toleration had succeeded too well, and, by not showing the sensitivity to religious sensibilities that his father had, the third Lord Baltimore sowed the seeds of his own undoing.[62]

The one group that seemed to have gained the least from toleration was the unchurched Anglicans. Although Charles maintained that their numbers were no greater than the Catholics, their population was rapidly increasing by the late seventeenth century. The immigrants of the 1670s and 1680s tended to be adherents of the Church of England and they found little in the way of institutionalized Anglicanism in Maryland. Under the proprietorship of Charles Calvert, Anglicans become a vocal and dissident minority, who made their complaints directly to English authorities.[63] In 1676 John Yeo, a Church of England minister in Maryland, wrote to the Archbishop of Canterbury to inform him of the "Deplorable state & condition of the Province of Maryland for want of an established ministry." He claimed that there were only three ministers who were conformable to the doctrine and discipline of the Church of England to serve the approximate 20,000 Anglicans scattered throughout Maryland. The result was that Anglicans "fell away" either to "Popery, Quakerism or Phanaticisme." In addition, he maintained that without an established Church "the lords day is prophaned, Religion despised, & all notorious vices committed," so that Maryland has "become a Sodom of uncleaness & a Pest house of inquity." Yeo wanted the archbishop to use his influence in the English government to lobby for the establishment of a Protestant ministry in Maryland. "A hue and crye," a particularly virulent anti-Catholic tract, was sent in the same year. Its anonymous author demanded to know why Anglicans must submit to Maryland's "arbitrary government" and thereby entangle "our innocent posterity under that tyrannicall yoake of papacy." Anglican unrest, combined with endemic anti-Catholicism, provided a real threat to toleration.[64]

The unchurched Anglicans seemed unwilling to accept the basic rules laid down by the Catholic Lords Baltimore. Given the relationship to which they were accustomed in England, Anglicans were quite uncomfortable with having their ministers "maintained by a voluntary contribution of those of their own persuasion," even though, as Charles Lord Baltimore pointed out, the situation was the same for "Presbiterians, Independents, Anabaptist, Quakers, & Roman Church." Lacking the missionary zeal of the Quakers and the affluence of the Catholics, Anglicans saw their only hope in a tax-supported institution. However, their efforts to secure legislative support for an established ministry failed. Dissatisfied on so many counts, the Anglicans were a continuing source of political unrest.[65]

Not all adherents to the Church of England were disgruntled. In an attempt to answer the charges that his government showed partiality "on all occasions towards those of the Popish Religion to the discouragement of his Majesties Protestant Subjects," in 1682 Baltimore produced a statement signed by twenty-five influential Anglicans. They acknowledged "the general freedom & priviledge which we and all persons whatsoever ... enjoy" under proprietary government. From their own observation, they knew that Baltimore's favors were impartially distributed without any respect to religious persuasion and that Protestants were well-represented in the government. However, perhaps because so many of the signees were related to the proprietor by marriage, their protestation had little effect with English authorities. Charles Calvert's departure from the province in 1684 accentuated developments that could not be overcome by declarations. It

Contemporary Perspectives on Religion in Maryland, 1669, 1676

... [D]ivine goodnesse hath beene pleased to Land my foot uppon a province off Virginia called Mary-Land which is a Province distinct from the government of Virginia: of which the Ld Baltemore is proprietor and governor. Under his Ldships goverment we enjoy a greate deale of liberty and Pticularly in matters of religion, wee have many that give obedience to the church of Roome, who have theire publique libery, our governour being of that Pswasion: wee have many also of the reformed religion, who have a long while lived as sheepe without a shepherd [T]he last yeare brought in a young man from Ireland, who hath already had good successe in his worke: ... how many young men are theire in England that want wages and worke too we cannot but judge itt their duty to come over and helpe us.

— **Letter of Matthew Hill to Richard Baxter, from Charles County, Mary-Land, 3 April 1669**

* * * * * * * * * *

O yee reverent Bishops in England Here lays the Keye of the work, and the popes service, why doe ye not take care for the sheep in Maryland, and send protestant pastores, as the pope doth to his papists, in America?

...

Wee confess a great many of us came in servants to others, but wee adventured owr lives for it, and got owr poore living with hard labour out of the ground in a terrible Willdernis, and som have advanced themselves much thereby: And so was my Lord Baltemore but an inferior Irish Lord, and as is sayth one of the Popes privy Agents in England.

— **From "Complaint from Heaven with a Huy and crye" (1676)**

is understandable that he would entrust his government to a group of deputy governors who were either relatives or Catholics. However, with the death or departure of a number of Protestants by 1688, his govenment seemed to fit the image projected by disgruntled Protestants.[66]

The Calvert design was based on gaining the loyalty of Marylanders of differing religious affiliations and tying them to the proprietary government. The Calverts had been successful to a remarkable degree among the Catholics and Quakers and to a lesser degree among Anglicans and other Protestant sects. But the success and visibility of the Catholics in the late 1680s, and the increasing anti-Catholicism of this period in England and America, worked against the continuation of their policy of toleration. Too many Marylanders were left out. For them Maryland had become a closed society that could only be opened by force of arms. The Protestant Revolution in Maryland destroyed the Catholic Calverts' bold experiment in religious toleration. With the final establishment of the Church of England in 1701, both Quakers and Catholics were excluded from full membership in Maryland society.[67]

Daring and resourceful, the Catholic Lords Baltimore had consistently ventured to rise above their age. Their effort to implement religious toleration cannot be diminished by its ultimate failure, for they pointed to the future. Their failure brings to mind a comment on recent politics by Richard N. Goodwin. "Of all human activities," Goodwin wrote,

> politics—the process of acquiring and using governmental or official power—is among the most responsive to shifting values and situations, always reflecting the dominant and visible themes of the human turbulence which creates it and which it attempts to govern. Hence politics cannot be understood or analyzed apart from the wider society which give it coloration and direc-

> tion. An artist may be an age ahead of his time. Even the greatest politician can only be a step or two ahead of his.... Actions and public words based on a more profound vision than this may suit a prophet, but not a politician. His material is the desires and attitudes of living people.[64]

Marylanders, and for that matter English men and women, were not ready for broadly-based religious toleration in the seventeenth century. English History provides comparable examples in the efforts of both James I and James II, who attempted
148 to extend toleration to Catholics and other dissenters through executive power. But neither of these Stuart kings, popularly identified with absolutism, could establish toleration, a concept which ran so contrary to public opinion. That the Catholic Lords Baltimore established and maintained toleration for as long as they did attests to their skills as proprietors of their colony. The failure of religious toleration came because too many of their subjects no longer saw the value of it. And this no Catholic Lord Baltimore could overcome.

REFERENCES

The author wishes to express his appreciation to Mary Croy for her research assistance and to the Reverend Eric McDermott, S.J., who generously shared his extensive research collection on early Maryland with the author.

1. The most exaggerated statement of this interpretation was made by the Catholic bishop, William T. Russell, in *Maryland: The Land of Sanctuary, A History of Religious Toleration from the First Settlement until the American Revolution* (Baltimore, 1907). The interpretation was mainstreamed into American history primarily by Charles M. Andrews, *The Colonial Period of American History*, 4 vols. (New Haven, 1932–1938), II, 279. For a recent statement, see Susan R. Falb, "Advice and Ascent: The Development of the Maryland Assembly, 1635–1689" (unpublished Ph.D. dissertation, Georgetown University, 1976), 292–295, 301. *Records of the English Province of the Society of Jesus*, ed. Henry Foley (7 vols. London, 1877–1893), III, 362. For an effort to manipulate the Roman bureaucracy by painting a dismal picture of English Catholic life, see the letters of the Discalced Carmelite Simon Stock to Propaganda Fide in Luca Codignola, *Terre D'America E Burocrazia Romana: Simon Stock, Propaganda Fide E la colonia de Lord Baltimore a Terranova, 1621–1649* (Venice, 1982), 107–176.
2. Expressed in an outrageous manner, this interpretation formed the basis for the argument of Episcopalian minister, C.E. Smith, in *Religion Under the Barons Baltimore* ... (Baltimore, 1899). More balanced statements were made by Alfred Pearce Dennis, "Lord Baltimore's Struggle with the Jesuits, 1634–1649," *Annual Report of the American Historical Association, 1900*, 2 vols. (Washington, D.C., 1901), I, 112, and Newton D. Mereness, *Maryland as a Proprietary Province* (New York, 1901), 423–437. For a recent assessment, stated in bold terms but without the usual religious bias, see J. Frederick Fausz, "'By Warre Upon Our Enemies and Kinde Usage of Our Friends': The Secular Context of Relgious Toleration in Maryland, 1620–1660" (unpublished essay in author's possession). For an early statement of anti-Catholicism in Maryland historiography see, John Gilmary Shea, "Maryland and the Controversies as to her Early History," *American Catholic Quarterly Review*, X (October, 1885), 658–677. As Babette May Levy noted, "Not a few articles and books treat Maryland's early History with due regard to the part religion played in the proprietary colony's varied fate during the upheavals in England's troubled seventeenth century. And a goodly portion of these essays reveal as much about their author's point of view, not to say prejudice, as they do about conditions in Maryland" ("Early Puritanism in the Southern and Island Colonies," *Proceedings of the American Antiquarian Society*, LXX [April, 1960], 221).
3. Thad W. Tate, "The Seventeenth-Century Chesapeake and Its Modern Historians," in *The Chesapeake in the Seventeenth-Century: Essays on Anglo-American Society Politics*, ed. Thad W. Tate and David L. Ammerman (Chapel Hill, 1979), 3–50.

   There was a flurry of interest in the origins of toleration at the time of the 300th anniversary of the colony's founding. See Matthew Page Andrews, "Separation of Church and State in Maryland," *The Catholic Historical Review*, XXI (July, 1935), 164–176, and J. Moss Ives, "The Catholic Contribution to Religious Liberty in Colonial America," *ibid.* (October, 1935), 283–298. Renewed interest in toleration is evidenced in John D. Krugler, "Lord Baltimore, Roman Catholics, and Toleration: Religious Policy in Maryland during the Early Catholic Years, 1634–1649," *ibid.*, LXV (January, 1979), 49–75; David W. Jordan, "'The Miracle of This Age': Maryland's Experiment in Religious Toleration," forthcoming in *The Historian*; and R.J. Lahey, "The Role of Religion in Lord Baltimore's Colonial Enterprise," *Maryland Historical Magazine*, 72 (Winter, 1977), 492–511, hereafter *MHM*.
4. For a 1635 Catholic vision of what Maryland could become, see *To Live Like Princes: "A Short Treatise Sett Downe in a Letter Written by R. W. to his Worthy Freind C.J.R. Concerning the New Plantation Now Erecting under the Right Ho[nora]ble the Lord Baltemore*, ed. John D. Krugler (Baltimore, 1976).
5. For an assessment of the Catholic intellectual background see, Thomas O'Brien Hanley, S.J., *Their Rights & Liberties: The beginnings of Religious And Political Freedom in Maryland* (Westminster, 1959).

6. Toleration was a practical necessity comparable to Catholic France's acceptance of the Edict of Nantes in 1598. As Owen Chadwick argued, the Edict was accepted "not because Catholic France affirmed toleration to be merely right, but because without the Edict France must be destroyed." *From Uniformity to Unity*, ed. G. F. Nutall and Owen Chadwick (London, 1962), 9.
7. J. Lecler asserted that "among all the countries that were divided by the Reformation ... England comes last as far as toleration is concerned." *Toleration and the Reformation*, trans. T. L. Westow, 2 vols. (London, 1960), II, 493. However, English legislation must be judged in the context of its enforcement, which was at best lax. On the penal legislation, see A. H. Forbes, "'Faith and true allegiance', The Law and Internal Security of England, 1559-1714: A Study of the Evolution of the Parliamentary Legislation and the Problem of its Local Enforcement" (unpublished Ph.D. dissertation, University of California—Los Angeles, 1960), *passim*, but especially, 82-90; and J. Anthony Williams, *Catholic Recusancy in Wiltshire, 1660-1791* (London, 1968), ch. 1.
8. *The Political Works of James I*, ed. Charles Howard McIlwain (Cambridge, 1918), 55. Conrad Russell, "Arguments for Religious Uniformity in England, 1530-1650," *Journal of Ecclesiastical History*, XVIII (October, 1967), 201-226.
9. The best general survey remains W. K. Jordan, *The Development of Religious Toleration in England*, 4 vols. (Cambridge, 1932-1940). However, Jordan is badly dated when it comes to his treatment of English Catholics.
10. John Miller, *Popery & Politics in England, 1660-1688* (Cambridge, 1973), ch. 14; Barry Coward, *The Stuart Age: A History of England, 1603-1714* (London, 1980), 318-320.
11. Carol Z. Weiner, "The Beleaguered Isle: A Study of Elizabethan and Early Jacobean Anti-Catholicism," *Past & Present*, 51 (May 1971), 27-62.
12. For George Calvert's career, see John D. Krugler, "Sir George Calvert's Resignation as Secretary of State and the Founding of Maryland," *MHM*, 68 (Fall, 1973), 239-254, and "'The Face of a Protestant, and the Heart of a Papist': A Reexamination of Sir George Calvert's Conversion to Roman Catholicism," *Journal of Church and State*, 20 (Autumn, 1978), 507-531.
13. John D. Krugler, "The Calvert Family, Catholicism, and Court Politics in Early Seventeenth-Century England," *The Historian*, LIII (May, 1981), 378-392; Lahey, "Role of Religion," 493.
14. Martin J. Havran, *The Catholics in Caroline England* (Stanford, 1962), ch. 6. John Bossy, "The English Catholic Community, 1603-1625," in *The Reign of James VI and I*, ed., Alan G. R. Smith (London, 1973), 101-102. Caroline M. Hibbard, "Early Stuart Catholicism: Revisions and Re-revisions," *The Journal of Modern History*, 52 (May, 1980), 14.
15. John Bossy, *The English Catholic Community, 1570-1850* (New York, 1976).
16. Public Record Office. State Papers 16/495. Keith Lindley, "The Lay Catholics of the Reign of Charles I," *Journal of Ecclesiastical History*, VIII (July, 1971), 206. In Durham, for example, Catholicism survived mainly among "gentry households with their dependent bodies of servants" (Mervyn James, *Family, Lineage and Civil Society: A Study of Society, Politics, and Mentality in the Durham Region, 1500-1640* [Oxford, 1974], 141-142).
17. Hibbard, "Early Stuart Catholicism," *Journal of Modern History* 52: 3-4.
18. Thomas Hughes, S.J., *History of the Society of Jesus in North America: Colonial and Federal*, 2 vols. (Cleveland, 1907), *Documents*, I, 3-5). "No excessive pressures on Catholics to emigrate for religion's sake existed after perhaps 1609, but there remained strong incentives to invest in business enterprise" (David Beers Quinn, *England and the Discovery of America, 1431-1620* [New York, 1974], 393.
19. *The Archives of Maryland*, ed. William Hand Browne *et al.*, 72 vols. to date (Baltimore, 1883-), V, 267-268. Hereafter cited as *Md. Arch.*
20. *A Declaration of the Lord Baltemore's Plantation in Maryland; Wherein is set forth how Englishmen may become Angels, the King's Dominions be extended and the adventurer attain Land and Gear; together with the other advantages of that Sweet Land* (London, 1633).
21. Russell R. Menard, "Economy and Society in Early Maryland" (unpublished Ph.D. dissertation, University of Iowa, 1975), 32-36.
22. *Md. Arch.*, V, 267-268. Catholics also sought guarantees. Catholic Thomas Cornwallis wrote that Baltimore knew that "my Security of Contiens was the first Condition that I expected from this Government" (Cornwallis to Baltimore, 16 April 1638, *The Calvert Papers*, 3 vols. [Baltimore, 1889-1899], I, 172-173).
23. Baltimore to Sir Thomas Wentworth, 10 January 1633/34, *The Earl of Strafforde's Letters and dispatches ...*, ed. W. Knowler, 2 vols. (London, 1739), I, 178-179; Edward Watkins to Privy Council, 29 October 1633, *Calendar of State Papers. Domestic Series of the Reign of Charles I ...*, ed. John Bruce *et al.*, 22 vols. (London, 1858-1893), *1633-1634*, 261; Menard, "Economy and Society," 37. The Venetian Ambassador reported the number as 800 (*Calendar of State Papers and Manuscripts Relating to English Affairs Existing in the Archives and Collections of Venice ...*, ed. Rawdon Brown *et al.*, 38 vols. [London, 1864-1947], *1632-1636*, 158).
24. *Narratives of Early Maryland, 1633-1684*, ed. Clayton Coleman Hall (New York, 1910), 118; Krugler, "Lord Baltimore, Roman Catholics, and Toleration," *Catholic Historical Review*, 63.
25. *Narratives of Early Maryland*, ed. Hall, 118; Baltimore to Wentworth, 10 January 1633/34, *Strafforde's Letters*, I, 178; "The Lord Baltemores Declaration to the Lords," *Calvert Papers*, I, 223-225; *To Live Like Princes*, ed. Krugler, 36.
26. Charles Calvert erred when he stated that "soone after the first planting" his father had a law enacted which guaranteed Christians "Liberty to Worshipp." Formal legislation did not come until 1649. *Md. Arch.*, V, 267.
27. Krugler, "Lord Baltimore, Roman Catholics, and

Toleration," *Catholic Historical Review*, 74–75; *Narratives of Early Maryland*, ed. Hall, 16.

28. *Md. Arch.*, I, 158; IV, 35–39. *Calvert Papers*, I, 163.

29. *Records of the Governor and Company of the Massachusetts Bay*, ed. Nathaniel B. Shurtleff, 5 vols. in 6. (Boston, 1853–1854), I, 79, 82; John David Krugler, "Puritan and Papist: Politics and Religion in Massachusetts and Maryland before the Restoration of Charles II," (unpublished Ph.D. dissertation, University of Illinois at Urbana-Champaign, 1971), ch. 5.

30. *Narratives of Early Maryland*, ed. Hall, 103.

31. *Md. Arch.*, I, 72–73, 82–83; Hanley, *Their Rights & Liberties*, ch. 5; Edwin W. Beitzell, "The Maryland Assembly of 1638/1639," *Chronicles of St. Mary's* 7 (1959), 396–401. 150

32. Father Edward Knott to Papal Nuncio in Belguim (Hughes, *Society of Jesus, text*, I, 255–256); *Narratives of Early Maryland*, ed. Hall, 118; *Records of the Society of Jesus*, ed. Foley, III, 363–364; *Calvert Papers*, I, 165–166; 217–218.

33. Lawrence C. Wroth, "The First Sixty Years of the Church of England in Maryland, 1632–1692," *MHM*, XI (March, 1916), 4, 12; George B. Scriven, "Religious Affiliation in Seventeenth Century Maryland," *Historical Magazine of the Protestant Episcopal Church*, XXV (September, 1956), 221, 222. There were only twenty-two Anglican clergy in Maryland before 1692 (Wroth, "First Sixty Years," *MHM*, 16; *Records of the Society of Jesus*, ed. Foley, III, 369–371).

34. *To Live Like Princes*, ed. Krugler, 38. Copley to Cecil Lord Baltimore, 3 April 1638, *Calvert Papers*, I, 21; Thomas Lord Arundel to Secretary of State Sir Francis Windebanke, 17 February 1638/39, P.R.O. State Papers 16/413/17; Krugler, "Lord Baltimore, Roman Catholics, and Toleration," *Catholic Historical Review*, 65–73. For a study very critical of the political leadership of Baltimore and Gov. Leonard Calvert, see Steven Douglas Crow, "'Left at Libertie': The Effects of the English Civil War and Interregnum on the American Colonies, 1640–1660" (unpublished Ph.D. dissertation, University of Wisconsin, 1974), 18–20, 23, 24.

35. *Records of the Society of Jesus*, ed. Foley, III, 381; John Winthrop, *The History of New England From 1630 to 1649*, ed. James Savage, 2 vols. (2nd ed., Boston, 1853), II, 72, 149; *Md. Arch.*, IV, 103, 204. The first encounter between the people of Massachusetts and the sailors of the *Dove*, who had been sent in 1634 to trade corn for fish, established something less than cordial relations. Winthrop reported that some of the Bay settlers aboard the Maryland vessel were reviled by the Maryland sailors who called them "holy brethren" and by cursing and swearing "most horribly" (*Journal*, ed. Savage, I, 172). Gibbons eventually relocated in Maryland. On 20 January 1650/51 Baltimore appointed him to the Council and named him "Admiral of our Province" (*Md. Arch.*, III, 261–262).

36. *Md. Arch.*, I, 270; IV, 262. Henry More, S.J., *Anglia Historia* (1645) in Hughes, *Society of Jesus, Doc.*, I, 125–126. Russell R. Menard, "Maryland's 'Time of Troubles': Sources of Political Disorder in Early St. Mary's," *MHM*, 76 (June, 1981), 124–140. For Baltimore's legal problems in England, see Krugler, "Puritan and Papist," 265–267, and James W. Vardaman, "Lord Baltimore, Parliament and Cromwell: A Problem of Church and State in Seventeenth-Century England," *Journal of Church and State*, 4 (May, 1962), 31–46.

37. *Md. Arch.*, III, 187, 201. In 1638 Copley complained that the office of sheriff was occupied by one "who hath formerly bin a persevante, and is now a chiefe Protestante" (*Calvert Papers*, I, 163).

38. *Md. Arch.*, III, 201.

39. In the words of Robert Beverley, Gov. Berkeley, "to prevent the infection from reaching that Country, made severe laws against the Puritans." (*The History and Present State of Virginia*, ed. Louis B. Wright [Charlottesville, 1968], 63).

40. *The Statutes at Large . . . of Virginia from the First Session of the Legislature in the Year 1649*, ed. William W. Hening, 13 vols. (Richmond, 1809–1823) I, 277, 341, 359; Winthrop, *Journal*, ed. Savage, II, 93–94, 407; Leonard Strong, *Babylons Fall in Maryland: A Fair Warning to Lord Baltamore or a Relation of an Assault made by divers Papists and Popish Officers of the Lord Baltamore's against the Protestants in Maryland* . . . (London, 1655), as reprinted in *MHM*, III (September, 1908), 229.

41. *Md. Arch.*, III, 85, 105, 117, 145, 174; I, 44–45, 210–213.

42. *Ibid.*, IV, 234, 404, 431. Dennis M. Moran, "Anti-Catholicism in Early Maryland Politics: The Puritan Influence," American Catholic Historical Society of Philadelphia, *Records*, LXI (September, 1950), 139–154.

43. Baltimore to Gov. Stone, 26 August 1649, *Md. Arch.*, I, 262–263. The extant records of the 1649 Assembly are incomplete. Only the results of the last day of the three week session remain. This means that any assessment of the Act must be tentative (Krugler "Puritan and Papist," 272–276).

44. Baltimore to Gov. Stone, 26 August 1649, *Md. Arch.*, I, 272. On the negative impact of this letter, see Crow, "'Left at Libertie'," 134–135.

45. *Md. Arch.*, I, 244. Much of the earlier historical literature is partisan in nature. Exponents of Catholic and Protestant viewpoints have claimed credit for the "liberal" aspects of the Act while attempting to pin the more severe aspects of the other religion (Smith, *Religion under the Baltimores*, 319; Russell, *Land of Sanctuary*, 201, 205). This assembly was not under a Puritan influence. The majority of Puritans were yet to enter Maryland. As far as the religious make-up of the assembly, it is probable that Catholics still dominated, but "an accurate reconstruction of the membership is impossible" (Falb, "Advice and Ascent," 309). This part of the Act should be compared to Baltimore's "An Act for Felonies," presented to the assembly in 1639 (*Md. Arch.*, I, 71–72).

46. *Md. Arch.*, I, 245–246. Baltimore undoubtedly added this last section to induce further Puritan migration. He may have been already negotiating with Robert Brooke, "a well-to-do English Puri-

tan" who intended "to transport himself his wife Eight sons and family and a Great Number of other Persons" to Maryland (*ibid.*, III, 237–241).

47. *Md. Arch.*, I, 246–247.
48. The document was signed on 17 April 1650 and was printed in John Langford, *A Just and Cleere Refutation of a False and Scandalous Pamphlet Entitled Babylons Fall in Maryland &c and a true discovery of certaine strange and inhumane proceedings of some ungratefull people in Maryland, towards those who formerly preserved them in time of their greatest distresse* ... (London, 1655), in *MHM*, IV (March, 1909), 63; *Md. Arch.*, I, 318–319; III, 257.
49. *The Lord Baltemore's Case, Concerning the Province of Maryland*... (London 1653), in *MHM*, IV (June, 1909), 171–172; *Md. Arch.*, III, 264, 271, 276, 311–312; "A Surrender of Virginia to the Parliamentary Commissioners, March 1651–52," *Virginia Magazine of History and Biography*, II (July, 1903), 34; Krugler, "Puritan and Papist," 281–288.
50. *Md. Arch.*, I, 340–341. How many Catholics remained in Maryland at this point is a matter of conjecture. John Hammond maintained "they are but few." *Hammond versus Heamonds or an Answer to an audacious Pamphlet, published by an impudent and ridiculous Fellow, named Roger Heamans* (London, 1656), in *MHM*, IV (September, 1909), 239.
51. *Md. Arch.*, III, 384, 424; Falb, "Advice and Ascent," 380–388.
52. *Md. Arch.*, XLI, 132–133, 144–146, 170–171, 566–567; Edwin Warfield Beitzell, *The Jesuit Missions of St. Mary's County, Maryland* (privately printed, 1959), 29.
53. *Md. Arch.*, XV, 13; George Alsop, *A Character of the Province of Mary-Land. Together with a Collection of Historical Letters* (London, 1666), in *Narratives of Early Maryland*, ed. Hall, 349.
54. *Md. Arch.*, V, 133; Kenneth L. Carroll, "Elizabeth Harris, the Founder of American Quakerism," *Quaker History*, LVIII (Autumn, 1968), 96–111, and "Persecution of Quakers in Early Maryland (1658–1661)," *ibid.*, LIII (Autumn, 1964), 78, 80.
55. Kenneth L. Carroll, "Quaker Opposition to the Establishment of a State Church in Maryland," *MHM*, LXV (Summer, 1970), 153. David W. Jordan, in describing Baltimore's willingness to extend religious freedom to the Quakers, called it "another calculated effort" to broaden his support ("'Gods Candle' within Government: Quakers and Politics in Early Maryland," *William and Mary Quarterly*, 3rd. ser., XXXIX [October, 1982], 632).
56. J. Reaney Kelly, *Quakers in the Founding of Anne Arundel County, Maryland* (Baltimore, 1963), 1.
57. David W. Jordan, "Maryland's Privy Council, 1637–1715," in *Law, Society, and Politics in Early Maryland*, ed. Aubrey C. Land, Lois Green Carr, and Edward C. Papenfuse (Baltimore, 1977), 76; Jordan, "Quakers and Politics," *WMQ*, 636–637, 645; Carroll, "Quaker Opposition," *MHM*, 155.
58. *Md. Arch.*, V, 133. Richard Shepherd, an English captain who traded in Maryland, dramatically overstated the situation when he claimed in 1681 that "there are thirty Protestants to one Papist" (*ibid.*, 301).
59. *United States Documents in the Propaganda Fide Archives: A Calendar*, ed. Finbar Kinneally, 1st series, 8 vols. to date (Washington, D.C., 1966—), III, 109, 203. For the politics of Propaganda Fide in the period of George Calvert's Newfoundland colony, see Codignola, *Terre d'America E Burocrazia Romana.* Agretti was on a special mission to examine the condition of ecclesiastical affairs in England. His report was dated 14 December 1669. The two Franciscans who arrived in 1673 may have been as a result of Baltimore's complaint (*Records of the Society of Jesus*, ed. Foley, III, 392). 151
60. Calvert to Lord Baltimore, 2 June 1673, *Calvert Papers*, I, 281–282. For the years 1671, 1672, 1673 and 1674 the Jesuits claimed 184 converts and 299 infant baptisms (*Records of the Society of Jesus*, ed. Foley, III, 392).
61. Commission to Charles Calvert, 14 September 1661, *Md. Arch.*, III, 439; Charles Calvert to Baltimore, 26 April 1672, *Calvert Papers*, I, 264–265.
62. Lois Green Carr and David W. Jordan, *Maryland's Revolution of Government, 1689–1692* (Ithaca, 1974), 221; Miller, *Popery and Politics*, ch. 8.
63. *Md. Arch.*, V, 267. David W. Jordan, "Political Stability and the Emergence of a Native Elite in Maryland," *Chesapeake in Seventeenth Century*, ed. Tate and Ammerman, 248.
64. *Md. Arch.*, V, 130–131; 143.
65. *Ibid.*, I, 404, 406; II, 86; V, 133. For a different perspective, see Wroth, "First Sixty Years," *MHM.*
66. *Md. Arch.*, V, 300, 353–355; Jordan, "Privy Council," *Law, Society, and Politics*, ed. Land, Carr, Papenfuse, 75.
67. Carr and Jordan, *Revolution*, 212–214, 218–219. For the petitions of eighteenth-century Maryland Catholics for equal participation with all other subjects "in All the Rights and Privileges" of government, see "Popery in Maryland," *The American Catholic Historical Researcher*, n.s., IV (April, 1908), 258–276, and the anonymous statement, "Liberty and Property or the Beauty of Maryland Displayed," in *United States Catholic Historical Magazine* III (1890), 237–263.
68. "The Shape of American Politics," *Commentary*, 43 (June 1967), 25.

IV The Crusade Against Catholicism

"Marylando-Hibernus": Charles Carroll the Settler, 1660-1720

Ronald Hoffman

THE Slieve Bloom Mountains meander for a distance of some fifteen miles along the southeastern border of County Offaly in the Irish midlands. West of the range the land is remote and sparsely populated, separated by the line of hills from the more populous and prosperous Dublin hinterland. The scrubby forests that once covered the mountains have been gone for centuries, but the ubiquitous peat still gives the ground a dark and somber hue. The terrain that is not bog is more suitable for pasture than for cultivation, and widely scattered herds of sheep and cattle graze peacefully on the hillsides. Yet the present-day tranquillity of this nearly deserted landscape belies its history, for from Tudor times until the beginning of the eighteenth century the Slieve Bloom Mountains were a battleground in the desperate struggle between the Gaelic Irish and the English for control of the destiny of Ireland. And it was in the hills and valleys of the Slieve Bloom, in the midst of that bitter conflict, that the story of the Maryland Carrolls—the family destined to produce Charles Carroll of Carrollton, the only Roman Catholic signer of the Declaration of Independence—began.

When the first Charles Carroll—the grandfather of Charles Carroll of Carrollton—came to Maryland in 1688 at the age of twenty-eight, he brought a fierce determination to reverse the fate that had befallen his Irish kin at the hands of the English. Given the sobriquet "Charles Carroll the Settler" by historians, the young man carried with him the burden of Protestant England's suppression of Catholic Ireland, and that burden shaped not only his personal history and his family's but also the history of Maryland in the first decades of the eighteenth century. During the years after his arrival in Maryland, Carroll was fully aware of the further decline of the relatives he had left behind in Ireland. Already reduced by the

Mr. Hoffman is a member of the Department of History at the University of Maryland, College Park. Versions of this article were presented to the Society of St. Brendan, Ennis, Ireland; the Washington Area Early American Seminar, University of Maryland, College Park; and the Columbia University Seminar in Early American History and Culture. The author wishes to express his appreciation to Peter J. Albert and Ira Berlin for perceptive criticism and to Eleanor S. Darcy, assistant editor of the Carroll Papers, for her work in discovering and disentangling the Irish genealogy of the Carrolls. He also thanks Sally D. Mason, associate editor of the Carroll Papers, for invaluable assistance in the researching and writing of this essay.

1680s from ownership of extensive lands to small holdings, Carroll's brothers rose to the banner of James II and suffered the fate of other Irish Jacobites. His younger brother Thomas was killed at the battle of the Boyne in 1690; his older brother Anthony and nephew Daniel later surrendered under the Treaty of Limerick and were subsequently attainted for treason.[1] By the early years of the eighteenth century, Charles Carroll's surviving kinsmen had been diminished to struggling farmers—mere shadows of what their forebears had been. So complete was the family's dispossession and so desperate their situation that by 1710 over three-fourths of the younger generation had left Ireland to join Carroll in Maryland.[2]

Driven by these Old World realities, the Settler was consumed by the
156 vision of reconstituting his family's economic and political fortunes in the Chesapeake. And he succeeded—but only partially. Charles Carroll went to his grave in 1720 the wealthiest man in Maryland, but he was also disenfranchised and thus politically powerless. Ironically, both the financial achievements he enjoyed and the political disabilities he suffered were immediate products of his Irish past and his reckless and implacable ambition.

I

The branch of Irish Carrolls that produced Charles Carroll settled in the parish of Litterluna, situated in the northeast section of the territory of Ely O'Carroll in the Irish midlands, during the twelfth century.[3] Displaced from this location as a result of land confiscations during the reign of James I, the family moved southwest into neighboring Shirkyran Parish, where by the time of the Irish rebellion of 1641—a bitter uprising that was ultimately crushed by Cromwell's forces between 1649 and 1652—the Settler's great-grandfather Daniel Carroll held some 1,773 acres of

[1] Genealogical Files in the possession of Gerald Carroll, descendent of Thomas Carroll (?-1690), London, England. Bernard Bailyn, *The Peopling of British North America: An Introduction* (New York, 1986), presents a stimulating and suggestive argument that emphasizes in part the contrast between the primitive cultural environment of the British mainland colonies during the 17th and early 18th centuries and the highly civilized European societies from which most white immigrants came. While Bailyn's conceptualization of the new settlements as "marchland" societies is valuable, the violence and disorder endemic to the colonial experience must have been distressingly familiar to Irish Catholic migrants whose history, 1593-1702, was a product of their bloody resistance to brutal Anglo-Protestant attempts to destroy their way of life.

[2] Genealogical Files, Charles Carroll of Carrollton Papers, Maryland Historical Society, Baltimore.

[3] The territory of Ely O'Carroll was located in the region shired as King's County in 1557 and known today as County Offaly (*Books of Survey and Distribution,* King's County, Dublin, Public Record Office, Ireland; Carroll-O'Carroll Genealogies, Md. Hist. Soc.). The Irish background of the Carrolls will be treated in detail in my forthcoming study of the family in Ireland and Maryland, 1660-1782.

profitable land.[4] This property qualified Daniel as a gentleman of substance, and although he was forced to forfeit ownership of his lands as a consequence of having participated on the wrong side of the 1641 revolt, he appears to have secured a lease from the new owners for a 136-acre tract called Aghagurty. This arrangement permitted Daniel, his son Anthony, and his grandson Daniel—who was Charles Carroll the Settler's father—to remain on at least that small portion of their former holdings as head tenants.[5] Thus the family into which the Settler was born in 1660 had already entered the downward trajectory of displacement and dispossession that within the sixty years of his lifetime would culminate in their complete social and economic reduction, a fate they shared with the vast majority of Ireland's Roman Catholic landowners. (See map.) *157*

Charles Carroll, the second son of Daniel Carroll, head tenant at Aghagurty, spent his boyhood in Ely O'Carroll. Despite his family's reduced circumstances, he managed to acquire a remarkable education. Leaving Ireland at a young age for schooling in France, he studied the humanities at Lille and the civil and canon law at Douai.[6] In May 1685 Carroll was admitted to London's Inner Temple, and three years later, in

[4] *Books of Survey and Distribution*, King's County, 59, 60, 77, P.R.O.I.; "Articles of Agreement between Garrett Dillon, Co. Westmeath, and Daniel Carroll of Ballimoneene," Nov. 3, 1638, Thrift Abstracts from the Calendar of Patent Rolls, P.R.O.I.; William Petty, "Hibernae Delineato" (maps based on the Down Survey 1652-1654), 1685. The 1,773-acre holding may have represented far less property than the family possessed at Litterluna before the planting of that area under James I in 1619. Some undocumented sources suggest that before that date, Charles Carroll the Settler's forebears may have controlled nearly 11,000 acres. While such an estate would have made them men of considerable substance, it should be kept in mind that the land lay in the Slieve Bloom Mountains, an extremely picturesque region but remote and poor even by the standards of 17th-century Ireland.

[5] It is quite possible that the Carrolls may also have recovered other portions of their holdings as a result of the "decree of innocence" received by Anthony Carroll of Aghagurty—Charles Carroll the Settler's grandfather—in 1662. Catholics judged to be "innocent Papists" by the court of claims—the seven commissioners charged with executing the Act of Settlement that redistributed Irish lands confiscated as a result of the 1641 rebellion—were either reinstated on their former property or compensated with equivalent land elsewhere. "Inrolments of Decrees of Innocents passed under the Act of Settlement; preserved in the Office of the Chief Remembrancer of the Exechequer, Dublin," *The Eleventh, Twelfth, and Thirteenth, Fourteenth, and Fifteenth Reports from the Commissioners Appointed by His Majesty to Execute the Measures Recommended in an Address of the House of Commons Respecting the Public Records of Ireland, 1821-1823, and 1824-1825* (London, 1824-1825), 528, 538. J. G. Simms, "The Restoration, 1660-85," in T. W. Moody, F. X. Martin, and F. J. Byrne, eds., *A New History of Ireland* (Oxford, 1976), III, 422-425.

[6] Charles Carroll's education was described by his son Charles Carroll of Annapolis in notes appended to the family pedigree in Carroll-O'Carroll Genealogies, Md. Hist. Soc.

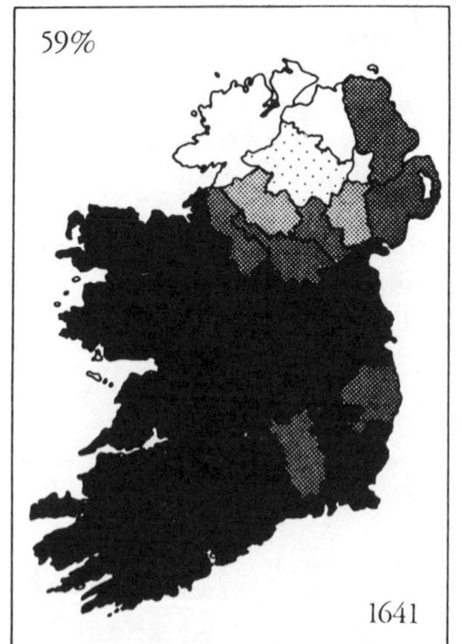

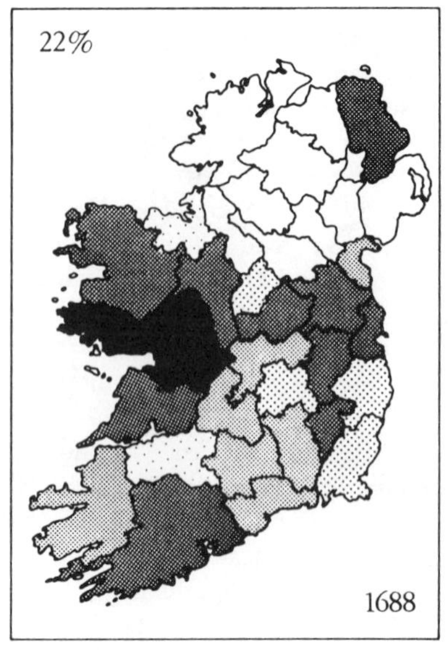

158

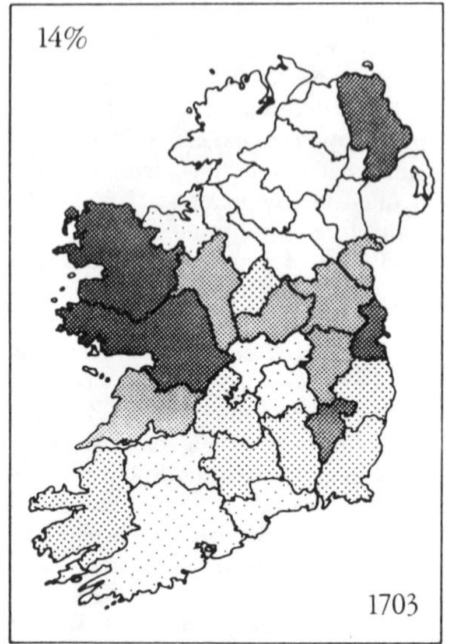

LAND OWNED BY CATHOLICS
1641, 1688, 1703
by counties

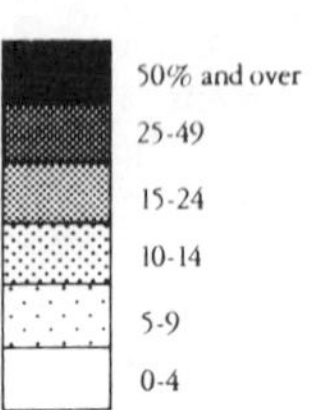

J.G. Simms, *The Williamite Confiscation in Ireland 1690-1703,* (London, Faber and Faber Ltd., 1956), 196. Reproduced by permission of Faber and Faber Ltd.

July 1688, he received a commission from Charles Calvert, third Lord Baltimore, as attorney general of Maryland.[7]

The circumstances surrounding Carroll's acquisition of this mid-level appointment were entwined with the brief respite enjoyed by Catholics under James II but in ways that are only vaguely understood. With James's accession in February 1685, Catholics unexpectedly found themselves readmitted to the powerful circles from which their religion had long excluded them. Among the first effects of James II's reign was the exoneration of several prominent Catholic peers who had been imprisoned in the Tower on the basis of accusations made by Titus Oates. One of these gentlemen—William Herbert, Lord Powis, whom the king elevated to the Privy Council in 1686—appears to have been critical for
Charles Carroll's career. According to an undocumented family tradition, 159
Carroll secured a position as Powis's clerk or secretary at some point during the mid-1680s. Powis is known to have had grave reservations about James's aggressive reinstatement of Catholics, and he is alleged to have communicated his misgivings to Carroll and to have recommended the young man to Calvert, the proprietor of Maryland.[8] Indeed, the legend maintains that Powis strongly urged Carroll to get out of England and then took action to help him do so. The onset of the Glorious Revolution within three months of Carroll's departure confirmed Powis's judgment. Carroll landed in Maryland on October 1, 1688.

The effects of the revolution reached across the ocean to cause major problems for Charles Carroll. Within a year of his arrival in Maryland, a related anti-proprietary Protestant revolt known as Coode's Rebellion deprived Roman Catholics of the right to hold office and confronted Carroll with the necessity of pursuing his goals as a private citizen. In this

[7] Indenture between James, Duke of Ormond, Lady Elizabeth his wife, and Anthony Carroll of Ballynvolvassy, Co. Tipperary, Apr. 17, 1683, D.5091, National Library of Ireland; Carroll Papers, MS206, 577c, Md. Hist. Soc.; notes by Charles Carroll of Annapolis appended to Carroll-O'Carroll Genealogies, Md. Hist. Soc.

[8] Originally published in John Carroll Brent's anecdotal *Biographical Sketch of the Most Rev. John Carroll, First Archbishop of Baltimore . . .* (Baltimore, 1843), 16, this story is repeated in Kate Mason Rowland's generally reliable biography of Charles Carroll of Carrollton with a citation to Brent (*The Life of Charles Carroll of Carrollton, 1737-1832, with His Correspondence and Public Papers,* 2 vols. [New York, 1898], I, 3-4). While I am still working to document a Carroll-Powis connection, Powis's ties to Maryland's proprietary family are a matter of record: his wife, Lady Elizabeth Somerset, was the niece of Sir John Somerset. Somerset's wife, Mary Arundell, was the sister of Anne Arundell (?-1649) and thus the aunt of Charles Calvert, 3d Lord Baltimore and proprietor of Maryland, 1675-1715. In addition, Powis was incarcerated in the Tower of London from 1678 until 1684, having been accused by Titus Oates of complicity in the "Popish plot." Jailed with Powis on the same charges and for the same period was Henry, Lord Arundell, first cousin to the proprietor. Leslie Stephen and Sidney Lee, eds., *Dictionary of National Biography* (New York, 1908-1909), IX, 682-683; Genealogical Files, Charles Carroll of Carrollton Papers, Md. Hist. Soc.

regard, it is important to understand how the Glorious Revolution changed the situation of Maryland's Catholics. Always a minority in the colony from its founding in 1634, Catholics accounted for approximately 25 percent of Maryland's 25,000 inhabitants in the late 1680s.[9] Concentrated primarily in the Western Shore counties of Charles and St. Mary's, and knit together by the missions and priests that served the faithful, most Catholics were small landowners whose lives differed little from those of their Protestant neighbors. However, a small but highly visible and quite wealthy elite bound to the proprietor by blood and marriage as well as by religion headed the Catholic community. By virtue of Lord Baltimore's favor, men from this group monopolized the most powerful and lucrative
160 offices in the colony's government. In 1688, for example, six of the eight men serving in the dual capacity of councillors to the governor and members of the upper house of assembly were Roman Catholics, and five of them were related both to the proprietor and to each other. This reality sorely rankled equally ambitious Protestants who considered non-Catholic domination of the lower house, as well as of county and local offices, insufficient compensation for a policy that denied them access to the top echelons of provincial power. In the spring of 1689 the uncertainties generated in Maryland by the triumph of a Protestant succession in England gave these men an opportunity to redress the balance of power in their favor. Led by a habitual troublemaker named John Coode, they concocted a "risinge in armes" that wrested the authority to govern Maryland from Lord Baltimore and transferred it to the English crown. Receiving royal support for their activities, Coode and his cohorts in the assembly consolidated their victory by enforcing oaths of allegiance, abhorrence, and supremacy that effectively barred Roman Catholics from holding office and restricted the kinds of courts in which they could practice law. Later, statutes were enacted that forbade Catholics to worship publicly or educate their children under schoolmasters of their own faith.[10] The message of these laws was clear to Maryland's Catholics. Henceforth, the religion they professed would make them vulnerable in the New World to the same kinds of threats and pressures that had constricted and endangered them in the Old.

Deeply angered by the course of events that so rudely thwarted his expectations, Charles Carroll the Settler did not accept the overthrow of the proprietor with good grace. His strident defiance of the rebellion's leaders, whom he characterized as "profligate wretches and men of scandalous lives," earned him two stays in the St. Mary's City jail,

[9] Lois Green Carr and David William Jordan, *Maryland's Revolution of Government, 1689-1692* (Ithaca, N.Y., 1974), 33, n. 64.

[10] The definitive study of this period of Maryland history is Carr and Jordan, *Maryland's Revolution of Government*, from which my brief description is drawn. See esp. 37, 39-40, 213. William Hand Browne *et al.*, eds., *Archives of Maryland: Proceedings and Acts of the General Assembly of Maryland* (Baltimore, 1883-1972), XXVI, 340-341.

confinements that must have been especially galling for a man who, upon his emigration, had changed the motto on his family crest from "In fide et in bello forte" ("Strong in faith and war") to "Ubicumque cum libertate" ("Anywhere so long as there be freedom").[11] Despite these difficulties, however, the Settler's position was far from hopeless because, although his benefactor Charles Calvert, third Lord Baltimore, had lost political control of the colony, he retained ownership of the land and rights to specific revenues. To protect and advance these interests the proprietor continued to maintain an active private establishment in Maryland, and Charles Carroll carved out a key role for himself in this organization, where he could serve without having to swear any objectionable oaths. Indeed, his accrual of offices in the proprietary establishment during the period of royal government in Maryland (1690-1715) attests both to his 161
ability and to his ambition—and to the growing esteem in which Calvert held his services.[12]

II

For a full appreciation of both the expectations that Charles Carroll brought to Maryland and his furious disappointment at being deprived of them in such short order, it is necessary to understand the character of the provincial society upon whose opportunities he intended to capitalize. At the time of his arrival most of the colony's land remained heavily forested, and a scraggly patchwork of settlements clung to the shore of the Chesapeake Bay and its tributary rivers and creeks. There were no towns of any size; the capital, though called St. Mary's City, was nothing more than a collection of primitive structures.[13] To this setting Carroll brought two distinct personal advantages: he was a free man rather than an indentured servant, and he came with the middle-level post of attorney general in the proprietary government, an office from which he could expect a return of some £50 sterling a year.[14] In a society where the gross annual income of ordinary planters ranged from £10 to £15—and frequently fell below that standard—he could therefore count upon a modest measure of comfort from his legal duties alone.[15] But even if the turn of events had not robbed him of his official position, Carroll would never have confined himself solely to that pursuit. The great planters, in what was still a rude frontier society, realized a gross yearly income of £200-250

[11] Browne *et al.*, eds., *Archives of Maryland,* VIII, 125.

[12] For the best analyses of how government functioned in Maryland during this period see Donnell MacClure Owings, *His Lordship's Patronage: Offices of Profit in Colonial Maryland* (Baltimore, 1953), and Lois Green Carr, "County Government in Maryland, 1689-1709" (Ph.D. diss., Harvard University, 1968).

[13] Lois Green Carr, " 'The Metropolis of Maryland': A Comment on Town Development along the Tobacco Coast," *Maryland Historical Magazine,* LXIX (1974), 124-125.

[14] Owings, *His Lordship's Patronage,* 43-44.

[15] Paul G. E. Clemens, *The Atlantic Economy and Colonial Maryland's Eastern Shore: From Tobacco to Grain* (Ithaca, N.Y., 1980), 87-89.

from their tobacco.[16] Moreover, by virtue of their other activities as merchants, creditors, lawyers, and local or provincial officeholders, the wealthiest of these men could expect to take in an additional £200-350 per annum, while placemen in the highest echelons of the governing establishment often managed to increase their gross incomes by £500 or more.[17] The Settler's behavior in Maryland unmistakably indicates that it was to these heights that he aspired.

It should be kept in mind, however, that although the incomes of Maryland's wealthiest men were substantial for the late seventeenth century, Carroll entered a society in which traditional economic and class distinctions were just beginning to become apparent. By the 1680s the

movement toward a propertied elite, encouraged by proprietary policy, was clearly underway, and the colony already contained distinguishable

[16] Gloria L. Main, *Tobacco Colony: Life in Early Maryland, 1650-1720* (Princeton, N.J., 1982), 84.

[17] Calculating the incomes of Maryland's wealthiest men for the last decade of the 17th century and the first decade of the 18th is extraordinarily difficult, but if I have erred, I believe I have done so on the conservative side. Gloria Main cites one wealthy planter, Joseph Chew, who in 1705 shipped two years' production of tobacco—150 hogsheads—and received a price in England of £449 (*Tobacco Colony,* 84). Certainly, the incomes of Maryland's greatest planters whose slaveholding and servant assets exceeded Chew's—he died in 1705 with 20, whereas seven years later, Henry Darnall's estate contained over 100—suggest that there were men who could produce more than 75 hogsheads annually. Further, since most wealth estimates for the colonial period are based on probate records, no hard figures exist for planters' yearly earnings from their mercantile pursuits. One way to approximate annual income from retailing in Maryland is to multiply capital investments in merchant goods as listed in probate inventories by a conservative rate of return—8%, a figure 2% higher than the legal interest rate. Thus planter-merchant Philemon Lloyd, the richest man of his time, who died in 1685 possessed of an inventory of mercantile goods worth £751, probably received a net return of at least £60 annually. The net return Lloyd earned through exporting tobacco—the year of his death he shipped nearly 200 hogsheads that he acquired through trade—certainly equaled his domestic business and probably exceeded it. The monies owed Lloyd's estate in 1685 approximated some £1,900 sterling, the interest on which probably returned him £100 a year. Talbot County Orphans Court Inventories 1635-1709, J.R. No. 1, 324-327, and Inventories and Accounts, Liber 9, 1686-1688, 244, all at the Maryland State Archives, Annapolis.

Regarding planters who were also lawyers, Lois Green Carr cites the case of William Stone of Prince George's County, who in the mid-1690s earned nearly £100 annually by practicing in three county courts ("County Government in Maryland, 1689-1709," 505-507). Lawyers plying their trade in higher courts presumably earned a minimum of £150 a year. A lawyer's income, it should be noted, was especially high because lawyers' fees represented net profit while a planter's return consisted of gross earnings minus his costs of production and shipping. Finally, the highest proprietary officeholders, who were expected to pay a percentage of their incomes to their patrons, could expect to earn anywhere from £200 to £300 or more from their posts. Owings, *His Lordship's Patronage,* 23-24, 34, 79.

groups of wealthy, middling, and poor planters. Still, such divisions were rudimentary, for virtually all of these planters shared a style of life that can only be described as crude, and even the richest of them preferred capital investments in land, slaves, livestock, and mercantile goods to expenditures for refinements or for improving their creature comforts.[18] Moreover, the religious and economic tensions expressed in the political turmoil of the early years of royal government, 1689-1692, tended to blur class distinctions, so that while the coming to power of the Protestants, combined with the spread of slavery, ultimately led to a society marked by recognized lines of division among the upper, middling, and meaner sort, the Maryland of the late 1680s remained in a state of flux. Equally important, the colony's system of proprietary governance had not hardened into a pattern of hierarchical authority. Political, socioeconomic, and 163
geographic mobility—even in the depressed economic situation of the 1680s—remained a reality, thereby retarding the development of deferential relationships. Similarly, while the coterie of Catholic officeholders attached to the proprietary family had used their ties to considerable personal advantage, they had not produced an intergenerational ruling elite, and their hold on power was so tenuous that Coode's Protestant rabble-rousers could displace them with little difficulty.[19]

[18] Research in probate records has shown that the most affluent late 17th-century Maryland planters resided in timber houses containing six modestly sized rooms, while their poorer neighbors inhabited one- or two-room structures. Members of the fledgling gentry tended to express their economic success by acquiring featherbeds and a variety of chairs—items rarely found in the homes of poor and middling planters—rather than through the possession of such objects as looking glasses, plate, clocks, pictures, and books that became badges of status among the elite during the "consumer revolution" that developed during the 18th century. (Lois Green Carr and Lorena S. Walsh, "Changing Life Styles in St. Mary's County," in Cary Carson, Ronald Hoffman, and Peter J. Albert, eds., *Of Consuming Interests: The Style of Life in the Eighteenth Century* [forthcoming]; Main, *Tobacco Colony,* chaps. 4-7.) For an able description and analysis of the Upper South see John J. McCusker and Russell R. Menard, *The Economy of British America, 1607-1789* (Chapel Hill, N.C., 1985), esp. chap. 6. The strength of their material on colonial Maryland rests in large measure on the fine work of a generation of scholars who have remarkably enriched our understanding: Lois Green Carr, Paul G. E. Clemens, Carville V. Earle, Allan Kulikoff, Gloria L. Main, Russell R. Menard, Edward C. Papenfuse, Gregory A. Stiverson, and Lorena S. Walsh.

[19] For a suggestive treatment of the patterns of officeholding in Maryland from 1660 to 1715 and the emergence of a governing elite, see David W. Jordan, "Political Stability and the Emergence of a Native Elite in Maryland," in Thad W. Tate and David L. Ammerman, eds., *The Chesapeake in the Seventeenth Century: Essays on Anglo-American Society* (Chapel Hill, N.C., 1979), 243-273. Although I agree with Allan Kulikoff's general conclusion in *Tobacco and Slaves: The Development of Southern Cultures in the Chesapeake, 1680-1800* (Chapel Hill, N.C., 1986), that a mature intergenerational gentry class did not blossom in Maryland until sometime after the first quarter of the 18th century, his analysis ascribes to that

This, then, was the milieu into which Charles Carroll the Settler came—a society open enough to offer ample opportunities to a young man on the make. His basic strategy for advancement was deceptively simple: he made a habit of marrying well. Surviving several months of what he described as a "hard seasoning"—a period of acclimatization to the colonial ecological environment that in Carroll's case happened to coincide with the overthrow of the proprietary government—he cushioned the blows dealt his original prospects by contracting a marriage in November 1689 with a wealthy widow named Martha Ridgely Underwood.[20] Several years his senior and the mother of four young children, Martha had come to Maryland as an indentured servant, but by 1671 she had married the man to whom she was bound—Robert Ridgely, a prominent attorney and holder of several provincial offices.[21] Upon Ridgely's death in 1681, Martha inherited a sizable estate consisting of two plantations—a dwelling plantation of 94 acres on St. Inigoe's Creek in St. Mary's County and a 1,200-acre tobacco plantation on Wicomico River in Somerset County—along with all of her husband's personal property, including household goods, plate, servants and slaves, livestock, and debts owed to him, totaling in value £500.[22] Sometime after 1683 Martha Ridgely married Anthony Underwood, a former bound servant and law clerk of her first husband.[23] At his death in

---

class a uniformity that did not exist. First, it is important to remember that in the colony in the 1680s—and even before—there were elitist individuals of recognizable power who conceived of themselves as gentlemen and thus superior to the common folk. The most powerful of these figures were wealthy, had close personal ties to the proprietor, and were Roman Catholics. As a result, they were deeply resented and, as Carr and Jordan have decisively shown in *Maryland's Revolution of Government,* they were replaced in the turmoil of Coode's Rebellion. However—and this is my second point—religious enmity continued to divide Maryland's nascent gentry as Protestants and Catholics vied for dominance during the period of royal government, 1690-1715, and although Protestants won a decisive political victory in 1718, the issue of religion persisted in influencing the development and character of the colony's gentry class until the eve of the American Revolution. While Roman Catholics remained a minority within the Maryland gentry, their substantial wealth and highly self-conscious ideology played an influential role in provincial life even though their religion sharply differentiated their status—and their sense of security—from that of their Protestant counterparts, a theme I will address more fully in my forthcoming study of the Carrolls.

[20] Browne *et al.*, eds., *Md. Archs.*, VIII, 126.

[21] For evidence of Martha Ridgely's servitude see Patents, Liber 16, 400-401, Md. State Archs. Robert Ridgely served as clerk of the council, 1664-1674, clerk of the lower house, 1671-1681, and clerk of the secretary's office and provincial court, 1670/1-1673, and acted as deputy secretary, 1671-1673. Owings, *His Lordship's Patronage,* 126, 128, 136, 138, 140.

[22] Will of Robert Ridgely, Wills, St. Mary's County, 1680, Liber 2, 162-166, and Inventories and Accounts, St. Mary's County, 1682, Liber 8, 295-302, Md. State Archs.

[23] Edward C. Papenfuse *et al.*, eds., *A Biographical Dictionary of the Maryland Legislature, 1635-1789,* II (Baltimore, 1985), 846. By 1687 Underwood had also

1689 Underwood left a personal estate—composed almost entirely of the property his wife had inherited from her first husband—worth nearly £550 sterling and about 2,000 acres.[24] Into this convenient breach stepped the enterprising and ambitious Charles Carroll, who happened to be the executor of Anthony Underwood's estate. On November 9, 1689, no more than six months after Underwood's demise, Carroll wed the well-provisioned Martha. The union was destined to be a short one. In November 1690, Martha Ridgely Underwood Carroll died in childbirth, followed three days later by her infant.[25]

The Ridgely-Underwood legacy was central to Carroll's rise to power and wealth.[26] Capitalizing upon the assets made available to him as the administrator of his wife's estate, the Settler acted quickly to establish
himself in trade: records of a suit filed against him in February 1692 for 165
illegally importing a sizable quantity of "Strong beer" and wine show that he operated a warehouse on St. Inigoe's Creek, the site of the Ridgely-Underwood dwelling plantation.[27] While it is unclear whether he was also able to make similar use of "Little Bellean," Martha's 1,200-acre Somerset County plantation, he certainly continued to occupy her St. Mary's County house. Anthony Underwood's inventory, filed by Carroll in 1692, evaluates the contents of that seven-room residence, including £11.01.06 of possessions—"Beds & furniture, Chairs, Tables &c"—in a chamber the administrator referred to as "my roome."[28]

---

been admitted to the St. Mary's and Calvert county courts and the Prerogative Court.

[24] Presumably, the 1,294 acres Martha received by Robert Ridgely's will were still intact. Underwood patented 700 acres on his own. *Ibid.* Inventories and Accounts, Liber 10, 320, 329, Md. State Archs.

[25] Charles Carroll, Bible Records, #49735, Filing Case A, Md. Hist. Soc.

[26] Carroll's obligations to his deceased wife's minor children appear to have been largely fulfilled by the turn of the century. By the terms of Robert Ridgely's will, Robert, Charles, William, and Martha Ridgely, all of whom were of age by 1701, received specific bequests separate from the provisions that made their mother the principal heir. Mrs. Ridgely was charged, however, with the children's maintenance and schooling until they reached their ages of majority, and from all indications Carroll assumed these responsibilities upon his wife's death. When the youngest child, his stepdaughter Martha, was removed from his care in 1692 and placed with a Protestant guardian, he readily agreed to continue to support her from the estate until she became 21. (Testamentary Proceedings 1692-1694, Liber 15, 24, Md. State Archs.) In March 1705 Carroll paid £6.6.8 to his stepdaughter, who had married a merchant named Lewis Duvall, and the same sum to one Thomas Underwood, "part heir" of William Ridgely, as "the filial portions" of their father's estate. Robert Ridgely, Jr., and his brother Charles had died in 1702 and 1705, respectively, and William's whereabouts were unknown; he had apparently left Maryland in 1698. Martha Ridgely Duvall died in 1709. *Ibid.*, Liber 19B, 14, 90-91.

[27] Carroll T. Bond, ed., *Proceedings of the Maryland Court of Appeals, 1695-1729* (Washington, D.C., 1933), I, 31. The Settler won the case on appeal in 1697.

[28] In addition to the main house, the Ridgely-Underwood plantation included at

The Settler's access to this inheritance—it is impossible to verify whether he ever permanently acquired any of Martha's property—shielded him from the most harmful practical effects of Protestant ascendance in Maryland. But, like other Catholics, he faced new proscriptions that limited his opportunities. His unwillingness to compromise his religious beliefs made his legal career vulnerable to the kinds of anti-Catholic restrictions long common in England. Clients continued to seek his services in the immediate aftermath of the overthrow of proprietary government, but Carroll and other attorneys of his faith were permitted to practice only in the Chancery and Prerogative courts following the formal institution of royal government in 1692.[29] Such restrictions, however, did
166 not prevent him from continuing to provide astute legal advice not only to the proprietor, Charles Calvert, but also to Calvert's cousin Col. Henry Darnall, Maryland's most powerful Catholic.[30]

Whether Carroll received any financial reward from the proprietor for his loyalty and counsel is unknown, and none of the legal maneuvers he suggested enabled Calvert to regain control of the government of Maryland. But his fearless efforts to protect proprietary interests brought him two enormously important benefits—Calvert's gratitude and, perhaps even more significant, the approbation and patronage of Darnall. Once again Carroll had positioned himself to the utmost advantage, and in February 1693/4 he moved decisively to consolidate his gains by marrying the colonel's fifteen-year-old daughter Mary, a girl less than half his age.

The opportunities this alliance brought Carroll can scarcely be exaggerated. Until the overthrow of the proprietary government, Darnall sat on the council, the colony's most powerful political body, served on the Board of Deputy Governors and the Land Council, was the proprietor's rent roll keeper, and held the two extremely lucrative offices of Lord Baltimore's agent and receiver general, and keeper of the great seal. Most significant, though Darnall, like all nonconforming Catholics, lost his political posts after 1689, he retained all his positions within the proprietor's private establishment, and the power and wealth that continued to flow from these posts made him indisputably one of the colony's dominant personalities.

---

least three outbuildings—a kitchen, a milk house that seems to have become a wash house by 1692, and a quarter that presumably housed Underwood's four servants and two slaves. A "store," usually a structure used for storage of new goods, appears in Ridgely's inventory but not in Underwood's, replaced perhaps by the Settler's warehouse on St. Inigoe's Creek. Inventories and Accounts, Liber 10-A, 1, and Liber 8, 295-302, Md. State Archs.; Papenfuse *et al.*, eds., *Biographical Dictionary,* II, 846; Main, *Tobacco Colony,* 294. By 1704, Martha's 1,200-acre Somerset County tract, "Little Bellean," had been broken up and sold. Rent Rolls, Somerset County, Liber 9, 32, Md. State Archs.

[29] Browne *et al.*, eds., *Md. Archs.*, VIII, 508, 448; Carr and Jordan, *Maryland's Revolution of Government,* 60, n. 35.

[30] Carr and Jordan, *Maryland's Revolution of Government,* 150.

Carroll had hardly recited his wedding vows when his fortunes took still another turn for the better. Darnall bestowed on his new son-in-law, whose abilities he recognized, two Prince George's County tracts totaling 1,381 acres.[31] Far more important, three months later, in May 1694, when Maryland's land office reopened, he appointed Carroll clerk, a position that carried a salary of approximately £100 a year and placed him at the strategic center of all land transactions.[32] This was precisely where Darnall needed a "point man" whom he could trust to protect not only the proprietor's interests but also those of Maryland's beleaguered Catholic gentry. In all, Henry Darnall had two sons, five stepsons, and six sons-in-law, but from the mid-1690s to the end of his life in 1711 his principal protégé was Charles Carroll.

III

Carroll's economic career exemplifies the classic pattern of broadly diversified Chesapeake entrepreneurs who built fortunes by combining strategic marriages with the activities of a planter, banker, lawyer, merchant, and proprietary officeholder. Land constituted the foundation of his wealth: when he died in 1720, Carroll owned 47,777 acres and was the largest landholder in the province. He also possessed a warrant for 20,000 additional acres, 10,000 of which were patented by his son Charles Carroll of Annapolis in 1723.[33] Conservatively, the Settler's acreage was worth £20,000.[34] He accumulated this estate by several methods. Nearly three-fifths of the land he held at the time of his death—26,413 acres—he had acquired by patent. He also owned 13,026 acres that he had purchased and another 12,249 obtained through mortgage foreclosures. Additionally, the records show that during his lifetime Carroll sold 7,418 acres that he had either bought or acquired by foreclosure. (See Table I.)

The chronological pattern of the Settler's land acquisitions was clearly related to the improved prospects that resulted from his second marriage and shows his ambition to build a landed estate. Beginning in 1696—two

[31] Warrants, Liber A-C, 373, Md. State Archs.

[32] Owings, *His Lordship's Patronage*, 169-170. The process of land acquisition in Maryland began with the payment of "caution money"—120 lbs. of tobacco per 100 acres—to the proprietor's agent and receiver general, who in 1694 was Henry Darnall. The agent then directed the clerk of the land office—in this case, Darnall's son-in-law Charles Carroll—to forward a warrant to the deputy surveyor for a tract to be laid out in a particular county. Following the survey and the approval of the certificate by the examiner general, the clerk of the land office drew up a patent confirming the tract. The patent then went to the keeper of the great seal—again, Henry Darnall—who affixed the proprietor's stamp and returned the document to the land office to be picked up by the patentee. *Ibid.*, 80-81; Carr and Jordan, *Maryland's Revolution of Government*, 36.

[33] This tract, called Carrollton, lay in western Prince George's, later Frederick County, between the Potomac and Monocacy rivers.

[34] Calculated on the basis of Paul Clemens's evaluation of the Lloyd family lands in 1733 (*Atlantic Economy*, 135, n. 18).

TABLE I BUILDING A LANDED ESTATE: CHARLES CARROLL THE SETTLER'S METHODS OF LAND ACQUISITION (IN ACRES)

County[a]	*Marriage and Inheritance*	*Patented*	*Purchased*	*Acquired by Foreclosure*	*Sold*	*Total in 1720*
Anne Arundel/Baltimore[b]		19,403	6,857	8,138	(3,573)	30,825
Calvert			1,380	1,240		2,620
Cecil		2,304	2,330	666	(3,109)	2,191
Dorchester		1,500				1,500
Kent				100		100
Prince George's	3,507[c]	1,806	1,850	1,105	(236)	8,032
Queen Anne's		1,000	500		(500)	1,000
St. Mary's		400	109			509
Talbot				1,000		1,000
Totals	3,507	26,413	13,026	12,249	(7,418)	47,777[d]

Sources: County land records—warrants, certificates of survey, and patents—located at the Maryland State Archives, Annapolis.

[a] The county boundaries are those in existence at the Settler's death.

[b] Because the boundary between western Anne Arundel County and western Baltimore County remained somewhat indefinite at the time of the Settler's death, his holdings in those counties have been grouped together. For example, Doohoregan Manor, the 7,000-acre tract at Elk Ridge that became the family's principal dwelling plantation, appears as part of Carroll's Baltimore County lands in his will, drawn in 1718, but was within the next decade recorded within the bounds of Anne Arundel County.

[c] Carroll received four tracts of land from his father-in-law, Henry Darnall. Two parcels, totaling 1,381 acres, were part of the Settler's marriage settlement with Darnall's daughter in 1693/4. Darnall willed him the other two in 1711. Warrants, Liber A-C, 373, and Anne Arundel Wills, Liber 13, 223, Md. State Archs.

[d] Not included in this total are three large manors upon which Carroll acquired the right to collect rents. Two of these tracts—Bashford Manor (1,500 acres) and St. Clement's Manor (11,000 acres)—were located in St. Mary's County. The third, Westwood Manor (1,600 acres), was in Charles County. The records available do not indicate whether the Settler ever realized any income from these properties. By mid-century, lawsuits in which his descendants were engaged over these lands indicated a long history of tenant refusal to acknowledge the Carroll family's claim to any rents. The tenants insisted up to the American Revolution that they held their properties as freeholds from owners previous to the Carrolls. (Chancery Court Records, Liber I.R. No. 4, 100-131, Md. State Archs.; "Answers of Tenants," Carroll-McTavish Papers, Md. Hist. Soc.) The Settler's will also mentions 20,000 acres of unpatented land in Prince George's County. Charles Carroll of Annapolis laid this tract out as Carrollton, 10,000 acres, in 1723.

years after he wed Mary Darnall—Carroll commenced actively purchasing land warrants, the first step in securing title to land. Between that year and 1700 he bought warrants for about 12,000-13,000 acres, although during these four years he only patented 3,900, including a 1,500-acre Eastern Shore property. The first significant increase in his steady process of accumulation occurred in 1702, when he patented 7,000 acres at Elk Ridge on the border of Baltimore and Anne Arundel counties, the nucleus of the property that was to become the family's principal dwelling plantation, Doohoregan Manor. The circumstances of its acquisition show how Carroll was able to use his powerful connections to advance his interests. Following his purchase in 1699 of a warrant for 7,000 acres, he waited three years before securing a patent on July 2, 1702. The next
month he left Maryland for an extended trip to England, where it appears 169
he so favorably impressed the proprietor that he returned to Maryland with a remarkable dispensation.[35] In a document issued on March 9, 1704, Lord Baltimore extended to Carroll the unique privilege of paying no quitrents on his 7,000-acre tract until his infant son Charles, for whom the land was intended, reached his age of majority some twenty years hence. The arrangement further provided that, even if the child died before reaching his twenty-first birthday, the dispensation would remain in effect until the date when the boy would have come of age.[36]

The next quantum leap in the Settler's accumulation of land occurred in 1711, the year his father-in-law, Henry Darnall, died. Once again, Carroll's personal loss was compensated by a distinct improvement in his economic position. He immediately assumed both of Darnall's important offices in the proprietor's private establishment, becoming agent and receiver general as well as keeper of the great seal, and he acted in these capacities for over a year until his official appointment to the posts in the fall of 1712. Collectively, the positions enhanced his potential income by £500 to £900 sterling annually and provided him with the resources to expand his planting and mercantile activities. Table II, charting on a yearly basis Carroll's acquisition of land during his thirty-two years in Maryland, shows that in the decade between Darnall's death and his own, he doubled the acreage he had acquired during his first two decades in the colony. Although a similar chronological calculation for Carroll's investment in slaves cannot be made, we know that at the time of his death he owned 112, half of whom were working hands. Valued at £1,931, Carroll's slaves resided on the quarters of his five plantations, where they produced tobacco, wheat, and corn, and tended livestock worth more than £600.[37]

Like his rate of land acquisition, Carroll's banking activities increased markedly after he assumed his father-in-law's offices in 1711. In a society

[35] Browne *et al.*, eds., *Md. Archs.*, XXV, 130.

[36] Patents, Liber DD #5, 711-712, Md. State Archs.

[37] Analysis of Charles Carroll's inventories by Victoria Allen, Charles Carroll of Carrollton Papers. The inventories are contained in the Carroll-McTavish Papers, Ledger X, Md. Hist. Soc.

TABLE II
CHARLES CARROLL THE SETTLER:
LAND ACQUISITIONS, 1693-1720

Year[a]	*Net Increase (Decrease) in Acreage*	*Cumulative Total*
1693	1,381	1,381
1694	2,000	3,381
1695		
1696	1,000	4,381
1697		
1698	900	5,281
1699		
1700		
1701	2	5,283
1702	8,000	13,283
1703		
1704	969	14,252
1705	282	14,534
1706	1,300	15,834
1707	4,210	20,044
1708	2,415	22,459
1709	800	23,259
1710	638	23,897
1711	11,218	35,115
1712	(2,575)	32,540
1713	5,276	37,816
1714	500	38,316
1715	3,913	42,229
1716	3,080	45,309
1717	980	46,289
1718	2,067	48,356
1719	(917)	47,439
1720	338	47,777

Sources: County land records—warrants, certificates of survey, and patents—located at the Md. State Archs. This table includes all of Carroll's land acquisitions, whether by marriage settlement, inheritance, patent, purchase, or foreclosure.

[a] Although Carroll acquired no lands during his first five years in Maryland, 1688-1692, he had access to and benefited from the real and personal property of his first wife, Martha Ridgely Underwood Carroll.

where liquid capital was always scarce, those who could provide credit performed a vital and extremely profitable service. After 1704 the interest rate on such transactions was regulated by law in Maryland at 8 percent per hundredweight when the loan was based on the colony's prime staple, tobacco, and 6 percent per hundred pounds sterling for cash.[38] Provincial Court and Anne Arundel County records indicate that Carroll was involved in the mortgage loan market as early as 1700, with a marked

[38] Browne *et al.*, eds., *Md. Archs.*, XXVI, 352.

increase occurring after 1705, and that by 1711 he had more mortgage loans outstanding than anyone else in Maryland—a total of thirty. His nearest competitor was one of his most important legal clients, the English merchant John Hyde. During the period 1700-1711, Hyde contracted only fourteen mortgages, although the cumulative value of his fewer loans totaled more than Carroll's many—£4,615 to £2,514.[39] It should be emphasized, however, that since many of these loans were repaid or foreclosed—most had a life of one to three years—neither lender had his entire cumulative total out at any one time.

Within two years of assuming Darnall's high proprietary offices, Carroll replaced Hyde as the colony's largest lender. In 1712 and 1713 Hyde made substantial loans totaling £1,704, but the Provincial Court deeds record no further activity on his part. By contrast, between 1711 and 1720 171
the Settler made twenty-four loans worth £4,464. Conceivably, since Hyde continued to be active in the Maryland tobacco trade, he may have lent money to Carroll, who in turn re-lent it at a higher rate.[40] The prospects for such an arrangement may have suggested themselves to Hyde as early as 1710, when the depression in the tobacco economy resulting from Queen Anne's War intimidated lenders. Creditors may well have been further deterred when the Maryland assembly in 1714 enacted a measure to restrict suits for the collection of debts worth up to £20 sterling or 2,000 pounds of tobacco exclusively to the county courts. Although Hyde's mortgage loans were much larger, the legislation combined with the severe economic depression to create a climate unpropitious for creditors.[41] In this situation Carroll's positions both as an accomplished lawyer well versed in representing mercantile interests—one court petition in 1714 referred to him as an "Attorny in fact for divers Merchants and others in Great Britain"—and as a high proprietary official would have offered Hyde considerable security.[42] Hyde indicated in a letter written several years earlier to a Maryland correspondent that Carroll was already extremely familiar with his operations in the colony. Explaining his refusal to advance further credit, Hyde wrote: "But Mr Carroll knows very well that I have such Sumes of money allready due to me in Maryland which I cannot gett in that I am not willing to runn any further."[43] Whatever the case, it is clear that while Carroll's income from

[39] Provincial Court Deeds, TL#2, PL#3, PL#6, TP#4, PL#5, Md. State Archs. I wish to thank Dr. Lorena S. Walsh for making her research into these records available to me.

[40] Aubrey C. Land believes that such practices had developed in Maryland by the 1730s (*The Dulanys of Maryland: A Biographical Study of Daniel Dulany, the Elder [1685-1753] and Daniel Dulany the Younger [1722-1797]* [Baltimore, 1955], 103).

[41] Browne *et al.*, eds., *Md. Archs.*, XXIV, 439-442. Alan Frederick Day, "A Social Study of Lawyers in Maryland, 1660-1775" (Ph.D. diss., Johns Hopkins University, 1977), 205-206.

[42] Browne *et al.*, eds., *Md. Archs.*, XXIX, 368.

[43] John Hyde to Lewes Duvall [London], Mar. 25, 1710, in John M. Hemphill II,

proprietary offices increased markedly after 1711, his substantial mortgage activities show that he found access to an even greater source of capital.

Besides lending money on mortgages, Carroll extended numerous loans. Although his personal accounts have not survived, the extent of the credit he advanced is revealed by his frequent recourse to the provincial courts in efforts to collect debts that ranged from £20 to £280 sterling. Carroll's strategies indicate his skill in using Maryland's legal system. Sometimes he attached the borrower's goods and chattels; in other instances he had defaulters incarcerated; and if the debtor had died, he sued the estate. Over the course of twenty years—from 1699 to 1718—Carroll brought sixty suits and received awards totaling £1,712 sterling,
172 over 2,300 pounds of tobacco, and £100 current money. In addition, in eight of these cases the records specify that he was allowed to collect more than 8,000 pounds of tobacco for his expense in bringing suit. (Similar costs were also granted in his other cases, but the exact amounts were not recorded.) Equally significant, in 1721, the first year after his death, Carroll's administrators brought suit in behalf of his estate for debts amounting to £2,200 sterling.[44]

While Carroll was prohibited from practicing law in the Provincial Court, he remained very active in the Chancery Court and also practiced, though much less frequently, in the Prerogative Court. Between 1695 and 1717, he represented 187 different clients in the Court of Chancery, which had jurisdiction over equity cases involving more than 1,200 pounds of tobacco or £5 sterling.[45] In the Prerogative Court, where probate cases were heard, Carroll represented twenty clients between 1694 and 1711. Undoubtedly, he concentrated his efforts on chancery cases because the fees were higher. In 1708 the Maryland assembly standardized the amount that lawyers could charge in chancery at 600 pounds of tobacco per case but allowed only 400 pounds in the Prerogative Court.[46] In that year Carroll carried his heaviest case load—forty clients—and thus earned a minimum of £100 sterling.[47] Presumably, Maryland's most able lawyers, Carroll among them, worked out private arrangements for higher fees despite the law. One thing is clear: his legal practice was exceptionally lucrative.[48] As an envious adversary noted

---

"Documents Relating to the Colonial Tobacco Trade," *Md. Hist. Mag.*, LII (1957), 156.

[44] Provincial Court Judgements, WT#3, TL#3, TB#2, PL#1, PL#2, PL#3, IO#1, VD#2, PL#4, TP#2, WG#1, Md. State Archs.

[45] Chancery Court Records, 1695-1717, Md. State Archs.

[46] Day, "Social Study of Lawyers," 203.

[47] Owings states in *His Lordship's Patronage*, 44, that 12,000 lbs. of tobacco equaled £50 sterling a year.

[48] Beyond court appearances there were a host of other services for which lawyers earned handsome fees not regulated by law. For example, they were paid retainers for drawing mortgages and bonds, drafting and recording legal forms, and

in 1718, Carroll acquired "a vast estate in this Province, by the Offices he formerly Employed, and his Practice in the Law."[49]

Carroll's mercantile activities proved similarly prosperous. The inventory of the goods in his Annapolis store at the time of his death suggests that he may well have been the richest merchant in the colony. The wide variety of items he carried included an extensive selection of dry goods, pewter, brass, hosiery, stays, bodices, upholstery, saddlery, jewelry, guns, glass, earthenware, sugar, stationery, cutlery, groceries, ironware, wigs, harnesses, spices, and rum, with a total value of £3,144 current money.[50] By contrast, Samuel Chew, a wealthy merchant-planter who died in 1718, possessed an inventory of "new goods" worth only £545, and Amos Garrett, who succeeded Carroll as Annapolis's major merchant, left a
mercantile inventory valued at £3,570 in 1727.[51] Moreover, Carroll's 173
nephew James Carroll (?-1729), who was extremely close to the family and had benefited from his uncle's sponsorship, invested profitably in the slave trade, and it is conceivable that the Settler also had a financial interest in such ventures.[52]

By 1715 or thereabouts Charles Carroll had become one of Maryland's most powerful men, and the inventory made of his possessions at his death vividly portrays his status. The total value of his assets, excluding land, amounted to £7,535, the largest personal estate ever probated in the colony to that time.[53] Two testamentary bonds, the instruments used to ensure that administrators did not steal from the legacies entrusted to them and usually calculated at twice the value of the estate, were taken out to secure the administration of the Settler's personal estate. The first was drawn in August 1720 in the amount of £60,000 sterling. The second, recorded in January 1720/1 when Carroll's "Executors in Chief," his sons Charles and Daniel, had returned to Maryland from their studies abroad, reduced the amount to £40,000. Apparently, the difference between the total appraised value of Carroll's personal estate and the £20,000 indicated by the bond represented debts owed the estate.[54]

---

for giving advice. Day, "Social Study of Lawyers," 223-225. Day's study is a remarkably rich analysis of Maryland's colonial legal profession.

[49] Browne *et al.*, eds., *Md. Archs.*, XXXIII, 120.

[50] Ledger X, Carroll-McTavish Papers, Md. Hist. Soc., and inventory analysis by Victoria Allen.

[51] Main, *Tobacco Colony,* 236. Analysis of the Inventory of Amos Garrett, courtesy of Dr. Jean Russo, Historic Annapolis, Inc.

[52] James Carroll's Account Book, Special Collections Division, Georgetown University Library, Washington, D.C.

[53] Although Charles Carroll the Settler's dates fall within the time span covered by Gloria L. Main's excellent study *Tobacco Colony,* his inventory is not on file at the Md. State Archs. and thus escaped her notice.

[54] Testamentary Proceedings, Liber 24, 283, 385, Md. State Archs. The appraisals of the various sectors of Charles Carroll the Settler's estate took place over a five-year period, beginning in Nov. 1721 with his Baltimore County quarter and ending in Dec. 1726 with the inventory of his goods and chattels on Poplar Island.

The variety and richness of the Settler's wearing apparel, the size of his house, and its elaborate furnishings indicate even more dramatically than the value of his estate the kind of presence he projected in Annapolis and provincial society. His wardrobe, worth £114, included eight suits, one of which was a splendid affair of "fine Cloath trimmed wth gold" worth £16, five wigs, a variety of breeches and waistcoats including a scarlet coat and pants, Holland shirts, silk stockings, a great coat, a "drab coat," a cloak, several pairs of shoes, half a dozen hats, a scabbard, and four nightgowns. Carroll's house contained eleven well-appointed rooms with not only such marks of gentility as featherbeds and chairs but also an array of refinements that signified a style of living virtually unequaled in Maryland at that period. There were eight portraits and five other pictures on the walls; there were looking glasses and clocks, and the service for dining included plate and fine linen, with separate utensils in the bed chamber for tea service. The well-equipped kitchen with its buttery and vault contained an assortment of kettles, pans, skillets, chafing dishes, and utensils—in short, a supply of implements more than sufficient for preparing meals of elegance and sophistication. The Settler's dwelling also housed a well-furnished chapel that may have served the Catholics of Annapolis as well as the Carroll family.[55]

IV

Charles Carroll had climbed to the economic pinnacle of his society by the beginning of the eighteenth century's second decade. As a result he was not only the most powerful Catholic in Maryland but also a dangerous rival for any official he chose to oppose. Yet—and this is an important consideration—he had never lost his insatiable—some would say fatal—desire for political power. And in 1715—nearly twenty-five years after he had been deprived of his original appointment as attorney general—the adjustments necessitated by the rapid turnover of the proprietorship and the return of the government of Maryland to the Lords Baltimore led the Settler to take steps to reclaim for Roman Catholics a share of the colony's public offices and to install himself on an equal footing with the governor. His chief opponent was Maryland's governor, John Hart, a Protestant Irishman and former captain in the British army who was as implacable a foe of Catholic ambitions as Carroll was their champion. Thus the stage was set to play out in Maryland the same bitter conflicts that during the

---

The appraisal of the Settler's Annapolis estate, by far his most substantial property in 1720, is dated May 2, 1723, a month to the day after the 21st birthday of his eldest son, Charles Carroll of Annapolis. The inventory of his Prince George's County quarters, Western Branch and Enfield Chace, was completed on Dec. 20, 1721, immediately after that of his Baltimore County establishment. A fifth appraisal, untitled, undated, and possibly incomplete, was probably for the supply plantation, later referred to as Annapolis quarter. Ledger X, Carroll-McTavish Papers, Md. Hist. Soc.

[55] Ledger X, Carroll-McTavish Papers, Md. Hist. Soc.

seventeenth century had destroyed Ireland's great Catholic landowners and driven Charles Carroll to the New World.

The unusually fluid political conditions that obtained both in England and in Maryland between 1714 and 1716 seemed to augur well for the success of Carroll's plans. Within two months of Queen Anne's death on August 1, 1714, the accession of her Hanoverian cousin George I reaffirmed the Protestant succession to the British throne. Stuart hopes were not entirely vanquished, however, and sentiment favoring the return of the "Old Pretender," who aspired to become James III, found expression in the "Fifteen Rebellion," a revolt that broke out in Scotland in September 1715. Although the threat was contained within six months, the Jacobite/anti-Jacobite passions it aroused persisted for some time and 175
had a particularly unsettling effect on politics in Maryland.

Maryland was especially vulnerable to the political and religious tensions inherent in the "Fifteen Rebellion" because problems of succession in the proprietorship in the spring of 1715 had already created uncertainties within the colony's government. Between early February and mid-April of that year, three different individuals held the title of Lord Baltimore. Charles Calvert, third Lord Baltimore, died on February 2, and was succeeded by his son Benedict Leonard Calvert, fourth Lord Baltimore, whose own death on April 16 left the title in the hands of his sixteen-year-old son Charles Calvert, fifth Lord Baltimore, and the young man's guardian Lord Guilford. Complicating matters further was the fact that, during this rapid turnover, the crown was in the process of returning the authority to govern Maryland, which it had held since 1690, to the Calverts. This arrangement had been negotiated by Benedict Leonard Calvert, who had perceived that such a restoration would never take place as long as the proprietor remained a Roman Catholic and had, in anticipation of his accession to the title, converted himself and his sons to the Anglican faith in 1713. This action so enraged his father that he cut off the apostate's allowance and refused to have anything further to do with him.[56] Nevertheless, on May 15, 1715, a month after Benedict Leonard's son Charles succeeded to his titles, the government of Maryland was restored to the proprietary family, an event proclaimed in the colony on December 27, 1715.

For Charles Carroll this combination of events—the accession of George I in 1714, the rapid turnover of the proprietorship, the restoration of the government of Maryland to the Calverts, and the loyalties exposed by the "Fifteen Rebellion"—posed enormously tempting opportunities

[56] Benedict Leonard Calvert to Robert Harley [Oct. 20, 1713], Charles Calvert to Benedict Leonard Calvert [Aug. 7, 1713], and Charles Calvert to Robert Harley, Dec. (?) 31, 1713, printed in Michael G. Hall, "Some Letters of Benedict Leonard Calvert," *William and Mary Quarterly*, 3d Ser., XVII (1960), 361, 362, 366; Memorial of Benedict Leonard Calvert to George I, Feb. 2, 1715, printed in J. Thomas Scharf, *History of Maryland from the Earliest Times to the Present Day*, 3 vols. (Baltimore, 1879), I, 379; Owings, *His Lordship's Patronage*, 113-114, 127.

and equally grave dangers. The colony's Catholics had been subject to a series of restrictions ever since the institution of royal government—they had lost the right to hold office, to practice law in certain courts, to worship publicly, and to educate their children in Catholic schools—but they had retained the franchise, provided they could meet the property requirements that applied to all male residents.[57] Though onerous, these restraints were far less disabling than the penal statutes that had been invoked against Catholics in England and Ireland since the seventeenth century. Indeed, from the perspective of Maryland's Protestant majority, the Catholic minority was being treated extraordinarily well and owed the governing powers a considerable debt of gratitude.[58] Yet, in spite of the fact that the Settler's situation in Maryland was, as he well knew, a massive
176 improvement over the desperate circumstances of his brother Anthony in Ireland, he was not content. Specifically, Carroll perceived in the restoration of the government of Maryland to the proprietary family—whose interests he had protected and promoted with unswerving loyalty for over a quarter of a century—an opportunity for Catholics to regain the privileges of officeholding that they had previously enjoyed under proprietary rule. Early in 1716 Carroll informed Governor Hart of his views and his intention to act upon them.[59]

For both personal and professional reasons Hart did not welcome this news. From the governor's arrival in the colony in May 1714 his encounters with Carroll had been testy. Hart clearly recognized Carroll as a rival, and he saw in the occasion of the colony's restoration to the Calverts an opportunity to underscore the considerable authority that his office possessed. Thus, on the day that the restoration was formally

[57] Browne *et al.*, eds., *Md. Archs.*, XXVI, 340-341, 431-432, 630-631. As of 1670, men possessing a 50-acre freehold or a visible estate of £40 could vote. Carr and Jordan, *Maryland's Revolution of Government*, 16.

[58] For a discussion of the penal laws in Ireland see J. C. Beckett, *The Making of Modern Ireland, 1603-1923*, 2d ed. (London, 1981), chap. 8; for the position of English Catholics during the 17th and early 18th centuries, John Bossy, *The English Catholic Community, 1570-1850* (New York, 1976), esp. chap. 7. English penal statutes, first enacted during the reign of Elizabeth I, formed the precedent for the later Irish legislation. Under the Elizabethan laws, which continued to be enforced and added to during the 17th and early 18th centuries, Catholics were prevented from voting, standing for Parliament, bearing arms, owning a horse worth more than £5, converting Protestants, and celebrating mass. The priesthood was outlawed, and attendance at Anglican services was made compulsory. The laws were extended after the Glorious Revolution and the penalties for disobedience increased, the most severe of which undermined Catholics' rights of inheritance. Although some recent scholarship suggests that English Catholics may have survived the period "far better than previously thought," the statutes "were sufficiently capable of reducing Catholics to a servile and deprived position" (Robert Blackey, "A War of Words: The Significance of the Propaganda Conflict between English Catholics and Protestants, 1715-1745," *Catholic Historical Review*, LVIII [1973], 535, n. 2, 536).

[59] Browne *et al.*, eds., *Md. Archs.*, XXXIII, 120.

proclaimed in Maryland—December 27, 1715—Hart required Carroll to surrender to him the proprietor's great seal, which, during the period of royal government, had been in the Settler's keeping as Lord Baltimore's chief agent in the colony.[60] While Hart may have enjoyed that moment, he had a totally different reaction when Carroll informed him shortly thereafter that he intended to travel to England to press the proprietor to return to Catholics the right to hold office. As Hart later recounted to the Maryland assembly, Carroll "shewed me a Representation, which was to be presented to their Lordships on behalf of the Roman Catholicks of this Province Importing that they Prayed to be Restored to what they alledged was their right of being Qualifyed for Offices in the Government, as they formerly had been." The governor's response was blunt: "I plainly told Mr Carroll that It was against the Laws of Great Britain & the Acts of 177
Assembly of this Province, & that I would Oppose it to the Utmost of my Power."[61] According to Hart—and it must be noted that this is his recollection set down two years after the event—the "Surprise & Indignation" with which he greeted Carroll's proposal persuaded that gentleman not to deliver the appeal to the proprietor, on condition that Hart keep what had passed between them confidential.[62]

Shortly after this incident, Carroll embarked for England, where he met on several occasions with proprietary officials, among them the young proprietor's guardian Lord Guilford. During these discussions, the Settler, in direct violation of his alleged agreement with Hart, urged restoring the rights to public office to Maryland Catholics.[63] Subsequent events indicate that his appeal fell on receptive ears: Carroll left England with a new commission from Lord Baltimore that, in addition to confirming him in all of his former proprietary posts, gave him substantial public power that challenged the governor's authority in two critical areas—control of the revenues for the support of government, and local patronage. A major confrontation with Hart thus became inevitable, as the Settler must have known, and the way in which he chose to unveil his new commission intensified the drama of the clash.

Reentering Maryland without fanfare, Carroll made no fuss about the

[60] During the period of royal government two great seals were used in Maryland—a crown seal for the government and the Calvert seal for all land transactions that fell within the domain of the proprietor's private establishment. With the restoration of the colony's government to the proprietor, the crown seal was discarded and the proprietor's emblem once again became Maryland's official seal.

[61] Browne *et al.*, eds., *Md. Archs.*, XXXIII, 120.

[62] *Ibid.*, 121.

[63] Accused by Hart some months later of "unfaithful Dealing on this Account," the Settler justified his behavior by maintaining he had not asked "that the Roman Catholicks might be Qualified for Imploym^{ts} but that they might not be Unqualifyed for them." Unimpressed by this fine distinction, the governor reported to the legislature that "So poor & Jesuiticall Evasion wants no Remark." Browne *et al.*, eds., *Md. Archs.*, XXXIII, 121.

fact that William Bladen, a Protestant, had assumed, along with the office of provincial attorney general, the duties of proprietary attorney general that had formerly been his. If this apparent acquiescence lulled Hart, his peace of mind was to be short-lived. On June 10, 1716, while the governor was absent from the capital, a couple of Irish servants fired two of Annapolis's "Great Guns on the Court House Hill" in honor of the Old Pretender's birthday, while other Jacobites drank openly to his health and spoke "contemptibly of the King."[64] Upon his return to Annapolis on June 15, Hart, horrified by the affront, issued a proclamation calling for the apprehension and punishment of the perpetrators of the "Traiterous Wicked Audacious & Insolent Action" and offering a reward of £20 sterling to anyone who discovered the culprits.[65] In less than a month the
178 offenders were taken into custody, tried, and convicted by a specially summoned court of oyer and terminer. The men who had fired the guns were whipped and pilloried, and two others who had toasted the pretender and denigrated the king—one of whom happened to be a kinsman of Carroll's named William Fitzredmond—were fined £100 sterling and committed to jail until they satisfied the penalty. On July 10, 1716, Charles Carroll thrust himself into the center of this agitated situation by informing the governor that "He had a Commission from the Lord Proprietary and his Guardian under the Lord Proprietary's Great Seal And that He would discharge those Fines which the Sherriff of Ann Arundel County was directed to receive."[66]

Enormously displeased by this unwelcome surprise, Hart immediately demanded to know by what authority Carroll—a professed Catholic—intended to act in a public capacity. The Settler answered by revealing the text of his new commission, which specifically continued him in his position as the proprietor's agent and receiver general, empowered him to act as escheator and naval officer, and to receive all fines and forfeitures. Moreover, as the commission stipulated, the proprietor had given Carroll the authority "to inspect into[,] Order[,] Manage & Account for all & every other Branch or Branches of our Revenue within our said Province."[67] In short, Carroll was to have control of both the proprietor's private revenues and all public monies intended for the support of government, including Hart's own salary![68]

For a man like Hart, whose pride and tenderness of ego equaled Carroll's, the situation was intolerable. Several years later, his sense of having been grossly insulted unsoothed by the passage of time, Hart charged that "I should have been by so Servile a Complyance Reduced to the Despicable Circumstance of Applying to him for my bread by Craving of him that Appointment their Lordships were pleased to nominate for my

[64] *Ibid.*, XXX, 373-374.
[65] *Ibid.*, 373.
[66] *Ibid.*, 374.
[67] *Ibid.*, 375-376.
[68] *Ibid.*, 376.

maintenance."[69] Perceiving Carroll's new powers as a calculated assault on duly constituted Protestant authority in Maryland and furious at the diminution of his own status implied in the granting of those powers, yet unable to deny the validity of the commission, Hart demanded that the Settler qualify himself for his public positions by swearing the oaths of allegiance and abjuration required by act of the assembly of all Maryland officeholders. Though apparently willing to swear allegiance, Carroll refused to take the oath of abjuration that denied all present and future Stuart claims to the English throne and affirmed the Protestant succession. Yet in spite of the fact that he had not sworn, Carroll proceeded to receive the fines and to order the release of the Annapolis prisoners.[70]

Scarcely able to contain his rage at this audacity, Hart on July 17 placed 179
the entire matter before the upper house of the assembly, informing that body that he considered the granting of this kind of authority "to any other Person but himself, especially to a Papist," to be "such a lessening of his Power & Dishonour to his Character that He has desired to be recalled unless He can be Restored to the full Authority he held under the Crown."[71] Accusing Carroll of having "deceived the Lord Proprietary in his tender age & also his Guardian" in order to obtain his expanded appointment, Hart reported that Carroll, "by virtue of his sd commission," had already required of him an accounting of the monies appropriated for the colony's defense, a request to which "His Excellency" had retorted that "He would as soon give him up his Hearts Blood."[72]

Hart thus launched a two-pronged counterattack. First, he sought to discredit his opponent's character by asking if the upper house did not agree with him that Carroll had "imposed upon the Lord Proprietary and his Guardian in obtaining such a commission."[73] Of the eight gentlemen present, only one—Philemon Lloyd—dissented from the governor's interpretation. It was Hart's second thrust, however, that held the potential for bringing the Settler down: was Carroll, asked the governor, capable of holding public office in Maryland without swearing the oath of abjuration? To this question the members of the upper house responded unanimously: having refused to swear one of the oaths "Enjoined by the Laws of Great Brittain and this Province," Mr. Carroll "is absolutely incapable of holding or Executing the af^{d} Commission as to any the powers therein Which do or may Concern the publick Affairs or Interest of this Province."[74]

In developing his strategy Carroll had made two critical miscalculations. First, he had failed to take into account the sustained and vigorous opposition Hart was prepared to mount against him—an opposition fueled

[69] *Ibid.*, XXXIII, 481.
[70] *Ibid.*, XXX, 376, 517.
[71] *Ibid.*, 377.
[72] *Ibid.*, 379.
[73] *Ibid.*, 378.
[74] *Ibid.*, 379.

by the governor's deep personal animosity. Second, the Settler seems not to have suspected that the proprietary support upon which the final success of his plan depended was really quite shallow. Once Hart, with the assembly's backing, focused the issue on Carroll's refusal to swear all of the oaths required of public officeholders, the challenger's downfall became inevitable, because the governor had struck at the Achilles heel of the newly Protestant proprietorship.[75] There was little chance that Lord Guilford and his minions, having held the reins of Maryland's government for scarcely a year, would risk what they had gained in behalf of a stubborn Irish Catholic Jacobite, no matter how much his loyal and diligent service had benefitted the proprietary family in the past.

Unable or unwilling to recognize these realities, Carroll continued to
180 challenge and provoke the governor. Early in August 1716, for example, he instructed Hart to send him the revenues due the proprietor from one of the major tonnage assessments, with the exception of £1,000, which he gave the governor leave to deduct "for your Excellency's Sallary." Next he advised Hart to use caution "in assenting to some Laws which I understand are prepared And whereby his Lordships Interest will evidently suffer detriment."[76] Outraged by what he regarded as thoroughly insolent behavior, the governor reported Carroll's requests to the assembly, declaring that he did not know what the gentleman meant by the word salary—that "being a Terme too mean and base to accept from a Subject by a person who has had the honour to serve the Crown in so many Imployments"—and asserting that as "protestant Governour" he would "disdain . . . to goe to a Virulent Papist to know when my family may have leave to Eat."[77] After considering Hart's complaints, the assembly concluded that Mr. Carroll had indeed "used a very undecent freedome with his Exn^{cy} . . . a ffreedome wee have never heared used before by any Subject to a Govr," and proceeded to enact a bill entitled "An Act for the better Security of the Peace and Safety of his Lordship's Government, and the Protestant Interest within this Province," which was designed to put Catholics firmly in their place.[78] By the terms of this law, all would-be officeholders had to qualify themselves by swearing the oaths of allegiance, abhorrence, and abjuration and publicly denying the doctrine of transubstantiation. Anyone who executed an office without so doing would be liable to a fine of £250 sterling and forfeiture of his office. Officeholders who violated their public trust by subsequently attending mass or any other "Popish Assembly, Conventicle or Meeting," or receiving the sacrament from a priest, would suffer the same penalties.[79]

With the assembly firmly behind him, Hart sat back to await a response from the proprietor to whom he had sent a detailed account of the

[75] Prov. Ct. Judgmts., VD#2, 139, Md. State Archs.

[76] Browne *et al.*, eds., *Md. Archs.*, XXX, 466.

[77] *Ibid.*, 599.

[78] *Ibid.*, 602.

[79] *Ibid.*, 617.

situation. He was not disappointed, for on February 20, 1717, notwithstanding nearly twenty-nine years of loyal service, Charles Carroll was cast aside. The proprietor revoked his commission and bestowed his office on a Protestant Calvert relative. There can be no doubt that Governor Hart took special pleasure in reading his lordship's letter to the assembly when it convened on April 22:

> As we Cannot Enough commend the Loyalty & Zeal you have shewn
> for his Majesty & the Succession in the Illustrious house of Hannover
> so none of those Laws to which we have Assented met with a more
> ready Confirmacōn of them than that, which makes it penall for men
> to Act in Imployments without takeing the Oaths to our Dread 181
> Sovereign King George Whereby Protestants & Papists may Clearly
> Perceive that your Lord & Propry is not as has been Maliciously
> suggested by some A Papist in Masquerade but a true Protestant of
> the Church of England in which faith he is Resolved to live & Die.[80]

To Hart's chagrin, however, his vanquished opponent had no intention of being a graceful loser. The Settler manifestly did not share the governor's view that, having been defeated, "the Gentlemen of the Romish Comunion" should "prudently consider their own Interest & Content themselves with the Lenity of the Governmts they live under who admitts them in this Province to an Equal share of Priviledges with the rest of their fellow Subjects the bearing of Offices alone Excepted."[81] Perhaps Carroll, having had his "Interest" so rudely thwarted in a way that left him bereft of any official recourse, saw no reason to count his blessings and behave in a prudent manner. Perhaps his disappointment was too bitter for a man of his pride to stomach without some form of retaliation. Perhaps his sense of outrage at what he perceived to be the injustice of his treatment was too great to be checked by reason. Whatever the motive, or combination of motives, the Settler reacted to his defeat by embarking on a course of action that ultimately deprived Maryland Catholics of the last of their civil "Priviledges"—the franchise—for the next half century.

The only record of Carroll's activities during 1717 and early 1718 is contained in the report Hart presented to the legislature on April 23, 1718. According to the governor, Maryland's Roman Catholics, under Carroll's direction, had mounted a concerted campaign "to Calumniate my Conduct, and by heaping of Indignities upon me, used their Utmost Efforts, thereby to Remove me from this Station. . . . I am informed," Hart told the assembly, "that a very large sume of money, was Subscribed for, by the Leading men of the Romish Community and some of them went as Emissaries to London And were very Active there against me, and Exclaimed in bitter Terms of my prosecuteing the Papists in this Province

[80] *Ibid.*, XXXIII, 4.
[81] *Ibid.*, 7.

and how Cruel a manner they were Treated in."[82] Determined to put the Settler and the Catholic faction down hard, the governor and his supporters secured two laws from the 1718 assembly. The first, "An Act repealing an act to prevent the growth of Popery," rescinded a range of provisions passed in 1704 that protected Catholics from the harsher restrictions on religious observance contained in the English penal laws. The second, adopted on April 29, 1718, deprived Catholics of the right to vote. In a memorial to the proprietor praying his assent to the legislation, the assembly justified the latter act on the ground that Carroll and his associates were currently conducting an organized effort to elect a representative to the lower house who would be sympathetic to their views.[83] The proprietor assented, and the law remained in effect until the
182 end of proprietary government in 1776.

The final scene in the political reduction of Maryland's Catholics occurred in April 1720. Hart, who continued to be annoyed by their repeated complaints to the proprietor of unremitting persecution under his administration, challenged a dozen of the faction's most prominent leaders to justify their accusation in public, before the assembly. He was particularly interested in hearing them defend their claim that Maryland's charter guaranteed to Catholics privileges equal to those of all other inhabitants. In Hart's view, "the Papists" did not "derive any Privileges here beyond what the Connivance of the Government may indulge them in."[84] The spokesmen summoned included Charles Carroll, his nephew James Carroll, his brothers-in-law Henry Darnall, Jr., and William Digges, Benjamin Hall, Clement Hill, Henry Darnall III, William Fitzredmond, Henry Wharton, Charles Digges, Maj. Nicholas Sewall, Richard Bennett, and Father Peter Atwood, a Jesuit priest. All were duly served with sheriff's warrants ordering them to appear before the assembly by April 16, 1720, but none of them did so, even though the majority were known to be in Annapolis. Their failure to present themselves completed Hart's victory. The assembly proceedings for April 19 record his triumph: "His Excellency and this House Observe on the foregoing proceedings That Although the most Eminent of the Papists were in Town at the time appointed Them to make good their pretentions, yet they have not thought fitt to appear then or at any time Since to offer any thing in Vindication of their pretended Rights, and therefore take this their Demeanour as a Tacit Acknowledgement that their Pretentions are Groundless and their Exclamations most unreasonable."[85]

The battle was over. In May 1720 Hart, having been replaced as governor, sailed for England. On July 1, 1720, Charles Carroll died, leaving his coreligionists and his descendants an ironic and compelling

[82] *Ibid.*, XXX, 121.
[83] *Ibid.*, XXXIII, 279.
[84] *Ibid.*, 484.
[85] *Ibid.*, 533.

legacy. To the former Carroll left the political disabilities that would bind Maryland Catholics until the coming of the American Revolution. To his heirs he bequeathed the most substantial estate ever created in Maryland to that time, a fierce tribal loyalty, and a tenacious memory. The Settler had traveled a long way from the foothills of his native Slieve Bloom Mountains to his grand house in Annapolis. But his personality and perception of the world bore the indelible imprint of the ruthless struggle over land and culture waged between his Gaelic forebears and the English and Irish Protestants intent on displacing them. Charles Carroll was raised in the crucible of that conflict, and his career in Maryland was marked—and ultimately marred—by his inflexible loyalty to that heritage.

The same defiant pride of lineage, stubborn clinging to his traditions, 183
and determination to work his will on the world that shaped Carroll's public behavior was equally evident in the more personal aspects of his life. For example, the sole possession he is known to have brought into Maryland with him in 1688 was, as described by his son Charles Carroll of Annapolis, "a little Irish Manuscript Book" containing the "Genealogies of the O'Carrolls," a document "which he strictly charged his Wife to deliver to me his son Charles."[86] Similarly, the Settler expressed the motivating continuity between his Irish memory and his Maryland ambitions in the names he bestowed on four major tracts of land he acquired in the colony. To his second sizable acquisition—1,000 acres in Baltimore County that he patented in January 1695/6—he gave the name Ely O'Carroll. A year later he patented 900 more acres in the same county, designating the parcel Litterluna after his family's ancestral parish, and in 1711 he named another 5,000 Baltimore County acres Clynmalira, recalling the territory of the O'Dempseys that lay northeast of ancient Ely O'Carroll. Most telling of all, Carroll named his largest single holding of 7,000 acres—the property destined to become his family's principal Maryland seat—Doohoregan, after a magnificent valley in the Slieve Bloom Mountains from which his family had been expelled.[87]

But the weightiest of Carroll's legacies was the mantle of responsibility he transferred to his second son, Charles, the young man who, upon the unexpected death of his older brother Henry in April 1719, became his family's principal link to the future. In the only personal letter of his that has been found, Carroll wrote to his two remaining sons, Charles, seventeen, and Daniel, ten—both of whom were abroad in school—about the duties now incumbent upon them as a result of their brother's grievous demise. Carroll's sorrow reinforced the stern message he directed to the older boy. As heir apparent, Charles was to bend firmly to the task of

[86] Notes by Charles Carroll of Annapolis included in Carroll-O'Carroll Genealogies, Md. Hist. Soc.

[87] Local historian Patrick Heaney of Cadamstowne, Litterluna Parish, County Offaly, gives the meaning of "Doohoregan" as "black fields of Regan." The color refers to the dark tone given the landscape by peat, which appeared to me on a recent visit to cover a good portion of the valley's level ground.

becoming his father's successor, remembering always who he was, from whence he came, and the burden of history he carried. Thus Carroll instructed his son to pray for his dead brother, visit his mother when she came to Europe, and "Vigorously prepare for the defense of your Universall Philosophy," dedicating the performance to him, as Henry had done. Significantly, the most important and enduring command was the one with which the Settler ended his letter: "I would," he ordered, "have you Stile your Self in your Thesis Marylando-Hibernus."[88]

[88] Charles Carroll the Settler to Sons Charles and Daniel, July 7, 1719, Carroll-McTavish Papers, Md. Hist. Soc.

ANTI-CATHOLICISM AS A POLITICAL TOOL IN MID-EIGHTEENTH-CENTURY MARYLAND

BY

TIMOTHY W. BOSWORTH*

I

Recent scholars have isolated a recurring belief in conspiracy throughout American history. This view of the world has been labeled differently depending upon the historian: David Brion Davis analyzed "themes of counter-subversion" during the 1830's and 1840's: Richard Hofstadter discovered a "paranoid style" in American political history; and John Higham has investigated a tradition of American nativism.[1] According to this conspiratorial outlook which is most commonly called nativism, "demonic forces" are almost on the verge of overturning civilization and an all-out crusade is necessary to smash them. What disturbs the nativist most about the conspirator is the secrecy which shields the inner workings of his organizations from public view; if loyal Americans are forbidden to see what the subversive is doing, he must be hiding something, and what he is hiding must be un-American. The enemy is considered particularly dangerous because no physical characteristics distinguish him from a member of true society.[2]

* Mr. Bosworth is a doctoral candidate in history at the University of Wisconsin, Madison. He wishes to thank Professors David S. Lovejoy and David C. Skaggs for their help in preparing this article.

[1] David Brion Davis, "Some Themes of Counter-Subversion: An Analysis of Anti-Masonic, Anti-Catholic, and Anti-Mormon Literature," *Mississippi Valley Historical Review*, XLVII (September, 1960), 205-224; Richard Hofstadter, *The Paranoid Style in American Politics and Other Essays* (New York, 1966); John Higham, "Another Look at Nativism," *Catholic Historical Review*, XLIV (July, 1958), 147-158. Nativism has been defined as "intense opposition to an internal minority on the grounds of its foreign (i.e. un-American) connections." John Higham, *Strangers in the Land*, 2d ed. (New York, 1970), p. 4.

[2] Davis, *op. cit.*, pp. 211-213.

The investigations of John Higham bolster Hofstadter's point that a "paranoid style" has been a constantly reappearing phenomenon in American history. Higham stated that "the kinds of accusations which nativists leveled against foreign elements remained relatively constant. Antiradical and anti-Catholic complaints in the twentieth century sounded much like those bruited in the eighteenth." Only the emotional intensity with which nativists have voiced their prejudices has changed, Higham found.[3]

The evidence indicates that a "paranoid style" was not uncommon in eighteenth-century Maryland. Protestants' references to Catholics
186 in provincial Maryland appeared quite similar to views expressed about "subversive" minority groups throughout American history.

Protestant legislators accused Catholics of eroding the foundations of social stability: the family, the church, the schools, and the government as early as the 1750's. Catholics were said to be but one potent arm of a vast international conspiracy taking direct orders from the pope and aid from the king of France. If these papists were not stopped, legislators cried, his Majesty's Protestant government would be overthrown; the precious rights and liberties of the British Empire cast down, and citizens of Maryland would be subjected to the slavery of Catholic despotism. To smash the plot and eradicate the Catholic danger, the lower house formulated a legislative program designed to deport the Jesuits and confiscate their lands. Protestant politicians, in attacking Catholics in this manner, appeared to be playing upon the fears and anxieties of their constituents to gain support in their "quest for power" over the proprietor and his Catholic friends. These lower house proposals met with stiff opposition from the upper house, however, and few of the lower house's intended measures ever became law.[4]

Protestant rhetoric was especially sharp between 1753 and 1758. In denouncing Catholics, Protestant Marylanders consistently referred to themselves as Englishmen, repeatedly voiced their love of England's rights and liberties which were being threatened, and continually

[3] Higham, "Another Look at Nativism," pp. 150-151. "If nativism was an ideological disease, perhaps we might best diagnose it by observing when it raged and when it slackened," *ibid.*, p. 150.

[4] For a detailed discussion of politics in Maryland during the eighteenth century see Charles A. Barker, *The Background of the Revolution in Maryland* (New Haven, 1940).

affirmed their loyalty to England and the British Empire. The persistent intensity of their outcries probably betrayed fundamental insecurities and tensions within the society. Anti-Catholicism did not exist in a vacuum, however; a number of factors interacted with it to create an extremely volatile mixture.

II

Readers of the *Maryland Gazette* during the middle eighteenth century might well have been insecure for a number of reasons. War seemed to be nearing home as France's military activity in the Ohio country appeared threateningly close. A menacing string of forts in the northwest by 1753 surrounded Maryland with "an immense Country in the possession of those restless and professed enemies to all Liberty the FRENCH."[5]

Maryland's tobacco prices were depressed too. By the eighteenth century, tobacco had penetrated to every level and area of life in Maryland. As Governor Benedict Leonard Calvert had remarked, "tobacco, as our staple, is our all."[6] Since the seventeenth century, Maryland's officials had been trying various remedies, but even by the 1750's Maryland residents were still complaining about the low price of their "trashy tobacco."[7]

Marylanders were also concerned about the economic drain of their proprietary government. Revenue syphoned off the economy and not returned to it in any way amounted to between fifteen and eighteen per cent of the province's purchasing power.[8] Residents of Charles

[5] Reply of Timothy Archtype to Thomas Type, *Maryland Gazette* (Annapolis), November 25, 1746. For an account of the French in the Ohio country see Howard H. Peckham, *The Colonial Wars, 1689-1762* (Chicago, 1964), pp. 120-128.

[6] Report of Governor Benedict Leonard Calvert in Barker, *op. cit.*, p. 71.

[7] Introduction to *Archives of Maryland*, L (1933), xiv-xx (hereafter cited as *Md. Arch.*); Avery O. Craven, *Soil Exhaustion as a Factor in the Agricultural History of Virginia and Maryland, 1606-1808* (Urbana, Illinois, 1926), p. 65. Tobacco quickly depleted the soil, and because it was so exclusively planted, fertilizers which would have restored the soil were not produced. By 1700 tobacco production per person had been reduced by one-half. *Ibid.*, p. 65. For an insightful account of the attempts to reform tobacco see Barker, *op. cit.*, pp. 70-99.

[8] These revenues fell into four kinds: quitrents, returns from land offices,

County objected that "the Fines, and Forfeitures arising by the Acts of this Province, instead of being applied for the support of the government, as by the said Acts intended, are pocketed by the proprietor."[9]

The potential uprising of such a large number of Negro slaves in Maryland had long been a source of worry. In 1740 Governor Samuel Ogle summarized the fears of many Marylanders when he commented upon the "Danger we must of Course be exposed to, from so large a Body of Slaves, [which] will always be very great, but particularly so in time of War."[10]

188 A final source of anxiety might well have been an intrenched Catholic elite; Maryland citizens complained about menacing Catholics on numerous occasions during the seventeenth and eighteenth centuries. One outburst was "Complaint from Heaven and a Huy and Crye out of Virginia and Maryland." This document, written in 1676, attacked the proprietor for his alleged participation in a Catholic plot to overthrow the Empire. In 1689, too, according to the author of "Mariland's Grievances Wiy The Have Taken Op Arms," Catholics, "ffrench & Northerne Indians" were scheming to overcome Protestants in Maryland. The writer of the tract indicted the proprietor for allowing "Priests and Jessuits [to live] in great wealth & splendor with the fauvorable asspect of the govermt . . . whilst the protestants and clergy [have been] wantinge maintenance & liveinge in poverty vnder the Contemptable lookes of the government." The latter document expressed the rationale of Coode's Rebellion which, precipitated by the Glorious Revolution of 1688 in England, overthrew the Catholic proprietor and brought royal government to Maryland.[11]

---

manor rents, and fines. For a detailed discussion of these see *ibid.*, pp. 140-153. Barker's calculations do not take into account the value of goods produced and consumed within the province, but they do suggest a bleak picture. Because much of the tax was levied in tobacco, the loss was more dearly felt. *Ibid.*, pp. 152-153.

[9] Petition of freemen of Charles County, Maryland, May 22, 1756, *Md. Arch.*, XXXI (1911), 122-123.

[10] Governor Ogle's opening address to the Assembly, April 23, 1740, *ibid.*, XL (1921), 425.

[11] *Ibid.*, V, 134-135; Beverly McAnear (ed.), "Maryland's Grievances Wiy The Have Taken Op Arms," *Journal of Southern History*, VIII (August, 1942), 401-404. The causes of the revolution have been examined in depth by Michael G. Kammen, "The Causes of the Maryland Revolution of 1689," *Mary-*

After 1689, the new Protestant regime established the Anglican Church and enacted a string of anti-Catholic laws; Catholics were prohibited from voting, holding office, and hearing Mass.[12] Catholicism was not outlawed, however, and evidence indicates that Catholics were usually left to themselves in matters of private religious worship.[13]

Throughout the eighteenth century, these anxieties were evidently heightened by anti-Catholic sentiment received from England. Anti-Catholicism was common in England,[14] spurred by the abortive rebellions of 1715 and 1745. According to an association signed by 6,735 people in Cornwall, England, "the Sone of a popish and abjur'd Pretender, having actually set up his standard, audaciously carries on an horrid and unnatural Rebellion, in conunction with wicked ill-designing and traiterous Persons, and supported by France, Spain, and Rome, the implacable Enemies to our Religion and Country, daringly avows his Intentions to dethrone our most gracious and only lawful Sovereign King George, subvert our Religion and Liberties."[15] These sentiments reached Maryland via the *Maryland Gazette*. Comments voiced later by delegates and the Anglican clergy during the 1750's indicate that at least some of the governing officials of Maryland took English anti-Catholicism seriously.

Thus, throughout the seventeenth and eighteenth centuries, Catholics found themselves subjugated to much abuse which blazed into bitter denunciation during certain critical periods. Many of the anti-Catholic outcries were merely reiterations of condemnation heard often during the seventeenth century. Although Catholics may have managed to live with relatively little disturbance despite official vilification in daily life, events of the 1740's and 1750's made anonymity for Catholics impossible.

---

land Historical Magazine, LV (December, 1960), 293-334, and Richard A. Gleissner, "Religious Causes of the Glorious Revolution in Maryland," *ibid.*, LXIV (Winter, 1969), 327-341.

[12] Francis X. Curran, *Catholics in Colonial Law* (Chicago, 1963), pp. 19-96, summarizes the laws against Catholics in Maryland between 1633 and 1718.

[13] John Tracy Ellis, *Catholics in Colonial America* (Baltimore, 1969), pp. 346-348; Barker, *op. cit.*, pp. 43-44; Albert Werline, *Problems of Church and State in Maryland During the Seventeenth and Eighteenth Centuries* (South Lancaster, Massachusetts, 1948), p. 56.

[14] Werline, *op. cit.*, p. 56.

[15] *Maryland Gazette* (Annapolis), January 15, 1746.

III

During the 1740's a series of events occurred which, in all likelihood, laid the kindling for the later anti-Catholic outburst. In 1740 Governor Ogle informed the Assembly of a "most wicked and dangerous [slave] Conspiracy to destroy his Majesty's Subjects within this Province and to possess themselves of the whole Country."[16] The governor also warned the Assembly that the French nearby were eager to invade Maryland should another rebellion cripple the colony. The issue soon became clouded with anti-Catholicism when the upper house blamed Roman Catholics for stirring the slaves to revolt. "We
190 have not the least doubt of the Truth of such cruel Designs having been in Agitation amongst the Negroes." To the upper house, such collusion implied grave danger for the safety of the province. French, Negroes, and Catholics were soon mentioned in the same phrase. Imploring the lower house to pass revenue bills, the upper house commented upon the colony's "War with Spain, the danger of being attacked by some French Colonies, the Insurrection of negroes and evil Dispositions of Papists."[17] The lower house in its usual cantankerous mood assured the upper house that all necessary means to protect the colony would be taken, but that the "punishment they Received we apprehend will Deter others from the like practice."[18] The matter might have dropped at this point had not two other events, occurring during the 1740's, added credibility to the upper house's anti-Catholic accusations.

The first of these was the rebellion in England of the pretender, whose grandfather had been ousted from the throne in 1688. News of this traumatic event reached Maryland in December, 1745. Images of bloodthirsty Catholics leaped from the pages of the *Maryland Gazette*. The Archbishop of York warned of the evil consequences which would follow should "Popery and Arbitrary Power come in upon us," and the Bishop of London instructed Maryland clergymen to "raise in your People a just abhorrence of Popery."[19] In the

[16] December 23, 1739, *Md. Arch.*, XXVIII (1908), 188.

[17] Governor Samuel Ogle's opening address to the Assembly, April 23, 1740, *ibid.*, XL (1921), 425, 457, 486.

[18] *Ibid.*, p. 523. The terms lower house and house of delegates will be used interchangeably.

[19] *Maryland Gazette* (Annapolis), January 21, 1746.

colony, Thomas Cradock, apparently following the bishop's orders, warned his congregation of the "heavy Yoak of Slavery and Bondage; which we must have submitted to had the Pretender and his Accomplices triumphed over us."[20] Governor Thomas Bladen instructed his county sheriffs to be wary for "Jesuits and other Popish Priests" who were trying to "pervert several of his Majesty's Protestant Subjects from their Religion and to alienate their Affections from his Majesty's Royal Person and Government," and to arraign any Catholic offenders found. Thus, by July, 1746, Marylanders were searching for Catholic subversives in their midst due to the "unnatural Rebellion broke out in Scotland."[21]

The second event, much closer to home, occurred in December, 1747, when an anonymous author, known only as "Z.L.," wailed in an open letter: "Oh! Conscience, Conscience at Length thou hast . . . forced me to throw down my Cursed Commission with these few lines of my too late Repentence and Confession of my Crimes." What Z.L. revealed was a covert Catholic conspiracy to re-establish the authority of the Catholic Church. Conspirators were carefully bound to secrecy by priests during Mass, and were enlisting the support of debtors. Details of the plot were tantalizingly omitted, but the writer supplied enough to indicate that the plot was secret, carefully conceived, and soon to be hatched.[22] The lower house was at least outwardly convinced, for in March, 1748, the delegates instructed tobacco inspectors to cease practices which cheated the people out of their money and drove them into debt."[23]

The lid had been raised. The contents of the box were numerous and varied, but each item convinced the beholders that something sinister was about to happen.

[20] Thomas Cradock, *Two Sermons* . . . (Annapolis, 1747), p. 10.

[21] Governor Thomas Bladen's Proclamation, July 13, 1746, *Md. Arch.*, XXXVIII (1908), 363.

[22] Z.L. to Governor Samuel Ogle, Letter of R.T.M., December 11, 1747, *ibid.*, XLVI (1929), 13-16.

[23] Lower house's proclamation, March 12, 1748, *ibid.*, p. 16. Precisely what was being done to cheat debtors is not clear. Nor is the document a clear indication that the threat was real. The importance of the document is that the threat was believed, or at least used.

IV

During the 1750's, Protestants in Maryland began an intensive witchhunt for Catholics in the province. According to Protestant rhetoric, Catholics were guilty of attacking society on four levels: the schools, the church, the family, and the government.

As Bernard Bailyn has noted, in early America schools were viewed as an important mainstay of society. Maryland apparently was no exception; the province's Protestants regarded their schools as essential in inculcating Anglican values in their children. According to provincial laws, children who were being raised in the Catholic faith
192 might be taken away from the parents and placed with Protestant families who would ensure that the children were brought up properly.[24]

In reaction to the anti-Catholicism which pervaded the province's schools, Maryland Catholics took two courses of action. First, they established a number of Catholic schools throughout the colony and attempted to keep them running as often as possible. Secondly, it became common for many of the richer Catholic families to send their children abroad for their education. This practice provoked bitter outcries from provincial Protestants.[25]

St. Omer's College in Flanders bore the brunt of the derision, and the lower house produced deposition after deposition to document the charge that various Catholic citizens were having their children educated in "their Superstitions and dangerous Principles."[26] Even more disturbing to Protestants was the fact that Catholics were trying to persuade Protestant families to have their offspring educated at St. Omer's.[27]

These accusations gained force from an underlying suspicion that

[24] Bernard Bailyn, *Education in the Forming of American Society: Needs and Opportunities for Study* (Chapel Hill, North Carolina, 1960); Ellen Hart Smith, *Charles Carroll of Carrollton* (Cambridge, Massachusetts, 1942), p. 29.

[25] *Ibid.*, pp. 29-30.

[26] Report of the Committee on Grievances, June 17, 1752, *Md. Arch.*, L (1933), 52. St. Omer's was considered to be French. The Committee of Grievances had been instituted by the lower house to investigate grievances voiced by the people. It is not clear, though, to what extent the committee's reports echoed the grievances of the people or to what extent the reports merely represented political rhetoric.

[27] Report of the Committee on Grievances, October 29, 1753, *ibid.*, pp. 199-200

the instructors at the French seminary were enlisting Catholic students in an international crusade to take over Protestant government in England and in North America. Probably King Louis's "Thanks to English Catholics" vividly reflected this prognosis. "'You have clearly demonstrated, to ME at least," the French monarch allegedly said, "that to promote my INTEREST, and aggrandize my FAMILY, you are ready to sacrifice your OWN COUNTRY, and to entail perpetual SLAVERY upon it." Louis also congratulated Catholics in England and North America on their "SAGACITY and CUNNING, . . . CRAFTINESS and ART." Finally, the king advised that although Catholic intrigues had been frustrated by the failure of the pretender's rebellions in Scotland, Catholic intentions must be achieved in "IMPERCEPTIBLE Ways," by creating jealousies, disaffection, and disloyalty. He instructed the Catholics to "MAKE A PROPERTY of the UNDERSTANDING of the People, as we MONARCHS make a Property of our SUBJECTS."[28]

Upon returning to the province, Catholics were supposedly determined to complete the task set before them in France. The Committee of Grievances attempted to prove that Catholic priests were in the back country conspiring to aid the French.[29] Overtly, Catholics were trying to keep Marylanders from enlisting in the militia. Singing disloyal songs and drinking the pretender's health, the committee claimed, papists along the Maryland frontier had seized a Virginia recruiting sergeant at the throat and forced him to release the Maryland recruits he had enlisted.[30]

Protestants also railed against the schools Catholics were keeping in Maryland. "Contrary to statutes, a Papist keeps a School for Education of Youth, within six, or seven Miles of Annapolis, the Seat of Government," complained the Committee on Grievances. This practice was particularly dangerous because the Catholic school masters were allegedly intending to expose the "great Danger of corrupt-

[28] *Maryland Gazette* (Annapolis), February 10, 1747. This excerpt from a British newspaper ostensibly proves the truth of the Protestant's charges. It is undoubtedly a fraud. It might even have been submitted as a satire upon current anti-Catholic attitudes in England.

[29] Report of the Committee on Grievances, June 17, 1752, *Md. Arch.*, L (1933), 52. See also *Maryland Gazette* (Annapolis), October 17, 1754.

[30] Report of the Committee on Grievances, May 21, 1754, *Md. Arch.*, L (1933), 487-488.

ing their Principles" to Protestant children.[31]

Catholics allegedly were attacking two other important institutions, the family and the church, major socializing agencies for Protestant children. The family implanted and reinforced socially acceptable attitudes and patterns of behavior in the child, thereby strengthening society's authority. Any attempt to interfere with a normal Anglican upbringing met with shrill denunciations.[32]

One of the Catholics' most deceitful practices, supposedly, was their attempts to interfere with Protestant family life. Protestants complained that priests were refusing to intermarry Catholics and Protes-
194 tants unless the Protestant spouse would either convert, which was preferable, or at least promise to raise any offspring "in the Romish Faith."[33] "Papists" even tried to undermine the family by destroying his household; "my Negroes are all perverted and turn'd Roman Catholic, unknown to [me]," wrote Thomas Reader. The old charge of Catholics stirring up slave rebellion was resurrected, and Catholics were again accused of having raised money to aid the pretender's abortive revolts.[34] Catholics, by attacking the stability of the family and household, appeared to be trying to attract children to their cause.

The church, too, served a distinct social role in early America:

[31] Report of the Committee on Grievances, June 17, 1752, *Md. Arch.*, L (1933), 51-52. According to Thomas Reader, he had been forced to send his children out of the colony for their education, "there being none but Romish Schoolmasters near him." Deposition of Thomas Reader, October 29, 1753, *ibid.*, p. 203. For other complaints about Popish schoolmasters see depositions of Archibald Standiford, Thomas Chase, Samuel Webb, April 28, 1757, *ibid.*, LV, 79-80; lower house to Governor Sharpe, May 2, 1757, *ibid.*, pp. 86-87; Petition of Freemen of Charles County, April 3, 1756, *ibid.*, XXXI (1941), 122-123; Petition of Freemen of [?] County, April 3, 1756, *ibid.*, p. 125; Address of the lower house to Governor Sharpe, May 2, 1757, *ibid.*, pp. 208-209; Report of the Committee on Grievances, April 28, 1757, *ibid.*, p. 209.

[32] Bailyn, *op. cit.*, p. 16.

[33] Numerous depositions were submitted to prove this charge. See "Report of the Parochial Clergy," October 29, 1753, *Md. Arch.*, L (1933), 199; Depositions of Samuel Clagett, Francis Waring, Thomas Reader, *ibid.*, pp. 200-204.

[34] Deposition of Thomas Reader, October 29, 1753, *Md. Arch.*, L (1933), 203. See also Lord Proprietary *vs.* John Thomas, William Fothergill, Bowlen, and Samuel Harrison, June 17, 1753, *ibid.*, pp. 56-58; lower house to Governor Sharpe, April 8, 1756, *ibid.*, LII (1935), 357.

> It furthered the introduction of the child into society by instructing him in the system of thought and imagery which underlay the culture's values and aim. It provided the highest sanctions for the accepted forms of behavior, and brought the child into close relationship with the intangible loyalties, the ethos and higher principles, of the society in which he lived.[35]

Again, Maryland apparently was no exception: Protestants sensed the importance of this social mechanism. Public preaching by Catholics was strictly proscribed, and priests were forbidden to hold public Mass. Nevertheless, Protestants complained of the evil intentions of Catholic priests. "Notorious and unreserved" preaching enabled Jesuits to spread their seditious doctrines, Protestants claimed. The priests were not content simply with preaching in the existing Catholic houses; the Catholics were trying to build new chapels where public activity would give the priests wider exposure.[36]

The ultimate objective of the "papist" conspiracy, supposedly, was the colony's government. Catholics aimed to subvert it at both its provincial and local levels. Catholics' plans were being facilitated by malignant officeholders who were only too eager to help the Jesuits betray the colony to the French. Particularly obnoxious in this respect were Charles Carroll of Annapolis and the Darnall brothers.[37]

Carroll, reputed to be a "powerful papist," was one of the wealthiest citizens of Maryland. He earned the dubious distinction of violating the rights of loyal Protestant Maryland citizens when by "treating, writing, and other artful Means" he tried to influence the elections of Anne Arundel, Prince George's, and Frederick Counties in favor of Catholics.[38]

Henry Darnall, attorney general of the province, had just recently converted from Catholicism in order to receive appointment to office, but the house of delegates was convinced that he was still Catholic

[35] Bailyn, *op. cit.*, p. 18.

[36] *Maryland Gazette* (Annapolis), October 17, 1754.

[37] Report of the Committee on Grievances, June 17, 1752, *Md. Arch.*, L (1933), 52-53; *Maryland Gazette* (Annapolis), October 17, 1754. In addition, the delegates were incensed because the governor had pardoned a number of supposed Roman Catholic prisoners. See also the address of Governor Sharpe to the lower house, July 8, 1755, *Md. Arch.*, LII (1935), 189-191; Governor Sharpe's address, April 24, 1756, *ibid.*, pp. 382-383.

[38] Report of the Committee on Grievances, June 17, 1752, *ibid.*, L (1933), 54.

in sentiment. After all, he still educated his children "in a Foreign Popish Seminary" indicating that he still believed in the "pernicious Principles of the Church of Rome." Therefore, he was not believed qualified to hold office.

John Darnall also continued to educate his children in Catholicism. Clerk of Frederick County and holder of several other provincial offices, he was suspected of helping Catholics there in aiding the French. The governor's assurances that the Darnalls were loyal and acceptable only convinced the delegates that the governor was not out for the county's best interests.[39]

196 Because of the way in which Maryland citizens viewed the French, the Catholic attempts to aid them appeared especially fearsome. The French were seen as Catholic despots out to enslave Maryland Protestants in their religion as well as in their government. According to one piece printed in the *Maryland Gazette*, "POPERY is a great Friend of ARBITRARY GOVERNMENT" and an "IMPIOUS, an ABSURD, a PERSECUTING, BLOOD-SHEDDING. Religion . . . Chiefly Calculated to support . . . tyrannical Power . . . opposite to true Christianity." The article described the French as "daring, insolent Enemies, of our Religion, our Government, of all that is dear and valuable to us as Protestants, as Men, as Free born BRITONS." The colonists saw French Catholicism as part of an over-all French scheme of aiming at "UNIVERSAL EMPIRE, or in other words, UNIVERSAL SLAVERY."[40] Political and religious slavery necessarily implied one another and were inevitable results should the French overcome Maryland.

Yet, the French did not escape so easily. They were accused of crimes of unspeakable cruelty and barbarity, even to their own countrymen. In France during the 1680's, one writer pointed out that "men and women were hung upon beams or Hooks in their Chimneys, by their Hair and Feet, and smoked with Whisps of wet Hay, 'til they were almost suffocated. . . . Others were thrown into Fires kindled on Purpose. . . . They stripp'd Men and Women nacked. and in that condition tied them together. Some were stuck with

[39] Lower house to Governor Sharpe, July 3, 1755, *ibid.*, p. 159; lower house to Governor Sharpe, April 8, 1756, *ibid.*, pp. 359-360; Horatio Sharpe to Calvert, July 9, 1775, *ibid.*, VII (1888), 240.

[40] *Maryland Gazette* (Annapolis), October 10, 1754; *ibid.*, January 14, 1746.

Pins from Head to Foot, cut with Pen knives, or taken by the nose with red hot Tongs, and in that Manner led about. . . . In some Places they would bind the Husband or Father Hand and Foot, and ravish the Wife or Daughter before their Faces."[41] If this is what happened to French Huguenots, Maryland's citizenry protested in horror, what would the French do to English Protestants? In answer, they invoked visions of "garments roll'd in blood" and "infants slain at the Mothers' Breast . . . of Families butchered in their Beds; or carried into Captivity."[42]

In addition, the French in the Ohio country supposedly enticed Maryland Jesuits to rebel by supplying them with arms. The evidence backing such charges was meager; Jesuits in Frederick County spent long periods away from their residences. No one knew for sure where they went during these times, but one could guess. A number of French-speaking gentlemen had been spotted conspiring with frontier Jesuits for extended periods. Attempting to stop these practices, the lower house ordered provincial magistrates to arrest all priests who could not account for their whereabouts, and moved to prohibit Roman Catholics from owning weapons. Also, Catholics were banned from the militia.[43] Nevertheless, fear persisted that Catholics were determined to "wash their Hands in the Blood of the Protestants," that Catholics wanted to take over Protestant pulpits, and that Catholics

[41] *Maryland Gazette* (Annapolis), August 29, 1754.

[42] *Ibid.*, October 30, 1755. Descriptions of what would happen should the French be victorious can also be found *ibid.*, December 26, 1754; March 17, 1757; message by upper house to lower house. March 24, 1755, *Md. Arch.*, LII (1935), 40, 43.

[43] According to John Veasy and Mr. Earle, Catholics had collected huge caches of arms. John Veasy and Mr. Earle to Governor, September 5, 1754, *Md. Arch.*, XXXI (1911), 47-49. Several documents reflect the belief that Catholics were absent from their places of abode and that French spies were abroad on the frontier. One John Jones affirmed that these men were really Frenchmen only posing as Catholic priests due to their "being too gay drest." Deposition of Thomas Reader, October 29, 1753, *ibid.*, L (1933), 203. Some "Gentlemen in Cecil County" asserted that Catholics were being armed by the French. September 5, 1754, *ibid.*, XXXI (1911), 48-49. Provisions were taken to seize arms from papists and to prohibit their services in the militia; Council resolution, March 3, 1755, *ibid.*, p. 54; "An Act for regulating the Militia of the Province of Maryland," May 22, 1756, *ibid.*, LII (1935), 450, 454, 460-461; "Recruiting Instructions to Colonel [?]. and the Officers under his Command," September 16, 1756, *ibid.*, p. 598.

were conferring with the French as to how best to carry out the rebellion.[44]

By the end of the 1750's, the conviction became confirmed that Catholics in the colony, aided by the French and sympathetic Maryland officials, were just about ready to topple the government, force Protestants to become Catholics or perish by refusing, erect the slavery of arbitrary government, and destroy British rights and liberties. Feelings were so heated that the slightest remark sometimes provoked violence.[45] In 1756 the lower house appraised the colony's situation as follows:

> 198 The present Discontents of the People are not owing to the Clamours of a few factious Men, as the Papists and their Abettors have suggested, but to one uniform and continued Scheme of the Papists themselves, either avowed or concealed as the Times and Occasions required, to subvert the Protestant Interest. And we cannot but be of Opinion that the open and unrestrained Practice of sending Youth to Foreign Popish Seminaries for Education has this pernicious Scheme in View; we therefore think it to be incumbent on a Protestant Legislature to guard against the Consequences of that dangerous Practice, as it is notorious that there is in those Seminaries a Root of Enmity irreconcilable to his Majesty's Government, and the Religion of his Kingdom.[46]

There apparently were grounds for these accusations. Catholic parents frequently sent their children to Catholic schools rather than Protestant schools and abroad to St. Omer's where they would be spared the Anglican education in Protestant schools. Catholics apparently were running schools in the province, preaching in public, and

[44] Deposition of Thomas Greaves, October 29, 1757, *ibid.*, L (1933), 201.

[45] Deposition of Robert Chesley, October 29, 1753, *ibid.*, L (1933), 204-205.

[46] Lower house to Governor Sharpe, April 8, 1756, *ibid.*, LII (1935), 357-358. For other statements of the plot and evil consequences of the "Growth of Popery within this Province," see Report of the Committee on Grievances, October 29, 1753; Report of the Committee on Grievances, March 5, 1754, *ibid.*, p. 419; Address to governor, March 6, 1754, *ibid.*, p. 422; lower house to Governor Sharpe, April 8, 1756, *ibid.*, LII (1935), 356-357; Governor Sharpe's address to lower house, April 24, 1756, *ibid.*, p. 387; "Petition of the Freeholders and Inhabitants of Calvert County," *ibid.*, pp. 668-669; Horatio Sharpe to William Sharpe, July 6, 1757, *ibid.*, IX (1890), 46; Petition of Freemen of [?] County, April 3, 1756, *ibid.*, XXXI (1911), 125; *Maryland Gazette* (Annapolis), October 17, 1754.

controlled more than their share of provincial offices.[47] There is little evidence, however, which would prove that Catholics were actively perverting the schools, weakening family stability, and attempting to subvert the government. Governor Horatio Sharpe, despite repeated attempts to uncover a Catholic conspiracy, consistently maintained that there was none. According to him, "none of the County Courts could, upon Strictist Enquiry, find that any of the Papists had behaved or expressed themselves in any unbecoming manner."[48] In addition, limited evidence indicates that Catholics were peaceful and kept to themselves as much as possible. According to one Catholic shopkeeper, "it goes here much as in England; where, by the severity of the times, we do little more than keep our own."[49] It seems reasonable, therefore, to conclude that there probably was not a plot.

Nevertheless, that there was not a plot is not in itself an important consideration. As Hofstadter pointed out, it is not the absence of verifiable facts which characterizes the paranoid style, but the leap in imagination that is made at critical points in narrating the evidence.[50] The important question to be answered is why Protestants said Catholics were subverting Maryland society. The discrepancy between Catholics' actions and Protestants interpretations of them suggest that politicians of the day were playing upon the fears and anxieties of their constituents and using the dispossessing of Catholics' land as a political tool in a "quest for power"[51] over the proprietor and his Catholic associates.

[47] Donell McClure Owings, *His Lordship's Patronage: Offices of Profit in Colonial Maryland* (Baltimore, 1953), pp. 112-486; Thomas O'Brien Hanley, "The Catholic and Anglican Gentry in Maryland Politics," *Historical Magazine of the Protestant Episcopal Church*, XXXVIII (June, 1969), 143-151.

[48] Horatio Sharpe to Lord Baltimore, December 16, 1758, *Md. Arch.*, IX (1890), 317. See also letter to Governor Sharpe, October 23, 1755, *ibid.*, XXXI (1911), 80; Horatio Sharpe to Calvert, December 26, 1757, *ibid.*, IX (1890), 117; Sharpe to Lord Baltimore, December 17, 1758, *ibid.*, p. 315; upper house to lower house, *ibid.*, LV (1938), 508-511.

[49] Thomas Hughes (ed.), *History of the Society of Jesus in North America: Colonial and Federal: Texts and Documents* (London, 1917), *Text*, II, 437.

[50] Hofstadter, *op. cit.*, p. 37.

[51] See Jack Greene, *The Quest for Power: The Lower House of Assembly in the Southern Royal Colonies, 1689-1776*, 2d ed. (New York, 1963), especially p. vi.

V

Maryland politics were indeed "convulsed" during the eighteenth century, but by more than anti-Catholicism.[52] The colony's government was polarized into opposing factions over the proper allocation of revenues traditionally belonging to the proprietor. The Court Party, consisting of the governor and members of the upper house, believed that these revenues should continue to go to the proprietor for his personal use, and that new taxes should be raised if the colony needed protection. In opposition, the Country Party, made up of the members of the lower house, felt that the colony's citizens were already too
200 highly taxed, and that the proprietary revenue should be returned to the colony to help provide a defense. By 1750, this conflict had become institutionalized; after 1753, the delegates refused to vote new taxes, arguing instead that existing revenues should be used to prosecute the war against the French and Indians.[53]

Although the lower house refused to pass new appropriations, it did not object to supporting the defense of the colony by using part of the proprietor's revenues. The house attempted to seize part of the proprietary income in two ways: defense bills and anti-Catholic legislation.

The lower house introduced a number of measures designed to provide for the colony's defense by diverting some of the proprietor's revenue to the possession of the colony. These measures were repeatedly turned down by the upper house because such funds were held to be solely the proprietor's. Bickering between the two factions sharpened between 1755 and 1756. The lower house probably reasoned that since the governor would be obligated to defend the colony, he might more easily bend to the delegates' wishes.[54] Nevertheless, the bills met severe opposition from members of the upper

[52] Barker, *op. cit.*, p. 155.

[53] For the governor's inability to get new taxes voted see Arthur M. Schlesinger, "Maryland's Share in the Last Intercolonial War," *Maryland Historical Magazine*, V (March, 1910), 46-57; for Governor Sharpe's opinion on the matter see Horatio Sharpe to William Pitt, April 18, 1759, *Md. Arch.*, IX, 334. The representatives had the power to act no new expenditures of public money, and they used it as a political lever to fight the proprietor in the few effective ways they could. Paul H. Giddens, "The French and Indian War in Maryland, 1753-1756," *Maryland Historical Magazine*, XXX (December, 1935), 281-310.

[54] Introduction to *Md. Arch.*, L (1933), x, xi-xx; *ibid.*, LII (1935), vii.

house in whose interest it was to protect the proprietor's economic concerns in the colony.

Frustrated in its attempts to pass its defense bills, the lower house tried a second approach. Utilizing information supplied by a number of Maryland clergymen, the lower house asserted that the Catholics were out to destroy the colony. Exploiting this issue, the lower house hoped to achieve the very goal which had proven unobtainable through its defense measures. The tools the house used were various repressive measures introduced between 1753 and 1758.

Anti-Catholic legislation fell roughly into two categories: the curtailment of Catholic immigration through a system of excessive duties and penalty fees, and the dispossessing of Catholics already within Maryland. According to the wording of the bills, they were passed to restrain a "dangerous intestine enemy" who would ruin the colony if not restricted. The bills were, on one level, submitted because of the anti-Catholicism stimulated by the war, but on another level, they were attempts to force the diversion of proprietary revenue into the defense treasury of the colony. In so doing, the lower house would gain a measure of power at the expense of the proprietor by dictating to him how he could spend his money.

Maryland had always taxed incoming Irish Catholic servants, but during the 1750's these restrictions were expanded to hysterical proportions. The underlying rationale for the new taxes was that "several Popish Priests, and Jesuits, have been lately imported into this Province, who have immediately resorted to the Western Frontiers . . . [to] give his Majesty's Enemies constant secret Intelligence of the Situation of Affairs in this Province." In conjunction with the French and Indians, the preamble of one bill stated, the Catholic immigrants would turn against Maryland's Protestants, establish "Tyranny and Slavery, both Ecclesiastical and Civil," and subvert "the happy constitution of the Government of this Province, and the Loss of Liberties and Properties of the good People thereof."[55]

An act passed the lower house on March 21, 1755, providing that masters of all incoming ships had to pay rates of as high as £500 for Catholics on board the masters' ships. The act further provided that any Catholics entering the province in any other manner must

[55] "An Act for preventing the Importation . . . of Papists," *ibid.*, LII (1935), 89.

report to a justice of the peace and pay a deposit of up to £200. If the Catholics tried to hide or cover up their religion, penalties of as much as £400 were specified. An important provision was that funds collected would go to support the county in which they were levied. Catholics were to prove their loyalty by taking the oaths of Abjuration and the Test. Should anyone fail to subscribe to them, he was assumed to be Catholic.[56]

The act met with reservations in the upper house where it received two readings, but the amount and distribution of fines were drastically amended. Fines were reduced by as much as three-quarters and
202 the method of payment was changed; the upper house version provided that fines were to go to the proprietor as a part of his revenues.[57] The upper house further stated that the act would not be in effect until the proprietor had seen it. Such arrangements obviously did not suit the lower house and the dispute continued throughout the decade.[58]

The Protestant crusade also took steps to prevent further growth of Catholicism within Maryland by attempting to dispossess the Catholic priests. The house of delegates had repeatedly shown its desire to punish Catholics since 1751, but "An Act for the Security of his Majesty's Dominion and to prevent the Growth of Popery within this province" did not reach the upper house until May 23, 1754.[59] The act's preamble cited the grievances which had been mouthed since 1752, that priests were gathering "as in a collegiate Manner,"

[56] For specific provisions of this act see "An Act for preventing the Importation of . . . Papists," March 21, 1755, *ibid.*, pp. 89-92. The oath of abjuration required one to repudiate the doctrines of the Catholic Church and the Test verified one's loyalty to England and the Anglican Church.

[57] Act to prevent the importation of papists, March 20, 1755, *ibid.*, p. 37.

[58] Amendments proposed to the act to prevent the importation of papists, May 18, 1756, *ibid.*, X, 286-290. The progress of the act through the legislature can be seen from the readings of the acts on May 17, 1756, November 3, 1757, November 24, 1757, December 16, 1757, November 4, 1757, November 5, 1757, November 25, 1757, May 5, 1758, April 6, 1758, April 20, 1758, April 21, 1758, May 4, 1758, May 5, 1758, May 6, 1758. See *ibid.*, LV (1938), 163, 175, 196-197, 252, 254, 287, 394, 522, 564, 608, 642, 644-645, 662, 665.

[59] "An Act to Prevent the Growth of Popery," May 29, 1751, *ibid.*, XLVI (1939), 521; upper house to lower house, June 8, 1751, *ibid.*, p. 534; passage of such an act, June 3, 1751, *ibid.*, p. 569. For the 32-19 affirmative vote on May 23, 1754, see *ibid.*, L (1933), 495.

saying public Mass, converting Protestants to Catholicism, perverting Negroes, and generally helping the French and Indians in every conceivable way. Therefore, the bill provided that all land held by Jesuits would be confiscated by the assembly and sold to the highest bidder, although those priests who had acquired title to land or property since October 1, 1751, would be allowed to sell their own land. The money from land sales would not go to the proprietor, however, but would go to defend the colony from the French and Indians. Catholic priests were also disbarred from owning or inheriting real or personal property of any sort.[60]

On May 30, the law was read before the upper house and promptly 203
denied, apparently without discussion. What was at issue was the status of the proprietor's revenues. The passage of this act would jeopardize that part of the proprietary income which was obtained from quitrents. Should the assembly have passed the bill, part of these earnings would have been denied him. Such a measure the upper house was determined not to enact.[61]

In 1756 the lower house tried again to circumscribe the Catholics' activities. After the usual exercises in anti-Catholicism in which the lower house stated the general need to "lay the Popish Priests and Jesuits (those great Enemies to our Laws, Liberties and Religion), under some more severe Restraint than they have heretofore been,"[62] the delegates moved to severely reduce Catholicism in Maryland. Both Catholics who sent children to St. Omer's and the children who went were disbarred from owning, inheriting, or passing on any real or personal property. The lower house also provided that schoolmasters had to be licensed Protestants; they levied heavy fines on priests who tried to convert Protestants and also upon Marylanders who subjected themselves to conversion; they fined heavily priests who made conversion to Catholicism a prerequisite to marriage; they made all non-property-holding priests register on pain of a £200 fine and made it illegal for them to acquire property; they

[60] "An Act for the Security of his Majesty's Dominion, and to prevent the Growth of Popery within this Province," May 30, 1754, *ibid.*, pp. 514-519.

[61] The act of May 30 was read twice before the upper house and turned down. Reading of the act, May 23, 1754, *ibid.*, p. 456; vetoing of the act, May 30, 1754, *ibid.*, p. 467.

[62] "An Act to prevent the Growth of Popery within this Province," May 22, 1756, *ibid.*, p. 441.

forced each priest to post a £500 bond for good behavior in addition to two personal references; they forbade foreign priests from preaching or risk a £100 fine; they prohibited priests from traveling through the colony in disguise, and they required Catholics to surrender all arms and ammunition except those essential for defense against the Indians. The lower house did, however, provide that those Catholics who would convert to Protestantism would be restored to all their rights and privileges. The bill was undoubtedly denied by the upper house.[63]

The session, nearly twice as long as the typical session, did not
204 close without a victory for the lower house;[64] the delegates managed a small, but impressive success in its quest to gain more power in running the government. The Supply Bill[65] of 1756 raised a tax of one shilling per hundred acres of land including His Lordship's manor lands, and under a special provision known to history as the "Double-Tax," the bill required Catholics to pay an extra one shilling per hundred acres. This was a very conservative win for the lower house in comparison with its earlier tries, but the delegates had made a clear victory in getting the upper house and governor to assent to the measure, for it authorized a part of the proprietor's revenues to go to fight the war. Governor Sharpe was somewhat skeptical as to whether the proprietor would accept the bill,[66] but Lord Baltimore finally approved the act for the period of its duration.

The lower house stated that the Catholics were being doubly taxed because they were not serving in the militia. Hence, Catholics should pay extra to support the colony's defense in lieu of military duty. This was an obvious screen, however, for earlier the lower house had prohibited Catholics from enlisting because they were considered

[63] For the provisions of the act see *ibid.*, pp. 441-449. There is no specific reference to the outcome of this act, but considering its provisions, it is difficult to see how anyone else could have consented to it. The fact that the act was not made law probably indicates that the upper house disapproved it.

[64] Barker, *op. cit.*, pp. 240-241.

[65] Its complete title was "An Act for Granting a Supply of Forty Thousand Pounds for his Majesty's Service, and striking Thirty-four Thousand and Fifteen Pounds Six Shillings Thereof, in Bills of Credit, and raising a Fund for Sinking the same." See provisions of the Supply Bill affecting Catholics, May 15, 1756, *Md. Arch.*, LII (1935), 508, 510.

[66] Horatio Sharpe to John Sharpe, May 27, 1756, *ibid.*, VI (1888), 429.

to be a liability. Catholics could be heavily fined even if they were caught loitering near a training area. Thus, Catholics were placed in an impossible situation; they were enjoined from militia service and then taxed because they were not helping actively to defend the colony.[67]

Evidently, the measure satisfied neither faction. The upper house and governor regretted the fifty to sixty-five per cent of the manor rents which would be lost to the proprietor. This represented not only a financial loss, but also a loss of the proprietor's power in that the Country Party gained a greater say in the running of the government. The lower house's discontent sprang from the feeling that the delegates should not have gone into conference with the upper house on a money bill. The delegates felt that money appropriations were their sole area of responsibility.[68]

In sum, during the 1750's the lower house tried to place into law those fears, suspicions, and beliefs which were in circulation throughout the colony, fears which had arisen from the French threat, political factionalism, the colony's large population of slaves, depressed tobacco economy, and the presence of a Catholic minority. Historians rarely have seen the double tax in this context; most have treated the measure and the Catholic "scare" which helped to produce it merely as a function of the French and Indian War and Maryland's often noted anti-Catholic feeling. Although these forces were undoubtedly very real, the measure, as well as the more extreme anti-Catholic legislation which preceded it, must be viewed as a part of the political factionalism of the period in which the Court and Country Parties vied for political power. When seen in this light, Charles A. Barker's statement that "only the military hazards of the months following Braddock's defeat can account for the enactment of such a law" must be seen as an oversimplification.[69]

After 1758, the belief in a Catholic plot rapidly disappeared as a major issue; public denunciations of Catholicism in the *Maryland Gazette* frequently printed earlier in the decade now lost their traditional prominence. In the legislature bickering continued, sometimes

[67] For the provisions of the Militia Act passed May 22, 1756, see *ibid.*, LII (1935), 460-461.

[68] Barker, *op. cit.*, pp. 241-242.

[69] *Ibid.*, pp. 240-241.

over "Romish or Jesuitical" people, but long dissertations on Catholic danger did not have the emotional appeal of the earlier language. Acts to prevent the importation of papists continued to be enacted as late as 1765.[70] These, too, were not supported with the same narrow-minded gusto as had characterized the earlier legislative adventures. While it cannot be said with certainty that no one viewed Catholics with suspicion or fear, at least these fears were not voiced with the same intensity or regularity. Passions had apparently subsided to the degree that the construction of a Catholic church (as opposed to the tolerated private chapels) in St. Mary's County occasioned no great
206 public outcry from Protestants.[71]

Why did the frenzy abate? The most important reason probably was that the military threat posed by the French and Indians had by this time subsided. Hence, the crisis was over, and the opportunity for leverage was no longer available to the lower house as it had been earlier.

VI

In a deep sense, the clamor against Catholicism was a statement of nationalism. Protestants attested to their love of and loyalty to the British Empire and the political and religious liberties which Maryland Protestants thought were implied.[72] "Romish" people appeared so dangerous because they seemed to threaten these benefits of being British and to pose Catholicism and arbitrary government as substitutes.

[70] Edwin W. Beitzell, "Newtown Hundred," *Maryland Historical Magazine*, LI (June, 1956), 130.

[71] See further considerations of these acts on March 23, 1762, April 9, 1762, March 24, 1762, March 25, 1762, April 18, 1762, November 19, 1763, November 22, 1763, November 11, 1763, *ibid.*, LVIII (1941), 14, 23, 90, 92-93, 95, 134, 264, 266, 321, 370, 382. An act was finally enacted on December 12, 1765. See *ibid.*, LIX (1942), 288.

[72] For a classic statement of nationalism see Hans Kohn, *Nationalism: Its Meaning and History* (New York, 1965), pp. 9-15. For its application to the American Colonies see Max Savelle, *Seeds of Liberty: The Genesis of the American Mind* (Seattle, 1965), pp. 567-568; Savelle, "Nationalism and Other Loyalties in the American Revolution," *American Historical Review*, LXVII (July, 1962), 901-923; Hans Kohn, *American Nationalism: An Interpretive Essay* (New York, 1957).

This attitude was commonly in print during the 1740's and 1750's. Thomas Cradock, after being accused of drinking the pretender's health, bitterly lashed out that he was "an ENGLISHMAN, a Protestant, a Minister of the Protestant Church."[73] According to Cradock, "we are Britons; . . . we are the Sons of those who valued Life less than Liberty, and readily gave their Blood to leave that Liberty, to their posterity."[74] The lower house described Marylanders as "People who enjoy the Rights and Privileges under a British government."[75] At least one outcry in the *Maryland Gazette* called attention to the religious and civil rights being endangered by Papists. According to "Jura,"

> We live in a Community, which for the Justice and equality of its Laws, and the Safety and Security of the Lives and Properties of its Members, is the Envy and Admiration of all Europe. . . . We live at a Time when Bold Rebellion rages in the Land.—Rebellion! against a Government founded on the Principles of Liberty, and exercised in the Spirit of it. —Rebellion! supported by the Tyranny of FRANCE, our Mortal Foe; instigated by the Bigottry and blind Superstition of ROME, our Jest and Derision; yet abetted—by ENGLISHMEN must I say? Shame! by ENGLISHMEN! By Men who, born and nourish'd in the Land of Liberty, yet act and live insensible to her charms; . . . and all for—what? For that Reproach to Reason, that Scandal to Humanity, the mere Nonsense and Wickedness of Jacobitism. Not SWEAR! Impossible! He who does not with all his Might oppose them, is not a Lover of Liberty; and every honorer of Truth and Virtue, who does not from his Soul abjure, detest, and scorn them, is guilty at least of Immorality, if not Impiety.[76]

It was upon this general feeling that the delegates were able to capitalize in their quest for power over the proprietor.

During the decade, the lower house came to suspect that the proprietary interest might also have been out to destroy English freedoms so precious to Marylanders. Much of this feeling probably arose because the Court Party had repeatedly turned down the lower house's defense and anti-Catholic measures. This suspicion could not have

[73] Cradock, *op. cit.*, p. ii.

[74] *Ibid.*, p. 5.

[75] Lower house message to upper house, May 10, 1740, *Md. Arch.*, XL (1921), 448.

[76] *Maryland Gazette* (Annapolis), April 2, 1752.

been allayed by the expressed attitude of Governor Sharpe. When the lower house questioned some of the governor's pardoning of criminals, the governor replied, "I will not suffer the undisputed and undoubted Rights of the supreme Magistrate in this Government, to be invaded or infringed upon by any Pretense whatsoever."[77] The lower house fumed in utter contempt, "this house has done what was incumbent upon them, as faithful and loyal Subjects towards making a Grant for his Majesty's Service, and the Defense and Security of this Province; and though their Endeavors . . . have been frustrated by the Non-Concurrence of the Upper House, they are conscious
208 the deplorable Circumstances which this unhappy Province may probably labour under through Want of such a Grant, cannot be imputed to" the lower house.[78]

Throughout these contentious 1740's and 1750's the Protestant Marylanders came to view both Catholics and the proprietary interest with a great deal of suspicion. Protestants soon found themselves defending British liberties from attack on two fronts. Opposition to the proprietor and to the Catholics often became mixed, and anti-Catholic measures often became anti-proprietary measures.

VII

Protestants in Maryland during the 1750's were evidently reacting to a set of insecurity-producing experiences: depressed tobacco prices, potentially rebellious slaves, fear of the French, and a suspiciously acting proprietor. In addition, the anti-Catholic sentiment existed in Maryland since the founding of the colony. The prospect of war with France, a Catholic nation, undoubtedly drew latent anti-Catholicism into the open and precipitated a Catholic scare. Politicians then seized upon this fear of Catholics, using the issue as a means to achieve a long pursued goal: a gain in power over the proprietary interest. In so doing, Protestants rationalized their actions to themselves in terms of the good Protestants defending the ancient rights and liberties of the British Empire against its enemies, the Catholics. The above might afford a workable model to describe a number of nativist episodes

[77] Governor Sharpe's Address to the lower house, July 8, 1755, *Md. Arch.*, LII (1935), 190-191.

[78] Lower house resolution, May 9, 1758, *ibid.*, LV (1938), 674.

in American history.

To explain the appearance of nativism in Maryland during the 1750's, one must ask why these Protestants held this particular set of attitudes.

In part, the answer lies in the English connection; a great deal of anti-Catholic sentiment crossed the ocean and was reprinted in the *Maryland Gazette.*

VIII

The events of the 1750's, then, constituted one short chapter in the 209
continuing efforts of the assembly to gain power over the proprietor. One of the means they chose was attempts to deprive the proprietor of his traditional sources of revenue by dispossessing his Catholic supporters of their estates. In this way, legislators could both gain additional control of provincial government, and at the same time weaken one of the proprietor's traditional bases of power. The delegates were exploiting their constituents' fears and anxieties, insecurities which evidently were produced by depressed tobacco prices, potentially rebellious slaves, latent anti-Catholicism, and fear of a war with France, a Catholic nation.

In their fight with the proprietor, Protestants triggered an early outburst of nativism. They rationalized their actions in terms of the good Protestants defending the ancient rights and liberties of the British empire against its enemy, "Popish" tyranny. Apparently at least some Maryland Protestants felt a need to demonstrate their allegiance to the ideals and institutions of the British empire.

It was less than a decade since the second Jacobite uprising. Anti-Catholicism became equated with loyalty to the Hanoverian monarchy. Thus, one could conveniently combine imperial allegiance, anti-proprietarianism, and Protestantism in a common cause.

Anti-Popery In Colonial Pennsylvania

IN THE mid-eighteenth century, Conrad Weiser, an otherwise broadminded Pennsylvania Indian agent, could discriminate in his will against one of his daughters merely because she had dared to marry a Roman Catholic. A religious seeker himself, Weiser, far from castigating himself as a bigot, very likely saw himself as a staunch defender of true religion.[1] He may have been uncertain about what he favored, but there was no uncertainty about what he opposed. Even though he lived in the most tolerant of the British North American colonies, Weiser also inhabited a society in which a hatred and fear of popery was common.

Anti-popery was grounded in an antipathy for Roman Catholicism which emerged in many European countries during the Protestant Reformation. It especially affected the lives of Englishmen in the sixteenth and seventeenth centuries during Britain's struggles to resolve her internal Protestant-Catholic and Protestant-Protestant turmoil. An insular kind of anti-papist paranoia also developed from England's conflicts with Catholic Spain, France, and Ireland. A product as well as a cause of emerging British national consciousness, anti-papist prejudices incorporated into law, education, and social patterning the stereotype of a consistently hostile, foreign, and anti-national threat. Anti-popery came to provide a peculiarly religious definition of national security in terms of defensive conflict with all the real and imagined agents of the Church of Rome.[2]

[1] J. Bennett Nolan, "Conrad Weiser's Inventory," *PMHB*, LVI (1932), 269. Weiser changed religions several times in the 1730's and 1740's. Theodore Tappert and John W. Doberstein, eds., *The Journals of Henry Melchior Muhlenberg* (Phila., 1942-58), I, 102-3, 143-4, 170, 172, 188-190.

[2] The struggles of England in those years assumed "an even more religious, more ideological character, exhibiting more sense of moral regeneration and missionary zeal" than that of her counterparts in central and eastern Europe. Richard S. Dunn,

As a popular nationalistic medium through which to mobilize the country against internal as well as external enemies, anti-popery possessed an amazing flexibility of application and thus was susceptible to being applied promiscuously by opportunists, or when social and political crises demanded a scapegoat. Almost anyone was liable to anti-papist accusations, depending on the ebb and flow of contests for political or theological supremacy. As such, anti-popery was often counterproductive in rooting out real internal enemies, but it did serve to define the boundaries of national allegiance.

The nationalistic element also facilitated the transference of anti-popery sentiments from England to all of her colonies. Despite their various differences with the mother-country, the initial ethnic composition 211 of the colonies almost dictated some cultural affinity, and bound those settlements in a union of sensitivity to every threat to England from Catholic France and Spain. That sensitivity, and that union, became even more intense in the eighteenth century as the colonies came to share in the military peril from traditional popish enemies.[3] In the

---

The Age of Religious Wars, 1559-1689 (N.Y., 1970), 47. Ray Allen Billington, in *The Protestant Crusade*, 1800-1860: *A Study of the Origins of American Nativism* (Chicago, 1964), 2, also argues that British hatred of Catholicism was due largely to the anti-national character of that religion,"for Catholicism was feared not only as an antagonistic theology, but also as a force through which the English government itself was to be overthrown." Anti-Catholicism was "a patriotic as well as religious concern." Anti-popery, then, contained an element which could be called nativism—a cultural trait which John Higham describes as "intense opposition to an internal minority on the ground of its foreign. . .connections." *Strangers in the Land*: *Patterns of American Nativism*, 1860-1925 (N.Y., 1970), 4. Higham sees anti-Catholicism as just one element in nativism, and not the other way around. Loyalty to Protestantism in England was wedded to patriotism in the person of Elizabeth I by the Act of Supremacy, by that sovereign's national popularity, and by the longing of the English for stability. Anti-nationalism and treason were fixed on Catholicism by the Rising of the North in 1569, by Pope Pius V's bull *Regnans in Excelsis* (1570) which released English subjects from allegiance to their sovereign, by the Spanish Armada of 1588, and by the 1605 Gunpowder Plot—a conspiracy by disaffected Catholics to blow up Parliament with King, Lords, and Commons inside. Henry Gee and William Hardy, eds., *Documents Illustrative of English Church History* (London, 1896), 442, 458; Philip Hughes, *The Reformation in England* (N.Y., 1954), III, 272, 418; Garrett Mattingly, *The Armada* (Boston, 1959); Philip Caraman, *Henry Garnet and the Gunpowder Plot* (N.Y., 1964). This relationship between Protestantism and patriotism was maintained in the colonies.

[3] To the question, "what Occasion there is at this Time of the Day [1731] for an Oration against Popery; is the Protestant Interest in any Hazard from that Quarter?" a Gentleman answered, "the Church Militant will never be out of Danger, and therefore she has Watchmen set upon her Walls. . . .The common Enemy is still in Being, and hath great Power in the World, . . .so that we have no Reason to be secure." *A Seasonable Caveat against Popery*: *or, an*

tolerant Quaker colony of Pennsylvania, that peril was compounded after the 1720's by the fear of cultural bastardization from increased foreign immigration, a fear that was used by political and religious factions in the colony in their contests for power.

But there was more to the continuance of anti-popery in the colonies than simple ethnocentrism or nationalism. Hostility to Catholicism remained strong in the colonies, and even reached a peak in the mid-eighteenth century, just as it was beginning to weaken in the mother-country. Also, during the height of anti-papist fervor in the 1750's, many American colonists did not hold their national or cultural ties to England so high as to prevent them from illegally trading with
212 Catholic France and Spain.

A more enduring and fundamental element in anti-popery was the intellectual component. This element, which cherished the values of reason and individualism, was a mixture of envy and disdain. Popery was held in awe and feared as an absolutist method for organizing people and holding fast to their thoughts, allegiances, and even their consciences. It was very effective in this because of its alleged freedom from rationality and individual choice, but these traits defined a corrupt system for Protestants. In the contest for souls, Protestanism would have to suffer losses and divisiveness as the price for right religion. Popery's authoritarian structure could appeal to those who opted for security over freedom in a world of turmoil;[4] its international organization could recruit those malcontents in every society who longed for participation in an entity greater than an unstable nation-state; its rituals

---

Essay on the Merchandise of Slaves and Souls of Men; Revelations XVIII, 13, with an Application Thereof to the Church of Rome, by A Gentleman (Boston, 1731; reprinted London, 1733) 3, 4-5. In 1765, Jonathan Mayhew wrote:

> The agents of Rome, ever restless and scheming, compass sea and land to make proselytes; going about continually from country to country, seeking whom they may devour: And, probably, there is no protestant country, in which there are not some of them, at least lurking, if they dare not discover themselves. We should not be ignorant of their devices; nor ever off our guard against them.

Jonathan Mayhew, *Popish Idolatry: A Discourse Delivered in the Chapel of Harvard-College in Cambridge, New England, May* 8, 1765 (Boston, 1765), 50-51.

[4] In comparing Catholic with Protestant faith, one anti-papist wrote "they believe the Scriptures to be the Word of God, and Christ to be the Son of God, because the Church of Rome doth tell them so." Ignotus, *Thirty Plain, but Sound Reasons Why Protestants Differ from Popery; to which are added thirty-four points held by many Papists, which were never yet rationally proved by any one of them* (London, 1688; reprinted 1851), 8.

could work on the emotions as well as "enslave" the mind;[5] and its sense-defying "trickery"(transubstantiation, Jesuitical mental reservation and undercover subversion, priestly absolution, papal indulgences, etc.)[6] could win over weak minds intrigued by the mysterious and magical. The time-tested appeal of such "charlatanry" and "idolatry" would forever "enslave" hordes of Catholics, and threatened to "seduce" many Protestant Englishmen confused by the proliferation of creeds and organizations and desirous of a faith beyond the postulates of reason alone. Thus, anti-popery erected as the chief defensive works of an evolving and troubled Protestantism what it admitted were its chief weaknesses in the battle for souls. Freedom from "superstition" and enforced religious conformity became for Protestant identity what freedom from Rome, Paris, and Madrid became for British national identity.[7] Yet, anti-papist preachers were ever on guard to prevent the

[5] On Catholic faith as enslavement, see the general arguement in A Gentleman, *A Seasonable Caveat*.

[6] Catholic mortuaries, rights of burial, relics, pilgrimages, canonization, vows, and Masses, prayers and indulgences for souls in Purgatory were also attacked as popish trickery. A Gentleman, *A Seasonable Caveat*, 7-12. The number of undercover Catholic missionaries in England was never very great. By 1578, there were only 50 seminarists—missionaries trained at the College des Prêtres Anglais in Douai, Flanders—operating in England, but their influence was magnified, for the Bishop of London complained in 1577 "that the papists marvelously increase in numbers and in obstinate withdrawal from church and services of God." Philip Hughes, *The Reformation in England* , III, 303. In all of Elizabeth's reign there were only 440 seminarists and a handful of Jesuits in England—too few effectively to subvert a total of 8,000 parishes. What was alarming was the fact that of the 183 executed by Elizabeth, 54 were converts to Catholicism, and 9 had been clergymen in the Established Church. Marvin R. O'Connell, *The Counter Reformation*, 1559-1610 (N.Y., 1974), 236-9.

[7] A Gentleman boasted that France, Spain, Italy, and parts of other nations "were left to wallow in the Filth and Mire of Popery, and are perishing in Antichristian Darkness even to this Day," and wondered with nationalistic and intellectual pride why those nations suffered themselves "to be thus grosly gull'd and abused, and not see thro' the Cheat to this Day." *A Seasonable Caveat*, 31-32. Perhaps the best summary of what popery meant for Englishmen and British colonials is contained in Jonathon Mayhew, *Popish Idolatry* (1765), 48-49:

Detestable as the idolatry of the church of Rome is, there are other of her principles and practices. . .which more immediately affect the peace and order of civil society, the honor of princes, and the liberty and common rights of mankind. Our controversy with her is not merely a religious one: It is not, on our part, only a defence of the worship of one God by one Mediator, in opposition to that of a thousand demons or idols; of the authority of the sacred oracles, in opposition to that of idle legends and traditions; and of sober reason in opposition to the grossest fanaticism: But a defence of our laws, liberties, and civil rights as men, in opposition to the proud claims and encroachments of ecclesiastical persons, who under the pretext of religion, and saving men's souls, would engross all power and property to themselves, and reduce us to the most abject slavery: It is a defence, . . .of the common rights of seeing, smelling, tasting; all

natural human tendency to slide back into a comfortable surrender to a sensual, but sense-defying, Catholicism; and they were naturally sensitive to the mixed blessing of denominationalism formed by emphasizing reason and celebrating the individual as the center of thought, belief, and action.[8]

Religious and political stability of a sort came to Britian with the establishment of the Church of England. Theologically and organizationally, Anglicanism was a "middle way," occupying a precarious position somewhere between Catholicism and the more radical forms of Protestantism.[9] Established in 1559 by the Act of Supremacy,

---

which popery attacks and undermines, by the doctrine of transubstantiation; and would take them from us, as a means of making us dutiful sons, or rather wretched slaves of the church. . . . we ought in reason and prudence to detest the church of Rome, in the same degree that we prize our freedom. . . . Popery and liberty are incompatible; at irreconcileable enmity with each other.

[8] The perception of Catholicism as sensual was perhaps best expressed by John Adams, who, after having visited Saint Mary's Catholic Church in Philadelphia, wrote:

This Afternoons Entertainment was to me most awfull and affecting. The poor Wretches, fingering their Beads, chanting Latin, not a Word of which they understood, their Pater Nosters and Ave Maria's. Their holy Water—their Crossing themselves perpetually—their Bowing to the Name of Jesus, wherever they hear it—their Bowings and Kneelings, and Genuflections before the Altar. The Dress of the Priest was rich with Lace—his Pulpit was Velvet and Gold. The Altar Piece was very rich—little Images and Crucifixes about—Wax Candles lighted up. But how shall I describe the Picture of our Saviour in a Frame of Marble over the Altar at full Length upon the Cross, in the Agonies, and the Blood dropping and streaming from his Wounds.

The Musick consisting of an organ, and a Choir of singers, went all the Afternoon, excepting sermon Time, and the Assembly chanted—most sweetly and exquisitely.

Here is every Thing which can lay hold of the Eye, Ear, and Imagination. Every Thing which can charm and bewitch the simple and ignorant. I wonder how Luther ever broke the spell.

John Adams to Abigail Adams, 9 October 1774, L.H. Butterfield, ed., *Adams Family Correspondence* (Cambridge, Mass., 1965), I, 166-7. The Protestant emphasis on reason was expressed in all anti-papist writings. Ignotus wrote that "Popery fighteth with sense and reason; The Papists would make men void of sense." *Thirty Plain, but Sound Reasons*, 12. William Sherlock, in *A Dissertation or Discourse concerning a Judge of Controversies in Matters of Religion* (London, 1686), 26, argued that the individual man had "the best evidence that he can possibly have for anything, that the consecrated bread and wine are still bread and wine, not flesh and blood; for all his senses tell him so."

[9] As William Sherlock argued, the Church of England justified her doctrines and practices both from Scripture and antiquity, while the Church of Rome "alleges antiquity to prove such doctrines and practices as the Scripture either condemns or knows nothing of." As for the Dissenters in England, Sherlock said that the Anglican dispute with them is "not about articles of faith, but the external modes and circumstances of worship, or the government and discipline of the Church." *A Dissertation or Discourse*, 22, 23.

which transferred to the crown any jurisdiction ever exercised or claimed by the pope, and by the Act of Uniformity, which imposed the rites and prayers of the 1552 Book of Common Prayer as the only lawful form of worship, the Church of England became wedded to the sovereign and came under attack from other Protestants for that marriage, and for having retained such vestiges of popery as bishops, vestments, candles, and the kneeling position for reception of the Lord's Supper.[10] As one non-Anglican Protestant put it,"The papacy was never abolished, . . .but transferred to the sovereign."[11] When several clergymen were suspended in 1565 for failure to wear the prescribed vestments, anti-papist voices were raised against the Church of England for this "new filth and restored relics of wretched popery."[12]

Anglicanism faced the dilemma of having to uphold the twin intellectual pillars of anti-popery, reason and individualism, while denying them in order to enforce the religious conformity deemed essential to the national welfare. As the state church with its destiny intricately bound up with the fate of the British nation, it shared in all the shocks to the realm from foreign Catholics and from internal dissidents. Along with the monarch, the Church of England was brought low by the Puritan Revolution, in which an effective use of anti-popery was made against it. Returned to a less lofty position of power with the Restoration of 1661, the Church of England faced an uneasy alliance with a monarchy gradually veering toward Roman Catholicism, and under attacks from Quakers and other Dissenters or Nonconformists.

The Anglican counter-attack accentuated the third element in anti-popery as it was passed on to the colonies—the element of utilitarianism. During the terrors of the alleged Popish Plot, characteristics which formerly had been used to identify and root out Catholics in England were attributed to members of the Society of Friends; and both groups were penalized under the same existing laws for non-attendance at Anglican services.[13] Ironically, in 1671, when King Charles II, in an

[10] O'Connell, *The Counter Reformation*, 154, 360-363; Roland H. Bainton, *The Reformation of the Sixteenth Century* (Boston, 1952), 183-210.

[11] H. Robinson, ed., *The Zurich Letters* (Cambridge, 1846), 246.

[12] O'Connell, *The Counter Reformation*, 155.

[13] A 1582 law which forced Papists to pay £20 monthly for absence from the Established Church, and a 1605 law giving the king the option of accepting that sum or all of the personal, and two-thirds of the real, estate of the accused, were used to penalize Quakers. In 1678, when Parliament was reassessing the laws against popery, an oath by which the penalty could be

apparent effort to assist Roman Catholics, suspended the execution of these laws, Quakers benefited as well. Nearly five hundred Friends who had been imprisoned, some for several years, were set free by the royal proclamation.[14]

The Quakers, of course, were thankful for their legal association with papists in this case, but they were frequently at pains to separate themselves from Catholics because of the theological confusion fostered by the laws and by the anti-papist charges of the Established Church. On January 22, 1678, William Penn felt compelled to point out to a Committee of Parliament:

> 216 I have not only been supposed a Papist, but a seminarist, a Jesuit, an emissary of Rome and in the pay of the Pope. . . .some zealous for the Protestant cause have been so far gone in this mistake as not only to think ill of us and to decline our conversation, but to take courage to themselves to prescribe us as a sort of concealed Papist. All laws have been let loose upon us, as if the design were not to reform but to destroy us, and that not for what we are, but for what we are not.[15]

Theologically, nothing could have been further from the truth than that Quakers and Catholics were doctrinally alike. Quakers' deep-seated antipathy for popery was vehemently expressed in George Fox's *The Arraignment of Popery*, Josiah Coale's *The Whore Unveiled, Or the Mystery of the Deceit of Rome Revealed*, Robert Barclay's *Anarchy of the Ranters, and other Libertines; the Hierarchy of the Romanists, and other Pretended Churches, equally refused and refuted*, and William Penn's own *A Seasonable Caveat against Popery*. Written in 1670, *A Seasonable Caveat*, while espousing Penn's unshakeable belief in religious toleration, nevertheless attacked the tenets of Catholicism as inconsistent with Scripture, right reason, and the opinions of the early Christians. Nine years later, Penn was still struggling to disentangle his beliefs from the net of popery which the penal laws and the Anglican clergy had cast around him. In *One Project for the Good of England—that is, Our Civil Union is our Civil Safety*, he argued that all English Protestants

---

avoided was proposed, but that did the Quakers little good, since they were in conscience opposed to the taking of oaths. Charles J. Stille, "Religious Tests in Provincial Pennsylvania," *PMHB*, IX (1885), 379; *RACHSP*[Records of the American Catholic Historical Society of Philadelphia], I (1884-6), 75-6.

[14] *Passages From the Life and Writings of William Penn* (Phila., 1882), 110.

[15] *Ibid.*, 201.

pledged their allegiance and subjection to the civil government alone, whereas Catholics owed their allegiance to the pope in Rome. Therefore, dissenting Protestants should not be persecuted, and they should be given the opportunity, by public declaration or test, to prove that they were not Catholics and alien threats to the nation. The declaration which he drew up denied the pope's authority to depose any sovereign or to absolve subjects of their allegiance to a sovereign, the pope's position as Christ's vicar on earth, the existence of Purgatory, transubstantiation in the Lord's Supper, and the lawfulness and efficacy of prayers to saints and images. Penn hoped that Parliament would set a day when this declaration would be required in every town and parish in England.[16]

Penn's efforts at establishing what should have been the self-evident 217
distinctions between Quakerism and Catholicism were nullified by the strength of anti-popery paranoia in England. The Quakers' doctrine of the Inward Light, their disregard for social and religious hierarchy, and their principle of religious toleration allowed them to be labelled as anarchic, destructive of the established religio-political order, and detrimental to a unified Protestant front to the inroads of popery. Anglicans charged Penn with being a papist or a Jesuit, or at least engaged in a treasonous correspondence with the Jesuits in Rome. Allegedly he had been bred at St. Omer's, the English Jesuit college, and had received Holy Orders at Rome. Since, obviously, Penn was married, which Catholic priests were not, he supposedly had received a dispensation from the pope for that purpose. Worst of all, Penn's intimacy at the court of James II, and his supposed influence with that papist sovereign, dragged him deeper into the anti-papist trap. In 1686, he defended his principle of toleration against the attacks of the Anglican Archbishop of Canterbury, John Tillottson. Penn argued

> I am a Catholic, though not a Roman. I have bowels for mankind, and dare not deny others, what I crave for myself. I mean liberty for the exercise of my religion, thinking, faith, piety, and providence a better security than force, and that if truth cannot prevail with her own weapons, all others will fail her.[17]

[16] *Ibid.*, 99, 212-213.
[17] *Ibid.*, 310, 313.

In 1687, and again in 1688, James II issued a declaration of liberty of conscience in England and forbade all tests and penalties for not attending Anglican worship. To the Anglicans this was tantamount to treason, for by weakening the revenues of the Established Church, he was threatening the state itself. To make matters worse, in 1688 he also permitted the Jesuits to erect a college in the Savoy in London, the friars to appear publicly in the dress of their order, and the Papal Nuncio d'Ada to enter Windsor with great pomp and ceremony. Popery indeed seemed to be in the ascendant, and, of course, Penn shared in the fallout. One of Penn's friends, William Popple, Secretary to the Board of Trade and Plantations, warned him of his peril. Penn responded that

218

> If the asserting of an impartial liberty of conscience, if doing to others as he would be done by, and an open avowing and a steady practicing of these things at all times and to all parties, will justly lay a man under the reflection of being a Jesuit or Papist of any sort, I must not only submit to the character, but embrace it too.[18]

Within a fortnight, however, James had been overthrown, William, Prince of Orange, had landed in England, and Penn was left exposed to popular indignation as one who had plotted to establish popery and arbitrary power in England. His planned second visit to his Pennsylvania domain had to be postponed for several years.

Penn remained under suspicion as a political and religious subversive until about 1695, and avoided the public during those years. During his enforced seclusion, he composed a tract entitled *A Key, Opening the Way to Every Capacity How to Distinguish the Religion Professed by the People Called Quakers From the Perversions and Misrepresentations of Their Adversaries* in which one of the errors attacked was "that the Quakers set up works, and meriting by works, like the papists, whereby justification by faith in Christ is laid aside."[19] Despite his efforts, however, the charge of theological similarity with popery would plague Penn and his Quaker followers, even in far away Pennsylvania, because it served the purposes of antagonistic groups in England and in the colony.

At a time when proprietary colonial grants were falling into disfavor

[18] *Ibid.*, 329-41, 347.
[19] *Ibid.*, 351-2, 361-2, 364, 368-383.

and when the Crown was attempting to bring all the colonies under direct royal control, every anti-papist accusation was not to be taken lightly. During his first visit to Pennsylvania in 1682, Penn had to be defended in London against charges that he was a papist and kept "a Jesuit to write his books."[20] According to Penn's 1682 Frame of Government, office-holding in Pennsylvania was open to all who expressed belief in the Christian God. In 1692, however, when Penn's rights of government in the colony were temporarily suspended, King William III demanded that all office-holders subscribe to the oath then in use in England. Quakers were permitted to make an affirmation; but because of the questionable legality of the demand, there was some resistance. Under pressure from Queen Anne in 1702, the Pennsylvania legislature complied, and all office holders took the oath or affirmation. In 1705, it was given statutory form by the Assembly.[21] The formula, duplicating the wording of English tests, required the prospective office-holder to swear or affirm,

> that I do from my heart abhor, detest and abjure as impious and heretical that damnable doctrine that Princes excommunicated or deprived by the Pope, or any authority of the See of Rome, may be deposed or murdered by their subjects or any other whatsoever.

He further had to

> solemnly and sincerely in the presence of God, profess, testify, and declare that I do believe that in the sacrament of the Lord's Supper, there is not any transsubstantiation of the elements of bread and wine into the body and blood of Christ, at or before the consecration thereof by any person whatsoever, and that the invocation or adoration of the Virgin Mary or any other saint, and the sacrifice of the Mass, as they are used in the Church of Rome, are superstitious and idolatrous.

Finally, there was the required admission that he

> solemnly in the presence of God, profess, testify and declare, that I do make this declaration and every part thereof in the plain and ordinary sense of the words now read to me as they are commonly understood by English Protestants without any dispensation already granted me for this purpose by the Pope, or

[20] Joseph L. J. Kirlin, *Catholicity in Philadelphia* (Phila., 1909), 12.

[21] John Tracy Ellis, *Catholics in Colonial America* (Baltimore, 1965), 371-2; Stille, "Religious Tests," 387-395.

> any person whatsoever, and without any hope of such dispensation from any person or authority, or without thinking that I am or may be acquitted before God or man, or any person or authority should dispense with or assume the same and declare the same null and void from the beginning.[22]

The declaration obviously took great pains to prevent surface conformity covering over all sorts of mental reservations which were believed to be resorted to by Jesuits and other papists.

The testimonies of faith contained in the declaration could have been lifted directly out of Penn's own proposed declaration of 1679. Quaker tolerance towards Catholics in Pennsylvania, however, seemed to ne-
220 gate that fact. Catholics were among the first settlers in the colony, and some of them were wealthy and achieved political influence.[23] Pennsylvania became a haven for Catholics driven out of New York by Leisler's Rebellion and for those who fled during the frequent anti-Catholic disturbances there.[24] After 1692, when Maryland prohibited public mass by statute, nowhere else in the British colonies except Pennsylvania could Catholics worship publicly, although there was no regular resident priest until 1729 and no official church building until 1732.

This liberality brought Penn increasing worry at a time when his affairs were in a shambles, with Penn actually spending part of 1708 in a London jail for debt. That year he wrote anxiously to his agent in the colony, James Logan, that

> Here is a complaint against your government that you suffer publick Mass in a scandalous manner. Pray send the matter of fact, for ill use is made against us here.[25]

[22] James T. Mitchell and Harry Flanders, eds., *The Statutes at Large of Pennsylvania from 1682 to 1801*, (Harrisburg, 1896), II, 219-220; Stille, "Religious Tests," 391.

[23] John Gray, alias Tatham, was a London "Gentleman" who came to Pennsylvania in 1685. He possessed extensive lands on both sides of the Delaware River, and for a short time served as Governor of New Jersey. His estate was valued at £3,765 at his death in 1700. Peter Dubuc was a French "gentleman" who settled in Philadelphia in the 1690's. The Philadelphia tax list of 1693 ranks him tenth among 705 taxpayers. Kirlin, *Catholicity*, 14-16.

[24] *RACHSP*, I (1884-6), 82; *Documents Relating to the Colonial History of the State of New York* (Albany, 1856-1887), II, 41, 71, III, 585-6, 609, 617, 674, 689; "Leisler's No Popery Revolt in New York," *ACHR* [American Catholic Historical Researches], XIV (July, 1897), 123-5; H.L. Osgood, *The American Colonies in the Seventeenth Century* (N.Y., 1907), III, 130-1; N. D. Mereness, *Maryland as a Proprietary Province* (N.Y., 1901), 38-42.

[25] 29 July 1708. Deborah Logan and Edward Armstrong, eds., *Correspondence between*

That one incident to which Penn refers, which involved the celebration surrounding the conversion to Catholicism of Lionel Brittin, an Anglican church warden in Philadelphia, and his son, was deemed "scandalous" because it confirmed anti-papists' fears of back-sliding into Catholicism among Protestants. Pennsylvania was obviously as vulnerable to the seductions of popery as was poor beleaguered England. The conversion was also sufficient proof of the errors of Quaker toleration, and prompted at least one Anglican clergyman to raise the familiar cry that Quakers and Catholics were in secret league with each other. Rev. John Talbot, minister of Saint Mary's Church in Burlington, New Jersey, complained that "Mass is set up and read publicly in Philadelphia, and several people are turned to it,"[26] and he stridently 221
reported to the Society for the Propagation of the Gospel that

> There's an Independency at Elizabethtown, Anabaptism at Burlington, and the Popish Mass at Philadelphia. I thought the Quakers would be the first to let it in, particularily Mr. Penn, for if he has any religion, 'tis that.[27]

The small group of Catholics in Pennsylvania at that time was usually not so ostentatious in their religious celebrations, meeting as they did in private houses, and only occasionally favored with the ministrations of an itinerant Maryland Jesuit.[28] That invisibility, however, only served to increase the anti-papists' fears that there were many more Catholics and Jesuits operating in a clandestine manner.[29] The major differences between sixteenth-century England and eighteenth-century Pennsylvania notwithstanding, the inherited prejudice against popery remained so strong that it could still magnify minor incidents into major crises.

Talbot's report, however, indicates that there was more to the

---

William Penn and James Logan (Phila., 1872), II, 294.

[26] Rev. John Talbot to Rev. George Keith, 14 February 1708, quoted in *ACHR*, new series, I (1905), 122.

[27] 10 January 1708, quoted in *RACHSP*, I (1884-6), 80.

[28] Kirlin, *Catholicity*, 31-2.

[29] This belief was popular in the colonies even before Penn's grant. In 1680, two Labadist ministers in passing through New York reported "We are in every one's eye and yet nobody knew what to make of us. . .Some declared we were French emissaries going through the land to spy it out; others, that we were Jesuits travelling over the country for the same purpose." Bartlett B. James and J. Franklin Jameson, eds., *Journal of Jasper Danckaerts*, 1679-1680 (N.Y., 1913), 249.

maintenance of anti-popery in Pennsylvania than mere inherited prejudice against an alien creed. Until the 1740's overt anti-popery was almost the exclusive preserve of the Anglican clergy. All Protestants, including the Quakers, shared an antagonism for popery, but only the Church of England felt compelled to use that popular medium to explain certain events. After the 1740's the Presbyterians joined the Anglicans on the anti-popery stage.

All religious organizations had some difficulty in adapting to the new and unexpected conditions in Pennsylvania, a society which was referred to as "hell for preachers."[30] The Anglican, and later the Presbyterian, Church, accustomed to state support in Europe, were especially disoriented. The Quakers and other sectarians, the pariahs of European society, seemed to fare much better in the New World. Unlike the churches, whose ministers were separated from laymen by education, vocation, and ordination, the sects chose their leaders from the congregation with no special qualifications. Weakened by the absence of a resident bishop with powers of ordination and discipline, the Anglicans were always hampered by a shortage of reputable ministers.

Every loss of souls to the Church of England in Pennsylvania was attributed to the political power of the Quakers and to their principle of toleration. Toleration was assailable because it opened the door to popery in the colony. When they were unsuccessful in installing one of their own as schoolmaster in Chester in 1741, the Anglicans argued that "the Quakers, with all their power and ill offices," had worked to drive him away and "set up another, not one of their own sort truly, but a native Irish biggoted Papist."[31] The specter of popery was used to explain "the thinness of Churches in this part of the world," as two Philadelphia Anglican ministers expressed it. "Great advantages are given to dissenting preachers and Romish priests, to seduce the people and add to their own numbers, already but too great."[32]

Even internal problems, arising more from the scarcity of preachers and the weakness of disciplinary agencies than anything else, were

[30] Gottlieb Mittelberger, *Journey to Pennsylvania*, ed. and trans. Oscar Handlin and John Clive (Cambridge, Mass., 1960), 48.

[31] Richard Backhouse to the Secretary of S.P.G., 25 July 1741, William S. Perry, ed., *Historical Collections Relating to the American Colonial Church*, (Hartford, Conn., 1871), II, 216.

[32] William Sturgeon and John Hughes to the Secretary of S.P.G., 23 March 1765, *ibid.*, II, 374. See also, *ibid.*, II, 4, 6, 68, 69, 82, 105, 135, 161, 162, 178, 182-3, 294, 358-9, 404-5.

explained in terms of the ancient popish threat and Quaker-Catholic collaboration. One Anglican priest, Francis Philipps, was accused in 1714 of having debauched three gentlewomen of Philadelphia. As the case wore on, however, defenders of Philipps appeared who argued that he was the victim of a popish conspiracy. Governor Charles Gookin and others pointed out that one of the accusers was "a reputed Roman Catholick," obviously insinuating that the testimony of a papist was not to be trusted.[33] Another defender asserting that Philipps "hath been vehemently abused and persecuted by a Popish crew," charged that the Anglican rector of Burlington, Rev. John Talbot, was "more like to be a Jesuit or a father confessor," and came to the conclusion that "the Quakers combined with the highflyers as so called but more fitly stiled 223
Papists to try our Minister by their illegal Laws."[34]

After Penn's death in 1718, Quaker-Catholic collaboration remained a fixture of anti-popery, and it was reinforced by the less invisible threats posed by increasing foreign immigration. In the 1720's, Pennsylvania began to be flooded with immigrant Redemptioners and convicts from the German Palatinate and from Northern Ireland. In 1728, Lieutenant Governor Patrick Gordon appealed to the Assembly to "provide a proper law against these crowds of Foreigners" and to "prevent the importation of Irish Papists and convicts." Yet, even though the Quaker Assembly responded by asserting that such action was necessary for "the Preservation both of Religious and Civil Rights of the People of this Province," the final bill omitted the word "Papists" and merely placed a duty on the importation of "Irish servants and Persons of Redemption."[35]

The prospect of increased foreign immigration seemed to present an internal security threat as well as a religous one during the frequent eighteenth-century wars of England against France and Spain and their Indian allies. The growing strategic importance of exposed Pennsylvania in those wars placed that colony in a position analagous to that of exposed England during the wars of religion. Thus, anti-popery gained added strength. Already in 1688, there had been reported the alleged connivance of "Papists" with the northern Indians to "cut off the

[33] Gov. Charles Gookin and Others to the Bishop of London, 7 March 1715, *ibid.*, II, 87.

[34] John Newberry to Mr. Vesey, 30 November 1715, *ibid.*, II, 95.

[35] *PCR* [Pennsylvania Colonial Records], I, 299, III, 546-7; *PA* [Pennsylvania Archives], 4th ser., I, 455, 896.

Protestants, or at least to reduce them to the See of Rome."[36] In 1710, the governor of Pennsylvania told the Provincial Council that a Peter Bezalion,"a Frenchman and a *Roman Catholic*, a trader among the Indians at Conestogue, had lately spoken some suspicious words and done some misdemeanor."[37] At councils held in 1721, and again in 1732, the government warned the Indians "not to be deluded by their Jesuits and Interpreters" who came among them speaking only of peace.[38]

Anti-papists' fears of internal enemies—or their use of those fears for political or denominational reasons—increased in spite of the scarcity of Catholics in Pennsylvania in the fifty-five years preceding the American
224 Revolution. There were only 37 of them in a Philadelphia numbering in 1732 a total of 12,000 persons.[39] One Anglican clergyman admitted in 1738 that "I know but four or five Papists in all my circuit," but he felt compelled to add that "there are many reputed ones in the quakers' Garb & Frequent their meetings."[40] In 1745 another Anglican minister complained that Philadelphia "is much infested with Popery," when in fact there were less than 140 Catholics in the whole county.[41] When there were less than 88 Catholics in Reading, a Protestant resident there worried because they were "very numerous in this County."[42] Anglican Provost William Smith of Philadelphia in 1759 reported that there were 10,000 Catholics in the colony out of a total population of 250,000, when existing records indicate that Catholics numbered only about 1,500.[43] National and religious antipathy, plus the unsettled state of affairs in a booming Pennsylvania, combined in anti-papist

[36] *PA*, 4th ser., I, 138, 141; *PCR*, I, 277, 279.

[37] *PCR*, II, 530.

[38] *PCR*, III, 129-130, 441.

[39] *RACHSP*, I (1884-6), 79.

[40] Richard Backhouse to the Secretary of S.P.G., 9 December 1738, Perry, ed., *Historical Collections*, II, 202.

[41] "This City [Phila.] is very much infested with Popery & sysmatical divisions among the Protestant Inhabitants & its influence spreads into the Country. There is scarce a Missionary but complains of one or other & many of both." Robert Jenney to the Secretary of S.P.G., 14 November 1745, *ibid.*, II, 236.

[42] J. Bennett Nolan, *The Foundation of the Town of Reading in Pennsylvania* (Reading, Pa., 1929), 152-6.

[43] Horace Wemyss Smith, *Life and Correspondence of the Rev. William Smith, D.D.* (Phila., 1879-80), I, 219; *PA*, IV, 144; "Report of Bishop Challoner to Rev. Dr. Stoner, Clergy Agent at Rome, September 14, 1756," *ACHR*, XIII (1896), 35.

exaggeration of the size and power of an internal "threat" of a group which comprised only .6% of the total population.

There were always sufficient visible reminders, however, to fuel anti-papist suspicions of the nearly invisible popish enemy. In 1733, for example, Catholics in Philadelphia erected their first official religious structure in any of the colonies, Saint Joseph's Church, immediately adjacent to the Quaker Almshouse. Complaints were soon made that such open display of popery was contrary to the laws of England. The Pennsylvania Council responded in 1734, however, that Penn's Charter of Privileges guaranteeing free exercise of religion antedated those laws passed in the reign of William III and had not been repealed.[44]

The symbolic significance inherent in the proximity of the two structures was not lost on anti-papists. In 1737, a British writer charged, in terms strongly reminiscent of the accusations made against William Penn in England, that

> In the town of Philadelphia. . .is a public Popish Chapel, where that religion has free and open exercise, and in it all the superstitious rites of that Church are as avowedly performed as those of the Church of England are in the royal chapel of Saint James. And this chapel is not only open upon fasts and festivals, but is so all day and every day in the week, and exceedingly frequented at all hours either for publick or private devotion, tho' it is fullest. . .at those times when the meeting house of the men of Saint Omers is thinnest, and so *vice versa*.[45]

After 1740, rumors of popish plots proliferated as Pennsylvania shared in the shocks of King George's War and the French and Indian War, as foreign immigration continued to transform the political and social complexion of the colony, and as schism wreaked temporary havoc on many church organizations while leaving the Quakers untouched.[46] At the beginning of both imperial wars, in 1740, and again in 1755, Quakers helped protect the recently constructed Saint Joseph's church from mobs of axe-wielding Presbyterians intent

[44] Kirlin, *Catholicity*, 32-4, 35, 39-40.

[45] *London Magazine and Monthly Chronologer*, 7 July 1737, quoted in *RACHSP*, I (1884-6), 83.

[46] Martin E. Lodge, "The Crisis of the Churches in the Middle Colonies, 1720-1750," *PMHB*, XCV (April, 1971), 202-216. See also, Frederick B. Tolles, "Quietism versus Enthusiasm: The Philadelphia Quakers and the Great Awakening," *PMHB*, LXXIX (1945), 26-49.

on destroying that concrete symbol of the inroads of popery in the colony.[47] Philadelphia newspapers in 1741 printed accounts of the trials and executions of those involved in an alleged Negro plot to burn New York City and massacre the white population, in which the supposed head conspirator, Anglican priest John Ury, was consistently described as "the Romish Priest."[48] George Whitefield's preaching in those years raised Anglican fears that he intended "to set up for the head of a sect" and that he was "supported under hand by deists & Jesuits or both."[49] Yet Whitefield was attacking the Anglican clergy as "Doctrinal Papists."[50] Still, twenty years later, Anglicans were explaining New
226 Light inroads by charging that "Romish Priests are busy among the people on the one hand and the Sectaries dependent on the Quaker on the other."[51] When Lutheran minister, Henry Melchior Muhlenberg, was on the point of setting out for South Carolina and Georgia, rumors circulated that his real purpose in going abroad was to celebrate Catholic mass for King George, who was said to have turned papist.[52] One Anglican minister in 1742 complained of the obstructions he and his colleagues met with in that "nursery of Jesuits," Pennsylvania. With great alarm he reported that

> no less than two priests are in Philadelphia, four in Conestoga. . .and what the end of Quaker power may prove we may painfully guess. Many Irish Papists turn Quaker and get into places as well as Germans.[53]

[47] Kirlin, *Catholicity*, 53; "Extracts from the Diary of Daniel Fisher, " *PMHB*, XVII (1893), 274.

[48] *Documents Relating to the Colonial History of the State of New York*, III, 198, 201; Kirlin, *Catholicity*, 54.

[49] Archibald Cummings to the Secretary of S.P.G., 29 August 1740, Perry, ed., *Historical Collections*, II, 203. At the same time in Connecticut, a group of Moravians was being persecuted because rumor had it that they were Jesuits in disguise working among the Indians. *Public Records of the Colony of Connecticut*, 1636-1776 (Hartford, Conn., 1850-1890), VIII, 521.

[50] Archibald Cummings to the Secretary of S.P.G., 31 July 1740, Perry, ed., *Historical Collections*, II, 210-211.

[51] William Smith to the Secretary of S.P.G., 26 August 1760, *ibid.*, II, 325-6.

[52] Tappert and Doberstein, eds., *Journals of Muhlenberg*, II, 693.

[53] Colin Campbell to the Secretary of S.P.G., 2 November 1742, quoted in *ACHR*, VI (1889), 183. Joseph Greaton, S.J., was the only resident Catholic priest in Pennsylvania from 1729 until 1741 when he was joined by Henry Neale, S.J., William Wappler, S.J., and Theodore Schneider, S.J. But by 1749, there was again only one priest—Robert Harding, S.J. In 1758, Ferdinand Farmer, S.J., arrived, but after 1772, when Harding died, he too was alone. In 1773, Robert Molyneux, S.J., joined Farmer. This small number of priests was

Every move of the imagined army of Catholic missionaries was scrutinized.[54]

By the 1740's Penn's sons, Richard and Thomas, had left the Society of Friends for the Church of England, the Quakers in Pennsylvania no longer comprised a majority of the population, and the immigration of Germans and Scots-Irish Presbyterians had complicated the social and political situation. The Presbyterians settled largely in the militarily exposed frontier areas and were therefore sensitive to issues of wartime defense. In addition, in 1740, Presbyterian clergymen were faced with increasing lay independence in church affairs, a situation which was exacerbated by the inability to provide enough ministers for the swelling Presbyterian population and by the turmoil created by the Great Awakening. Scots-Irish Presbyterians, led by William Allen, joined with the Anglicans and the Proprietors in attacks on the Quaker party in the Assembly for refusing to pass a militia law and otherwise provide for defense against the Catholic French and their Indian allies on the frontier. On the other side, the Germans, who by 1755 comprised nearly one-half of the population of Pennsylvania, consistently supported the continuance of Quaker power.[55]

Other colonies also believed they recognized the implications of Quaker policies and German immigration, and that perception contributed to the maintenance of anti-popery. In March, 1744, Governor Lewis Morris of New Jersey expressed his anxiety to Governor George Clinton of New York that

> They have there [Pa.] a popish chapel and numbers of Irish and Germans that are Papists and I am told that should the French appear and 1500 to 2000 men, they would in that Province soon get ten or twelve thousands together, which

---

responsible for five far-flung churches and congregations in seven Pennsylvania counties, eleven New Jersey counties, one in Delaware, and one in New York. They were thus almost constantly on the road. Kirlin, *Catholicity*, 26-7, 45, 47, 74, 94, 96, 97.

[54] Richard Backhouse reported in 1742 that "in Lancaster there is a priest settled, and they have bought some lots and are building a Mass House" and "there is another itinerant priest that goes back in the Country." Six years later, he was alarmed that "as to ye Papists, we find more in numbers, than ye particular number of Families I us'd to mention in my *Notitia Parochialis*," but "how many more, it is impossible for me to tell." Backhouse to the Secretary of S.P.G., 14 June 1742 and 26 June 1748, Perry, ed., *Historical Collections*, II, 232, 252. Richard Locke at Lancaster wrote in that same year that "the country is so much overrun with Jesuitism, Moravians and New Lights." Locke to S.P.G., 29 September 1748, *ibid.*, II, 253.

[55] Theodore Thayer, *Pennsylvania Politics and the Growth of Democracy*, 1740-1776 (Harrisburg, Pa., 1953), 11-19, 36; Lodge, "The Crisis of the Churches," 202-216.

would in that case, be not a little dangerous to these and neighboring colonies.[56]

When Charles Edward Stuart invaded England in 1745, more evidence appeared of a trans-Atlantic papist conspiracy. On January 8, Lieutenant Governor George Thomas informed the Pennsylvania Assembly that "a most unnatural Rebellion had broke out, . . . in favor of a Popish Pretender, supported by France and Spain."[57] On April 24, the "Covenanted Presbyterians in America" assembled in Philadelphia, and resolved that

> 228 we being threatened with trouble by a Popish Pretender and with the Indians going with the French we judge our indispensable duty immediately to draw up ourselves in companies to exercise, in order to prepare for war, if necessary called thereto for the defence of our sacred and civil rights.[58]

Pennsylvania rejoiced when the Battle of Culloden proved the undoing of Bonnie Prince Charlie. Governor Thomas proclaimed July 24, 1746, a day of thanksgiving for the "completest victory over ungrateful and rebellious subjects encouraged and supported by our ancient and inveterate enemies, the French and Spaniards" and by "that monster of Iniquity the Court of Rome."[59] The churches of Pennsylvania, like those of England, held services of thanksgiving for the fortuitous discovery of the Jacobite plot "first hatched in hell, and afterwards nursed in Rome."[60] On August 24, George Whitefield, only lately having been under suspicion as a Jesuit collaborator, harangued his listeners in Philadelphia concerning their happy deliverance from the rule of the Pretender, the loss of English liberty, and vassalage to Rome. If England had failed, he queried,

> how soon would whole swarms of monks, dominicans and friars, like so many locusts, have overspread and plagued the nation; with what winged speed would foreign titular bishops have posted over, in order to take possession of their respective sees? How quickly would our universities have been filled with youths who have been sent abroad by their popish parents, in order to drink in

[56] Quoted in Kirlin, *Catholicity*, 55.

[57] *PCR*, V, 6.

[58] Quoted in Kirlin, *Catholicity*, 57.

[59] Kirlin, *Catholicity*, 57.

[60] George Whitefield, *Works* (London, 1771), V, 82.

all the superstitions of the church of Rome."[61]

Even Benjamin Franklin was caught up in the contagion. " 'Tis well known," he argued in *Plain Truth on the present state of the City of Philadelphia* written in 1747, "that we have a number of the same religion with those who of late encouraged the French to invade the Mother-country." A major source of danger to Pennsylvania, he continued, was the Six Nations because of their conversion by French missionaries. To stave off the threat, Pennsylvanians had to rely upon the children of those brave people who in former times had "made so glorious a stand for our religion and liberties, when invaded by a powerful French army, joined by Irish Catholics, under a bigoted 229
Popish King."[62] Similarly, in 1748 Lieutenant Colonel Thomas James appealed to the militia to uphold "the Glory, Strength and Prop of a Protestant Government. . .the Protestant Religion Conscientiously held in its Purity" lest it be "trodden under foot by the bloody and tyrannical power of Popery." It was well-known, he added, that

> we have numerous, or rather numberless enemies amongst us, many of them fed at our tables, and nursed at our bosoms, as it were, who are ill-wishers to the Protestant interest, and may, if they have an opportunity, rise to such a height in rebellion that neither Church discipline nor civil law can quash them.[63]

The near-hysteria nourished by the sense of impotency in the face of an invisible and uncontrollable, yet "self-evident" internal enemy reached its peak with the outbreak of the French and Indian War. New Light clergymen, such as George Whitefield and Gilbert Tennent, portrayed French activity on the frontier as part of a papal conspiracy.[64] William Smith, an Anglican, in sermons and in his pamphlet *A Brief State of the Province of Pennsylvania*, constantly belabored the supposed threat of Irish and German Pennsylvanians uniting with the French and Indians to cut the throats of all good

[61] *Ibid.*, V, 82, 84.

[62] Benjamin Franklin, *Plain Truth on the present state of the City of Philadelphia* (Phila., 1747).

[63] Reported in *Pennsylvania Gazette*, 13 June 1754.

[64] *Pennsylvania Journal*, 25 December 1754; Sister Mary Augustina Ray, *American Opinion of Roman Catholicism in the Eighteenth Century* (New York, 1936), 95 n. 90.

Protestants.[65] Many sober citizens reared in the tradition of anti-popery, while admitting Smith's exaggerations, agreed with his overall accusations.[66] Political writers, such as Philanthropos, addressed the colony through the newspapers. "Can we endure the thought," he asked rhetorically,

> of having our children enslaved by the Church of Rome and forced contrary to the Light of their Minds, either to comply with all its idolatrous superstitions or fall a sacrifice to the cruel and bloody zeal of bigotted Priests, and their blinded Followers, who think they do God a good service by cutting off such as they call Heretics from the face of the earth, and such, in their esteem, are all those who are not of their Community. Nor will it afford us a more agreeable
> 230 prospect to view the tender offspring of our dear children, whom Priestly Rage has murdered, sitting at the feet of those inhuman butchers and meekly receiving for divine Truths, all the monstrous Tenets of that anti-Christian Church; and how cutting the consideration, that we ourselves should be accessory to all those intolerable Evils.[67]

The Pennsylvania press also helped to spread the contagion by reprinting inflammatory sermons and addresses from other colonies and from England.[68]

The Justices of Berks County expressed their alarm in an address to the governor on July 23, 1755. Some Catholics had allegedly shown great joy at the news of Braddock's defeat, and, the petition demanded that they should be disarmed or otherwise controlled. The Justices reported that around Goshenhoppen, where the Catholics had a "magnificent chapel," thirty Indians were lurking, "well armed with Guns and Swords or Cutlasses." It was further rumored that the priests who administered to Reading and Goshenhoppen every four weeks had told their congregations that they would not be returning for nine weeks, an absence interpreted as occasioned by a visit to Fort Duquesne to consult with the French for some treasonous purpose. The Justices concluded by complaining that it was

[65] *Pennsylvania Gazette*, 24, June 1755; William Smith, *A Brief State of the Province of Pennsylvania* (London, 1755); Horace W. Smith, ed., *Works of William Smith* (Phila., 1803), II, 20, 22, 91, 107.

[66] Thomas Graeme to Thomas Penn, 1 July 1755, quoted in Kirlin, *Catholicity*, 79-80.

[67] *Pennsylvania Gazette*, 5 September 1754.

[68] *Pennsylvania Gazette*, 29 August 1754 and 1 May 1755. Other anti-popery polemics from England were carried in the same newspaper on June 12 and July 17, 1755.

> a great Unhappiness at this Time to the other People of this Province that the Papists should keep Arms in their Houses, against which the Protestants are not prepared, who therefore are subject to a Massacre whenever the Papists are ready.[69]

The Assembly took no action on this petition because a committee of investigation reported that the Indians at Goshenhoppen—six warriors with their wives and children—were beggars, the recipients of Catholic Rev. Theodore Schneider's charity. Again in October, another alarm was raised as thirteen-hundred French and Indians were said to be approaching, and again investigation proved that the rumor was unfounded.[70]

These rumors were grounded in the real shock of British military defeat in the first years of the war, and anti-popery provided a more palatable explanation than British military blunders. The nationalistic, theological, and opportunistic components of the stereotype provided a buffer against harsh reality. But that perennial bugbear of Protestantism, a sense of moral guilt, also provided its share. The advance of popery was seen as punishment for moral failing. In a sense, the internal enemy which had to be expurgated was guilt over failure in colonial society taken advantage of by French Catholics. Failure to gain converts, failure to combat religious indifference, and failure to hold the allegiance of the Indians were explainable both as the result of popish machinations, and as the cause of the ascendancy of popery over true religion. One frontier Anglican minister seemed to understand this when he lamented that British traders had consistently cheated the Indians while "the French always paid them well for their Skins, &c.; built houses for them; instructed their children and took care of their wives when they went to war." He added sadly that

> While the French were industrious in sending Priests and Jesuits among them, to convert them to Popery, we did nothing but send a set of abandon'd profligate men to trade with them who defrauded and cheated them, and practic'd every vice among them that can be named, which set the English and the Protestant Religion in such a disadvantageous light, that we have reason to fear they detest the name of both.[71]

[69] *PCR*, VI, 503, 533.

[70] H.W.Kriebal, "The Schwenkfelders in Pennsylvania," *Pennsylvania German Society Proceedings*, XII (1902), 141-2.

[71] Thomas Barton to the Secretary of S.P.G., 8 November 1756, Perry, ed., *Historical*

Paranoia regarding internal enemies was also augmented by ethnic fear and political opportunism. Among others, Benjamin Franklin had long been concerned with the enormous immigration of Germans into the colony. In 1752 he had recommended that all non-English speaking people should be barred from holding civil or military office. He also believed the importation of German books should be prohibited, that all legal documents should be in English only, that a quota should be placed on German immigration, and that intermarriage should be encouraged to force the Germans to assimilate more rapidly. In addition, he proposed that English schools be established among the Germans to Anglicize the children of these clannish people.[72]

William Smith believed that there were already 100,000 Germans in a total population of 250,000, and knew "nothing that will hinder them, either from soon being able to give us Law and Language, or else by joining with the French, to eject all the English Inhabitants." He bemoaned, in *A Brief State*, of the

> extraordinary indulgence and privileges granted to Papists in this Province—privileges plainly repugnant to all our political interests considered as a frontier colony, bordering on the French and one half of the people an uncultivated Race of Germans, liable to be seduced by every enterprising Jesuit, having almost no Protestant clergy among them to put them on their guard and warn them against Popery. . . .

He argued that the French "have turned their hopes upon this great body of Germans" and therefore had sent Jesuit missionaries among them "to persuade them over to the Popish religion" and "draw them over to the French in multitudes." Despite the fact that only .9% of the Germans in Pennsylvania were Catholics, Smith claimed that

> there are near one-fourth of the Germans supposed to be Roman Catholics who cannot be supposed friends to any design for defending the country against the French. Many are Moravians who hold some tenets and customs. . .very much akin to those of the Roman Catholics.[73]

Collections, II, 280.

[72] Thayer, *Pennsylvania Politics*, 35.

[73] Quotations from William Smith, *A Brief State*. Statistics on Catholic Germans are found in *PCR*, VII, 447. Thomas Barton agreed with Smith's accusations. On 8 November 1762, he wrote to the S.P.G. that "Popery has gained considerable ground in Pennsylvania of late years. The professors of that Religion here are chiefly Germans who are constantly supplied with missionarys from the Society of Jesus, as they are pleased to stile themselves. One of that order

Other Anglican ministers confirmed Smith's speculations, but were perhaps more upset that in all of Pennsylvania by 1764 only one-fiftieth of the people belonged to the Church of England.[74]

The result of all this furor over supposed internal enemies was twofold. For one, a society for English schools among the Germans was established, with Benjamin Franklin, William Smith, William Allen, and Conrad Weiser among the trustees. Many Germans, including influential editor Christopher Sauer, opposed the idea, and by 1756 the experiment had failed. The Quakers also opposed the project because they sensed, and rightly so, that under the guise of war-time defense, cultural homogeneity, and anti-Catholicism lay a political stratagem by the Proprietary party to separate the German vote from the Quakers. Indeed, as William Smith had already said, if the Germans were properly instructed, "so as to be capable of using their own judgment in matters of Government, they would no more be misled by Acts of a Quaker preacher, than a lurking French priest."[75] In Smith, British colonial ethnocentrism was taken to the extreme of identifying good judgment in religion and politics as a byproduct of the English language.

Secondly, generations of fruitless searching for hidden popish enemies manifested itself in a witch-hunt for subversive Catholics in Pennsylvania. The first victims were the 454 French Acadians deported from their homeland by the British and dumped in Philadelphia in November 1755. Many Pennsylvanians feared that these newcomers would join with their fellow countrymen on the frontier and accomplish some pincer-like aggression along with the imagined swarms of Irish and German Catholics already in the colony. These Acadians were at first quartered in "neutral huts" in Philadelphia, where Anthony Benezet, a Quaker, and Rev. Robert Harding, a Catholic, cared for them. Later they were distributed throughout the province, one family to each township.[76] On March 21, 1757, five of the exiles were arrested at the

---

resides in this place [Lancaster], and had influence enough last Summer to get a very elegant Chapel of hewn Stone erected in this Town. Their behaviour in outward appearance is quiet and inoffensive; but they have been often suspected during this war of communicating intelligence to the Enemies of our Religion and Country." Perry, ed., *Historical Collections*, II, 343.

[74] George Craig to the Secretary of S.P.G., 3 September 1764, Perry, ed., *Historical Collections*, II, 361.

[75] Thayer, *Pennsylvania Politics*, 36.

[76] Lawrence Henry Gipson, *The Great War for the Empire* (London, 1946), VI, 242-344;

request of Lord Loudoun as fomenters of treasonous mischief. After serving time on a prison ship, they were allowed to return to Philadelphia in 1758, where the arrival of such "bigoted papists" proved "*very* disagreeable to the people."[77] Despite anti-papists' fears, the conditions of the Acadians' confinement and the rapid reduction of their numbers by disease eliminated them as a real internal threat.

In 1756, the story of another popish plot was concocted on the basis of allegedly treasonous correspondence. Certain persons in the colony were purported to be designing to sell out England's interests to the French.[78] Rumors surrounding the plot spread far, for on July 9, Sir
234 George Hardy, governor of New York, wrote to Pennsylvania's Governor Robert Morris that he was "rather Inclined to think the Treasonable Correspondence must have been carried on by some Roman Catholics." Hardy had learned, he explained, that "you have an ingenious Jesuit in Philadelphia."[79]

The tensions of war merely stimulated further an audience already conditioned to accept when the *American Magazine, or Monthly Chronicle for the British Colonies* warned Pennsylvanians of the number and wealth of the Jesuits in Maryland, and the danger of having such a stronghold of popery in the very heart of the colonies.[80] Many believed the truth of the relationships drawn in a 1764 cartoon: a house being destroyed by fire, Indians killing settlers, and a Quaker astride a Catholic Priest.[81] Already in 1755, the Catholic church in Philadelphia had been narrowly saved from destruction by a mob; but on December 15, 1760, the Catholic church in Lancaster was completely destroyed by enraged Protestants.[82]

The legislature was finally moved to action by popular pressure. Catholics were disarmed, disallowed from serving in the militia, forced to pay double taxes, and those residing in the colony were registered so

---

PCR, VII, 5-20, 44, 45, 239, 241, 293, 446; *PA*, II, 573, III, 565-8, 4th ser., I, 549, 554, 579; W.B. Reed, "The Acadian Exiles, or French Neutrals, in Pennsylvania, to which is appended A Relation of their Misfortunes by John Baptiste Galeron," *Memoirs of the Historical Society of Pennsylvania*, VI (1858), 285, 289.

[77] *PCR*, VII, 32; Gipson, *The Great War*, VI, 310-318.

[78] Intercepted correspondence is in *RACHSP*, X (1899), 208-221.

[79] *PA*, II, 694.

[80] October 1757-October 1758, 345, 352-4, 510.

[81] Plate in Thayer, *Pennsylvania Politics*, facing p. 89.

[82] *Pennsylvania Gazette*, 25 December 1760.

that their every movement could be scrutinized.[83] Recruiting instructions forbade the enlistment of non-Englishmen unless they could definitely be identified as Protestants. Spies were everywhere busily earning their informer's reward and summoning unoffending citizens before the courts.[84] For example, the Irish extraction of Indian traders George Croghan and Francis Campbell was enough to bring them under suspicion.[85] The Assembly even attempted to prohibit Catholics from holding land in the colony, but this measure was blocked by the governor. The Assembly did succeed, however, in preventing Catholic settlement in a planned western buffer colony.[86]

Overt harrying of suspected papists declined once the French threat
was removed from North America by the Peace of Paris. Colonists took 235
pride in membership in the victorious British empire. Anglican optimism for a resolution of their long-standing institutional problems in Pennsylvania soared in the post-war period as clergymen eyed the newly-won lands in Canada as their salvation from the unfair competition of the sectarians in Pennsylvania.[87] Rev. Thomas Barton recommended to the S.P.G. that "the lands lately belonging to the Romish

[83] *PA*, III, 131-2, 144-5. The militia act was disallowed by George III for unrelated reasons. The return of April 28, 1757, showed 1,365 Catholics in Pennsylvania: 949 Germans and 416 Irish and English. *PCR*, VII, 447.

[84] *PA*, 2nd ser., II, 594-5; *PCR*, II, 344; *PA*, III, 16-17.

[85] *PA*, II, 114, 228-9, 694; C.H.Browning, "Francis Campbell," *PMHB*, XXVII (1904), 63.

[86] *PCR*, IX, 596. Only Catholics who were British citizens could hold land in Pennsylvania. Foreign Catholics were barred from naturalization, and therefore from owning land. This impediment was circumvented by an English or Irish Catholic holding land in trust for the foreigner. Kirlin, *Catholicity*, 58 n. 3. Even though barred from holding land in the province, a foreign Catholic like Joseph Cauffman, who arrived from Germany in 1749, could become a large investor in lands in Philadelphia, Chester, Bucks, Westmoreland, Indiana, Blair, and Montgomery Counties. Theodore F. Rodenbough, ***Autumn Leaves from Family Trees*** (New York, 1892), 13-14. In at least one case, that of Simon Rüffner, a foreign practicing Catholic took the oath of allegiance to the Crown and to the Church of England, and so was allowed to purchase land. Jane S. Sweinberger, ***Ruffners of Pennsylvania and Collateral Lines***, 1743-1978 (San Diego, Calif., 1979), 16-24.

[87] "It is the unanimous opinion of all here who wish well to the preservation & enlargement of the Church, that in the Settlement of our late conquests in America application should be made in the very beginning for the allotment of Lands towards the support of a Clergy regularly ordained in our Church, after the example of the French, who constantly pursued this scheme in Canada, & thereby maintained a numerous Body of priests and Jesuits, who are over zealous and active in proselyting [sic] the Natives and sowing among them the seeds of prejudice and antipathy against the British." Alexander Murray to the Secretary of S.P.G., 25 January 1764, Perry, ed., *Historical Collections*, II, 357.

Clergy in Canada, are sufficient to support a Bishop in America, and a number of Missionaries in the new Conquests, without adding to the burden of the Mother Country."[88]

In such an atmosphere, there was a positive shift away from anti-papist diatribes by the Anglican clergy. Even William Smith began referring to Catholic Father Harding as "a worthy Jesuit" and insisted that Harding "was always in good Terms with us."[89] Charges of Quaker-Catholic collaboration ceased because Anglican leaders perceived their real enemy now to be the more numerous Presbyterians who, as Smith asserted in 1768, "from one end of the Continent to the other are attacking the Church about American Bishops."[90] His colleague in Newcastle County, Philip Reading, contended that "Our present danger indeed doth not arise so much from the avowed designs of Papists against the Church, but from the attempts of Dissenters of various kinds."[91] Once again the Church of England found itself on the receiving end of anti-papist attacks as she had in sixteenth and seventeenth-century England.

The extreme aggressiveness of non-Anglicans against the establishment of an episcopacy in America was just one aspect of a growing alienation in the colonies with certain developments in the mother-country. Just when trans-Atlantic national and cultural bonds seemed the strongest, Protestants in Pennsylvania and other colonies thought they perceived a definite back-sliding into the errors of popery in England. Already there were ominous rumblings out of New England.[92]

As in its earlier phases, intellectual or religious anti-popery was inseparable from anti-popery grounded in social and political sources. Attempts by the mother-country in the 1760's to make the colonies more productive within the mercantilist system appeared to many to signal a shift toward centralization and a limitation of Protestant individualism.

[88] Barton to the Secretary of S.P.G., 16 November 1764, *ibid.*, II, 368.

[89] Smith to the Lord Bishop of London, 13 October 1773, *ibid.*, II, 462.

[90] William Smith to the Secretary of S.P.G., 6 May 1768, *ibid.*, II, 427. Hugh Neill also complained that "The Dissenters very well know that the sending of a Bishop to America would contribute more to the increase of the Church here than all the money that has been raised by the Venerable Society for the Propagation of the Gospel." Neill to the Secretary of S.P.G., 19 May 1766, *ibid.*, II, 405.

[91] Philip Reading to the Secretary of S.P.G., 15 March 1775, *ibid.*, II, 469.

[92] Jonathon Mayhew, *Popish Idolatry*, 50.

The spectre of Charles I and James II was raised again. An emerging yet incoherent resistance movement began to identify nationally and culturally no longer with Great Britain in general, but with British dissidents; and both opposition groups justified themselves by claiming a greater purity and consistency with traditional Protestant English values.[93]

The Quebec Act of 1774 provided a confirmation of American fears and a whipping boy for American and English demagogues. The law activated all the components of the traditional anti-papist stereotype which for generations had provided easy explanations for complex issues, security in a changing society, comfortable links to some glorious national past, and powerful political weapons in the hands of opportunists. The Act stirred up a new wave of ferocious anti-popery producing a temporary unifying element for all the disparate provincial resistance movements.[94]

One London agitator opened his attack on the Bill with "if this don't rouse the most lethargic man amongst you I shall be amazed."[95] Another Englishman prodded the well-known sensitivities of his Pennsylvania readers, in particular frontier Presbyterians, by asking "Must Protestants mourn while Papists rejoice? We believe to keep a large body of Popish Canadians in *terrorem* against our Protestant Brethren in America the true ground and principle of the Bill."[96] Pennsylvania newspapers carried the story of the king's encounter with the London mob as he rode to Parliament to sign the Act, their jeers and their suspicion that the case of the sword of state contained in reality a popish crucifix.[97] The *Pennsylvania Packet* printed a widely circulated English ballad, "A New Song," representing "Goody" North singing a lullaby "to the foundling brat, the Popish Quebec Bill." The last stanza read

> Then heigh for the penance and pardons,
> And heigh for the faggots and fires;

[93] Pauline Maier, *From Resistance to Revolution: Colonial Radicals and the Development of American Opposition to Britain*, 1765-1776 (New York, 1972), 161-248.

[94] "Selections from the Letter-Books of Thomas Wharton of Philadelphia, 1773-1783," *PMHB*, XXXIII (1909), 319, 441, XXXIV (1910), 41; Anne Izard Deas, ed., *Correspondence of Mr. Ralph Izard of South Carolina*, 1774-1804 (New York, 1844), I, 28; *ACHR*, VI (Oct., 1889), 147, VII-VIII (1911-12), 391.

[95] *Pennsylvania Gazette*, 28 September 1774.

[96] Tribunus, "Letter to the King," 30 June 1774, *London Evening Post*, in *Pennsylvania Gazette*, 16 September 1774.

[97] *Pennsylvania Gazette*, 24 August 1774.

And heigh for the Popish Church wardens,
And heigh for the Priests and the Friars;
And heigh for the rareshew relics,
To follow my Canada Bill-e,
With all the Pope's mountebank tricks;
So prithee, my baby, lie still-e.
Then up with the Papists, up, up,
And down with the Protestants, down-e;
Here we go backwards and forwards,
All for the good of the crown-e.[98]

Pennsylvania opponents of the Bill deplored the Quebec Act as
238 "openly countenancing Popish conspiracies" designed solely for the destruction of Protestant Americans by Catholic Canadians.[99] "We may live," one writer declared, "to see our churches converted into mass houses and our lands plundered by tythes for the support of the Popish clergy." The logical outcome of the Act was that "the Inquisition may erect her standard in Pennsylvania and the city may yet experience the carnage of St. Bartholomew's Day."[100] Fulfillment of this prophecy seemed near when several Pennsylvania newspapers reported that a popish army of thirty thousand Canadians was being formed to subdue colonial troublemakers.[101] One writer illustrated what might be expected from the change in Canada by reviewing the persecution of Protestants in Europe in the previous two centuries. All that remained to make the resemblance complete was "to introduce the inquisition at Quebec, and to erect Lord North's statue at Boston, in the posture of the Duke of Alva's at Antwerp, trampling upon the expiring liberties of America."[102]

Sermons against the Act were preached throughout the colony, and the Presbyterian clergy of Pennsylvania appealed to the memory of past warfare against popery in their *Address to the Ministers and Presbyterian Congregations in North Carolina*.[103] An "Association of Protestant

[98] *Pennsylvania Packet*, 29 August 1774.

[99] *Pennsylvania Journal*, 5 October 1774.

[100] *Pennsylvania Packet*, 31 October 1774.

[101] *Pennsylvania Gazette*, 19 October 1774; *Pennsylvania Journal*, 2 November 1774. See also *Pennsylvania Gazette*, 14 September, 12 October 1774; *Pennsylvania Journal*, 14 September, 5 October 1774; *Pennsylvania Packet*, 19 August 1774.

[102] *Pennsylvania Gazette*, 21 & 28 September 1774, 26 July 1775.

[103] *The State Records of North Carolina* (Goldsboro, N. Car., 1886-1907), X, 86, 222.

School Boys" canvassed Philadelphia collecting tea with which to feed "a BONFIRE on the memorable fifth day of [November], commonly called GUNPOWDER PLOT DAY." The bonfire was to commemorate the revival of an old custom "of exhibiting a piece of pageantry, to show their abhorrence and destestation of the *Pope*, Pretender, etc., and such of their *Adherents* as would overthrow the GOOD OLD ENGLISH CONSTITUTION."[104] Even the American Philosophical Society discontinued its meetings in protest against the "Bill for establishing popery and arbitrary power in Quebec."[105] Thomas Paine exclaimed "An aim of Parliament was to subvert the Protestant Religion" by "the Roman Catholic Religion not tolerated but established."[106] The newly formed Continental Congress "in order that their Religion, Laws and Liberties may not be subverted" drew up appeals to the King and to the people of Great Britain. These addresses expressed astonishment "that a British Parliament should ever consent to establish in that country, a Religion that has deluged your Island in blood and dispersed Impiety, Bigotry, Persecution, Murder and Rebellion through every part of the World."[107]

The colonies thus began their separation from the mother-country by using the same arguments that had helped establish British national identity in the sixteenth century. In a sense, the tradition of anti-popery facilitated the creation of a new nation by permitting England to be cast off as morally corrupt and by allowing colonists to proudly assert that they were the real guardians of a Protestant ideal that had been lost elsewhere. The stereotype was universal enough, even in tolerant Pennsylvania, to provide the necessary bonding element for the resistance movement. It also allowed the labelling of pro-British sympathizers as internal enemies detrimental to both civil and religious freedom.

But anti-popery had served several functions even before the Revolution. It existed at two levels. The first was the level of actual theological differences and real fear of the destruction of Protestantism. As such, it should have provided a unifying element for a Protestantism wracked

[104] *Pennsylvania Journal*, 9 November 1774.

[105] *Early Proceedings of the American Philosophical Society for the Promotion of Useful Knowledge*, 1744-1838 (Phila., 1884), 87.

[106] Quoted in *ACHR*, new ser., II (1906), 10.

[107] Worthington Chauncey Ford, ed., *Journals of the Continental Congress*, 1774-1789 (Wash., D.C., 1904-1931), I, 28, 44.

by internal divisions and insecurities in a besieged England and later in a seemingly besieged Pennsylvania. Anti-popery did not perform that function because of a second level of significance, an amazing adaptability in the hands of individuals and groups vying for power and influence in an uncertain world. In England, anti-popery was used by the civil government to consolidate its power, by radical Protestants to destroy the established Church of England, and by the Anglicans to discredit religious dissidents. In early Pennsylvania, anti-popery was used by the Church of England to rectify an imbalance Anglicans perceived as stemming from a misguided tolerance and Quaker political and religious dominance, by Presbyterians living in the exposed backcountry to
240 force the Quaker Assembly to provide for defence, and by the religious supporters of the Proprietary party in their campaign against the Quakers. In the agitation preceding the Revolution, Presbyterians used the prevalence of anti-popish sentiment to stymie Anglican efforts to obtain an American bishop, and resisters of British imperial decrees focused on the Quebec Act as a dangerous example of Romish tyranny by the mother-country herself.

Anti-popery, however, was a response as well as a tool. That was most evident in the tendency of anti-papists to exaggerate the numbers and influence of Catholics in the colony and to search for internal enemies where very few could be found. For a people disconcerted by ethnic and religious pluralism and an unstable political balance, the evils and power of popery were something certain on which to rely, even at the expense of denying one of the major bulwarks of Protestantism—the evidence of the senses. Actual persecution of Catholics in Pennsylvania was rare. Prejudices became virulent only when social change, foreign entanglements, and increases in alien immigration seemed to threaten an established order. Only during the French and Indian War, when a real French threat was imminent and some Pennsylvanians sensed the moral failings of British colonial policy towards the Indian, did overt social and political persecution of Catholics result.

Villanova Univeristy JOSEPH J. CASINO

V Building An American Catholic Church

THE VISION OF JOHN CARROLL

JAMES HENNESEY

But this you may be assured of; that no authority derived from Propaganda will ever be admitted here; that the Catholick Clergy & Laity here know that the only connexion they ought to have with Rome is to acknowledge the Pope as Spiritual head of the Church; that no Congregation existing in his States shall be allowed to exercise any share of his Spiritual authority here; that no Bishop Vicar Apostolical shall be admitted, and if we are to have a Bishop he shall not be *in partibus* (a refined Roman political contrivance), but an ordinary national Bishop, in whose appointment Rome shall have no share.[1]

THE DATE WAS APRIL 10, 1784. The writer was John Carroll. He was angry that plans for church government in the new United States of North America were being made in Europe in trilateral conversations involving the Roman Congregation for the Propagation of the Faith, Pope Pius VI's nuncio at Versailles, and Dr. Benjamin Franklin, the American Congress's representative at the court of King Louis XVI of France. Congress itself had even been asked, and had declined, to have its say in the matter, and just at a time when it boasted not a single Catholic member. The one group ignored in the whole proceedings was the "Catholick Clergy & Laity," and the priest who was fast becoming that group's most visible and articulate spokesman was unhappy about it. A man with a solid grasp of theology and of church history, he was about to be given the opportunity to put his ideas and his abilities at the service of the community with which he had cast his lot in 1774 after over a quarter-century on the Continent and as chaplain in English country-houses. On June 9, 1784 an official letter from Rome

---

[1] John Carroll to Charles Plowden, Maryland, April 10, 1784, in Thomas Hughes, S. J., *History of the Society of Jesus in North America, Colonial and Federal* (4 vols., London and New York: Longmans Green, 1907–1917), Documents, I, II, 619–620. Plowden (1743–1821) was Carroll's principal English correspondent. He was later Master of Novices (1803) and Provincial and Rector of Stonyhurst College in the restored English Jesuit Province.

named John Carroll, forty-nine years of age, native of Upper Marlboro in Prince George's County, Maryland, onetime member of the now suppressed Society of Jesus, to the position of Ecclesiastical Superior of the Mission in the thirteen United States of North America. The American Catholics' ties to the Catholic Church in England and to the Vicar Apostolic of the London District were formally severed. Five years later Carroll became first Bishop of Baltimore and first Roman Catholic bishop in the United States. He did not become a vicar apostolic. He became an ordinary national bishop, and he was nominated for that office by vote of the priests of the new diocese.[2]

It is sometimes thought sufficient explanation of Carroll's harsh early
244 strictures on Propaganda—the missionary arm of the pope's Roman Curia—to say that he reacted as did many Jesuits of his era, who were persuaded that influential staff members in that particular congregation had played a large part in events which led to the suppression of the Jesuit order by Pope Clement XIV in 1773. There is considerable truth in the judgment. Carroll harbored no great affection either for Pope Clement or for Propaganda. But to stop there in analyzing him is to miss the rich greatness of the man who, more than any other single person, shaped the structural foundations of Catholicism in the United States.

This country's first bishop was notable for theological breadth and for a deep sense of historical consciousness. Profoundly aware that he lived in a country both geographically and psychologically different from the European world of his youth and education, he was still steeped in, and lived out of, the Christian and Catholic historical tradition. He understood and willingly shared in the American Revolutionary experience, just as he also understood, but rejected, the revolutionary experience of France a decade later. He was a Jesuit, in fact for twenty years and in spirit for another forty-two. His conviction of the vision of Ignatius Loyola, coupled with a realistic awareness of the difficulties successive generations of Jesuits have had incarnating that vision in their lives, had an enormous impact on him. Both factors, his historical sense of the Church and his integration of Ignatius's approach to reality, played their parts in shaping his vision of the church he worked to establish in the new United States.

Of Carroll's deep and continuing love for the Society of Jesus there can be no doubt. In September, 1773, he had written home to Maryland of the

---

[2] John Carroll (1735–1815) was the son of Daniel Carroll, an Irish immigrant and planter in Maryland, and of European-educated Eleanor Darnall, member of an old Maryland English family. After preliminary schooling at the Jesuits' Bohemia Manor school in northeastern Maryland, he travelled in the summer of 1748 to the college at St. Omer in French Flanders, and from there went "up the hill" to the English Jesuit novitiate at Watten in 1753. After studies and ordination at Liege he was assigned to the Great College at Bruges, to which the St. Omer college had been transferred after the expulsion of all Jesuits from France in 1763. He was Prefect of the Sodality at Bruges when the entire Jesuit order was suppressed in 1773. In America he became Superior of the Mission (1784), Bishop (1789) and Archbishop (1808) of Baltimore.

"fatal stroke," as a result of which "our so long persecuted, and, I must add, holy society is no more." "Is it possible," he wondered

> that Divine Providence should permit to such an end [*sic*], a body wholly devoted, and I will still aver, with the most disinterested charity, in procuring every comfort and advantage to their neighbours, whether by preaching, teaching, catechizing, missions, visiting hospitals, prisons, and every other function of spiritual and corporal mercy?

"Such I have beheld it," the letter continued, "in every part of my travels, the first of all ecclesiastical bodies in the esteem and confidence of the faithful, and certainly the most laborious."[3] John Carroll guided his life according to the ideals set him by St. Ignatius Loyola for sixty-two years. 245
In 1811, when he was nearly seventy-seven years old, some of his brethren, blissfully careless of the niceties of canon law and the delicacy of their own position as members of the still not wholly restored Society, accused Carroll, by then Archbishop of Baltimore, of disaffection towards their order. He replied with a scorching letter to the then Jesuit Superior of the Mission, Charles Neale, in which he stated in no uncertain terms that he was sure he loved the Society "more than you do, because I knew it much better." Convinced of Ignatius's fundamental vision, he had clear ideas as to how it ought to be implemented, and he took the occasion to read the Superior a lecture on the subject:

> For those [Jesuit] Constitutions I believe no one feels more respect or a higher estimate of their wisdom, not merely because I love the Society, with the most filial tenderness, but because I have studied their excellence, and in varying countries and circumstances have had the happiness of observing their effects in transforming the minds and hearts of those, who embraced them as their rules of life. Everywhere they answered the most religious purposes of their author. Wherever these Constitutions were observed in their letter and spirit, they raised men eminent in their knowledge for defending the church, & illustrating its history and doctrines; great masters of a spiritual life; zealous & disinterested labourers in all the functions of zeal, & evangelical ministry, distinguished for their talents, success and reputation in the education of youth; studious of every improvement, which might advance the glory of God; solicitous to recommend themselves to the first pastors of the Church, by their cooperation in whatever might conduce to the salvation of souls.[4]

Carroll's affection for the religious order to which he belonged lasted to the end of his days, but never blinded him to a realistic appreciation of Jesuit merits and demerits. His criticism could be particularly sharp when it

---

[3] Carroll to ?, Bruges, September 11, 1773, in Thomas O'Brien Hanley, S.J., ed., *The John Carroll Papers* (3 vols., Notre Dame and London: University of Notre Dame Press, 1976), I, 32. Cited hereafter as JCP.

[4] Carroll to Charles Neale, Baltimore, November 5, 1811, JCP, III, 159–160. Neale (1751–1823), one of four brothers who were Jesuits, had been a novice in 1773. He re-entered the Society in 1805 and twice served as Superior of the Mission. He brought the first Carmelite community to the United States and governed the Jesuit mission from his residence at their convent in Port Tobacco, Maryland.

bore on what he perceived as corporate failure to live up to the Society's primitive ideals. Writing, for example, in 1803, to his former faculty colleague at the Great College of Bruges, Charles Plowden, he paid tribute to the learning of the English secular clergy: "It must be owned, that for more than a century, we have been greatly eclipsed by the Gentlemen of Doway; witness Hawarden, Manning, Walton, Challenor, Butler, & now Milner & Coombs." In a revealing glimpse of education as he had experienced it in the English Jesuit scholasticate of Liege in the 1750s and 60s, he was frank in analyzing the reasons for Jesuit intellectual inferiority. Nothing had mattered at Liege except memorizing the professors' lectures. The approach to learning was a narrow one:

246 It seemed to me that at Liege far from encouraging young men to extend the circle of their knowledge, the heads of the College esteemed no merit but that of the study of their dictates. The little of Greek which had been learned at S. Omer or Bruges, was suffered to perish; the Hebrew lesson was a mere mockery; even the cultivation of Latin elegance was thrown aside; and as to our native language, there was scarcely a book of it in the Library worthy of being studied. No modern author of any science or in any language was introduced into it.

The consequences were inevitable: "Thus genius and talent were cramped, & a habit of inapplication was acquired, which few escaped."[5]

John Carroll was one Liege alumnus whose genius and talent were not cramped. Nor could he easily understand those who carried over into their later lives in America the intellectual torpor induced by the Liege scholasticate. In 1800 he told Plowden that "amongst our few remaining brethren here"

there are some, whose violence will listen to no lessons of moderation; & others, whose knowledge & observations are too confined to comprehend that anything useful can be learned, beyond what they know; or that any change of circumstances should suggest improvements suitable to times & situations, or cause the smallest deviation from the track, in which they once walked themselves.[6]

Fortunately for the church which he was called to shape, Carroll was exactly the opposite of that type. In *An Address to the Roman Catholics of the United States of America by a Catholic Clergyman* (Annapolis: Frederick Green, 1784) he showed himself well read, not only in classic patristic and medieval sources, but in contemporary theologians both Catholic and Protestant. He also indicated his own attitude on the key question of freedom of inquiry. The *Address* was written in answer to a challenge from his kinsman and fellow ex-Jesuit Charles Wharton, now an Anglican minister. Wharton had pointed to the annual publication each Holy Thursday, in papal bulls beginning *In Coena Domini*, of lists of ecclesiastical censures, including those incurred by Catholics who read prohibited books. Carroll found it hard to take the charge seriously. He

[5] Carroll to Plowden, Baltimore, February 12, 1803, JCP, II, 409.

[6] Carroll to Plowden, Washington, September 3, 1800, JCP, II, 318.

reminded his cousin that "the Bull not only was never received into, but was expressly rejected from almost every Catholic state," where "the very alleging of its authority was resented as an encroachment on national independence." "Thoughout his extensive acquaintance with Catholics," he asked, had not Wharton known them "to read Protestant authors without hesitation or reproof?"[7] The long list of authors cited by Carroll stands as evidence of his own position in the matter.

Openness of spirit in theological questions remained a constant in Carroll's vision. In an 1804 letter to Charles Plowden's more conservative brother Robert, he hoped that Jesuits in a restored Society of Jesus would no longer be bound by the precept of Claudio Acquaviva (Father General of the Jesuits from 1581–1615) which obliged them to "combat constantly the 247
doctrine of the powerful body of Thomists" by upholding the so-called Molinist approach in controversies about grace. Carroll preferred no restriction other "than that of the Orthodox doctrine in the Catholic church."[8] He never wavered in his option for breadth of vision. In the last summer of his life, writing to recommend a new set of textbooks to the Jesuit Superior in Maryland, John Grassi, he told him: "I am indeed anxious for a uniform system of divinity amongst us, allowing however all the liberty of opinion granted by the Church."[9] Nor was theological learning to lie fallow. He had already urged Grassi to make sure that candidates for ordination: "cultivate very much the study of our native language, the rules of elegant composition in it, the reading of the best Christian orators, ancient and modern, the use & application of the holy Scriptures."[10] All of this, of course, was to be an aid to sermon preparation, in which seminarians were to be exercised regularly. Carroll's theological vision was not only open and comprehensive. It was also very practical.

A key element in John Carroll's understanding of the spirit of St. Ignatius is contained in the eulogy of the Jesuit Constitutions which he sent to Charles Neale in 1811: Jesuits should be ". . . solicitous to recommend themselves to the first pastors of the Church, by their cooperation in whatever might conduce to the salvation of souls." He had put it more bluntly in 1787: "Religious orders in the Church are only auxiliaries to the Ecclesiastical Hierarchy established by Christ."[11] His own life's work, for its final quarter-century, was to be first pastor of the church in the United States. In that role, he expected Jesuits and others to cooperate with him.

---

[7] The text of the *Address* is in JCP, I, 82–144. Wharton (1748–1833) played a prominent role in organizing the Episcopal Church in the United States. He had become a Jesuit in 1766 and a priest in 1772. He left the Roman Catholic Church in 1784.

[8] Carroll to Robert Plowden, Washington, August 14, 1804, JCP, II, 448.

[9] Carroll to Grassi, Baltimore, August 25, 1815, JCP, III, 357. Grassi (1775–1849), had been first destined for the Siberian Mission, then for China, and finally came to Georgetown, where he was President as well as Mission Superior. He returned to Italy in 1817 and died as Assistant for Italy to Jesuit Father General Jan Roothaan.

[10] Carroll to Grassi, Baltimore, March 8, 1813, JCP, III, 218.

[11] Carroll *et al.* to the Gentlemen of the Southern District, n.p., n.d., JCP, I, 228.

He also moved to a more considered appreciation of the broader cooperation demanded for the good of the universal church. His attitude toward the Roman Congregation for the Propagation of the Faith mellowed, and in 1809 he shared with Charles Plowden his hope that a similar metamorphosis would take place generally among Jesuits and that there might be the:

> most cordial cooperation and understanding with the Directors and alumni of the College of the Propaganda, and other establishments of a similar nature, instead of wrapping up ourselves in our own plans without endeavouring to profit by the experience, lessons, or influence, of men engaged in pursuits similar to our own.

248 "The more I study the life of S. Ignatius," he continued, "the more I am convinced that such was his spirit."[12]

It was with attitudes like these that Carroll approached the task of building the Catholic Church in America. As far back as 1787, arguing with the conservative country pastors of southern Maryland who opposed plans to finance the academy projected at Georgetown and the regularization of episcopal government, he and his supporters had emphasized that they lived on "such an extensive continent" that means beyond those which had sufficed in Maryland's "counties" had to be taken. In 1791, the new Bishop of Baltimore traced for Charles Plowden another dimension of the question. For well over a thousand years Europe and Latin Christianity had been very nearly convertible terms. But the church was now planted in a land not only extensive, but with no political center of gravity in the old Continent:

> Our distance, tho not so great, if geometrically measured, as S. America, Goa and China, yet in a political light is much greater. S. America, & the Portugese possessions in Africa & Asia have, thro' their metropolitical countries, an intermediate connexion with Rome; and the missionaries in China are almost all Europeans.

The case with the United States was different:

> . . . we have no European metropolis, and our Clergy will soon be neither Europeans, nor have European connexions. There will be the danger of a propensity to a schismatical separation from the centre of unity.[13]

It was in this context, consciously understood, that John Carroll worked out, in theory and in practice, his understanding of a national church within the Roman communion.

The United States with which Bishop Carroll had to cope was a difficult setting for episcopal ministry. Anti-papist feeling, endemic in the English heritage and then magnified on the frontier in days of French and Indian wars, was never far below the surface of life. Episcopal church polity—having a bishop—had not been possible in colonial times, even in

---

[12] Carroll to Plowden, Baltimore, June 2, 1809, JCP, III, 87.

[13] Carroll to Plowden, Baltimore, October 12, 1791, JCP, I, 524.

the Established Church. "Diocesan bishops," Congregationalist preacher Jonathan Mayhew warned, were "a pernicious set of men, both to church and state," and "people have no security against being priest-ridden but by keeping all imperious bishops and other clergymen who love to lord it over God's heritage from getting their feet into the stirrup at all."[14] The extent to which democratic ideas could, or should, be incorporated in Catholic church government was unclear, and this was one of the problems which Carroll faced. He had certain advantages of position and experience to help him. His cousin, Charles (of Carrollton) and his brother Daniel served in the Continental Congress. One was a signer of the Declaration of Independence, the other of the Federal Constitution. The bishop himself had
undertaken a fruitless mission to Quebec on behalf of Congress in the 249
spring of 1776. His companions, all signers of the Declaration the following summer, were Samuel Chase, Benjamin Franklin and his cousin Charles. There was another advantage. The colonial Catholic community had contributed to the Revolution. Although there were Catholic Tories among the Scots highlanders of the Mohawk Valley and hard by Independence Hall in Philadelphia, the French Alliance and the more numerous American Catholics in Patriot ranks had lessened, although hardly eliminated, anti-Catholic feeling. John Carroll could remind the editor of *Columbian Magazine* in 1787 that "Freedom and Independence, acquired by the united efforts and cemented with the mingled blood of Catholic and Protestant fellow-citizens, should be equally enjoyed by all."[15] Still, whatever smacked of foreign interference was suspiciously resented in the world's first emerging nation. Consciousness of that feeling conditioned Carroll's carefulness about Propaganda's involvement in American church affairs. But there was more. He exhibited at times a startling sense for the mood of the nineteenth century that was to come. But he was at base an eighteenth-century Catholic. His ecclesiology—his understanding of the way in which the church is put together—antedated the romantic neo-ultramontanism which would exalt the papal role to new heights within a half-century of the old archbishop's death.

A document crucial to understanding Carroll's thought on the church is the letter which he wrote sometime late in 1784 to Ferdinand Farmer, pastor at Philadelphia, about his new appointment from Rome. He was unhappy that he had been designated Superior at the pleasure of the Congregation for the Propagation of the Faith. His basic objection was that "the Clergy here consider themselves as a national Clergy, & not as missioners." As such, they were "competent to the choice of their Ecclesiastical Superior, and only wanting that spiritual connexion with the

---

[14] Carl Bridenbaugh, *Mitre and Sceptre: Transatlantic Faiths, Ideas, Personalities, and Politics, 1689–1775* (New York: Oxford University Press, 1967), pp. 241, 99–100.

[15] Carroll to Editor, New Jersey, September 1, 1787, in JCP, I, 259. The letter appeared in *The Columbian Magazine, or Monthly Miscellany*, I (December, 1787), 881–882.

holy See, which shall be an evidence of our sincere attachment to & union with it." Carroll's whole theory of "church," as opposed to "mission," is there. He spelled it out at greater length, adding the element of civil recognition as a factor:

> By the Constitution, our Religion has acquired equal rights & privileges with that of other Christians: we form not a fluctuating body of labourers in Christ's vineyard, sent hither, & removeable at the will of a Superior; but a permanent body of national Clergy, with sufficient powers to form our own system of internal government, &, I think, to chuse our own Superior, & a very just claim to have all necessary Spiritual authority communicated to him, on his being presented as regularly and canonically chosen by us.[16]

250 A vicariate-apostolic would not fill the bill. "A refined Roman political contrivance," he called the system of a titular bishop who exercised authority in the pope's and not in his own name. This judgment reflected a longstanding English Catholic prejudice.[17] Carroll wanted a church in communion with the Bishop and See of Rome, internally autonomous, self-perpetuating, and free of dependence on any foreign jurisdiction. This led him to discussions, both theoretical and practical, on such topics as the establishment of a national clergy and their education, the choice of bishops and pastors, the jurisdictional relationship within the universal Church of the Roman and the various national churches, the teaching authority of pope and of ecumenical council, and the use of the vernacular in the liturgy.

Carroll's years as Superior and Bishop were bedeviled by a plague of wandering clergy, secular and regular, "a medley of clerical characters," he called them, who came to America to try their fortune. He was determined to replace them with a regular body of priests, preferably trained at home and not in Europe. Nostalgically he thought at an early stage of staffing the parishes in Maryland, Pennsylvania and perhaps Virginia with ex-Jesuits, and as late as 1808 he wrote to the Jesuit Superior,

---

[16] Carroll to Ferdinand Farmer, n.p., n.d., JCP, I, 155. Farmer (1720–1786), a Württemberger and onetime medical student, had been a member of the Upper German Jesuit Province. He came to Pennsylvania in 1752 and was a missionary there and in New Jersey and New York, as well as a member of the American Philosphical Society and a trustee of the University of Pennsylvania. He had reservations about Carroll's theology of church: "Another objection I cannot help making is to the idea of our being a body of clergy and no more Missionaries, for I cannot conceive how we could be a body without a Bishop for a head. . . . Our voluntary union *in spiritualibus* cannot constitute us a canonical body of clergy unless declared and bound as such either by the superior pastor, or rather by a Bishop set over us by him." (Farmer to Carroll, Philadelphia, January 1, 1785, in *American Catholic Historical Researches*, 28 [1888], 29).

[17] The English priests of the "Old Chapter" had explained the problem to King James II in 1685: "By a Bishop who is an Ordinary is meant one who hath power in Himself to govern the flock over which he is sett, according to the common received Rules or Canons of the Church, and is not revocable at pleasure. On the contrary a Vicar is one who hath no power in himselfe, but only the Use or Exercise of the power of the Person whose substitute he is . . . to whom therefore he is at all times accountable as using purely *his* Power, and both that and himselfe revocable att pleasure. (Basil Hemphill, O.S.B., *The Early Vicars Apostolic of England, 1685–1750* [London: Burns, Oates, 1954], pp. 7–8).

Robert Molyneux:

> My heart bleeds so much for the Catholics of the State of Ohio, of Vincennes, Detroit & c., places bedewed with the sweat of Jesuits, and first established with their labours, that I feel a strong impulse to send other sons of S. Ignatius to cultivate the same soil.[18]

But above all he was a realist, and the needs of the church came first. "We can not," he once reminded the priests of southern Maryland, "put such a clog on people's dispositions, as to leave no door for admittance to Holy Orders, but thro' that of the Jesuit novitiate."[19] His great contribution to development of a national clergy was the bringing of the Sulpicians and the opening of St. Mary's Seminary, Baltimore, in 1791. 251

Ferdinand Farmer took the new Superior to task in 1785 on the central role in historical Catholic polity of the local bishop. Carroll needed no reminder. He was anti-episcopalist neither in theory nor in practice. On the contrary, he had a "high" concept of the function of bishops on both local and universal levels in the church. But before he came to that stage, there was the problem of how bishops should be chosen. There could be no question of participation by civil government, as was the well-nigh general custom in Europe. Public authorities and legislators in the United States were mostly "discordant Religionists" (that is, not Catholics). Direct papal appointment would "create more jealousy in our government, than even in France, Germany, or Spain."[20] "I wish sincerely," he told Plowden, "that Bishops may be elected, at this distance from Rome, by a select body of Clergy."[21] He was himself nominated by ballot of the clergy, and his name was the only one submitted to Rome. Over the years several proposals for an electoral body representing the priests were made. None was put into practice. Local problems, the dislocations caused by the Napoleonic wars, and high-level ecclesiastical meddling in both Dublin and Rome combined to postpone a permanent solution, but Carroll's concerns made it plain that for him autonomy was the natural condition of a national church and that such a state was more consonant with the historical tradition and discipline of Catholic Christianity.

The first Bishop of Baltimore's understanding of a national church was reflected both in the way in which he dealt with internal situations and in his appreciation of relationships with Rome. Locally, his concern for preparation of good preachers has already been mentioned. He was a strong advocate of replacing Latin in the liturgy with the various national

---

[18] Carroll to Robert Molyneux, Baltimore, June 19, 1808, JCP, III, 64. Molyneux (1738–1808), a Lancashire man, was first Superior of the restored Jesuit order in the United States. Carroll described him as "my oldest friend, after my relation & companion to St. Omers in my childhood, Mr. Chs. Carroll of Carrollton." (Carroll to Plowden, Baltimore, February 21, 1809, JCP, III, 81).

[19] See above, n. 11.

[20] See above, n. 16, p. 157.

[21] Carroll to Plowden, n.p., n.d. [1792], JCP, I, 548.

languages. Along with "the Extent and Boundaries of the Spiritual Jurisdiction of the Holy See," he ranked "the use of the Latin Tongue in the publick Liturgy" as "the greatest Obstacles" to Christian unity and to the spread of Catholicism in the United States.[22] He was also open to congregational participation in parish government, although frustrated in efforts to devise a formula which would not turn Catholic parishes into "distinct & independent Societies" like those of New England's Congregational Presbyterians.[23] In any case, he stoutly maintained that "the laity are neither the source of spiritual jurisdiction nor can stop its course."[24] But these were not the only ways in which he worked to establish an identity for the church with no European metropolis. A project
252 to which he devoted considerable effort was Matthew Carey's publication at Philadelphia in 1790 of the Douai English version of the Bible. He took twenty subscriptions for himself and relentlessly dunned others to enter subscriptions and then to pay them off. The "Carey Bible" was designed to play a significant role in shaping the American Catholic community.[25]

Communion with the Bishop and See of Rome was fundamental in Carroll's vision of the church, but his nuances were not quite those with which the twentieth century Catholic has been familiar. The "Roman church" meant for him the local church of Rome, not the universal church, although he readily acknowledged that see's prerogatives in relation to the rest of the church. The Roman church was mother and mistress of all churches and obedience was owed its bishop. The spiritual supremacy of the Vicar of Christ was

> an essential tenet of our religion . . . the bond of our union, which cements and keeps together, in the profession of the same faith, and in the celebration of the same solemn and public worship, and under one uniform government, established by Jesus Christ, and perpetuated by succeeding pastors, so many different nations, so distant from each other, and unconnected in every other respect.[26]

---

[22] Carroll to Joseph Berington, Maryland, near George-town, July 10, 1784, JCP, I, 148. Berington (1743–1827) was an English Catholic controversialist and a great adversary of Carroll's friend Charles Plowden.

[23] Carroll to Dominick Lynch and Thomas Stoughton, Rock Creek, January 24, 1786, JCP, I, 204. Lynch (1754–1825) and Stoughton (1748–1826) were brothers-in-law, partners in the importing business and founding trustees of St. Peter's Church, New York City. The congregation was largely Irish, but included Dutch, French, Spanish and Portuguese also. An early report on the New York situation is found in a letter to Propaganda from the first resident pastor, Charles Maurice Whelan, O.F.M. Cap. (1741–1806), New York, January 28, 1785 (Archives of the Congregation for the Propagation of the Faith, Rome, Scritt, rif. Amer. Sett., I, fol. 425–8).

[24] Carroll to James Kernan, Secretary of the Congregation of Charleston, South Carolina, n.p., August 15, 1805, JCP, II, 485.

[25] "The First American Catholic Bible," *American Catholic Historical Researches*, 3 (1887), 64–68; Lawrence F. Flick, "Selections from the Correspondence of the Deceased Matthew Carey," *Records of the American Catholic Historical Society of Philadelphia*, 9 (1898), 352–384; Joseph Jackson, "First Catholic Bible Printed in America," *ibid.*, 56 (1945), 18–25.

[26] Carroll to the Congregation of Holy Trinity Church in Philadelphia, n.p., February 22, 1787, JCP, II, 202.

His ecclesiology on this point was that of Robert Bellarmine. By divine appointment the Bishop of Rome was head of the universal church, and the see of St. Peter the center of ecclesiastical unity, he had told his Roman agent John Thorpe in 1785.[27]

Carroll lived before the First Vatican Council spelled out the details of papal supremacy. He saw the relationship between Rome and a local bishop differently than did the council fathers a half-century after his death. In the 1784 *Address* he stated as the constant belief of Catholics that the church's infallibility resided "in the body of bishops, united and agreeing with their head, the bishop of Rome." Emphasis was on the episcopal college. The opinion, of which he was aware, that the pope, as Christ's vicar, was infallible even without a council, he noted as something with 253
which "faith has no concern, every one being at liberty to adopt or reject it, as the reasons for or against may affect him."[28] Rome was the center of ecclesiastical unity, but in the eighteenth century ecclesiology of John Carroll individual bishops in their dioceses and the body of bishops in the universal church loomed very large.[29]

With Bishop Carroll the structured life of the Roman Catholic Church in the United States began. He was a thoughtful, intelligent man, versed in the church's history and knowledgeable in its theological tradition. A born aristocrat, he freely admitted the appeal of Edmund Burke's ideas, particularly when, as he saw it, "furious democracy" ran amok in the French Revolution. At the same time he was a child of the American Revolution, and nothing was clearer to him than that it was his task to incarnate the church in a world that was distinctively new. He was very much a son of Ignatius Loyola and caught up in that saint's vision of hard, intelligent service. Among his American contemporaries in the church he was without peer. There was no divided *magisterium* in Baltimore. The Bishop was plainly the chief theologian of the diocese. At the same time he was an active pastor, throughout the diocese and in the cathedral parish, and that into his eightieth year.

Carroll's life had begun in British colonial America and seemed at first destined to run its course, as did the lives of many other American-born Jesuits of the time, in the Flanders colleges or in one of the English

---

[27] Carroll to John Thorpe, Maryland, near George-town, February 17, 1785, JCP, I, 163. Thorpe (1726–1792), an English ex-Jesuit, had been a member of the College of Penitentiaries at St. Peter's Basilica until the Jesuit suppression. He remained in Rome as an art collector for English Catholic gentry and agent at the Holy See for English and American ex-Jesuits. He is said to have died of a burst bladder, suffered while waiting for an audience at a curial office.

[28] JCP, I, 105–106.

[29] Carroll's position—holding for the church's infallibility, but declaring the papal infallibility apart from a council was only a disputed theological opinion—actually lined him up as a conservative. For a discussion of varying Catholic theological views on the question, see Franz Xaver Bantle, *Unfehlbarkheit der Kirche in Aufklärung und Romantik. Eine dogmengeschichtliche Untersuchung für die Zeit der Wende vom 18. zum 19. Jahrhundert* (Freiburg, Basel and Vienna: Verlag Herder, 1976).

chaplaincies. Clement XIV and the Continental Congress changed all that, the first by his suppression of the Jesuits in 1773 and the second by its Declaration of Independence in 1776. John Carroll's vision, to its immense benefit, was placed at the service of the church in the United States. In the canonical sense of the term he became the church's ordinary national bishop. In every other respect he was quite extraordinary.

THE CATHOLIC MINORITY IN THE UNITED STATES, 1789-1821*

By Thomas T. McAvoy, C.S.C.

Catholic England commemorates this year the centenary of the reestablishment of her hierarchy which Cardinal Newman glorified as the "Second Spring." All Catholics in the English-speaking world rejoice in the resurrection of Catholicism in England. Long before 1850, however, there existed another Catholic hierarchy in the English-speaking world which seems destined to play a far greater role in the history of the Church. We in this country celebrated our centenary of a Catholic hierarchy nearly sixty years ago—in 1889. Further, the American Catholic hierarchy is not one merely tolerated but is freer and more self-sustained than any other hierarchy in the English-speaking world. Several times since 1889 have Europeans turned to American Catholicism both hopefully and critically; and today that hope and criticism of American Catholicism are openly renewed by friend and foe in the press of Europe.[1] Present day American Catholicism, in its material condition and its social influence, is the product of many forces and of many types of people. But I think that its chief and peculiar characteristics are the products of American conditions which began to form the spirit of our Catholic minority[2] in the United States almost from the very day the United States became a nation.

The late Monsignor Peter Guilday liked to point out the amaz-

*This paper was read at the Annual Public Meeting of the Society, held at the Park Lane Hotel, New York City, on December 5, 1950. Dr. McAvoy is head of the Department of History in the University of Notre Dame, Notre Dame, Indiana.

[1]Some examples of this critical attitude can be found in such articles as "Le Catholicisme aux États Unis," by Georges Escoulin in *Le Monde*, Jan. 10, 11, 12, 1950; "American Catholics Revisited," by Erik von Kuehnelt-Leddihn in *The Tablet* (London), April 22, 1950; and "Kirchliches Leben in Amerika," by "Ein Laie" in *Schweizer Rundschau* (Einsiedeln), March, 1946, 887-95.

[2]I have considered the Catholic minority in other periods in "The Formation of the Catholic Minority in the United States, 1820-1860," *Review of Politics*, X (January, 1948), 13-34; "Bishop John Lancaster Spalding and the Catholic Minority (1877-1908)," *ibid.*, XII (January, 1950), 3-19; and "The Anguish of the Catholic Minority," *American Ecclesiastical Review*, CXXI (November, 1949), 380-85.

ing parallels in dates between the events of American civil and American Catholic history. Certainly the fact that John Carroll was named the first Bishop of Baltimore the same year that George Washington became the first President of the United States would indicate that between the two executives there might be some connection which history, however, will not support. Yet, the parallel in time has some parallel in significance if one considers that the critical era in American history between the ratification of the Articles of Confederation in 1781 and the inauguration of Washington under the Constitution is almost coterminus with the
256 period in which the orphaned missions in the former English colonies changed from a group of scattered missioners into the first formal diocesan organization in the new country. One may carry the comparisons too far; yet there is one other obvious parallel. The Constitution was still but a piece of paper when Washington reached New York to take office; similarly, the Catholic Church in the United States was little more than a blueprint when Bishop John Carroll returned to Baltimore after his consecration in England to form his diocesan organization.

The group of missioners to which the new Bishop returned had as its nucleus a remarkable body of men, mostly former members of the English province of the Society of Jesus.[8] In the history of these Jesuits, as in so many other trials of the Church, can be found a story of a disaster turned into a blessing. For, just as a few years later the tragic exile of a remarkable group of French priests during the French Revolution brought the blessings of their missionary zeal to the new American diocese, so the dissolution of the English province of the Jesuits in 1773 released these American members of the province from a closer bond of a religious community, enabling them to become the nucleus of the first diocesan organization in the United States. I do not wish to imply that ceasing to be Jesuits made them more suitable for their grand work, rather that their having been Jesuits insured to them a uniformly exacting formation which is the best assurance of sus-

[8]Thomas Hughes, S.J., *History of the Society of Jesus in North America, Colonial and Federal,* 4 vols. (New York, 1910), contains the most authentic account of these Jesuits and documentary material on their activities.

tained zeal. And having been once a community, they found it easier to unite into a diocesan organization even when their numbers were increased by the added membership of Franciscans, Dominicans, and secular clergy. As a matter of fact, under the inspiration of Father John Carroll after the suppression of the Society the former Jesuits had drawn up a plan of government to preserve their unity and to handle the properties by which they were supported. This Select Body of the Clergy was eventually incorporated in Maryland in 1792 as the Corporation of the Roman Catholic Clergy of Maryland and it was to this organization that Carroll first appealed as Bishop of Baltimore. 257

It is true that formal attachment to a bishop or to a diocese alone did not make American Catholics members of the Church. The French in the Illinois country and in New England, the Irish in the port towns of Charleston, Norfolk, New York, and Boston were members of the Church but they were not yet formally members of the unit just beginning to be the Catholic Church in the United States. The appointment of 1789, indeed, had given Bishop Carroll jurisdiction throughout the territory of the United States; still his effective jurisdiction at the start was dependent upon those clergy who were united with this group of Maryland clergymen, and the American Catholic body as an effective force centered in the missions under the care of these priests. These Maryland clergymen, while waiting for the Holy See to decide their future, had extended the benefits of their organization to the other missioners who came to work in the missions of Maryland and Pennsylvania, thus constituting the nucleus of the first diocese. Later on this central body would attract and absorb these smaller drops of Catholic life in the west and north and south, but during the remaining episcopate of John Carroll and his immediate successors it was this central body of Maryland and Pennsylvania Catholics which developed certain important characteristics that were in time to mark the Catholic minority in the United States as we know it today. Although the overwhelming numbers of later immigrants and the magnitude of the later Catholic growth have modified that inheritance, the full importance of the Catholic role in

American history can be measured in terms of the plans and goals set up by these early Catholic leaders.

These generalizations are very simple; but the tasks of Bishop Carroll were difficult and complicated. There were practically no Catholic communities and the problem of reaching the thousands of baptized Catholics in the coast towns, on pioneer farms, or in western settlements with a handful of priests of varying ages and nationalities called first for the drawing together of a functioning organization. If one more parallel to civil history may be permitted, just as George Washington as the first President was great
258 not by any striking manifestation of daring but by his being a great administrator, so the character of John Carroll seemed to fit him for his great administrative burden of harmonizing many diverse groups and submitting to discipline the irregular elements to be found in this missionary country. He was an American whose Anglo-Irish Catholic ancestry[4] made him readily sympathetic to American independence. He had had the advantage of education and travel abroad during which he had been a direct witness of the intrigues leading to the suppression of his religious society. This experience had given him an acute sensitiveness to human weaknesses in religious organizations. He was a member of a family of some means, able to meet the social and political leaders of his Maryland countryside on equal terms. He had demonstrated his civil loyalty as a member of the Commission to Canada during the American Revolution. Physically he seems to have been a man of moderate height, soft lines, and pleasant countenance.[5] As the missionary of Rock Creek and as the Bishop of Baltimore he was able to meet amiably Catholic and non-Catholic alike, although he did not hesitate on occasion to attack a defaulting missionary[6] or

[4]Peter Guilday, *The Life and Times of John Carroll, Archbishop of Baltimore (1785-1815)*, 2 vols. (New York, 1922), I, 2-6. Guilday repeats most of the information in John Gilmary Shea's *Life and Times of John Carroll* (New York, 1888) with much new documentary material. I have referred to Guilday rather than to the sources he has used.

[5]Letter of Jeanne and Rebecca Carroll to James F. Edwards, December 10, 1885, describing family accounts of Archbishop Carroll's appearance, Carroll-Brent papers in the Archives of the University of Notre Dame.

[6]Carroll's *Address to the Roman Catholics of the United States of America* (Annapolis, 1784), was written against an apostate cousin, the Rev. Charles Wharton.

to write against any anti-Catholic article in the press[7] of the day a letter of protest in which he claimed for Catholics the liberties they had helped to win in the Revolution.

But his problems as Bishop did not involve so much those outside the Church as they did the internal organization of the new diocese. One might say that the Catholic group of about 30,000 souls—scarcely one per cent of the population of nearly four millions of the new country—was a minor concern of their Protestant neighbors. This indifference of most Americans of that early period about the existence of the Catholic group is so clear to us today that the earlier fear of these missioners that the appointment of a bishop would bring down upon them persecution seems rather a symbol of the defeatism they had inherited from their English Catholicism than a fear based upon any actual threat of persecution. Generally speaking, as Orestes A. Brownson has pointed out, for most Americans of 1789 Roman Catholics "were not then sufficiently numerous in the country to be counted"[8] and excited no great fear. Consequently, Bishop Carroll's chief problems were not concerned with any external persecution but in harmonizing the varying elements and bringing into unity the scattered members of his newly formed diocese.

All together within the limits of his new diocese of the territory of the United States Bishop Carroll had fewer than thirty-five priests who were scattered from the Illinois country in the west to Boston in the east and from Savannah in the south to Albany in the north. There are no accurate lists of the Catholics who were in the United States at that time. His flock included the French in the west who had formerly been under the jurisdiction of Quebec, Irish who had lately arrived in the ports of entry along the coast, other French who had fled the insurrections in the West Indies or the mother revolution in France, and German settlers in Pennsylvania, besides the original English group of Maryland.

---

[7]Carroll claimed authorship of a letter defending Catholics that appeared in *The Columbian Magazine* (December, 1787), cf., Guilday, *op. cit.*, I, 113-4, and *American Catholic Historical Researches*, XV (April, 1898), 62-4.

[8]*Brownson's Quarterly Review*, II (third series, October, 1854), 475; and *ibid.*, II (first series, October, 1845), 536. See also E. B. Greene, *Religion and the State* (New York, 1941), 107-10.

Outside of a few families in this Maryland-Pennsylvania group, and an occasional French or Spanish consul, his flock had little of this world's wealth.

The nucleus of his clergy was the former members of the Society of Jesus who had organized the Select Body of the Clergy and incorporated their property under the laws of Maryland. Although this organization was formed by the former Jesuits primarily to preserve their property and to regulate their government and sustenance until the restoration of the Society of Jesus, other clergy working in the missions of Pennsylvania, Maryland and
260 Virginia had been admitted to membership and granted salaries from the estates owned by the corporation.[9] As a former Jesuit, Father John Carroll had played an important part in the formation of this corporation but he did so merely as a member of the group. His appointment as Prefect Apostolic and later his election as Bishop did not give him any greater power or position in the corporation. Although he shared the ex-Jesuits' hope for the restoration of the Society and sympathized with their efforts to preserve their property until the restoration, John Carroll, as the appointee of the Holy See to the new see of Baltimore, had to think first of his new position and prefer the diocese and the permanent diocesan organization to the welfare of his former confreres.

There were times when the new Bishop found this position midway between his former brethren and the other clergy of the diocese very trying.[10] Dissatisfied clergy accused him falsely of using his office to discriminate in favor of his former Jesuit confreres while some members of the Society felt that he was taking for his diocese properties that rightfully belonged to the Jesuits. Carroll at first had to depend financially for the most part on his Select Body of the Clergy because few of his Catholic families could afford the funds necessary to build churches and to support his clergy. Eventually, he knew that the growth of the diocese must come from the meager contributions of the flock; never-

---

[9]Hughes, *op. cit.*, *Documents,* I, Part II, 691-3.
[10]*Ibid.*, 854-6.

theless, as can be seen in his first diocesan synod in 1791,[11] the core of his diocesan organization remained for some time the members of this Select Body of the Clergy. Most of these had already grown old on the missions. Although Carroll knew that he must secure additional clergymen to help him, he must have been pleased to have such experienced missionaries as Father Robert Molyneux, Father John Ashton, Father Francis Beeston, Father Francis Graessel and others to assist him. And there were others whose zeal and loyalty made possible the spiritual care of distant missions and the new immigrants in the ports. Among these there were the Dominicans, Francis Anthony Fleming and William O'Brien, the first of newly arrived Sulpicians, Fathers Francis Nagot, Anthony Garnier and John Tessier, and a few other secular clergymen such as the New England convert, Father John Thayer. The Select Body of the Clergy had granted the Bishop an annual salary and supported their own members on the missions, but in New York, Philadelphia, Charleston, Norfolk, Boston and certain other communities there were forming small congregations with resident clergymen whose chief support came from the contributions of the faithful.

Carroll's immediate task, as shown in the first Synod which met in Baltimore in 1791, was to establish his spiritual jurisdiction and to make clear to his clergy and their flocks that the diocese of Baltimore had superseded the Select Body of the Clergy or any other organization. On this basis the Synod turned then to those rules for the administration of the Sacraments and for the public services which were to be proper to the United States. In this, the Synod warned the priests against adopting American customs not befitting their dignity. For a while Carroll took over the three districts formerly set up by the Select Body of the Clergy, making the superiors of the northern and southern districts his vicars general and sending other vicars to the scattered missions beyond the Allegheny Mountains. To prepare additional priests for his diocese Carroll aided the establishment of Georgetown College in

---

[11]Peter Guilday, *A History of the Councils of Baltimore (1791-1884)* (New York, 1932), treats of this synod of 1791, 60-71.

the District of Columbia and the Sulpician Seminary of St. Mary's in Baltimore.

Carroll's first episcopal activities concerning Philadelphia, New York, and Boston and particularly his visitations to these distant towns were undertaken to maintain order and discipline against disobedient clergymen and rebellious trustees. Beyond the needs of pastoral instruction, the problems of the new bishop had little to do with dogma; one might say that any fears that Rome may have felt of the rise of heresy in the Americans' desire for a national organization were mostly groundless. Despite the Gallican
262 training of so many of the early American prelates[12] probably the chief characteristic of American Catholicism from this early day has been its constant devotion to papal authority. Neither was American Catholicism of that day troubled with problems of civil politics. Even though there were still some state laws which did not follow the Federal rule laid down in the First Amendment of the Constitution and which discriminated against Roman Catholics,[13] there was no tendency on the part of the Federal government to interfere in the administration of the Church nor any effort by the clergy to seek political favors. The lack of numbers gave the Catholics of that day little inclination to bring their religion into politics and the social position of Catholics was determined chiefly by the circumstances of their birth and property. The major public problem of the new bishop was to help his flock adopt the proper traditions in conformity with its position as the first Catholic minority enjoying liberty in the modern English-speaking world.

From their English tradition the dominant Catholic group in Maryland and Pennsylvania seemed reconciled to a minority role in a country whose literature, political theory, and social institutions had come from the mother country. Their fear of the effects of having a bishop, their promise of loyalty to Washington, and their hesitancy about external manifestations of Catholic worship

---

[12]Orestes A. Brownson makes the most pointed charge of Gallicanism in his article on Archbishop Martin John Spalding in *Brownson's Quarterly Review*, II (last series, January, 1874), 111.

[13]Guilday, *Carroll*, I, 110-15.

were products of English traditions and colonial persecution. These English traditions were in time to be modified partly by the practice of American freedom but chiefly by the coming of Irish and other immigrants from countries where Catholicism was still supreme. The efforts of the Carrolls, the Brents, and the Digges in Maryland, of Thomas Fitzsimons, Matthew Carey, and Robert Walsh of Philadelphia and of some other Catholics to achieve political and social position showed that in their minds their Catholicism was in no way a badge of inferiority. But these acted, as Catholics have usually acted in social and political matters in the United States, as individuals. Bishop Carroll, while he had at heart the 263
salvation of the individual Catholic, had as his major concern institutional Catholicism, the formal and public Catholic organization. He and his immediate successors aided and witnessed the delineation of the first role of the Catholic minority in the United States. During the next fifty years the Catholic population was notably increased by Irish immigration and by conversion, but the number of Catholics was not sufficiently large to cause any general alarm among non-Catholics. New priests were ordained, others came from Europe, new dioceses were created but in general the Catholic minority in the United States at the beginning of the 1820's was chiefly an Anglo-American Catholic minority, increased at the edges by French and Irish immigration but culturally an American group with its centers in the seminaries and colleges of Maryland and the District of Columbia.

In the thirty years after Carroll's appointment the Catholic minority acquired certain definite characteristics which were to be modified by the events of the later nineteenth century but which must be studied if one is to understand the role of the Catholic minority then and in later American history. The great problem in the history of the Catholic Church in the United States was not the development of any special dogmatic or moral theory but the working out, in the newly won freedom of the United States, of certain substitutes for civil establishment and the other political relationships that had accompanied the growth of the Church in Western Europe.

Most of these characteristics of the Catholic minority were the product of American conditions. Perhaps the most notable characteristic of the new diocese—a deep respect for episcopal power—was the direct result of the problems that had beset Father John Carroll during his brief career as Prefect Apostolic[14] without full episcopal powers. During that brief time the disturbing activities of the former chaplains of the French fleet, Father Claudius de LaPoterie and Father Louis Rousselet in Boston,[15] the schism of Father Andrew Nugent[16] in New York, and the other rapidly occurring difficulties the Prefect Apostolic met in establishing his
264 authority in local situations, as well as the growing need of additional clergymen, quickly convinced the majority of the Select Body of the Clergy and Father Carroll himself of the need of episcopal authority if Catholicism was to remain vital in the American missions. The fact that the Select Body sought and obtained from Rome permission to elect its own bishop because of the fear of foreign influences merely served to emphasize this confidence in hierarchical order. In turn the high character of Bishop Carroll and his fearless action after his consecration in settling local disorders gave to the Catholic doctrine of sacred orders a practical importance in American Catholic life. Later on, the recognition of the great distances separating the increasing groups of Catholic settlers caused Carrol to urge the establishment in 1808[17] of additional episcopal sees at Boston, New York, Philadelphia and Bardstown and the provision for continuity in the central see of Baltimore by the coadjutorship of Leonard Neale. From this early period the major unit of the Catholic Church in the United States has been the bishop with his flock no matter what were the geographical or national divisions of the dioceses. This is, of course, the normal unit of Church government but it has been particularly important in the United States where American freedom from political or nationalist connections has emphasized the spiritual character of the Church's mission.

---

[14]Cf. *ibid.*, 202-342.

[15]Robert H. Lord, John E. Sexton and Edward T. Harrington, *History of the Archdiocese of Boston,* 3 vols. (New York, 1944), I, 375-446.

[16]Guilday, *Carroll,* I, 262-82.

[17]*Ibid.*, II, 567-601.

Bishop Carroll had at his command many remarkable priests whose fidelity in mission work and willingness to take over the difficult assignments made his efforts fruitful. Among these, besides the old Maryland Jesuits, must be recognized the Dominicans, Fleming and O'Brien, some Franciscans, some Augustinians and the Sulpicians. From these Rome chose most of the early bishops, such as Bishops John Cheverus of Boston, Michael Egan, O.F.M., of Philadelphia, and Benedict Joseph Flaget, S.S., of Bardstown and his own coadjutor, Leonard Neale. The failure of efforts by interested persons to establish rival and independent bishoprics, such as the proposed bishopric of the Ohio Company and the one proposed for the Oneida Indians,[18] and the attempted schismatic bishopric of Virginia[19] served again to emphasize the important role the American bishop was to retain in the history of the Church in the United States.

Only once was this respect for the episcopate endangered, when confusion and intrigue caused the appointment in 1820[20] of three Irish bishops to the sees of Philadelphia, Richmond and Charleston without consultation with the Maryland-Pennsylvania clergy. Archbishop Ambrose Maréchal in the spirit of Carroll went immediately to Rome to explain the true condition of the American missions and to prevent the recurrence of similar errors. Of these three Irish appointees, Bishop Patrick Kelley of Richmond soon resigned, Bishop Henry Conwell of Philadelphia later was displaced by the more capable Bishop Francis Kenrick, and Bishop John England, although not of the tradition of Carroll, became himself a glory of the American episcopate. And Rome made provision for American nominations for future vacant American sees.

Next in importance to the problem of episcopal authority in the newly organized Church was the management of the temporal goods of the Church. At the outset of American independence

---

[18]*Ibid.*, 392-418.

[19]Peter Guilday, *The Catholic Church in Virginia (1815-1822)* (New York, 1924), treats of the Norfolk schism in Chapters IV and V.

[20]Peter Guilday, *The Life and Times of John England*, 2 vols. (New York, 1927), treats of Maréchal in volume one, particularly of his differences with England. I do not entirely agree with his interpretation of the character of Maréchal, cf., I, 283-98.

the American missions had the advantage of the corporation of the Select Body of the Clergy. Although the purpose of that corporation was the preservation of the property for the benefit of the Society which they hoped would soon be restored, the immediate benefits were felt by the whole Catholic body of Maryland and Pennsylvania as yet too poor to support its own clergy. In later decades France, Germany, and Austria were to furnish funds for the American missionary effort but during the critical period of foundation the first diocese drew its support from this corporation. Bishop Carroll sought immediately to enable his
266 diocesan organization to carry its own burdens and began to distinguish between what belonged to the members of the Society soon to be restored and what belonged to the diocesan organization. There was for many years, especially after the restoration of the Jesuits, a minor controversy[21] between the Bishop and the Society about the proper division of the goods of the Church between the diocese and the Jesuits, but the welfare of the missions was never permitted to suffer from the dispute. The material welfare of the diocesan organizations was one of the chief problems of the American episcopate.

But there was a greater controversy over the question of Church property decided during these first decades. With the Church in the United States really politically free there arose the possibility of some civil organization to take the place of the State and to care for the property and material welfare of the Church. In American law the Church was not recognized as such and while this fact freed Bishop Carroll and his co-workers from political interference it did hamper him in legally controlling the properties of the Church.[22] Carroll alone was not financially able to build the churches needed to provide services for his flock scattered so widely from Maine to Georgia and from the Atlantic to the Mississippi. Outside of contributions from the Select Body of the Clergy in Maryland and an occasional gift of French or Spanish

---

[21]Hughes gives many documents on this controversy, *op. cit., Documents,* I, Part II, 822-1008.

[22]Peter Guilday, "Trusteeism," *Historical Records and Studies,* XVII (March, 1928), 7-73.

consuls, the self-sacrifices of the laity alone made possible the erection of modest churches or chapels in communities where Catholics were more numerous. But while these Catholic laymen were providing the churches, they also felt the desire, particularly where national prejudices were involved, to demand some control of the church even to the appointment of the pastor. An important factor in this tendency was the American process of incorporation by which the trustees of the corporation were recognized as having the ownership of the property.[23] Either ecclesiastical property had to be incorporated in the name of the bishop, involving certain difficulties of inheritance, or in the name of the trustees of the corporation. The latter custom was the usual way among most Protestant congregations in the country and even had some European Catholic antecedents in the managers of the *fabrique* of the church and in the right of patronage obtained in many cases by trustees or benefactors of the church. In establishing the American tradition Carroll and his successors had two antecedents. The first was that of the ex-Jesuits and their Select Body of the Clergy who supported their mission from the proceeds of their own plantations without contributions from the faithful, but such a plan could not care for the growing number of missionaries and chapels. Consequently, Bishop Carroll and the other bishops were increasingly dependent upon the second means, the contributions of the faithful. At first Carroll, lacking sufficient clergy and funds to establish regular parishes and impressed with the zeal of many Catholic laymen, was content to let the lay trustees incorporate the church property, usually with the existing pastor as a member of the board. Soon, however, personal jealousies between clergymen and between the laymen, national prejudices, and wilful disobedience produced an outbreak of schismatics in Boston, New York, Philadelphia, Baltimore, Norfolk, and Charleston, sometimes with the trustees demanding the appointment of pastors

---

[23]Cf. Patrick J. Dignan, *A History of the Legal Incorporation of Church Property in the United States (1784-1932)* (Washington, 1933), and Edward Louis Heston, C.S.C., *The Alienation of Church Property in the United States* (Washington, 1941) for canonical treatments of these controversies.

and at other times with the pastors defying the bishops. Carroll himself at first appealed to the religious sense of the rebellious trustees and clergymen and when that appeal failed he imposed suspensions upon disobedient clergymen, interdicts upon alienated churches, and excommunication upon rebellious trustees. By the time of his death in 1815 Carroll had begun to assert ecclesiastical authority over the property of the churches. His successor, Archbishop Leonard Neale, and after him Archbishop Ambrose Maréchal, continued the struggle during their regimes; but only after the Roman intervention in the Philadelphia controversy, by which the freedom of the bishops in
268 spiritual matters was demanded, was the conflict fully resolved. The principle of episcopal control of church property set forth by Pope Pius VII was later incorporated in the decrees of the Baltimore Councils and eventually the episcopal authority over the temporal goods of the church was enforced despite the American problem of incorporation.

Only in the perspective of time do we realize the importance of the proper solution of this conflict. Because of the intervention of Rome[24] in the case of Bishop Henry Conwell of Philadelphia, in which the concessions of the aged Bishop to the trustees were cancelled, and because the Catholic solution of the problem in insisting on episcopal control seemed so diverse from that in the Protestant congregations, it might seem that the Catholic solution departed from American democratic ideals. Actually the solution preserved the full religious liberty of the Church in the only way consonant with the religious freedom of the United States. The American Catholic way was not the way of the established churches of Europe, neither did it make the Church beholden to the accidental holders of temporal power in the person of non-spiritual trustees who would be hampered by material and political considerations. The Catholic Church in America by this decision has been free to devote its means to sacramental good and spiritual purposes. While there have been local lapses from the decision of Carroll,

[24]A translation of the papal letter of Pope Pius VII on the trustee controversy is given in the *Records of the American Catholic Historical Society*, XXV (December, 1914), 325-30.

Neale and Maréchal in which national prejudices have embroiled for a time the material welfare of the Church in racial or political divisions, the liberty of the Church in this country to devote all its resources to religious purposes and its independence from political chicanery was a direct result of this victory of the bishops in these early days over local pressure, national and racial prejudice, and political interference. Trusteeism[25] was an unfortunate name for the conflict because so many of the trustees were and have always been very zealous for the welfare of the Church. Similarly the preservation of the material liberty of the Church has been wrongly pictured as a rejection of American democratic methods[26] 269
instead of the fulfillment of the principle of religious liberty under the Constitution.

A third characteristic of the Catholic minority in the United States began to take shape in the years immediately before John Carroll became bishop. Undoubtedly the efforts of the ex-Jesuits in Maryland to preserve their properties for the day of the restoration of their Society played an essential part in determining the source of leadership of the early Catholic minority, and John Carroll became unwittingly the chief figure during his lifetime in a struggle to determine whether there was really to be a distinctively American church organization or not. This was not a question of doctrine nor a question of loyalty to the Holy See. It was the question whether in this new country with its distinctive culture and tradition the Church would find the proper milieu for growth and expansion. As Archbishop John Hughes later pointed out,[27] those who claimed that the Catholic Church would lose its membership once the Catholic immigrant reached the freedom of American shores could find their answer especially in the loyalty and increased numbers among the descendants of the Maryland Catholics. These English and American Catholics, and among them should be in-

---

[25]Hugh J. Nolan, *The Most Rev. Francis Patrick Kenrick, Third Bishop of Baltimore, 1830-1851* (Philadelphia, 1948), 61-101.

[26]Henry K. Rowe, *The History of Religion in the United States* (New York, 1928), 117-9, and Willard L. Sperry, *Religion in America* (New York, 1946), 207-8.

[27]*Complete Works of Most Rev. John Hughes, D.D., Archbishop of New York*, 2 vols. (New York, 1865), II, 127-29.

cluded the older Irish, French and German families, became the cultural leaders of the Catholic minority. For while to those immigrants who had no special attraction towards the dominant English character of the American people the fact that the country was dominantly Protestant was actually a reason for attempting to make the Catholic body separate from the dominant culture, it was chiefly to Carroll, Neale, and Maréchal that we owe the establishment of the tradition of an American Catholicism in which American democracy and Anglo-American culture formed the nucleus of Catholic intellectual leadership in the United States.
270 This development began in this early period.

At first after the Revolution, when the English bishops no longer cared to administer faculties to the American missions and the American clergy feared the effect of the appointment of a bishop from abroad in the republican United States, the Maryland clergymen under the leadership of Carroll asked for the appointment of a superior of their own choosing to preside over their governing Chapter. A fortuitous series of exchanges between the American minister in Paris, Benjamin Franklin, and the Papal Secretary of State through the Papal Nuncio in Paris had led to the appointment of John Carroll as that superior. In this first appointment Carroll was not the choice of his fellow missioners, who nominated Father John Lewis, but he had been a prominent member of the Select Body of the Clergy, the nucleus of the future diocesan organization. To his fellow missioners, however, once Rome had appointed him Prefect Apostolic, Carroll was for them now the proper ecclesiastical superior who would combine the qualities of American rule to safeguard the liberties and the property of the Catholic minority and the needed episcopal authority. Accepting the urgency of the situation Rome granted special permission for the American clergy to elect their bishop and Carroll was elected by his fellow priests as the first Bishop of Baltimore.

Of course the manner of election had no effect on the dignity or the power of the new bishop but the American election of Carroll did effect two things. First it eliminated the fear of the American missionaries that they would become the appendage of a foreign

hierarchy[28] to the damage of their civil and social position in the newly declared republic. More important, however, was the recognition of the Anglo-American group, centered in Maryland and Pennsylvania as the nucleus of the future American Catholicism. Behind Bishop John Carroll was a tradition of American Catholicism already one hundred and fifty years old. Also, before Carroll's appointment prominent Maryland Catholics had publicly expressed the loyalty of American Catholics to the new government in their letter to George Washington, and the first President had in turn given assurances that their fellow Americans would respect the rights of the Catholics in recognition of their 271
share in the Revolution. Further, in the person of the first Bishop non-Catholic Americans found a fellow American of recognized loyalty. Thus, within a short time the assertion of Carroll's authority in the trustee controversies and his action against national schisms meant not only the assertion of his spiritual power but also the assertion as a fact that the Church in the United States was to be American in its civil and social aspects. Carroll's appointment also gave to this nucleus of American Catholics the dominant position in the Church in the United States.

This cultural leadership was not always acknowledged. The Anglo-American group was never heavily reinforced except among the American converts. Yet, the French and Irish in Boston, the Irish in New York and Norfolk, the Germans in Baltimore and Philadelphia soon learned from Carroll that the Catholic congregations in this country were expected to give up their foreign allegiances and customs and to get in line with the American group not only in spiritual matters but in language, custom and loyalty.[29] Nor did the character of this loyalty change when the French priest,

---

[28]Jules A. Baisnee, *France and the Establishment of the American Catholic Hierarchy, the Myth of French Interference (1783-1784)* (Baltimore, 1934), rejects the charges of Guilday in his *Carroll,* I, 178-201, and Shea in his *Carroll,* 212-24, that the French tried to gain control over the American Church. Guilday and Carroll do refer to the efforts of Archbishop Troy of Dublin to interfere later in American episcopal appointments but without attaching as great an importance to them.

[29]Father John Carroll so wrote to the French and Irish in Boston just before leaving for England for his consecration, urging them to "strive to form, not Irish, nor English, or French Congregations & Churches, but Catholic-American Congregations & Churches." Lord, Sexton and Harrington, *op. cit.,* I, 431.

Ambrose Maréchal, succeeded Leonard Neale to the archiepiscopal see of Baltimore. For a short time in the appointment of Bishop Henry Conwell to Philadelphia, Bishop Patrick Kelley to Richmond and Bishop John England to Charleston, the cultural unity of the American Catholic group was threatened, but the energy of Maréchal who went to Rome itself to stop foreign intrigue finally secured permanently the cultural unity of the Church in the United States. Time and the flow of later European immigration did submerge the Anglo-American cultural leadership but whether the actual leaders were English, French, Irish, or German in
272 ancestry, the cultural unity and the dominance of an American loyalty once established during these first decades has been constant in American Catholicism.

During these thirty years, from the time John Carroll returned from England to Baltimore as its first Bishop until Ambrose Maréchal returned from Rome in 1821, the essential characteristics of the American Catholic minority in the United States had been established. During the next few decades the great influx of Irish and German immigrants was to make difficult the maintenance of these three dominant qualities of American Catholicism. The lack of episcopal chapters and the failure to develop any strong national organization among the American bishops have served to emphasize the dominance of episcopal authority in American Catholicism. This has been emphasized also in the liberty of American bishops in the control of church property secured amid the trustee controversies of these early decades. This control is the chief point of criticism of those who profess to fear the Church and is the envy of Protestant organizations who must pay heavy tribute to those who manage the material goods of their congregations. The dominance of the Anglo-American cultural group in the Church has been the hardest of these three characteristics to maintain because of the overwhelming waves of immigrants who become culturally American only in succeeding generations. But these characteristics did survive, although it must be added that the later immigrants rejecting the defeatism of the old Anglo-American minority added to the original qualities new strength and vigour so greatly needed in the face of the nativist persecutions and the poverty of immigrant life.

VI American Catholics And Religious Pluralism

AMERICAN CATHOLICS AND RELIGIOUS PLURALISM, 1775-1820*

Joseph P. Chinnici

PRECIS

Between 1775 and 1820, some American Catholics participated in and uniquely incarnated the struggle of the European Catholic Enlightenment to respond to the forces of political, intellectual, and religious pluralism in both state and church. Because of the inheritance of church-state unity, European Catholic thinkers could not evolve an adequate definition of toleration which distinguished between religious liberty in the civil sphere and complete doctrinal indifference. The notion of a social contract made by a diversity of believers was impossible. In the British Isles, because of their minority status and the philosophical inheritance of John Locke, Catholics moved beyond the continental view but received no opportunity to realize their plans.

In contrast, the Roman Catholic Church in the United States, led by John Carroll, accepted the Enlightenment notions of civil contract, separation of church and state, and anthropology of rights. This acceptance encouraged Roman Catholics to take a positive stance toward religious pluralism. Some supported ecumenical approaches in liturgical life and sacramental practice. They reinterpreted the phrase *extra ecclesiam nulla est salus* in an irenic way. This was a singular combination of Enlightenment anthropology and Roman Catholic doctrine and practice. Under pressure from increased immigration, the rise of a "no popery" campaign, and a changing mentality, this enlightened Roman Catholic program in the United States collapsed by 1830. Today the fundamental basis of the position has been revived, and if we are to continue ecumenical discussion we should see the political, anthropological, ecclesiological, and apologetic questions as interrelated.

The Catholic Church in Lebanon, Pennsylvania, first opened its doors on July 23, 1810. Jesuit priest John William Beschter, who had immigrated to the United States from Flanders in 1807, presided at the ceremonies. He preached, once in German and once in English, to a mixed congregation of Catholics and Protestants. Three Lutheran, three Reformed, and one Moravian minister listened attentively as Beschter spoke on Protestant misrepresentations of Cathol-

*The opportunity for researching this material was made possible by the gracious assistance of a summer stipend from the National Endowment for the Humanities.

Joseph P. Chinnici (Roman Catholic) is Associate Professor of Church History at the Franciscan School of Theology of the ecumenical Graduate Theological Union in Berkeley, CA. A Franciscan priest of the Province of Saint Barbara, he holds an M.A. from the Graduate Theological Union, an M.Div. from the Franciscan School of Theology, and a D.Phil. (1976) from Oxford University. He studied at the Center for the Study of American Catholicism at Notre Dame during the Summer of 1978, and had an N.E.H. Summer Stipend in 1977. His most recent publications include an article on American Catholic devotional works (1791-1866) in *Theological Studies* (June, 1979), and *The English Catholic Enlightenment* (Patmos Press, 1980).

icism and the solidity with which Christ had built his church. After the services, all of the clergy dined at the home of the local Lutheran minister.[1]

This scene, although curious by our present standards, was not unusual in the early years of American Catholicism. Lebanon was the world written in miniature and testified to the impact of national and religious pluralism on the internal composition and external practices of Catholicism. From 1785, when Charles Whelan noted the diversity of religious persuasions and nationalities in his own parish in New York, until 1822, when Louis du Bourg reported that Catholics frequently attended Protestant churches in order to hear about moral principles, America realized a unique experience in Western Christendom.[2] Filippo Filicchi reported to Propaganda Fide with some amazement in 1794 that
276 the government and manner of thinking of Americans left Catholics in perfect tranquility; many were predisposed to accept false ideas of Catholicism; still, generosity characterized the souls of Americans, a generosity which extended to giving all citizens equal status and accepting "that each religion be accepted by God" (*che qualunque Religione sea accetta a Dio*).[3] A similar awareness of novelty pervaded many other reports about the American religious scene.[4] If Enlightened Europeans had first conceived the ideals of civil toleration, some degree of pastoral pluralism within the church, and a type of common Christianity, those dreams began to take flesh in the New World. The argument of this article will be that, from 1775 until 1820, some American Catholics participated in and incarnated in a unique way the European Catholic Enlightenment's struggle to respond to the forces of religious pluralism in both state and church. What will be described are two of the major concerns of the American Catholic Enlightenment. In order to understand this a brief description of the European background is necessary.

---

[1]John William Beschter to John Carroll, August 6, 1810, Archives of the Archdiocese of Baltimore (AAB), IQB.

[2]Charles Whelan to Your Eminence, January 28, 1785, Archives of the Sacred Congregation of the Propogation of the Faith, Scriture Riferite nei Congressi (SRC), America Centrale, 1776-1790, vol. 2, fols. 442, 443. Louis DuBourg, "Notice sur l'etat actuel de la Mission de la Louisiana," Derniere Édition, Turin, 1822, p. 40, SRC, America Settentrionale, 1792-1830, vol. 2, fols. 649-683.

[3]Filippo Filicchi to Cardinal Antonelli, 1794, SRC, America Centrale, 1791-1817, vol. 3, fol. 47.

[4]Cf. Stephen Theodore Badin to Propaganda, June 7, 1805, SRC, America Centrale, vol. 3, fol. 291-294; Felice de Andreis to Propaganda, September 5, 1817, ibid., fols. 623-624; Edward Fenwick to Nicholas Sewall, April 2, 1830, Letters of Bishops and Cardinals, 1753-1853, fol. 297, Archives of the English Province of the Society of Jesus, Farm Street, London (ESJ); John Austin Hill to the Rev. M. Scott, April 12, 1825, vol. 25, fols. 143-144, ESJ.

The Context: The European Catholic Enlightenment

Recent studies in eighteenth-century European Catholicism have isolated a group of thinkers who attempted to bridge the ever-widening gap between the Roman Catholic Church and the social and intellectual forces of the Enlightenment. These people were, in Emile Appolis's phrase, "enlightened Catholics,"[5] not Jansenists or *Zelanti* (the term used to characterize those Catholics who were excessively attached to the prerogatives of the papacy and the curial party). Although concerned to protect the national traditions of their churches, they were loyal to Rome and cosmopolitan in outlook, forming an international group of critics, historians, and theologians. Building on the speculative foundations articulated by Jacques Benigne Bossuet (1627-1704), Claude Fleury (1640-1725), and Jean Mabillon (1632-1707), a reconciliation was proposed between Catholicism and the Enlightenment by such men as Ludovico Muratori (1672-1750), Giovanni Lami (1697-1770), and Giovanni Bottari (1689-1775) in Italy; Jean-Baptiste Demangeot (1742-1830) in France; Eusebius Amort (1692-1775) in Germany; and Arthur O'Leary (1729-1802), Joseph Berington (1743-1827), and John Fletcher (1766-1845) in the British Isles. They did this in such diverse areas as scientific criteria for miracles, the reasonableness of Church authority, the rejection of baroque piety, historical criticism, suppression of the Inquisition, and clerical education. In various degrees these people combined the philosophical traditions of Descartes, Newton, and Locke, with a Gallican conciliar ecclesiology and a Jansenist desire for practical reform. They rejected the dominant model of post-Tridentine Catholicism. Within the context of the eighteenth century, the Enlightenment challenged Catholics to both a project of intelligibility—an attempt to make Catholic belief and practice understandable to the Age of Reason—and a socio-political anthropology, a redefinition of the structures of church and state in terms of the new view of the person.

One major reality which structured the thought of this Catholic Enlightenment was political, intellectual, and religious pluralism. The underlying tension of the age was the relationship between the part and the whole. For a person of Enlightenment mentality, society was built on individual consent; the state incorporated different religious persuasions; the Catholic Church consisted of national traditions united to Rome; the methodology of natural science represented the rejection of tradition and the application of individual critical reason to inherited positions. An anthropological preoccupation with the particular supported all of these views. They raised in an ever-acute form the central question: How could the integrity of the singular (individual rights,

---

[5] Emile Appolis, *Le "Tiers Parti" Catholique Au XVIIIe Siècle (Entre Jansénistes et Zelanti)* (Paris: A & J Picard, 1960). Cf. F. G. Dreyfus, *Societés et Mentalités A Mayence dans la seconde moitie du XVIIIe Siècle* (Paris, 1968); Bernard Plongeron, *Théologie et Politique au Siècle des Lumières, 1770-1820* (Droz, 1973); "Recherches sur L'Aufklarung Catholique en Europe Occidentale (1770-1830)," *Revue d'Histoire Moderne et Contemporaine*, October-December, 1967, pp. 555-605.

individual consent, individual participation, individual reason) be reconciled with the demands of the whole?

In the religious sphere, European thinkers searched for a theory and praxis which could deal with this central issue of pluralism from the time of Hugo Grotius' (1583-1645) *Via ad Pacem Ecclesiasticam* and John Locke's *Essay on Toleration* (1680) to Justinus Febronius' *De Statu Ecclesiae* (1763) and Joseph II's Edict of Toleration (1781). They labored to formulate a consistent intellectual approach which integrated Catholic Church teaching, ecclesiology, and social philosophy with the reality of religious pluralism and the emerging socio-political anthropology. Theologians influenced by the Erasmian irenical tradition attempted to move beyond the accoutrements of a baroque religion to distin-
278 guish between the essentials and accidentals of faith, to stress national traditions and independence from the Roman curia, and to promote ecumenism. In short, they wanted to make room for the individual within the structure of post-Reformation Catholicism. They also stressed the international community of peoples and the rights of individual conscience. Thus, the reality of pluralism and the Enlightenment's view of the person raised at least two interconnected but distinct religious questions: How could a civil diversity of faiths be recognized without either destroying the social fabric or denying the necessity of "one, true religion"? How could reconciliation and social harmony be promoted between denominational traditions? The questions cut across the social, ecumenical, and ecclesial areas of the Catholic mentality. The following sections will consider how these questions were formulated in Catholic Europe and how they were dealt with in America.

Religious Pluralism and the Question of Toleration

The problem of toleration in eighteenth-century Europe has been surveyed many times.[6] It was the social issue of the period. For the members of the Catholic Enlightenment, ecclesiological conciliarists, Catholic Church reformers, and humanist philosophers, the central anthropological notion which structured their thought was *contract*. This idea balanced a limited government with the rights of individual conscience. In the area of politics, contract came to imply an anthropology of rights, the acceptance of constitutionalism, and the separation of church and state. This in turn meant a positive concept of religious freedom. Toleration was a personal right, not a governmental concession. The consistency of this view was manifested most clearly in the thought of John Locke. For

[6]Cf. Ursula Henriques, *Religious Toleration in England 1787-1833* (London: Routledge and Kegan Paul, 1961); Joseph Lecler, "Religious Freedom: An Historical Survey," *Concilium* 47 (1969): 3-20; Charles H. O'Brien, "Ideas of Religious Toleration at the Time of Joseph II. A Study of Enlightenment among Catholics in Austria," *Transactions of the American Philosophical Society*, New Series, vol. 59, part 7 (1969).

Catholics a problem arose when these ideas with their underlying anthropology were applied to the socio-religious sphere. How could they be reconciled with the inherited notions of Christendom? Did the positive acceptance of civil toleration imply religious indifference?

Bernard Plongeron has shown that Catholics in France and Italy rejected any positive notion of toleration.[7] The maximum opening which they made to an Enlightenment socio-political anthropology was to recognize toleration as a civil possibility and to distinguish it from theological intolerance. In the practical order, religious pluralism was a princely concession; liberty of conscience was not an inalienable right. In Austria, especially with the radical supporters of Joseph II's Edict of Toleration, there was an attempt to move beyond this
position by rooting religious liberty in natural law. This resulted in a unique type 279
of credal rationalism. It accepted religious pluralism by substituting the philosopher's notion of "natural religion" for revealed truth and by making the former the religion of the state. In all three countries the inheritance of state jurisdictionalism and royal absolutism blocked the discovery of any possible synthesis between the notion of contract as applied to state and to church. There could exist no middle term between toleration as concession and toleration as religious indifference. Ecumenical coexistence in the civil order could only be accepted passively by an established church or encouraged actively by a state whose religion dissolved the tenets of traditional Catholicism.

The reason for this impasse was the inability to conceive of a consistent political anthropology which reconciled dogmatic truth, separation of church and state, and constitutionalism. The notion of a social contract made by a diversity of believers was impossible. Civil order could not exist without Christendom. Ultimately, the Enlightenment and Catholicism as it was understood at the time were antithetical. As a result there could be no positive social response to religious pluralism. The crux of the issue lay in the relationship between toleration, social contract, and church-state cooperation. The imbroglio came to fruition in 1789.

The significance of the Enlightened Catholic movement in the British Isles lay precisely in its ability to overcome the difficulties caused by the European inheritance of state absolutism. In England and Ireland religious pluralism could be dealt with in a positive way.[8] Arthur O'Leary, Joseph Berington, and John Fletcher inherited a position of minority status within an established church order, a vibrant tradition of constitutionalism, and a socio-political theory which secularized the state. Since church and state were separate, civil religious liberty could be accepted without acknowledging doctrinal indifference. Fletcher summarized the basic position on toleration in this way:

---

[7]"Recherches"; for Austria, see O'Brien, "Ideas of Religious Toleration."

[8]For this and what follows, cf. Joseph Chinnici, "English Catholic Tradition and the Vatican II *Declaration on Religious Freedom*," *The Clergy Review* 60 (August 1975): 487-498; "John Lingard and the English Catholic Enlightenment," unpublished D. Phil. dissertation, Oxford, 1976.

> Catholic intolerance, in speculation, is a steadiness of belief, and a refusal to compound with error. In practice, it is the care with which the shepherd attends his flock; and the vigilance, by which he withholds contagion from it. . . .
>
> Whoever believes, that any other kind of intolerance is necessary, or approves of any other mode of conduct, believes and approves what the catholic religion neither teaches, nor recommends. . . .
>
> [the church] does not wield the sword of human justice. . . . [It's censures] neither affect life, liberty nor property. The power of the church is spiritual; and the punishments, which she employs are, like her authority, spiritual only.[9]

280

Joseph Berington indicated the Lockian political foundations of this view in his *State and Behaviour of English Catholics*. He wrote that no religion should be established by form of law. "At all events, what has state-policy to do with the concern of a man's conscience? If he obeys the laws of his country, and performs the duties of a subject, the demands of the civil magistrate are complied with."[10] In its most consistent form this position presupposed separation of church and state and constitutionalism. Socially, it saw religious pluralism as a reality which could facilitate the pursuit of truth. Toleration was not a concession but a human right:

> *Liberty of thought* is essential to human nature. Take that away, and man, his organization alone excepted, will not be superior to the ass which browses on the thistles, or to the thistle which vegetates from the earth. It is that only which he can strictly call his own, because no created power can deprive him of it.[11]

Because of the penal status of Catholicism in the British Isles, Berington, O'Leary, and Fletcher were never able to articulate a completely consistent theory of government. In various degrees they wavered between a moderate and a radical Whig stance. Their underlying unity lay in a common presupposed view of the person. Berington and O'Leary relied heavily on a theory of natural rights and contract. They spoke in terms of the individual: "life," "liberty," "the power to accumulate a fortune," "the rights of nature," "social compact," "conscience," "rights anterior to society," "delegated authority," "liberty of thought," etc.[12] John Fletcher, although he was considerably closer to the

[9]John Fletcher, *Reflections on the Spirit etc. etc. of Religious Controversy* (London: Keating, Brown and Keating, 1804), pp. 232, 233, 234-235; cf. Arthur O'Leary, *The Works of Rev. Arthur O'Leary, O.S.F.*, edited by a Clergyman of Massachusetts (Boston: Patrick Donahoe, 1868), p. 215.

[10]*The State and Behaviour of English Catholics From the Reformation to the Year 1870 with A View of their Present Numbers, Wealth, Character, etc.* (London: R. Faulder, 1780), pp. 141, 184. O'Leary and Fletcher were much more reluctant to advocate full separation of church and state.

[11]Ibid., p. 139.

[12]Cf. ibid., pp. 138-142, 186-188; O'Leary, *Works*, pp. 207-253.

continental view, still advocated separation of church and state and gave toleration a positive basis in the rights of conscience.[13] The thinking of these men enabled them to reconcile Catholic Church teaching with the notion of civil contract. Their political anthropology facilitated an integrated approach to the Enlightenment and Catholicism. The reflections on religious pluralism were indicative of a deeper view. Unfortunately, these people never received an opportunity to see their theories put into practice. That chance was given only to their friends across the Atlantic.

Enlightened Catholicism in the United States

Most American Catholics recognized the startling newness of their governmental revolution, its acceptance of toleration as a human right, and its complete separation of church and state. Some used their Maryland tradition and continental Enlightenment background to articulate a coherent response to these social forces. They dealt with religious pluralism in a positive way. In doing so, they moved beyond the position of their co-religionists in France, Itlay, and Austria, and more fully realized the ideas of Berington, Fletcher, and O'Leary. The most notable of these American Catholics was John Carroll. His approach to the separation of church and state is well known. Here it must be considered only from the standpoint of toleration and an Enlightenment anthropology.

The leader of the Roman Catholic Church in America clearly accepted the Enlightenment's notion of civil contract and its anthropology of individual rights. Carroll agreed explicitly with O'Leary, Berington, and Fletcher.[14] Positive references to civil and religious liberty and the separation of church and state are scattered throughout his writings and correspondence. He expressed his views most clearly in newspaper controversies in 1787 and 1789. In these publications Carroll spoke about "every natural right," "rights of conscience," "equal liberty," "the common rights of nature," "civil and religious liberty," "rights legally acquired," "the rights of conscience and liberty of religion," "free participation of equal rights," and "the great principle of religious freedom."[15] He had taken a similar stance in his controversy with Charles Wharton in 1784 and in his *Journal of European Tour* (1771-1772) he noted the ideas of "original equality," and their "common rights of mankind."[16] Carroll definitely conceived

---

[13]Cf. *Sermons on Various Religious and Moral Subjects for All the Sundays after Pentecost: With Illustrations* (Newcastle: Edward Walker, 1810), vol. 1, pp. 131-143, 343, 360.

[14]Cf. John Carroll to Joseph Berington, July 10, 1784, in Thomas O'Brien Hanley, S.J., editor, *The John Carroll Papers* (Notre Dame: University of Notre Dame, 1976), vol. 1, p. 148; Carroll to O'Leary (1787), ibid., vol. 1, pp. 224-226; Carroll to Charles Plowden, December 5, 1808, ibid., vol. 3, p. 73.

[15]Cf. ibid., vol. 1, pp. 259-261, 365-368.

[16]Ibid., vol. 1, pp. 140, 19.

of toleration as a positive right, not a concession, and he carefully distinguished it from religious indifference.[17] In all his writings the Marylander separated the spiritual from the temporal.[18] Although he was by no means a radical Whig, he noted that he had "contracted the language of a Republican."[19] Carroll based good government on the "just concurrence of all" and on the "general agreement of the nation and on the respective rights of the different orders of the community."[20] He disagreed with Edmund Burke and believed that the latter's principles went "almost to persuade mankind to suffer every evil, rather than attempt a change."[21]

John Carroll's stance on toleration and church and state enabled him, as it
282 did his English counterparts, to accept in a positive way the social reality of religious pluralism. Instead of merely acquiescing in its existence or granting it as a pragmatic concession, he saw it as an opportunity to pursue a fuller and deeper Catholic truth. Carroll's anthropology of rights necessitated seeing the "other," despite his religious beliefs, as a fellow citizen, one to be approached within the context of respect, not concession. To do this was to place the Catholic Church in the midst of the Enlightenment world. Carroll wrote in his response to Wharton:

> . . . if we have the wisdom and temper to preserve [civil and religious liberty], America may come to exhibit a proof to the world, that general and equal toleration, by giving a free circulation to fair argument, is the most effectual method to bring all denominations of christians to an unity of faith.[22]

The Catholic prelate reiterated the same position in a letter to Charles Plowden.[23] He best stated the view when he wrote to Joseph Berington:

> You have expressed on the Subject of Toleration those Sentiments, which I have long wished to see come strongly recommended from eminent writers of our Religion; and which I am well persuaded, are the only sentiments, that can ever establish, by being generally adopted, a reasonable system of universal Forbearance, and Charity amongst Christians of every Denomination. Indeed their Operation may extend much farther; and as you have observed, such an

---

[17]Carroll to Charles Plowden, February 28, 1779, ibid., vol. 1, p. 53; Carroll to John Thorpe, February 17, 1785, ibid., vol. 1, p. 164; Carroll to Charles Plowden, February 24, 1790, ibid., vol. 1, p. 432; Carroll to John Troy, July 12, 1794, ibid., vol. 2, p. 121.

[18]Carroll to Charles Plowden, February 27, 1785, ibid., vol. 1, p. 168; Carroll to Andrew Nugent, July 18, 1786, ibid., vol. 1, p. 215; Carroll to Robert Plowden, March 2, 1798, ibid., vol. 2, p. 232.

[19]Carroll to Charles Plowden, February 20, 1782, ibid., vol. 1, p. 65.

[20]"Plan of Clergy Organization," ibid., vol. 1, p. 60; Carroll to Charles Plowden, April 30, 1792, ibid., vol. 2, p. 41.

[21]Carroll to Charles Plowden, March 21, 1791, ibid., vol. 1, p. 501.

[22]Ibid., vol. 1, p. 140.

[23]Carroll to Charles Plowden, October 12, 1791, ibid., vol. 1, pp. 522-524.

> unlimited Toleration giving an open Field to the Display of Truth and fair argument may greatly contribute to bring mankind to an unity of Opinion on matters of Religious Concern.[24]

Carroll revealed the consistency of his views in a 1797 letter reflecting on Francis Plowden's *Jura Anglorum* (1792).[25] Plowden's work confined the papacy to spiritual concerns and defended liberty of conscience. The English layperson openly advocated the Lockian theory of contractural government. His work identified him as an advocate of the Catholic Enlightenment in England, a member of the Cisalpine group led by Joseph Berington. Presupposing separation of church and state, *Jura Anglorum* argued that excommunication from the Catholic Church could produce no civil effect. Francis' brother, Robert, dis- 283
agreed with this approach. Carroll wrote to Robert expressing his concurrence with *Jura Anglorum*, especially in its theory of toleration:

> . . . the point of difference (between us) is in your doctrine concerning the lawfulness (&) propriety of suppressing, by force of severities, heresies, which are attempted to be introduced into states, where the true religion was before universally prevalent. The plausible reasons may be adduced in favor of this, & it may be defended by arguments *ex natura rei*; yet considering the grounds for retaliation, which this doctrine suggests, & the cruelties, which it would provoke; and considering likewise the language of scripture and tradition, I do not think, that J. Christ ever impowered his church to recur to the means of force & bloodshed, for the preservation of faith against error. My idea, in this, as in every other lawful defence, is, *ut fiat cum moderamine inculpatae tutelae*; that the means be proportioned to the attack; persuasion, argument, coersion by spiritual censures, unless force of arms be used against the friends of truth; if our enemies recur to these, then indeed the same weapons may be used to repel & destroy the invaders.[26]

This short paragraph summarized John Carroll's disagreement with the European continental tradition of toleration and the consequences of his view for religious pluralism. The Marylander placed his relationships with non-Catholics on the basis of spiritual persuasion, not civil coercion. Robert Plowden, working from a different political anthropology—one which rejected natural rights, contract, and the secularized state—advocated the interference of the state in the religious concerns of individuals. Carroll's approach was ecumenical to its core because of its foundation in the Enlightenment view of the person. Once church and state were separated, religious amity became a primary value.

---

[24]Carroll to Berington, July 10, 1784, ibid., vol. 1, p. 148.

[25]Francis Plowden, *Jura Anglorum, The Rights of Englishmen* (London, 1792).

[26]Carroll to Robert Plowden, July 7, 1797, in Hanley, *Carroll Papers*, vol. 2, p. 219. Cf. Carroll to John Troy, July 12, 1794, ibid., vol. 2, p. 121; Carroll to Charles Plowden, September 3, 1800, ibid., vol. 2, p. 319.

This meant "the need to conform with others whenever it is possible without detriment to faith and the precepts of the Church."[27]

Although he has left us the largest body of writings, Carroll was definitely not alone in his beliefs. He shared a common colonial tradition and European education with many of his fellow Catholics.[28] Previous studies have indicated the widespread exposure of Marylanders to the ideas of the French Enlightenment.[29] Their English roots are also well known. Carroll's close collaboration with his fellow priests, the acceptance of his plan of clergy organization, his election to the bishopric, and his popularity as a leader indicate the universality of his views. It should be noted that the writings of Arthur O'Leary and Joseph Berington were well accepted in the United States.[30] John Fletcher's *Reflections*
284 *on the Spirit etc. etc. of Religious Controversy* (1804) achieved a total advance sale of 1,118 copies. Carroll himself read it at least four times.[31] The work was a *tour de force* of eighteenth-century reasoning. Fletcher sought "to unite the divided; and to show that divisions are the effect of misunderstanding, interest, or passion." He wrote "to implore benevolence, to instruct ignorance; or to enlighten prejudice." For Carroll, Fletcher, and many others, "nothing is more compatible with truth, than liberality. United, they possess an irrestible influence over the mind, that is controlled by reason: for while truth strikes the understanding, liberality gains the heart."[32] To a greater degree than has been realized, American Catholics participated in the mentality of the Enlightenment. A Lockian socio-political anthropology enabled them to approach religious pluralism in a positive way.

Religious Pluralism and Ecumenism

Once American Catholics adopted an Enlightenment anthropology and accepted religious pluralism as a civil right, their relationships with Protestants changed. People searched for an apologetics of convergence. Since the individual conscience, which in the eighteenth century meant "reason," had to be per-

---

[27]Carroll to Hyacinth Gerdil, December, 1795, ibid., vol. 2, p. 160.

[28]Cf. T. G. Holt, "Americans at St. Omers, Bruges and Liege," *Stonyhurst Magazine*, 1976, pp. 243-247; Thomas O'Brien Hanley, *The American Revolution and Religion, Maryland 1770-1800* (Washington, DC: Catholic University of America, 1971), pp. 171-193.

[29]Thomas O'Brien Hanley, "Young Mr. Carroll and Montesquieu," *Maryland Historical Magazine* 58 (December, 1963): 394-418.

[30]Cf. Robert Gorman, *Catholic Apologetical Literature in the United States (1784-1858)* (Washington, DC: Catholic University of America, 1939), pp. 58-61; Joseph M. Finotti, *Bibliographia Catholica Americana. A List of Works Written By Catholic Authors, and Published in the United States, Part I, 1784-1820* (New York: The Catholic Publication House, 1872).

[31]Cf. Peter Guilday, "Two Catholic Best Sellers," *America* 54 (1935): 177-179; Carroll to Charles Plowden, December 5, 1808, in Hanley, *Carroll Papers*, vol. 3, p. 73.

[32]Fletcher, *Reflections*, pp. iii, 85.

suaded and could not be coerced into external belief, church practice began to be approached in a "reasonable" way. Intelligibility became a dominant concern. Because the state no longer had the support of an established church, Christians pursued a policy of common doctrine in order to promote social harmony. In both areas American Catholics tried to meet the Enlightenment's challenge to relate the church to the world. Only two examples need be given here: the American Catholic approach to worship, and the understanding of the doctrine of church membership.

There is no doubt that the heady wine of legal toleration and the underlying Enlightenment mentality led Catholics and Protestants to mix in an unprecedented way in Revolutionary America. This included some type of common 285
attendance at liturgical events. Ecclesial assemblies themselves became religiously pluralistic. John Carroll described a typical missionary scene in this way:

> To pass thro' a village, where a Roman Catholic Clergyman was never seen before; to borrow of the parson the use of his meeting house, or church in order to preach a sermon; to go or send about the village, giving notice at every house, that a priest is to preach at a certain hour, and there to enlarge on the doctrines of our Church; this is a mode adopted by some amongst us for the propagation of religion.[33]

Although Carroll worked to establish a parish system and opposed Protestant ministers' officiating at mixed marriages and preaching from Catholic pulpits,[34] there is evidence that considerable latitude existed when Catholics were officiating. This has been well documented by Joseph Agonito.[35]

Given this type of social reality, John Carroll and many of his priests sanctioned sacramental practices which would encourage Protestants to convert. Priests consciously departed from universal Catholic Church law and tried to tailor religious practices to ecumenical needs, to foster an apologetics of convergence. In 1784, Carroll considered Latin in the liturgy to be one of the greatest "obstacles, with Christians of other Denominations, to a thorough union with us; or at least, to a much more general Diffusion of our Religion, particularly in N. America."[36] He definitely wanted an alteration in discipline, and most of his clergy agreed. The Catholic leader shared his anxiety with friends in England in 1790. Robert Plowden reported that at that time Carroll believed

---

[33]John Carroll to Charles Plowden, April 30, 1792, in Hanley, *Carroll Papers*, vol. 2, p. 40.

[34]Carroll to Francis Beeston, Nov. 16, 1791, ibid., vol. 1, pp. 545-546; Carroll to Charles Carroll, July 15, 1800, ibid., vol. 2. p. 310; Carroll to William Vousdan, September 10, 1801, ibid., vol. 2, p. 362.

[35]"Ecumenical Stirrings: Catholic-Protestant Relations during the Episcopacy of John Carroll," *Church History*, vol. 45, no. 3 (September, 1976), pp. 358-373.

[36]Carroll to Joseph Berington, July 10, 1784, in Hanley, *Carroll Papers*, vol. 1, p. 148. For clergy agreement, see Carroll to Berington, September 29, 1786, ibid., vol. 1, p. 219.

that such a change in Catholic Church discipline would exceed his powers as a bishop. Traditional historiography has left the issue at that point.[37]

John Carroll apparently allowed some use of the vernacular in the liturgy when he returned from England. Robert Plowden wrote to Carroll in 1799:

> In fact only a few months before I was positively assured by a clergyman of my acquaintance, a man of first rate abilities in point of theological knowledge, that yr Ldsp was making alterations in the administration of the Sacraments, contrary to the laws of the Church, and whatever arguments I cd offer to correct the false notion he had imbibed, my words were of no avail; he had been assured of the fact, he said, by his friends in London, & so it must
> 286 be.[38]

This letter in itself is ambiguous. It neither mentions the type of changes that were made nor proves that they were made. Still, the 1810 regulations of the bishops' meeting indicate that there was frequent use of the vernacular in the administration of the sacraments.[39] Article nine noted that the form of the sacraments was to be kept in Latin, but other prayers could be in English.

In 1821, Stephen Dubisson, a priest working at St. Patrick's in Washington, complained to Archbishop Marechal that:

> Rev. Mr. Matthews [the pastor] uses for internments, and likewise frequently for baptisms, the English translation of the Roman Ritual instead of the Latin Original, on account of the late Right Revd. Archbishop Carroll's having formerly so stated. This is quite contrary to the universal practice of the Catholic Church, and I am pressingly invited to adopt the opposite mode of acting. Yet, as I do not wish really to introduce new forms in this congregation, nor in general to appear as differing from Mr. Matthews in the administration of the sacred rites, I respectfully beg of Your Grace to let me know what your sentiment is on the subject.[40]

Unfortunately, Archbishop Marechal's response is not extant, but apparently the practice continued. In 1828, Bishop Rosati wrote to the Sacred Congregation:

> Can priests use the English language for the administration of Baptism, Matrimony, Extreme Unction and in the prayers established for burial? Such use exists in some dioceses, a use which certain bishops foster by their own example.[41]

---

[37]Robert Plowden, *A Letter to A Roman Catholic Clergyman Upon Theological Inaccuracy* (London: J. P. Coghlan, 1795), pp. 150-151.

[38]March 10, 1799, AAB, 6S7.

[39]"Provincial Council Resolutions," in Hanley, *Carroll Papers*, vol. 3, p. 133, no. 9.

[40]August 30, 1821, AAB, 16B1.

[41]SRC, America Centrale, 1827-1828, IV, fol. 527 as cited in Thomas F. Casey, *The Sacred Congregation of Propaganda Fide and the Revision of the First Provincial Council of*

Further evidence indicates that this use of the vernacular in the administration of the sacraments and burial rites started with Carroll's knowledge and approval. The purpose of the change in practice was to make the services intelligible to both Catholics and Protestants. This was taking an Enlightenment anthropology to its practical conclusions. In 1806, the Rev. Pierre Babade, a Sulpician teaching at St. Mary's Seminary, voiced his opposition to this custom. He turned the argument of the Enlightened Catholics on end. Babade maintained to the Prefect of Propaganda that Latin should be used because it was the only language which could unite Catholics of so many European backgrounds. The Sulpician included the following description in his letter:

> Nevertheless, today we see that a pastor of Baltimore and certain 287
> other fellow priests of ours, under the eyes of the bishop and with his approval, administer the sacraments and perform ecclesiastical rites (e.g. for burial, etc.) in the English language, which more often than not seems ridiculous and inharmonious. . . .
>
> So likewise, when we recently attended the funeral of a certain friend together with the bishop and several priests, we were not only amazed, seeing ourselves associated in a serious and religious ceremony with heretical ministers who had been invited, [unclear] but above all because the priest, old and full of piety, at the introduction of the body into church before it was taken to the burial place, recited the prayers assigned in the ritual for burial in the English language, and, even though he was surrounded by a large group of priests, no one responded to the versicles because this innovation was displeasing to them.[42]

Such innovations extended even to the Eucharist. There the priest recited the "*miseratur* [sic], *indulgentiam*," and other prayers in English.[43]

The impact of a positive acceptance of religious pluralism on ecumenical relations was also evident in the attempt of Enlightened American Catholics to broaden the traditional understanding of church membership. Within the context of an anthropology of rights, fellow citizens were worthy of respect as individuals; they were endowed with the natural light of reason and therefore possessed some insight into truth. Here the Enlightenment revealed its innate optimism.[44] In addition, Catholics mixed with Protestants so frequently and with enough amicability that it became difficult to criticize the other's faith in any ultimate way. The acceptance of religious pluralism possessed a natural dynamism toward religious indifference. Given their notion of toleration, many

---

Baltimore (1829-1830) (Rome: Universitatis Gregorianae, 1957), p. 133, fn. 47. Translation from the Latin by courtesy of Michael Guinan, O.F.M.

[42]Archives of the Sacred Congregation of the Propagation of the Faith, November 21, 1806, Atti della Congregatione Particolare de 4 Marzo, 1808, America Settentrionale, 145, fol. 105r. Translation from the Latin.

[43]Ibid.

[44]Cf. Fletcher, *Reflections*, *passim*.

Catholics were forced to ask how the phrase *extra ecclesiam nulla est salus* should be interpreted.

The source material for the Carroll period amply testifies to the concern of Catholics for a more nuanced understanding of the traditional doctrine of "one, true Church." People attempted to walk the thin line between ecclesiological exclusivism and doctrinal indifference. In 1794, Fillippo Filicchi recognized the need for an apologetic work suited to the reality of religious pluralism. There was a need to show that true worship occurred only in the Roman Church, but this should be done with the greatest gentleness, without the point of the argument offending the other churches by its bad conclusions. With respect to
288 the question of *extra ecclesiam* the Italian wrote:

> . . . and in determining the necessity of being Catholic to obtain Eternal Life it would be necessary to urge a desire of finding this important Truth, and of pointing out the easiest and most certain means of finding it; the Americans do not know how to forgive, they say, that lack of charity which they presuppose in us, of not wishing them to be saved because they are not actually Catholics, when really they desire with love only to know and to follow through that which they intend, nothing other than the Truth.[45]

In 1805 Pere Babade complained about the prevalence of "religious indifference" among the American clergy. According to the Sulpician, many persons of important dignity and authority among them adopted a conciliatory manner of speaking. They believed that Protestants could maintain good faith and invincible ignorance even when they conversed and argued with Catholics and still did not convert. Many priests held that it was impossible to judge a Protestant's final end and his or her good or bad faith.[46]

Felice de Andreis, another Italian, cited an example of religious indifference among the Protestants:

> The other day I heard that one of these groups which are called "congregations" were looking for a priest, and when they did not find him, a Protestant minister went there. My God![47]

Catholics could not help but be concerned about this problem. The apologetic works of the period contain numerous references to the issue. The writings of John Gother, James Mumford, William Pilling, Joseph Berington, Arthur O'Leary, John Carroll, Stephen Badin, Demetrius Gallitzen, and Roger Baxter

---

[45]Filippo Filicchi to Cardinal Antonelli, 1794, SRC, America Centrale, 1791-1817, vol. 3, fol. 49rv. Translation from the Italian.

[46]Petrum Babade, S.S., to Congregation, November 16, 1805, Atti della Congregations Particolare de 4 Marzo, 1808, America Settentrionale, 145, fols. 101-102.

[47]Felice de Andreis to Propaganda, August 26, 1816, SRC, America Centrale, 1791-1817, vol. 3, fols. 494-495. Translation from the Italian.

dealt with the question explicitly.[48] A *Catechism on the Foundations of the Christian Faith*, issued with Carroll's approbation in 1811, contained a long footnote on the subject.[49]

The material indicates that there were two distinct approaches to the ecclesiological question posed by religious pluralism. Those who generally opposed any type of Enlightenment accommodation held firmly to the usual interpretation that only invincible ignorance and inevitable necessity excused one from belonging to the only true church existing which is "really Catholic." The seventeenth-century English apologists Mumford and Gother were very strict. The former spoke of the necessity of the "one true Faith" and equated "Church" with "Roman Church."[50] Gother included among the disbelievers "heathens, infidels, all heretics and schismatics." "Whosoever obstinately and 289
willfully is separated from her [the Roman Catholic Church] is in the same distance separated from Christ himself."[51] This basic approach continued in the works of Pilling, Badin, and Gallitzen. Richard Challoner's earliest apologetic work, reprinted in Philadelphia in 1789, also argued that "the whole visible Church of Christ, is but in one communion: of which heretics and schismatics are no part." Excepting the case of invincible ignorance, "whatsoever christian is out of the true church . . . is out of the church."[52] Pere Babade also wrote from this perspective in his 1805 letter to Propaganda.

The common foundation for all of these people was a preoccupation with the institutional elements in the church. Their anthropological starting point was society, not the individual. They exhibited the Counter-Reformation's apologetic concern for structure and order and viewed "Church" in a socio-political way. Because of this, *extra ecclesiam nulla est salus* could only be interpreted in the strictest possible sense. Such a position prevented any positive theological

---

[48]John Gother, *A Papist Mis-Represented and Represented; or, A Two-Fold Character of Popery* (Dublin: R. Cross, 1806), pp. 163-174; James Mumford, *The Question of Questions, which Rightly Resolv'd Resolves All Our Questions on Religion. This Question is, Who Ought to be our Judge in all these Differences?* (London: Henry Hills, 1686/7), p. 526; William Pilling, *A Caveat Addressed to the Catholics of Worcester, against the Insinuating Letter of Mr. Wharton* (London: J. P. Coghlan, 1785), pp. 7-10; Berington, *State and Behaviour*, pp. 155-156; Arthur O'Leary, *A Review of the Important Controversy Between Dr. Carroll and the Reverend Messrs. Wharton and Hawkins, Including a Defence of the Conduct of Pope Clement XIV (Gaganelli) in Suppressing a late religious Order: In A Letter to A Gentleman* (London: P. Keating, 1786), pp. 34-49; John Carroll, *An Address to the Roman Catholics of the United States of America*, 1784, in Hanley, *Carroll Papers*, vol. 1, pp. 87-92; Badin, *The Real Principles of Roman Catholics, In Reference to God and the Country* (Bardstown: F. Peniston, 1805), pp. 7, 28; Gallitzen, *A Defence of Catholic Principles, A Letter to a Protestant Minister* (Winchester, VA: John Heiskell, 1818), pp. 102-109; Baxter, *The Most Important Tenets of the Roman Catholic Church Fairly Explained* (Washington, DC: Davis and Force, 1820), pp. 9-13.

[49](New York, 1811), pp. 100-102.

[50]Mumford, *Question*, pp. 526, 374, 524.

[51]Gother, *Papist*, pp. 164, 173-174.

[52]*The Unerring Authority of the Catholic Church In Matters of Faith, Maintained against the exceptions of a late author, in his answer to a letter on the subject of Infallibility; or, A Theological Dissertation* . . . (Philadelphia: T. Lloyd, 1789), pp. 34, 52.

response to religious pluralism. The concern for apologetics excluded a catholic approach to the pluralistic forces of Enlightenment.

In light of this view, the open approach of some other Roman Catholics becomes particularly significant and indicates their acceptance of an Enlightenment mentality. To some extent Pere Babade's complaints were well taken. Joseph Berington, Arthur O'Leary, John Carroll, and Roger Baxter seemed to reflect a popular mentality when they argued that *extra ecclesiam* had to be interpreted in the broadest possible sense. Carroll agreed with Berington when the latter wrote:

> Religion certainly is an affair of very serious consideration. When
> 290 therefore a man, either neglects to inform himself, or when informed, refuses to follow the convictions of his mind, such a one we say, is not in the way of Salvation. After mature enquiries, if I am convinced that the religion of England is the only true one, am I not obliged to become a Protestant? In similar circumstances, must not you likewise declare yourself a Catholic? Our meaning is, that no one can be saved out of the true Church, and as we consider the evidence of the truth of our religion to be great, that he who will not embrace the truth, when he sees it, deserves not to be happy.[53]

Given the Counter-Reformation interpretation of ecclesiology, this position necessitated a redefinition of "Church." In the controversy with Wharton, Carroll agreed that to be a member of the Roman Catholic Church and to be in communion with it were two distinct realities. Communion implied adherence to creed, sacraments, and institutional structure; membership implied a sincere heart seeking true religion and an unfeigned disposition to embrace the truth. He based his distinction, one which was to be popular in the nineteenth century, on Robert Bellarmine.[54] Arthur O'Leary elucidated the position further when he stated that all persons became children of the Catholic Church by baptism; many were members of the Catholic Church unknown to themselves.[55] Carroll denied that he "*absolutely excludes from the honourable appellation of Christians, all who are not within the pale of his church.*" In fact, he maintained, the direct opposite of this was true.[56] Roger Baxter summarized the view in 1820:

> Although those, who sincerely profess dissenting creeds, containing the essentials of christianity, do not belong to the Catholic church in the eyes of men, they do nevertheless belong to her in the sight of God, and, as such, are real members of the church. By baptism, by whomsoever or wheresoever it be given, they are initiated into the

---

[53]Berington, *State and Behaviour*, pp. 155-156; Carroll, in Hanley, *Carroll Papers*, vol. 1, p. 88.

[54]Hanley, *Carroll Papers*, vol. 1, p. 87. For background see Yves M.-J. Congar, *Sainte Église, Études et approaches ecclésiologiques* (Paris: Editions du Cerf, 1963), pp. 417-432.

[55]O'Leary, *A Review*, pp. 42-43.

[56]"An Answer to Strictures on an Extraordinary Signature," November 21, 1792, in Hanley, *Carroll Papers*, vol. 2, pp. 70-71.

> church of Christ, (and the Catholic church deems herself that church;) and as by the supposition, they have never wilfully and obstinately rejected any known tenet of divine faith, they still remain members of that church.[57]

The important factor in all of the arguments was that "Church" in *extra ecclesiam* could be understood in a non-institutional way. In his "Sermon on Membership in the Church" Carroll implied a sharp distinction between Church and Kingdom.[58] It should be noted that Carroll relied on Augustine, whose thought inspired most of the Enlightened Catholics. The intricacies of the theological position need not be considered here. The Catholic leader even went beyond the usual argumentation when he wrote that since people could be saved without baptism, and baptism was necessary to belong to the Catholic Church, therefore Catholics "not only *may*, but *are obliged* to believe, that *out of our communion* salvation may be obtained."[59]

It is not surprising that such a radical position—the acceptance of which was quite widespread, if we are to believe Babade—upset people. One Italian accused Carroll of departing from the fundamental principles of theology.[60] In the context of this sermon, however, the significance of these interpretations of *extra ecclesiam* lay in the anthropology which supported them and the opening which they provided to a truly ecumenical outlook. The Enlightenment position of Carroll and others tended to dissolve the distinction between material and formal heresy. Why? Because the Enlightenment mentality was primarily focussed on individual faith, the particular appropriation of truth, not the abstract notion of "objective truth." The insistance on baptism as incorporating people into the church was the natural corollary of this interpretation. Socially, the first of the sacraments dealt with the initial relationship between the individual and the community, with the state of the person before and after entrance into society. To focus on baptism was also to recognize the sacrament common to all Christian traditions, to promote in this way an apologetics of convergence. Carroll and others thus joined a civil anthropology of freedom of conscience with a theology which adequately responded to the social need for harmony and the accomplished fact of religious pluralism. The position tightroped its way between doctrinal indifference and ecclesiological exclusivism. It reached toward a synthesis between the Enlightenment and Catholicism.

Within the context of the European Enlightenment, the program of intelligibility which American Catholics adopted appears to have been unique. After the Revolutionary War, Carroll and his fellow priests were in a position to implement some of the ideas of their continental counterparts. Many Europeans had

---

[57] Baxter, *Most Important Tenets*, p. 11.

[58] Hanley, *Carroll Papers*, vol. 2, pp. 373-374.

[59] *An Address*, in ibid., vol. 1, p. 89.

[60] Carroll to Charles Plowden, January 22, 1787 and February 28, 1787, in ibid., vol. 1, p. 244.

argued for a vernacular liturgy, but in the practical order their position came to be equated with Jansenist reform tendencies. Only among American Catholics, removed from regular communication with Rome, assured of government non-interference, and led by Carroll, could such a program actually be attempted. English, German, and French Catholics also struggled with the meaning of *extra ecclesiam*, but the American separation of church and state forced Catholics there to reflect on it in an explicitly ecumenical way. The Anglo-Saxon ability to distinguish toleration from complete religious indifference encouraged an approach which could remain integrally Catholic yet still accommodate Protestants. The result in both areas was a unique blend of Catholic doctrine and
292 Enlightenment anthropology, a singular attempt to respond creatively to the forces of religious pluralism.

Enlightened Catholicism Today

Unfortunately, this enlightened Catholic program of intelligibility did not perdure beyond the first quarter of the nineteenth century.[61] Although a similar anthropology characterized the thought of Isaac Thomas Hecker, and a few late-nineteenth-century American Catholics adopted the ecclesiological stance, the forces which shaped the immigrant Catholic Church insured that Carroll's tradition would not dominate.[62] Increased immigration from France, Ireland, and Germany relegated the original Anglo-American Catholic nucleus to a position of relative unimportance within the Roman Catholic Church. A growing self-consciousness on the part of the Protestant majority and periodic "no popery" campaigns precluded ecumenical developments.[63] Ecclesiologically, the passage from a missionary to an institutionalized parochial structure severely limited Catholic-Protestant interaction. The foremost American Catholic apologists of the nineteenth century, heavily influenced by European Ultramontanism, stressed disciplinary uniformity. In a similar vein, the legislation of the Councils of Baltimore (1829-1866) insisted on the adoption of the Roman ritual.[64]

---

[61]It lasted only slightly longer in portions of Germany. Cf. Leonard Swidler, *Aufklärung Catholicism, 1750-1850* (Missoula, MT: Scholars Press, 1978).

[62]Cf. Joseph Francis Gower, "The 'New Apologetics' of Isaac Thomas Hecker (1819-88): Catholicity and American Culture," unpublished Ph.D. thesis, University of Notre Dame, 1978; and Margaret Mary Reher, "The Church and the Kingdom of God in America: The Ecclesiology of the Americanists," unpublished Ph.D. thesis, Fordham University, 1972. On the immigrant church see Jay P. Dolan, *The Immigrant Church* (Baltimore: Johns Hopkins University Press, 1975).

[63]Ray Allen Billington, *The Protestant Crusade 1800-1860* (Chicago: Quadrangle Books, 1964); John Higham, *Strangers in the Land, Patterns of American Nativism, 1860-1925* (New York: Atheneum, 1969); Thomas T. McAvoy, C.S.C., *A History of the Catholic Church in the United States* (Notre Dame: University of Notre Dame Press, 1969).

[64]This is a complex development which needs to be explored more fully. For some indications, see Peter Guilday, *A History of the Councils of Baltimore (1791-1884)* (New

However, if the argument of this article is correct, then the most important reasons for the loss of a creative approach to religious pluralism lay much deeper than external developments. What was involved in the change was a fundamental transformation of mentality. Firstly, American Catholic thinkers lost contact with the Enlightenment tradition of church-state separation. They ceased to distinguish civil toleration from religious indifference. The writings of Martin John Spalding and Francis Patrick Kenrick implied the indirect temporal power thesis of the European Ultramontanes.[65] Correspondingly, after 1830, the earlier understanding of the person changed dramatically. John Carroll had presupposed individual rights and the basic integrity of reason. In contrast, devotional writings, bishops' statements, and apologetic works indicate that a pessimistic view of the person dominated the immigrant Roman Catholic community. The notion of contract lost popularity; society itself bestowed individual rights. As John Hughes wrote: "All that is good is due to Christianity [i.e., Catholicism]—all that is evil . . . to the perverse exercise of men's free will." "Man is naturally evil."[66] Both the new view of church and state and the pessimistic anthropology necessitated an apologetics of authority and imputation not one of convergence.

Today, the fundamental basis on which the enlightened Catholic position rested has been revived. The emergence of Catholics into positions of social prominence has broken the sociological hold of the immigrant Catholic Church.[67] The work of John Courtney Murray on religious liberty has encouraged a positive acceptance of church-state separation and a distinction between civil toleration and religious indifference. The Second Vatican Council's *Declaration on Religious Freedom* accepted an anthropology of contract. As a result, the door has been opened to ecumenical discussion, and an apologetics of convergence has emerged. It is hoped that this article has shown how these

---

York: The Macmillan Co., 1932); James Hennesey, S.J., "The Baltimore Council of 1866: An American Syllabus," *Records of the American Catholic Historical Society of Philadelphia*, vol. 76, no. 3 (September, 1965), pp. 157-173; and Br. David Spalding, C.F.X., "Martin John Spalding, Legislator," *Records of the American Catholic Historical Society of Philadelphia*, vol. 75, no. 3 (September, 1964), pp. 131-160.

[65]Cf. *Theses ex Universa Theologia et Jure Publico Ecclesiastico quas auspicibus et patronis Eminentissimis Patribus S. Consilii P. F. Publice Propugnandas Suscipit Joh. Martinus Spalding Kentuckiensis eiusdem S. Consilii Alumnus XVI* (Rome: In Collegio Urbano, 1834); F. P. Kenrick, *Theologicae Dogmaticae, Tractatus Tres, De Revelatione, de Ecclesia, et de Verbo Dei* (Philadelphia: L. Johnson, 1839). Kenrick's position was much more nuanced than that of Spalding. The former was more willing to distinguish civil from spiritual concerns and struggled with how they were to interrelate. Still, the struggle itself was indicative of a shift in mentality from the Carroll period.

[66]Laurence Kehoe, ed., *The Complete Works of the Most Rev. John Hughes, D.D.* (New York: The American News Co., 1864), I, II, 112; I, IV, 9. Cf. a typical devotional work, *True Piety; or, The Day Well Spent, Being A Catholic Manual of Chosen Prayers, Devout Practices, and Solid Instructions*, By A Catholic Clergyman of Baltimore (Baltimore: Warner & Hanna, 1809).

[67]Cf. Andrew M. Greeley, *The American Catholic: A Social Portrait* (New York: Basic Books, Inc., 1977).

political, anthropological, ecclesiological, and apologetic questions are historically interconnected. If ecumenical progress is to endure, these fundamental areas must be seen as mutually supportive. Discussion can no longer consider them in isolation. What is involved is a complete mentality; what is demanded is a restructuring of our approach to the person and our view of the church. American Catholics themselves would do well to reconsider their past and thus draw out of their history realities "both new and old."

Ecumenical Stirrings: Catholic-Protestant Relations during the Episcopacy of John Carroll

JOSEPH AGONITO

In 1790, the year John Carroll was consecrated as the first Roman Catholic Bishop of Baltimore, the Catholic population numbered less than 40,000—a very distinct minority in a country of nearly 4,000,000 people. As a small group living in a society overwhelmingly composed of Protestants, Catholics could not avoid mixing with those of different faiths in their everyday life.[1] Carroll viewed such contacts with mixed feelings. As a native American he understood that so many of his countrymen considered his church, however wrongly, an "alien" institution. He resented most the accusation that the allegiance that Catholics owed to Rome 295 detracted from their attachment to the United States. He could only hope, then, that through daily contact with Catholics, Protestants would come to realize that their fears and suspicions were groundless. Still, for Carroll there were dangers as well from such meetings, for established relationships must not become so close that Catholics fall prey to the errors of Protestant thought or come to view "all religions as equally acceptable to God and salutary to men."[2]

Despite such dangers to the faith, however, Carroll cautioned against Catholic withdrawal from Protestant society lest such actions alienate non-Catholics "from our doctrines and rites, for, as they outnumber us and are more influential, they may, at some time, be inclined to renew the iniquitous laws against us."[3] Actually, Carroll need not have feared a renewed persecution of Catholics, for their position had improved during the revolutionary era. Protestant Americans found it increasingly difficult to maintain an intolerant system against a religion whose members had proven their loyalty during the long struggle for independence. Furthermore, the spirit of the Declaration of Independence, with its stress on the natural rights of all men, supported the movement to extend religious freedom to all denominations. As a result, then, of the liberalizing forces set loose by the American Revolution various states emancipated the small band of Catholics from the oppressive penal legislation of the colonial period which had denied them their basic political and religious rights. Catholics could now worship freely and, in several states, they gained as well full political equality. In some states, though, old prejudices remained, and Catholics still suffered from laws which barred them from voting and officeholding.[4]

1. Gerald Shaughnessy, *Has the Immigrant Kept the Faith? A Study of Immigration and Catholic Church Growth in the United States 1790-1920* (New York: Macmillan Company, 1925), pp. 36-38.
2. John Carroll, "First Sermon as Bishop of Baltimore," 12 December 1790, Maryland Province Archives of the Society of Jesus, Baltimore (hereafter MPA).
3. Carroll to Cardinal Hyacinth Gerdil, Prefect of the Roman Congregation for the Propagation of the Faith, December 1795, John Carroll Papers. Father Thomas O'Brien Hanley of Baltimore, editor of the John Carroll Papers, provided me with a typescript, microfilm copy of Archbishop Carroll's correspondence. All references to the John Carroll Papers—hereafter JCP—are from this source.
4. For a thorough study of the position of Catholics during the revolutionary era consult Sister Mary Augustina Ray, *American Opinion of Roman Cathlicism in the Eighteenth Century* (New York: Columbia University Press, 1936), chap. 7, "The Tradition in the Pre-Revolutionary Decade," pp. 263-310; chap. 8, "The Revolution," pp. 310-350; and chap. 9, "Making the Constitutions," pp. 350-394.

Mr. Agonito is professor of history in Onondaga Community College, Syracuse, New York.

The granting of religious and political liberties to Catholics did not imply any significant change in Protestant America's attitude toward Roman Catholicism as a religion, for which there still existed considerable disdain. The postwar years witnessed a tempering, not an abandonment, of anti-Catholic sentiment. Still, there was no denying that in practice many Americans had grown more tolerant of Catholics. The word "Catholic" no longer connoted all that was bad, and these Americans had to grudgingly admit that even a Roman Catholic "might be a desirable neighbor, a devoted friend, a loyal citizen."[5]

Public opinion of Catholics had mellowed, and John Carroll was to find out, to his pleasant surprise, how much had changed even in that bastion of anti-Catholicism, Puritan New England. Carroll visited Boston in the early summer of 1791. Many Bostonians gave him a warm welcome, and they invited him to several large functions.[6] Carroll wrote enthusiastically to his good friend and fellow Jesuit,
296 Charles Plowden: "It is wonderful to tell, what great civilities have been done to me in this town, where a few years ago a popish priest was thought to be the greatest monster in the creation."[7] The warm reception given to Carroll, however, was out of respect for his person and not for the religion which he represented. Reverend Jeremy Belknap made this point clear to his correspondent Ebenezer Hazard: "Bishop Carroll is here yet, and I assure you is treated with the greatest attention and respect by most of our distinguished characters; but the cause which he meant to serve is not the foundation of this respect: it is wholly owing to his personal character."[8]

Carroll was perceptive enough to realize that despite the fine reception he had received in Boston the prejudice against his religion and its adherents was so deep-rooted that it would take a long time before it disappeared.[9] Events in New England later demonstrated the accuracy of this observation.

In the town of Newcastle, District of Maine, James Kavanagh and Matthew Cottrell, two respectable merchants, maintained a chapel for Catholic worship. Along with Father Francis Anthony Matignon, pastor of the Church of the Holy Cross in Boston, they decided in 1799 to challenge in the courts the Massachusetts State Constitution of 1785 and subsequent laws of the General Court, which compelled Catholics to support with their taxes Congregational churches and ministers. The case was taken all the way to the State Supreme Court which ruled against Matignon.[10] According to Father Jean Lefebvre de Cheverus, Matignon's assistant at

5. Ibid., pp. 310, 348-349; Thomas O'Brien Hanley, *The American Revolution and Religion: Maryland 1700-1800* (Washington, D. C.: Catholic University of America Press, 1971), pp. 210-214 shows the improved image of Catholics in Maryland.
6. Carroll attended a dinner in honor of the Ancient and Honorable Artillery Company (6 June 1791), where he gave "thanks" at the banquet at Faneuil Hall. Reverend John Eliot noted in his interleaved almanac for that day, "An elegant entertainment at the hall, where a clergyman of the C. of England (Rev. Dr. Parker) and a Romish Bp. acted as Chaplains. How would our Fathers have stared! Tempora mutantur etc., and much to the credit of modern times." Quoted in Percival Merritt, "Sketches of the Three Earliest Roman Catholic Priests in Boston," *Publications of the Colonial Society of Massachusetts* 25 (1923): 205-206.
7. Carroll to Plowden, 11 June 1791, MPA, Box 202-B36.
8. As quoted in Robert H. Lord, John E. Sexton, and Edward T. Harrington, *History of the Archdiocese of Boston*, 3 vols. (New York: Sheed and Ward, 1944), 1:457.
9. Carroll to Cardinal Leonardo Antonelli, Prefect of the Roman Congregation for the Propagation of the Faith, 27 February 1785, JCP: Carroll to Guiseppe Doria Pamphili, Apostolic Nuncio at Paris, 27 February 1785, JCP; Hanley, *American Revolution and Religion*, p. 214.
10. For a full account of this incident see Matignon's letter to Carroll, 16 March 1801, Archives of the Archdiocese of Baltimore (hereafter AAB), Case 5-H4. A good secondary account of this controversy is William Leo Lucey, *Edward Kavanagh: Catholic,*

Holy Cross, the judges lectured Matignon on the proper place of Catholics in New England: "'The Constitution [of Massachusetts],'" said they, "'obliges everyone to contribute for the support of *Protestant* ministers and *them alone*. Papists are only tolerated and as long as their ministers behave well, we shall not disturb them. But let them expect no more than that.'"[11]

Despite these continuing signs of animosity, Catholics were encouraged not to isolate themselves from their Protestant neighbors. This would not only have been impractical in a society composed largely of non-Catholics, but also highly undesirable. There was no other way for the church, her doctrines, and rites to become known and understood except by Catholics involving themselves in Protestant society. Hopefully, a better understanding of Catholicism and Catholics would diminish prejudice. So, in countless ways, in private and public life, Catholics and Protestants touched each other's lives, thereby marking the beginnings of an ecu- 297
menical movement between the two faiths.

The small number of Catholics scattered throughout Protestant America, the scarcity of religious buildings, and the shortage of priests often led to novel situations. Catholic priests frequently celebrated religious services in Protestant churches or homes. Carroll described to Plowden one approach to preaching the gospel, which some of the clergy were compelled to adopt:

> To pass thro' a village, where a Roman Catholic clergyman was never seen before, to borrow of the parson the use of his meeting house, or church, in order to preach a sermon; to go or send about the village, giving notice at every house, that a priest is to preach at a certain hour, and there to enlarge on the doctrines of the Church.[12]

Father John Thayer, a former Congregationalist minister and convert to Catholicism, celebrated the first mass in Salem, Massachusetts in the home of Reverend William Bently, pastor of the town's Unitarian church.[13] In distant Kentucky Father Stephen Theodore Badin remarked that for want of chapels Catholic priests preached in Protestant churches.[14] Carroll, however, professed a reluctance to allow Protestants to celebrate services in a Catholic church. When William Vousdan, a resident of Adams County, Mississippi Territory, requested permission to allow a Presbyterian minister to make use of the Catholic church, Carroll explained the reasons for his disapproval:

> Catholic churches are dedicated to God for purpose of the most adorable sacrifice of the law of grace; and many august prayers & ceremonies, consecrated by their antiquity are used for their sanctification. After this, would it be justifiable to make our altars & church resound with doctrines, reviling & reprobating that holy sacrifice, & all the rites of our religion? Would not those holy places be profaned, & the character of sanctity acquired by their consecration be effaced, by their becoming the seminaries of error & false doctrines?[15]

Sometimes, the shortage of priests and facilities led Catholics to participate in

Statesman, Diplomat from Maine 1795-1844 (Francestown, New Hampshire: Marshall Jones Company, 1947), pp. 31-38.

11. Cheverus to Carroll, 10 March 1801, AAB, Case 2-N3.
12. Carroll to Plowden, 30 April 1792, MPA, Box 202-B42.
13. William Bentley, *The Diary of William Bentley*, 4 vols. (Salem, Massachusetts: Essex Institute, 1905-1914), 1:161-162, 165-166. Bentley was a generous and tolerant person. He assisted Thayer in finding the few Catholics that lived in Salem. When no Catholic family could be found to maintain Thayer while in the town, Bentley offered his own house to the visiting priest.
14. Stephen Theodore Badin, "Origin and Progress of the Missions of Kentucky," *Catholic World* 21 (September 1875): 830-831.
15. Extract of an Answer. Carroll to William Vousdan, 10 September 1801, AAB, Case 8A-Y6.

Protestant services. Father Simon William Gabriel Bruté said that the Catholics at Emmitsburg, Maryland sometimes attended the religious meetings of the Presbyterians, which were held in the open fields.[16] Thayer wrote Carroll that he had to reproach a Mr. Barry, a Catholic living in Albany, New York "for paying for a pew in the Protestant church and for bringing up all his family in that religion."[17] Barry was evidently not the only Catholic in Albany to frequent a Protestant church. The trustees of the Catholic church in that city lamented to Carroll that the failure to provide a resident pastor had a harmful effect, since several members of the priestless congregation attended Protestant churches.[18]

Protestants returned the visits of their Catholic neighbors by frequently participating in Catholic religious services. They often attended Catholic mass (either out of curiosity or sincere interest), and this was as true on the frontier as in the urban churches of the east. When the Trappist Fathers built a chapel in the Casey
298 Creek area in Kentucky, several Protestant families attended mass on Sundays and feastdays.[19] While making a trip to Baltimore, Benedict Joseph Flaget, the Bishop of Bardstown, Kentucky, noted the several occasions when Protestants came to hear mass which he celebrated in private homes. Later, when Flaget visited Vincennes, Indiana and preached a sermon in English, many Protestant settlers attended the service.[20] In Boston Protestants attended Sunday service at the Church of the Holy Cross to hear the eloquent sermons of the learned Cheverus.[21] At St. Peter's Church in New York City, Father Anthony Kohlman expressed his pleasure that non-Catholics came to Sunday mass.[22] Further south at St. Peter's in Baltimore, Protestants came to see John Carroll celebrate his first mass as Bishop upon his return from England where he had gone for his consecration.[23]

On one occasion Protestants were more than mere spectators. In Detroit Father Gabriel Richard allowed them to participate in the procession of the Corpus Christi by holding the ribbons of the canopy under which the Blessed Sacrament was carried. Joseph-Octave Plessis, Bishop of Quebec, who recorded the event on his visit to Detroit, observed that not all of Richard's parishioners approved of this step. "The Abbé Richard," Plessis added, "justifies his conduct by what the Bishop of Baltimore has given as a principle to his clergy: to do towards Protestants all that might draw them to the Catholic Church, an excellent principle as long as it does not violate the essential rules."[24]

It must have come as a surprise to those Protestants visiting a Catholic church

16. Simon William Gabriel Bruté, "Bishop Bruté's Account of Religion at Emmitsburg, Md.," *American Catholic Historical Society of Philadelphia Researches* 15 (January 1898): 89.
17. Thayer to Carroll, 4 October 1797, AAB, Case 8B-I6.
18. Trustees of the Catholic Church in Albany to Carroll, 26 April 1802, AAB, Case 11A-A5.
19. Joseph Durand, "Epistle or Diary of the Reverend Marie Joseph Durand," trans. Ella M. E. Flick, *Records of the American Catholic Historical Society of Philadelphia* 26 (December 1915): 331. (hereafter *Records*).
20. Benedict Joseph Flaget, "Bishop Flaget's Diary," trans. William J. Howlett, *Records* 29 (September 1919): 240, 244; Thomas T. McAvoy, *The Catholic Church in Indiana 1789-1834* (New York: Columbia University Press, 1940), p. 128.
21. Anthony Filicchi to Elizabeth Bayley Seton, 8 October 1804, printed in Elizabeth Seton, *Memoirs, Letters, and Journal of Elizabeth Seton*, ed. and comp. Robert Seton, 2 vols. (New York: P. O'Shea, 1869), 1:200-201.
22. Francis X. Curran, "The Jesuit Colony in New York 1808-1817," *Historical Records and Studies* 42 (1954): 58-59.
23. Peter Keenan Guilday, *The Life and Times of John Carroll: Archbishop of Baltimore 1735-1815* (New York: The Encyclopedia Press, 1922), p. 384.
24. As quoted in Sister M. Dolorita Mast, *Always the Priest: The Life of Gabriel Richard* (Baltimore: Helicon Press, 1965), p. 144.

to hear the choir singing Protestant hymns, or to see hanging on the walls religious paintings by non-Catholics. John Aitken, a Protestant, published the first compilation of sacred songs for use in Catholic churches in the United States. Aitken included a considerable number of Protestant-composed songs in his collection.[25] Benjamin Carr, an Episcopalian, published another collection of sacred songs for use in Catholic churches—a work which he dedicated to Bishop Carroll. Carr also included Protestant hymns in this work. For a number of years he served as organist and choir-master at St. Mary's and St. Augustine's in Philadelphia.[26]

As for non-Catholic paintings in the churches, Father John Grassi, an Italian Jesuit who was President of Georgetown from 1812-1817, made this revealing remark:

> The good impression produced upon the people by sacred pictures cannot be sufficiently described. . . . But unfortunately, paintings are rare and of little artistic merit, the production generally of non-Catholic pencils: I make particular mention of this circumstance, because the observation has been made by many, that non-Catholic painters do not succeed in imparting to their work that air of piety which helps so much to excite devotion.[27]

Protestants did more than come to Catholic churches for mass or sermons. Sometimes, especially in the more remote areas, they called upon the priests to perform religious services. Flaget noted that at the request of a Protestant couple he baptized their three children.[28] In New Orleans, where there was no Episcopalian ministry, several couples requested Father Lewis Sibourd to bless their marriage.[29] Closer to home, in St. Mary's County, Maryland, Father James Van Huffel married several Protestant couples who did not want to go before the Methodist minister.[30] And Catholic couples, much to the dismay of Bishop Carroll and Father Grassi, had Protestant ministers perform the wedding ceremony.[31]

Since Protestants often contributed their money, land, and labor to the establishing of Catholic churches, they may not have felt so strange entering a Catholic church, or calling upon the services of a priest. In Boston non-Catholics contributed $3,453 towards the building of Holy Cross Church. It was accordingly only appropriate for them to attend the dedication ceremony of the new church performed by Bishop Carroll on September 29, 1803.[32] When Father Charles Maurice Whelan made plans to build a Catholic church in New York City he ap-

25. John Aitken, *A Compilation of the Litanies and Vespers, Hymns and Anthems, as they are Sung in the Catholic Church* (Philadelphia: By the Author, 1787); Erwin Esser Nemmers, *Twenty Centuries of Catholic Church Music* (Milwaukee: The Bruce Publishing Company, 1948), p. 166; H. T. Henry, "A Philadelphia Choir Book of 1817," *Records* 26 (September 1915): 219-221.
26. Benjamin Carr, *Masses, Vespers, Litanies, Hymns, Psalms, Anthems, & Motets, Composed, Selected and Arranged for the use of the Catholic Churches in the United States of America* (Philadelphia 1808); Nemmers, *Twenty Centuries of Catholic Church Music*, p. 168; Joseph L. J. Kirlin, *Catholicity in Philadelphia* (Philadelphia: John Jos. McVey, 1909), pp. 191-192; Jane Campbell, "Notes on a Few Old Catholic Hymnbooks," *Records* 31 (June 1920): 132-133. Campbell pointed out that Carr's hymnbook was used in the choirs at St. Mary's and St. Augustine's churches, Philadelphia. Copies of Carr's work were purchased by Bishop Carroll, Michael Egan, Bishop of Philadelphia, and by DuBourg, President of Mount St. Mary's College at Emmitsburg, Maryland.
27. John Grassi, "The Catholic Religion in the United States in 1818," *Researches* 8 (1891): 105.
28. Flaget, "Bishop Flaget's Diary," pp. 46, 48, 160.
29. Sibourd to Carroll, 12 February 1812, AAB, Case 7-R4.
30. VanRuffell to Carroll, February 11, 1811, AAB, Case 8-P7.
31. Carroll to Francis Beeston, Secretary to the Diocesan Synod, 16 November 1791, AAB, Case 9-E2; Grassi, "The Catholic Religion in the United States in 1818," p. 107.
32. Lord, Sexton, and Harrington, *History of the Archdiocese of Boston*, 1:581-584; Arthur J. Connolly, "Rev. Francis A. Matignon, First Pastor of Holy Cross, Boston," *United States Catholic Historical Magazine* 3 (1890): 143.

pealed successfully to the Protestants for funds.[33] The Catholics of Alexandria, Virginia turned to Protestants for financial assistance in establishing their church; and so did the Catholics of rural Chambersburg, Pennsylvania.[34]

Kentucky Catholics were equally indebted to their Protestant neighbors for financial help. Badin built the churches of St. Peter's in Lexington and St. Louis in Louisville with generous assistance from non-Catholics. In the case of St. Peter's two of Badin's close Protestant friends helped to circulate the list; as for St. Louis, Badin remarked that nine-tenths of the subscribers were Protestants.[35] The most magnificent church structure in Kentucky was St. Joseph's Cathedral in Bardstown. Protestants contributed nearly $10,000 for the erecting of the Cathedral, and three non-Catholics served on the Board of Directors to oversee the work.[36] The Protestants of Bardstown may have assisted in this project by a desire to have an impressive edifice grace their town. Father John Baptist Mary
300 David, Superior of St. Thomas Seminary in Kentucky, told Bruté that the Protestants "have said openly that if it were a question of a small church, they would not contribute willingly, but that if we wanted to build a good, large substantial church, they would contribute generously."[37]

In some cases, instead of money, Protestants offered land and services for the building of Catholic churches. Several churches in Kentucky were established on land donated by non-Catholics.[38] And when ground was broken on March 31, 1788 for the building of Holy Trinity Church, Philadelphia (a German-Catholic parish), the German Lutherans of the city contributed their time, labor, and materials, all free of charge.[39] Ethnic ties, and the fact that the German-Catholics of Holy Trinity were challenging Bishop Carroll's authority, may have persuaded the Lutherans to assist their fellow-countrymen.

Having contributed so much in time, land, and money for the building of Catholic churches, it almost seemed natural for Protestants to become members of the Board of Trustees, which governed the temporal concerns of the churches. This actually happened. The Church of St. Louis in Louisville, Kentucky, built largely with the support of non-Catholics, contained two Protestants on its Board of Trustees.[40] As Badin told Carroll these two Protestant trustees were his friends:

> I received this day a letter of Mr. Fairbairn giving his assent that the Church of St. Louis be built on his lots: but some of the trustees who are Protestants (mirabile dictu) want to procure a five acres lot, that a Priest may also be ac-

33. Father Ferdinand Farmer to Carroll, 10 May 1785, AAB, Case 3-P9.
34. Trustees of the Catholic Church in Alexandria, Virginia to Carroll, 20 June 1810, AAB, Case 10-A5; Patrick Campbell to Matthew Carey, 8 August 1812, printed in "Selections from the Correspondence of the Deceased Matthew Carey, Writer, Printer, Publisher," *Records* 9 (September 1898): 345.
35. Sister Mary Ramona Mattingly, *The Catholic Church on the Kentucky Frontier 1785-1812* (Washington, D. C.: Catholic University of America Press, 1936), pp. 89, 92.
36. Flaget to Plessis, 18 June 1816, printed in Lionel Lindsay, trans. and ed., "Correspondence between Bishop Plessis of Quebec, Canada and Bishop Flaget of Bardstown, Ky. 1811-1833," *Records* 18 (March 1907): 24; Sister M. Columba Fox, *The Life of the Right Reverend John Baptist Mary David 1761-1841* (New York: United States Catholic Historical Society, 1925), p. 85.
37. David to Bruté, 18 July 1811, Notre Dame Archives, Joseph Herman Schauinger Transcripts (Private collection).
38. Mattingly, *Catholic Church on the Kentucky Frontier*, pp. 96, 98-99, 101.
39. Francis Hertkorn, *A Retrospect of Holy Trinity Parish 1789-1814* (Philadelphia: F. McManus, Jr. and Company, 1914), pp. 29-30.
40. Mattingly, *Catholic Church on the Kentucky Frontier*, p. 92; Joseph Herman Schauinger, *Stephen Theodore Badin, Priest in the Wilderness* (Milwaukee: Bruce Publishing Company, 1956), p. 148.

> commodated. If all the Catholics are not my friends, I am amply compensated by the friendship of many non-Catholics of respectability.[41]

In some cases, especially on the frontier, Protestants gave money and land for the building of Catholic churches for speculative reasons only. Father Charles Nerinckx, pioneer priest in Kentucky, explained to his relatives in Belgium why Protestants gave land for Catholic churches: "These people know that the Catholics follow their priests, and that by those they would gain settlers and have a chance to sell the public lands."[42] Grassi supported Nerinckx's analysis that land was often given for speculative purposes:

> The settlers in newly opened sections are most anxious to have churches and missionaries; many landholders also, even Protestants, offer hundreds of acres gratis for this purpose, not through any special zeal for religion, but simply as a matter of speculation. For people prefer to settle in places where they can easily procure the helps of religion, and hence the land increases in value.[43] 301

Whatever the reasons—piety or speculation—Protestants contributed to the building of Catholic churches, but there are few, if any, incidents where Catholics reciprocated. According to Édouard de Mondesir, a French Sulpician who came to America in 1791, "nos frèrer de l'Eglise romaine r'en auraient pas fait autant en faveur des dissidents . . . . Jamais un romain ne contribuait a l'erection d'un prêche hérétique."[44]

There was considerable contact between Catholics and Protestants in the area of education. John Carroll cooperated with Protestant clergymen in the establishment and governance of two non-denominational colleges—Washington and St. John's—chartered by the Maryland Legislature in the 1780s. The colleges were open equally to students, faculty, and administrators of all religious persuasions, and though nondenominational, a religious quality permeated the academic program.[45] Carroll served as a member (later President) of the Board of Trustees for St. John's College; and Washington College, which he also supported, conferred on him a Doctor of Divinity degree in 1785.[46] Despite the dangers, which Carroll felt existed for the morals of young Catholics attending mixed schools, he supported these institutions and praised an educational approach that spread "liberal and tolerating principles" by recognizing academic ability instead of religious affiliation.[47] Since Catholics in the early 1780s lacked the means to establish their own schools, Carroll argued that they could receive the rudiments of an education at Washington College; and even after the founding of Georgetown he still viewed St. John's as a place where Georgetown graduates could "puruse their higher studies of law, medicine, etc."[48] For a time Carroll tried to recruit Catholic faculty mem-

41. Badin to Carroll, 3 October 1810, AAB, Case 1-J10.
42. Nerinckx to relatives in Belgium, September 1805, quoted in William J. Howlett, *Life of Reverend Charles Nerinckx* (Techny, Illinois: Mission Press, 1915), p. 119.
43. Grassi, "The Catholic Religion in the United States in 1818," p. 103.
44. Édouard de Mondésir, *Souvenir d'Édouard de Mondésir* (Baltimore: Johns Hopkins Press, 1942), p. 48.
45. Hanley, *American Revolution and Religion*, pp. 216-217.
46. Carroll to Plowden, 24 February 1790, MPA, Box 202-B26; Bernard C. Steiner, *History of Education in Maryland* (Washington, D. C.: United States Government Printing Office, 1894), pp. 101-102; Carroll to Visitors and Governors of Washington College, 1 July 1785, JCP.
47. Carroll to Farmer, December 1784, JCP; Carroll to Plowden, 27 February 1785, MPA, Box 202-B8; Carroll to the Visitors and Governors of Washington College, 1 July 1785, JCP.
48. Carroll to Farmer, December 1784, JCP; Carroll to Plowden, 24 February 1790, MPA, Box 202-B26. The founding of Georgetown College by John Carroll did not imply a repudiation of the Maryland experiment in education, though Carroll did become more critical of Washington and St. John's colleges during the late 1780s. It was, above all,

bers—even fellow Jesuits—for the Maryland colleges. "To me it appears," he noted to a friend, "that it may be of much service not only to learning, but to true Religion, to have some of the professorships filled by R. C. men of letters & virtue: and if one or two of them were in orders, it would be so much the better."[49] Carroll saw Catholic participation in the life of these schools in ecumenical terms. As he explained to a doubting Father Ferdinand Farmer, "Being admitted to equal toleration, must we not concur in public measures, & avoid separating ourselves from the community? Shall we not otherwise be marked, as forming distinct views, & raise a dislike which may terminate in consequences very disagreeable to us."[50]

Catholics and Protestants attended each other's schools. The lack of, or dissatisfaction with, existing Catholic schools forced Catholics to attend non-Catholic schools. John Lee, the son of the Catholic governor of Maryland, went to Harvard,
302 much to the regret of Matignon, who feared for the boy's religion.[51] Apparently Carroll did not object since he wrote a letter of recommendation for John Lee to Samuel Willard, the President of Harvard College.[52] When Georgetown suffered a decline in the 1800s, many parents withdrew their children and sent them to Protestant schools.[53] The same thing happened at the New York Literary Institution, founded by the Jesuits in 1808, where the severity of one member of the staff turned away young boys who probably went on to Protestant schools.[54]

Protestants, in turn, attended most of the Catholic schools. Within the first years of their existence the New York Literary Institution, Georgetown, and St. Mary's College, Baltimore, admitted Protestant boys.[55] Likewise, St. Joseph's Academy at Emmitsburg, Maryland (founded by Elizabeth Bayley Seton, a convert to Catholicism), the Ursuline Convent School in New York City, and the school founded by the Sisters of Loretto in Kentucky, admitted Protestant girls.[56] The general rule in such cases was that Protestant students abided by the moral discipline of the college, except that they were free to attend their own places of worship.[57]

Not all Catholic educators favored the idea of having Protestants attend Catholic schools. Mr. Thomas Kelly tried to persuade Mrs. Seton from sending her children to St. Mary's because there were too many Protestant students there, which

Carroll's need for an American trained clergy and his growing belief that the faith of young boys could be best safeguarded in a Catholic college that led him to establish Georgetown. John Carroll, "First Sermon as Bishop of Baltimore," 12 December 1790, MPA; Bishop Carroll's "Pastoral to the Catholics of United States," 28 May 1792, MPA; John M. Daly, *Georgetown University: Origin and Early Years* (Washington, D. C.: Georgetown University Press, 1957), pp. 26, 31-32, 34, 47, 51, 76-77; Hanley, *American Revolution and Religion* pp. 218-19.

49. Carroll to Joseph Edenshink April-June 1785, JCP.
50. Carroll to Farmer, December 1784, JCP.
51. Lord, Sexton, and Harrington, *History of the Archdiocese of Boston*, 1:603-604.
52. Carroll to Samuel Willard, President of Harvard College, 14 May 1804, JCP.
53. Charles Sewall to Nicholas Sewall, 29 July 1803, printed in Thomas Aloysius Hughes, *History of the Society of Jesus in North America: Documents* (London: Longmans, Green, and Company, 1910), 1, pt. 2:798-799.
54. Father James Wallace to Grassi, 21 September 1812, MPA, Box 202-C16.
55. Father Anthony Kohlman to Father William Strickland, 28 November 1810, MPA, Box 4-S2; Kohlman to Grassi, 26 July 1809, MPA, Box 203-N4; MS. Brother John McElroy, "Diary," 1 January 1813 to 4 September 1815, pp. 2, 59-60, Georgetown University Archives, Box 521-9; Joseph William Ruane, *The Beginning of the Society of St. Sulpice in the United States 1791-1829* (Washington: Catholic University of America Press, 1935), pp. 121-122.
56. Annabelle M. Melville, *Elizabeth Bayley Seton 1774-1821* (New York: Charles Scribner's Sons, 1951), p. 221; Kohlman to Grassi, 18 May 1813, MPA, Box 204-Z16; Howlett, *Life of Reverend Charles Nerinckx*, p. 267.
57. Copy of a Proposal for Estalishibng an Academy at Georgetown 1788, MPA, Box 65-Z1.

might have an adverse effect on the religious life of her boys.[58] Father John Dubois, a teacher at Mount St. Mary's, Emmitsburg, Maryland, advised Mother Seton (who had established her own religious order, the Sisters of Charity) not to admit Protestant girls into her school, but St. Joseph's did not adopt this policy.[59] Father James Wallace, a Jesuit, regretted that the debt-burdened New York Literary Institution had to take in Protestants, for "they are a curse to any Catholic institution."[60] The Sulpicians looked with disfavor on Father Louis Guillaume Valentin DuBourg for accepting Protestants at St. Mary's College. Father Jacques-André Emery, Superior of the Society of St. Sulpice, wrote DuBourg that he could not approve of this practice. He had taken up the matter with Pope Pius VII who "gave a sign of disapprobation by turning his head." Cardinal Leonardo Antonelli, Prefect of the Roman Congregation for the Propagation of the Faith, with whom Emery also consulted, disapproved even more strenuously. Emery eventually changed his position and accepted St. Mary's as a Sulpician institution. He did so, in great part, to satisfy Carroll, who did not object to the admission of Protestants into the college.[61] In fact, as Carroll told Plowden, "I believe that the general effect will be beneficial."[62]

Catholics and Protestants also worked together in the political realm. In 1785 John Carroll and other Catholics collaborated with several Protestant groups in opposing the "Clergy Bill," proposed by the Maryland House of Delegates. The bill would have laid a general and equal tax for the support of all Christian ministers, each taxable inhabitant (with certain exceptions) designating the denomination and minister of his choice.[63] Fearful that the bill was "calculated to create a predominant and irresistible influence in favor of the Protestant Episcopal Church," Carroll joined forces with like-minded Presbyterians, Methodists, Quakers, and Anabaptists in working to defeat the proposed bill. "We have all smarted," he told Plowden, "heretofore under the lash of an established church and shall therefore be on our guard against every approach towards it. All other denominations were formerly subject to pay a heavy tax to the Clergy of the Ch. of England."[64] As regards the Clergy Bill past experiences of oppression by the established Church of England had created sympathetic and working bonds between Catholics and dissenting, Protestant churches.

An interesting chapter in Catholic-Protestant relations concerned John Thayer and Charles Henry Wharton, the two most significant converts respectively to the Catholic and Protestant faith. The Thayer-Wharton cases tested ecumenical relations which, however, proved sufficiently strong to survive the strain that such conversions placed on inter-faith harmony. John Thayer was born in Boston on May 15, 1758. After receiving an honorary A. B. degree from Yale in 1779, Thayer was licensed to preach (though not ordained) in the Congregational Church. After the war he embarked for Europe where, as a result of theological debates with

58. Kelly to Seton, 8 April 1806, printed in Seton, *Memoirs, Letters, and Journal of Elizabeth Seton*, 1:244-246.
59. Melville, *Elizabeth Bayley Seton*, p. 221.
60. Wallace to Grassi, 21 September 1812, MPA, Box 203-C16; Wallace to Grassi, 1 July 1813, MPA, Box 204-W1.
61. Emery to DuBourg, 26 February 1804, quoted in Ruane, *The Beginning of the Society of St. Sulpice in the United States*, pp. 121-123.
62. Carroll to Plowden, 10 January 1808, Guilday Collection, Catholic University of America Archives.
63. A copy of the proposed bill, with John Carroll's marginal notes, can be found in AAB, Special Case C-A9.
64. Carroll to Plowden, 27 February 1785, MPA, Box 202-B8; Hanley, *American Revolution and Religion*, pp. 64-68, 212-213.

priests in France and Italy—and personal knowledge of a reputed miracle, Thayer entered the Catholic Church on May 25, 1783.[65] Thayer studied for the priesthood at the Seminary of St. Sulpice in Paris and soon after receiving ordination (June 2, 1787) he returned to Boston so as to convert his Protestant countrymen to the "true faith."[66]

Carroll's European friends—perhaps uncomfortable with the ways of a former Protestant—warned him about Thayer's faults. From Rome Father John Thorpe cautioned, "It will be necessary to have a priest of friendly eye over Mr. John Thayer . . . . his passion for more independence than any apostle in God's church ever had or desired, may involve himself and others in great difficulties."[67] Nonetheless, ever in need of priests, Carroll welcomed Thayer to America, though it was not long before he expressed some misgivings about this distinguished con-
304 vert-priest. Thayer arrived in Boston on January 4, 1790 and by his own account was well received. He informed Carroll: "The reception which I've received from the Governor, from the ministers, from my family and in fine from all classes of people is the most flattering & is an omen perhaps of good sucess tho I'm prepared for and expect opposition."[68]

There was, understandably, as Thayer expected, some opposition to this Protestant-turned-Catholic who came to convince Puritan Boston of the true religion. Some called him "John Turncoat"; others, like the editor Noah Webster and the distinguished Lawyer John Gardiner, ridiculed the priests' character, conversion, and faith.[69] All things considered, though, Puritan Boston treated Thayer with more tolerance and charity than it would have shown to a convert priest years earlier.[70] Thayer was not an easy person to live with. Aggressive, uncompromising, and tactless, he quarreled with his fellow priests and parishioners, and engaged in sharp, polemical debates with Protestants.[71] Thayer's conduct in Boston deeply disturbed Bishop Carroll, who complained to Plowden, "I am afraid that Mr. Thayer wants that spirit of accommodation, & perhaps of humility, which is so essentially requisite for a labourer in the Lord's vineyard."[72] Carroll ordered Thayer to cease engaging his fellow-priest and Protestant divines in the public press. Thayer's conduct threatened to undo all of Bishop Carroll's efforts to create a model

65. Richard J. Purcell, "Thayer, John," *Dictionary of American Biography*, 9, pt. 2: 406-407; Percival Merritt, "Sketches of the Three Earliest Roman Catholic Priests in Boston," *Publications of the Colonial Society of Massachusetts* 25 (1923):211-215; Arthur T. Connolly, "Historical Sketch of the Rev. John Thayer, Boston's First Native Born Priest," *United States Catholic Historical Magazine* 2 (July, 1888): 261-265; Lord, Sexton, and Harrington, *History of the Archdiocese of Boston*, 1:358-367.

66. John Thayer, *An Account of the Conversion of the Reverend John Thayer* (Baltimore: William Goddard, 1788), p. 16.

67. Father John Thorpe to Carroll, 11 August 1790, AAB, Case 8B-K6; see Father William Strickland to Carroll, May 1789, AAB, Case 8-A6 and Plowden to Carroll, 13 November 1787, AAB, Case 6-K5.

68. Thayer to Carroll, 6 January 1790, AAB, Case 8B-H1.

69. Guilday, *John Carroll*, p. 424; Purcell, "Thayer," p. 407; Merritt, "Sketches," p. 223; John Gardiner's attack on Thayer is printed in John Thayer, *Controversy Between the Rev. John Thayer and the Rev. George Lesslie* (Newburyport: John Mycall, 1793), pp. 108-112; Noah Webster, *American Magazine* (September 1788) 1:738-739.

70. Guilday, *John Carroll*, p. 423; Merritt, "Sketches," pp. 215-219; Purcell, "Thayer," p. 407; Connolly, "John Thayer," p. 267.

71. Purcell, "Thayer," p. 407; Merritt, "Sketches," p. 229.

72. Carroll to Plowden, 16 March 1790, MPA, Box 202-B27. After visiting Boston to heal the split in the congregation between the followers of Thayer and Father Louis de Rousslet, Carroll complained to Plowden, "I am very sorry not to have here a clergyman of amiable, conciliatory manners, as well as real ability," Carroll to Plowden, 11 June 1791, MPA, Box 202-B36.

Catholic church in Boston free of scandal and to establish good relations with the Protestant community.[73]

When Carroll sent Father Matignon as pastor of the Catholic church in Boston, Thayer assumed the life of a missionary priest. He spent the next several years serving various congregations in the eastern United States, always restless, apparently never satisfied, and exasperating Carroll in the process.[74] Finally, in 1799, Carroll sent Thayer to frontier Kentucky where the controversial priest managed to cause further disturbances. Badin (Carroll's Vicar-General in Kentucky) complained to Carroll that Thayer's polemical style antagonized Protestants: "He preached here some sermons that have gained him applause, but in his controversial discourses he is too harsh for the freemen of Kentucky; in one of them he calls the Methodists *fools* & I could not prevail on him to soften the expression, which has offended many hearers."[75] 305

Even more damaging to interfaith relations were the charges that Thayer committed indiscreet acts with members of the opposite sex. Several women complained that Thayer kissed and embraced them in the church or confessional and Badin rejected as ill-founded Thayer's defense that he was merely carrying on the traditional Christian kiss-of-peace.[76] A Mrs. Jameston, who actually filed a complaint against Thayer with a local Justice of the Peace, alleged that the priest had made improper advances towards her in the confessional.[77] News of the Jameston "affair" spread throughout Kentucky and was even reported in Maryland.[78] Badin and Carroll were shocked at the scandal that such "incidents" caused to the Catholic church and to the damaging impact they had on interfaith relations.[79] Protestants reproached Catholics with "countenancing a scandalous man for their Pastor."[80] As a result of the Jameston "affair" Protestants renewed their long-standing criticism of priestly celibacy and confession. One legislator told Badin that "priests should be married & then would be better men."[81] And even though Badin kept the confession door widely open another Protestant raised "calumnies against him as well."[82] The Thayer "incident" apparently revived ancient grievances that Protestants harbored against Catholics, though they lacked the vituperation of earlier days.[83] Badin (with Carroll's support) suspended Thayer from all priestly func-

73. Carroll to Thayer, 22 February 1791, JCP. Carroll to Plowden, 3 February 1781, MPA, Box 202-B34. While recognizing, at this time, Thayer's good qualities—his piety and defense of the faith—Carroll regretted that the convert-priest was not "more gentle in dealing with heretics, and with his own flock as well." Carroll to Antonelli, 17 June 1793, JCP.
74. Carroll to Thayer, 12 August 1794, JCP; Carroll to Thayer, 5 July 1796, JCP; Merritt, "Sketches," pp. 224-227; Purcell, "Thayer," p. 407.
75. Badin to Carroll, 4 February 1800, AAB, Case 1-F1.
76. Henry Clarvos to Badin, 26 December 1800, AAB, Special Case A-H11; Badin to Carroll, 25 February 1801, AAB, Special Case A-H8; Badin to Carroll, 9 March 1801, AAB, Special Case A-H16; Badin to Carroll, 5 May 1801, AAB, Special Case A-H2.
77. A copy of Mrs. Jameston's "Affidavit," dated 11 January 1801 can be found in AAB, Special Case A-H9. It would appear from Badin's correspondence that the case did not move beyond the local level and no legal action was taken against Thayer.
78. Badin to Carroll, 9 March 1801, AAB, Special Case A-H16; Carroll to Badin, 18 March 1801, JCP.
79. Carroll to Badin, January 1801, JCP; Carroll to Badin, 18 March 1801, JCP; Badin to Carroll, 28 October 1800, AAB, Special Case A-H15.
80. Badin to Carroll 5 May 1801, AAB, Special Case A-H2.
81. Badin to Carroll, 28 October 1800, AAB, Special Case A-H15.
82. Badin to Carroll, 3 November 1801, AAB, Special Case A-H12.
83. John Martin Spalding, *Sketches of the Early Catholic Missions of Kentucky* (Baltimore: John Murphy Company, 1844), p. 47, narrates the story of Father Whelan, the first Catholic priest to serve in Kentucky. Whelan was sued for slander by some of his parishioners, and the jury which found him guilty fined the priest five hundred pounds with imprisonment until paid. Fortunately, Whelan did not go to jail since one

tions and the censure brought peace to the congregation of Scott City and satisfied the moral sensibilities of Protestant critics.[84] Thayer left Kentucky under a cloud of suspicion, spending his last days in Ireland.

Carroll was relieved by Thayer's departure, for the controversial convert-priest by his polemical debates threatened the harmony between the different denominations which Carroll encouraged. How Catholic priests should act in their debates and relationships with Protestants Carroll demonstrated in the Wharton affair. Charles Henry Wharton (1748-1833) was born into an old Maryland Catholic family. After completing his studies in Jesuit colleges on the continent, he entered the Society of Jesus and was ordained on September 19, 1772. He then spent several significant years as chaplain to the Roman Catholics of Worcester, England —and it was here that he began to question his faith. Wharton returned to Maryland in 1783 under suspicion, though he was warmly defended by his friend and
306 distant relative John Carroll. Within a year Wharton announced (much to Carroll's amazement) that he would enter the ministry of the Protestant Episcopal Church.[85] He published at the same time a polished and dignified apologia in which he rejected as cruel the Catholic "doctrine" that "outside of the Church there is no salvation."[86] While Protestants momentarily exulted over Wharton's conversion and treatise, they did not exploit the affair.[87]

John Carroll felt compelled to reply to Wharton's charges which, he told Plowden, constituted a "malignant invective & misrepresentation of our tenets."[88] He was reluctant to engage in debate, especially if it "would disturb the harmony now subsisting amongst all christians in this country, so blessed with civil and religious liberty." Yet he understood the need to rebut Wharton's erroneous conclusions which, if not corrected, would embitter Protestants against Catholics and disturb the peaceful relations that existed in the United States among all religious groups.[89] In his work Carroll rejected Wharton's narrow interpretation and argued instead for a broad definition on what constitued "membership" in the "church," so that it included, under certain conditions, baptized non-Catholics and non-Christians as well.[90] When Wharton wrote a reply Carroll refused to continue the debate, ever reluctant to revive the religious controversy.[91]

John Carroll harbored no ill-feelings towards this former Jesuit who converted to the Episcopal faith. And Wharton maintained throughout his life a warm feel-

of his "detractors" stood bail. Years later, Father Badin spent a night with a man named Ferguson who had served on that jury. Ferguson, not knowing Badin was a priest, said to him of that case: "they [the jurous] had tried very hard to have the priest hanged, but were sorry that they could find no law for it." See also Spalding, p. 26, n., and pp. 119-120 for further examples of anti-Catholicism.

84. Badin to Members of the Congregation of Scott City, Kentucky, 13 March 1801, AAB, Special Case A-H7; Carroll to Badin, 18 March 1801, JCP; Badin to Carroll, 5 May 1801, AAB, Special Case A-H2.
85. For a biographical sketch of Wharton consult George Washington Doane, ed., *The Remains of the Rev. Charles Henry Wharton with a Memoir of His Life*, 2 vols. (Philadelphia, 1834), 1:xiii-xxxix; Harris Elwood Starr, "Wharton, Charles Henry," *Dictionary of American Biography*, 9, pt. 2:26-27; Carroll to Plowden, 26 September 1783, MPA, Box 202-B5; Carroll to Plowden, 10 April 1784, MPA, Box 202-B6.
86. Charles Henry Wharton, *A Letter to the Roman Catholics of the City of Worcester* (Philadelphia: Robert Aitken, 1784), pp. 7, 9-10, 13.
87. Carroll to Plowden, 27 February 1785, MPA, Box 202-B8; Hanley, *American Revolution and Religion*, pp. 214-215.
88. Carroll to Plowden, 18 September 1784, MPA, Box 202-B7.
89. John Carroll, *An Address to the Roman Catholics of the United States of America* (Annapolis: Frederick Green, 1784), pp. 11, 114.
90. Ibid., pp. 11, 15-17.
91. Carroll to Plowden, 29 June 1785, MPA, Box 202-B9; Carroll to Berington, 29 September 1786, JCP.

ing for John Carroll. Years later, after Carroll's death, Bruté wrote a harsh note to Wharton, urging him to undo the scandal he had caused by returning to the Catholic church. Wharton's reply is instructive and reveals how successfully Bishop Carroll had cultivated charitable relations with Protestants:

> The feelings which your letter excited, would not have partaken of anything like resentment, had you not mentioned my venerable relative and former friend, Archbishop Carroll, as countenancing your denunciations and abuse. I knew him well. I loved him during his lifetime, and shall revere him during my own. . . . He was too well acquainted with the sacred rights of conscience, and the anomalies of the human mind, to condemn the exercise of the first, or wish to regulate the latter by the standard of his own opinions; much less would he have presumed to consign them both to perdition.[92]

Frequent contact between Catholics and Protestants often led to fast bonds of friendship for many of the clergy. Father Peter Helbron, financially pressed and persecuted by several prominent Catholics of Philadelphia, turned to a Prot- 307
estant friend who loaned him $50.[93] When certain Catholics accused Father Demetrius Augustine Gallitzin of appropriating a sum of money for his own personal use, many of his Protestant neighbors, with whom he was friendly, "shewed as much indignation at the base, malicious and foul steps that are a taking, as some of the most zealous Catholics."[94] In Kentucky Badin numbered among his friends laymen such as Colonel Joe H. Daviess (for whom he composed a Latin poem on his friend's death in the War of 1812) and clergymen like the Presbyterian minister, Reverend Moore.[95] And in Boston the generous and warm Matignon and Cheverus counted innumerable Protestants—clerical and lay—as their good friends.[96]

The Catholic laity carried their relationships with Protestants beyond the bounds of mere friendship. In many cases Catholics married Protestants—and this was understandable in a land where Catholics were far outnumbered by those of different faiths. Carroll explained to Plowden the situation as it existed in America:

> Here our Catholics are so mixed with Protestants in all the intercourse of civil society, and business public and private, that the abuse of intermarriage is almost universal; and it surpasses my ability to design any effective bar against it—No general prohibition can be enacted, without reducing many of the faithful to live in a state of celibacy, as in sundry places there would be no choice for them of Catholic matches.[97]

As some of the clergy understood, there simply were not enough young Catholic men or women available—and often Catholics had to look outside the fold for suitable partners.[98]

Carroll knew the problem first hand, for several of his own relatives had married non-Catholics, often to the detriment of their faith.[99] Many of the children of Dominick Lynch, a prominent Catholic resident of New York City, married Protestants, and few of their children remained Catholic.[100] Father Joseph Pierre

92. Wharton to Burté, 20 April 1816, in Doane, *Remains of Charles Henry Wharton*, 2:xiii.
93. Helbron to Carroll, 19 April 1800, AAB, Case 4-E2.
94. Gallitzin to Carroll, 11 May 1807, AAB, Case 8A-06.
95. Badin to Carroll, 2 March 1797, AAB, Case 1-E7; Schauinger, *Stephen Theodore Badin, Priest in the Wilderness*, p. 79.
96. Lord, Sexton, and Harrington, *History of the Archdiocese of Boston*, 1:763, 765, 767; Annabelle M. Melville, *Jean Lefebvre de Cheverus 1768-1836* (Milwaukee: Bruce Publishing Company, 1958), pp. 135-136, 140-142.
97. Carroll to Plowden, 12 February 1803, Stonyhurst Archives.
98. Carroll to James Barry, 8 April 1806, AAB, Case 9-C6; Matignon to Carroll, 19 March 1801, AAB, Case 5-H5.
99. Bishop Carroll to Charles Carroll, 15 July 1800, AAB, Case 9-F2; Carroll to James Barry, 8 April 1806, AAB, Case 9-C6.

Picot de Clorivière complained to Carroll that the coldness of the trustees of St. Mary's Church, Charleston resulted from their being married to Protestants.[101] James Patrick Oeller, a son of the leading trustee of Holy Trinity Church, Philadelphia, married a Baptist woman and left the church.[102]

If mixed marriages were unavoidable in the United States, they were nonetheless undesirable and condemned by the clergy as detrimental to the faith of the Catholic partner and the children. In a "Sermon on Marriage" Carroll argued that the spiritual and temporal ends of marriage were best reached when both partners were Catholics.[103] While Carroll admitted that sometimes some good resulted from these marriages, more often than not, the Catholic partner grew cool towards his faith, and the children "thro the discordancy of the religious sentiments of (the) parents . . . grow up without attachment to any, and become an easy prey to infidelity or indifferentism."[104] Carroll's fears were shared by Grassi, who considered
308 mixed marriages as troublesome to religion, for "sometimes the husband hinders his wife from frequenting the Sacraments, sometimes the wife does not allow the children to be reared in the faith."[105]

The problem of mixed marriage was viewed as so serious to religion that Carroll and the clergy took up the question at the first Diocesan Synod of the Clergy, meeting in Baltimore, November 7-11, 1791. The Synod urged priests to try and prevent Catholics from marrying non-Catholics, but since this appeared unlikely because of conditions prevailing in America, the Synod established the following regulations to guide priests in questions of mixed marriages: (a) admonish Catholics of the dangers resulting from such unions; (b) inquire whether the non-Catholic party will promise "not to put any obstacles to having all the children from the marriage educated in the true Religion"; (c) if the priest forsees that by not performing the ceremony the couple would go before a non-Catholic minister then he should marry them; (d) but these marriages "may not be sanctioned with the blessing which is prescribed in the Roman Ritual."[106]

Despite the work of the Synod, Catholics continued to marry non-Catholics and Protestant ministers often performed the ceremony. Such practices constituted a serious breach of Catholic discipline. Marriages so contracted were not recognized as valid by the church.[107] Carroll felt compelled to speak out strongly against Catholics marrying before non-Catholic ministers. In a "Circular Letter on Christian Marriage" he declared that those Catholics who did so "rendered themselves guilty of a sacrilegious profanation of a most holy institution." Carroll instructed the clergy to inform all those who had been (or would be) married before any other than a priest, that they "cannot be admitted to reconciliation and the Sacraments, till they shall agree to make public acknowledgement of their disobedience, before the assembled congregations, and beg pardon for the scandal they have given."[108]

100. Thomas F. Meehan, "Some Pioneer Catholic Laymen in New York—Dominick Lynch and Cornelus Heeney," *Historical Records and Studies* 4 (October, 1906): 285, 290-291.
101. Clorivière to Carroll, 2 November 1813, AAB, Case 2-Q6.
102. Martin I. J. Griffin, *History of the Right Reverend Michael Egan, First Bishop of Philadelphia* (Philadelphia: The Author, 1893), p. 29.
103. Bishop Carroll, "Sermon on Marriage," 17 January 1802, John Carroll Collection, Catholic University of America Archives.
104. Carroll to Plowden, 12 February 1803, Guilday Collection; Carroll to James Barry, 8 April 1806, AAB, Case 9-C6.
105. Grassi, "The Catholic Religion in the United States in 1818," p. 107.
106. Synod of the Clergy, Third Session, No. 16, AAB, Case 9A-L.
107. Grassi, "The Catholic Religion in the United States in 1818," p. 107.
108. Carroll to Father Francis Beeston, Secretary to the Diocesan Synod, 16 November 1791,

Protestants did not favor mixed marriages either. The tradition of discouraging marriages with Catholics, which stemmed from the Reformation, carried over into the eighteenth century.[109] Reverend William Endfield, in an often printed treatise on marriage, considered mixed marriages as a major factor in causing unhappy marriages and divorce.[110] Reverend Stephen West reminded his fellow Presbyterians that, according to the Westminister Confession, it was the "duty of Christians to marry *only in the Lord;* and, therefore, such as profess the true reformed religion, should not marry with infidels, *papists* [italics mine], or other idolators."[111] The Methodists expelled from their society those who married with "unawakened persons." Thomas Coke and Francis Asbury, two prominent Methodists, explained what their church meant by the term "unawakened person":

> By the word unawakened . . . we mean one whom we could not in conscience admit into society. We do not prohibit our people from marrying persons who
> are not of our society, provided such persons have the form, and are seeking the 309
> power of godliness; but, if they marry persons who do not come up to this description, we shall be obliged to purge our society of them. And even in a doubtful case, the member of our society shall be put back upon trial.[112]

Presumedly the Methodists would have designated the Catholics, who did not subscribe to the theology of Protestantism, as "unawakened persons."[113]

The mixed marriage question clearly indicated the boundaries beyond which neither religious group could, or would, go. While Protestants mingled more freely with Catholics during these years, in the end they could not easily forgo their age-old objections against the Roman Catholic Church. (Witness the renewed attack on the evils of "Papism" in the Dudleian lectures delivered at Harvard during the 1780s.)[114] Catholics, in turn, harbored their own lingering suspicions and prejudice. They still referred harshly to Protestants as "heretics" and to the Protestant religion as possessing limited value and truth. In short, Catholics believed that they alone possessed the one, true religion, and no amount of personal contact or friendship with Protestants could change that inescapable truth.[115]

Still, the postwar years marked an unique period in American Catholic relations with Protestants, a bright though brief moment between the darkness of the colonial period when Catholics suffered political and religious persecution and the violent Nativist movement of the middle nineteenth century. It was a time of ecu-

AAB, Case 9-E2. See Carroll to Father Claude Florent Bouchard de la Poterie, 24 December 1788, AAB, Case 9A-G3, in which Carroll insists on "subjecting to a public penance" (not merely a "public acknowledgment") those who marry before a Protestant minister.

109. George Elliot Howard, *A History of Matrimonial Institutions*, 3 vols. (Chicago: University of Chicago Press, 1904), 1:391-392.

110. William Endfield, *An Essay on Marriage* (Philadelphia: Zachariah Poulson, 1788), p. 5.

111. Stephen West, *The Duty and Obligations of Christians to Marry Only in the Lord* (Hartford: Watson and Goodwin, 1778), p. 18; *The Constitution of the Presbyterian Church in America* (Philadelphia: Robert Aitken, 1797), chap. xxiv.

112. Thomas Coke and Francis Asbury, *The Doctrines and Discipline of the Methodist Episcopal Church in America*, 10th ed. (Philadelphia: Henry Tuckniss, 1798), pp. 156-157.

113. In a letter to Alexander M'Caine, dated 30 August 1804, Francis Asbury castigated the Roman Catholic Church as follows: "I have lately seen David Simpson's plea for religion. The greatest of all, it is England's warning. He proves that the Church of England is as anti-Christian as the Church of Rome. He has confirmed me in my opinion." Printed in Francis Asbury, *The Journals and Letters of Francis Asbury*, ed. Elmer T. Clark, J. Manning Potts, and Jacob S. Payton, 3 vols. (Nashville: Abingdon Press, 1958), 3:300-301.

114. Ray, *American Opinion of Roman Catholicism*, pp. 378-380.

115. I have developed this theme at length in my dissertation, "The Building of an American Catholic Church: The Episcopacy of John Carroll," (Ph.D. diss.: Syracuse University, 1972), chap. 9, "Catholic Opinion of Protestants and Protestantism," pp. 179-204.

menism when Protestants, tempering their anti-Catholic sentiment, became more tolerant and charitable towards Catholics; and when Catholics, emerging from the catacombs of the penal era, entered more freely into Protestant society and discovered that even here, among their "separated-brethren," some good could be found.[116]

Catholic leaders, like Bishop Carroll, could only hope that in these everyday contacts Protestants would lose some of their fear, distrust, and dislike of Catholics, and for a brief period of time this appeared to happen. Unfortunately, Carroll's hopes for the future were dashed when the anti-Catholicism of many Protestants, subdued during the postwar years, surfaced again in the middle years of the nineteenth century as waves of Catholic immigrants poured into this country.

116. Flaget to his brother, 21 March 1811, Mount St. Mary's Seminary Archives, Joseph Herman Schauinger Transcript (Private collection); Memorial of Haroldite supporters to
310 Carroll, 22 January 1812, AAB, Case 4-M7; Louis Guillaume Valentin DuBourg, *St. Mary's Seminary and Catholics at Large Vindicated Against the Pastoral Letters of the Ministers, Bishops, and of the Presbytery of Baltimore* (Baltimore: Bernard Dornin, 1811), p. 43; see also *The Catholic Religion Vindicated* (n. p.: the author, 1813), p. 57.

VII The Foundation Of American Catholic Education

The "Carroll Catechism"–A Primary Component of the American Catholic Catechetical Tradition *

CHARLES J. CARMODY

As we approach the bi-centennial of our national existence, many aspects of the American experience are being examined in their origins. Accordingly, this essay is related to the beginnings of the Roman Catholic Catechesis in the United States and is particularly concerned with what came to be known as the "Carroll Catechism."[1] The "Carroll" is the initial text of American Catholic religious education and, to date, its most long-lived material, used as the basis of almost all subsequent major American catechisms. The "Carroll" is truly a primary component of the American Catholic catechetical tradition. 313

This essay will proceed through five parts: I) the American origins of the "Carroll Catechism," II) the British antecedents of the American text, III) the American redactions of the British text, IV) the continuing presence of "Carroll" in American Catholic religious education, and finally, V) selections reproduced from the text of the "Carroll Catechism."

I. THE AMERICAN ORIGINS OF THE "CARROLL CATECHISM"

The earliest monuments of the Catechesis in North America are understandably Spanish and French. Acknowledging this prior Catholic presence, it must be said the American Church, as it has developed to the present, grew from small nuclei of Roman Catholics that settled in the English colonies.[2] The spiritual care of these peoples was largely the responsibility of the English Jesuits.[3] However publicly or covertly these priests ministered, catechizing was one of their principal pastoral concerns, but, in implementing their catechetical efforts, the colonial clergy had to obtain printed instructional materials from abroad.[4] This dependence on European publishers continued until the arrival of Father Robert J. Molyneaux in Philadelphia *ca.* 1771. Among his many accomplishments there, Molyneaux initiated and greatly promoted the printing of

[1] This essay is an expansion of material found in Charles J. Carmody, "The Roman Catholic Catechesis in the United States, 1784-1930: A Study of Its Theory, Development, and Materials" (Ph.D. dissertation, Loyola University of Chicago, 1975—University Microfilm: 75-14504).

[2] Cf. John Tracy Ellis, *Catholics in Colonial America* (Baltimore and Dublin: Helicon Press, 1963), pp. 315-59 (Maryland), 360-80 (New York, Pennsylvania).

[3] The English Jesuits began their work in Maryland in 1634 and in Pennsylvania informally from 1706 and more formally from about 1734. From 1741 a number of German Jesuits worked in Pennsylvania.

[4] For more on this, cf. Charles J. Carmody, "The Origins of the Roman Catholic Catechesis in the United States (1776-1799)," *Journal of the Midwest History of Education Society,* III (1975), 1-14. (Hereinafter cited as Carmody, "Origins.") Cf. also a very interesting note in Thomas Hughes, *History of the Society of Jesus in North America, Colonial and Federal. Text, Volume II, from 1645 till 1773* (London, New York, *et alibi:* Longmans, Green, and Co., (1917), p. 517, n. 7 (1)).

* PART V HAS BEEN OMMITED FROM THE GARLAND EDITION.

Catholic books.[5] That greater freedom traditionally enjoyed by Catholics in Quaker Pennsylvania included freedom to print. Most of what we know of the Philadelphia priest's printing efforts must be gleaned from a series of letters he wrote to Father John Carroll from 1784 into 1786.[6]

After a very confused situation regarding just who had canonical jurisdiction over Catholics in the English colonies and later in the thirteen United States, the Holy See appointed Father John Carroll (1784) Prefect Apostolic of the nascent American Church.[7] Among the many matters discussed in the correspondence cited above, Molyneaux reported on his printing activity to the American Prefect. He shows himself to be greatly interested in providing instructional and devotional literature for the children and adults of the various American Catholic clusters. His references are often cryptic, but they give a clue to those catechetical
314 materials Father Molyneaux had caused to be published.[8]

Among these catechetical references, the Philadelphia priest four times variously refers to "the Catechism," or "a Cath. Catechism," or "the Short Abridgement," or finally "the short Abstract of the Doway Catechism." His references are loose and confusing, but in the judgement of the present writer, they all refer to what came to be known as the "Carroll Catechism." In the spring of 1785, Molyneaux wrote Carroll, "I send you a sample of the Catechism lately printed by Wm. Spotswood."[9] At the end of the same year, he explained that this 1785 catechism was the same as "the short abridgement, wch. I had printed some years ago by Bell."[10] In this same letter, he informed the Prefect, "there is now printing a Spelling Primer for Children with a Cath. Catechism annexed." In the final letter of the series, written in early 1786, Molyneaux added a postscript in which he wrote, "I forgot whether I informed you that the short abstract of the Doway Catechism is again reprinted, and to be had either annexed to a spelling book or without."[11]

Unfortunately, the Bell (*ca.* 1775) or Spotswood (1785, 1786) imprints are not known to be extant, but Evans[12] lists the data of the primer-catechism:

---

[5] Biographical material on Father Molyneaux can be found under his name in *Dictionary of American Biography* (XIII) and *New Catholic Encyclopedia* (IX). He was born in Lancashire in 1738. He joined the Society in 1757. He studied and taught in the Jesuit institutions of Flanders. Shortly after his ordination, he arrived in Philadelphia in 1771, where he remained until *ca.* 1788. He rejoined the Society of Jesus as it came to be restored in the United States (1805). In 1806, he was confirmed as its first American superior. He served twice as president of Georgetown College before his death in 1808. Cf. also below, n.22.

[6] Archives of the Archdiocese of Baltimore, Case 5: K5—K17, L1. A number of these letters were published in the *American Catholic Historical Researches,* n.s., VII (July, 1912), 267-78.

[7] Cf. Peter Guilday, *The Life and Times of John Carroll* (reprint; Westminster, Md.: Newman Press, 1965), pp. 163-64 and *A History of the Council of Baltimore* (New York: Macmillan Company, 1932), pp. 37-49. Some of this confusion resulted from the papal suppression of the Society of Jesus (1773-1814). Both Carroll and Molyneaux had been priests of the suppressed Society and friends from their days together in Flanders.

[8] Cf. Philadelphia imprints from 1774-1788 listed in Wilfred Parsons, *Early Catholic Americana: A List of Books and Other Works by Catholic Authors in the United States, 1729-1830* (New York: Macmillan Company, 1939); also Carmody, "Origins," pp. 4-11.

[9] AAB, Case 5: K8, Philadelphia, n.d. [*ca.* April, 1785].

[10] AAB, Case 5: K15, Philadelphia, December 27, 1785.

[11] AAB, Case 5: L1, Philadelphia, February 25, 1786.

[12] Cf. No. 19967 in Charles Evans, *American Bibliography* [*etc.*], (24 vols.; Chicago: Printed by the author by Blackley Press, *et alii,* 1903-1959), VII, 65. Evans took the data from an advertisement in *Pennsylvania Herald,* July 12, 1786 (Clifford K. Shipton and James

The Roman Catholic Primer, to which is added with approbation a short abridgement of Christian Doctrine with a short daily exercise; also further instructions, from the French Catechism of John Joseph Languet, formerly Archbishop of Sens. Philadelphia: Printed and sold by W. Spotswood, Frontstreet, between Market and Chestnut streets, 1786. It is practically certain that Molyneaux's edition of *A Short Abridgement of Christian Doctrine* is preserved in extant cetechisms bearing almost the same title but characterized as the twelfth (1793), thirteenth (1795), fourteenth (1798), fifteenth (1803), and sixteenth (1806) editions, all of which are listed in part IV of this essay. These various imprints are all presented as having been printed "with approbation." Since Carroll was the proper authority to give this approbation, the American *A Short Abridgement of Christian Doctrine* came to be known as the "Carroll Catechism." Bernard Dornin in his 1806 edition (cf. part IV) presented it as "recom- 315
mended to the Catholics of the United States by the Right Rev. Bishop Carroll." Most of these editions, referred to here, also claim to have been "newly revised for use in the United States." In time, some erroneously thought Bishop Carroll had actually put the catechism together. Some contemporary scholars also see this to have been the case. In the judgement of the present writer, the first bishop composed nothing in the way of a catechism, although he was capable of doing so. Neither did he do any compiling, nor abridging, nor any active selecting of catechetical materials. The "Carroll Catechism" resulted from Molyneaux's activity albeit "with approbation." What is the "Carroll" *textus receptus*, however, clearly has a British antecedent and several notable American redactions.

II. The British Antecedents of the American Text

The First English catechisms of the Counter-Reform emerged from the continent, where large numbers of Catholics had gone, in and after 1559, "recusing" to take the religious oath prescribed by the Acts of Supremacy and Uniformity. Of the many recusant catechisms,[13] the greatest, in terms of contemporary and long-range influence, is that summary authored by Henry Tuberville in 1649.[14] It came to be called, seemingly from the start, the "Dovvay Catechism." In time, need for a smaller instructional aid produced *An Abstract of the Doway Catechism*.[15] It cannot be said to have had an author but rather an editor, but his identity has not been determined.

E. Mooney, *National Index of American Imprints Through 1800. The Short Title Evans*, [Worcester, Mass.: American Antiquarian Society and Barre Publishers, 1969], II, 745.)

[13] Cf. G. Carmody, "Origins," pp. 2-4.

[14] *An Abridgment of Christian Doctrine. With Proofs of Scripture for Points Controverted. Catechistically explain'd. By Way of Question and Answer. By H. T.*, (Doway: n.p., 1648). This initial edition and a later one (Basel: n.p., 1680) are held at Newberry Library (Chicago). Other editions (Doway; n.p. 1661 and London: n.p., 1701) are held at Memorial Library, University of Notre Dame.

[15] The earliest edition of the *Abstract* (Doway: n.p., 1682) examined by the present writer is held at Newberry Library; a later and more expanded edition (Doway: M. Mairesse, 1697) was examined on microfilm by courtesy of the British Museum (B.M. 3504 a 26).

In 1728, a new *catechismus minor* appeared for English-speaking Catholics, entitled *A Short Abridgement of Christian Doctrine.*[16] A careful examination of this text shows it is taken from Tuberville's *An Abridgement of Christian Doctrine;* hence, its title. The 1728 *A Short Abridgement* contains some 200 question/answer units taken from the Doway Catechism and its *Abstract*. The units, however, have been rearranged and largely rewritten, in a then more current style. Additional material is also interspersed. Just who redid the Doway material in this 1728 form is not known and is a topic for further research. At any rate, *A Short Abridgement* proved very popular for use with younger children; so popular, that it was expanded for use with older children and some adults.

In 1741, Dr. Richard Challoner was consecrated titular Bishop of Derbe and
316 Coadjutor to the Vicar Apostolic of the London District (Vicariate Apostolic); in 1758 he became full vicar.[17] In addition to his pastoral-administrative work, Challoner's literary output was very large; much of it, revisions of the older recusant classics. In 1759, he produced *An Abridgement of the Christian Doctrine, revised and enlarged by R. C. and published for the use of the L—n District,* (n.p., 1759).[18] The London Vicar greatly preserved the 1729 text but made many stylistic changes, rewrote some units, and added new ones; he also added, as additional chapters, "The Christian's Rule of Life" and "The Christian's Daily Exercise."[19] Another edition of the Challoner revision appeared some twelve years later, *An Abridgement of Christian Doctrine, revised and enlarged by R. C.* (St. Omers: H. F. Boubers, 1772).[20] This 1772 imprint contains only stylistic changes made here and there in the language. Burton makes reference to additional printings of the Challoner revision (1775 and 1777) by the London printer Coughlan,[21] but the present writer has been unable to find these; perhaps these later editions contained further slight revisions. At any rate, Challoner did preserve the classic 1729 text, which (with continued revision) became England's famous "Penny Catechism," used until quite recently in religious education of English and Welsh Catholics, and those of Scotland as well.

---

[16] *The Little Catechism or A Short Abridgement of Christian Doctrine* (London: n.p., 1728)—examined on microfilm by courtesy of the British Museum (B.M. 3504 aa 24). The little that has been written on the English-speaking Catechesis makes no mention of this work. It seems to be the direct link between the Doway Catechism, its *Abstract,* and latter English-language catechetical materials.

[17] The yet definitive work on Challoner is Edwin Burton, *The Life and Times of Richard Challoner* (2 vols.; London: Longmans, Green, and Co., 1909). For a critical list of his published works, cf. *ibid.,* II, 323-39.

[18] Examined on microfilm by courtesy of the British Museum (B.M. 1490 bb 17 [1]). Burton and Challoner's other biographers make no mention of this early revision.

[19] The "Rule of Life" seems to be an original piece; but the "Daily Exercise" was taken from the later editions of the Doway *Abstract* (cf. above, n.15).

[20] Examined on photocopy by the great courtesy of Oscott College, Sutton Coldfield, England.

[21] Cf. Burton, *Challoner,* II, 337. The present writer was able to examine an 1815 edition (London: Keating Brown & Co., 1815) by courtesy of the British Museum (B.M. 3504 dg. 14 1). He was also able to examine all subsequent editions, obtained from several sources. It

III. The American Redactions of the British Text

Just which of the above British texts Father Molyneaux chose to have reprinted in Philadelphia by Bell (*ca.* 1775) and Spotswood (1785, 1786) is uncertain. As noted above, his title-references to these publications are loose and confusing. But again, it is practically certain that the text of Molyneaux's catechismal imprints is preserved in those earliest extant editions of the "Carroll Catechism" (12th-16th) published from 1793 to 1806 (cf. part IV). It is clear, however, that these last editions are definitely based on one of the Challoner revisions. The present writer was able to make this judgement after he received the British texts (cf. part II) from English repositories and made a textual comparison with the earliest extant editions of the "Carroll" (cf. part IV). 317

The "Carroll" editions of the 1790's all claim to have been "newly revised for use in the United States." This last phrase might suggest substantial revision, but this is not the case; there are, however, redactions in the American text. In making a textual comparison of the 1795 "Carroll"[22] with the 1772 Challoner,[23] the following differences can be ascertained.

The first difference is that the 1795 "Carroll" uses New Testament quotations from a different English version than that used in the 1772 Challoner. Further investigation showed that the American text quotes from the 1752 Challoner revision of the Rheims New Testament (1582).[24] It is surprising to find that the 1759 and 1772 revisions of *A Short Abridgement* do not use Challoner's own revisions of the Rheims New Testament but rather retain the scriptural quotations as they appear in the classic 1728 text. The 1728 text, however, uses an English version of the New Testament other than the "Rhemes" version.[25]

The 1795 "Carroll" and the 1772 Challoner both divide the catechismal text itself into seven chapters. A chapter by chapter analysis reveals some dozen differences, but most of them are small stylistic variances of language that could be reasonably credited to the American typesetter. A few differences, however,

---

[22] *A Short Abridgment of Christian Doctrine, Newly Revised for the Use of the Catholic Church in the United States of America. To Which Is Added, A Short Daily Exercise, The Thirteenth Edition, with Approbation,* (Baltimore: Printed by Samuel Sower, 1795). This 1795 edition is verbally identical with the earliest extant edition of the *American Short Abridgment* (12th ed.; Georgetown: James Doyle, 1793). The 1793 edition was examined at Georgetown University Library; the 1795, at Woodstock College Library (then in Manhattan). It should be noted that Father Molyneaux (cf. above n. 5) was president of Georgetown in 1793.

[23] Cf. above, n. 20.

[24] For information on the various revisions of the New Testament made by Challoner, cf. Hugh Pope and Sebastian Bullough, "The History of the Rheims-Doway Version" in *A Catholic Commentary on Holy Scripture,* ed. Bernard Orchard *et alii* (New York: Thomas Nelson & Sons, 1953), pp. 34-39. A similar article by Bullough can be found in *New Catholic Encyclopedia,* II, 465-67.

[25] Cf. above, nn. 16, 18, 20; also *New Testament of Jesus Christ* [*etc.*], (Rhemes: John Fogny, 1582). The New Testament quotations used in the 1728, 1752, and 1772 editions of the *Abridgment* greatly resemble the versions of [Cornelius Nary], *New Testament of Our Lord and Saviour Jesus Christ* [*etc.*], (n.p., 1718) and that of [Robert Witham], *Annotations of the New Testament of Jesus Christ* [*etc.*], (n.p., 1730). The 1815 edition of the *Abridgment* (cf. above, n. 21) contains the Challoner revisions of the Rheims text. For this essay, the 1582 Rheims and 1730 Witham were examined at the Newberry Library; the 1718 Nary, at the Regenstein Library of the University of Chicago.

are definitely editorial. In Chapter I, the American redactor removed the British text's question/answer unit "What is Faith?" and reintegrated its material in Chapter VII with the treatment of the theological virtues. At the end of a long Chapter II, the "Carroll" adds the element "omission" to its definition of sin and the words "whereby we beg for good things, and to be freed from evil" to its definition of prayer. In Chapter IV, when answering what is forbidden by the ninth commandment, the American text changes the British "irregular motions of the flesh" to "irregular motions of concupiscence." In Chapter VI, in defining Extreme Unction, the more exact British "It is the anointing of the sick, with prayers for the forgiveness of their sins" is changed by the American redactor to "it is a sacrament which gives grace to die well." The 1795 American text also lacks reference to the classic proof-text from Jas. 5:14-15, but later
318 editions of the "Carroll" restore it in full to the unit on Extreme Unction.

The most surprising American redaction is found in Chapter V, "Of the Commandments of the Church." The Commandments of the Church have a long history in catechismal literature, but they are often slightly variously rendered. Now and then one hears from Catholics of a continental background and education that it is only in the United States that the element of "contributing to the support of one's pastor" is included in the ecclesial mandates. This is not true. The idea of *personally* supporting the pastor or the works of the parish has a long history in the Commandments of the Church as they have been presented in the English-speaking Catechesis. The historical reasons for this should be well known. The mandate of church support is not found in the first of the recusant catechisms, that of Laurence Vaux (*A Catechisme,* Louvain, n.p., 1567). Vaux, however, did not treat the newer problems of the day in his text. Subsequent recusant catechisms do include the mandate "to tythe" in the Commandments of the Church. The Doway Catechism stresses the "tything" concept as do all the catechisms sprung from it. The 1772 British text gives the third Commandment of the Church as "to pay Tithes to our Pastor." The 1795 American redaction removes this mandate from its listing. It further divides the British text's first commandment into Commandments 1. and 2., in order to keep six mandates. The present author found this redaction most surprising, considering that John Carroll in his first report to Rome (1784)[26] had pointed out there was a problem of church support in the United States; further he had seen to it that there was strongly worded legislation on the obligation of *personally* supporting the Church put into the decrees of the First National Synod (1791)[27] and stressed this same idea in his first national pastoral.[28] The elimination of the church support mandate in the 1795 "Carroll" may have been an anachronism, retained from the initial "Carroll" printed by Bell (*ca.*

[26] Carroll reported to the *S.C. de Propaganda Fide,* March 1, 1785; for the report, cf. John Tracy Ellis, *Documents of American Catholic History* (reprint: 2 vols.; Chicago: Henry Regnery Company, 1967), I, 147-50. (Hereinafter cited as Ellis, *Documents.*) Cf. below, n. 30.

[27] Cf. Statute No. 23 in "Statuta Synodi Baltimorensis Anno 1791 Celebratae," *Concilia Provincialia Baltimori Habita, Ab anno 1829 usque ad annum 1849* (*ed. alt.;* Baltimore: John Murphy & Co., 1851), pp. 12-28.

[28] Cf. Peter Guilday, ed., *National Pastorals of the American Hierarchy (1792-1919)* (reprint; Westminster, Md.: Newman Press, 1954). pp. 6-8. (Hereinafter cited as Guilday, *National Pastorals.*)

1775).[29] The clergy and churches were more supported by benefice-type funding at that time.[30] After 1800, the church support mandate was added to the "Carroll" text, and two additional question/answer units were written to explain it.[31] Not surprisingly, the mandate on fasting and abstaining, as explicated "according to the Custom of England" in the British text, was changed by the American redactor to fit the observances as kept "in this Diocese." The 1795 "Carroll" does not include the British Chapter VIII, "The Christian's Rule of Life" and greatly rewrites and reduces the British Chapter IX, "The Christian's Daily Exercise."[32]

The final American redaction is most interesting. The American editor, apparently Molyneaux, added "A Fuller Instruction concerning the Holy Eucharist and Communion, Translated from the French Catechism of John-Joseph
Languet, formerly Archbishop of Sens." This appendix greatly adds to the brief 319
Eucharistic material of the *Abridgement* itself. The inclusion of these units from the catechism of the anti-Jansenist prelate Jean-Joseph Languet de Villeneuve de Gergy, Archbishop (1730-50) of Sens and formerly of Soisson,[33] is significant in that it contravenes the strictures of Jansenist piety against the frequent reception of Holy Communion. Its inclusion in the "Carroll Catechism" seems to reflect the historic Jesuit reaction against Jansenism and further evidences that from the beginning of its organized life (and prior to it) the thrust in the American Church has been in the direction of frequent Holy Communion.[34] The Languet material appears in all extant editions of the "Carroll" and was subsumed into later major American catechisms in one way or another. The present writer did not know of Languet and his catechism until after he had first examined the "Carroll" text and then further consulted French reference sources. After putting a number of factors together, it became clear that Molyneaux must have been familiar with the Languet catechism from his years in Flanders[35] and

---

[29] Cf. above, n. 10.

[30] Carroll explained to *Propaganda* (as above, n. 26):

> Priests are maintained chiefly from the proceeds of the estates; elsewhere by the liberality of the Catholics. There is properly no ecclesiastical property here; for the property by which the priests are supported, is held in the names of the individuals and transferred by will to devisees. This course was rendered necessary when the Catholic religion was cramped here by laws, and no remedy has yet been founded for this difficulty, although we made an earnest effort last year (Ellis, *Documents,* I, 150).

A very great number of documents concerning the Jesuit properties in Maryland and Pennsylvania are contained in Thomas Hughes, *History of the Society of Jesus in North America, Colonial and Federal. Documents* (1 vol. in 2 parts; London, New York, *et alii*: Longmans, Green, and Co., 1908-10), Sections II-VIII. Material on the support question in Pennsylvania can be found in Martin I. J. Griffin, "The Sir John James Fund," *American Catholic Historical Society of Philadelphia Records,* VIII (1898), 195-209.

[31] In the editions of the "Carroll" listed below in part IV, the 1801 (Albany) and the 1806 (New York) editions carry the tithing commandment. The 1803 (Boston) edition does not. The two added question/answer units on Church support appeared in the "Carroll" at least by the 1818 (Baltimore) edition. The pertinent material, extracted from this last edition, is appended at the end of part V.

[32] Cf. above, n. 19.

[33] Cf. J. Carreyre, "Languet de Villeneuve de Gergy, Jean-Joseph," *Dictionnaire de théologie catolique,* IX, 2602-06. Languet had a career filled with controversy, largely concerning Jansenism. His catechism was the subject of one related controversy; the published documents of which, pro and con, fill three large tomes (Paris, 1742).

[34] All major American catechisms have favored frequent reception.

[35] Cf. above, n. 5.

quite possibly brought a copy with him on coming to America. The present writer, however, was unable to find the Languet catechism in an American repository and could not obtain a microfilm of the material from European sources. Several years after these original inquiries, the present writer was greatly surprised to find in Porter[36] that Languet's *Catéchisme de Sens* was mandated for use in the Diocese of Quebec from 1753 and had been printed at Quebec in 1765, the first imprint of book-length to be published in Canada. Through the extraordinary kindness of the *Bibliothèque St. Sulpice* (Montreal), this writer was able to examine the original 1765 imprint.[37] While examining the *Catéchisme de Sens,* it became clear where Molyneaux got his material for the "fuller instruction" that he appended to the "Carroll." The question yet remains: did Molyneaux use a Canadian or European imprint of Languet as the direct source
320 of his extraction? There may have been a greater connection between Philadelphia and Quebec, in terms of early catechetical materials, than is yet apparent.

IV. The Continuing Presence of the "Carroll" in American Catholic Religious Education

The "Carroll Catechism" was published "with approbation," but Carroll never seems to have prescribed it for use in the United States.[38] It did not carry a *mandement,* for instance, in the manner of the French diocesan catechisms.[39] Further, the First National Synod of 1791 does not mention the catechism in its catechetical legislation.[40] The fact remains, however, that the "Carroll" was

[36] Fernand Porter, *L'Institution catéchistique au Canada, deux siècles de formation religieuse, 1633-1833* (Montreal: Les Editions Franciscaines, 1949), 109ff. In the same scholarly work, there is correspondence discussing the adoption of the British *Abridgment* (*le catéchisme de Londres*) for the English-speaking Catholics of the Diocese of Quebec; one of the reasons adduced for its adoption was *"parce qu'il s'enseigné dans les Etats-Unis"* and it would become *"alors le catéchisme de l'Amerique Septentrionale"* (pp. 126-30). Father Porter graciously answered inquiries from the present writer and has sent additional material which will be valuable for future research into the early English-speaking Catechesis of the United States and Canada.

[37] *Catéchisme du Diocèse de Sens, Par Monseigneur Jean-Joseph Languet, Archêveque de Sens* (Quebec: Chez Brown & Gilmore, 1765). A second edition was printed in 1766. A third edition, slightly changed, was authorized by Mgr. Jean-Oliver Briand (*Catéchisme a l'usage du Diocèse de Quebec* [Montreal: Chez Fleury Mesplet & Charles Berger, 1777]). William Brown and Thomas Gilmore had come from Philadelphia to Quebec in 1764. Fleury Mesplet had come from Philadelphia to Montreal in 1776. Mesplet, for several years, acted as printer and also agent of the Continental Congress in that body's efforts to win French Canada.

[38] In the manner of the English vicars apostolic, Carroll would be slow to "prescribe" where it was not necessary. There really would be no doubt that a question/answer catechism was the proper catechetical material to be published and used. Carroll and Molyneaux worked within the epoch of the catechism—a 400-year era when catechesis and catechism were convertible terms.

[39] Usually the *mandement de M. L'Evêque* presented the catechism *"pour être seul enseigné" dan son diocèse"* (p.e.s.e.d.s.d.). Often too, the *mandement* contained instruction on how to catechize. The present writer has been unable to find such pedagogical material published for English-speaking Catholics in the eighteenth century. Later references, however, have suggested to him that Henri-Marie Boudon's *La Science sacrée du catéchisme* [etc.] (Paris: J.T. Herissant, 1749) may have been influential in England, Ireland, and America.

[40] In his March 1, 1785 report to *Propaganda* (as above, in n. 26), Carroll discusses the "abuses that have grown among Catholics":

> Then among other things, a general lack of care in instructing their children and especially the negro slaves in their religion, as these people are kept constantly at work, so that they rarely hear any instructions from the priest, unless they can spend a short time with one . . . (Ellis, *Documents,* I, 149).

the common catechism of English-speaking Catholics in the United States for many generations. The following list of editions published demonstrates this:[41]

A Short Abridgment of Christian Doctrine. Newly Revised for the Use of the Catholic Church in the United States of America, To Which Is Added a Short Daily Exercise.

Philadelphia: Robert Bell, *ca.* 1775.
Philadelphia: William Spotswood, 1785, 1786.
*12th ed. Georgetown: James Doyle, 1793.
*13th ed. Baltimore: Samuel Sower, 1795.
*14th ed. Baltimore: Michael Duffy, 1798.
*12th ed. [sic]. Albany: Charles R. and George Webster, 1801.
*15th ed. Boston: Manning & Loring, 1803.
Baltimore: John W. Butler, 1805. 321
*16th ed. New York: Bernard Dornin, 1806.
n.p.: 1812, 1815.
*Philadelphia: William Fry, 1816 [printed with Bazeley, C. W. *Arithmetical Rules*].
Baltimore n.p. [Fielding Lucas Jr.?], 1818 [hymns added].
*Philadelphia: For the Proprietor, 1823.
Baltimore: Fielding Lucas Jr., 1825, 1826 [?], 1836 [?], 1841. [There are extant, other Lucas eds. undated, as was his custom].
Lancaster, Pa.: H. W. Villee, 1831.
*Philadelphia: n.p. [Eugene Cummiskey?], 1835.
*New York: J. Doyle, 1839.
Baltimore: n.p., 1846.
New York: E. Dunigan, 1849, 1855.
New York: n.p., 1873.
*Philadelphia: Eugene Cummiskey, 1878.

The above listing concerns the publishing of the "Carroll" in its own proper form. The initial catechism, however, was incorporated into other subsequent catechisms either in whole or in part. Sections of the "Carroll" were subsumed in the various editions of the Bardstown Catechism (1812, 1825, 1853, 1854) compiled by Bishop John Baptist David. The whole "Carroll" was incorporated, as Part I, in Bishop Benedict Fenwick's Boston Catechism (1828, 1835, 1839, 1843, 1846, 1858). Fenwick's compilation was widely used in New England and other parts of the United States. The *General Catechism of Christian Doctrine* (1853, 1858, 1859, 1862, 1865, 1867, 1869, 1872, 1875, 1884) emerged from the First Plenary Council of Baltimore. Compiled by Bishop John Timon of Buffalo, the *General* was a redaction of the Boston Catechism. The *General Catechism* contained the entire text of "Carroll." With the support of Archbishop Martin J. Spalding of Baltimore, Father John Henry McCaffrey presented his *Catechism of Christian Doctrine for General Use* (1865, 1866, 1869) for official adoption by the Second Plenary Council. In McCaffrey, the "Carroll

The Synod of 1791 put forth strong catechetical demands; cf. Statutes Nos. 10, 15, 17, 18 (as above in n. 27). Cf. also Carmody, *Origins*, pp. 13-14.

[41] The title given here is the most characteristic one used by the various imprints. Editions marked with an asterisk (*) have been examined by the present writer in various repositories. Editions without the asterisk have been encountered in various bibliographies and in several nineteenth-century sources.

Catechism" was completely maintained among the parts added. This was done in response to the request of a number of bishops that "the catechism of the venerable Archbishop Carroll be preserved." The Fathers of 1866, for various reasons, did not adopt McCaffrey and the *General* continued to be used. When the Third Plenary Council met in 1884, the desire was strong for a new national catechism. Accordingly, *A Catechism of Christian Doctrine, Prepared and Enjoined by the Third Plenary Council of Baltimore* was published in 1885. Largely, if not totally, the compilation of Bishop John Lancaster Spalding, the Baltimore Catechism was most comprehensively used in the United States until well after World War II. Practically the whole "Carroll" is reproduced in the Baltimore text, although often slightly rewritten.[42] The "Carroll" is truly a primary component of the American Catholic catechetical tradition.

322

[42] A textual analysis of the Baltimore Catechism shows its compilers used McCaffrey's catechism (cf. above) as one of their principal sources.

The Main Sheet Anchor: John Carroll and Catholic Higher Education*

Philip Gleason

John Carroll was disturbed about the future of Catholicism as he surveyed the scene in the aftermath of the American Revolution. As a supporter of the patriot movement he was pleased that the policy of religious toleration allowed Catholics to participate fully
in the political life of the new nation. No doubt he also perceived 323
that the wartime alliance with Catholic France had done much to improve the status of the church among his countrymen. But these positive features were outweighed by the disorganization of the church and the apathy of her ministers. There were only about two dozen priests in the new republic, several of whom were too old to be of any use. But even the younger ones seemed listless and demoralized.

Perhaps the disruptions of the wartime era contributed to the demoralization of the Catholic clergy, but something that happened just before the American Revolution was at the root of it. In 1773 Pope Clement XIV's brief *Dominus ac Redemptor* solemnly and publicly terminated the existence of the Society of Jesus.[1] The Jesuit missioners who constituted the whole of the American clergy were accustomed to attacks upon their society, but this was different. The papal action signified a complete repudiation by the supreme authority in the church of the religious body to which they had dedicated their lives. The effect was shattering. John Carroll, a veteran of sixteen years in the society, was plunged into near despair. In his initial shock he longed for the delivery of "immediate death"; because of the suppression, he quit Europe and returned to his native America where he lived for several years in semiretirement before fully recovering his equilibrium. The sense of loss was still vivid more than a decade later when the American ex-Jesuits described the time of the suppression as "that doleful era

---

* An abbreviated version of this paper was presented to the symposium on *John Carroll and American Independence,* held at John Carroll University, Cleveland, Ohio, October 10, 1975.

[1] Cf. William V. Bangert, *A History of the Society of Jesus* (St. Louis, 1972), chap. 6.

. . . when we were torn from our dear Mother . . . [and left orphaned], oppressed with grief, [and] uncertain of our future destiny."[2]

Beyond its effect on the individuals involved, the suppression of the Jesuit order, followed immediately by the Revolutionary War, left the church in America completely without leadership or effective authority. Since the 1630's the Jesuits had furnished virtually all the missioners for the English mainland colonies. It was the English Jesuit superior who really had charge of the Catholic church in English-speaking North America despite a hazily defined
324 authority that the Vicar Apostolic of London was supposed to hold over the colonial American Catholics. The tenuous connection with London was broken when America gained her independence, and since the Society of Jesus was no more, Catholics in the new nation were in a strictly autocephalic condition—the church in America literally had no head, no structure, no organized means to mobilize its resources for the tasks that lay ahead. Indeed, the very security of its material resources was precarious since the title to church properties—that is, the chapels, dwellings, and farms that previously belonged to the Jesuits—was now held by the various individual priests in their own names, any one of whom could dispose of what he held as he saw fit.[3]

This was the state of affairs that disturbed Carroll and convinced him that something had to be done. Since no one else was doing it, Carroll himself took the initiative. Although he had no official position of leadership, he drafted a plan of organization in 1782 and submitted it to his fellow priests for their consideration. It was a constitution-making period, and Carroll's plan furnished the basis on which the ex-Jesuits of Maryland and Pennsylvania came together in a series of meetings and worked out a kind of provisional

---

[2] The quotation is from John Carroll *et al.* to the Rev. Gentlemen of the Southern District, Feb., 1787, as given in Thomas Hughes, *A History of the Society of Jesus in North America, Documents*, vol. I, pt. 2 (New York, 1910), p. 605. *Ibid.*, pp. 676-79, establishes the date of this letter. (Hughes' two volumes of documents are continuously paginated and will be cited simply as *Documents.*) For Carroll's personal reaction to the suppression of the Jesuits, see John Carroll Brent, *Biographical Sketch of the Most Rev. John Carroll* (Baltimore, 1843), pp. 25-26; Annabelle Melville, *John Carroll of Baltimore* (New York, 1955), pp. 35-37. Peter Guilday, *The Life and Times of John Carroll*, 2 vols. (New York, 1922), I: 43-56, describes the suppression as it affected the English Jesuit Province of which Carroll was a member.

[3] Cf. Guilday, *Carroll*, I, chaps. 10-12.

constitution for the church in America. In October of 1784 they formally approved an organizational structure variously known as the Chapter, the Select Body of the Clergy, or the Clergy Corporation. This institution made it possible for the clergy to reach collective decisions on the management of ex-Jesuit properties and to determine jointly the manner in which the revenues accruing from those properties should be employed for the general good of the church. The arrangement was designed to care for the "temporalities" of the church, not questions of spiritual jurisdiction such as the assignment of ministers to different localities. John Carroll's leadership in devising this system, and the standing he enjoyed in
the community, resulted in his being selected as the spiritual head 325
of the American church, first as superior of the mission in 1784 and finally as the first American bishop in 1789.[4]

In those heroic days when there problems on every hand and the first foundations were still being laid, one could hardly suppose that Carroll would devote much of his attention to such refinements as colleges for Catholic youth. Even today, when the brick-and-mortar stage is long past, few bishops have time to concern themselves very actively in the field of higher education. But we know that John Carroll did think often and earnestly about higher education because he wrote about it frequently and because his thoughts were translated into action. Moreover, his words and actions reveal something even more surprising—that he regarded the establishment of a college as essential to the survival and growth of the church. From the very beginning of his active concern for the future of American Catholicism, Carroll repeatedly stated that a college was the object nearest his heart. In 1785, when he was already actively promoting the idea among his clerical brethren, he declared that the founding of a college and afterward a seminary were indispensably necessary to "give consistency to our religious views in this country." The following year, 1786, Carroll persuaded the Select Body of Clergy to commit itself to the project of which he personally assumed direction. Progress was slow, but the school eventually came into being at Georgetown and the present-day uni-

[4] Guilday, *Carroll,* I, chaps. 12, 14, 19; Melville, *Carroll,* chaps. 6, 8; John M. Daley, *Georgetown University: Origin and Early Years* (Washington, 1957), pp. 21-35, covers these developments and relates them to Georgetown's beginnings in admirably clear and concise fashion. Hughes' *Documents,* pp. 601-97, contains a wealth of primary materials, but the organization is difficult to follow.

versity rightfully claims John Carroll as its founder.[5]

What we find, then, is that the first bishop made it his first item of business to establish the first Catholic college, and that he called the college "our main sheet anchor for Religion."[6] This discovery seems so surprising that it demands explanation. Why did John Carroll think of a Catholic college as so essential? What role did the college play in the life of the church that made it so important? With these questions in mind let us review Carroll's association with Catholic higher education.

326

I

For this purpose, Carroll's life falls into three distinct periods. The first extends from his birth in 1735 to 1774 when the thirty-nine-year-old former Jesuit returned to America after the suppression of his beloved society. Since Carroll spent most of this period in and around various Jesuit institutions of learning in Europe, he was intimately acquainted with Catholic higher education abroad, both as a student and as a priest who found in it his ministry.

Carroll's formal education began with a year or two of studies at a short-lived Jesuit school at Bohemia Manor in northeastern Maryland. But at age thirteen he crossed the Atlantic to pursue higher studies at the college of St. Omers, a school run by the English Jesuits and located in French Flanders only fifteen miles or so from Calais. Here he finished his basic classical education and then entered the Jesuit novitiate at the nearby town of Watten. Upon completion of this two-year program of spiritual formation, Carroll took the vows that made him officially a member of the Society of Jesus at age twenty-two.

The chronology of the next epoch of Carroll's life is uncertain, but it seems he was not ordained to the priesthood until 1769, when he was thirty-four years of age.[7] Before ordination the English Jesuits usually spent six or seven years studying philosophy and theology at their scholasticate at Liège, but this period of study was

---

[5] See the letters of Carroll to Charles Plowden, Sept. 26, 1783, and Dec. 15, 1785, in *The John Carroll Papers*, edited by Thomas O'Brien Hanley. 3 vols. (Notre Dame, 1976), I: 78, 198. (Hereafter cited as *Carroll Papers*.) See Daley, *Georgetown*, chaps. 2-3, for Carroll's role in Georgetown's founding.

[6] Carroll to Charles Plowden, Oct. 23, 1789. *Carroll Papers*, I: 390.

[7] Cf. Melville, *Carroll*, pp. 15-16, 20; Guilday, *Carroll*, I: 31.

broken up by stints of teaching or by other duties connected with the society's activities.[8] Hence a long lapse of time between first vows and ordination was not unusual. Carroll's life apparently followed this pattern. We know that he taught philosophy at Liège in the early 1760's, that he spent two years as tutor and companion to a young English Catholic nobleman who was making the Grand Tour, and that he was at the Jesuit college at Bruges when the society was suppressed in 1773.

The schools in which Carroll lived and worked were key institutions in the life of English-speaking Catholics. From the time of Queen Elizabeth I, who established Protestantism as the official
religion of the land, the English Catholics had maintained scores
of convents, schools, and seminaries on the continent.[9] The area of present-day Belgium was a favorite site for these establishments because it was close to England and was at the time under the control of Spain, the leading Catholic power. The seminary at Douai, founded in 1568 by Cardinal William Allen, was the oldest and most important institution preparing priests for the English mission. Although designed primarily as a seminary, Douai also accepted lay students. During the latter part of the eighteenth century only a quarter of its lower-level students proceeded to the priesthood, so Douai also played an important role in the education of the English Catholic lay elite.[10] St. Omers, established in 1593, was intended from the first as a school for the laity, but its founder anticipated that a smaller group of "picked men" might be attracted to the religious life while in school and continue on to higher studies as members of the Society of Jesus. And this is what in fact took place —about the same proportion of St. Omers' boys became priests as at Douai.[11]

---

[8] Cf. Bernard Basset, *The English Jesuits, from Campion to Martindale* (New York, 1968), pp. 288-97, 311.

[9] Peter Guilday, *The English Catholic Refugees on the Continent 1558-1795* (London, 1914), p. 40, lists some sixty such institutions.

[10] On Douai see Guilday, *English Catholic Refugees,* chaps. 4, 9; Edwin H. Burton, *The Life and Times of Bishop Challoner (1691-1781),* 2 vols. (London, 1909); A. F. C. Beales, *Education Under Penalty; English Catholic Education from the Reformation to the Fall of James II, 1547-1689* (London, 1963); and especially P. R. Harris, "The English College, Douai, 1750-1794," *Recusant History,* 10 (April, 1969), 79-95; and P. R. Harris (ed.), *Douai College Documents, 1639-1794,* vol. 63 of Catholic Record Society Publications, Records Series (n. p., 1972). Marvin R. O'Connell, *The Counter Reformation, 1559-1610* (New York, 1974), p. 236, says 440 priests went from Douai to England in Elizabeth's reign.

[11] On St. Omers (also spelled St. Omer from the town in Flanders where

The reason for all this activity on the continent was, of course, that the Roman Catholic faith was proscribed in England. Catholics could not hold office or practice their religion publicly. After 1585 it was a crime punishable by death for a priest merely to enter England, and niney-eight priests from Douai alone were executed during Elizabeth's reign—not to mention a smaller number of Jesuits and priests ordained at other continental seminaries.[12] No Catholic school or seminary could be maintained in England; eventually stiff penalties were enacted even for sending children abroad to Catholic academies or colleges. Enforcement was not 328 too rigorous, however, and despite the risks involved the English Catholics sent a steady stream of youngsters over the Channel, often bidding them good-bye for years at the tender age of ten or thereabouts.[13] Parents who made this sort of sacrifice obviously placed a high premium on assuring a Catholic education for their children, and for them the continental schools took on crucial importance in their struggle to maintain the faith, as nurseries of their champions and martyrs, and as pledges of their determination to survive.

The Catholics of colonial Maryland shared this intense devotion to the continental schools and developed their own tradition of sustained loyalty to St. Omers. This Jesuit school rather than any other was their focus because the priests who accompanied the first settlers in Maryland were Jesuits. Indeed, Father Andrew White, known as the "Apostle of Maryland," was one of the first group of students to attend St. Omers, and from the earliest days a two-way traffic existed between the Chesapeake colony and the school in Flanders. Already in 1685 two boys from Maryland anticipated the path that John Carroll was to follow by entering the Jesuit

the school was located) see Guilday, *English Catholic Refugees,* pp. 138-45; Beales, *Education Under Penalty,* esp. pp. 69-70, for the phrase "picked men"; Hubert Chadwick, *St. Omers to Stonyhurst* (London, 1962), is the fullest account; John Gerard, *Stonyhurst College, Centenary Record* (Belfast, 1894), has some interesting material and illustrations of St. Omers. (St. Omers became Stonyhurst when moved to England in 1794 by revolutionary upheavals in the Low Countries.)

[12] O'Connell, *Counter Reformation,* p. 236. *Ibid.,* p. 239, gives 183 as the total number of Catholics executed during Elizabeth's reign, excluding those implicated in plots against the government. Guilday, *English Catholic Refugees,* p. 26, says twenty-three Jesuits were executed in England from 1577 to 1681.

[13] B. Elliott, "Some Notes on Catholic Education Abroad," *Recusant History,* 7 (April, 1964), 250, 254.

novitiate after completing their course at St. Omers.[14]

There does not seem to be any record of how many "Marylandians" went to St. Omers, but by the mid-eighteenth century a loosely organized system existed for escorting youngsters to the continental schools, transmitting payments, forwarding instructions for their care and so on. The names of some thirty-five Maryland families turn up in the records of the agent who handled these matters in London. We also know that young girls from Maryland attended convent schools in no fewer than ten towns in France and the Low Countries, and that some of them entered the religious life in those places.[15]

As one of the leading Catholic families in the colony, the Carrolls shared fully in the devotion to St. Omers. Three of John Carroll's uncles went there in the early eighteenth century, one of whom lost his life at sea on the homeward trip. John's older brother, Daniel, spent six years at St. Omers; Charles Carroll made the ocean crossing in the same group with his cousin, John, and the two were schoolmates for several years at St. Omers.[16]

Generations of Carrolls thus demonstrated their commitment to Catholic institutions of higher education. John Carroll himself dedicated his life as a priest to the Society of Jesus, which specialized in education; and had it not been dissolved in 1773, he might well have lived out his life as a teacher or administrator in Jesuit colleges. When the suppression of the society brought this phase of his life to a close, it left him with a fund of experience on which he could draw in America.

---

[14] On White see Basset, *English Jesuits,* pp. 183-84; Chadwick, *St. Omers,* p. 21. Beales, *Education Under Penalty,* pp. 168-69, reports on Maryland boys at St. Omers and their advancing to the Jesuit novitiate by 1685. Cf. also Henry Foley, *Records of the English Province of the Society of Jesus,* 7 vols. (London, 1877-83), III: 394.

[15] Cf. Thomas Hughes, "Educational Convoys to Europe in the Olden Times," *American Ecclesiastical Review,* 29 (1903), 24-39; Hughes, *History of the Society of Jesus in North America, Text,* II: 523 n, 524 n. For the use of the term "Marylandian" see Charles Carroll to his parents, March 22, 1750, manuscript letter in Maryland Historical Society. These interesting letters which Charles Carroll wrote home to his family while studying at St. Omers and other continental schools have been published in *Maryland Historical Magazine,* 10 (1915), 143 ff., and subsequent issues.

[16] Thomas O'Brien Hanley, *Charles Carroll of Carrollton* (Washington, 1970), is the fullest discussion of the continental education of the Carrolls and in particular of Charles Carroll of Carrollton.

II

The second phase of John Carroll's involvement with Catholic higher education coincides roughly with the decade of the 1780's. These years also form a distinct epoch in his life, spanning as they do his emergence as the leader of the church in America and culminating in his consecration in 1790 as the first bishop of Baltimore. This decade was the period of Carroll's strongest statements about the essential importance of a Catholic college and of his drive to bring such an institution into being. In 1783 he called a college "the object nearest my heart" and three years later he persuaded
330 the Select Body of the Clergy to commit itself to the erection of a college. Over the next five years Carroll threw himself into every aspect of the effort to realize that goal. He solicited contributions, watched over the selection of the site and the construction of the building, sought to attract a strong president and faculty from among his friends in Europe, and personally drafted the plan of organization and studies to be followed.[17]

In November, 1791, Carroll had the satisfaction of seeing Georgetown academy (as it was called at first)[18] open its doors to students and begin its long and honorable career as a Catholic institution of learning. By that time a second educational establishment was also in operation in Baltimore. Its existence was a completely gratuitous act of providence as far as Carroll was concerned; he had not sought its foundation and it cost him nothing.

The background of this place, which came to be known as St. Mary's Seminary, is as follows:[19] When Carroll was in England for his consecration as bishop in 1790, he received from Father James A. Emery, superior of the Society of St. Sulpice in Paris, a remarkable proposal. Emery wanted to send some of his men to establish,

[17] Daley, *Georgetown*, chaps. 2-3.

[18] On April 23, 1790, Carroll wrote to the Papal Nuncio in Lisbon: "I have been working for several years to form a college, or rather this school; for I dare not dignify it with the name of College . . ." (*Carroll Papers*, I: 438). The term Georgetown College came into use in 1796 or 1797. See Daley, *Georgetown*, p. 92; and John Gilmary Shea, *History of Georgetown University* (New York, 1891), p. 23.

[19] Joseph W. Ruane, *The Beginnings of the Society of St. Sulpice in the United States (1791-1829)* (Washington, 1935), pp. 12-36. Father Vincent Eaton of the Sulpician Archives in Baltimore tells me that the name "St. Mary's Seminary" did not come into use until after St. Mary's College (discussed later) was founded in 1799. In this article, I have simply called it the Baltimore Seminary.

at their own expense, a seminary for the new diocese of Baltimore. Carroll was rather embarrassed by the offer since he did not see how he could reasonably encourage the Sulpicians to found a seminary in a diocese that had no seminarians and no immediate prospects of getting any. But Emery pressed the offer because he wanted at least one Sulpician establishment somewhere safely removed from the storms of the French Revolution, which had already resulted in legislation reducing the church to a department of the state and which threatened greater evils for the future. After thinking things over, Carroll was delighted to take advantage of the opportunity to acquire so potentially valuable an institution, especially since the Sulpicians were willing to send some seminarians of their own and to permit priests not needed in the seminary to work as missionaries among the French-speaking Catholics of the Ohio Valley. An agreement was therefore worked out in London and the first group of Sulpicians—four priests and five seminarians—reached Baltimore a year later. Here they established their seminary in a house converted from its earlier use as a tavern.

Within a period of less than ten years, Carroll had thus created a college and a seminary, the first building blocks of what was to become the imposing edifice of American Catholic higher education. The question we must now try to answer is, Why? Why did Carroll give a college such high priority? Why did he consider higher education so important that he gave it greater emphasis than any other project at the very outset of his efforts to organize the church in America?

The answer to these questions is very clear; Carroll himself states it in the plainest terms. There was a critical shortage of priests and the founding of a college was the first step toward overcoming that shortage by raising up a native American clergy. Eventually it was to be followed by the establishment of a seminary, since the college by itself was not sufficient to train priests. But the college had to come first for two reasons: it was needed to provide the basic classical education on which training in philosophy and theology would build and it would serve as a recruiting agency for the priesthood.

From his earliest statements on the subject Carroll linked the projected college with the need to assure "a succession of laborers in this vineyard"; this was what he had in mind in calling it "our

main sheet anchor for Religion."[20] In his first pastoral letter as bishop he alluded to Georgetown's role in preparing "a constant supply of zealous and able pastors . . . acquainted with the tempers, manners, and government of the people" whom they were to serve.[21] During the first year of Georgetown's operation he confided to three different correspondents his prayerful hope that "providence will attract many of the students . . . to the service of the church and that it will become a nursery for the seminary [in Baltimore]."[22] It was in responding to Emery's offer to establish a Sulpician seminary, however, that Carroll stated most explicitly the role of Georgetown in the preparation of clerics. After informing
332 Emery that he had no seminary, Carroll continued:

> I have worked for three or four years to form an establishment for the education of Catholic youth in *belles lettres* and the principles of religion. This literary establishment is on the point of opening for the reception of youth. When I conceived the idea their instruction was not my principal object. I proposed to form there students for an ecclesiastical seminary which will be prepared while the youths are making their first studies.[23]

This statement leaves little room for doubt as to Carroll's motives in founding Georgetown. It may, however, strike some persons today as reflecting a very inadequate appreciation of the true values of higher education—as being too vocationally oriented, if not downright anti-intellectual. This is, I think, a quite misguided kind of reaction. But since Richard Hofstadter interpreted the religious motivation of early American college founders as evidence of anti-intellectualism, and since the leading authority on the history of Catholic colleges, Edward J. Power, implies that Catholics were even more anti-intellectual in this respect than their Protestant counterparts, the point must be met.[24] Fundamentally, of course, the issue hinges on the view one takes of the nature of intellectual

[20] Carroll to Charles Plowden, Sept. 26, 1783, and Oct. 23, 1789. *Carroll Papers*, I: 78, 390.

[21] Peter Guilday, *The National Pastorals of the American Hierarchy (1792-1919)* (Westminster, Md., 1954 [reprint]), pp. 4-5.

[22] Carroll to Jean Hubert, Jan. 20, 1792; Carroll to Cardinal Antonelli, April 23, 1792; Carroll to Charles Plowden, April 30, 1792. *Carroll Papers*, II: 6, 27, 39.

[23] Ruane, *St. Sulpice*, p. 25.

[24] Cf. Richard Hofstadter, *Anti-intellectualism in American Life* (New York, 1963), esp. pp. 72 ff., 90, 101 ff., 105-06; Edward J. Power, *Catholic Higher Education in America, A History* (New York, 1972), pp. 46-54.

activity and how it relates to other spheres of life, especially, in this case, religion and education. This is not the place for a theoretical analysis of such matters, but two more restricted lines of argument can be offered to defend Carroll against the imputation of anti-intellectualism.

In the first place, the charge simply doesn't fit the personality of John Carroll. No one acquainted with the thoughtful, reflective mind that Carroll's letters reveal could accept even the implication that such a person was anti-intellectual. On the contrary, Carroll was a highly cultivated man with a lively appreciation of learning. He valued the college for what it would do in awakening the minds of young men and diffusing knowledge among them. Indeed, he mentioned these points specifically in answering the objections raised by some of his clerical brethren to the project of establishing a college; he insisted that these considerations would make a college worthwhile even though none of the students should "take to the Church."[25] Many years later he urged the president of Georgetown to make it his constant concern to stimulate the faculty to "a passion for study, reading, and litterary (sic) improvement" for, once having caught this passion, "they will infuse the same insensibly into their pupils."[26]

Carroll had fairly stringent intellectual standards and he did not deceive himself when Georgetown, or other Catholic institutions, failed to meet them. He frankly admitted that some of Georgetown's administrators, though very worthy men, were not academically qualified for their responsibilities.[27] And in writing to Father Charles Plowden, an English friend and former Jesuit confrere, about the education they both had received in the Jesuit houses in Belgium, Carroll sounded like a latter-day critic of Catholic intellectual life. The Jesuits had been eclipsed by graduates of Douai, Carroll asserted, because the society did not require its young scholastics "to extend the circle of their knowledge," but let them get through merely by memorizing the lectures they had taken down in dictation. The study of languages was neglected and modern writers ignored; as a result, Carroll concluded, "genius and talents were cramped, and a habit of inapplication was acquired, which few escaped."[28]

[25] Daley, *Georgetown*, p. 42.
[26] Carroll to John Grassi, Oct. 30, 1812. *Carroll Papers*; III: 204.
[27] Carroll to William Strickland, April 2, 1808. *Carroll Papers*, III: 53.
[28] Carroll to Charles Plowden, Feb. 12, 1803. *Carroll Papers*, II: 409.

Carroll regarded the Sulpicians as models of priestly virtue, but he was not uncritical of their methods of seminary education. In 1804 he expressed doubt that the "mode of studies" they employed was "calculated to produce eminent scholars"; with characteristic realism he added that little could be done about it "till time and opportunity give the means of introducing a more solid and comprehensive system of education." Some years later, when Simon Gabriel Bruté was assigned to teach theology at the Baltimore seminary, Carroll heartily approved because "it is important to the interests of religion to form some at least of our young clergymen to erudition; to teach them to acquire biblical, theological, and
334 Ecclesiastico-historical knowledge in an eminent degree. Who but Mr. Bruté," he asked, "can be their guide in these pursuits?"[29]

But while Carroll valued scholarship he did not found Georgetown out of any abstract commitment to culture or learning. He was, let us recall, a man struggling to meet the most fundamental organizational needs of the religion in which he was a believer. Why should he involve himself in so laborious an undertaking as founding a college if that project promised nothing more immediately rewarding than a diffuse elevation of the intellectual tone of the Catholic community? It would be most unreasonable to expect him to do any such thing, or to accuse him of anti-intellectualism for not having such a motivation in founding a college. Carroll had to take first things first, and one of the very first things the church in America needed was priests. If a college could help produce them— and he was sure it could—he would do his best to establish one. The cultural and intellectual goods that would flow from the college were excellent, to be sure, but they were secondary, a kind of bonus.

This, then, is the second line of argument to defend Carroll against the implication of anti-intellectualism—namely, the argument that it was perfectly reasonable, intellectually very defensible, for him to regard Georgetown's function in helping to create an American priesthood as the primary value of the institution. The priesthood is uniquely important in the Catholic religion. For

---

This letter and other items used in this section are also quoted in Melville, *Carroll*, pp. 152-55, a perceptive treatment of Carroll's views on education.

[29] Carroll to Charles Plowden, Dec. 7, 1804; Carroll to John Dubois, Dec. 22, 1811. *Carroll Papers*, II: 461; III: 165.

whatever may be said today about Catholicism's being overly clericalized, the fact is that without a priest the faithful cannot worship through the Mass in the manner that the church prescribes, nor can they have access to the means of spiritual assistance she offers, i.e., the sacraments. A people denied the Mass and the sacraments may keep the faith alive, but the Catholic Church is not fully present among them. And a "prolonged absence of priests from a country guarantees the Catholic Church's demise," as Marvin O'Connell has recently pointed out in discussing the plight of Catholics in Elizabethan England.[30] Recognizing this fact, Elizabeth's government forbade priests to enter England and hunted them down when they did. The Catholic exiles on the continent likewise realized that priests were the key to survival, and therefore founded seminaries and sent their graduates back to England despite peril of rack and rope.

Happily, there was no persecution to contend with in the new American states of the 1780's but the opposite condition created its own exigent needs. That is, the very condition of "universal toleration throughout this immense country" spurred the rapid growth of the Catholic population and the consequent demand for more priests. In the same letter in which he spoke of a college as the object nearest his heart, Carroll also reported that the "innumerable R. Cats. going & ready to go into the new regions bordering on the Mississippi . . . [were] impatiently clamorous for Clergymen to attend them."[31] Eighteen months later Carroll was still distressed by the fear that the French Catholics of the Mississippi valley were "destitute of priests." And when he reported to Rome on the condition of the American Church in 1785, Carroll knew of only one priest to serve all the Catholics in New York, and but twenty-four others along the Atlantic seaboard.[32] Several of the latter group were superannuated and useless; two of them died within the

---

[30] O'Connell, *Counter Reformation*, p. 235.

[31] Carroll to Charles Plowden, Sept. 26, 1783. *Carroll Papers*, I: 78. (This letter also contains Carroll's reference to "universal toleration . . .")

[32] Carroll's "Report for the Eminent Cardinal Antonelli Concerning the State of Religion in the United States of America," dated March 1, 1785, gives the numbers of priests. Text available in John Tracy Ellis, ed., *Documents of American Catholic History* (Milwaukee, 1956), pp. 152-54, and *Carroll Papers*, I: 179-82. Guilday, *Carroll*, I: 301-05, identifies these priests of 1785. *Ibid.*, chap. 17, discusses some of Carroll's problems concerning the clergy.

year.[33] Clearly some way had to be found to increase the numbers of priests.

Europe proved to be the crucial supplier of clerical manpower, and continued to be such long after institutions were at hand to train American vocations. But Carroll's experience with volunteer clerics from Europe was well calculated to make him long the more ardently for priests whose background he knew and whose training he had confidence in. Between 1785 and 1790 thirty European priests turned up in the United States; most were good and useful men, but enough of them were trouble-making "missionary ad-
336 venturers" to cause Carroll endless grief.[34] "You cannot conceive the trouble I suffer . . . from the medley of clerical characters coming from different quarters . . . and seeking employment here," he lamented to Charles Plowden, adding mournfully, "I cannot avoid employing some of them, & they soon begin to create disturbances."[35] Considering that the broils created by these ecclesiastical vagrants often ended in local schisms, one can understand more readily Carroll's desire to lessen his dependence on European volunteers.

But even if all the recruits from the Old World had been sacerdotal jewels, their numbers would not suffice for the needs at hand. Again and again Carroll found himself in the kind of straits he described for Plowden two months before Georgetown opened its doors:

> Kentucky is not yet supplied. I am obliged to have recourse to Ireland for it; & expect two priests from thence to go thither. Two wanted in Georgia; one in N. Carolina; four or five in different parts of Maryland & Pennsylvania.[36]

Nothing testifies better to "the dreadful want of priests" than

---

[33] Carroll to Cardinal Antonelli, March 13, 1786. *Carroll Papers,* I: 209.

[34] Carroll to Cardinal Antonelli, Sept. 27, 1790, gives the figure of thirty priests; Carroll to Francis Beeston, March 22, 1788, refers to "missionary adventurers." *Carroll Papers,* I: 468, 292.

[35] Carroll to Charles Plowden, Oct. 23, 1789. A few months later (Feb. 24, 1790), Carroll told Plowden that some of the European priests "have proved turbulent, ambitious, interested, and they unite much ignorance with consummate assurance." *Carroll Papers,* I: 389, 431.

[36] Carroll to Charles Plowden, Sept. 3, 1791. In the same letter Carroll wrote: "We really want some good German priests to make amends for the very indifferent cargoes of Friars and Capucins [sic], we have had from that Quarter" (*Carroll Papers,* I: 517, 516).

the work load borne by Carroll personally.[37] Although his correspondence to Rome, to friends and benefactors in Europe, and to priests and congregations throughout the whole country was prodigious in volume, and although he often found it necessary to make copies of both incoming and outgoing letters, Carroll had no copyist or secretary for the first twenty-one years of his episcopacy. Smothered under this mountain of correspondence, he could say with simple truth, "my whole life . . . is taken up writing letters."[38] And why did he not have a secretary? Because only a priest whom he trusted completely could handle the confidential matters that came to him daily, "and unfortunately, such is the scarcity of ministers of the Sanctuary that I cannot or I dare not withdraw a single one of them from the duties of a life devoted entirely to the salvation of the neighbor, to teaching and administering the sacraments. . . ."[39] Not until he was seventy-five years old did Carroll call upon one of his priests to act his secretary and to take over the duties of the cathedral parish which the archbishop was then personally attending to.[40]

If it is established that Carroll wanted a college primarily to recruit and prepare clergymen (an aim which he shared, of course, with all the early founders of Protestant colleges), and if enough has been said about whether such a motivation was anti-intellectual, the next question that presents itself is this: what model guided Carroll's efforts to set up a college? How did he combine his European experience and his understanding of the American situation in drawing up the plans for Georgetown? An inquiry into these matters has reference not only to the case of Georgetown itself, but also by implication to the larger question of how much Catholic colleges differed from Protestant and secular schools in structure and program.

---

[37] Carroll used the expression "dreadful want of priests" in a letter to John Grassi, Sept. 25, 1815. This was only three months before his death. *Carroll Papers,* III: 360.

[38] Carroll to Charles Plowden, Sept. 24, 1796. *Carroll Papers,* II: 187.

[39] Carroll to John Peemans, June 2, 1807. *Carroll Papers,* III: 23.

[40] Carroll to the Trustees at Alexandria, Va., July 5, 1810; Carroll to Charles Neale, Sept. 11, 1810. *Carroll Papers,* III: 118-19, 120-21. Carroll to Cardinal Litta, July 17, 1815, reports him as being again without a secretary. *Carroll Papers,* III: 346. For other items referring to Carroll's work load, see his letters to Charles Plowden, Sept. 3, 1791, Sept. 3, 1800, March 12, 1802, and Dec. 7, 1804. *Carroll Papers,* I: 517; II: 316-17, 382, 460. See also Carroll to Matthew Carey, Jan. 19, 1792, and Carroll to Elizabeth Seton, May 23, 1807, which amusingly relates the kind of interruption he sometimes ex-

The short answer to the question is that St. Omers was undoubtedly the model for Georgetown. But while Carroll's continental experience was decisive in the shaping of the college, he was also sensitive to the need to adapt to American conditions.

From the evidence available, it is impossible to determine how thoroughly Carroll knew the arrangements and methods of non-Catholic colleges in America. We can be sure, however, that he had some acquaintance with them, for he was associated with several non-Catholic schools. These associations came about because Carroll, as a respected public figure, was called upon to lend his name to various projects in higher education. In 1784 he was asked to
338 be one of the original trustees of St. John's College, Annapolis; he received an honorary degree from another institution about the same date; many years later he helped to found Baltimore College, and in 1813 he declined the post of provost of the University of Maryland.[41]

His numerous associations with interdenominational educational ventures have perhaps contributed to the erroneous belief that Carroll did not at first intend to establish a Catholic college, but rather planned to make use of non-Catholic institutions for the collegiate preparation of seminary prospects.[42] It is true that he did espouse this alternative for a time, but it was not his original plan; and although he saw certain advantages in it, he came to the conclusion that a Catholic college was the preferable option.

The situation was this. When the idea of setting up a Catholic college was first broached around 1783, persons whose judgment Carroll respected (he called them "our most intelligent friends") threw cold water on it. The idea was unworkable, they said, because Catholics were too poor to erect such a school and lacked the manpower to staff it. In the light of this adverse reaction Car-

---

perienced in his letter writing. In this case, two drunken persons "found access to [his] study." *Carroll Papers,* II: 5; III: 22.

[41] Melville, *Carroll,* pp. 151-52. He was also associated with two other secondary-level schools in Baltimore.

[42] See, for example, William J. McGucken, *The Jesuits and Education* (Milwaukee, 1932), p. 63; and Power, *Catholic Higher Education,* pp. 16-18. The original source of the error is likely the fact that Carroll mentions this alternative plan in his 1785 report to Cardinal Antonelli, which received early attention in such works as John Gilmary Shea, *Life and Times of the Most Rev. John Carroll* (New York, 1888), pp. 260-61; and James A. Burns, *The Principles, Origin and Establishment of the Catholic School System in the United States* (New York, 1912), p. 153. (Burns' volume was first published in 1908.)

roll felt that "the only reasonable prospect of raising up a succession of ministers for the service of Religion" was to try to recruit one or two Catholic graduates each year from the colleges of Philadelphia and Maryland. These young men could then be trained for the ministry by just two priests: the one who handled their instruction in theology must be a man of learning and abilities, Carroll said; but their spiritual formation could be guided by a priest too advanced in years for more active duty on the missions.[43]

While the great saving in manpower and expense made this plan attractive, Carroll also regarded it as having serious drawbacks.
But asking "are we able to do anything better?" he went on to point 339
out another argument in its favor, one that has a very modern ring:

> Being admitted to equal toleration, must we not concur in public measures, & avoid separating ourselves from the Community? Shall we not otherwise be marked as forming distinct views, & raise a dislike which may terminate in consequences very disagreeable to us?[44]

When he voiced these sentiments in December, 1784, Carroll had already been approached to cooperate in the establishment of St. John's College, Annapolis. In the course of the next six months he referred several times to the alternative plan and encouraged Catholic professors he knew in Europe to apply for positions in the existing colleges in Philadelphia and Maryland, noting that he personally had some influence with their administrators and that "my recommendation would have some weight."[45] But after midsummer of 1785 no more is heard of this plan; Carroll reverted to his original project of starting a Catholic college. When St. John's College opened in 1789, Carroll told his friend Plowden that Catholics would derive no benefit from it except as a place where "our young lads, who have finished their Grammar education at Georgetown . . . [may] pursue their higher studies of law, medicine, etc. In other respects," he added, "it will be hurtful to our Institution."[46]

---

[43] Carroll to Ferdinand Farmer, Dec., 1784. *Carroll Papers*, I: 158.

[44] *Ibid.*

[45] Carroll Report to Antonelli, March 1, 1785; Carroll to Joseph Edenshink, April-June, 1785; Carroll to Leonard Neale, June 17, 1785. *Carroll Papers*, I: 181, 186, 190.

[46] Carroll to Charles Plowden, Feb. 24, 1790. *Carroll Papers*, I: 431.

We can only speculate about why Carroll returned to his original idea. Presumably some more positive indications as to its feasibility overcame the discouraging advice given by his consultants. There is also evidence that Carroll may have lost some of his confidence about the prospects of amicable cooperation with non-Catholics. In June of 1785—about the same time he stopped talking about the alternative plan—Carroll saw signs of a recrudescence of religious antagonisms; and a year later he referred to "a Sourness in the minds of our protestant Brethren."[47]

Having determined to pursue his original goal of a Catholic college, Carroll inevitably thought along the lines of the continental
340 schools with which he had been so intimately associated for more than twenty-five years. The general purpose of Georgetown was identical with that of St. Omers—both were intended to provide a basic humanistic education for a Catholic lay elite, and at the same time recruit a smaller group who would go on to seminary training elsewhere. Carroll laid greater emphasis on the latter function, but he was conscious of both. Since he wanted a school that would do for American Catholics what St. Omers did for their English brethren, it was only natural for him to look to St. Omers as his model.

Carroll nowhere stated that he was patterning Georgetown after St. Omers, and we need not assume that he had St. Omers consciously in mind as he sketched out the organization and methods to be followed at Georgetown. However, the document in which he specified these matters exhibits so many parallels with St. Omers, and corresponds so closely to what we know of Jesuit educational methods in general, that the conclusion is inescapable that Carroll was drawing on this tradition, and not on contemporary American models, when he sat down to work out the details of Georgetown's administrative structure and academic program.

The scope of the program laid out in the document (which dates from the late 1780's or early 1790's) corresponds precisely to what was known in the Jesuit tradition as a *humanities* program.[48]

---

[47] Carroll to Charles Plowden, June 29, 1785, in which Carroll says he is not going to continue his controversy with Charles Wharton "least [sic] it should add fuel to some sparks of religious animosity, which are visible at present amongst us." In a letter to Joseph Berington, Sept. 29, 1786, Carroll refers to "sourness," which he had noted earlier but which had since subsided. *Carroll Papers,* I: 191, 217.

[48] This much corrected and interwritten draft is in Carroll's handwriting. It is item 9A N3 in the Archives of the Archiocese of Baltimore. Daley,

As it was originally put together in the days of St. Ignatius, the Jesuit humanities program comprised a sequence of studies lasting five or six years, the purpose of which was to give the student fluency in the use of the classical languages, especially Latin.[49] By the eighteenth century, vernacular languages, mathematics, and some natural and social science had been added, but the study of Latin and Greek remained the core of the humanities program. Students had to be literate in the vernacular before entering the humanities course, but they were quite young, usually between nine and twelve years of age. They finished their humanities somewhere between the ages of fourteen and eighteen, and at this point their college education was completed. If a young man wished to pursue a professional career in law, medicine, or the church, his further studies were thought of as comprising the university level of his education. Thus a St. Omers boy who wished to become a priest went to the Jesuit scholasticate at Liège for philosophy and theology; only the humanities was provided by the college at St. Omers.[50]

In its first promotional flyer, Georgetown promised to educate students in "the several Branches of Classical Learning" that would prepare them for university-level studies.[51] Carroll's organizational plan filled in the details by listing Latin, Greek, English, mathematics ("the elements and useful branches"), geography, and French (if

---

Georgetown, pp. 53 ff., 68 ff., discusses it and dates it about 1788; Hanley dates it in 1791 in *Carroll Papers*, I: 482-87. For Jesuit use of the term *humanities* see Chadwick, *St. Omers*, p. 72: Beales, *Education Under Penalty*, p. 147; Burton, *Challoner*, I: 16.

[49] Cf. Allen P. Farrell, *The Jesuit Code of Liberal Education* (Milwaukee, 1938), and George E. Ganss, *Saint Ignatius' Idea of a Jesuit University* (Milwaukee, 1954), for detailed scholarly treatment of early Jesuit education.

[50] Chadwick, *St. Omers*, pp. 69 ff., discusses curriculum; cf. also Gerard, *Stonyhurst*, p. 24. Ganss, *St. Ignatius' Idea*, pp. 31 ff., discusses the relation of college and university. At Douai, students could go from humanities all the way through theological studies in the same institution. The same was also possible in some of the Jesuit institutions to judge from John Dury's 1645 "Description of a Transmarine School" in T. Corcoran, *Studies in the History of Classical Teaching, Irish and Continental, 1500-1700* (New York, 1911), p. 236.

[51] Ellis, *Documents*, pp. 172-73, reproduces this prospectus and dates it 1789; Daley, *Georgetown*, p. 35 quotes from it, but dates it about 1786 (see p. 322, index under heading "Prospectus of 1786"). Carroll's remarks, quoted above at footnote 46, also indicate that Georgetown was designed for "Grammar education," or humanities, as a preparation for "higher studies," or university studies, in law, medicine etc.

there was a demand for it) as the subjects to be covered.[52] The entering students had to know how to read and write, and were to be at least eight years of age. Carroll did not specify how long the full course would take, but it is clear from the terminology employed that he was thinking of the five- or six-year Jesuit humanities program.

A particularly revealing passage runs as follows:

> The masters of the respective classes if Clergymen (excepting the Master of English) shall advance with their scholars, till they commence Poetry. (Quaere—shall they conduct them on to Poetry &
> 342 Rhetorick? or shall the professors of those branches always remain the same?)

Though probably unintelligible to those not familiar with the old Jesuit system, these remarks show that Carroll was using the same names for the last two classes of the humanities programs as those in vogue at St. Omers and Douai, i.e., Poetry and Rhetoric. The passage is also of interest because it reveals that he intended to follow the standard Jesuit practice of having the teacher move up with the boys in his group as they advanced from one stage to the next higher one in their struggle to master the grammar and syntax of the classic languages.[53] The "Quaere"—Carroll's question to himself—indicates that he was undecided whether this practice should carry over into the last two classes which aimed at imparting literary and oratorical effectiveness to the student's use of Latin and, to a lesser extent, of Greek.

The fact that the English teacher was specifically noted as an exceptional case in the quoted passage, as well as Carroll's stress on the importance of English elsewhere in his plan, shows that he gave careful thought to the study of the vernacular. In part this doubtless arose from an appreciation of what American students needed, but it also reflected a contemporary trend in Jesuit education. The same is true of geography, a subject mentioned twice in Carroll's plan, which was incorporated into the Jesuit humanities course in the eighteenth century.[54] But while he was fully abreast

[52] The following discussion is based on Carroll's organizational plan (see footnote 48) which will not be cited further.

[53] Beales, *Education Under Penalty*, p. 172, calls the practice of having the teacher move up with his class the core of the Jesuit system.

[54] Cf. Farrell, *Jesuit Code*, pp. 365-76; François de Dainville, "L'Enseignement de l'histoire et de la geographie et le Ratio Studiorum," *Analecta Gregoriana*, 70 (1954), 123-56.

of these modifications of the Jesuit program, a remark he let slip about "the mere English teacher," and his uncertainties about how to handle geography, indicate that Carroll regarded these subjects as secondary elements in a basically classical curriculum.

The teaching procedures outlined by Carroll likewise testify to the Jesuit lineage of Georgetown. The instructional device known as "prelection," which became almost the trademark of Jesuit teaching, was succinctly described by Carroll (who did not use the term) in these words: "The Master himself shall explain aloud the lessons for the following day; & accompany the explanation with proper remarks."[55] In calling for "repetitions" on Saturday (i.e.,
recitations reviewing the week's work) Carroll reproduced the 343
practice followed at St. Omers. And in requiring "public exhibitions" of student work (translating, answering questions, declaiming compositions, etc.) he was continuing a feature of Jesuit pedagogy that dated back more than two centuries. At certain of these periodic exhibitions, the class ranking of the students was read out by the president, or prefect of studies, who glossed the reading with appropriate comments of praise or censure of individual students. Carroll describes this ceremony, but fails to mention the Latin formula with which it was introduced; we know, however, that the formula in use at St. Omers was one recommended for Jesuit schools as early as the 1560's.[56]

Carroll considered American colleges notoriously deficient in discipline, or, as he put it, in enforcing the duties of religion and good manners.[57] Hence it is only reasonable to infer that he drew on his knowledge of the strict boarding school tradition of St. Omers in listing twelve guidelines for the behavior of Georgetown students. The opening sentence of this list epitomizes its overall thrust: "Their first duty must be obedience & docility." The seventh item which prescribed "some peculiar badge in their dress, without which they are never to appear in public," hints at a uniform such

---

[55] The Jesuit historian Thomas Hughes called prelection the "typical form of Jesuit instruction" (Hughes, *Loyola and the Educational System of the Jesuits* [New York, 1901], p. 232). Cf. also Ganss, *St. Ignatius' Idea*, pp. 100-101 n., on prelection.

[56] The formula beginning "Quod felix faustumque sit . . ." was suggested in the early 1560's by Father Jerome Nadal. See Farrell, *Jesuit Code*, p. 84. Chadwick, *St. Omers*, p. 133, says "this well-known formula" survived at Stonyhurst until after 1900.

[57] Carroll to Charles Plowden, Jan. 22-Feb. 28, 1787. *Carroll Papers*, I: 241.

as was in vogue at both St. Omers and Douai. Carroll later added a marginal note to his organizational scheme saying that this requirement was suspended for the present; around 1797, however, Georgetown's third president, who had a flair for public relations, introduced an eye-catching uniform consisting of blue coat and trousers, and a red waistcoat with large yellow buttons.[58]

Carroll earnestly besought his former Jesuit confreres in Europe to send him both teachers and an able president from among their numbers. This would indicate that he had in mind a college much like the ones these men were familiar with in Flanders. Moreover, it is clear from his organizational sketch and other sources[59] that
344 Carroll envisioned using upper-level clerical students as teachers of the college classes in precisely the same manner as this practice was followed at St. Omers and Douai. He did not anticipate having any clerics to use in this fashion at the beginning, since they would not yet have worked their way up through the system. As matters turned out, however, one of Georgetown's first professors was just such a seminarian-teacher. Jean de Mondésir, one of the seminarians who came with the first group of Sulpicians, was drafted to serve on Georgetown's faculty; his own studies for the priesthood were thereby delayed almost five years.[60]

The foregoing evidence shows that Georgetown closely resembled St. Omers, which is to say it resembled any European Jesuit college, since St. Omers was but a local variation of a highly standardized system. Perhaps the most distinctive feature of St. Omers in the Jesuit spectrum was that it had always been a boarding school, whereas the Jesuits definitely preferred day schools and nearly all of their colleges were strictly for day students. But a strong trend toward boarding schools in the late eighteenth and early nineteenth centuries brought other colleges more closely into

---

[58] Daley, *Georgetown*, pp. 55, 89, for Georgetown's uniform; Chadwick, *St. Omers*, pp. 233-39, for a discussion which describes the uniform used at Douai also. Cf. *ibid.*, pp. 85-86, for reference to "the excessive surveillance" at St. Omers. For the strict discipline at Douai, see Harris, *Douai Documents*, pp. 165-69.

[59] For example, Carroll to Charles Plowden, Jan. 22-Feb. 28, 1787. *Carroll Papers*, I: 241. For use of theology students as teachers at Douai, see Harris, *Douai Documents*, p. 139; and Burton, *Challoner*, I: 33, 35.

[60] Daley, *Georgetown*, pp. 68, 93: Ruane, *St. Sulpice*, p. 40; cf. also *Souvenirs D'Edouard de Mondésir* (Baltimore, 1942).

line with the system that had long prevailed at St. Omers.[61]

Although Georgetown conformed to the residential pattern of other American colleges, it differed sharply in one respect from American Protestant institutions patterned after Cambridge University. In the continental tradition from which Georgetown stemmed a college was an institution that took very young boys and put them through a five- or six-year program that combined what we would now think of as secondary education with the first two years or so of college-level work.[62] In the English Protestant tradition, however, the boys were older when they entered college, and had already completed their secondary work at a different school; their college program was only four years in length, and included studies in philosophy and theology that were regarded on the continent as belonging to the university level of education.[63]

This latter pattern is so dominant today that we think of it as the natural arrangement for a collegiate institution—indeed, as the only kind of institution that is "really" a college—and we therefore assume that American Catholic educators started out from the beginning with the intention of setting up this sort of four-year, post-secondary institution. But that assumption is wrong. As the foregoing analysis has shown, Carroll did not have that kind of college in mind when he planned Georgetown. His college, and other early Catholic schools, were based on a different understanding of what a college properly was, and it required a long and painful process of adjustment before they were brought into line with the prevailing American pattern.

But while Carroll was working from the continental Catholic

---

[61] Presuppression Jesuit colleges "were in the very great majority day schools," according to John W. Padberg, *Colleges in Controversy; the Jesuit Schools in France from Revival to Suppression, 1815-1880* (Cambridge, Mass., 1969), p. 126. Cf. also Farrell, *Jesuit Code*, p. 60. For the transition to boarding schools, see Philippe Ariès, *Centuries of Childhood* (Vintage, 1965), pp. 269-85.

[62] Cf. McGucken, *Jesuits and Education*, p. 78; John W. Donahue, *Jesuit Education* (New York, 1963), pp. 34 ff.

[63] Harvard, and other American colleges, "followed the English universities in enriching the Arts curriculum [i.e., the undergraduate program] at the expense of the higher faculties, and making the last three years of the Arts course in effect a professional course in Theology" (Samuel Eliot Morison, *The Founding of Harvard College* [Cambridge, Mass., 1935], p. 146). Cf. *ibid.*, pp. 60-62, 144-46, for the ages of students, the number of years in the college course, and a comparison with continental universities.

tradition,[64] he was perfectly willing to make the adjustments that were needed for the United States. He stated the principle most explicitly in describing to Plowden the kind of president he wanted for Georgetown. He knew the college president would be the key figure in winning public confidence, and since there was no one suitable at hand, he hoped Plowden could locate for him a mature and experienced educator in Europe. Carroll emphasized, however, that this person must be "capable of abstracting his mind from the methods used in the colleges, where he has lived, so as to adopt only as much of them, as is suited to the circumstances of this country, and of substituting such others as are better adapted to the
346 views and inclinations of those with whom he has to deal."[65]

One of the areas where a modification was needed was in the arrangement for ownership and control of the college. Since the Select Body of the Clergy was the constituted body having authority over all existing ecclesiastical resources, Carroll improvised a plan whereby the Select Body chose from among its members a board of directors, or visitors, in whom control of the college was vested.[66] The president was to be appointed by this board, and was responsible to it. In his draft plan for the college he left a couple of points unsettled on the division of authority between the board and the president; but in spite of the jurisdictional ambiguities, this arrangement provided a framework for Georgetown's governance for more than two decades. It might also be noted that this *ad hoc* system shared the characteristic feature of American college governance of the time—viz., ultimate authority over the college was vested in an external, nonacademic board that was primarily com-

---

[64] Carroll asked Cardinal Antonelli (March 13, 1786) for a plan of studies for the college and seminary that Carroll hoped to create in America. (See Daley, *Georgetown*, pp. 32-33, and *Carroll Papers*, I: 209.) No plan was sent, however (see Daley, *Georgetown*, p. 44); hence there is no justification for the conclusion drawn by Power, *Catholic Higher Education*, pp. 53-54, that Roman influence affected Georgetown and, through it, other Catholic colleges.

[65] Carroll to Charles Plowden, Jan. 22-Feb. 28, 1787. *Carroll Papers*, I: 242.

[66] This arrangement is outlined in Carroll's organizational plan cited above at note 48. Cf. also Daley, *Georgetown*, pp. 54-55. The Resolves of the Chapter, or the Select Body of the Clergy, Nov. 13-22, 1786, at which the decision was formally taken to establish Georgetown, provided for the appointment from the Clergy of five Directors who were to supervise the enterprise, appoint a president, masters, tutors, and so on. Cf. Hughes, *Documents*, pp. 665-66. For later deliberation on the same points, see *ibid.*, p. 695.

mitted to religious rather than educational goals.[67]

The most notable adaptation made by Carroll to American circumstances was in the admission of non-Catholic students to Georgetown. The prospectus of 1786 announced the policy in these words:

> Agreeably to the liberal Principle of our Constitution, the Seminary [i.e., Georgetown] will be open to Students of every religious profession. They, who, in this Respect differ from the Superintendent of the Academy, will be at Liberty to frequent the places of Worship and Instruction appointed by their Parents; but with Respect to their moral Conduct, all must be subjected to general and uniform Discipline.[68]

Carroll says nothing further on this subject in his organizational sketch, but it is clear he was still thinking of a student body composed of both Catholics and Protestants.[69] Georgetown did in fact admit non-Catholic students, as did virtually every other American Catholic college for the next half-century. It was a policy that made good practical sense since it enlarged the potential clientele of the school, but Carroll was doubtless quite sincere in relating it to "the liberal Principle of our Constitution." He was committed to the American style of church-state separation and had a genuinely irenic temperament. Having so recently considered encouraging the attendance of Catholic youth at Protestant institutions, he had no hesitation about the intermixing of Catholic and Protestant boys at Georgetown.

Tensions sometimes developed, however, when Protestant parents complained that their sons were being subjected to proselytizing efforts. Commenting on this matter just a few weeks before his death, Carroll linked the problem to the inexperience of some of Georgetown's European Jesuits with the religious pluralism of American society. Intimating to Plowden that the charges might well be true, Carroll added: "It is not uncommon for those [Cath-

---

[67] Cf. Jurgen Herbst, "The First Three American Colleges: Schools of the Reformation," *Perspectives in American History*, 8 (1974), 7-52.

[68] Ellis, *Documents*, p. 172.

[69] The fifth heading of Carroll's organizational plan for Georgetown (see note 48) reads: "The special duties of and the attention to be given to Cat. students in their religious instruction." This page was left blank, but the fact that Carroll included it as a supplement to the earlier section dealing with "The duties and discipline to be observed by all scholars" indicates he assumed that the Catholic students would be a special subgroup within the student body.

olics], who never associated with, or were very conversant with other religionists, to be sometimes indiscreet and abrupt in disputation against their errors."[70] Tact in dealing with the separated brethren was, in Carroll's view, an adjustment required by the conditions of American society, and one very congenial to him personally.

Student discipline was another area where experience taught Carroll that modifications of European practice were in order. Despite much reflection, he was never able to resolve the contradiction that, although religion and morality seemed to require severe restraint of the liberties of students, "yet that very restraint operates
348 against the effects intended by it" since "on being delivered from it, young men . . . burst out of confinement into licentiousness, and give way to errors and vices, which with more acquaintance with the manners and language of the world, they would have avoided." But whatever his theoretical perplexity, Carroll observed that the kind of discipline outlined in his organizational plan worked great mischief when put into effect by men less prudent than himself. In 1802 he told Plowden that Georgetown suffered from "too monastic" a system of discipline: "some rigourous regulations not calculated for the meridian of America" unduly cramped "that liberty which all here will lay claim to" and resulted in a loss of students. Making the same point six years later, Carroll specifically linked it to the need for a recently arrived European Jesuit to "become more informed of the customs of this Country."[71]

III

The foregoing discussion has carried us considerably beyond the temporal boundaries of the second period of Carroll's association with higher education, not merely in noting the adjustments he thought necessary but in several other areas as well. While this overlapping indicates that the division into periods is somewhat

---

[70] Carroll to Charles Plowden, Oct. 13, 1815. *Carroll Papers,* III: 368.

[71] Carroll to Charles Plowden, March 12, 1802; Carroll to William Strickland, April 2, 1808. *Carroll Papers,* II: 383; III: 53. In 1815 Carroll remarked in a different context that the European Jesuits at Georgetown, although "good religious men," too often lacked the discernment "to estimate the difference between the American character and that of the Countries which they left" (Carroll to Charles Plowden, June 25-July 24, 1815. *Carroll Papers,* III: 338). Cf. Daley, *Georgetown,* pp. 113-15, 149.

artificial, yet there was a real change in Carroll's relationship to the college and seminary after these institutions were once set up and operating under their own administrators. As bishop and later archbishop he still provided the guiding aegis under which these schools developed—and other new ones were initiated—but he had too many other responsibilities to give them much attention or to concern himself more than occasionally with their operation. Hence the third phase of his association with Catholic higher education, which we can think of as extending from 1791 to his death in 1815, is more detached.

Carroll always retained a keen interest in Georgetown's affairs. 349
He also played a key role in its development, especially in its early years, by making priests and seminarians available to serve as teachers and officers of the college. Although he cherished the place dearly, he could assess its merits and prospects quite realistically. He was disappointed in its failure, at first, to produce vocations for the seminary, and he criticized the rigidity and other defects of its leadership. At one time he even proposed closing the college temporarily because it was in such a "state of depression."[72]

A perennially troublesome ambiguity concerned the relationship of Georgetown to the Society of Jesus.[73] All the American Jesuits had signed the document submitting to the suppression of the society in 1773, but they were aware that a remnant of the order continued to exist in Prussia and White Russia because the rulers of those territories would not permit publication of the official papal brief of suppression. This fact encouraged the hopes of some who anticipated an early reconstitution of the society. Rumors of an impending restoration were already circulating when Carroll opened his campaign to organize the Select Body of the Clergy and to establish a college. The Select Body was originally composed exclusively of former Jesuits, the more conservative of whom felt that its proper role was simply to maintain intact the holdings of the old Society of Jesus against the happy day, soon to come, when

[72] Daley, *Georgetown*, chaps. 4-8; p. 135, for the proposal to close the college. In 1797, for example, the president of Georgetown appealed to Carroll to transfer a priest from his present assignment to the college. In this case, Carroll did not comply. See William DuBourg to John Carroll, May 22, 1797, in Archives of Georgetown University.

[73] Daley, *Georgetown*, pp. 28 ff., 39-43, 121-53, 187-88, is indispensable for the following account. Hughes, *Documents*, pp. 665-85, 744-63, 849-53, contains valuable material but it is difficult to use. Cf. also Melville, *Carroll*, esp. pp. 249-58, and Guilday, *Carroll*, II, chap. 27.

it would be officially reestablished. These Jesuit loyalists, as we might call them, had serious reservations about setting up the college at all, since it would constitute a heavy drain on the resources which they considered as being only temporarily under the makeshift jurisdiction of the Select Body. Carroll's persuasiveness overcame the objections of this group, but the establishment of the hierarchy (in the person, of course, of John Carroll), the coming of the Sulpicians and other priests, and the admission of clergymen not formerly Jesuits to the Select Body, all created new sources of tension and disagreement.

Carroll himself was profoundly attached to the Society of Jesus
350 and longed to see it reconstituted. But he took a strict constructionist view of what had to be done to reconstitute it. The pope had terminated the existence of the old society in the most solemn manner, and Carroll held that only an equally formal reversal of that action by the same supreme authority could bring the society back into being. Hence he was not satisfied when, in 1801, the pope confirmed the existence of the society in Russia and permitted individual priests in other countries to aggregate themselves to it. Although he allowed the priests of his diocese who wished to affiliate themselves to the Jesuits in Russia to do so, Carroll did not consider that the society was established on a firm canonical basis.[74] Doubting that the Jesuits were fully reconstituted as a religious institute within the church, Carroll was uncertain whether an institution such as a college properly *could* be entrusted to them; but he was categorically sure that Georgetown *had not* been entrusted to them simply by virtue of the fact that some of the individuals associated with the college chose to become Jesuits. However, he anticipated that it *would* in the future become a Jesuit institution in the full sense when the order was duly restored, and as non-Jesuits were replaced by Jesuits in the Select Body of the Clergy through the process of attrition. In the meantime, he urgently requested the Jesuit authorities in Europe to send men to staff it because the college was desperately in need of reinvigoration.

Georgetown's status was especially ambiguous in the last decade of Carroll's life, that is, between 1805 when the so-called partial restoration of the Society of Jesus took effect in America, and 1814

[74] On this point see Daley, *Georgetown*, pp. 122, 128, 132, 146-47. Cf. also Carroll to Robert Plowden, Dec. 12, 1813; Carroll to Marmaduke Stone, Jan. 31, 1814. *Carroll Papers*, III: 248-50, 255-56.

when the papal brief *Sollicitudo Omnium Ecclesiarum* provided the kind of solemn public reestablishment that Carroll believed necessary.[75] Some of his ex-Jesuit confreres had always considered his position unduly conservative and very likely attributed it to his being influenced by the interests of his episcopal office; moreover, they resented what they interpreted as his favoritism toward the Sulpician fathers. The coming of European Jesuits after 1806 also complicated the picture. These included some very able men, such as John Grassi, whom the historian of Georgetown calls its second founder, and Anthony Kohlmann, who headed the Jesuit mission in New York City for a time and created a successful school there. But these newcomers did not always grasp the complexities of the ecclesiastical situation in America right away; they also had something of the enthusiasm of recently commissioned apostles and perhaps even a tinge of presumptuousness in their dealings with the courtly old gentleman in Baltimore. But in spite of the frictions arising inevitably in a situation of ambiguous and overlapping spheres of authority, the archbishop's relations with these men were marked by mutual regard, especially in the case of John Grassi who recognized in Carroll "rare goodness of heart."[76]

Nor did these tensions mean that Georgetown ever lost first place in Carroll's affections. In 1813, for example, the Jesuits had to choose between Georgetown and Kohlmann's flourishing New York Literary Institute because they lacked the manpower to keep both places open. Carroll unhesitatingly ruled in favor of Georgetown. And on an earlier occasion, he expressed his personal chagrin that Georgetown was so much "eclipsed" in the public

---

[75] Although Daley, *Georgetown*, pp. 120, 132, indicates that Georgetown became a Jesuit institution in 1806, the Jesuit president, John Grassi, was still asking for complete control of the school in 1813, and didn't seem to get it until 1815 (*ibid.*, p. 184). Carroll stated in a letter to John Grassi Oct. 27, 1811, that Georgetown was "in no sense, a property, or house of the Society." And to the Jesuit general in 1814 he wrote: "For since the college is a new foundation, it never belonged to the Society; nor could it be handed over to the Society under the circumstances . . . [because the Society] has no corporate existence; and it cannot have one till the Holy See officially abrogates the Brief [of suppression] of Clement XIV which had full effect in this country." Carroll to Thaddeus Brzozowski, Jan. 28, 1814. Carroll to John Grassi, July 9, 1812, maintains the Jesuit general had no authority to appoint Grassi president of Georgetown. *Carroll Papers*, III: 158, 253, 185.

[76] Daley, *Georgetown*, pp. 152-53, and chap. 8. Francis X. Curran, "The Jesuit Colony in New York, 1808-1817," *Historical Records and Studies*, 43 (1954), 51-97, is the best account of Kohlmann's first years in America.

estimation by a college operated by the Sulpicians in Baltimore.[77]

Although Carroll might reveal such feelings to an old Jesuit comrade, he had the highest respect for the Sulpician fathers and treated them with so much consideration that some of the ex-Jesuits felt he was preferring them over his former confreres.[78] Since they were headquartered in Baltimore, he was in close touch with the Sulpicians; and because they had so few seminary students, the bishop used several of them for ordinary pastoral work, at which they performed admirably. Carroll also depended heavily on the French clerics to staff Georgetown in the days of its infancy. This service was rendered at some cost to the Sulpicians, since the use
352 of their seminarians as college teachers cut deeply into their tiny student body; moreover, two of the seminarians lost their vocations while teaching at Georgetown and a third died of a lung ailment. And in addition to the seminarians, priests of St. Sulpice filled the offices of president and vice-president at Georgetown between 1796 and 1799.[79]

While the Sulpicians were thus making themselves indispensable to Carroll, their superior in Paris, Father Emery, was growing more uneasy. The special work of the Society of St. Sulpice was the education and spiritual formation of priests. But what was going on in America? There his subjects were staffing frontier missions and teaching Latin grammar to adolescent boys, some of whom were Protestants, while their seminary stood virtually empty. Small wonder that he thought of calling them back to France after the religious prospects began to improve there. A misunderstanding that arose over rivalry between Georgetown and Sulpician educational efforts precipitated his decision and created a painful dilemma for Carroll.

What caused the ill feeling was the establishment by the Sulpicians of a college in Baltimore in 1799 which the Georgetown men quite naturally looked upon as a competitor. St. Mary's College,

---

77 Daley, *Georgetown,* pp. 174-79, 181; Carroll to Robert Molyneaux, May 22, 1807. *Carroll Papers,* III: 20-21.

78 Daley, *Georgetown,* p. 111. Cf. also Charles Sewall to John Carroll, Dec. 15, 1800, Archives of the Archdiocese of Baltimore. Note Carroll's comment on this letter. *Carroll Papers,* II: 332.

79 Cf. Ruane, *St. Sulpice,* esp. pp. 40-43. The two priests at Georgetown were William DuBourg and Benedict J. Flaget. Cf. John M. Tessier's "Epoques du Seminaire de Baltimore," given as an appendix in James J. Kortendick, "The History of St. Mary's College, Baltimore, 1799-1852" (M. A. thesis, Catholic University of America, 1942), pp. 145-46, 147.

as the new place was called, unquestionably represented a departure from the previous arrangement (theoretically advantageous to both) whereby Georgetown was to offer college work and serve as a feeder to the seminary, while the Sulpicians were to confine themselves to seminary-level work and provide teachers for Georgetown. In justification for their action, however, the Sulpicians could point out that the benefits of the previous arrangement had been unequally divided: from 1791 through 1799 not one ecclesiastical prospect had come from Georgetown, while the Sulpicians had supplied five seminarians (from a total of fourteen) and two priests to teach at Georgetown.[80] After an eight-year trial of this (to them) unsatisfactory system, the Sulpicians might reasonably have felt that they had more to gain by setting up their own feeder school directly under their own supervision. But although they later offered this justification, it seems doubtful that they would have taken the step but for the boldness and dynamism of one man. William Louis Valentine DuBourg, the Sulpician who guided Georgetown as president from October 1796 to December 1798, founded St. Mary's College in August of 1799.

DuBourg, one of the most fascinating characters in the history of American Catholicism, had a profound impact on Catholic higher education.[81] He came to Baltimore as a refugee from the French Revolution in 1794 and joined the Society of St. Sulpice there the following year. One year later he was chosen president of Georgetown, almost certainly at the instance of Carroll, who described him at the time as a man of abilities and "most pleasing character" and who added many years later that he was a person of

---

[80] Ruane, *St. Sulpice*, pp. 40-43, gives a list of the seminary's students which shows that before 1800 none came from Georgetown, although five seminarians taught there. Ruane's work (chaps. 2-3) is the best source for this whole episode, Cf. also Hughes, *Documents*, pp. 744-68, for pertinent materials and a different viewpoint.

[81] Annabelle Melville is presently at work on a much needed biography of DuBourg. He was associated not only with Georgetown and St. Mary's College, but also with Mother Seton's school at Emmitsburg, with Mount St. Mary's College, and with the beginnings of St. Louis University; he also brought to this country the first Vincentian fathers who established a number of seminaries and colleges.

"an active and towering genius."[82] DuBourg was thirty years of age when he became president of Georgetown. He seems to have been a dazzling personality whose intelligence, charm, and generous imagination at first overwhelmed all who came in contact with him, and carried all obstacles before him; yet in time his character proved flawed by a defect in solidity and staying power. As with many another man of expansive vision, DuBourg had the reputation of running up enormous debts; he was later said to have left a debt of $20,000 at Georgetown, which was sufficient in itself to disturb the directors of that place. What was far worse was that he somehow gave them the impression that he was trying to displace them
354 and turn the college over to the "gentlemen of the Seminary."[83]

Perhaps it was simply that DuBourg's flamboyant approach lent itself to misinterpretation, but Carroll suspected that "national attachments" were at the root of the problem. DuBourg, for his part, was "too fond of introducing his countrymen into every department" of the college; while on the other hand, "the Directors had too strong prejudices against everything which was derived in any shape from France."[84] American feeling against France was high at the time because of several foreign policy issues, but the Sulpician refugees should not have been blamed for the misdeeds of a government from which they fled. Very likely that was not crucial, in any case, for there are indications that at least some of the Select Body of the Clergy entertained misgivings about the Sulpicians several years earlier.[85] Indeed, it would have been contrary to human nature had this not been the case. For besides the national and

[82] Carroll to Charles Plowden, Sept. 24, 1796, and Jan. 10, 1808. *Carroll Papers,* II: 189; III: 37. Carroll to Charles Plowden, Dec. 12, 1813, describes DuBourg as "A priest of great talent, but delighting more in brilliancy than solidity" (*Carroll Papers,* III: 247). Cf. also Hughes, *Documents,* pp. 754, 799, 801.

[83] Hughes, *Documents,* p. 537 n., for debt; *ibid.,* p. 753, for alleged plan to take over Georgetown. Shea, *Life of Carroll,* p. 670, says rather harshly that DuBourg, although a brilliant and learned man, "lacked courage and firmness." DuBourg's vacillations in his career in Louisiana are treated critically in William Barnaby Faherty, *Dream by the River, Two Centuries of Saint Louis Catholicism, 1766-1967* (St. Louis, 1973), pp. 13-32.

[84] Carroll to Charles Plowden, Dec. 11, 1798. *Carroll Papers,* II: 248. Cf. Hughes, *Documents,* p. 754.

[85] Carroll noted on the back of a letter he received in 1796 that it contained "anecdotes respecting the appointment of Mr. DuBourg to the presidency of G. T. College" (*Carroll Papers,* II: 190). Melville, *Carroll,* pp. 145-47, stresses the anti-French feeling stemming from the XYZ Affair and the Quasi-War with France.

linguistic differences, the viewpoint of the Jesuit loyalists has to be taken into consideration. Their religious order, grievously wronged and officially dead, could not lift its head or recruit a single member. Suddenly here were the Sulpician refugees in their midst, unfortunate perhaps but ubiquitous, reaping the harvest planted by generations of Jesuit laborers in the vineyard, supported by properties that had once belonged solely to the Society of Jesus, intruding themselves into the college erected at such cost and loading it with debts. Small wonder that the directors of Georgetown were "not . . . on the best of terms" with DuBourg; and if national feeling was involved, it probably stood for a good deal besides nationality.

Whatever the mix of causes, DuBourg found the situation impossible and resigned as president in December, 1798. While they were probably relieved to be rid of him, the directors might have found it somewhat irritating that the students gave DuBourg a big send-off, that two or three of them left Georgetown with him, and that the simultaneous departure of the other Sulpician teacher-administrator left Georgetown with a staffing problem.[86] Three months later it was the Sulpicians' turn to be annoyed by the demand that they hand back to the Select Body the management of one of the former Jesuit estates that had been entrusted to them five years earlier.[87] But these irritants were only a prelude to the crisis that erupted when, in the summer of 1799, DuBourg returned from a brief foray to Cuba with three youngsters whose education he proposed to continue in Baltimore. Other Spanish- and French-speaking families sent their sons, and St. Mary's College became a reality by the fall term of the same year. Within a period of eight months, DuBourg had changed from being the president of Georgetown to being the founder of a rival college.[88]

Carroll was displeased by the opening of St. Mary's College; he did not prohibit the undertaking, but at first limited the number of students DuBourg could accept. It was also understood that St. Mary's would take only French or Spanish boys. The Georgetown authorities, however, interpreted Carroll's action as a blessing upon the new venture. And since the bishop was willing to acquiesce in what they regarded as an improper encroachment on their educa-

---

[86] Daley, *Georgetown*, pp. 100-01; Tessier's "Epoques" in Kortendick, "St. Mary's College," p. 147, and in Hughes, *Documents*, p. 765.

[87] See Ruane, *St. Sulpice*, pp. 68-85, 225-31, for this tangled matter.

[88] *Ibid.*, pp. 99-104.

tional territory, they apparently felt free to retaliate by entering upon seminary-level work at Georgetown. Thus, instead of sending a half-dozen ecclesiastical prospects to Baltimore, they determined to keep them at Georgetown and provide there the instruction in philosophy that constituted the first stage of seminary studies.[89]

This move quite exasperated Carroll. To Plowden, who was his safety valve on this occasion, he repeated his conviction that "national prejudices" were at the bottom of it. He also touched on the narrow-mindedness of some of the former Jesuits, and pointed out that Georgetown did not even have a man qualified to teach
356 philosophy "without disgracing himself and the College." Such was his annoyance that he interpreted the Georgetown decision as an infringement of his episcopal prerogative to direct the education of clerics in his diocese.[90]

By now the degree of ill will generated had convinced Father Emery in Paris that it was time for his subjects to come home. "[We] can no longer think of establishing a seminary conducted by French priests," he wrote, adding:

> I see a depth of rivalry and jealousy which I did not at all conceive, I did not even suspect, but which, once perceived, demands infinite consideration. They write that we are not proper for educating young Americans, and that may be the truth. Perhaps it is fitting that Americans be educated by Americans?[91]

Carroll had given a good deal of thought to the kind of education suitable for American priests and, while he did not consider the Sulpicians perfect, thought they were incomparably the best available. He was appalled at the prospect of losing them and implored Father Emery "by the bowels of Our Lord not to take them all away."[92] Several of the Sulpicians, including DuBourg, themselves wished to stay in America and were permitted to do so; the others were called back to France in 1803.

By this time tempers had cooled considerably. The Sulpicians

---

[89] *Ibid.*, pp. 104 ff.; precis of letter Carroll to James Emery, Aug. 1800, *Carroll Papers,* II: 313-14; Hughes, *Documents,* pp. 797, 777.

[90] Carroll to Charles Plowden, Sept. 3, 1800. *Carroll Papers,* II: 318-19. The relevant passages of this letter are also reproduced in Hughes, *Documents,* pp. 757-60, with fuller annotation.

[91] Ruane, *St. Sulpice,* pp. 50-51, 114.

[92] Carroll to James Emery, Sept., 1801, in Ruane, *St. Sulpice,* p. 49, and in *Carroll Papers,* II: 358.

made several gestures of conciliation, one of which, ironically enough, was that they provided the man who taught philosophy at Georgetown the first year it was offered there![93] Carroll, of course, deplored the differences that existed between two valued groups of his miniscule force of clergymen. At first he was most irritated by the Georgetown actions, but in 1803 DuBourg took the provocative step of admitting Americans to his college, not just Spanish and French, thus making it more directly competitive with Georgetown. Carroll, then, could not fully endorse the position of either faction, but he understood the pressures bearing on both and did his best to encourage more amicable relations between them.[94]

In spite of the strains, the two centers of Catholic educational endeavor managed to get along together. Vocations increased in a heartening way, assuring the continuation of the Baltimore seminary; and Georgetown contributed eight of these ecclesiastical students to the seminary between 1800 and 1810.[95] The older college itself had only the most precarious grip on existence for a number of years, but the restoration of the Jesuits assured its long-term prospects by providing a continuing source of manpower. St. Mary's College flourished under DuBourg's leadership until 1812, when he was tapped for the difficult job of bringing order to the church in the Louisiana Territory. After DuBourg's time, the college continued to play an honorable role in the life of Baltimore until 1852 when the Sulpicians withdrew from the field of secular education and confined themselves strictly to seminary work. Rather ironically in view of the earlier difficulties with Georgetown, the Jesuits' newly founded Loyola College inherited the clientele of St. Mary's College.

IV

Several other Catholic colleges, seminaries, and girls' academies were founded during Carroll's lifetime, but his connections with them were not direct or sustained enough to warrant treatment

---

93 Ruane, *St. Sulpice*, pp. 87, 114-21; Hughes, *Documents*, pp. 793-95.

94 Carroll told Charles Plowden, Dec. 7, 1804, that Emery had "not behaved well to me" in recalling his subject of France. Writing to Robert Molyneaux, Feb. 25, 1807, he accused the Sulpicians of being too devoted to their own establishments and not having sufficient regard for "the general cause of religion" (*Carroll Papers*, II: 461; III: 10).

95 See the list given in Ruane, *St. Sulpice*, pp. 55-66.

here. Georgetown, the Baltimore seminary, and St. Mary's College were the institutions with which he was most closely associated. Some brief comments on what that story suggests about the beginnings of American Catholic higher education in general and about Carroll as a person may now be in order.

In the first place, the crucial role played by Carroll in founding Georgetown, and by DuBourg in the origin of St. Mary's College, highlights the pivotal importance of leadership in the history of higher education. Institutions like colleges and universities often seem to have a life of their own; they strike us as somehow operating independently of the individuals who compose them, and it is hard
358 for us to convince ourselves that any one person makes much difference in their destiny. But leadership is always important, and at the beginning it is indispensable. Without John Carroll, Georgetown simply would not have come into being when it did; in its early years it was almost literally the lengthened shadow of one man.

Secondly, the foregoing account underlines the close connection between college and seminary in the early years of American Catholic higher education. The connection is observable both in motivation and in practice. Carroll's purpose in founding Georgetown illustrates the former; the mutual interdependence that was theoretically supposed to exist between Georgetown and the Baltimore seminary (and which did exist in some degree) illustrates the latter. The establishment of St. Mary's College as a feeder for the seminary threw into even sharper relief the symbiotic relationship between Catholic collegiate education and the professional training of clergymen. And this close association continued until the middle decades of the nineteenth century.

Thirdly, the comparison of Georgetown with St. Omers (and the European Jesuit schools generally) locates the beginning of American Catholic higher education in a specific tradition. At the same time, it also helps us to identify some of the organizational anomalies that plagued the adjustment of Catholic colleges to American norms for over a century. Consideration of Georgetown's departures from the Catholic continental model, however, reveals that this process of adjustment to the American environment began right at the beginning.

Finally, the differences of opinion between Carroll and the Jesuits over the status of Georgetown, and the friction between Georgetown and the Sulpicians, are symptomatic of endemic stresses in the Catholic system of church-sponsored higher education. The case of Carroll and the Jesuits illustrates the jurisdictional ambiguities and overlapping spheres of authority that arose from having two quasi-distinct chains of command: that of the episcopacy, and that of the religious community. The difficulties between Georgetown and the Sulpicians are witness to the tensions that sometimes developed between different religious communities. This case also illustrates the range and variety of factors that could be involved in such rivalries. Individual personalities (notably that of DuBourg), national and linguistic sensibilities, loyalties to different religious orders, and the imperative demands of institutional self-preservation all played a role in the imbroglio centering around St. Mary's College.

Carroll's actions doubtless left some of the parties to that controversy dissatisfied. Yet the impression that emerges from a study of his whole career as it touches on higher education is a very favorable one. To me he seems a wise and good man. Through birth and family connection he enjoyed the advantages of wealth, rank, and education, but he proved worthy of the privileges that came to him unearned. His leadership in the 1780's combined insight into the problems of the church, the ability to devise practical measures to meet them, the courage to put those measures to the test of action, the tact and diplomacy to win support for his plans, and a sensitive feeling for the milieu in which the whole undertaking was carried on. He never shrank from the burdens of responsibility, or of sheer irksome toil, that were thrust upon him by the project on which he was engaged. He was prudent in what he attempted, but persistent in seeing it through—a kind of paragon of activist moderation. To a friend like Charles Plowden he must have been a treasure; it is difficult to believe he had enemies, but to those who differed with him he tried to be as mild and forebearing as the nature of the issue would permit. There is a serenity that shines through the bustle of his activities and the minor tempests that swirled around him. He possessed in eminent degree the enlarged views, the breadth of sympathy, so much admired by the men of his time. And while remaining anchored in his religious faith and his personal commitments, he was hospitable to new ideas and ready to adjust to new situations.

According to David Knowles, the historian may measure a man's character by asking whether his life is guided by principle rather than self-interest, whether he shows love for his fellow men, whether he puts justice before expediency, and whether he is sincere and truthful.[96] In the case of John Carroll, the answers we can give to those questions are such as to display what Knowles would call "his moral worth, his loveliness."

---

[96] David Knowles, *The Historian and Character* (Cambridge, 1963), pp. 13-14.

VIII The Struggle Within Early American Catholicism

THE LAITY'S UNDERSTANDING OF THE TRUSTEE SYSTEM, 1785-1855

BY
PATRICK CAREY*

Historians of American Catholicism have generally interpreted trusteeism, one of the most turbulent struggles of Catholicism during the national period, as an heretical and rebellious attempt by lay and clerical trustees to control the temporal and sometimes the spiritual welfare of the local congregation.[1] Trusteeism, in this interpretation, arose when Catholic laymen purchased property, built churches, and formed themselves into religious associations or corporations by electing lay representatives from their parish community for the legal protection of their property. Many times these lay trustees understood by such legal incorporation that they had the right not only to hold and to manage all ecclesiastical temporalities but also to appoint and dismiss their pastors at will. As a result of their attitudes, the bishops and sometimes the pastors vigorously opposed the trustees.

This description of the trustee experience does not adequately represent the various historical roots of the trustee system, nor does it describe the numerous sources of conflict which the system produced within the American Church. The interpretation, moreover, has been based almost exclusively upon an analysis of episcopal perceptions of the movement. The trustees' understanding of the campaign has only rarely been put forward.[2] This paper will present trusteeism from the trustees' perception, using their own numerous pamphlets, letters,

* Mr. Carey is currently teaching at Gustavus Adolphus College, St. Peter, Minnesota, and will be an assistant professor of theology in Marquette University beginning in September.

[1] Thomas T. McAvoy, C.S.C., *A History of the Catholic Church in the United States* (Notre Dame, Indiana, 1969), p. 115; cf. also G. C. Treacy, "The Evils of Trusteeism," *Historical Records and Studies*, VIII (1915), 136-156; Peter Guilday, "Trusteeism," *ibid.*, XVIII (1928), 14-73; Robert F. McNamara, "Trusteeism in the Atlantic States, 1785-1863," *Catholic Historical Review*, XXX (July, 1944), 135-154; Alfred G. Stritch, "Trusteeism in the Old Northwest, 1800-1850," *ibid.*, 155-164.

[2] See, e.g., V. J. Fecher, S.V.D., *A Study of the Movement for German National Parishes in Philadelphia and Baltimore (1787-1802)* ("Analecta Gregoriana," Vol. LXXVII, Series Facultatis Historiae Ecclesiasticae, Sectio B, No. 11 [Rome, 1955]).

broadsides, and newspaper articles. The study concentrates upon the trustees' views, prescinding as much as possible from the personal hostilities of the period and from theological judgments on the trustees' positions. From their perspective, trusteeism can be defined as a lay and clerical movement to adapt the European Catholic Church to American culture by identifying that Church with American republicanism.[3] The controversies, dissensions, and schisms which this campaign produced, therefore, resulted more from conflicting perceptions of and programs for accommodating Catholicism to American republicanism than from lay and clerical insubordination.

364 This study examines trusteeism within a broader cultural context than has been previously attempted. It outlines first the extent and duration of the trustees' campaign, and briefly describes their system and their position within their local communities. Second, it analyzes the American cultural conditions, the transplanted European Catholic experiences, and the theological perceptions which contributed to the rise and development of the movement.

Trusteeism and the Trustees

The trustee movement permeated the American Catholic experience in the years immediately following the American Revolution. Although the struggles of the campaign were local (arising out of specific parish problems), they were also national in scope because the trustees were responding to conditions common to most of the American Catholic communities. The trustees throughout the United States never built a national organization, but they did communicate with one another intermittently, and for a period they tried to unite various local movements into a national effort. Since trusteeism arose as a response to American conditions, it is no wonder that it developed in almost every major city and parish in the United States, from New York to Charleston to New Orleans.

The trustee campaign was not only extensive; it was also persistent. It began in New York City at Saint Peter's Church in 1785 and continued until 1815 with occasional conflicts. From 1815 to 1829, i.e.,

[3] In this paper the term "trustees" refers to clerical as well as lay trustees, unless otherwise indicated. Parish priests and laity were part of the trustee system. A more comprehensive analysis of the history of trusteeism would demand, among other things, an extensive examination of both episcopal and trustee perceptions of the movement. Such is not possible in this study. I am working on a more comprehensive history.

from the death of Archbishop John Carroll until the First Provincial Council of Baltimore, it achieved its most widespread support, articulate expression, as well as its most hostile dissensions. Because of the Baltimore council's statutes against it, the hostility of nativism, and the increase of uneducated Catholic immigrants, the movement lost most of its former vigor; but it still continued from 1829 to 1855 to create frictions in New Orleans, in New York State, and in isolated areas of the Old Northwest. After 1855, even though the trustee system lingered on, the crusade had little significant force within American Catholicism. The unresolved ideological conflicts of the movement, however, erupted periodically in a variety of new forms during the nineteenth and twentieth centuries and even continue here and there to disturb the contemporary Church.

While the trustee endeavor was extensive and tenacious, one may ask if it represented the Catholic population at the time. The bishops of the period, as well as historians who have accepted episcopal judgments, accused the dissenting trustees of representing a tiny minority of the Catholic population. By the nature of the system, however, the trustees in every parish represented at least one-half of the pewholder population. Whenever dissensions or schisms erupted, the same trustees who had precipitated the crises continued to be elected by a majority of the parishioners throughout the periods of strife. It would seem, therefore, that the trustee effort, which is primarily associated (in this paper) with the dissenting trustees' campaign, had the support of the majority of pewholders of their congregations.[4]

Those who led the trustee crusade were, as already noted, both clergy and laity. The lay trustees were not, as were many of their immigrant countrymen after the 1830's, from the poorer and uneducated classes. Some of them were wealthy, but most were middle-class professionals, e.g., physicians, lawyers, publishers, business executives, and skilled laborers. As their numerous published pamphlets and letters indicate, the articulate leaders were mostly immigrants of some years of experience in the United States, and some, as in Philadelphia, were native-born Americans. They were, moreover,

[4] It is difficult to examine the numerical support for the dissenting trustees without over-extending the present study. In 1822 the dissenting trustees of Saint Mary's in Philadelphia, to give but one example, were elected by a majority of 497 to 437 during the crisis there. See Ignatius Reynolds (ed.), *The Works of the Right Reverend John England* (5 vols.; Baltimore, 1849), V, 110. Hereafter cited as "England, *Works*."

men of American and foreign governmental experiences; had administrative and business skills; were well-educated or self-taught men who knew a number of languages and were capable of reading and interpreting the sources of theology. Although a few were rebellious malcontents, most were responsible leaders (acknowledged so by their parish elections) who disagreed with some of the clergy on the relationship of the Catholic Church to the new situation created by the American political and cultural environment.

The clerical trustees, like the lay, were mostly immigrants from different national backgrounds. Their various immigrant experiences
366 influenced their different approaches to the laity and their divergent views of the future organization of American Catholicism. Some trustee pastors vehemently opposed the lay trustees in their attempts to establish a republican government in the parish; others supported lay leadership and publicly advocated such a system. Still others were conveniently ambivalent toward the trustee movement, favoring it when it supported them and rejecting it when it opposed them. Under the banner of trusteeism, moreover, a few of the clergy tried to advance their own prestige and self-interests; in the process, they violated ecclesiastical discipline, purposely deceived their lay congregations and ecclesiastical superiors, falsely charged some of the hierarchy and members of their own congregations with immorality, scandalized many of the people with public drunkenness, or obstinately refused to resolve conflicts within their congregations by peaceful compromises. These different types of clerical trustees provided a positive leadership, a critical reaction, and indeed at times a destructive force in the movement to adapt Catholicism to American conditions.

American Conditions

The immigrant factor in American society, while it was not a direct cause of the trustee system, was a contributing force in the trustee conflicts. In the 1780's and 1790's, German national feelings conditioned the trustee disputes at Holy Trinity Church in Philadelphia and at Saint John's Church in Baltimore. After this period, Irish nationalism surfaced in the trustee controversies. From 1808 to 1820, the newly appointed bishops—except for Richard Luke Concanen and John Connolly of New York, and Michael Egan of Philadelphia—were either of French origin or had French sympathies. Irish Catholic laymen and priests felt that the French dominated the hierarchy and that they planned to control it in the future. In addition to protesting French supervision of the American Church, the Irish criticized their French pastors for their inability, among other things, to use the English language fluently.

Nationalism was also intensified by a French aristocratic conception and exercise of ecclesiastical authority, and by Irish republican opposition to that authority. These attitudes contributed greatly to the frictions in the southern cities of Norfolk and Charleston where the Irish laity were in the majority from 1800 to 1820. In these cities the nationalistic hostility was more pronounced than in most other places because French pastors had replaced Irish priests and because the French Archbishop of Baltimore, Ambrose Maréchal, exercised his authority in a decisive, if not authoritarian, way.[5] The Irish in Charleston, e.g., complained to the archbishop that they had left their homeland in search of religious freedom and they felt that his arbitrary exercise of authority had threatened that freedom.[6] Thus, nationalistic antagonisms were responsible in intensifying the trustee conflicts.

Nationalistic hostilities, however, were not, as some historians have suggested,[7] responsible for all the dissensions of trusteeism. The trustee disputes in New York City and in Saint Mary's Parish in Philadelphia during the late eighteenth and early nineteenth centuries were primarily among divergent Irish factions. In Buffalo and other parts of upper New York State in the early 1840's and 1850's, the cultural differences were merely incidental to the controversies. In New Orleans during the 1820's and 1840's, the trustee disturbances were not significantly intensified by the various national backgrounds. It would seem that too much weight has been given to the nationalistic basis of this early American Catholic turbulence. Most certainly, national differences did contribute to the controversies; but certain historians, reared in a Church conscious of the later national struggles, have tended to read the earlier dissensions almost exclusively in light of their own consciousness and experience of later developments.

[5] Ronin J. Murtha, O.S.B., "The Life of the Most Reverend Ambrose Maréchal, Third Archbishop of Baltimore, 1768-1828" (unpublished Ph.D. dissertation, The Catholic University of America, 1965), p. 301.

[6] Memorial of Charleston Trustees to Archbishop Ambrose Maréchal, December 7, 1817, quoted in Peter Guilday, *The Life and Times of John England* (2 vols.; New York, 1927), I, 223.

[7] See, e.g., McAvoy, *op. cit.*, p. 131.

Although immigration and national differences contributed to the trustee conflicts, the primary source of trusteeism was the general diaspora condition of American Catholicism during the national period. Catholics existed as a tiny minority within a predominantly Protestant culture which was hostile to Catholic tenets and religious life; the Church survived in many places without the benefit of clergy, with a low religious profile, an independence from the hierarchy, a sense of lay initiative, and at the same time with an acceptance of the democratic and republican political ideologies and institutions.

The diaspora conditions are revealed most clearly in the absence of
368 clergy in many of the parishes and the resulting lay initiative and lay leadership. A few large cities had permanent Catholic pastors. Others had only occasional visiting or missionary priests to serve them. Under such circumstances lay men and women were primarily responsible for the religious and spiritual needs of the few Catholics as well as for the temporal affairs of the local congregations. When a lay community was large and prosperous enough, as in New York City in 1785, laymen formed themselves into Catholic communities, elected their leaders, i.e., the trustees, purchased a plot of ground, built a church, and took full financial and legal responsibility for the temporalities of parish life. The lay trustees frequently felt that since they had initiated and formed the Catholic congregation in their community, they should have some say about how the Church was to be governed; they also believed that they had a right to draw up a "job description" for the priest who would serve them, listing what they considered necessary personal and professional qualifications.[8] Even after they had received a full-time pastor they felt they had a personal responsibility for the congregation's "earthly and heavenly happiness."[9]

Lay initiative was likewise manifested when lay men and women became the spiritual supervisors of their communities, leading Catholics in prayer meetings, Bible readings, and other quasi-liturgical services, and helping to organize the religious instructions of their

[8] Jasper Moran of Norfolk to Archbishop John Carroll, February 24, 1815. In Archives of the Archdiocese of Baltimore, hereafter cited as AAB. Letter also found in Jasper Moran, *A Vindicatory Address; or an Appeal to the Calm Feelings and Unbiased Judgements of the Roman Catholics of Norfolk, Portsmouth, and Their Vicinity* (Norfolk, 1817), p. 55.

[9] Norfolk Trustees to Archbishop Leonard Neale, April 4, 1816, in Neale's papers, Case 12-F1, AAB.

children.[10] In 1816 and 1817, e.g., in the absence of a priest in Saint Louis, the trustees not only led the congregation in prayers on Sundays and holydays, but also performed the burial services.[11] In 1833 the entire American episcopate acknowledged the perseverance and courage of these lay Catholics who had "with firm faith preserved the sacred deposit and transmitted it to their children."[12] Thus, the general diaspora experience of American Catholicism and the necessity of historical circumstances gave rise to the spirit of lay responsibility in the Church. These conditions gave the laymen a taste for the possibilities of lay power in the local congregation, to such an extent that later they would only grudgingly surrender control.

The diaspora experience was reinforced by a lack of national or even diocesan organizational structure and unity. John Carroll was appointed superior of the American Catholic missions in 1784, was not elected Bishop of Baltimore until 1789, and was not consecrated until 1790. By that time laymen had already secured legal control of many congregations in the United States. Distance from Baltimore, lack of good communications, and difficulty of travel, moreover, aided the initiative of lay Catholics in developing their own form of parish government, even after Baltimore was established as a diocese. These problems were relieved somewhat in 1808 with the erection of four dioceses in Bardstown, Boston, New York, and Philadelphia. Bishops were not consecrated for these dioceses, however, until 1810, and New York did not receive its first resident bishop until 1815. This underdeveloped state of ecclesiastical organization was fertile ground for implanting the seeds of lay initiative.

Trusteeism arose not only as a result of the general diaspora circumstances of American Catholicism, but also in response to American legal structures—particularly laws regarding the incorporation of voluntary societies. American law recognized the churches as voluntary associations. The "prevailing" legal policy during the first third of the nineteenth century, one historian has noted, was based on the idea that "the civil power should treat all the religious organizations

[10] "Diurnal of the Right Rev. John England, First Bishop of Charleston, South Carolina, 1820-1823," *Records of the American Catholic Historical Society*, VI (1895), 39, 46, 49, 55, 217.

[11] Paul C. Schulte, *The Catholic Heritage of Saint Louis: A History of the Old Cathedral Parish, St. Louis, Mo.* (St. Louis, 1934), p. 87.

[12] Peter Guilday (ed.), *The National Pastorals of the American Hierarchy (1792-1919)* (Washington, D.C., 1923), p. 73.

alike by doing as little as possible for any of them and forcing all to conform to one procedure." The "one procedure" favored the "sectarian conception" of the Church which presupposed voluntary membership.[13] When Catholic laymen, therefore, incorporated themselves into communities, elected their trustees, and secured their properties under the trustee system, they were acting according to American law. The trustees' interpretation of American voluntaryism supported their legal control of ecclesiastical temporalities (even though the courts did not always accept their interpretations) and promoted their call for participation in ecclesiastical government. They believed that
370 because they freely supported the church, they naturally had a right to a say in its government. Their cry was: no financial support without representation.[14]

The American legal system also provided a forum for highlighting the conflicts which arose between the clergy and laity. Repeatedly from 1815 to 1855, from New York to Louisiana, lay and clerical trustees appealed to the federal government, to state legislatures, and to the courts to protect them from what they considered the unjust and "foreign," i.e., either Roman or episcopal, decisions and interventions regarding their civil rights—particularly those respecting their property rights and their personal reputations.[15] The bishops and the anti-trustee clergy responded to these appeals by issuing countersuits. At times, laymen either took their bishops to court, as in Philadelphia in the 1820's, for legal settlements or fought to have their original parish contracts of incorporation changed to favor the trustees exclusively, as in New Orleans in the 1840's.[16] In many of their appeals, the laymen were within their legal rights and, therefore, won their cases.

In some suits, however, they lost—especially when they sought absolute control of property, or when they asked for decisions respecting

[13] Patrick J. Dignan, *A History of the Legal Incorporation of Catholic Church Property in the United States (1784-1932)* (New York, 1935), p. 142.

[14] John F. Oliveira Fernandez, *Letter Addressed to the Most Reverend Leonard Neale, Archbishop of Baltimore by a Member of the Roman Catholic Congregation of Norfolk in Virginia* (Norfolk, 1816), p. 15, n. 11.

[15] Peter Guilday, *The Catholic Church in Virginia (1815-1822)* ("United States Catholic Historical Society Monograph Series," Vol. VIII [New York, 1924]), pp. 93-101; see also England, *Works*, V, 227.

[16] Alfonso Comeau, C.S.C., "A Study of the Trustee Problem in the St. Louis Cathedral Church of New Orleans, Louisiana, 1842-1844," *Louisiana Historical Quarterly*, XXXI (1948), 897-972.

their authority within the discipline of the Catholic Church. In some cases, when the federal government became involved in matters which related solely to the internal discipline of the Church, Bishop John England of Charleston was quick to remind government officials of the principle of the separation of Church and State, and to outline the temporal and spiritual realms of jurisdiction proper to the Church in a free society.[17] England felt that the lay and clerical appeals to the government were misguided; they were not, in his opinion, the result of a correct understanding of the American Constitution and republican ideology.[18]

Like Bishop England, most American Catholics were loyal to democracy and republican political institutions.[19] That loyalty was another major influence upon the development of the trustee movement. When the Catholic laity organized themselves into parishes (although they were not canonical parishes) they naturally copied the principles of American government in administering their own congregations. The trustees believed they were accommodating European Catholic practice to American republican institutions when they incorporated elements of lay representation in the government of their local parishes; they did not believe that they had changed Catholic doctrine or discipline significantly by doing so.[20] They constantly professed their belief in the sovereignty of the people and felt that what was sound and practical for political life was likewise appropriate for the temporal government of their parish life.[21] Thus, they asserted that American democracy should be adopted by the Catholic Church. They wanted the Church to acknowledge the laity's right to choose their own lay representatives for Church government, to participate in the selection of their pastors, and to dismiss them if they abused

[17] England, *Works*, V, 133.

[18] *Ibid.*, V, 163.

[19] Thomas T. McAvoy, C.S.C., "The Catholic Minority in the United States, 1789-1821," *Historical Records and Studies*, XXXIX-XL (1952), 48.

[20] Fernandez, *op. cit.*, p. 16, n. 11. One or two trustees asserted, contrary to Catholic teaching, that ecclesiastical government was based upon human and not divine principles; but the majority accepted Catholic doctrine on episcopal government. In a number of cases, however, trustees rejected specific episcopal commands, not because they rejected the office of episcopacy but because they considered the mandates an abuse of episcopal power. Failure to separate the trustees' perceptions of ecclesiastical government from their periodic practice of rejecting specific episcopal commands has caused some historians to attribute to most trustees heretical principles they did not accept.

[21] Dignan, *op. cit.*, p. 107.

their authority, were scandalous to the general public, or were incompetent in their ministry.[22] John Hughes, a priest in Philadelphia in the 1820's, noted that the laity of many of the parishes there sometimes showed more interest in the yearly elections of their lay trustees than they did in the national presidential elections. He believed that this local manifestation of the democratic spirit was particularly foreign to the spirit of Catholicism because of the annual disturbances such elections created.[23] Regardless of the turmoil they sometimes caused, the elections manifested, in the trustees' minds, the compatibility of Catholicism and democratic republicanism.

372 In a variety of ways, the dominant Protestant congregational polity and lay-centered theology also seem to have played their part in the rise of trusteeism. For obvious reasons, Catholic laymen themselves never acknowledged their indebtedness to their Protestant neighbors for the development of their own peculiar system of lay trusteeism. They were particularly careful not to arouse the hostility of their Protestant neighbors during the early days of the nineteenth century. In fact, they called their fellow parishioners to

> live in peace, charity and friendship with each other . . . and as common children of God, no matter how differently educated we may be, in the various doctrines of FAITH which is an affair for HIM alone to judge of—Not for us poor weak mortals to be disputing or contending about.[24]

As a tiny minority, the Catholic laymen overlooked theological differences and tried to conform as much as possible to the ways of the Protestant ecclesiastical structures. In 1817, for example, the Norfolk trustees petitioned Rome for a new diocese in Virginia and suggested a new form of government for the diocese; the appeal revealed a direct dependence upon the model of government used by the Protestant Episcopal Church in Virginia.[25] Similar trustee proposals indicate a strong tendency to identify early nineteenth-century Catholicism with some American Protestant ecclesiastical values.

The trustees' understanding of how separation of Church and State should affect American Catholicism contributed, even more than the Protestant influences, to the extent and duration of their campaign. According to Father Thadeus O'Meally, a Philadelphia trusteeist, the

[22] Fernandez, *op. cit.*, p. 26, n. 9; see also Guilday, *Virginia*, p. 55.

[23] John R. G. Hassard, *Life of the Most Reverend John Hughes, First Archbishop of New York* (New York, 1866), p. 65.

[24] Moran, *A Vindicatory Address*, p. 53.

[25] Guilday, *Virginia*, pp. 45-59.

"peculiar situation" of the separation of Church and State was the "only natural order of things."[26] As a consequence of this new experience, many trustees advocated a radical division between temporal and spiritual government within the Church itself. They supported their position with numerous theological sources which they interpreted in light of their experiences. Dr. John Fernandez, a Norfolk trustee, quoted what he believed were Jean Gerson's views on the separation of the spiritual and temporal authorities, and maintained that the clergy had no temporal, but only spiritual, powers in the Church; the temporal affairs, therefore, were to be administered exclusively by the laity.[27]

Fernandez believed that since the pope had no authority within the secular sphere, it could be said to a greater degree that neither did the priests in the local parish nor the bishops in the dioceses.[28] Other trustees looked to Scripture to support their views that Jesus Christ had given the Church only spiritual authority. Christ repeatedly told his disciples that "His kingdom is not of this world," and Saint Paul believed that priests were ordained for things "pertaining to God." After examining passages like these, Richard Meade, a Philadelphia trustee, argued that "the spiritual and temporal government of the church are distinct."[29]

According to the trustees, the "temporal" meant anything which was not permanent, absolute, or part of the divinely established constitution and doctrine of the Church; it was all those things which were changeable or adaptable, anything which had previously been altered in the Church's history or anything which pertained to ecclesiastical administration of temporalities—even the practice of appointing and dismissing pastors. Ecclesiastical administration, in particular, was historically conditioned. That the appointment of pastors, for example, was not an article of faith and, therefore, not part of the spiritual or sacramental dimension of the Church was, for

[26] Thadeus O'Meally, *A Series of Letters Relating to the Late Attempt at a Reconciliation between the Members of the Congregations of St. Mary's and St. Joseph's with a Brief Notice of the Present State of the Controversy between Them* (Philadelphia, 1825), p. 33.

[27] Fernandez, *op. cit.*, p. 5, n. 3.

[28] James Lucas to Archbishop Neale, February 8, 1816, in Neale's papers, AAB; cf. Guilday, *Virginia*, p. 11.

[29] Richard Meade, *An Address to the Roman Catholics of the City of Philadelphia, in Reply to Mr. Harold's Address* (Philadelphia, 1823), p. 10; cf. also Moran, *op. cit.*, p. 27.

the trustees, clearly proven from the fact that

> had the church ever considered the appointment of pastors to livings or benefices an article of faith, the right would not, or could not have been conceded to lay patrons in all catholic countries.[30]

While the temporal belonged to the time-conditioned areas of ecclesiastical government, the "spiritual" belonged only to what Christ had explicitly commanded or what was clearly evident in the Scriptures about the nature of the Church. The episcopacy, ordination to the priesthood, and the sacramental system, e.g., were properly spiritual.

374 The trustees' radical separation of the spiritual and temporal strengthened their contention that all human powers whether in Church or State had to be checked and balanced. The trustees, like their Puritan neighbors, believed in the corruptibility of all human power. They frequently referred to ecclesiastical despotism and the weakness of human nature. They were careful to distinguish, therefore, between divine and human authority. These beliefs led them to conceive of a church in which there would be a constitutional balance of powers. They saw the laity as one pole of power within the Church; their authority, they believed, would check that of the clergy.

European Catholic Experiences

European as well as American factors influenced the persistence of trusteeism. The papacy, the Irish Catholic campaign against the British government's desire for a veto in the selection of bishops, the Irish Catholic experience of congregationalism, and the European practice of the right of patronage—these elements of European Catholicism aided the trustee movement in one way or another.

From 1784 to 1820 the papal government was not always well informed on American circumstances and, therefore, unwittingly assisted the development of the trustee campaign. American lay and clerical trustees frequently asked the papacy to arbitrate disputes between themselves and their bishops. Roman officials at times granted some trustees privileges and promises which their bishops had denied. By such grants the trustees were, unknown to the Roman officials,

[30] *Address of the Trustees of St. Mary's Church to their Fellow Citizens . . . on a Late Attempt at a Reconciliation between the Contending Parties of the Congregation of Said Church* (Philadelphia, 1823), p. 12.

encouraged in their opposition to the bishops. When some of these favorable decisions were later reversed in Rome because of American episcopal protests, the trustees rejected the reversed judgments—as the American episcopacy had opposed the first determinations favoring the trustees. Until 1820, however, the trustees had generally won favorable decisions from the papacy. In response to the trustees' petitions, for example, the Congregation de Propaganda Fide supported the trustees' claims for the right of patronage,[31] created new dioceses, and appointed Irish bishops to Philadelphia and the two new Dioceses of Richmond and Charleston. After 1820, because of increased episcopal opposition to the trustees, Rome began to deny the trustees' demands and supported the American episcopal position. For the first few years, however, at a time when the American Church's future organization was still uncertain, Rome's participation in the trustee affair seems to have strengthened the trustees' campaign to adjust the American Church to democracy.

During the most volatile period of trusteeism (1815-1829), the Irish Catholic anti-veto movement also influenced the trustees' cause.[32] From 1808 to 1816 the British Government tried to obtain from the Holy See the right to veto appointments to the Irish episcopacy. Many Irish laity and clergy, led by Daniel O'Connell, rejected the move and eventually won the struggle to have the bishops selected within Ireland without British participation. Many of the trustees were either Irish Americans or sympathizers with the Irish Catholic campaign; they were well informed on the issues involved in the Irish cause and appropriated much of the Irish anti-veto ideology to support their own demands. The trustees in Philadelphia, in particular, saw the similarity between the Irish Catholic anti-veto crusade and the trustee movement. In their minds, both were struggles of a people for local control of their Church. The Irish struggle was an attempt to preserve the independence of the national Irish Catholic Church, i.e., to keep it free from British and Roman influence and interference.

[31] Even though the American bishops rejected the *jus patronatus* in the 1829 statutes of the council of Baltimore, Rome never opposed it absolutely as a possibility for the future and suggested that the American bishops change their original legislation to include this possibility. See *Concilia Provincialia, Baltimori habita ab anno 1829, usque ad annum 1840* (Baltimore, 1842), pp. 60, 69. See also Thomas F. Casey, *The Sacred Congregation de Propaganda Fide and the Revision of the First Provincial Council of Baltimore (1829-1830)* ("Analecta Gregoriana," Vol. LXXXVIII, Series Facultatis Historiae Ecclesiasticae, Sectio B, No. 15 [Rome, 1957]), pp. 77-82.

[32] On the veto see Guilday, *Life of England*, I, 98-124.

The trustee cause was the movement of American Catholic clergy and laity to establish a national Church on the grounds of lay and clerical participation in local ecclesiastical government. One trustee asked: "Why should the Catholics of America be less alive to the honour of their national church than the Catholics of Ireland?"[33]

Those who opposed the trustees also used the Irish Catholic question to support their claims. For them, the Irish rejection of the veto was the victory of the spiritual, i.e., ecclesiastical, over the temporal, i.e., governmental, authority. According to the anti-trustees, when Irish Catholics thwarted the British government's attempt to win the
376 veto, they were resisting the interference of the laity (i.e., lay government) in ecclesiastical government and administration. The trustees denied this interpretation of the event by pointing out that while the argument may have been justified when applied to the Irish or, for that matter, to any European Catholic Church, it could not be justified for the American Church. The latter had to differ from the Irish and European Church simply because the circumstances of political and ecclesiastical life in the United States differed so greatly from those in Ireland or Europe. In the United States, republican government was a new adventure and, therefore, the Catholic Church here had to have a new organization corresponding to these new circumstances. Thus, the trustees' interpretation of Irish Catholic events clearly contributed to the questions raised during the debates.

The immigrant trustees' experience of parish life in Ireland also seems to have affected their support of the congregational elements of the trustee movement. During the penal days and the first part of the nineteenth century, Irish Catholicism, much like American Catholicism, was predominantly a congregational-centered Catholicism, even though the Irish did not choose their pastors. During this period, many of the parishes, and particularly the Irish clergy, had a local autonomy which they did not enjoy in the later nineteenth century. To be sure, the Irish Church did have an episcopal structure, but the bishops did not have the same power and control over Irish ecclesiastical life that they would gradually gain during the middle years of the nineteenth century. Thus, the Irish Catholic experience of congregationalism prepared the Irish immigrants for the American Protestant and Catholic experience of congregationalism. The immigrants found it easy, therefore, to adjust to the American experience and to see that experience as a continuation of their own Irish Catholicism.

[33] O'Meally, *op. cit.*, p. 34.

Even the conflicts between the clergy and the laity were not entirely new for the Irish, as statutes of Irish episcopal synods indicate.[34]

The European practice of patronage also supported the trustee cause. Many of the trustees—Irish as well as Spanish, French, German, and Portuguese—had experienced the practice of the right of patronage in their former countries and knew the ecclesiastical laws regarding its regulation. The German trustees of Philadelphia in 1787, the Irish of Norfolk, Charleston, and Philadelphia from 1815 to 1829, the Spanish and French of New Orleans in the 1820's and 1840's, and the Germans of Buffalo, New York, in the 1840's and 1850's used the European experiences and ecclesiastical codes to support their claims for a right to participate in the selection of their pastors. Until 1829 there were no ecclesiastical laws in the United States forbidding the practice and, therefore, the trustees' *jus patronatus* arguments were another part of their program for accommodating the European Church to American politics and law. They believed that the right of patronage in the United States could not be exactly the same as that in Europe because of the new political circumstances in the United States.[35] They acknowledged the differences between European and American styles of government and felt that what had been given to European Catholic monarchs, i.e., the right of patronage, should be granted to all the American Catholics since the people themselves were sovereign in this country. What they were seeking was not diametrically opposed to their European experiences. They believed that even though the European right was usually associated with a fixed, permanent, and unalienable fund for the support of the pastor,[36] it could not be so in the United States because of the American circumstances. They believed, however, that the ecclesiastical laws could be accommodated to the American spirit of voluntaryism without doing violence to the European law, and that that spirit would provide a financial permanence even more as-

[34] The Provincial Council of Tuam in 1817 legislated against the *jus patronatus* and the problems it had caused in the clergy-laity relations in the province. See *Acta et Decreta Sacrorum Conciliorum Recentiorum Collectio Lacensis* (7 vols.; Freiburg, 1875), III, 761-762. On Irish anticlericalism, see also Robert Burns, "Parson, Priests and the People: The Rise of Irish Anti-Clericalism, 1785-89," *Church History*, XXXI (1962), 151-163.

[35] Fernandez, *op. cit.*, p. 16, n. 11.

[36] The episcopal argument against the right was based upon the fact that the right demanded such. See M. Bernetta Brislen, O.S.F., "The Episcopacy of Leonard Neale," *Historical Records and Studies*, XXXIV (1945), 32.

suring than the European practices.[37] Thus, they based their claims upon the necessity of adapting church law to American practices.

Theological Perceptions

Although European Catholic experiences as well as American circumstances created and conditioned trusteeism, the primary motivating force behind the movement was the trustees' own theological perceptions of the Church and its relationship to society. Contrary to common historical descriptions, trusteeism was a theological as well as a cultural, moral, social, legal, and disciplinary problem.[38] The
378 trustees, at least, saw that the American environment called for a new understanding of the Church and the roles of the layman, priest, and bishop. They were well aware that they were fighting for a new vision of the Church.

The new American experiences and the "spirit of inquiry" drove many trustees to a study of the history of the Church, canon law, the Scriptures, and theology.[39] In the process of their search, as already noted in some of the trustee arguments mentioned above, they discovered historical precedents and theologians to support their views of the Church and its relationship to society.

The idea and practice of adaptation, they discovered, was nothing new. Using arguments from historical precedent, therefore, the trustees called for the establishment of a "National Catholic Church" which would reflect the customs, laws, and political ideas of the country. They believed that the wisdom of the Church had always varied its discipline and government "to suit the times and circumstances, and which we have every right to insist upon being adopted [*sic*] to our peculiar situation."[40] The American Church should maintain its continuity with the European Church, but it should also be

[37] Thadeus O'Meally, *An Address Explanatory and Vindicatory to Both Parties of the Congregation of St. Mary's* (Philadelphia, 1824), p. 62.

[38] Many historians have argued that there were no ideological issues involved in the dissensions. Celestine J. Nuesse, *The Social Thought of American Catholics 1634-1829* (Washington, D.C., 1945), p. 176, e.g., maintained that the quarrels of the period were purely personal and administrative; they did not involve "adherence even to erroneous principles." Cf. also McAvoy, *History*, pp. 75, 131; Guilday, *Life of England*, I, 164-282.

[39] [Thadeus O'Meally], *Reflections on the Dissension actually Existing in St. Mary's Congregation. By a Roman Catholic* (Philadelphia, 1824), p. 3.

[40] *Address of the Lay Trustees to the Congregation of St. Mary's Church on the Subject of the Approaching Election* (Philadelphia, 1822), p. 24.

consistent with the republican and democratic character of the American people. According to Dr. Matthew O'Driscoll, a Charleston trustee, American Catholics should

> rear a National American Church, with liberties consonant to the spirit of the Government, under which they live; yet, in due obedience in essentials to the Pontifical Hierarchy, and which will add a new and dignified column to the Vatican.[41]

The trustees' call for a newly structured national Church was directly influenced by the example of their Protestant neighbors. The trustees suggested that the Catholic Church, like the Protestant Episcopal
Church, could change its European institutions to meet the demands 379
of the new age.[42]

The new age was republican. The trustees were loyal republicans. Their loyalty, however, created ideological tensions. "The elan vital of republicanism," according to Winthrop Hudson, "is democracy, freedom, discussion, persuasion, conviction, faith."[43] American Protestants saw these characteristics as incompatible with Catholicism. As much as they tried, Catholics were not able to answer the Protestant charge.

Because they did not, or could not, create an acceptable synthesis between republicanism and Catholicism, many Catholics divided the intellectual world in two: in one part they placed revealed religion, in the other, political truths.[44] What resulted, therefore, was an unresolved conflict between the values of American Catholicism and those of republican society. The trustees were attempting to overcome these ideological tensions. Thus, they suggested that the Church at the parish, diocesan, and national levels should adopt the democratic and republican framework of the United States Constitution.[45] In their study of the sources of theology they had discovered that democracy and common responsibility within the Church were elements consis-

[41] O'Driscoll to Ambrose Maréchal, December 15, 1817, in Maréchal's papers, Case 15-S6, AAB.

[42] *Address of the Trustees of St. Mary's Church to their Fellow Citizens . . . on a Late Attempt at a Reconciliation between the Contending Parties of the Congregation of Said Church*, p. 4.

[43] Winthrop Hudson, *The Great Tradition of the American Churches* (New York, 1963), p. 75.

[44] This is the opinion of Alexis de Tocqueville, *Democracy in America*, ed. J. P. Mayer and Max Lerner; trans. George Lawrence (New York, 1966), p. 266.

[45] Guilday, *Virginia*, pp. 45-59.

tent with the gospel, church history, and the views of some Catholic theologians such as Nicholas of Cusa.[46] The trustees found their own views of republicanism and Catholicism to be in conformity with Catholic tradition. Thus, they proposed a program for adaptation which was more an identification with American social and legal experiences than it was a simple accommodation.

The American Catholic Church, in the trustees' vision, was to be a republican Church. While most of the trustees accepted the episcopacy as an essential office in the Catholic Church, they emphasized the communal rather than the hierarchical character of Catholicism. 380 They believed that in the Church, as in the State, the people were sovereign. The Church was the people, therefore, and not solely the hierarchy.[47] Using Saint Cyprian and Nicholas of Cusa, the trustees described the Church as the "Great Association and Union of Christians" and stressed the local independence of the American Church.[48] This communal emphasis clashed with the bishops' hierarchical conception.

Within the ecclesial communion, according to the trustees, the clergy and the laity had radically different ministries. As already noted, the clergy were responsible for the spiritual affairs and the laity for the temporal. As many letters to their bishops indicate, the trustees wanted holy and pious priests, but especially evangelical clergy who could preach fluently, thereby impress the general population, and by so doing attract large numbers of converts to Catholicism.[49] The trustees' evangelical conception collided with the bishops' sacramental-hierarchical perceptions of the priesthood.

The trustees' views of the lay status and role in the Church also differed from that of the episcopacy. The American nativists had accused the Catholic laity of being priest-ridden. They believed that Catholic laymen could not be good democratic citizens because they were schooled in a church controlled by an authoritarian hierarchy and by a clergy subservient to that authority. The articulate Catholic trustees, therefore, wanted to appear before their nativist neighbors

[46] Fernandez, *op. cit.*, p. 10, n. 5.

[47] Servandus Mier, *The Opinion of the Rt. Rev. Servandus A. Mier . . . On Certain Queries Proposed to Him by the Rev. William Hogan* (Philadelphia, 1821), p. 9.

[48] Fernandez, *op. cit.*, p. 30, n. 29.; cf. also *A Letter to the Roman Catholics of Philadelphia and the United States, By a Friend to the Civil and Religious Liberties of Man* (1st ed.; Philadelphia, 1822), p. 50.

[49] Guilday, *Virginia*, p. xxxii.

as independent of clerical domination and yet as loyal Roman Catholics. Their perceptions of the lay role, however, were not simply an accommodation to nativist charges. They believed that their rights to control ecclesiastical temporalities, to elect their pastors, to judge and to hold them accountable for their ministries, and to be able to remove unreasonable or incompetent pastors were consistent with sound, but forgotten, Catholic theological traditions.

The trustees saw the necessity of accommodating the Catholic Church to the American experience in such a way that the layman would be viewed as a free, responsible, participating, and democratic citizen within the ecclesial communion. They tried to show that they were socially, politically, and religiously free of clerical control and obedient only to reasonable ecclesiastical authority. They believed this perception of the laity's role was consistent with the early Church's conception.[50] Many of the bishops saw the laymen more in terms of their passive responsibility in the Church and interpreted the articulate layman's desire for ecclesiastical independence as rebelliousness. According to the trustees, however, their emancipation campaign was an attempt to define a new role for themselves within the Catholic Church.

Thus, from the trustees' perspective, trusteeism was a crusade to adapt the European Catholic Church to American culture by identifying that Church with American republicanism. It arose as a response to American circumstances, transplanted European Catholic experiences, and theological perceptions more than as a consequence of lay and clerical rebellion. The dissensions of trusteeism, moreover, were the product of conflicting views of the relationship of the Catholic Church to American conditions as much as they were the result of personality conflicts or hostile class and nationality differences.

Even though the trustees failed to move the American Church to identify itself with republican ways, they saw, nevertheless, the necessity of some kind of change in the Catholic Church's relationship with the modern democratic world. Because they saw this necessity, they raised questions about lay and clerical participation in the decision-making processes of the local, diocesan, and national Church. These practical and theological questions have never really been satisfactorily resolved within the American Church. The tensions which these questions created were submerged by nativism,

[50] Fernandez, *op. cit.*, p. 10, n. 5.

Catholic defensiveness, and episcopal legislation; thus, the ideological conflicts of trusteeism have reappeared in new forms throughout the history of American Catholicism. This fact is borne out in the contemporary Church by the friction between some Catholic parish councils and their clerical leaderships.[51] In the future, a thorough study of trusteeism could reveal to contemporary theologians and church leaders not only the problems but also some directions for resolving the practical and ideological tensions between Catholicism and American republicanism.

382 [51] For reports on the dissensions within the parish of the Good Shepherd in Alexandria, Virginia, where the accusation of "trusteeism" has been raised, see *National Catholic Reporter,* October 11, 1974, p. 3; December 6, 1974, p. 1; December 27, 1974, p. 1; January 10, 1975, p. 15; February 7, 1975, p. 2; January 23, 1976, p. 2; January 30, 1976, p. 1; February 13, 1976, p. 3; February 27, 1976, p. 20. For similar conflicts see *ibid.,* March 7, 1975; March 14, 1975; November 1, 1974; December 20, 1974.

Two Episcopal Views of Lay-Clerical Conflicts: 1785-1860

By PATRICK CAREY*

American Catholic bishops have had divergent attitudes toward the laity's role in the church. Nowhere is this more clearly evident than in the bishops' approaches to the trustee conflicts from 1785 to 1860. Historians of American Catholicism have generally presented the episcopal response as a united front against the "evils of trusteeism."[1] True, the bishops unanimously rejected the excesses and abuses of the trustee system, but they differed greatly in precisely what they rejected and in their style of opposition. Historians have not always presented these differences. A close examination of representative episcopal responses to trusteeism shows at least two divergent kinds of opposition, revealing different approaches to the laity and their role in the church, and demonstrates that the bishops' attitudes were shaped by their perceptions of the relationship of the Catholic Church to democracy.

Bishops John Carroll and John England are examples of a republican approach to the lay trustees. Both saw the necessity of incorporating the laity into the administration and ministry of the church, but they rejected what they considered the trustees' excessive demands for lay control of ecclesiastical temporalities and clerical appointments. Their views were governed, in part, by their attempts to relate the Catholic Church to the American form of democracy. They believed that the Catholic Church should appropriate elements of American democracy in its administration while retaining the centrality of episcopal authority.

Bishops Leonard Neale, Ambrose Marechal, Henry Conwell and John Hughes represent a monarchical response to the trustees. They vigorously opposed the trustees for interfering in what they considered essentially clerical roles in the church and rejected the trustees' demands for participation as radical innovations in the church's administration. Some of these bishops, furthermore, perceived the trustee system itself as inherently evil. Their opposition to the trustees was based upon their attempt to establish the Catholic structures of the *ancien regime* in the United States. For them, this meant that the Catholic Church had to reject accommodations to democracy and implant episcopal monarchy in the church's government. Their view of adaptation and episcopal

*Assistant Professor of Religion, Carleton College, Northfield, Minn.

monarchy left little room for active lay participation in ecclesiastical affairs. These two episcopal attitudes must now be examined in greater detail.

Republican Opposition

From the beginning of John Carroll's appointment as Superior of the American missions in 1784 to the end of John Hughes' episcopal ministry in New York in 1863, American Catholic clergy and the lay trustees fought numerous battles with each other over, among other things, the nature and exercise of ecclesiastical authority in the American Church. Carroll first tangled with trustees in 1786, when he tried to settle such a dispute in St. Peter's parish in New York City. From 1787 to 1797, he contended with the trustees of Holy Trinity in Philadelphia and St. John's in Baltimore, and from 1802 to 1815 with those of St. Mary's in Charleston. His specific responses to the trustees of each parish differed because the situation in each case varied. An analysis of his correspondence with trustees reveals that his approach in all cases was firm, but conciliatory.

Carroll usually responded with hesitation at the onset of the trustee controversies. Upon being notified of conflicts in a parish between the clergy and the laity, he frequently waited for the troubles to settle themselves. Many times he deferred intervention until he realized that a solution to the disputes could be solved only by outside mediation.[2] When he finally did enter the hostilities, he preferred a rational discussion of the issues to a reliance upon episcopal *fiat* in order to solve the dissensions. Throughout the conflicts, he consistently rejected some of the trustees' demands,[3] but responded favorably to others—especially their call for lay participation in local church administration.[4] Unlike some of his successors, moreover, he did not reject the trustee system as inherently evil;[5] nor did he presume that the trustees were attempting to overthrow ecclesiastical authority. He did warn some Philadelphia trustees, however, that they would suffer his vigorous opposition if they persisted obstinately in their erroneous demands for control of the local parish church.[6]

Carroll approached the trustees as men of intelligence who did not properly understand the principle of authority in the Catholic Church. The problem of trusteeism for Carroll was one of ignorance, not one of lay rebellion. Thus, he saw his office as educator, not as disciplinarian. Through his letters to the trustees, therefore, he attempted to show them that his opposition to their excessive claims was based upon church discipline and theology. In his first letter to the New York City trustees on January 25, 1786, he outlined his disciplinary and theological objections to the trustees' claim that they had the right to appoint and dismiss pastors. He declared that the church's discipline in this country did not acknowledge the trustee cause because as of 1786 there were no legally established parishes and, therefore, no duly-constituted pastors and no congregational right to select clergy. The clergy who served the laity in the American congregations "are but voluntary labourers in the vineyard of Christ, not vested with ordinary jurisdiction annexed to their office, but receiving it as a delegated and extra-hierarchical commission."[7]

According to Carroll, the church's theology also prohibited lay appointments or dismissals of the clergy. He asserted that if the trustees' claims were acknowledged "the unity and catholicity of our church would be at an end." Their demand flowed more from the polity of the "congregational Presbyterians [sic] . . . of New England" than from that of the Catholic Church.[8] In another letter, Carroll noted that by making such a claim the trustees were "exchanging the doctrines of the Catholic Church for those of Luther and Calvin."[9]

Throughout the trustee debates, Carroll presented the traditional Catholic argument that all the sacramental and evangelical priestly functions were "in their nature entirely spiritual" and that they would "never be within the jurisdiction of, or subject to the dispensation of the laity, but were committed by Christ to the Apostles alone, and to their successors in the government of their respective churches."[10] Moreover, Carroll, as did his successors, equated conferring the power of orders with appointing pastors to their parishes. Both were spiritual functions, in Carroll's opinion, and, therefore, both were derived "not from human authority, or institutions of civil government, but from the same divine origin as the apostles themselves."[11] Thus, Carroll's primary argument against the trustees' claims was based upon his understanding of church authority.

Having stated his objections to the trustees' claims, Carroll was careful to show that he shared some of their views on the relationship of the Catholic Church to the American Republic. In 1786, for example, he promised the New York City trustees that their desires for lay participation and representation in the government of the church would one day be realized in the United States. In fact, the trustees could be assured that the government of the Catholic Church would be suitably likened to that of the American system of government.

> Wherever parishes are established no doubt proper regard (and such as is suitable to our governments) will be had to rights of the congregation in the mode of election and

> representation; and even now I shall ever pay to their wishes every deference consistent with the general welfare of religion.[12]

Carroll perceived that the *élan vital* of trusteeism was a proper mode of adapting the Catholic Church to the new circumstances of democratic government. On this point, he was most conciliatory to the trustees, even though he did not share their specific solution to the problems—i.e., full lay responsibility for electing pastors as well as full lay control of ecclesiastical temporalities. He did, however, see the necessity of accommodating the church's structures at the local parish level to the republican attitudes and institutions of the American people. He
386 accepted the conflicts of trusteeism, therefore, as part of the necessary tension involved in adapting the European Church to a new environment. The very fact that Carroll enacted no laws against trusteeism at the Baltimore Synod in 1790 and at the episcopal meeting in 1810—i.e., at a time when trusteeism had already created a number of disturbances in the American Catholic Church—reveals to some extent his acceptance of the trustee system and his belief that the troubles of trusteeism were a necessary part of the struggle of accommodation. Bishop John Hughes, perhaps the most forceful trustee opponent of the era, saw Carroll's attitude in this way. Hughes believed that Carroll

> wished to assimilate, as far as possible the outward administration of the Catholic Church property in a way which would harmonize with the democratic principles on which the new government was founded. With this view he authorized and instituted the system of lay trustees in Catholic congregations.[13]

Although Carroll did not, as Hughes maintained, "authorize and institute" the trustee system (it developed independent of Carroll's participation), he did accept the system as a viable way of accommodating the church to the American situation.[14]

While Carroll's episcopal successors repeated his theological and disciplinary arguments against the trustees, only Bishop John England of Charleston, South Carolina, followed his conciliatory form of opposition. England's opposition to the trustees, however, was not exclusively theological or disciplinary, nor was his conciliation merely an acceptance of the trustees' desire to accommodate the church to American republicanism. He saw that the proper way to oppose the trustees' excesses and to accept their valid desires was to create a legal structure of diocesan government which would constitutionally guarantee both. England believed that the Catholic Church in the United States lacked a proper legal structure and that that was the source of the difficulties between the clergy and the trustees.

By the time England came to the United States in 1820, the conflicts of trusteeism had reached the point of white heat. Carroll's episcopal successors and suffragans had demanded that the trustees give unconditional submission to episcopal mandates regarding parish administration and clerical appointments. This attitude hardened the trustees' opposition to episcopal authority and deepened their sense of lay independence. After Carroll's death in 1815, therefore, the lay trustees began a concerted campaign in this country and in the Roman ecclesiastical courts against what they considered ecclesiastical despotism. England's response to this situation in his own diocese and in that of others was a mixture of assertiveness and conciliation. He demanded a recognition of episcopal authority in the administration of all ecclesiastical affairs, but he also acknowledged the necessity of lay ministry and cooperation in church government. Like Carroll, he listened to the demands of his democratic-minded laity and sought their assistance in solving the conflicts between the laity and the clergy. Unlike Carroll, however, he did not see the trustee conflicts as a manifestation of lay ignorance of church discipline. The core of the problem was structural. Neither the laity nor the clergy (Carroll included) had attempted to adapt Catholic Church laws to the American legal system in such a way as to eliminate unnecessary conflicts over power and authority in the local Catholic communities. The laity, on the one hand, had used the American legal system to protect their rights over property and persons in the church without regard for clerical rights. The clergy, on the other hand, used episcopal mandate and ecclesiastical discipline rather than the American legal system to acknowledge their rights and duties within the church. What was needed, in England's opinion, was a written constitution, legally accepted by both clergy and laity, which would precisely define and limit the respective rights and duties of each group within ecclesiastical government.[15]

Shortly after his arrival in the United States, therefore, England consulted the laity and clergy of his diocese, studied the federal constitution and the legal constitutions of other churches, examined canon law, and combined both the American legal structures and Catholic discipline into a written constitution which successfully governed his diocese for more than twenty years. The constitution was a masterpiece of legal ingenuity; it carefully adapted the government of the European Catholic Church to the political and legal realities of American democracy and protected clerical rights and responsibilities as well as those of the laity in the administration of the parish and diocesan church. Moreover, it satisfied the laity and the clergy of his diocese and met the demands of Catholic theology and discipline. It was conciliatory; but, unlike Carroll's personal conciliation, it provided a definite legal structure for solving practical conflicts.

According to England, the successful administration of a diocesan church in a modern democracy demanded the participation and cooperation of the laity as well as the clergy. Decisions could be made with more universal acceptance and therefore implemented with more effectiveness if the whole church participated through elected representatives in the process of ecclesiastical government. The Charleston Diocesan Constitution served these purposes and revealed England's respect for lay and clerical opinion. Personal conciliation
388 based upon structured adaptation to democracy, therefore, was the key to England's successful solution to trusteeism. England's solution, however, was not followed by the American church.[16]

Monarchical Opposition

American Catholicism followed the leadership of Bishops Leonard Neale, Ambrose Maréchal, Henry Conwell and John Hughes in determining the position of the laity in the church. Their approach to the trustees was monarchical. While trying to uphold the centrality of episcopal and clerical government, these bishops aggressively rejected the trustees' attempts to identify Catholicism and American republicanism and thereby eventually diminished active lay participation in the administration of the American Catholic Church.

In 1796, as Vicar General of the Diocese of Baltimore, Leonard Neale absolutely opposed the trustees' demands, called them immoral and rebellious heretics, and advanced a rigid view of episcopal authority in the government of the church in this country. He used ridicule as well as canon law to defeat the trustees of Holy Trinity in Philadelphia when they tried to base their claims for lay participation in the church upon the right of patronage.

> Ah! my brethren, it is thus that you expose yourselves to the laughter and pity of a discerning public, by spouting forth terms which you understood not and repeating the reveries of an illiterate and factious leader, who will never reflect honor on you. The truth is you have no *jus patronatus:* you can have none because your church has no *Fixed, Permanent and Unalienable* fund for the support of a Pastor. Such is the doctrine of the Council of Trent.[17]

As Archbishop of Baltimore, Neale continued to use this argument against the trustees of Norfolk, Virginia and Charleston, South Carolina. Only the bishop could appoint and remove a priest, he maintained, and that he could do at will, "revocable at will."[18] Neale believed that the trustees could be bridled only by a strong show of episcopal power. Like Carroll, he rejected the trustees and the trustee system because they reflected the Protestant influences.

> The Presbiterian [sic] system puts the Vestrymen over the clergyman, but the Catholic system places the clergyman over the vestrymen whom he appoints and dismisses at will.[19]

Neale disregarded the trustees' American republican sympathies and suggested that rather than holding elections for parish trustees the pastor alone should choose certain members of the congregation to help him manage the temporal affairs of the parish.[20] Clearly, this move was not calculated to win a hearing from the republican trustees and many of the members of the Catholic parishes.

In Neale's perception (and in actual fact), the trustees had both the financial and legal power "to frustrate the most genuine views of the Pastor on all occasions." That power appeared to him to be unjust and, as he called it, "a fair inversion of the order of nature, which forbids the head to become the tail."[21] For Neale, therefore, trusteeism was a power struggle—a contest for the right to exercise authority in the church's government. He could see the trustees in no other light. They had usurped episcopal and pastoral authority, and had introduced Protestant practices into church government. By opposing the trustees the way he did and by referring to lay elections and representation in the parish as manifestations of Protestantism, Neale (as other clergy would after him) unwittingly gave the American Protestants reasons to suspect the practical and ideological compatibility of American republicanism and Catholicism. Thereby too, he advanced the identification of Americanism and Protestantism.

Like Neale, Bishop Ambrose Maréchal identified the trustees' desires to appropriate republican principles and practices in the government of the church with Protestantism.[22] For Maréchal, the trustees and their clerical supporters were "enemies of the church of Christ," "impious men," given over to "impiety and vice"—particularly to drunkenness and the "drunkenness of ambition;" but they represented only a minority of each parish.[23] Most important of all, the trustees' programs and principles reminded Maréchal, as they did many of the French émigre clergy, of the leaders of the French Revolution.

> They [trustees] possess the same customs, principles, and turbulent passions which imbued those impious men who tried to overthrow the altars of Christ in the abominable French Revolution.[24]

While Maréchal rejected the trustees as immoral and rebellious leaders of a faction in the church, he did not absolutely oppose the trustee system, as Neale had done. He believed the system would not be dangerous to Catholicism if the original parish constitutions would limit the trustees' powers. The system could work if it protected clerical independence and episcopal supervision as well as lay and clerical cooperation in the management of the church's temporal affairs.[25] Unlike England, however, Maréchal never attempted to construct such a conciliatory system within his own diocese. Perhaps the hostilities of the various trustee schisms prevented him from any conciliatory restructuring of the system.

390 Bishop Henry Conwell of Philadelphia, like Maréchal, considered lay and clerical trustees who opposed him to be immoral, "not practical Catholics."[26] Before he arrived in the United States in 1820, he had heard that the Catholics in his diocese were in "great confusion" and that "anarchy prevailed" in many of the parishes in the country.[27] He felt that the trustees' demands were part of a revolutionary campaign and believed that "revolutionary movements tend always to disorder."[28] At first he held that if the leaders of the church acceded anything to the trustees such concessions "would unhinge the hierarchy, undermine church government, destroy subordination, and subvert all rule and order in the church here [Philadelphia] and elsewhere, throughout the United States."[29] Like Maréchal, Conwell saw the lay-clerical conflicts as an American manifestation of the French Revolution. His was a European perception of an American experience.

After a period of prolonged hostility between himself and the trustees, Conwell drew up a contract with the trustees which recognized the trustees' right to participate in the selection of a pastor or to reject an episcopal appointment. Propaganda Fide ruled the agreement incompatible with Catholic doctrine and discipline and eventually removed Conwell from the episcopal jurisdiction of Philadelphia. Conwell's authoritarian opposition to the trustees and his later injudicious attempt to create peace in the diocese intensified the nativists' rejection of Catholicism as utterly incompatible with American republican ways.

The Philadelphia controversies schooled many of the American clergy in their opposition to trusteeism. None was more adamant, consistent and effective in that opposition than Bishop John Hughes of New York. Like his episcopal predecessors, he rejected the trustees as rebels against Catholic doctrine and discipline; but he saved his strongest attacks for the system itself. According to Hughes, the system was allowed to develop only because of the new circumstances of religious freedom in the United States. Because of that fragile new experiment, the first bishops considered it neither "practicable" nor "expedient" to enforce the full impact of Catholic Church law. The bishops, therefore, tolerated the evolution of trusteeism, even though the church did not approve it. They "merely bore with" it until a "better order could be introduced."[30] In the 1840's, Hughes believed the time had come in New York for a "return to the ordinary and regular discipline of the church."[31] He abolished the trustee system, therefore, and brought American Catholic discipline into conformity with the "ancient" discipline. Thereby, he also rejected the trustees' attempts to accommodate the church to the American environment.

According to Hughes, the trustee system was inherently hostile to *391*
Catholicism for at least three reasons. It was "altogether injurious to religion"[32] because it occasioned contentions and scandals.[33] It had also hindered the trustees' own religious character and piety. Hughes maintained that he never knew a trustee "to retire from office a better Catholic, or a more pious man" than he was before he entered the office. In fact, many who had become trustees had lost their religious feelings and their faith by serving in that capacity.[34] The trustees' financial mismanagement was the third reason for the system's inherent evils. Hughes felt that the system itself was responsible for the misappropriation of ecclesiastical property and for ecclesiastical debts. The trustees failed because they acted as officials of an organization and did not take individual and personal responsibility for their actions. They could always look to their successors to pay for the debts they incurred while in office. Also, they attempted to draw large congregations to pay for their debts by accepting pastors whose only qualification was evangelical eloquence. Moreover, the lay members of a congregation had a "natural repugnance" to contributing to laymen for eccesiastical purposes.[35]

According to Hughes, the financial affairs of a parish or a diocese could be more efficiently and more effectively managed by a priest or the bishop because they understood better "the account which is to be rendered to God for its just administration." Likewise, the clergy were better suited to take personal and individual responsibility for finances than were the laity because they were ordained for a life-time commitment to the church's administration. The clergy's mismanagement (were that to occur), morever, would be readily known by the congregation.[36] The clergy's administration, furthermore, would be responsible to higher ecclesiastical authorities. In the case of the trustee system, however, neither the ecclesiastical nor the civil laws were capable of "fixing or determining the responsibility of mismanaging or wasting ecclesiastical property. The only penalty that we have hitherto known is to decline re-electing those who may have so mismanaged." Hughes' solution to the abuses of trusteeism, therefore, was to abolish the system (which was an imitation of the "lofty human wisdom" displayed in the "ecclesiastical polity of modern sects") and to restore temporal management to the episcopacy.[37] Hughes stands out in American Catholic history as the chief opponent of the trustee system and lay involvement in ecclesiastical administration, and the primary advocate for a rigid conformity of the American Catholic Church's organization to that of the European Catholic Church.

Hughes' opposition to the trustees and his form of adaptation
392 represented the dominant episcopal attitude of the early nineteenth century. Supported by theology and canon law, Baltimore conciliar legislation, and a large number of immigrant clergy and laity, he eventually won the fight against the trustees and established the monarchical episcopacy as the sole governing body in the diocesan church in the United States. His was a Pyrrhic victory, however. The development of a powerful episcopacy had a twofold effect upon American Catholicism. On the one hand, it eventually healed many of the schisms, restored clerical freedom in the parishes, and created an effective Catholic leadership which united the immigrant Catholics during the mass immigrant invasion of New York. On the other hand, that development created an almost unchecked clerical domination in the parish and diocesan church, fanned the fires of Nativism, reduced the laity to a passive role in the church, and revealed the Catholic Church as incompatible with democratic and republican institutions.

In the 1890's, years after the trustee crisis, Bishop John Lancaster Spalding declared that the negative episcopal reaction to the trustees, necessary as it may have been, "tended to make laymen more or less indifferent to our religious wants, because of the concentration of the whole management of the affairs of the Church in the hands of ecclesiastics." When Spalding wrote this mild indictment, the organization of the church was "so perfect" that bishops no longer needed to fear lay involvement in the work of the church. He proposed, therefore, that the hierarchy of his day enlist "the intelligent co-operation of the clergy and laity for the furtherance of Catholic interests" in this country. For this purpose, he suggested the establishment of an annual or bi-annual lay and clerical congress similar to that of the German Generalversammlung.[38] The suggestion was analogous to those made by a number of lay and clerical trustees in the early nineteenth century.[39] Like Carroll and England, Spalding favored a church structure which accommodated itself to American republican institutions and utilized the talents and experiences of the clergy and laity.

Like Spalding, present-day church leaders continue to look back upon the trustee experience when discussing the role of the laity in the church. Like their early nineteenth century predecessors, they evaluate that experience in different ways. In 1954, for example, Archbishop Robert Dwyer wrote that the episcopal reaction to the trustees "reduced almost to a minimum" lay participation in the mission of the church.[40] He regretted the effect. More recently, in December of 1974, Bishop Thomas J. Welsh saw the conflicts between laity and clergy in his diocese as "the old trustee battle all over again."[41] For him, that seems to 393
have meant lay insubordination and a denial of clerical authority.

When contemporary church leaders return to the trustee experience, they may well be reminded that there were at least two different episcopal perceptions of the lay-clerical conflicts, reflecting two divergent approaches to adapting the Catholic Church to the American environment as well as two distinct methods of approaching the laity. While the republicans recognized that the primary intent of the trustee movement was an adaptation that was basically justified but too thoroughly identified with American republicanism, Protestant doctrine and discipline, the monarchists feared that the primary motive was a revolutionary attempt to gain power over the clergy by absolutely controlling the church's welfare.

For the most part, historians of American Catholicism have accepted the monarchical judgment on trusteeism. Most recently, the *New Catholic Encyclopedia*, for example, presented trusteeism as lay insubordination.[42] This judgment does not adequately describe the lay-clerical conflicts or the different episcopal approaches to the contentions. Divergent American Catholic perceptions of the church's relationship to a modern democracy are the primary source of the dissenstions and the principal reason for the different episcopal attitudes to the laity. The episcopal responses to lay-clerical tensions have not been monolithic, as some historians have indicated.

If past episcopal attitudes to lay participation varied because of different perceptions of the relationship of the Catholic Church to democratic societies, we may suspect that current episcopal responses to the laity are governed by similar conceptions. Perhaps a more thorough investigation of the American experience and current American Catholic views of the relationship of the church to society could give the contemporary church helpful insights into the foundations of lay and clerical conflicts in a democratic world. Such a study could also direct contemporary theologians and canon lawyers in designing ecclesiologies and church structures which could more adequately resolve the tensions and provide a more effective basis for implementing the Second Vatican Council's vision of the local church.

FOOTNOTES

1. See, e.g., G. C. Treacy, "The Evils of Trusteeism," *Historical Records and Studies*, VIII (1915), 136-156.

2. John Carroll to Holy Trinity Parish, February 22, 1797, quoted in [Henry Conwell], *A Concatenation of Speeches, Memoirs, Deeds, and Memorable References Relative to St. Mary's Church in Philadelphia Submitted to Consideration* (Philadelphia, 1824), p. 73.

3. *Ibid.*, pp. 77, 81; see also John Carroll to the New York City Trustees, January 25,

1786, quoted in Peter Guilday, *The Life and Times of John Carroll* (Westminster, Maryland: The Newman Press, 1954), pp. 264-67.

4. In 1787, Carroll denied that the Holy Trinity Trustees had the right of patronage, but he was not absolutely opposed to the idea of patronage under specific conditions. See Martin I. J. Griffin, "The Church of the Holy Trinity, Philadelphia," *Records of the American Catholic Historical Society*, XXI (1910), 9-10, 32. An undated, unsigned document in the Carroll Papers in the Woodstock Jesuit Archives reveals that Carroll accepted (at least at one time) the possibility of the *jus patronatus* in the United States and acknowledged the layman's right of presentation. The document is a sample contract between a layman and the Catholic Church. It reads, in part, as follows: "I, N.N., give and bequeath my farm situated (at such a place) with all its appurtenances to N. N., his heirs or assigns forever; in trust however for the residence, sole use and maintenance of a Roman Catholic Priest, to be presented by the aforesaid N. N., his heirs and assigns, and approved by the Roman Catholic Bishop for the time being . . ." See Thomas Hughes (ed.), *History of the Society of Jesus in North America, Colonial and Federal. Documents* (New York: Longmans, Green and Co., 1910), Part II, 828-829.

5. Carroll accepted the trustee system as a workable way of involving all the members of the congregation in the government of the local church. See John Carroll to the Vestry of the Catholic Church of Charleston, S.C., September 15, 1811, in *United States Catholic Miscellany*, January 14, 1822, pp. 23-24. He did prescribe, however, that the senior clergyman of each parish be an *ex officio* member of the Board of Trustees and that he should be president of the board.

6. Conwell, *A Concatenation*, p. 81.

7. Carroll to New York City Trustees, January 25, 1786, quoted in Guilday, *Carroll*, p. 265.

8. *Ibid.*, p. 266.

9. Conwell, *A Concatenation*, p. 77; Carroll, as many bishops after him, believed that the trustees manifested a number of Protestant principles. In addition to appointing pastors, some trustees, in Carroll's opinion, had "declared themselves independent of it [papacy] as of a *foreign jurisdiction*." Carroll was careful to proclaim, however, that the obedience owed to the papacy was "purely spiritual" and had nothing to do with civil affairs. The pope had no temporal jurisdiction in this country.

10. Conwell, *A Concatenation*, p. 75.

11. *Ibid.*, p. 76; cf. also Carroll to New York City Trustees, October, 1787 in Guilday, *Carroll*, pp. 278-281. The trustees never claimed that they had a right to confer sacramental orders, only that they had a right to select pastors who were already ordained. The right of selecting they considered a temporal not a spiritual function of the church. The bishops, however, considered the ordination and appointment of the clergy as spiritual functions and gave them equal theological significance in the heat of the conflicts.

12. Carroll to New York City Trustees, January 25, 1786, in Guilday, *Carroll*, p. 264-267.

13. Lawrence Kehoe (ed.), *Complete Works of the Most Rev. John Hughes, D.D., Archbishop of New York; comprising his sermons, letters, lectures, speeches, etc.* (2 vols; New York: L. Kehoe, 1865), II, 550. Hughes, of course, did not agree with Carroll's view of accommodation. He was only one of a number of American clergymen who did not

share Carroll's perceptions. John Anthony Grassi, one of Carroll's fellow Jesuits, believed that Carroll was partially responsible for the problems of trusteeism. "In the eyes of some," Grassi noted, "he [Carroll] was not cautious enough in his choice of confidants, and he was prone to give in to Protestants more than he should have done, and to appoint trustees over churches when he could have done well without them, and so have averted all the troubles which our missions suffered at the hands of those same persons, with damage even to religion." See. T. Hughes, *History of Society of Jesus*, Part II, p. 838, n. 46.

14. Archbishop Ambrose Maréchal also believed that Carroll "defended the [trustee] system" for many years. After so many schisms, however, he "regretted very much that he had ever permitted it." The bulk of evidence suggests that Carroll regretted the abuses of the system, but not the system itself. Commenting upon Maréchal's opinion, John Tracy Ellis noted that it was more accurate to say that Carroll "had rather tolerated and tried to work along with the lay trustee control of church properties than to say that he had defended it."See John Tracy Ellis (ed.), *Documents of American Catholic History* (Milwaukee: The Bruce Publishing Co., 1962), p. 216.

15. On the Constitution, see Ignatius A. Reynolds (ed.), *The Works of the Right Rev. John England* (5 vols.; Baltimore: John Murphy and Co., 1849), V, 91-110.

16. England's solution was almost unanimously opposed by the episcopacy of his time. See Peter Guilday, *The Life and Times of John England* (2 vols.; New York: The America Press, 1927), I, 350-52.

17. Leonard Neale to Trustees of Holy Trinity, December 8, 1796, in M. Bernetta Brislen, "The Episcopacy of Leonard Neale," *Historical Records and Studies*, XXXIV (1941), 32.

18. Neale to Rev. James Lucas, Norfolk, March 6, 1816, quoted in Treacy, *Historical Records and Studies*, VIII, 147.

19. Neale to Lucas, April 19, 1816, in Archbishop Neale's papers in the Archives of the Archdiocese of Baltimore.

20. *Ibid.*; cf. also, Neale to Norfolk Trustees, January 14, 1817, in Brislen, *Historical Records and Studies*, XXXIV, 71-72.

21. Neale to Norfolk Trustees, July 5, 1816, in Brislen, *Historical Records and Studies*, XXXIV, 67; Neale to Lucas, March 26, 1817, *ibid.*, 74.

22. "Archbishop Maréchal's Report to Propaganda, October 16, 1818," in Ellis, *Documents*, p. 214; cf. also, Maréchal to Charleston Trustees, January 9, 1818, in Guilday, *England*, I, 227.

23. "Marechal's Report," Ellis, *Documents*, pp. 208-09, 212, 218-19. The trustees, by the nature of their elected office, represented the majority of the pew holders of a parish. The fact that some trustees were elected year after year, even during the most turbulent times, indicates that their principles and programs were shared by a majority of the pew holders.

24. *Ibid.*, p. 218; cf. also, Ambrose Maréchal, *Pastoral Letter to the Roman Catholics of Norfolk* (Baltimore, September 28, 1819), p. 43, n.

25. "Marechal's Report," p. 216.

26. Martin I. J. Griffin, "The Life of Bishop Conwell," *Records of the American Catholic Historical Society*, XXV (1914), 155.

27. William Hogan, *An Address to the Congregation of St. Mary's Church Philadelphia* (Philadelphia, 1821), pp. 18-19.

28. *Ibid.*, p. 21.

29. *Ibid.*, p. 20.

30. John Hughes, *Pastoral Letter of the Right Rev. Dr. Hughes to the Clergy and Laity of the Diocese of New York* (New York: George Mitchell, 1842), p. 5. This argument probably lent weight to the Nativist charge that Catholicism would change American republicanism once it became strong enough in the country.

31. *Ibid.*, p. 5.

32. *Ibid.*, p. 8.

33. *Ibid.*, p. 9.

34. *Ibid.*, p. 8.

35. *Ibid.*, p. 9.

36. Hughes does not indicate how the clergy were to be accountable to the laity in financial matters, he simply asserts that it would be so. The laity, he maintained, could rely upon clerical integrity and honesty.

37. Hughes, *Pastoral*, p. 13.

38. John Lancaster Spalding, *The Religious Mission of the Irish People and Catholic Colonization* (6th ed.; New York: Christian Press Association Publication Co., 1897), p. 141.

39. See, e.g., Thadeus O'Meally, *A Series of Letters Relating to the Late Attempt at a Reconciliation Between the Members of the Congregations of St. Mary's and St. Joseph's with a Brief Notice of the Present State of the Controversy Between them* (Philadelphia: William Brown, 1825), p. 36; *A Republication of Two Addresses, Lately Published in Philadelphia, The First by a Committee of St. Mary's Church on Reform of Church Discipline, the Second by a Layman of St. Mary's Congregation in Reply to the Same with Introductory Remarks by a Layman of New York* (New York: William Grattan, 1821), p. 5.

40. Robert Dwyer, "The American Laity," *Commonweal* LX (August 27, 1954), 503.

41. As reported in *National Catholic Reporter*, December 27, 1974, p. 1.

42. R. F. McNamara, "Trusteeism," *New Catholic Encyclopedia*, XIV, 323.

IX American Catholicism Turned Upside Down

A Critical Period in American Catholicism

Jay P. Dolan

Historians are fond of looking back over the panorama of the past and writing about periods of cultural change that altered the continuity of history. The *age of discovery* and the *rise of the city* are phrases that describe such pivotal epochs. These are not Madison Avenue-inspired book titles, but legitimate interpretative descriptions of past ages that provide a key to understanding the development of American civilization. Although the history of American Catholicism does not lend itself to such epochal descriptions, interpretative concepts are applicable in this area of study as well and they can provide useful keys to the analysis of the past.

One critical age in American Catholic history developed during the middle decades of the nineteenth century. This was a time of transformation for all Americans. In the opinion of Ralph Waldo Emerson, a "new race" was emerging and a new consciousness had appeared.[1] John Hughes, the bishop of New York from 1838 to 1864, evidenced a similar awareness and described this age as a "time of foundation" for American Catholicism.[2] John Gilmary Shea, a pioneer Catholic historian, also sensed the uniqueness of the period and believed that the Catholic Church was "acquiring a more settled form" during these years of passage.[3] The rise of the city and the beginnings of industrialization were altering the landscape of the nation and changing the shape of religion. Catholicism was not immune to this change and what happened during this time of foundation would condition the pattern of the future.

In 1815 fewer than 200,000 Catholics lived in the United States and they were "chiefly an Anglo-American minority increased at the edges by French and Irish immigration but culturally an American group."[4] Fifty years later the Roman Catholic Church was the

---

[1] Ralph Waldo Emerson, *Complete Works*, X, *Lectures and Biographical Sketches* (Boston, 1883), 326.

[2] Archives of Archdiocese of New York (hereafter AANY), Bishop John Hughes to Society for the Propagation of the Faith, January 23, 1845.

[3] *New York Times*, December 10, 1852.

[4] Thomas T. McAvoy, "The Catholic Minority in the United States 1789-1821," *Historical Records and Studies*, XXXIX-XL (1952), 41; Gerald Shaughnessy, *Has the Immigrant Kept the Faith?* (New York, 1925), p. 262.

largest single denomination in the country, numbering more than three and one-half million members.[5] Immigration had changed its cultural complexion and Irish and German features supplanted Anglo-American trademarks. Archbishop John Carroll had died in 1815 and his death marked the passing of an age. During his episcopacy, 1790-1815, American Catholicism evidenced a degree of patrician culture and, though hardship and poverty were not absent, they were overshadowed by the culture and class of leading Catholic laity and clergy.[6] By the end of the Civil War Catholics could look back to the age of Carroll with nostalgic pride, but the immigrant newcomers held little in common with their patrician ancestors.

During this age of transformation the nation was undergoing a rapid urbanization and by 1870 26 percent of the population lived in the city.[7] Through a continual flow of immigrants the Catholic Church became increasingly identified with the urban frontier; this urbanization of the Church, at the critical time of its foundation, was an important element in the shaping of religion. By focusing on this dimension of the Church one may well discover the missing link for an interpretative study of American Catholicism.

In the city the Church faced common problems and resorted to similar solutions. St. Louis, Cincinnati, Baltimore, Philadelphia and New York were separated from one another by mountains and rivers but a common environment, the urban frontier, bound them more closely together than they would have liked to admit. The formation of the Church in these different cities was substantially identical, even given the variety of ethnic groups in each locale. What was emerging during these decades of transition was a pattern of organizational life that would define Catholicism for the next one hundred years.

To illustrate this thesis by focusing on several cities would demand a full-length study, but what follows is very indicative proof of the transformation of the Church in the middle decades of the nineteenth century. The selection of New York is by design since it was the center of a new Catholicism emerging in the United States. Moreover, what emerged in New York was not unique,

[5] Shaughnessy, p. 154.

[6] Joseph A. Agonito, "The Buildings of an American Catholic Church: The Episcopacy of John Carroll," (Ph.D. diss., Syracuse University, 1972), is a recent study of this period.

[7] David Ward, *Cities and Immigrants* (New York, 1971), p. 6.

rather it was the most conspicuous example of what was taking place in many cities across the nation.

During these years of passage immigration swelled the population of New York City and intensified the ethnic variety of the community. The city had always been distinguished for its variety of peoples, but the nineteenth-century immigration of foreign-born newcomers transformed it into what Walt Whitman described in 1865 as a "city of the world" where all races and lands of the earth gathered together.[8] The Church had to adapt to this new influx of immigrants with the result that it ultimately altered its concept of the neighborhood parish.

As New Yorkers ushered in the new year of 1815, Catholics 401
could boast of only one parish church, with a second one scheduled to open in a few months. Both parishes served a variety of nationalities with services in English, French and German languages, but the mingling of national groups in the same parish was not a happy arrangement.[9] Throughout the episcopacy of John Carroll the Church in the United States had sought to develop Catholic American parishes. As Bishop Carroll put it, Catholics should form "not Irish, nor English or French Congregations, but Catholic-American Congregations and Churches."[10] This ideal of a Catholic American Church remained very conspicuous throughout the century, but the polyglot nature of the community was a force that could not be overcome by the rhetoric of Americanization. In the words of one New York priest, Rev. Jeremiah Cummings,

> The Irish find it difficult to discard their affection for everything that concerns Old Hybernia and thus would like to establish here an Irish Catholic Church. Germans stay on their own and do not want to have anything to do with the Irish. Frenchmen, in many instances, would like indeed a Roman, Apostolic Catholic Church, but would like to dress her up *a la francaise.*[11]

---

[8] Walt Whitman, "City of Ships," *Leaves of Grass,* ed. John Kouwenhoven (New York, 1950), p. 233.

[9] See Peter Guilday, "Trusteeism," *Historical Records and Studies,* XVIII (1928), 7-73.

[10] Robert H. Lord, John E. Sexton and Edward T. Harrington, *History of the Archdiocese of Boston* (New York, 1944), I, 431.

[11] Archives of the University of Notre Dame (hereafter AUND), Scritture Riferite nei Congressi: America Centrale dal Canada all'istmo di Panama (hereafter Scritture), XIV, LETTER 226, Rev. Jeremiah Cummings to Prefect of Propaganda Fide, November 24, 1847, f. 639.

As a result of this ethnic consciousness the Church eventually adopted the concept of a national parish, or a congregation organized principally along the lines of language rather than territorial boundaries. Such an adaptation enabled the Church to avoid the conflict latent in an ethnically mixed parish and it provided a convenient way to meet the particular religious needs of foreign-born Catholics.

In 1865 thirty-two Catholic churches dotted the landscape of New York. Included in this number were eight German-language parishes and one French parish; the remaining twenty-three churches were made up of English-speaking Irish immigrants and
402 a remnant of American-born Catholics.[12] An Italian parish had already been formed in 1857, but it was dissolved after three years; in 1866 it would reopen. A church for Negro Catholics was also being proposed at this time, but it would not come to pass until 1883.[13] The organization of ethnic parishes was not unique to New York and during these years of transition church law eventually sanctioned the idea in many American dioceses. The ideal of a Catholic American congregation was disappearing and despite protests against catering to the foreignness of Catholic immigrants, the ethnic parish became a distinguishing trademark of American Catholicism. With the arrival of new immigrants in the late nineteenth century it continued to serve as a convenient bridge between the cultures of the Old and New worlds. When church authorities ignored the peculiar desires of these newcomers and delayed the formation of national parishes, conflict inevitably arose and many immigrants abandoned the Church to form their own national churches. This was especially true among Eastern European immigrants.

Closely connected to the development of ethnic parishes was the rise of the parochial school. Since 1800 St. Peter's Church had sponsored a parish school and as new parishes appeared some type

---

[12] See *Historical Records Survey. Inventory of the Church Archives in New York City,* II: *The Roman Catholic Church* (New York, 1941), 50-68, for brief history of the origins of city parishes.

[13] AUND, Scritture, XVII, LETTER 1080, Louis Binsse to Prefect of Propaganda Fide, March 16, 1857, f. 873; Scritture, XVIII, LETTER 1703, Rev. Antonio Sanguinette to Prefect of Propaganda Fide, October 27, 1860; Thomas F. Meehan, "Mission Work Among Colored Catholics," *Historical Records and Studies,* VIII (1915), 122-23.

of school generally followed.[14] But these schools were more the result of a particular parish's endeavors and not part of any organized plan. By 1865 the situation had changed considerably and New York Catholics had opted for a parochial school system. The principal catalyst for this development was the controversy over the control of education in New York City that dragged on from 1840 to 1842.[15] Catholics emerged from this debate defeated in their attempts to gain public funds for parochial schools. Moreover, the Protestant sectarianism of New York's public schools forced Catholics to admit "that the benefits of public education are not for us";[16] after 1842 the bishop of New York, John Hughes, led the campaign to establish a network of parish schools. In his words, the time had come "to build the school house first and the church afterwards."[17] As expected new schools appeared, and by 1865 75 percent of the city parishes were supporting a parochial school.[18]

It is clear that Catholics in New York, as well as in many other cities, had committed themselves to a separate educational system by the middle of the nineteenth century. Later decades built on this foundation and Italian, Polish and other immigrant communities followed the direction of their Irish and German predecessors. The school and the church were but two dimensions of the ethnic parish and they both served the same end—to preserve the religious heritage of immigrant newcomers. They reinforced the cohesion of ethnic communities and aided them in adapting to the New World by delaying the breakdown and disintegration awaiting them in the face of the culture demands of the new society.

Another aspect of the transformation of the Church in the city was the development of extraparochial institutions. In the early nineteenth century the parish was the center of religious life, but as the city expanded at a rapid rate the Church more and more began to organize its apostolate around specific interests rather than specific parishes. Since no one parish could provide for the needs

---

[14] Leo R. Ryan, *Old St. Peter's: The Mother Church of Catholic New York* (New York, 1935), pp. 236 ff.

[15] See Vincent P. Lannie, *Public Money and Parochial Education: Bishop Hughes, Governor Seward and the New York School Controversy* (Cleveland, 1968) for the history of this controversy.

[16] *Address of the Roman Catholics to their Fellow Citizens of the City and State of New York* (New York, 1840), p. 8.

[17] Pastoral Letter of November 15, 1850, cited in Lawrence Kehoe, *Complete Works of the Most Reverend John Hughes* (New York, 1865), II, 715.

[18] *Sadlier's Catholic Almanac 1864* (New York, 1864), pp. 85-87.

of an increasingly large number of Catholics, extraparochial institutions emerged and they directed their particular apostolate to Catholics scattered throughout the city, regardless of what parish they belonged to. Such specific apostolates as hospital work, care for orphans and guidance for delinquent women were institutionalized at this time; like the school and the church, they too were organized along ethnic lines.[19] Catholic colleges also began to appear to supplement the education offered in parochial schools. They appealed to a city-wide population and were particularly attractive to children "of the wealthier families."[20] By 1865 New York Catholics were supporting three men's colleges, three boarding schools for girls and a boys' academy as well as numerous female day academies. Twenty-five years earlier only two girls' academies were in operation.[21]

The increasing urbanization of the Church fostered this development of extraparochial institutions. For all practical purposes the parish was limited to care for the needs of its own parishioners and the limitation of financial resources prevented it from undertaking any extraparochial programs. But an expanding city placed new demands on the Church. Hospitals, asylums and orphanages were needed and the multiplication of such public institutions emphasized the demand. The Protestant sectarian atmosphere of these facilities served to dramatize the need for parallel Catholic organizations. As one Catholic put it, in public hospitals Catholics "were surrounded by Infidels, Apostates and even around enemies of religion, circumstances which rendered those institutions anything but desirable for a Catholic who wished to prepare for eternity."[22] The increase in the number of Catholics and the presence of a growing middle-class constituency furnished the financial resources necessary to establish such a city-wide apostolate; the growth in the number of female religious orders provided the personnel needed to staff the institutions. The result was that by 1865 the parish no longer defined the apostolate of urban Catholicism; an extra-

---

[19] See George P. Jacoby, *Catholic Child Care in Nineteenth Century New York* (Washington, D.C., 1941) for a history of some of these institutions.

[20] Quoted in John R. G. Hassard, *Life of the Most Rev. John Hughes* (New York, 1866), p. 215.

[21] *The Metropolitan Catholic Almanac and Laity's Directory 1840* (New York, 1840), pp. 149-51; *Sadlier's Catholic Almanac 1864*, pp. 88-90.

[22] AANY, Claims of the Fathers and the Congregation of the Church of the Most Holy Redeemer, New York, to St. Francis Hospital, Fifth Street, New York, July 20, 1868.

parochial structure had emerged and together with the parish it became one of the distinctive trademarks of the Church in the city.

As the city was increasing in size and number urban life naturally became more complex. Social, political and economic changes generated problems that overwhelmed New Yorkers. During the middle decades of the century, old problems were magnified and new ones were created. The old ways of city government were no longer adequate "to cope with the problems of a modern urban-industrial society" and into the void stepped William Marcy Tweed and the big city political machine.[23] A similar phenomenon was taking place in the Church.

Like the city the Church was outgrowing its old style of government. In earlier years the administration of church affairs was identified with one or two parishes, but the expansion of the city forced the Church to develop a new mode of government. New parishes had to be organized, religious education became increasingly necessary, numerous sick had to be cared for and such concerns surpassed the resources of a parish-oriented government. These were demands common throughout the city and they had to be met on a city-wide basis. A decentralized parochial form of government was no longer viable in a city undergoing rapid change. Decisions had to be made that transcended parish loyalties and causes had to be defended that affected all Catholics. A changing society emphasized the need to centralize and control the administration of church affairs. Bishop John Hughes recognized this and in 1852 appointed Father Thomas Preston as the chancellor of the diocese.[24] Preston was to establish a chancery office and organize the administrative aspects of church life. Dispensations from church marriage laws had to pass through his office and pastors had to submit financial and spiritual reports to the chancery. Gradually the administration of church affairs became centralized around the bishop and his chancellor; episcopal control increased in proportion to the degree of centralization and what ultimately emerged was the rule of one man, Bishop John Hughes.

In 1850 no one had to ask who ruled the Church in New York. John Hughes was boss. He believed that the city demanded a "new mode of government" in the Church and of necessity he had to be

---

[23] Alexander B. Callow, Jr., *The Tweed Ring* (New York, 1966), p. 4.

[24] AANY, Diary of Archbishop's Secretary, December 24, 1852.

both "bishop and chief."[25] He saw his task as one of molding the diversity of Catholics into "one dough to be leavened by the spirit of Catholic faith and of Catholic union" and he ruled New York's Germans, Irish, French and Italians with an equally firm hand.[26] He would interdict German parishes if necessary, dismiss Irish priests with haste and defend his churches with armed guards.

The school controversy of 1840 provides a good example of how Hughes exercised this "new mode of government." It was an issue that affected all parishes and a unified front had to be organized against the city government. Hughes became the rallying point for New York Catholics and the two-year debate succeeded in strengthening his leadership role. Divisions among Catholics were glossed over and parish loyalties were put aside. Hughes united the people in an opposition party and his militant stance gained him national acclaim and enhanced his authority in New York.

Hughes's struggle with lay trusteeism also illustrated his style of rule. In earlier years lay trustees held a firm grip on church government since it was centered in the parish where trustees were in control. The trustees could dismiss pastors for the slightest reason and their decisions often ignited parish feuds. Strong episcopal control was lacking and weak, aging bishops were no match for militant trustees. When John Hughes arrived in New York in 1838, he immediately challenged the control of the lay trustees. "I made war on the whole system," he said, and within a few years he had succeeded in breaking the grip of lay trustees on church government.[27] The trustees had met their match and as far as Hughes was concerned, they were handmaids and not decision-makers; in his opinion, "episcopal authority came from above and not from below and Catholics did their duty when they obeyed their bishop."[28]

The weakening of lay trusteeism shifted decision-making to the clergy and ultimately to the bishop. At one time laymen exercised a close control over parochial education and freely hired and fired instructors. By mid-century the administration of Catholic schools

---

[25] AUND, Scritture, XVIII, LETTER 1417, John Hughes to Prefect of Propaganda Fide, March 23, 1858, f. 527-28.

[26] *Ibid.*

[27] Rev. Henry J. Browne, "The Archdiocese of New York a Century Ago: A Memoir of Archbishop Hughes," *Historical Records and Studies*, XXXIX-XL (1952), 139.

[28] AANY, Diary of Archbishop's Secretary, May 12, 1850.

was passing rapidly into the hands of the clergy; in 1861 church law made the pastor the parish superintendent of education.[29] Lay men and women remained as teachers, but they no longer exercised the administrative control that their predecessors enjoyed. The position of the laity had been relocated and they found themselves at the bottom of the pyramid of church government. The bishop stood at the top and presided over ecclesiastical affairs while the laity were left to pay, pray and obey.

Squeezed between bishop and laity was the priest. In earlier years he was able to act quite independently of a distant bishop or a weak superior; if he had to struggle with authority, it was more often with lay trustees. As episcopal control increased, however, the authority of the priest shrunk. "The will of the bishop is the only law," a priest complained and this was certainly true in New York.[30] But priests did not acquiesce easily. They appealed to tradition and to canon law; the confused state of legal affairs in American Catholicism provided them with some leverage, or so they thought. But in New York John Hughes was boss and when some clergy discussed the necessity of priests' rights, Hughes told them "that he would teach them County Monaghan canon law; he would send them back to the bog whence they came."[31]

The emergence of boss rule in the Church was a phenomenon fostered by the urbanization of Catholicism. The variety of national groups demanded a degree of control to prevent schism in the Church; at the same time the rapid expansion of the city required a new mode of government to consolidate church affairs. Boss rule effectively met these needs and John Hughes was not reluctant to exercise this function. He ruled like an Irish chieftain and the Irish respect for the hierarchy of power made his task all the easier.[32]

Catholic theology in the nineteenth century certainly encouraged the development of strong episcopal control. Pius IX consolidated the authority of the Church in the papacy and the First Vatican

[29] *Concilium Provinciale, Neo-Eboracense III* (New York, 1862), *decretum I;* Sister Patricia Ann Reilly, O.P., "The Administration of Parish Schools in the Archdiocese of New York, 1800-1900," *Historical Records and Studies,* XLIV (1956), 45 ff.

[30] Quoted in Colman J. Barry, *The Catholic Church and German Americans* (Washington, D. C., 1953), p. 17.

[31] AANY, Diary of Rev. Richard Burtsell, July 26, 1865.

[32] See Nathan Glazer and Daniel P. Moynihan, *Beyond the Melting Pot* (Cambridge, Mass., 1963), pp. 226-27.

Council strengthened his position as supreme ruler.[33] This model of monarchical authority became normative on the local level where each bishop was pope in his own diocese. Urbanization in Europe and America, however, facilitated the role of pope and bishop. Large cities were developing and the Church needed to form a new style of government to control rapidly expanding communities. Though theology provided the rationale, urbanization emphasized the need for a new mode of government. This was especially true in the United States where Catholicism was taking shape at a time when cities were expanding at an unprecedented rate. Since it was predominantly an urban Church, the need for control and centralization was even more pronounced. Thus, boss rule appeared at a time when it was theologically justified and culturally necessary with the happy result that it effectively united the diverse elements of urban Catholicism.

During these years of transition another change took place that was more subtle than the incarnation of power in one man. This transformation had to do with the image of the priest. In the early decades of the century the prevailing image was that of a minister to the poor and to the sick. The priest's principal duties were hearing confessions, visiting the sick and preaching. Though some priests did not live up to the model, a sufficient number did to justify such an image.[34]

As the Church began building new churches and schools, the priest gradually became a minister of brick and mortar. In 1853 a papal visitor to the United States, Archbishop Gaetano Bedini, noticed this trait. He observed that the "most outstanding priest is the one that has built the most churches and begun the most institutions."[35] Bedini believed that this emphasis could be traced to the American desire for demonstrative success. Large churches, like private mansions, were prestigious symbols. For an immigrant church in an alien culture, such monuments enhanced the image of the community as well as the reputation of the priest-builder.[36] When a priest of the brick-and-mortar tradition died, the eulogy focused on his building accomplishments and he was remembered

---

[33] See Roger Aubert, *Le Pontificat de Pie IX* (nouvelle ed.; Paris, 1963).

[34] Such duties were extolled in the Catholic press, *e.g.*, *Freeman's Journal*, February 19, 1848.

[35] James F. Connelly, *The Visit of Archbishop Gaetano Bedini* (Rome, 1960), p. 244.

[36] *Ibid.*

not only as a good and zealous priest, but also as a man of excellent business habits.[37]

The income of the priest supported this emphasis on material success. The salary of a pastor at mid-century was $600 a year and an assistant pastor received a salary of $400.[38] Added to this were stipends offered for Masses, weddings and funerals which averaged as much as $1,000 a year for each priest.[39] For an unmarried man receiving his room and board, this was a relatively high income. It certainly placed the priest in an income bracket that was higher than most of his parishioners' and, as one priest remarked, many were able "to live luxuriantly."[40]

Unusual affluence was not limited to the clergy. The Church 409
itself was becoming increasingly wealthy and this development stood in dramatic contrast to earlier years when it labored under widespread indebtedness. In 1829, the bishop of New York, Jean Dubois, was forced to write letters to European aid societies begging for funds and despite advancing age he traveled to Rome and Lyons to plead his case.[41] John Hughes wrote many urgent pleas for aid and also returned to the old country in search of money.[42] But the large increase in Catholics and the rise of middle-class entrepreneurs expanded the resources of the Church. Later, begging letters became more modest and less urgent. When John Hughes was planning St. Patrick's Cathedral in 1858, a church, he said, "that may be worthy of our increasing numbers, intelligence and wealth," he sought one hundred Catholics who would contribute $1000 each to the building campaign. Although he was not totally successful, he did raise $73,000 in a short period of time from the more well-to-do members of the Church.[43] Seventeen

---

[37] See George W. Potter, *To the Golden Door* (Boston, 1960), p. 362.

[38] Circular Letter of Bishop John Hughes to the Clergy, *Freeman's Journal*, July 5, 1845; also, AANY, financial reports of various parishes.

[39] AANY, Diary of Rev. Richard Burtsell, May 25, 1865; priests were also urged to draw up wills so that their estates would go to the use of the poor and the church, *Concilium Provinciale, Neo-Eboracense III, decretum VI;* such a decree would suggest that priests had the means to accumulate an estate during their lifetime.

[40] AANY, Diary of Rev. Richard Burtsell, May 12, 1865.

[41] Charles G. Herbermann, "The Rt. Rev. John Dubois, D.D., Third Bishop of New York," *Historical Records and Studies,* I (1899), 318.

[42] Hassard, *Life of Hughes,* pp. 206 ff.

[43] John M. Farley, *History of St. Patrick's Cathedral* (New York, 1908), p. 120.

years earlier a yearlong campaign for funds was able to raise only $17,000 throughout the city.

Signs of new wealth appeared in parish churches as remodeling and refurnishing embellished the achievements of the past. Vestments from France and imported works of art appeared on the scene with greater frequency.[44] In earlier years Catholics were not so ostentatious. In a sermon given at the dedication of St. Nicholas Church in 1835 the speaker pointed out that "its plain construction will furnish nothing to elicit admiration. It will neither be planned by power nor achieved by wealth."[45] He was not exaggerating either since the small building could seat only one hundred people,
410 had no bell tower and only one altar; the priest lived in the basement.[46] The new German church of Most Holy Redeemer, built in 1851, elicited an entirely different response. Its size and grandeur were something Catholics boasted of and its bell tower proudly stood out along the skyline of the Lower East Side. St. Patrick's Cathedral was the ultimate sign of arrival and financial stability. Rivaling the churches in Europe, its grandeur appeared worthy of the "numbers, intelligence and wealth" of New York Catholics.

In 1820 the Church owned very little property in New York and it could claim only two modestly built churches. Forty years later thirty Catholic churches were scattered throughout the city and their combined property value totaled over a million and a half dollars ($1,505,600); only the Presbyterians and the Episcopalians surpassed the Catholics in landed wealth.[47] By 1858 the educational system represented almost a two-million-dollar investment.[48] Thus, in a relatively short period of time the Church had moved from borderline bankruptcy to landed wealth. Pride had replaced modesty and architectural grandeur and financial resources were signs of success that all Americans understood.

---

[44] AANY, Diary of Rev. Richard Burtsell, October 15, 1865; many parish histories witness to this transformation, *e.g., Souvenir of the Golden Jubilee of St. Bridgid's Church* (New York, 1899), pp. 15-17.

[45] John Gilmary Shea, *The Catholic Churches of New York City* (New York, 1878), pp. 538-39.

[46] Joseph Wuest, C.SS.R., *Annales Congregationis S. S. Redemptoris Provinciae Americae. Supplementum* (Ilchester, Md., 1903), I, 399.

[47] *U. S. Census 1860, Statistics of the U. S. in 1860* (Washington, D.C., 1866), Part II, pp. 431-33.

[48] Edward M. Connors, *Church-State Relationships in Education in the State of New York* (Washington, D.C., 1951), p. 46, note 137.

As the Church in the city was changing, it was acquiring a new mentality that shaped this transformation. In the early decades of the century, New York Catholics followed a policy of accommodation with the American culture; the anti-Catholic crusade of the 1840's and 1850's changed this policy. A militant Protestantism challenged the Americanism of Catholics and forced the immigrant Church to back away from any accommodation with urban institutions. Separate schools, hospitals and orphanages became necessary as far as Catholics were concerned; defensive apologetic sermons strengthened this separatist stance; the pervasive presence of Protestant missionaries, seemingly eager to gain converts, tended
to justify the withdrawal. The city government, rooted in a Prot- 411
estant past, could not meet the needs of an expanding community and so Catholics developed their own institutions. Their large numbers, their financial resources and a strong authoritarian leader eventually made the Church a citadel in the city that politicians learned to reckon with and Protestants could not ignore.

Forced to withdraw from an unfriendly society, the Church concentrated on building up its own internal strength. But the manner in which this took place is significant. Faced with the bewildering world of an expanding city where the old ways of doing things were inadequate, the Church willy-nilly adopted a new style of operation. The diversity of city life, magnified with the influx of immigrants, made the ethnic parish a normative institution. More than ever before the Church was becoming a community of immigrants and its task was to preserve the faith of the newcomers. The parish as well as the school served this end. As neighborhood institutions they formed an island community in the strange new world. They were a link with the past and in a changing society they furnished a desired measure of stability. Rather than reforming the parish to meet the demands of a new environment, Catholics transplanted the church of the old country to the American city. They strengthened it and fashioned a citadel in the city where they could escape from the cultural demands of the new society.

The big city also forced the Church to adopt a "new mode of government." Each parish was a little island, but the Church had to create a network of control lest these communities become too autonomous. It achieved this through the centralization of authority and the exercise of boss rule. Diocesan synods formulated a body of legislation binding on all Catholics and this reinforced the pattern of centralization.[49] Unity in the midst of plurality was the goal; the achievement of the Church during these years of transition was the formation of a system of control by which this aim might be realized. The anti-Catholic crusades only made the task easier by cementing the bonds of union among Catholics; as John Hughes said, nativism "tended powerfully to unite Catholics"; as bishop he could have wished for nothing better.[50]

During this time of foundation the Church inevitably adopted a conservative stance toward society. Its task was to conserve the faith rather than transform society. As an immigrant institution it had no choice other than to step into the future looking back-
412 ward. A modern urban society determined how it would carry the past into the future and the immigrant forced it to keep its eye fixed on the rear-view mirror. In subsequent years the city increasingly defined the shape of the nation and new immigrants forced the Church to continue its policy of consolidation rather than accommodation. The decade of the 1920's brought an end to large-scale immigration and only then did the Church begin "a long process of adjustment to a situation in which the immigrant no longer determined the church's basic stance."[51] But the patterns of the past were too firmly fixed to be uprooted easily and it was not until the 1960's that substantial change took place. Up until then the Church had followed the course charted out in the middle of the nineteenth century. The importance of this critical period in the history of American Catholicism can be measured by this century of influence, not only in New York, but also across the nation.

---

[49] John J. Considine, "The History of Canonical Legislation in the Diocese and Province of New York 1842-1861" (M.A. thesis, Catholic University, 1947), is a general study of the New York council during Hughes's episcopacy.

[50] Browne, "The Archdiocese of New York," p. 179.

[51] Sydney E. Ahlstrom, *A Religious History of American People* (New Haven, 1972), p. 1007.

The Heritage of
American Catholicisim

1. EDWARD R. KANTOWICZ, EDITOR
   MODERN AMERICAN CATHOLICISM, 1900-1965:
   SELECTED HISTORICAL ESSAYS
   New York 1988

2. DOLORES LIPTAK, R.S.M., EDITOR
   A CHURCH OF MANY CULTURES:
   SELECTED HISTORICAL ESSAYS ON ETHNIC AMERICAN CATHOLICISIM
   New York 1988

3. TIMOTHY J. MEAGHER, EDITOR
   URBAN AMERICAN CATHOLICISM:
   THE CULTURE AND IDENTITY OF THE AMERICAN CATHOLIC PEOPLE
   New York 1988

4. BRIAN MITCHELL, EDITOR
   BUILDING THE AMERICAN CATHOLIC CITY:
   PARISHES AND INSTITUTIONS
   New York 1988

5. MICHAEL J. PERKO, S.J., EDITOR
   ENLIGHTENING THE NEXT GENERATION:
   CATHOLICS AND THEIR SCHOOLS, 1830-1980
   New York 1988

6. WILLIAM PORTIER, EDITOR
   THE ENCULTURATION OF AMERICAN CATHOLICISM, 1820-1900:
   SELECTED HISTORICAL ESSAYS
   New York 1988

7. Timothy Walch, editor
Early American Catholicism, 1634-1820:
Selected Historical Essays
New York 1988

8. Joseph M. White, editor
The American Catholic Religious Life:
Selected Historical Essays
New York 1988

9. Robert F. Trisco
Bishops and Their Priests in the United States, 1789-1918
New York 1988

10. Joseph Agonito
The Building of an American Catholic Church:
The Episcopacy of John Carroll
New York 1988

11. Robert N. Barger
John Lancaster Spalding:
Catholic Educator and Social Emissary
New York 1988

12. Christine M. Bochen
The Journey to Rome:
Conversion Literature by Nineteenth-Century American Catholics
New York 1988

13. Martin J. Bredeck
Imperfect Apostles:
"The Commonweal" and the American Catholic Laity, 1924-1976
New York 1988

14. Jeffrey M. Burns
American Catholics and the Family Crisis, 1930-1962:
The Ideological and Organizational Response
New York 1988

15. Alfred J. Ede
The Lay Crusade for a Christian America:
A Study of the American Federation of Catholic Societies, 1900-1919
New York 1988

16. Jo Renee Formicol
The American Catholic Church and Its Role in the Formulation of United States Human Rights Foreign Policy, 1945-1978
New York 1988

17. Thomas J. Jonas
The Divided Mind:
American Catholic Evangelsts in the 1890s
Foreword by Martin E. Marty
New York 1988

18. Martin J. Kirk
The Spirituality of Isaac Thomas Hecker:
Reconciling the American Character and the Catholic Faith
New York 1988

19. Norlene M. Kunkel
Bishop Bernard J. McQuaid and Catholic Education
New York 1988

20. James M. McDonnell
Orestes A. Brownson and Nineteenth-Century Catholic Education
New York 1988

21. Elizabeth McKeown
War and Welfare:
American Catholics and World War I
New York 1988

22. Barbara Misner, s. c. s. c.
"Highly Respectable and Accomplished Ladies:"
Catholic Women Religious in America 1790-1850
New York 1988

23. Benita A. Moore
Escape into a Labyrinth:
F. Scott Fitzgerald, Catholic Sensibility, and the American Way
New York 1988

24. Marilyn Wenzke Nickels
Black Catholic Protest
and the Federated Colored Catholics, 1917-1933:
Three Perspectives on Racial Justice
New York 1988

25. David L. Salvaterra
American Catholicism and the Intellectual Life, 1880-1920
New York 1988

26. Helena Sanfilippo, r. s. m.
Inner Wealth and Outward Splendor:
New England Transcendentalists View the Roman Catholic Church
New York 1988

27. Fayette Breaux Veverka
"For God and Country:"
Catholic Schooling in the 1920s
New York 1988

28. Timothy Walch
The Diverse Origins of American Catholic Education:
Chicago, Milwaukee, and the Nation
New York 1988